AUTODESK® 3DS MAX® 8
REVEALED

AUTODESK® 3DS MAX® 8
REVEALED

Max Dutton and Rob Doran

Autodesk® 3ds Max® 8 Revealed

Max Dutton and Rob Doran

Managing Editor:
Marjorie Hunt

Product Managers:
Jane Hosie-Bounar, Megan Belanger

Associate Product Manager:
Shana Rosenthal

Editorial Assistant:
Janine Tangney

Production Editor:
Pamela Elizian

Contributing Author:
Jeanne Herring

Developmental Editors:
Jane Hosie-Bounar, Jeanne Herring

Marketing Manager:
Joy Stark

Marketing Coordinators:
Jordan Casey
Melissa Marcoux

Composition House:
Integra—Pondicherry, India

QA Manuscript Reviewer:
John Freitas

Cover Design:
Steve Deschene

COPYRIGHT © 2006 Thomson Course Technology, a division of Thomson Learning, Inc. Thomson Learning™ is a trademark used herein under license.

Printed in the United States of America

2 3 4 5 6 7 8 9 PH 09 08 07 06

For more information, contact Thomson Course Technology, 25 Thomson Place, Boston, Massachusetts 02210.

Or find us on the World Wide Web at: www.courseptr.com

ALL RIGHTS RESERVED. No part of this work covered by the copyright hereon may be reproduced or used in any form or by any means—graphic, electronic, or mechanical, including photocopying, recording, taping, Web distribution, or information storage and retrieval systems—without the written permission of the publisher.

For permission to use material from this text or product, contact us by

Tel (800) 730-2214
Fax (800) 730-2215

www.thomsonrights.com

Trademarks
Some of the product names and company names used in this book have been used for identification purposes only and may be trademarks or registered trademarks of their respective manufacturers and sellers.

Autodesk and 3ds Max are registered trademarks of Autodesk, Inc. in the United States and/or other countries. Third-party products, services, company names, logos, design, titles, words, or phrases within these materials may be trademarks of their respective owners.

Disclaimer
Thomson Course Technology reserves the right to revise this publication and make changes from time to time in its content without notice.

ISBN 0-619-27343-7

Library of Congress Catalog Card Number: 2005930008

Revealed Series Vision

The *Revealed* series is your guide to today's hottest multimedia applications. These comprehensive books teach the skills behind the application, showing you how to apply smart design principles to multimedia products such as dynamic graphics, animation, Web sites, software authoring tools, and digital video.

A team of design professionals including multimedia instructors, students, authors, and editors worked together to create this series. We recognized the unique needs of the multimedia market and created a series that gives you comprehensive step-by-step instructions and offers an in-depth explanation of the "why" behind a skill, all in a clear, visually-based layout.

It was our goal to create a book that speaks directly to the multimedia and design community—one of the most rapidly growing computer fields today. We feel that *Autodesk 3ds Max 8, Revealed* does just that—with sophisticated content and an instructive book design.

—The *Revealed* Series

Authors' Visions

First and foremost, I would like to acknowledge the hard-working people at Thomson Course Technology for making this book come alive. Jane Hosie-Bounar has taught me so much about the process of writing a book. Jeanne Herring, who worked with me on my chapters, is an amazing woman simply for the fact that she can tolerate my voice for so much time. She is also one of the most talented, hardworking women I have ever met. Marjorie Hunt has been incredible at orchestrating this project. She picked it up when it was already under-way and really helped move it along. Thanks also to the academic reviewers who looked at the early chapters in this book, including John Sledd, Greg Johnson, Arnaud Ehgner, Fred Boye, and Kevin Lee.

I could not have done this without the support of my wife Kim and the delightful distractions of my children. They have really helped me keep what is left of my sanity.

Throughout my life I have been inspired by my mother's writing and my father's artwork. They are the main reasons I got involved in writing this book.

—Max Dutton

There are many people I would like to thank for making my contribution to this book possible. First I would like to thank my wife Mara and sons Luke and Brendan for allowing me to write this book. The many hours spent writing was too much time away from you guys. Without your love and support it would not have been possible. Thank you Mom and Roisin for watching the kids; without your help this book could not have been written. Thanks Max for bringing me into your book. That was very cool, dude!

I would also like to thank all of the people at Course Technology who have worked so diligently to make this book what it is. Without superwoman extraordinaire, Jeanne Herring, working so tirelessly to edit my chapters, they would have been pretty lame. Thank you Jeanne for continually demanding more, and holding my hand through the process. I would also like to thank product manager Jane Hosie-Bounar for giving me the green light. Without you there at the beginning I would not have known where to start. Both of you kept me going, and gave me words of encouragement exactly when I needed them most. Thanks. I would also like to thank Quality Assurance guru John Freitas for being the most anal-retentive man in the world. His amazing attention to detail made the lessons in this book iron-clad and error-free.

Thank you, Professor Patrick Aievoli for giving me an extension on my final paper so I could finish this book. I'll get that to you soon.

I would also like to thank the many 3D artists whose books I have learned from over the years, and those of you who have shown me the cool stuff: Ted Boardman, Michelle Bousquet, Kim Lee, Michael McCarthy, Steve Schain and Alex Monteiro. And thank you Pia Maffai for failing me on my first DCT go-round. That was a great help!

—Rob Doran

Introduction to Autodesk 3ds Max 8

Welcome to *Autodesk 3ds Max 8, Revealed*. This book offers creative tutorials, concise instructions, and complete coverage of basic to intermediate 3ds Max skills, helping you use the many tools in 3ds Max to first model objects, and then use cameras, lighting, special effects, rendering, and particles to create basic—but stunning—animations. Use this book as you learn 3ds Max, and then use it later as your own reference guide.

This text is organized into ten chapters and an online MaxScript Appendix.

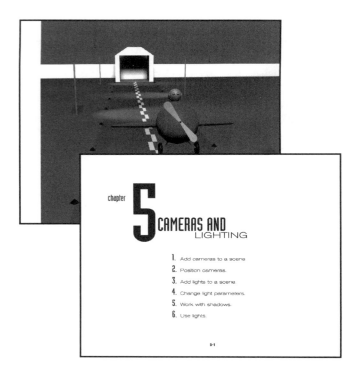

What You'll Do

A What You'll Do figure begins every lesson. This figure gives you an at-a-glance look at what you'll do in the chapter, either by showing you the current project or a tool you'll be using.

Comprehensive Conceptual Lessons

Before jumping into instructions, in-depth conceptual information tells you "why" skills are applied. This book provides the "how" and "why" through the use of professional examples. Also included in the text are tips and sidebars to help you work more efficiently and creatively, or to teach you a bit about the history or design philosophy behind the skill you are using.

Step-by-Step Instructions

This book combines in-depth conceptual information with concise steps to help you learn 3ds Max 8. Each set of steps guides you through a lesson where you will create, modify, or enhance a 3ds Max scene file. Step references to large images and quick step summaries round out the lessons.

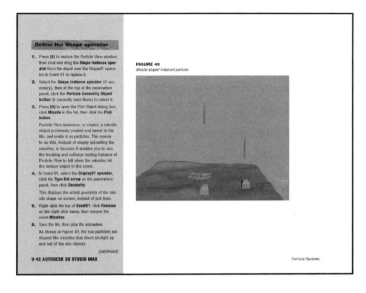

Chapter Summaries

This book contains chapter summaries that highlight the key tasks and terms that you learn in each chapter. You can use the summaries as a quick refresher should you find you need to review information you learned earlier in the book.

BRIEF CONTENTS

Chapter 1   Introducing Autodesk 3ds Max 8
Lesson 1   Explore the Interface   1-4
2   Work with Viewports   1-14
3   Work with the Main Toolbar   1-24
4   Explore the Command Panel   1-28
5   Work with the Track Bar   1-32
6   Customize the 3ds Max Interface   1-36
7   Use the Help Menu and the Hotkey Map   1-40

Chapter 2   Building and Modifying Objects
Lesson 1   Create Standard Primitives   2-4
2   Select Objects   2-12
3   Move, Rotate, and Scale Objects   2-20
4   Modify a Polygon Object   2-32
5   Work with Segments   2-38
6   Apply Modifiers   2-42
7   Clone Objects   2-52
8   Link and Group Objects   2-60
9   Work with Pivot Points   2-68
10   Use Snapping Tools   2-76
11   Align Objects   2-84

Chapter 3   Modeling
Lesson 1   Understand Editable Polygons   3-4
2   Apply Modifiers to Subobjects   3-18
3   Understand Normals   3-24
4   Chamfer, Extrude, and Bevel Objects   3-30
5   Use Paint Deformation and Soft Selection   3-44
6   Create and Connect Vertices, Edges, and Polygons   3-56
7   Model Efficiently   3-72
8   Model a Character   3-82
9   Understand Splines   3-92
10   Edit Splines   3-102
11   Model with Splines   3-112

Chapter 4   Materials and Maps
Lesson 1   Understand Materials   4-4
2   Apply Materials   4-10
3   Edit Materials   4-20
4   Understand and Assign Maps   4-30
5   Navigate Materials and Maps   4-40
6   Map Basic Shader Components   4-46
7   Map Other Standard Material Components   4-58

Chapter 5   Cameras and Lighting
Lesson 1   Add Cameras to a Scene   5-4
2   Position Cameras   5-12
3   Add Lights to a Scene   5-20
4   Adjust Light Parameters   5-30
5   Work with Shadows   5-44
6   Use Lights   5-48

Chapter 6   Animation
Lesson 1   Animate with Auto Key   6-4
2   Animate with Set Key   6-18
3   Configure Animation Timing   6-22
4   Edit Keys   6-32
5   Use the Dope Sheet   6-38
6   Use the Curve Editor   6-42
7   Assign Animation Controllers   6-52
8   Assign Animation Constraints   6-60

Chapter 7   Rendering
Lesson 1   What Is Rendering?   7-4
2   Render with ActiveShade   7-8
3   Understanding File Output   7-14
4   Create and Save Renderings   7-18
5   Use the Print Size Wizard   7-30

Chapter 8   Bones and Inverse Kinematics
Lesson 1   Create Bones   8-4
2   Create Bones within a Character Mesh   8-10
3   Edit Bones   8-16
4   Apply Inverse Kinematics   8-26
5   Use Skin   8-38
6   Animate Bones   8-48

Chapter 9   Particle Systems
Lesson 1   Work with Particle Systems   9-4
2   Use Space Warps   9-16
3   Create Materials for Particles   9-26
4   Work with Particle Flow   9-32
5   Use Material Operators   9-52

Chapter 10   Effects
Lesson 1   Add Atmospheric Effects   10-4
2   Adjust Atmospheric Effect Parameters   10-12
3   Understand Rendering Effects   10-22
4   Apply Lens Effects   10-26
5   Apply Depth-of-Field and Blur Effects   10-34
6   Apply Hair and Fur   10-46

Glossary   1
Index   9

ix

CHAPTER 1: INTRODUCING AUTODESK 3DS MAX 8

LESSON 1
Explore the Interface 1-4
Starting 3ds Max and Exploring
the Menus 1-4
Exploring the Main Toolbar
and the reactor Toolbar 1-7
Exploring the Viewports 1-7
Exploring the Command Panel 1-8
Exploring the Track Bar Timeline 1-10
Tasks Start 3ds Max and save a file 1-11
       Resize a viewport, create a new scene, and
       reset 3ds Max 1-12

LESSON 2
Work with Viewports 1-14
What Are Viewports? 1-14
Changing Viewports 1-14
Using the Viewport Controls
to Adjust a View 1-16
Using Axonometric Viewport Controls 1-16
Using Perspective Viewport Controls 1-17
Changing Display Options 1-17
Working with Grids 1-18
Tasks Change viewports 1-20
       Use viewport controls 1-21
       Change display options 1-22
       Work with grids 1-23

LESSON 3
Work with the Main Toolbar 1-24
Exploring and Positioning
the Main Toolbar 1-24
Tasks Explore and position
       the Main toolbar 1-26

LESSON 4
Explore the Command Panel 1-28
Understanding the Sections of the
Command Panel 1-28
Create Panel 1-28
Modify Panel 1-28
Hierarchy Panel 1-30
Motion Panel 1-31
Display Panel 1-31
Utilities Panel 1-31

LESSON 5
Work with the Track Bar 1-32
What Is a Track Bar? 1-32
Using the Time Slider
and Time Controls 1-32
Task Use the time slider and time controls to
      navigate an animation 1-34

LESSON 6
Customize the 3ds Max Interface 1-36
Hiding Toolbars and Panels 1-36
Switching to a Preset Custom UI 1-36
Restoring the Default User Interface 1-37
Tasks Hide toolbars and panels 1-38
       Switch to a Custom UI 1-38
       Restore the default user interface 1-38

LESSON 7
**Use the Help Menu
and the Hotkey Map** 1-40
Task Use Help and the Hotkey Map 1-42

CHAPTER 2 — BUILDING AND MODIFYING OBJECTS

LESSON 1
Create Standard Primitives 2-4
Creating Planes and Spheres 2-4
Creating Boxes, Cylinders, and Pyramids 2-6
Creating Cones, Tubes, and Toruses 2-6
Creating a Teapot 2-7
Using the Creation Method Rollout 2-8
Tasks Create a sphere and a box 2-9
  Create a tube 2-10
  Create a teapot from edge to edge 2-11

LESSON 2
Select Objects 2-12
Using the Select Object Tool 2-12
Selecting by Name 2-13
Creating Selection Sets 2-14
Tasks Select multiple objects by clicking 2-16
  Select multiple objects using a selection region 2-17
  Select objects by name 2-18
  Create and use a selection set 2-19

LESSON 3
Move, Rotate, and Scale Objects 2-20
Understanding Axes and Transform Gizmos 2-20
Using the Move Tool 2-21
Using the Rotate Tool 2-22
Using the Scale Tool 2-23
Using Transform Type-In Boxes 2-25
Tasks Move an object 2-26
  Rotate an object 2-28
  Scale an object 2-29
  Use the Transform Type-In to transform an object 2-30

LESSON 4
Modify a Polygon Object 2-32
Renaming and Recoloring an Object 2-32
Changing the Parameters of an Object 2-32
Setting Smooth, Slice, and Hemisphere Parameters 2-33
Tasks Rename and recolor an object 2-35
  Modify the parameters of a box 2-35
  Modify the parameters of a sphere 2-36
  Modify the parameters of a cone 2-37

LESSON 5
Work with Segments 2-38
Understanding Segments 2-38
Adjusting the Segments on an Object 2-38
Tasks Adjust the segments on an object 2-40
  Adjust the sides on an object 2-41

LESSON 6
Apply Modifiers 2-42
Understanding the Modifier Stack 2-42
Working with the Modifier Stack 2-44
Applying Modifiers to Multiple Objects 2-45
Tasks Apply modifiers to an object 2-47
  Work with the modifier stack 2-48
  Copy a modifier to another object 2-50
  Apply modifiers to a group of objects 2-51

LESSON 7
Clone Objects 2-52
Cloning an Object 2-52
Creating a Transformational Clone 2-53
Creating an Array 2-53
Tasks Clone an object 2-56
  Create a transformational clone 2-57
  Create an array 2-58

LESSON 8
Link and Group Objects 2-60
Linking Objects 2-60
Grouping Objects 2-62
Tasks Link and unlink objects 2-64
  Create a link hierarchy 2-65
  Group and ungroup objects 2-66
  Create and explode a nested group 2-67

LESSON 9
Work with Pivot Points 2-68
Understanding Pivot Points 2-68
Repositioning a Pivot Point in Relation to Its Object 2-68
Repositioning an Object in Relation to Its Pivot Point 2-70
Using the Affect Hierarchy Only Button 2-71
Tasks Reposition an object's pivot point 2-72
  Reorient an object in relation to its pivot point 2-73
  Rotate the links between objects in a hierarchy 2-74

LESSON 10
Use Snapping Tools 2-76
Using 3D Snap 2-76
Using Angle Snap 2-78
Using Percent Snap 2-78
Using Spinner Snap 2-79
Tasks Use 3D Snap to create and position an object 2-80
  Use Angle Snap to rotate an object 2-81
  Use Percent Snap to scale an object 2-82
  Use Spinner Snap to change an object's parameters 2-83

LESSON 11
Align Objects 2-84
Aligning Objects with the Align Tool 2-84
Using the Quick Align Tool 2-85
Using the Clone and Align tool 2-86
Tasks Align objects by position 2-88
  Align objects by orientation and scale 2-89
  Use the Quick Align tool 2-90
  Clone and align objects 2-91

CHAPTER 3: MODELING

LESSON 1
Understand Editable Polygons 3-4
Understanding Editable Polygons 3-4
Converting an Object into an Editable Poly 3-4
Accessing Subobject Levels 3-6
Selecting Editable Poly Subobjects 3-7
Using Other Options in the Selection Rollout 3-9
Tasks Convert primitives into editable polys 3-10
    Review subobject levels 3-11
    Select single and multiple editable poly subobjects 3-12
    Select multiple subobjects 3-14
    Grow and shrink a selection area 3-15
    Transform subobjects 3-16

LESSON 2
Apply Modifiers to Subobjects 3-18
Applying Modifiers to Editable Poly Subobjects 3-18
Using the Mesh Select Modifier 3-19
Tasks Apply and adjust subobject modifiers 3-21
    Use the Mesh Select modifier 3-22

LESSON 3
Understand Normals 3-24
Understanding Normals 3-24
Flipping Normals 3-25
Tasks View normals 3-27
    Flip normals 3-29

LESSON 4
Chamfer, Extrude, and Bevel Objects 3-30
Chamfering an Object 3-30
Extruding an Object 3-33
Beveling an Object 3-36
Tasks Chamfer a vertex and two edges 3-37
    Chamfer a border 3-38
    Extrude polygons 3-39
    Extrude vertices and edges 3-40
    Bevel polygons 3-42

LESSON 5
Use Paint Deformation and Soft Selection 3-44
Using Paint Deformation 3-44
Deforming an Object Using Soft Selection 3-47
Tasks Push and pull vertices 3-50
    Relax pulled vertices 3-51
    Use soft selection when moving a vertex 3-52
    Paint soft selection 3-54

LESSON 6
Create and Connect Vertices, Edges, and Polygons 3-56
Creating New Vertices, Edges, and Polygons 3-56
Connecting Vertices and Edges 3-57
Welding Vertices 3-58
Slicing and Cutting Polygons 3-59
Bridging Borders and Polygons 3-61
Tasks Create a vertex, edge, and polygon 3-64
    Connect vertices and edges 3-66
    Weld vertices 3-67
    Slice and cut an object 3-68
    Bridge borders and polygons 3-70

LESSON 7
Model Efficiently 3-72
Applying the MeshSmooth Modifier 3-72
Modeling with a Reference 3-73
Applying the Symmetry Modifier 3-74
Using XRef Objects 3-75
Tasks Apply the MeshSmooth modifier 3-77
    Model using a reference 3-78
    Apply the Symmetry modifier 3-79
    Add an XRef object to a scene 3-80

LESSON 8
Model a Character 3-82
Modeling a Character 3-82
Tasks Create character torso 3-84
    Create arms and hands 3-86
    Create fingers 3-88
    Add finishing touches 3-91

LESSON 9
Understand Splines 3-92
Creating Paths 3-93
Creating Shapes 3-94
Using the Creation Method Rollout 3-96
Tasks Create a line, arc, and helix 3-98
    Create a rectangle, donut, and NGon 3-99
    Create a text spline 3-100
    Create a line with smooth vertices 3-101

LESSON 10
Edit Splines 3-102
Modifying Spline Parameters 3-102
Converting a Spline into an Editable Spline 3-104
Converting Vertices, Segments, and Splines 3-105
Inserting Vertices 3-107
Tasks Modify parameters of an arc and star 3-108
    Convert splines to editable splines 3-109
    Convert vertices and segments 3-109
    Insert vertices 3-111

LESSON 11
Model with Splines 3-112
Extruding Splines 3-112
Applying the Lathe Modifier 3-113
Creating Loft Objects 3-114
Deforming Loft Objects 3-116
Tasks Extrude splines 3-118
    Apply the Lathe modifier to a spline 3-119
    Create a loft object 3-121
    Deform a loft object 3-122

CHAPTER 4: MATERIALS AND MAPS

LESSON 1
Understand Materials 4-4
Understanding Materials 4-4
Understanding Material Types 4-6
Understanding Shaders 4-7
Understanding Rendering 4-8
Task   Render a scene 4-9

LESSON 2
Apply Materials 4-10
Using the Material Editor 4-10
Viewing Materials in Sample Slots 4-10
Applying Material to a Sample Slot 4-11
Applying Material to an Object 4-13
Tasks   View materials in sample slots 4-15
Apply material to sample slots 4-16
Apply material to objects in a scene 4-18

LESSON 3
Edit Materials 4-20
Editing Basic Shader Parameters 4-20
Editing Material Color 4-21
Editing the Specular Level of a Material 4-23
Editing the Self-Illumination
and Opacity of a Material 4-24
Tasks   Edit basic shader parameters 4-25
Edit material color 4-26
Edit specular level and glossiness
of a material 4-27
Edit self-illumination and opacity 4-28

LESSON 4
Understand and Assign Maps 4-30
Understanding Maps 4-30
Assigning Maps to Material Components 4-31
Deactivating or Removing a Map 4-34

Instancing, Copying, and Swapping
a Map 4-34
Tasks   Assign maps to material components 4-35
Deactivate and remove a map 4-37
Copy maps between components 4-38

LESSON 5
Navigate Materials and Maps 4-40
Navigating with the Material/Map
Navigator 4-40
Navigating Within the Material Editor 4-41
Tasks   Navigate with the Material/Maps
Navigator 4-43
Navigate with the Material Editor 4-45

LESSON 6
Map Basic Shader Components 4-46
Mapping Color Components of Standard
Material 4-46
Mapping Specular Highlight Components 4-47
Mapping Self-Illumination and Opacity 4-48
Editing Map Parameters 4-48
Tasks   Map diffuse color 4-50
Map specular highlight components 4-52
Map self-illumination and opacity 4-54
Edit map parameters 4-55
Assign a map to another map 4-57

LESSON 7
**Map Other Standard
Material Components** 4-58
Understanding Map Reflection 4-58
Understanding Map Refraction 4-59

Understanding Map Bumpiness 4-60
Mapping the Filter Color 4-61
Tasks   Map reflection 4-62
Map refraction 4-64
Map bumpiness 4-65
Map filter color 4-66

CHAPTER 5: CAMERAS AND LIGHTING

LESSON 1
Add Cameras to a Scene 5-4
Understanding Cameras 5-4
Creating Cameras 5-5
Adjusting Camera Parameters 5-7
Tasks Create cameras in a scene 5-9
        Adjust camera parameters 5-10

LESSON 2
Position Cameras 5-12
Changing a Viewport
into a Camera Viewport 5-12
Positioning a Camera 5-12
Using Safe Frames 5-15
Tasks Change viewports into
        Camera viewports 5-16
        Position cameras 5-17
        Use Safe Frames 5-19

LESSON 3
Add Lights to a Scene 5-20
Exploring Standard Light Types 5-20
Adding Lights to a Scene 5-21
Tasks Insert spotlights 5-25
        Insert a directional light 5-27
        Insert an omni light 5-28

LESSON 4
Adjust Light Parameters 5-30
Changing Light Intensity and Color 5-30
Adjusting Cone and Cylinder Parameters 5-31
Using Decay and Attenuation 5-33
Instancing Lights 5-35
Tasks Change light intensity 5-36
        Adjust hotspot and falloff 5-37
        Use Overshoot to light a scene 5-38
        Use attenuation 5-39
        Use decay 5-41
        Instance lights 5-42

LESSON 5
Work with Shadows 5-44
Modifying Shadow Parameters 5-44
Mapping a Shadow 5-45
Tasks Modify shadow parameters 5-46
        Map a shadow 5-47

LESSON 6
Use Lights 5-48
Controlling How Light Affects Surfaces 5-48
Projecting a Map with a Light 5-49
Tasks Control how light affects surfaces 5-52
        Project a map with a light 5-54

CHAPTER 6 ANIMATION

LESSON 1
Animate with Auto Key 6-4
Understanding Animation 6-4
Setting Keyframes with Auto Key 6-5
Displaying Trajectories 6-6
Playing an Animation 6-7
What Can Be Animated? 6-7
Tasks Set keyframes with Auto Key 6-8
　　　　Animate cameras 6-10
　　　　Animate modifiers 6-11
　　　　Animate materials 6-13
　　　　Animate creation parameters 6-14
　　　　Animate lights 6-16

LESSON 2
Animate with Set Key 6-18
Setting Keyframes with Set Key 6-18
Filtering Keys 6-19
Tasks Filter keys 6-20
　　　　Set keyframes with Set Key 6-20

LESSON 3
Configure Animation Timing 6-22
Setting the Frame Rate 6-22
Setting the Active Time Segment 6-22
Re-scaling Time 6-24
Changing the Time Display 6-24
Editing Playback Properties 6-25
Tasks Set the frame rate 6-26
　　　　Set the active time segment 6-27
　　　　Re-scale time 6-28
　　　　Change the time display 6-29
　　　　Edit playback properties 6-30

LESSON 4
Edit Keys 6-32
Selecting and Moving Keys 6-32
Cloning and Deleting Keys 6-33
Editing Key Properties 6-34
Tasks Select and move keys 6-35
　　　　Clone and delete keys 6-36
　　　　Edit key properties 6-37

LESSON 5
Use the Dope Sheet 6-38
Understanding the Dope Sheet 6-38
Adjusting Keys 6-38
Tasks Adjust a key in the Dope Sheet 6-40
　　　　Adjust parent keys and their children 6-41

LESSON 6
Use the Curve Editor 6-42
Understanding the Curve Editor 6-42
Understanding Tangent Types 6-43
Changing Tangent Types 6-44
Adjusting Key Timing and Values 6-45
Adding Keys 6-46
Tasks Examine keys in the Curve Editor 6-47
　　　　Adjust timing and values 6-49
　　　　Adjust In and Out tangents 6-50
　　　　Add and move a key 6-51

LESSON 7
Assign Animation Controllers 6-52
Understanding Animation Controllers 6-52
Assigning Animation Controllers 6-53
Tasks Create an animation loop 6-55
　　　　Assign a controller using the Motion panel 6-57
　　　　Assign a controller using the Curve Editor 6-58

LESSON 8
Assign Animation Constraints 6-60
Understanding Constraints 6-60
Assigning a Constraint 6-61
Using a List Controller 6-62
Tasks Assign the LookAt constraint 6-64
　　　　Assign the Path constraint 6-66
　　　　Adjust path options 6-67
　　　　Use a List controller 6-68

CHAPTER 7 RENDERING

LESSON 1
What Is Rendering? 7-4
What Is Rendering? 7-4
Understanding Renderers 7-6

LESSON 2
Render with ActiveShade 7-8
Understanding ActiveShade Rendering 7-8
Initializing the ActiveShade Window 7-10
Tasks Use ActiveShade rendering 7-11
Initialize ActiveShade rendering 7-12
Update a region of the ActiveShade viewport 7-13

LESSON 3
Understanding File Output 7-14
Understanding File Formats 7-14
Choosing a Video Codec 7-14
Determining Image Resolution 7-17

LESSON 4
Create and Save Renderings 7-18
Using the Render Scene Dialog Box 7-18
Adjusting Common Parameters 7-19
Adjusting Output Size 7-21
Designating Render Output 7-22
Rendering a Scene 7-22
Rendering an Image File Sequence 7-23
Tasks Adjust output options 7-25
Designate an output file type 7-26
Render an image file sequence 7-28

LESSON 5
Use the Print Size Wizard 7-30
Understanding Image Resolution and DPI 7-30
Paper Size Settings 7-30
Rendering the Image 7-32
Task Render with the Print Size Wizard 7-33

CHAPTER 8: BONES AND INVERSE KINEMATICS

LESSON 1
Create Bones 8-4
Understanding Bones 8-4
Creating Bones with the Create Panel 8-4
Moving and Rotating Bones 8-6
Tasks Create bones with the Create panel 8-7
Move and rotate bones 8-8

LESSON 2
Create Bones within a Character Mesh 8-10
Working with the Dragonbird Character 8-10
Making the Mesh See-Through 8-10
Freezing and Unfreezing the Mesh 8-11
Creating Bones Using
the Bone Tools Floater 8-12
Changing the Names of Bones 8-12
Tasks Make the mesh see-through
and freeze it 8-13
Create bones with the Bone
Tools floater 8-14
Change the names of bones 8-15

LESSON 3
Edit Bones 8-16
Why Edit Bones? 8-16
Repositioning Pivot Points 8-17
Changing a Bone's Size and Shape 8-17
Adding and Editing Fins 8-18
Tasks Reposition pivot points 8-20
Change a bone's size and shape 8-21
Add and edit fins 8-22
Complete a skeletal rig 8-24

LESSON 4
Apply Inverse Kinematics 8-26
Understanding Inverse Kinematics (IK)
Chains 8-26
Applying IK to Bones 8-26
Using the SplineIK Solver 8-28

Creating and Linking Dummy Objects 8-28
Tasks Rotate the wings using
forward kinematics 8-30
Apply an IK solver to bones 8-30
Create a spline 8-31
Use the SplineIK Solver 8-33
Create and link dummy objects 8-34
Create and link a master control 8-36

LESSON 5
Use Skin 8-38
Understanding Skinning 8-38
Working with Envelopes 8-39
Testing the Deformation 8-40
Weighting Vertices Manually 8-40
Tasks Apply the Skin modifier 8-42
Test the skin deformation 8-43
Adjust skin envelopes 8-44
Adjust vertex weight manually 8-46

LESSON 6
Animate Bones 8-48
Animating the Dragonbird 8-48
Looping Animation 8-49
Secondary Motion 8-49
Tasks Animate the wings 8-50
Add secondary motion to the wings 8-52
Create a loop cycle 8-53
Animate position and rotation 8-54
Complete the animation 8-56

CHAPTER 9: PARTICLE SYSTEMS

LESSON 1
Work with Particle Systems 9-4
What Is a Particle System? 9-4
Creating a Non-Event-Driven
Particle System 9-5
Adjust Spray and Snow Parameters 9-7
Adjust Super Spray, Blizzard, PArray, and
PCloud Parameters 9-9
Tasks Create a non-event-driven
           particle system 9-11
           Adjust Spray parameters 9-11
           Create a Super Spray and adjust
           basic parameters 9-13
           Adjust particle generation parameters 9-14

LESSON 2
Use Space Warps 9-16
Understanding Space Warps 9-16
Creating and Modifying Space Warps 9-16
Tasks Create a Blizzard particle system 9-19
           Adjust the Blizzard parameters 9-20
           Create and modify a Gravity
           space warp 9-22
           Create and modify a spherical
           deflector 9-23
           Create and modify a planar deflector 9-25

LESSON 3
Create Materials for Particles 9-26
Building a Material to Apply to Particles 9-26
Applying a Material to Particles 9-26
Tasks Change the particle type 9-28
           Build and apply a material to particles 9-29

LESSON 4
Work with Particle Flow 9-32
What Is Particle Flow? 9-32
Creating a Particle Flow System 9-32
Understand and Use Particle View 9-34
Add and Define Operators and Tests 9-35
Wiring Events Together 9-36
Splitting Particles Between Events 9-37
Tasks Create a Particle Flow 9-38
           Define the Birth operator 9-39
           Define the Position operator 9-40
           Define the Speed and Rotation
           operators 9-41
           Define the Shape operator 9-42
           Add and define the Find Target test 9-43
           Wire events together 9-44
           Split particles between events 9-46
           Apply space warps to
           event-driven particles 9-48
           Define a Scale operator 9-49

LESSON 5
Use Material Operators 9-52
Understanding Material Operators 9-52
Assigning the Particle Age Map 9-52
Tasks Add and define a Material
           Static operator 9-54
           Setting up particles for material 9-55
           Assign a Particle Age
           map to a material 9-57
           Assign maps to the Particle Age map 9-57
           Add and define the
           Material Dynamic operator 9-59
           Create and assign the Smoke
           material 9-60

CHAPTER 10 EFFECTS

LESSON 1
Add Atmospheric Effects 10-4
Understanding Atmospheric Effects 10-4
Creating an Atmospheric Apparatus 10-5
Adding an Effect to an Object 10-6
Tasks Create an atmospheric apparatus 10-7
 Add a fire effect 10-9
 Add a volume light 10-10

LESSON 2
Adjust Atmospheric Effect Parameters 10-12
Locating an Effect's Parameters 10-12
Adjusting Fire Effect Parameters 10-12
Adjusting Volume Light Parameters 10-14
Adjusting Fog and Volume
Fog Parameters 10-15
Tasks Adjust fire parameters 10-17
 Adjust volume light parameters 10-19
 Add layered fog and adjust
 its parameters 10-20

LESSON 3
Understand Rendering Effects 10-22
What Are Rendering Effects? 10-22
Adding a Rendering Effect 10-23
Previewing Effects Interactively 10-24

LESSON 4
Apply Lens Effects 10-26
Understanding Lens Effects 10-26
Applying Lens Effect
Elements to Objects 10-28
Tasks Add a Glow effect 10-30
 Preview effects interactively 10-31
 Add a Star effect 10-32

LESSON 5
Apply Depth-of-Field and Blur Effects 10-34
Understanding Multi-Pass Rendering 10-34
Generating Depth-of-Field Effects 10-35
Understanding Motion Blur 10-37
Generating Motion Blur Effects 10-37
Tasks Use multi-pass rendering effects 10-40
 Render Object Motion Blur 10-42
 Render Image Motion Blur 10-44

LESSON 6
Apply Hair and Fur 10-46
Creating Hair and Fur 10-46
Adjusting Hair Parameters 10-48
Styling Hair 10-49
Cutting Hair 10-51
Rendering Hair 10-52
Tasks Apply the Hair and Fur modifier 10-53
 Adjust the hair parameters 10-54
 Style the hair 10-55
 Scale the hair 10-56
 Cut the hair 10-57

Glossary 1
Index 9

Intended Audience

This text is designed for the beginner or intermediate user who wants to learn how to use 3ds Max 8. The book is designed to provide basic and in-depth material that not only educates, but also encourages you to explore the nuances of this exciting program.

Approach

The text allows you to work at your own pace through step-by-step tutorials. A concept is presented and the process is explained, followed by the actual steps. To learn the most from the use of the text, you should adopt the following habits:

- Proceed slowly: Accuracy and comprehension are more important than speed.
- Understand what is happening with each step before you continue to the next step.
- After finishing a skill, ask yourself if you could do it on your own, without referring to the steps. If the answer is no, review the steps.

Icons, Buttons, and Pointers

Symbols for icons, buttons, and pointers are shown in the step each time they are used.

Data Files

To complete some of the lessons in this book, you need to obtain the necessary Data Files. You can download the Data Files for the steps at the following URL: *www.courseptr.com/downloads*. Once you have downloaded the files, select where to store them, such as the hard drive, a network server, or a USB storage device. The instructions in the lessons will refer to "the drive and folder where your Data Files are stored" when referring to the Data Files for the book.

Map and Texture Files

This book also uses map and texture files from 3ds Max. Depending on your version of the software, you might not have the Bitmap or JPG file suggested in the book. If this is the case, simply choose another file. Keep in mind that if you do, your screen won't match the figures in the book exactly.

Bonus Online Material

This book also includes bonus online material that you can access at *www.courseptr.com/downloads* or *www.course.com/revealed*. Online material includes a bibliography of books that will help you delve deeper into an understanding of things like lighting a scene or working with particles. Also included is a 3ds MaxScript Appendix, which provides an introduction to working with the 3ds Max scripting language.

chapter 1

INTRODUCING
AUTODESK 3DS MAX 8

1. Explore the interface.

2. Work with viewports.

3. Work with the Main toolbar.

4. Explore the Command panel.

5. Work with the track bar.

6. Customize the 3ds Max interface.

7. Use the Help menu and the Hotkey Map.

chapter 1
INTRODUCING 3DS MAX 8

Autodesk 3d Studio Max (3ds Max) is one of the world's leading three-dimensional (3D) modeling, rendering, and animation software packages. 3ds Max has many different uses. For example, you can think of it as a full movie studio at your fingertips, where you can use it for animation and visual effects for film or television. You can also use 3ds Max to develop video games. For architects and mechanical engineers, it provides the tools to render an architectural design for visualization, or to help a customer succeed at even the most complex mechanical assembly.

QUICKTIP

You can learn more about Autodesk and see examples of the work of some experienced 3ds Max users by going to the Autodesk 3ds Max Web site at *www4.discreet.com/3dsmax* and clicking Showcase.

3ds Max combines a visual effects engine with animation tools, letting you design 3D models using textures and lights, and then animate and render your models in scenes. It is a sophisticated piece of software that requires some dedication for you to become proficient. In fact, at first, the software might seem overwhelming, but if you take the time to explore and experiment, you will find it is quite rewarding to overcome the challenge.

Tools You'll Use

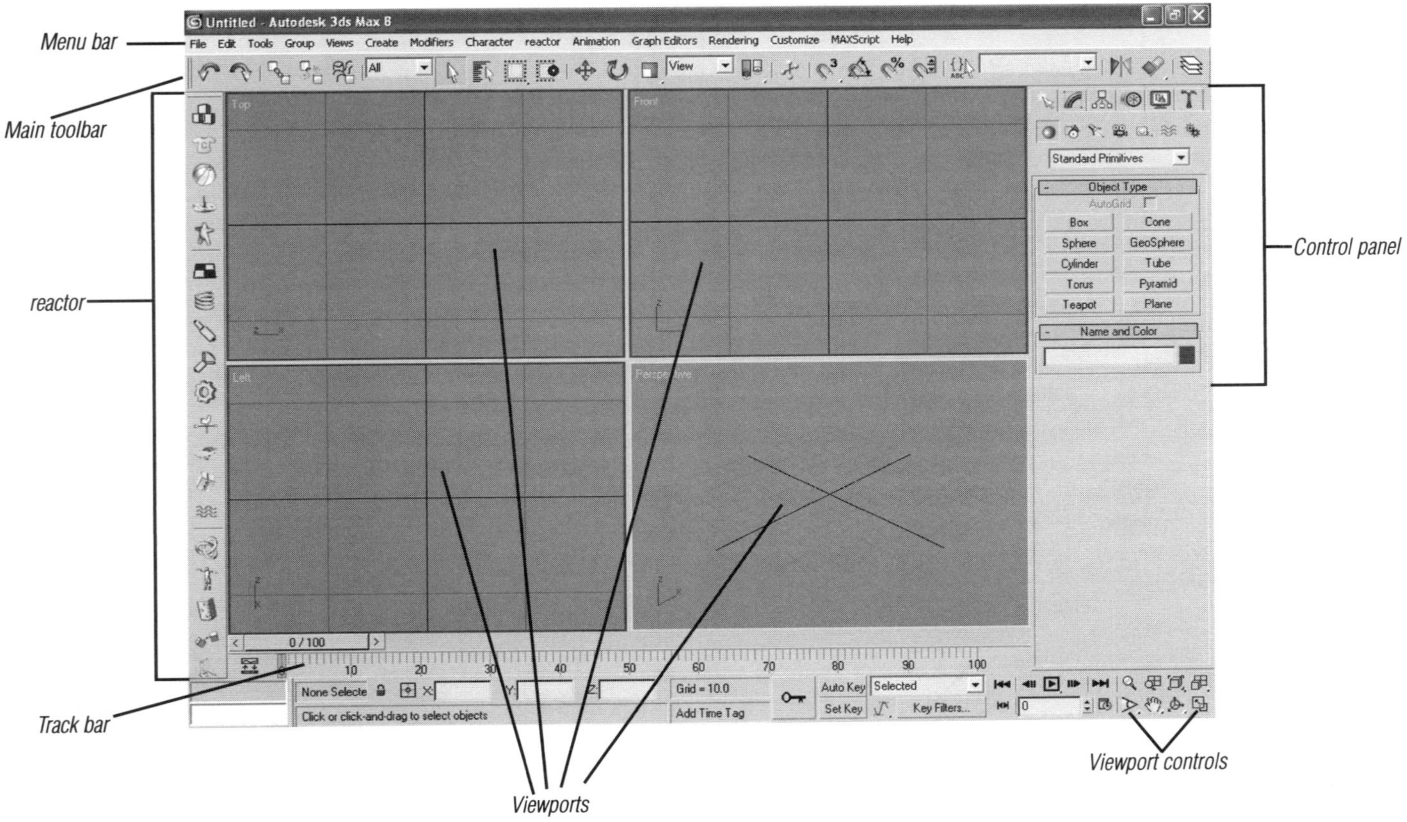

LESSON 1

EXPLORE THE INTERFACE

What You'll Do

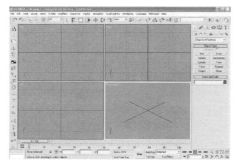

In this lesson, you will explore many of the elements of the 3ds Max interface, including its viewports, menu bar, toolbars, and the Command panel.

Starting 3ds Max and Exploring the Menus

Because of its many elements, the 3ds Max interface can be a bit confusing at first glance. However, if you understand the basic layout, you'll soon see that the program has a very efficient design. As shown in Figure 1, when you first start 3ds Max, it opens with four viewports displayed: Top, Front, Perspective, and Left.

Viewports let you look at a scene from different angles and dimensions. They are an important part of the 3ds Max interface, and will be discussed in detail throughout this book.

3ds Max displays its menu bar along the top of the program window. Each command on this menu opens another menu or lets you perform a task. One of the most important tasks you can perform is to save your work. The Save command can be found on the File menu, shown in Figure 2. From the File menu, you can also choose to Reset the program so that

the 3ds Max interface is laid out the way it was the first time you used the program. When you have finished working with a file, the Reset command closes whatever you were working on and refreshes the program window by reverting to the default display settings. The Reset dialog box is shown in Figure 3.

It is important to note that the New command on the File menu has a different function than the Reset command. The Reset command returns everything to the default settings and opens a new, blank file. The New command gives you three options in the New Scene dialog box shown in Figure 4:

- **Keep Objects and Hierarchy** creates a new file with all of the objects and relationships (or hierarchy) in the current file preserved. Hierarchy is discussed in chapter 2, and later in this book.
- **Keep Objects** creates a new file using the existing objects, but does not retain their hierarchy.

- **New All** creates a new, blank file, much like the Reset command does. However, it does not return 3ds Max to its default interface settings. For example, if you have resized the viewports or moved the Command panel, those settings stay the same when you create the new file.

The File menu also includes the Save As command, which lets you save your changes to a file with a new name. You will save files frequently as you progress through the exercises in this book. As you use 3ds Max, you will often spend hours working on a scene. As you progress, you'll want to save as many versions as you can with different names so you don't put all of your eggs in one basket. For example, if the file is corrupted or

FIGURE 1
3d studio Max interface

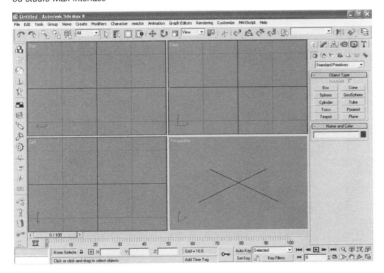

FIGURE 2
File menu

FIGURE 3
Reset dialog box

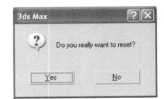

FIGURE 4
New Scene dialog box

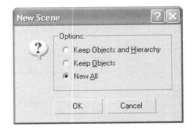

Lesson 1 Explore the Interface

damaged in any way, saving multiple versions allows you to revert to an earlier version. Even if a file has not been corrupted, there's a chance you'll make too many changes for the Undo feature to record. Reverting to the previous version of the file would then be a good option. In the Save File As dialog box shown in Figure 5, you'll notice a plus sign (+) to the right of the File name text box. Clicking this button after you type a file name results in the original file being saved as *filename*01, with subsequent files saved as *filename*02, *filename*03, *filename*04, and so on.

You can open a file in 3ds Max by choosing Open on the File menu, navigating to the drive and directory where your 3ds Max files are stored, and then clicking Open. (By default, 3ds Max stores files in a directory called Scenes.) To open a file with which you have recently worked, you click File, click Open Recent, and then choose from the list of recently opened files.

FIGURE 5
Save File As dialog box

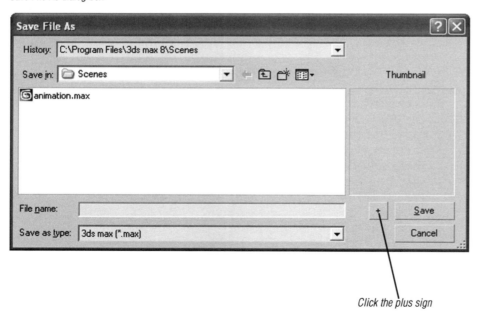

Click the plus sign

Exploring the Main Toolbar and the reactor Toolbar

The Main toolbar, shown in Figure 6, appears under the menu bar. These tools provide shortcuts for certain commands and tasks. Notice the Undo and Redo tools on the left. You have probably used similar tools in another application. The Undo tool lets you undo changes you have made to a file, and the Redo tool redoes a task you have undone. The Main toolbar is also home to the Select and Move tool (which allows you to both select and move objects), the Select and Rotate tool (which allows you to both select and rotate objects), and the Select and Uniform Scale tool (which allows you to both select and resize objects).

On the left side of the 3ds Max window, you will find the **reactor** toolbar, shown in Figure 7. The 3ds Max reactor has tools for simulating physical forces inside 3ds Max scenes. It includes powerful tools that let you simulate things such as collisions, gravity, wind, and more in your animations.

QUICKTIP

You can set the number of Undo levels on the General tab of the Preference Settings dialog box. To open this dialog box, select Preferences from the Customize menu.

Exploring the Viewports

In the center of the program window are four windows called "viewports." The viewports are a major feature of 3ds Max because they allow you to see what you are creating from many different angles and

FIGURE 7
reactor toolbar

FIGURE 6
Main toolbar

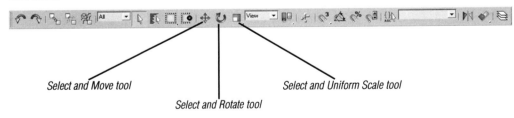

Select and Move tool
Select and Rotate tool
Select and Uniform Scale tool

Lesson 1 Explore the Interface

AUTODESK 3D STUDIO MAX 1-7

perspectives. As shown in Figure 8, each viewport includes a **grid**, which helps you align and place objects in your scene. Each viewport also displays a label in the upper-left corner. Depending on how you work, you can choose to display all viewports, or just selected viewports. You can resize a viewport by dragging its border to make it larger or smaller. You can also click and drag the center of your screen (where all four viewports meet) to resize viewports. To change them back to their default size or arrangement, right-click in the center of all the viewports, and choose Reset Layout.

QUICKTIP
You can also display the Asset Browser in a viewport pane, which lets you access files on your computer and on the Web.

Exploring the Command Panel
On the right side of the screen is the Command panel, shown in Figure 9.

The Command panel provides the tools that let you create, edit, and modify your scene. By default, 3ds Max opens with the Command panel for Standard Primitives displayed. **Standard primitives** are some of the basic geometric shapes you will use as you design your scenes. You will learn more about standard primitives in Chapter 2.

You can expand the Command panel by clicking the border of the Command panel where it meets the viewports and dragging

FIGURE 8
3ds Max viewports with grids displayed

FIGURE 9
Command panel with Standard Primitives displayed

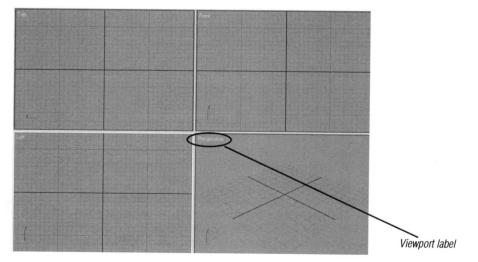

to the left. This is useful if you are working on something in the panel and you cannot see a specific parameter. By expanding the panel, you can view all of the parameters. You can also right-click the top of the Command panel and select Float to put the Command panel in its own resizable and movable window, called a **floating palette**, as shown in Figure 10. Finally, you can dock the Command panel on either side of the window by right-clicking and choosing Dock, and then selecting Right or Left. Figure 11 shows the Command panel docked on the left.

QUICKTIP

If you cannot return 3ds Max to its default configuration by docking and moving toolbars, click Customize on the menu bar, click Revert to Startup Layout, and then click Yes.

FIGURE 10
Floating Command panel

FIGURE 11
Command panel docked on the left

Lesson 1 Explore the Interface

AUTODESK 3D STUDIO MAX 1-9

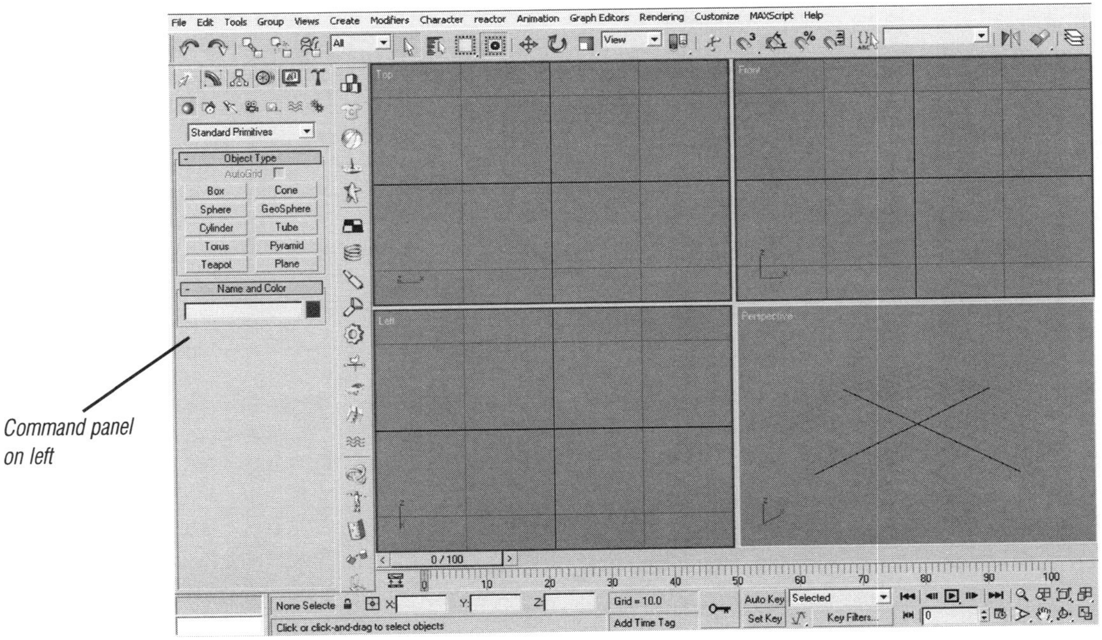

Exploring the Track Bar Timeline

On the bottom of the 3ds Max window, you see the track bar, also called the timeline, shown in Figure 12. By default, the **track bar** displays the frames in a scene, from 1 to 100. Each **frame** shows the scene at a different point in time. Notice the VCR-like controls to the right of the track bar timeline. These controls let you navigate from one frame to the next. You can always tell what frame of the animation you are viewing by looking at the **time slider**. The time slider displays two numbers: The number on the left is the number of the frame currently displayed in the viewports. The number on the right represents the total number of frames in your animation.

If you have only a static object in your scene, nothing happens when you run your animation using the VCR controls, but if your object changes or moves over the course of the animation, each frame is different in order to show the motion or the change. The track bar and its timeline are discussed further in Lesson 5, "Work with the Track Bar." Animation, keys, and keyframes will be explained in more depth in Chapter 6, "Animation."

QUICKTIP
Much of the 3ds max interface can be completely customized to suit your needs, using commands on the Customize menu. You can move menus, add or remove features, change the colors of interface elements, or even remove interface elements. Unless the steps in this book direct you to do otherwise, you should not make modifications to the interface or your screen will not match the figures in this book.

FIGURE 12
3ds Max track bar and time slider

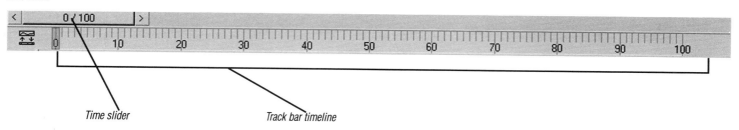

Time slider

Track bar timeline

1-10 AUTODESK 3D STUDIO MAX

Introducing 3ds Max 8

FIGURE 13
Save File As dialog box

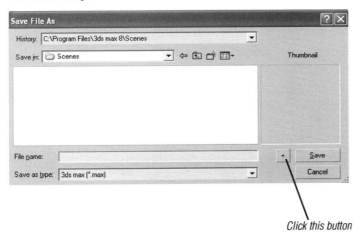

Click this button

FIGURE 14
File name displayed in 3ds Max title bar

File name

Start 3ds Max and save a file

1. Click **Start** on the taskbar, click **All Programs**, click **Autodesk**, click **3ds Max 8**, then click **3ds Max 8**.

   3ds Max starts and displays the default 3ds Max interface.

2. Click **File** on the menu bar, then click **Save**.

   The Save File As dialog box opens, as shown in Figure 13.

3. Navigate to the drive and directory where your Data Files are stored, type **myfile** in the File name text box, then click **+** (plus sign).

   3ds Max saves the file, adds an 01 to the file name, and displays the file name in the title bar, as shown in Figure 14.

4. Click **File** on the menu bar, then click **Save As**.

5. In the Save File As dialog box, click **+** (the plus sign).

   3ds Max saves the file as myfile02.max.

You started 3ds Max 8, and then saved a file using a feature that assigns consecutive numbers to different versions.

AUTODESK 3D STUDIO MAX 1-11

Lesson 1 Explore the Interface

Resize a viewport, create a new scene, and reset 3ds Max

1. Click in the Perspective viewport to activate it (if necessary).

   The active viewport in 3ds Max has a yellow border.

2. Point to the left border of the Perspective viewport until a two-headed arrow appears, then drag left.

   The Perspective viewport and the Front viewport take up more room in the interface, as shown in Figure 15.

3. Point to the upper-left corner of the Perspective viewport until you see a four-headed arrow, then drag up and left, as shown in Figure 16.

   The Perspective viewport fills most of the application window.

4. Click **Sphere** in the Command panel, then click and drag in the Perspective viewport to create a sphere.

   A sphere appears in the viewport.

5. Click **File** on the menu bar, click **Save**, click **File** on the menu bar again, then click **New**.

   The New Scene dialog box asks you if you want to keep objects and hierarchy, keep just the objects, or create a new scene with no objects.

   (continued)

FIGURE 15
Resized Perspective and Front viewports

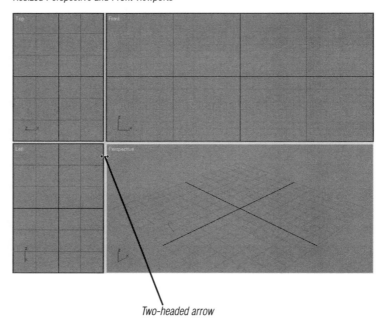

Two-headed arrow

1-12 AUTODESK 3D STUDIO MAX

Introducing 3ds Max 8

FIGURE 16
Resizing the Perspective viewport

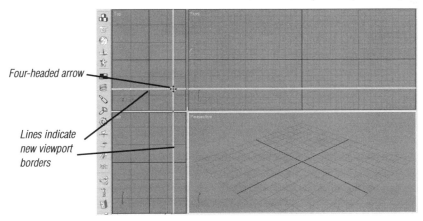

Four-headed arrow

Lines indicate new viewport borders

FIGURE 17
Resetting 3ds Max

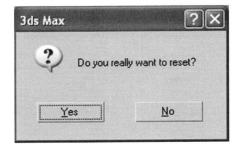

5. Click **Keep Objects**, then click **OK**.

   3ds Max opens a new untitled file containing the sphere you created, but does not change the interface settings. The Perspective viewport still fills the window.

6. Click **File,** click **Reset**, then click **No**.

   3ds Max asks if you're sure you want to reset the scene, as shown in Figure 17.

7. Click **Yes**.

   3ds Max refreshes the interface, and displays the viewports and the toolbars as they were when you first started the application. It also opens a new, untitled file.

You resized the viewports, created a new scene, and then reset the application to return it to its default settings and open a new file.

AUTODESK 3D STUDIO MAX 1-13

LESSON 2

WORK WITH VIEWPORTS

What You'll Do

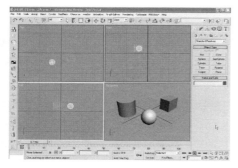

In this lesson, you will explore the different viewports in 3ds Max. You will also learn the difference between a perspective view and an axonometric or orthographic view.

What Are Viewports?

Viewports are essentially your windows to the 3D world. The viewports allow you to see your scene from many angles at one time to help you navigate 3D space. Each viewport has a label in the upper-left corner that tells you which view you are looking through.

There are two basic types of views in 3ds Max, as shown in Figure 18:

- A **perspective view** displays all three dimensions at once, resulting in a view that is not flat. Some examples of this kind of view are the Camera, Perspective, and Isometric User views.
- An **axonometric view** is a flat, two-dimensional (2D) view of your scene, displayed without perspective. A straight-on axonometric view of a scene, without any rotation, is called an **orthographic view**. Top, Bottom, Front, Back, Left, and Right are all orthographic views. When you are working in 3ds Max, you would typically use an orthographic view to create and place the objects in your scene, and then switch to a perspective view to see how the scene looks in three dimensions.

There are also two additional view types in 3ds Max: camera and light. You will work with these view types in Chapter 5, "Cameras and Lighting."

Changing Viewports

To change the view displayed in a particular viewport, you first need to activate it by clicking anywhere in the viewport. When you activate a viewport, the viewport border is displayed in yellow. After you have activated a viewport, you can then press [V] to display a list of all the different viewing angles, as shown in Figure 19.

You can also change a viewport by right-clicking the viewport label in the upper-left corner of the viewport. When you do, a right-click menu appears. Change the view by choosing Views and then the viewport name, as shown in Figure 20.

FIGURE 18
Orthographic versus perspective view

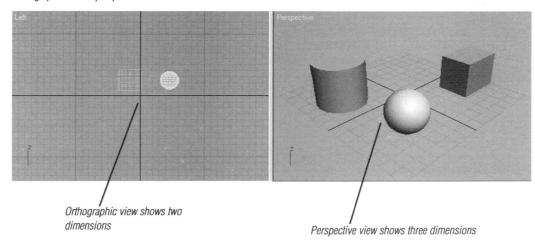

Orthographic view shows two dimensions

Perspective view shows three dimensions

FIGURE 19
List of available views

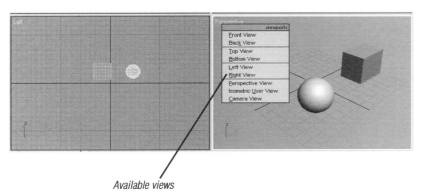

Available views

FIGURE 20
Right-click and choose a view from the list

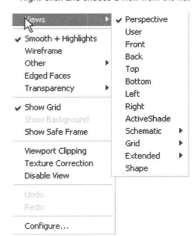

Lesson 2   Work with Viewports

AUTODESK 3D STUDIO MAX 1-15

QUICKTIP

When you activate a viewport, you can click with either the left or right mouse button. However, it is a good habit to use the right mouse button. If you use the left mouse button, you may deselect an object you want to work with. The right mouse button always maintains your selections.

Using the Viewport Controls to Adjust a View

The **viewport controls** in the lower-right section of the 3ds Max window let you look at your scene from different angles and from different distances. The controls change depending on the view you are using. Viewport controls let you change the way you look at a scene, but they do not actually change the position of any object in the scene.

Using Axonometric Viewport Controls

The following are the common axonometric (Front, Back, Left, Right, Top, Bottom) viewport controls, shown in Figure 21:

- **Zoom** lets you get closer to (or farther away from) the objects in your scene. To use Zoom, you click the Zoom button, then drag up in a viewport to zoom in, and down to zoom out.
- **Zoom All** lets you zoom in and out of all of your viewports at once.
- **Zoom Extents** fills your active viewport with all the objects you have in your scene. If you click Zoom Extents and hold down your mouse button, you can also choose **Zoom Extents Selected**, which is handy for locating an object that might get lost in a scene. First, you need to select an object with the Select by Name tool on the Main toolbar, and then click the Zoom Extents Selected tool to fill the viewport with the selected object or objects.
- **Zoom Extents All** is very similar to the Zoom Extents tool. However, it zooms all the viewports. If you click Zoom Extents All and hold down your mouse button, you can also choose **Zoom Extents All Selected**, which is similar to the Zoom Extents Selected tool, except that it zooms all the viewports.

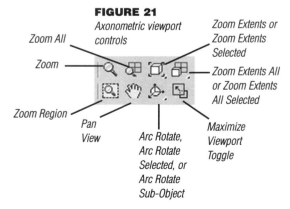

FIGURE 21
Axonometric viewport controls

Zoom All
Zoom
Zoom Region
Pan View
Arc Rotate, Arc Rotate Selected, or Arc Rotate Sub-Object
Zoom Extents or Zoom Extents Selected
Zoom Extents All or Zoom Extents All Selected
Maximize Viewport Toggle

- **Zoom Region** lets you drag a **marquee** around a region that you would like to zoom. A marquee is essentially a selection box.
- **Pan View** moves your viewport angle to the left, right, up, or down. You can do this quickly by simply holding down the middle-mouse button (with no keys pressed and without rolling the wheel) and moving your mouse.
- **Arc Rotate** gives you the ability to rotate the scene around the center of the view. If you click Arc Rotate and hold down your mouse button, you can also choose **Arc Rotate Selected**, which lets you rotate around the center of an object by using the object's center as a pivot point, or **Arc Rotate Sub-Object**, which lets you rotate around the center of a subobject. Subobjects will be explained in Chapter 3, "Modeling."
- **Maximize Viewport Toggle** maximizes your active viewport. Clicking this tool a second time returns all viewports to their original sizes.

Using Perspective Viewport Controls

Perspective viewports have many of the controls that axonometric viewports have, with a few differences, as shown in Figure 22:

- **Field-of-View** allows more of your scene to be visible in the viewport. This tool should be used with caution. It changes the active camera focal lens and the Field-of-View at the same time, and could distort your scene.
- **Walk Through** gives you the ability to have the "first person shooter" style of navigation. By selecting this option and using keys on your keyboard, you can travel forward ↑, backward ↓, up ([Shift] ↑), down ([Shift] ↓), and you can pivot left and right with the mouse. It is an efficient way to move if you are familiar with this style of gaming. It is also only available in the perspective and camera views.

QUICKTIP

This chapter gives an overview of the viewport controls. You will work with them extensively throughout this book as you create and edit your scenes.

Changing Display Options

When you first begin to create objects in 3ds Max, you will notice that three of the four viewports display the objects as a wireframe mesh, while the Perspective viewport displays the objects as shaded. A **wireframe mesh** displays an object as if it has been traced, but not filled in, as shown in Figure 23. Displaying objects this way conserves memory, and also makes it easier to precisely place your objects in the

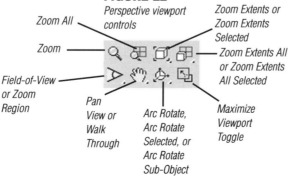

FIGURE 22
Perspective viewport controls

Zoom All
Zoom
Field-of-View or Zoom Region
Pan View or Walk Through
Arc Rotate, Arc Rotate Selected, or Arc Rotate Sub-Object
Zoom Extents or Zoom Extents Selected
Zoom Extents All or Zoom Extents All Selected
Maximize Viewport Toggle

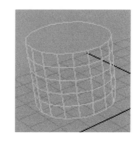

FIGURE 23
Wireframe mesh

Lesson 2 Work with Viewports

AUTODESK 3D STUDIO MAX 1-17

scene. Furthermore, it lets you see each object's basic elements, or sub-components, making it easier to model a complicated scene.

Three of the most common ways to view the objects in your scene are Wireframe, Shaded, and Edged Faces. To switch display options, activate a wireframe viewport (any of the default viewports except Perspective), and right-click the name of the viewport. Notice that in the orthographic views, Wireframe is already selected, as shown in Figure 24. Smooth + Highlights is the default display for Perspective view, but you can also use it in any of the other views. Figure 25 shows Smooth + Highlights applied to the Left and Perspective views, and Wireframe applied to the Top and Front views.

QUICKTIP

You can toggle between Wireframe and Smooth + Highlights by pressing [F3].

The Edged faces option is a very useful way to view your objects when you are modeling. This displays a wireframe on top of the Shaded view. To access the Edged Faces command, the objects in your scene need to be shaded. Then you can right-click the viewport name and select Edged Faces from the menu. A sphere with Edged Faces turned on is shown in Figure 26.

QUICKTIP

You can turn Edged Faces on and off using the [F4] key.

Working with Grids

Grids represent the center of your 3D universe. When you create an object in a viewport, it is automatically created

FIGURE 24
Wireframe selected on right-click menu

FIGURE 25
Smooth + Highlights and Wireframe applied to different views

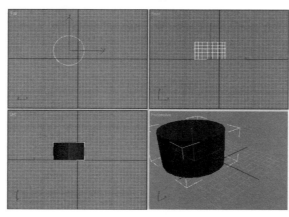

FIGURE 26
Sphere with Edged Faces

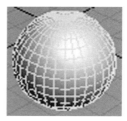

1-18 AUTODESK 3D STUDIO MAX

on a grid. This helps you understand where the object exists in space, or in the world of your scene, when it is created. Grids can appear in every viewport, as shown in Figure 27. You can turn them on or off using the Grids, Show Home Grid command on the Views menu or by pressing [G]. Grids can be very useful when you are trying to establish distance between objects. The grid in the Perspective viewport is commonly referred to as the **home grid**.

You will notice that the x-, y-, and z-axes displayed in the lower-left corner of the viewport are aligned to the home grid. This representation of the x-, y-, and z-axes is called the **axis tripod**. As you work, you can use the axis tripod to get an idea of which direction an object is traveling in space. The home grid you see in the Perspective viewport is also very handy in determining where the ground is in your scene. As you look at your objects from different angles, you can use the grid as a way of determining if all your objects rest on the same plane.

> **QUICK**TIP
> Remember that grids will not appear in your finished scene. They are simply available to guide you as you create and position complex objects and figures.

> **QUICK**TIP
> If you have worked with a different 3D animation package, the axis tripod might look unusual to you. Other packages use the "Right hand rule," where the y-axis points up and the z-axis represents depth. In 3ds Max, the z-axis points up and the y-axis represents depth.

FIGURE 27
Grids in 3ds Max

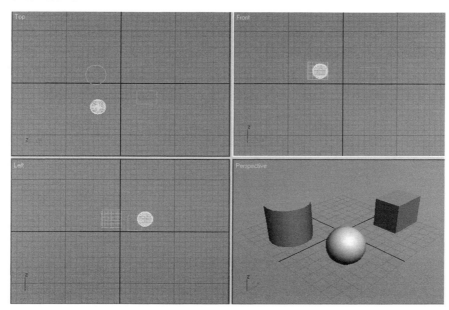

Lesson 2 Work with Viewports

AUTODESK 3D STUDIO MAX 1-19

Change viewports

1. Click **File** on the menu bar, then click **Open**.
2. Navigate to the drive and directory where your Data Files are stored, click the file named **MAX01-01.max**, then click **Open**.

   3ds Max displays a file with three standard primitive objects, a cylinder, a sphere, and a box.
3. Activate the Top viewport by right-clicking its center.

   Notice that the viewport's border is now yellow.
4. Press **[F]** to display the Front viewport, press **[L]** to display the Left viewport, press **[T]** to display the Top viewport, then press **[P]** to display a Perspective viewport.

   This Perspective viewport looks different from the lower-right Perspective viewport for two reasons: Wireframe is turned on, and you are looking at the scene from the top, as shown in Figure 28.
5. Press **[T]** to return the viewport display to Top.

   Notice how your viewport label changes, and how the viewport shows different angles of the scene.

   (continued)

FIGURE 28
A different Perspective viewport displayed

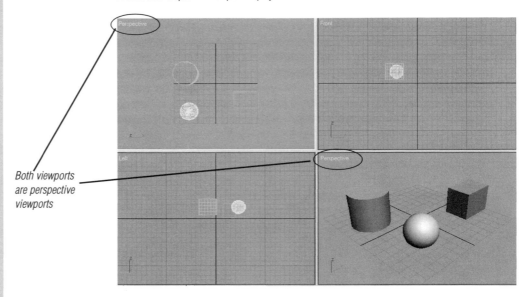

Both viewports are perspective viewports

1-20 AUTODESK 3D STUDIO MAX

Introducing 3ds Max 8

FIGURE 29
Zooming in on the Top viewport

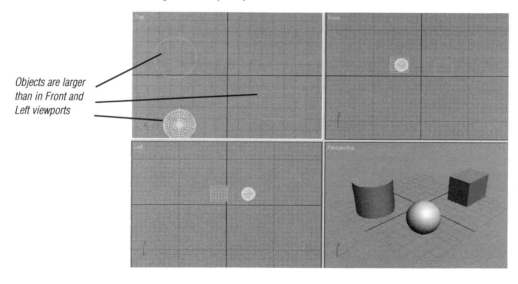

Objects are larger than in Front and Left viewports

6. Press **[Shift][Z]** four times to use the Undo feature to cycle through the most recent viewports you displayed.

    Every viewport change has been recorded and [Shift][Z] undoes those changes.

7. Click **File** on the menu bar, click **Reset**, then click **Yes**.

    Notice how all of your views have been reset and they all look like you just started 3ds Max.

You changed the display of the viewports, undid your changes using the keyboard shortcut, and then reset the 3ds Max interface.

Use viewport controls

1. Click **File** on the menu bar, click **Open Recent**, then click **MAX01-01.max** from the drive and directory where your Data Files are stored.

2. Click the **Zoom button**, click in the Top viewport, then drag up to zoom in on the scene.

    Notice that although you zoom in on the Top viewport, the other viewports do not change, as shown in Figure 29.

3. Click in the Perspective viewport, then drag down to zoom out from the scene.

(continued)

4. Click the **Maximize Viewport Toggle button** , click the **Zoom button** , then click in the maximized viewport, and drag up until your screen resembles Figure 30.

5. Click the **Maximize Viewport Toggle button** to display all four viewports.

   All four viewports are displayed, and the Perspective viewport is no longer maximized.

   You opened a recently viewed file, then used the viewport controls to change the way the file was displayed in the viewports, although you did not change the file itself.

Change display options

1. Right-click the **Front viewport label**, then click **Smooth + Highlights** on the menu.

   The objects are shaded and no longer have a wireframe, as shown in Figure 31.

2. Press **[F3]** to redisplay the wireframe.

3. Click in the Perspective viewport, right-click the **Perspective viewport label**, then click **Edged Faces**.

   As shown in Figure 32, the objects in the viewport now have edged faces in addition to the shading.

4. Right-click the **Perspective viewport label**, then click **Wireframe**.

   The viewport displays the objects as wireframes.

   (continued)

FIGURE 30
Zooming in on the Perspective viewport

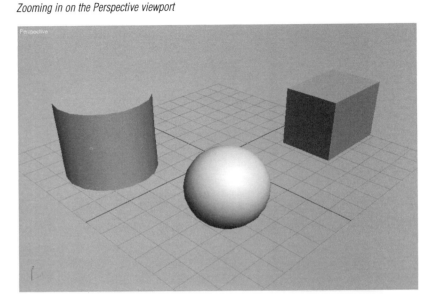

FIGURE 31
Shaded objects in the Front viewport

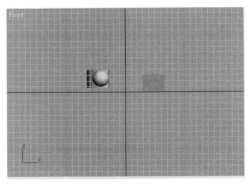

1-22 AUTODESK 3D STUDIO MAX

Introducing 3ds Max 8

FIGURE 32
Edged faces in the Perspective viewport

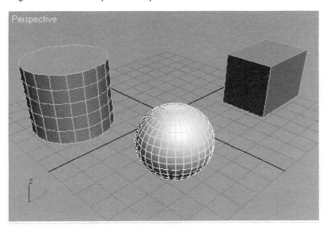

FIGURE 33
Perspective viewport without the grid displayed

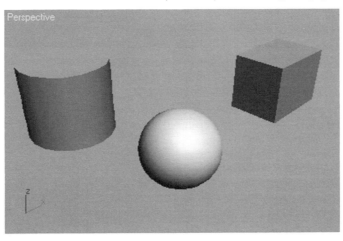

5. Right-click the **Perspective viewport label**, then click **Smooth + Highlights**.
6. Right-click the **Perspective viewport label**, then click **Edged Faces** to deselect it.

   The objects appear the way they were originally displayed, shaded and without edged faces.

You used different display options to see viewport objects rendered different ways.

Work with grids

1. Click in the Perspective viewport (if necessary), then press **[G]**.

   The grid is no longer displayed in the viewport, as shown in Figure 33.

2. Press **[G]**, then click in the Top viewport.

   The grid is displayed once again in the Perspective viewport.

3. Press **[G]** two times.

   The grid disappears and then reappears in the Top viewport.

4. Click **File** on the menu bar, click **Reset**, then click **Yes**.

You turned on and off the display of grids in the different viewports.

LESSON 3

WORK WITH THE
MAIN TOOLBAR

What You'll Do

 In this lesson, you will work with the Main toolbar, repositioning it on the screen and exploring some of its tools.

The Main toolbar is essentially a series of shortcuts. As you become more familiar with 3ds Max, you will find many of the tools on the Main toolbar also appear as commands on the menu bar. For instance, look at the first two tools, Undo and Redo. The Undo and Redo commands are on the Edit menu, but it is quicker to click the buttons on the Main toolbar when you want to undo or redo any changes you've made to your scene.

Exploring and Positioning the Main Toolbar

Figure 34 shows the tools found on the Main toolbar. As you work with 3ds Max, you will become more comfortable with different tools and their functions. Notice that some of the tools are grouped and expanded, and some are not. The expanded tools are grouped together because they are all related. For instance, look at the Selection shape tools. Each tool provides a different shape for your selection. They belong together because you use all of them to select objects.

Notice that all of the grouped tools have a small triangle in the lower-right side of the tool that appears at the top of the drop-down list of tools. To display the expanded list, simply point to the tool, and then click and hold down your mouse button.

QUICKTIP
You need to make sure you hold down the mouse button; if you just click, you activate the current button.

If your display is not set up to show the entire Main toolbar, you can slide the toolbar left and right by positioning the mouse pointer over empty space on the Main toolbar. When you do this, the mouse pointer changes shape to a hand. Click and drag the hand to either side and the toolbar slides, as shown in Figure 35.

QUICKTIP
If you can't see the entire Main toolbar, the screen resolution is probably too low. See "Read This Before You Begin" at the beginning of this book for information on screen resolution.

If you right-click on the far-left side of the Main toolbar, you'll see a menu that includes the Float command, which lets you display the Main toolbar as a floating window. You can resize the window and position it anywhere on your screen.

You can also choose the Dock option, which anchors the Main toolbar on the left, right, top, or bottom of the screen. If you click the Main toolbar handle shown in Figure 36, you can drag to manually reposition the Main toolbar anywhere on the screen. As you drag, you'll see the outline of the toolbar move with the mouse. The outline indicates where the Main toolbar will be repositioned when you release the mouse button.

FIGURE 34
Main toolbar

Selection Shape tools

FIGURE 35
Sliding the Main toolbar

Hand icon lets you slide toolbar

FIGURE 36
Main toolbar handle

Toolbar handle is here

Lesson 3 Work with the Main Toolbar

AUTODESK 3D STUDIO MAX 1-25

Explore and position the Main toolbar

1. Click and hold the **Rectangular Selection Region tool** as shown in Figure 37.

   3ds Max displays the group of related tools for selecting regions with different shapes.

2. Release the mouse button, then point to a blank area of the Main toolbar until the mouse pointer becomes a hand shape.

3. Click and drag to the left until the Quick Render (Production) tool appears on the right side of the toolbar, as shown in Figure 38.

FIGURE 37
Displaying related tools

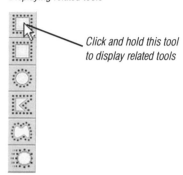

Click and hold this tool to display related tools

1-26 AUTODESK 3D STUDIO MAX

Introducing 3ds Max 8

FIGURE 38
Quick Render (Production) tool in the redisplayed toolbar

Quick Render (Production) tool

4. Right-click the far left side of the toolbar, click **Dock**, then click **Top**.

    The toolbar appears in its default position at the top of the screen.

    TIP You can also go to the menu bar and click Customize, Load Custom UI Scheme, and DefaultUI.ui to reset the window and reposition the toolbar. The Reset command will not return the toolbar to its default position.

You displayed a list of related tools by holding down the Rectangular Selection Region tool. You also slid the Main toolbar left to display the right-most tool, and then changed the position of the toolbar using different options.

LESSON 4

EXPLORE THE
COMMAND PANEL

What You'll Do

In this lesson, you will see an overview of all of the different panels available from the Command panel in 3ds Max.

Understanding the Sections of the Command Panel

By default, the Command panel is located on the right side of the 3ds Max window. The Command panel is broken into six different panels. You display each panel by clicking its icon, shown in Figure 39. The icons include Create, Modify, Hierarchy, Motion, Display, and Utilities. Each has several different features, grouped by category. This lesson provides a basic overview of each of the panels accessible from the Command panel.

Create Panel

The Create panel, shown in Figure 40, is where you go to create just about anything you need in your scene. It is broken into different categories: Geometry, Shapes, Lights, Cameras, Helpers, Space Warps, and Systems. Many of the categories have subcategories. For instance, when you look in the geometry section, you notice the Standard Primitives drop-down list.

Under that, you find many other types of geometry, such as Extended Primitives and Compound objects. The Create panel provides visual representations of functions and commands that are also available on the Create menu. In this book, the focus will usually be on the panels, not the menu.

QUICKTIP

If you try to create an object using the menu, 3ds Max switches to the correct panel and highlights the appropriate tool.

Modify Panel

After you create an object, you can open the Modify panel shown in Figure 41 to change it. You can rename the object, apply **modifiers** (which change an object's surface by deforming it in a specified way), adjust parameters, and more in this panel. The Modify panel is another way of viewing detailed information about your selected object. For example, you can see information such as the object's name.

Each object is given a default name based on its type (such as Sphere01). Every object is also assigned a display color by default that can be changed in the Modify panel. Some of the other things you can modify are the physical parameters of the object, such as its size or number of segments. These parameters are sometimes shared, and sometimes unique to an object. For instance, you can modify a teapot by turning its body, handle, spout, and lid on and off. A box object would have no use for these specific parameters.

FIGURE 40
Create panel

FIGURE 41
Modify panel

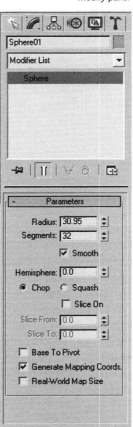

FIGURE 39
Panel display buttons for the Command panel

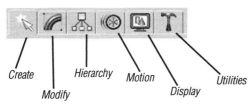

Lesson 4 Explore the Command Panel

AUTODESK 3D STUDIO MAX 1-29

Hierarchy Panel

The Hierarchy panel, shown in Figure 42, is broken into three major sections. You will be using this panel in different parts of the book. This section merely provides an overview.

- **Pivot** allows you to change the **pivot point** of an object. A **pivot point** is essentially the point around which an object rotates. Pivot points will be explained in depth in Chapter 2, "Building and Modifying Objects."
- **IK (Inverse Kinematics)** lets you apply limitations to objects. For example, you can limit the amount an object may rotate or move. This is also where you can fine-tune parent-child relationships. A **parent-child relationship** determines how two or more objects interact with each other. For example, a **parent** object controls its children. IK is covered in Chapter 7, "Working with Bones and Inverse Kinematics."
- Link Info lets you lock an object by enabling or disabling the ability to move, rotate, or scale an object along different axes. Locks come in handy when you are animating an object. Animation is covered in Chapter 6, "Animation."

In addition to Locks, the Hierarchy panel also has an **Inherit** section. Inherit is used only when two objects are linked together, as in a parent-child relationship. When you move, rotate, or scale the parent object, the child follows.

FIGURE 42
Hierarchy panel

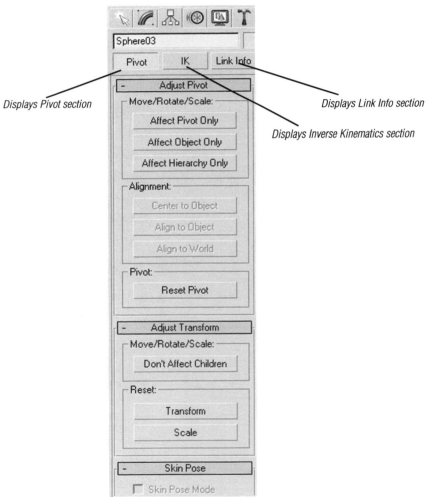

Displays Pivot section

Displays Link Info section

Displays Inverse Kinematics section

1-30 AUTODESK 3D STUDIO MAX

Introducing 3ds Max 8

Motion Panel

The **Motion panel** is broken into two major sections.
- The **Parameters** section lets you assign and adjust controllers that are applied to an object. In this panel, you can also create (and remove) keyframes for individual basic transformations such as moving, rotating, and scaling. You can also fine-tune the keyframes here and change the way keyframes interact with each other.
- The **Trajectories** section lets you animate an object to follow a path instead of manually moving the object around your viewport to create an animation path. The Motion panel will be covered in greater detail later in this book.

Display Panel

The Display panel is where you specify how an object should be displayed in your viewports. This includes changing the object's name and display color. You can also hide and unhide objects, or freeze and unfreeze objects here. A **frozen object** cannot be selected or adjusted in any way. Freezing an object helps in complicated scenes where some geometry might overlap.

Right under the Freeze options are the Display options, which help you determine how your selected object will be displayed in the viewport. For example, the See-Through option is very helpful for working on objects because you can quickly make an object somewhat translucent as you work on it.

Hiding objects gives you the ability to temporarily get rid of things you don't need to see at the moment. This tool is useful for building complicated scenes with many objects that can interfere with one another.

Utilities Panel

The Utilities panel is where "all the other stuff" goes. It is home to several additional features in 3d studio Max. Some of the features include **reactor**, also available as a toolbar, where you can make objects collide with one another, apply gravity, and make objects float, among other things. Another feature you can find in the Utilities panel is the **Asset Browser**, which is a utility that allows you to navigate the drives and directories on your computer to look for **assets** (such as other scenes, images, or exported objects), or even to the Web, where you can download files (such as textures) for your animation. **MAXScripting** is also available on this panel. (The Appendix, "MAXScripting," is devoted to writing and using scripts in 3ds Max.) If you click the More button on this panel, 3ds Max displays a dialog box that lists several more utilities.

This chapter has covered only the most basic features of the Control Panel. You'll use the more advanced features as you proceed through the book.

LESSON 5

WORK WITH THE TRACK BAR

What You'll Do

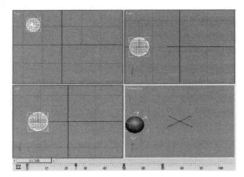

 In this lesson, you will work with the track bar to run a simple animation and understand how the track bar's timeline works.

What Is a Track Bar?

The track bar, or timeline, is located at the bottom of the window, as shown in Figure 43. Each tick on the **timeline** represents a frame in your animation. Think of your animation as a children's flipbook. When you flip through the pages in the book, the result is an animation. On the timeline in 3ds Max, each frame would represent a page in the flipbook.

The track bar also displays the keys for the selected object. **Keys** mark significant changes to an object or to its position in a scene. For example, if an object moves from point A to point B in your scene as the scene plays, 3ds Max inserts a **key** on the timeline at the start of the animation (0) and a key in the timeline when the object reaches point B (for example, at 50). Together, these two keys are called a **keyframe** in 3ds Max. In this example, 3ds Max automatically animates the object to get it from point A to point B by the time it reaches 50 on the timeline.

Using the Time Slider and Time Controls

The **time slider** (also referred to as the **playhead**) is located on the timeline. Inside the time slider you will see two numbers. The first number represents the frame you are currently viewing. The second number shows how many frames you have in your timeline. You can grab the time slider and **scrub** it left and right as you preview your animation. You can also type a value to be taken to a specific frame. In addition to using the time slider, you can use the time controls located to the right of the timeline.

The VCR-like controls in the lower-right side of the interface are called **time controls**, and are designed to help you navigate your animation. All of the controls (except the Jump to frame text box) have keyboard equivalents.

- **Go to Start** takes you to the first frame of the animation. The keyboard shortcut is [Home].

- **Previous Frame** allows you to step back one frame at a time. The keyboard shortcut is [,] (the comma key). When you turn on Key mode with the Key Mode Toggle button, this button changes to the **Previous Key** button, which takes you to the previous key on the timeline, as shown in Figure 44.
- **Play/Pause Animation** allows you to play or pause your animation. The keyboard shortcut is [/] (the slash key). Grouped under this button is the **Play/Pause Selected Animation** button.
- **Next Frame** allows you to step forward one frame at a time. The keyboard shortcut is [.] (the period key). When you turn on Key mode with the Key Mode Toggle button, this button changes to the **Next Key** button, which takes you to the next key on the timeline, also shown in Figure 44.
- **Go to End** takes you to the last frame of the animation. The keyboard shortcut is [End].
- **Jump to Frame** lets you type a specific frame number to navigate to that frame.
- **Key Mode** is a toggle, which means that you can turn it on and off by clicking its button. When Key mode is on, the Next Frame and Previous Frame buttons change so that you can navigate your timeline by jumping from keyframe to keyframe instead of frame to frame. This feature is handy when you are fine-tuning your animations.

FIGURE 43
Track bar timeline

Time slider

FIGURE 44
Frame navigation buttons change to Key navigation buttons

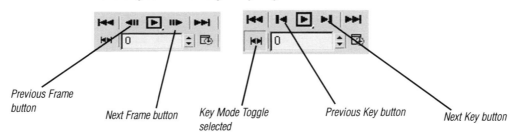

Previous Frame button

Next Frame button

Key Mode Toggle selected

Previous Key button

Next Key button

Lesson 5 *Work with the Track Bar*

Use the time slider and time controls to navigate an animation

1. Open the scene **MAX01-02** from the drive and folder where your Data Files are stored.

   The scene displays a single, unselected sphere. There are no keyframes on the track bar, as shown in Figure 45.

2. Use any viewport to click the **sphere** in the scene to select it.

   The track bar timeline displays keyframes, as shown in Figure 46.

   TIP If you select the sphere and then press [Spacebar], you have activated the selection lock feature. You cannot deselect the object until you press [Spacebar] again.

3. Click the **Play Animation button** ▶, then click the **Pause Animation button** ❚❚ after the animation has played a few times.

   The animation, which moves the sphere around the scene, plays, and then pauses.

FIGURE 45
No keyframes displayed

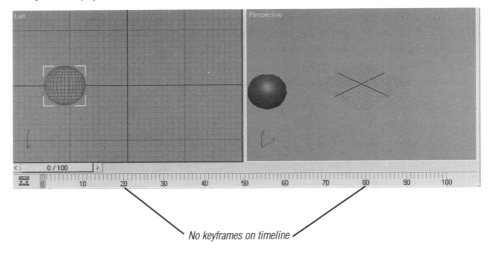

No keyframes on timeline

FIGURE 46
Keyframes for selected object

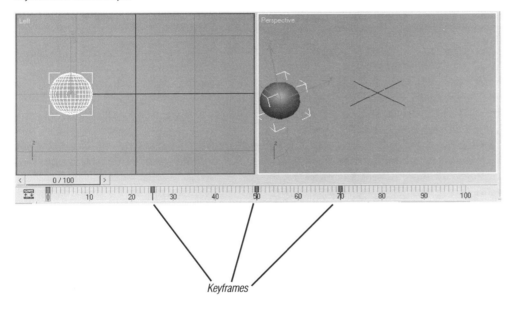

Keyframes

4. Click the **Next Frame button** ▸ five times to move forward five frames, and then click the **Previous Frame button** ◂ five times to move back five frames.
5. Click the **Key Mode Toggle button** ▸▸ to turn on Key mode, then click the **Next Key button** ▸▮ four times.

   The animation jumps to the next key, not the next frame, each time you click it.
6. Click the **Previous Key button** ▮◂ four times, then click the **Key Mode Toggle button** ▸▸ to turn off Key mode.

You used the time slider and the time controls to move forward and backward in an animation. You moved from frame to frame, and then from key to key

Lesson 5 Work with the Track Bar

AUTODESK 3D STUDIO MAX 1-35

LESSON 6

CUSTOMIZE THE
3DS MAX INTERFACE

What You'll Do

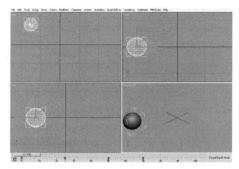

▶ *In this lesson, you will learn how to customize the 3ds Max user interface.*

Hiding Toolbars and Panels

Most of the elements in the 3ds Max interface can be hidden. The quickest way to do this is to enter Expert mode by pressing [Ctrl][x]. **Expert mode**, shown in Figure 47, hides all user interface (UI) elements except the menu bar, viewports, and track bar. In Expert mode, you must rely primarily on keyboard shortcuts and the **quad menus** that appear when you right-click in a viewport. Expert mode is beyond the scope

FIGURE 47
Expert mode

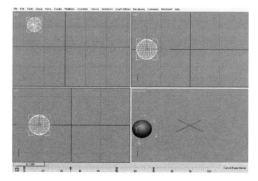

of this book. However, another way to hide elements in the interface is to click Customize on the menu bar, and then choose Show UI to display a list of elements to show or hide, as shown in Figure 48.

Switching to a Preset Custom UI

3ds Max comes with four preset Custom UI (User Interface) schemes from which you can choose. You use the Custom UI and Defaults Switcher command on the

Customize menu to preview these options. The Switcher is shown in Figure 49. It provides a description of the UI option you have highlighted, as well as a preview of the UI.

Restoring the Default User Interface

When you are first learning 3ds Max, you should use the default layout that appears when you start the software. If 3ds Max ever looks dramatically different when you start it, you can revert to the default layout by clicking Customize on the menu bar, clicking Load Custom UI Scheme, and then clicking DefaultUI.ui. This loads the interface that is used in this book. As you become more familiar with the software, you might want to change your interface to something other than the default UI.

QUICKTIP

The Revert to Startup Layout command on the Customize menu displays the user interface the way it appeared when you started 3ds Max for the current session. It does not necessarily revert to the default user interface.

For much of this book, you will be using the default user interface. Don't change user interface settings unless you are instructed to do so or your screen will not match the figures in this book.

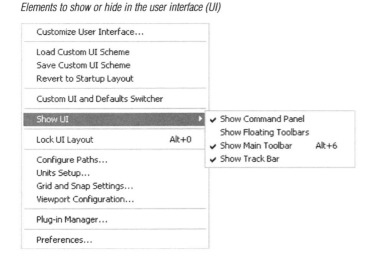

FIGURE 48
Elements to show or hide in the user interface (UI)

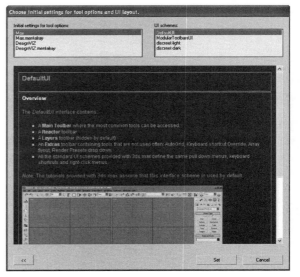

FIGURE 49
Custom UI and Defaults Switcher

Lesson 6 Customize the 3ds Max Interface

AUTODESK 3D STUDIO MAX 1-37

Hide toolbars and panels

1. Open **MAX01-02** from the drive and folder where your Data Files are stored (if necessary), then press **[Ctrl][x]**.

   3ds Max switches to Expert Mode, as shown in Figure 50.

2. Press **[Ctrl][x]**.

   3ds Max redisplays the toolbars and panels it hid in Expert Mode.

3. Click **Customize** on the menu bar, then click **Show UI**.

4. Click **Show Command Panel** to deselect it.

   The 3ds Max Command panel is hidden, as shown in Figure 51.

5. Click **Customize**, click **Show UI**, then click **Show Main Toolbar**.

   3ds Max hides the Main toolbar.

You switched Expert mode on and off, and then hid other user interface elements.

Switch to a Custom UI

1. Click **Customize** on the menu bar, then click **Custom UI and Defaults Switcher**.

   3ds Max displays the Switcher dialog box.

2. Click **discreet-dark** under UI Schemes, click **Set**, then click **OK**.

   The user interface changes to dark, as shown in Figure 52.

FIGURE 50
Expert mode

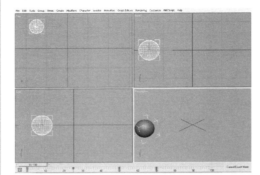

FIGURE 51
Command panel hidden

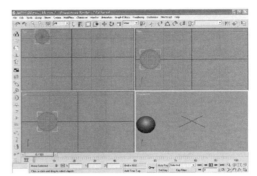

FIGURE 52
Discreet-dark user interface

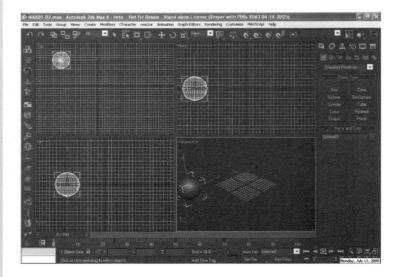

1-38 AUTODESK 3D STUDIO MAX

Introducing 3ds Max 8

FIGURE 53
Load Custom UI Scheme dialog box

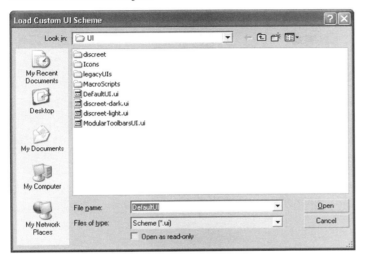

Loading a customized user interface

Many people who use 3d studio Max might use the software for a specific purpose. For example, one person might need a particular interface to create dynamic simulations, while another person might do a lot of character animation with Character Studio. Not only that, but one person might use the software in more than one way, depending on the project. Not only can you customize the 3ds Max interface, you can save those settings so that you can load the interface that meets your needs at the moment. To save a customized user interface, click Customize on the menu bar, click Save Custom UI Scheme, type a name in the File name text box, and then click Save. When you do so, you are presented with the Custom Scheme dialog box. Select the elements you want to include in your custom UI, and then click OK.

Restore the default user interface

1. Click **Customize** on the menu bar, then click **Load Custom UI Scheme**.

   3ds Max displays the Load Custom UI Scheme dialog box, shown in Figure 53.

2. Click **DefaultUI.ui**, then click **Open**.

   The user interface returns to its default settings.

You loaded the default user interface to undo the changes you made to the display of user interface elements.

LESSON 7

USE THE HELP MENU AND
THE HOTKEY MAP

What You'll Do

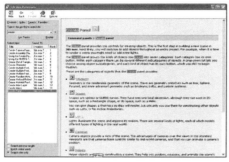

▶ *In this lesson, you will learn how to use the Help menu and the Hotkey map.*

If you are new to animation and to 3ds Max, you will frequently use the 3ds Max User Reference. When you click Help on the menu bar, the options shown in Figure 54 appear. You can also access Help by pressing [F1]. When you press [F1] in the middle of a task—for example, after you have clicked one of the standard primitives on the Create panel—3ds Max displays **context-sensitive Help** that gives you information about the task at hand.

The User Reference is set up like other online Help systems. It includes panels titled Contents, Index, Search, and Favorites. The Contents panel lists all the topics in the User Reference. To open a topic, you double-click the topic name. The Index provides an alphabetical listing of all of the keywords in the User Reference. You can scroll through the Index using the scroll bar on the right side of the list, or you can type the first few letters of a word to jump toward it. You can use the Search panel to type a term or keyword. When you press [Enter], 3ds Max displays a list of all of the Help topics that use that word. Finally, you can use the Favorites panel to keep a list of Help topics you plan to use frequently. Clicking the Add button on the bottom of the Favorites panel adds the currently selected topic to the list for quick display later.

QUICKTIP

You can use Boolean operators—the words AND, OR, NEAR, and NOT—to narrow a search to reduce the list of results 3ds Max Help displays. For example, if you want to find information about the sphere standard primitive, type "primitive AND sphere" to find topics that deal specifically with the Sphere standard primitive.

If you have used earlier versions of 3ds Max, the New Features Guide can provide you very useful information. If you use MAXScript to add functionality or add a process to 3ds Max, the MAXScript Reference will be invaluable. (Scripting is covered in the Appendix.) You can also use Help to find tutorials for specific features or tasks, or to find updates and additional help on the Web.

You can also open the Hotkey Map shown in Figure 55. To use the map, roll the mouse over different keys on the keyboard to see their hotkey functions. This feature is probably more useful for seasoned users of 3ds Max who need a refresher on which keys do what. Many of the hotkeys map to functions with which the novice user would not be familiar. A better way to find hotkeys for commands is to search for the command in the User Reference and see which hotkey maps to it. For example, if you display the Select All topic, you'll see that the shortcut, or hotkey, for selecting all the objects in a scene is [Ctrl][A], as shown in Figure 56.

QUICKTIP

You can also create your own keyboard shortcuts in 3ds Max using the Keyboard panel of the Customize User Interface dialog box, where 3ds Max functions are broken down into groups and categories. It is not advised that you do this until you are comfortable with 3ds Max. This book will often refer to the default keyboard shortcuts that ship with the software. If you start editing the keyboard shortcuts in this dialog box, you might accidentally delete or alter those that already exist.

FIGURE 54
Help menu options

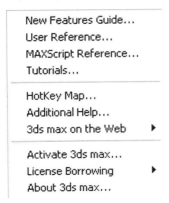

FIGURE 56
Keyboard shortcut in Help topic

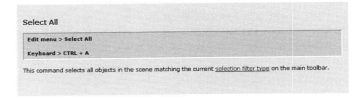

FIGURE 55
Hotkey Map

Lesson 7   Use the Help Menu and the Hotkey Map

AUTODESK 3D STUDIO MAX 1-41

Use Help and the Hotkey Map

1. Click **Help**, click **User Reference,** then click the **Search tab** (if necessary).

2. Type **create** in the Type in the word(s) to search for text box, click **Search titles only** at the bottom of the window to select it (if necessary), deselect **Search previous results** (if necessary), deselect **Match similar words** (if necessary), then click **List Topics**.

3. Double-click **Create Panel** in the list of topics to select it and open it.

   | **TIP** You may need to scroll to see the topic.

   3ds Max displays the selected Help topic on the right. The word "create" is highlighted wherever it appears in the text, as shown in Figure 57.

4. Click the 3ds Max Reference **Close button** ⊠, click **Help** on the menu bar, then click **Hotkey Map**.

   3ds Max displays the Hotkey Map.

   (continued)

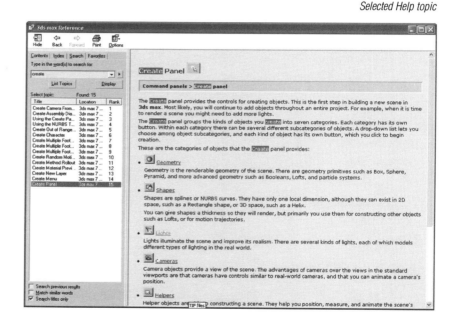

FIGURE 57
Selected Help topic

1-42 AUTODESK 3D STUDIO MAX

Introducing 3ds Max 8

FIGURE 58
Hotkey Map for the letter "O"

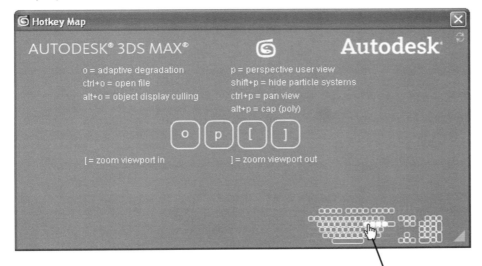

Point to O on keyboard

5. Point to the letter **O** on the Hotkey Map, as shown in Figure 58.

   3ds Max shows which commands or tasks the keys O, P, [, and] perform.

6. Point to other parts of the keyboard to see what the other keys do.

7. Click the Hotkey Map **Close button**.

8. Click **File,** click **Exit,** then click **No** to close the file and to close 3ds Max.

   The Data File and 3ds Max both close.

You explored Help and the Hotkey Map, and then closed the file and 3ds Max.

CHAPTER SUMMARY

In this chapter, you explored the 3ds Max interface and worked with some of its features. You learned the difference between the Reset command, which closes the current file and reverts the display to the default settings, and the New command on the File menu, which gives you three options for starting a new file: Keep Objects and Hierarchy creates a new file with all of the current file's objects and their relationships preserved; Keep Objects creates a new file using the existing objects but doesn't retain their hierarchy; New All creates a new, blank file but does not revert 3ds Max to its default settings. You also learned how to move between and resize viewports. You explored the Main toolbar and and the Command panel. You also used the track bar to run an animation. You customized the 3ds Max interface, learned how to apply a preset interface, and how to revert to the default 3ds Max interface. Finally, you used the Help menu and Hotkey map to investigate the different options for getting Help in 3ds Max.

What You Have Learned

- How to start 3ds Max
- How to open and save a scene
- How to Reset the display
- How to open a new file with different setting options
- How to navigate and resize the viewports
- How to use the viewport controls
- How to change the display of objects in a viewport from Wireframe to Smooth + Highlights
- How to display edged faces on an object
- How to work with grids
- How to use tools on the Main toolbar and change its position in the interface
- How to work with the track bar
- How to customize the user interface
- How to use the Help system and Hotkey map

Key Terms

Scene   The 3ds Max term for a file. Scenes in 3ds Max have a .max extension.

Viewports   3ds Max windows that let you look at a scene from up to four different angles.

Grid   A viewport feature that lets you align and place objects in your scene.

Track bar   A bar at the bottom of the window that lets you navigate between frames in a scene.

Perspective view   A viewport view that displays a scene in three dimensions.

Orthographic view   A viewport view that displays a flat, two-dimensional view of your scene.

Command panel   "Command central" for 3ds Max. You use it to create and modify objects, assign object hierarchy, and use many other features to create and modify the objects in your scene.

Track bar   Displays the frames in a scene, from 1 to 100 (by default).

Keys   Reference points in your animation. 3ds Max automatically draws all motion between the keys in an animation.

Frame   Shows a scene at a single point in time. An animation has multiple frames.

chapter 2
BUILDING AND MODIFYING OBJECTS

1. Create standard primitives.
2. Select objects.
3. Move, rotate, and scale objects.
4. Modify a polygon object.
5. Work with segments.
6. Apply modifiers.
7. Clone objects.
8. Link and group objects.
9. Work with pivot points.
10. Use snapping tools.
11. Align objects.

chapter 2 BUILDING AND MODIFYING OBJECTS

In this chapter, you'll begin to see the power of 3ds Max as you create, modify, and manipulate basic objects called "standard primitives." Standard primitives are very simple geometric shapes that are easy to create. You can use them as a starting point for drawing complex objects and then modify them until they look like something completely different.

There are a number of basic tools you need to understand in order to work with and manipulate standard primitive objects as well as more complex objects. Becoming familiar with these tools—such as tools for selecting, moving, rotating, and scaling—will help you create complex objects that look exactly the way you want. In this chapter, you will also learn how to change the most basic aspects of objects, such as their names and physical parameters, the location of their pivot points, or the number of segments that appear on their surfaces.

You can transform simple objects in 3ds Max by applying modifiers. You can also create and work with multiple objects that affect each other or are affected by the same action, whether they are clones of each other, combined in a group, or linked together in a parent-child relationship. Finally, you'll become more familiar with snapping and alignment tools that enable you to more precisely control the transformation and positioning you want the objects in your scenes to have.

Tools You'll Use

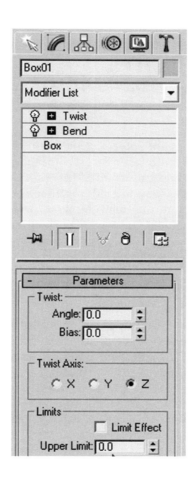
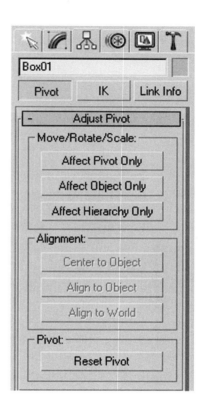

LESSON 1

CREATE STANDARD PRIMITIVES

What You'll Do

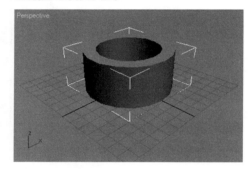

In this lesson, you will learn about the standard polygon primitive shapes available in 3ds Max and how to create each shape using the Create panel and viewports.

Standard polygon primitives are the building blocks for most of the things you will create in 3ds Max. These basic geometric shapes come in handy when you are trying to replicate something. All of the standard polygon primitives have different **parameters**, or settings, so it is helpful to work with each one to get familiar with it.

The process of creating realistic-looking objects in 3ds Max is called **modeling**. For the most part, you use standard polygon primitives to help you model. This is the most common type of modeling in 3ds Max, and it is referred to as **polygon modeling**. For example, the object shown in Figure 1 was created starting with a sphere standard polygon primitive. Polygon modeling will be explained in depth in Chapter 3, "Modeling."

QUICKTIP

In the 3ds Max interface, standard polygon primitives are referred to as standard primitives. This book uses the same shorthand, and will refer to standard polygon primitives as standard primitives.

Standard primitives are located on the Create panel, under the Geometry category, as shown in Figure 2. If you reset 3ds Max, the standard primitives are automatically visible. Notice the list of buttons: Box, Cone, Sphere, GeoSphere, Cylinder, Tube, Torus, Pyramid, Teapot, and Plane. These are your standard primitives. Figure 3 shows what each standard primitive looks like in 3ds Max.

To create a standard primitive, first click the button for the primitive, and then click and drag in the Top viewport to create the object. If you create an object in any viewport other than the Top, the object does not stand up straight in the Perspective home grid.

Creating Planes and Spheres

The simplest primitives to create are planes and spheres. A plane is a flat surface, often used in modeling as ground or as a surface upon which an object can rest. It has only length and width parameters; none for height. To create a plane, click the Plane button on the Create panel, click and drag in the Top viewport, and then click to complete the drawing. The plane appears as a rectangle in the Top viewport and looks like a flat surface in the Perspective viewport.

QUICKTIP
If you view a plane from underneath the home grid in the Perspective viewport, it is invisible.

To create a sphere, you need only set its radius. Click either the Sphere button or GeoSphere button in the Create panel, click and drag in the Top viewport to set the radius, and then click to complete the creation. The sphere appears as a circle in the Top viewport, and as a three-dimensional sphere in the Perspective viewport. The difference between a sphere and a geosphere is in the polygons used to create the surface of each, as shown in Figure 4. **Polygons** are closed sequences of three or more edges connected by a surface. The wireframe of a sphere's surface has poles and looks like the

FIGURE 1
Model with Sphere primitive as basis

Courtesy Miguel Miraldo www.blackbox.pt

FIGURE 2
Geometry category on the Create panel

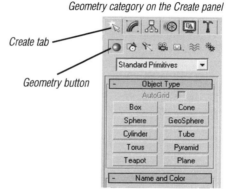

FIGURE 3
Standard polygon primitives

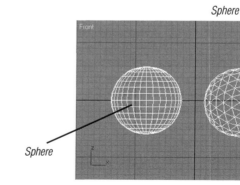

FIGURE 4
Sphere versus GeoSphere

Lesson 1   Create Standard Primitives

AUTODESK 3D STUDIO MAX 2-5

longitude and latitude lines on a globe; the polygons created by these lines have four sides, are irregular in shape, and are different sizes from one another. A geosphere's surface is made of equal-sized, triangular polygons. This difference becomes important when you are deciding which type of primitive to use during modeling.

Creating Boxes, Cylinders, and Pyramids

Other standard primitives call for more than one click and drag to create the shape. Boxes, cylinders, and pyramids each require that you set the foundation parameters first (length x width or, for a cylinder, radius) and then create the height. For instance, to create a box, click the Box button on the Create panel, and then click and drag in the Top viewport to create the foundation (length × width). Next, let go of the mouse button and move the mouse pointer either up or down to create the height of the Box either above or below the foundation, as shown in Figure 5. Click again to end the creation of the Box.

QUICKTIP

Pressing the [Ctrl] key when creating a box keeps the length and width of the box the same. It does not affect the height. You will notice that the [Ctrl] key works differently, depending on the standard primitive you are creating. For example, hold down [Ctrl] while you are creating a plane, and it will be a square and be drawn from the center.

This same process applies to both the cylinder and the pyramid primitives: click the Cylinder or Pyramid button on the Create panel, click and drag in the Top viewport to create the foundation, release the mouse button and drag up or down to create the height, and then click to complete.

Creating Cones, Tubes, and Toruses

The cone, tube, and torus also require more complex sets of steps to create, because each has more than one radius that needs to be set. To create a cone, click the Cone button, click and drag in the Top viewport to set the radius of the foundation: release the mouse button and drag up or down to

FIGURE 5
Creating a box in the Top viewport

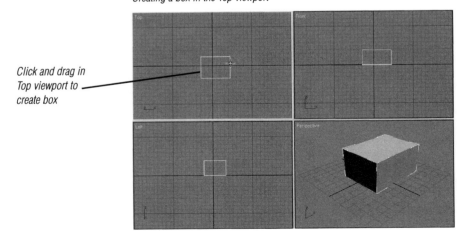

Click and drag in Top viewport to create box

create the height of the cone; click and drag up or down to set the radius of the upper surface of the cone, as shown in Figure 6, and then click to complete. Note that unlike a pyramid, a cone is rounded and doesn't necessarily come to a point, although you can make it do so if you want.

To create a tube, click the Tube button, click and drag in the Top viewport to set the outer radius of the foundation, release the mouse button and drag up or down to set the inner radius of the tube, click and drag up or down to set the height of the tube, and then click to complete. A torus is created by the same process as a tube after clicking the Torus button, except that you don't have to drag up or down to create the height of the torus. The height is automatically determined by the distance between its inner and outer radius.

Creating a Teapot

The teapot primitive is not a standard geometric shape, so the reason for its inclusion in the set of standard primitives isn't obvious. The teapot, or "**Utah Teapot**," was first created by a computer graphics researcher named Martin Newell, who worked at the University of Utah in 1975. Because of its irregular curves, as well as the hole in the handle, and the way it casts a shadow upon itself, it provided an excellent model for testing advances in 3D graphics. Newell's colleague, James Blinn, made slight modifications to the teapot model, and it has been used in one form or another by 3D modelers ever since. The originators of 3ds Max adopted this model and used a teapot to demonstrate new abilities in the software as they were developed. The teapot was an excellent way to test how new materials, lighting, and other elements looked on an irregularly shaped real-world object. Over time, the teapot has become a classic part of 3ds Max, and its availability here will be of great use as you continue to use the software. To create a teapot, click the

FIGURE 6
Creating a cone in the Top viewport

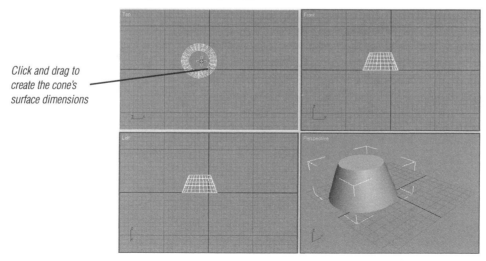

Click and drag to create the cone's surface dimensions

Teapot button, click and drag in the Top viewport to create the teapot, and then click to complete creation. The proportions of the teapot are already set so no additional clicking and dragging to create height is needed.

Using the Creation Method Rollout

When you click and drag to create a primitive in the Top viewport, the point from which the primitive is created is determined by the option selected in the Creation Method rollout. When you create a box, for example, the default option selected in the Creation Method rollout is Box. Thus when you click and drag to create the box's foundation, the resulting box stretches from the location of your first click to the location of your second click; you drag again to set the height. If you click the Cube option in the Creation Method rollout, however, you will create a box with sides of equal length; your first click is the center of the box, and your second is its outer edge. The height is the same as the length and width and is created automatically, as shown in Figure 7.

The Creation Method rollouts for the Plane and Pyramid primitives operate the same way. The default creation method option for a Pyramid is Base/Apex; click the Center option to create a foundation with sides of equal length. For a plane, click the Square option (default is Rectangle) in the rollout to create a plane with sides of equal length.

For the Sphere, GeoSphere, Cone, Cylinder, Tube, Torus, and Teapot primitives, by default the Center option in the Creation Method rollout is selected, and your first click in the viewport denotes the object's center. Click the Edge option (or, for geospheres, click the Diameter option) if you want to draw the object from edge to edge (click to click) instead of from the center out.

FIGURE 7
Using the Cube creation method

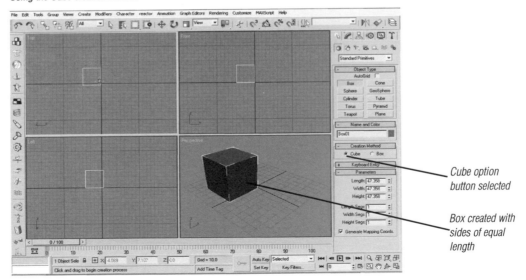

Cube option button selected

Box created with sides of equal length

2-8 AUTODESK 3D STUDIO MAX

Building and Modifying Objects

FIGURE 8
Sphere created in viewports

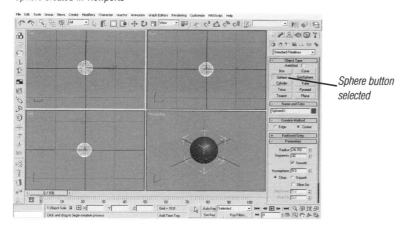

Sphere button selected

FIGURE 9
Box foundation created in viewports

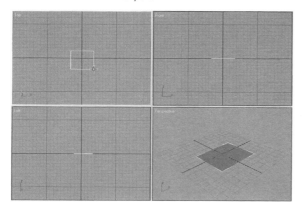

FIGURE 10
Completed box

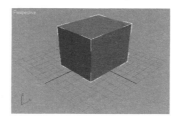

Create a sphere and a box

1. Start 3ds Max 7, then click the **Create tab** (if necessary) to open the Create panel.

   The Create panel is displayed on the right side of the screen.

2. Click the **Sphere button** on the Create panel, then click and drag in the Top viewport to create a sphere about one inch wide, as shown in Figure 8.

   The sphere appears in the Top, Left, Front, and Perspective viewports.

3. Click **File**, click **Reset**, click **No**, then click **Yes** to reset 3ds Max to its default settings.

4. On the Create panel, click the **Box button**, click in the Top viewport and drag down and to the right about one inch.

   The foundation for a box appears in the Top viewport as a rectangle, in the Perspective viewport as a plane, and in the Left and Front viewports as a line. See Figure 9.

5. Release the mouse button, drag up about one inch, then click to complete the box.

   After you add height to the box, it appears as a rectangle in the Top, Left, and Front viewports, and as a box in the Perspective viewport, as shown in Figure 10.

6. Reset 3ds Max without saving the file.

You created a sphere and a three-dimensional box by clicking and dragging in the Top viewport.

Lesson 1   Create Standard Primitives

AUTODESK 3D STUDIO MAX 2-9

Create a tube

1. On the Create panel, click the **Tube button**.
2. Click in the Top viewport, drag down and to the right about one-half inch, then release the mouse button.

   Your first click and drag in the viewport defines the outer radius for the tube.
3. Drag up about one-half inch, then click.

   The inner radius for the tube is defined, as shown in Figure 11.
4. Drag up about one-half inch to determine the height of the tube (similar to that shown in Figure 12), then click again to complete the tube.
5. Reset 3ds Max without saving.

You clicked and dragged in the Top viewport in order to define the inner radius, outer radius, and height of a tube.

FIGURE 11
Inner radius of tube created

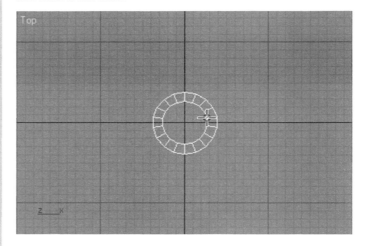

FIGURE 12
Completed tube

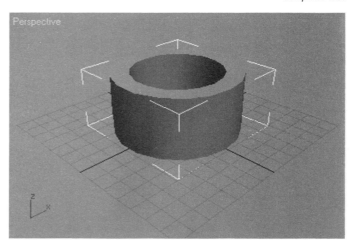

FIGURE 13
Create panel

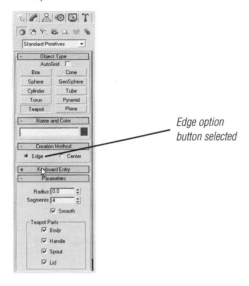

Edge option button selected

FIGURE 14
Completed teapot

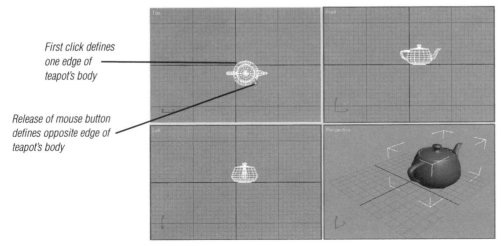

First click defines one edge of teapot's body

Release of mouse button defines opposite edge of teapot's body

Create a teapot from edge to edge

1. On the Create panel, click the **Teapot button**.
2. In the Creation Method rollout on the Create panel, click the **Edge option button**, as shown in Figure 13.
3. Click in the center of the Top viewport, drag down and to the right about one inch, then release the mouse button.

   A teapot is created in the viewports, as shown in Figure 14. Because you selected the Edge option in the Creation Method rollout, your first click determines where one edge of the teapot's body appears; after you drag, your release of the mouse button determines where the opposite edge of the teapot's body appears.

4. Reset 3ds Max without saving.

You used the Edge option in the Creation Method rollout to create a teapot from edge to edge by clicking and dragging in the Top viewport.

Lesson 1 Create Standard Primitives

AUTODESK 3D STUDIO MAX 2-11

LESSON 2

SELECT
OBJECTS

What You'll Do

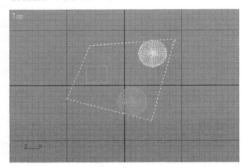

▶ *In this lesson, you will explore the different methods for selecting an object or set of objects. You will also learn how to create selection sets.*

To make modifications to an object or set of objects you have created in a scene, you must select the object or objects. This makes the object or objects active and available for manipulation. You can tell that an object is selected because its border in each of the viewports is white. 3ds Max provides several methods for selecting objects, all available from the Main toolbar.

Using the Select Object Tool

The Select Object tool on the Main toolbar enables you to select any object in your scene by clicking it. To select an object, click the Select Object tool (or press [q]), then click the object. If you have multiple objects to select, hold [Ctrl] down while clicking each object.

QUICKTIP

In 3ds Max, do *not* press the [Shift] key to add objects to a selection. The [Shift] key duplicates objects if you drag while it is pressed.

When you are selecting objects that all reside near each other in a scene, you might find that using a **selection region** is the most efficient way to select. As shown in Figure 15, a selection region is a shape with a dashed-line border that appears as you click and drag over an area with the Select Object Tool active. By default the selection region shape is a rectangle, but there are other options available from the Selection Region flyout, as shown in Figure 16. Click and hold the Selection Region button, then click the Circular Section Region button to change the selection region shape to a circle. The Fence Selection Region button enables you to click multiple times to create a "fence" around the objects you want selected. Click the Lasso Selection Region button to draw an irregular shape around the objects you want to select. Click the Paint Selection Region button to move the pointer, now a circle, like a paintbrush over the objects you want to select.

The Window/Crossing Selection toggle button on the Main toolbar determines how objects are selected when you use a selection region. By default, the toggle is set to **Crossing mode**, which means that any objects that are within or *cross* the selection region boundaries you create are selected. Click the toggle button to change to **Window mode** (the button turns yellow and the black circle appears within the dotted square outline); in this mode, only those objects that are entirely within the selection region are selected.

Selecting by Name

Every object that you create in a scene is assigned a name by default, and you can give specific names to objects as well. When you are building a scene with a lot of objects that overlap, or that are just hard to find, you might want to use the Select by Name tool to select an object or group of objects. To do

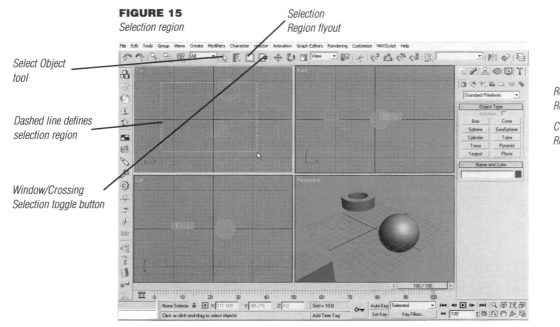

FIGURE 15
Selection region

FIGURE 16
Selection Region flyout

Lesson 2   Select Objects

AUTODESK 3D STUDIO MAX 2-13

this, click the Select by Name tool on the Main toolbar (or press [h]) to open the Select Objects dialog box, as shown in Figure 17. On the left side of the dialog box is a list of the names of the objects that are in the scene; any that are already selected are highlighted in blue. To select an object, click the object's name in the list, and then click Select. Press the [Ctrl] key to select multiple objects one at a time. To select all of the objects in the list, click the All button below the list. To deselect all selected objects in the list, click the None button below the list. If you want to select only those items that are not already selected and deselect any that are, click the Invert button under the list.

On the right side of the dialog box are options for viewing the objects in the list. You can sort the list alphabetically or by object type, color, or size. In the List Types area beneath the Sort area, you can choose which types of objects from your scene should be shown in the list. In a complex scene, this can help you narrow down the items in the list that you need and make the selection process much simpler.

Creating Selection Sets

As you are working on a scene, you might find yourself selecting the same group of objects over and over again, or a group of objects that you need to work on continuously might be somewhat hard to access. In both cases, you can create a **selection set**, or predefined group of selected objects, to make it easier to select the objects you need. To create a selection set, simply select the objects that you want to be in the set, and then click in the Named Selection Sets box on the Main toolbar, as shown in Figure 17. Type a name for the selection set into the box, and then press [Enter]. As you continue to work on the scene, when you want to select a selection set that you have created, click the Named Selection Sets list arrow, then click the name of the selection set you need. You can also select a selection set by clicking the Select by Name tool, clicking the Selection Sets list

FIGURE 17
Named Selection Tools and Select Objects dialog box

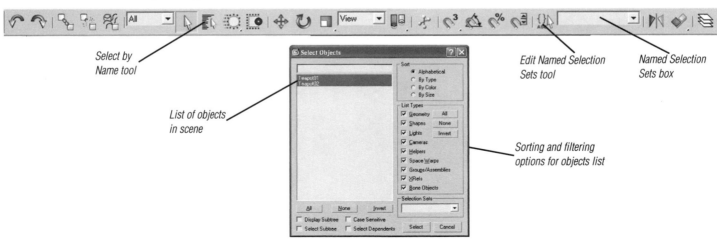

arrow in the Select Objects dialog box, and then clicking the name of the selection set you want. The objects in the selection set you click are highlighted in the list on the left side of the Select Objects dialog box.

After you have created a selection set or sets, you might want to edit the contents of the set. Click the Edit Named Selection Sets tool on the Main toolbar to open the Named Selection Sets dialog box. Click the Create New Set button to create a new selection set, or select a set and click the Remove button to remove it from the list; click the Add Selected Objects button or Subtract Selected Objects button to add items selected in the viewports to the set selected in the dialog box; click the Select Objects in Set button to select the items in the highlighted set; click the Select by Name button to select objects on-screen to add to a set; and click the Highlight Selected Objects button to show objects and selection sets that are currently selected in a font color different from unselected objects.

QUICKTIP

In addition to the Select Object and the Select by Name tools, you will find three other frequently used selection tools on the Main toolbar: the Select and Move tool, the Select and Rotate tool, and the Select and Scale tool. Because they function as more than just methods of selection, these tools are all covered in detail in Lesson 3, "Move, Rotate, and Scale Objects."

Select multiple objects by clicking

1. Create a box and two spheres similar in size and location to those shown in the Top viewport in Figure 18.
2. Click the **Select Object tool** on the Main toolbar, then click the **box** in the Top viewport.

   The box becomes white in the Top, Left, and Front viewports, indicating it is selected. In the Perspective viewport, white brackets appear around the box.
3. Press **[Ctrl]**, then click each of the two spheres to select them, as shown in Figure 19.

   All three objects are selected.
4. Click in the Top viewport away from the objects to deselect all of them, then save the file as **Selection Tools**.

You created three objects, selected each object one after the other by clicking, and then deselected the objects.

FIGURE 18
Box and two spheres in Top viewport

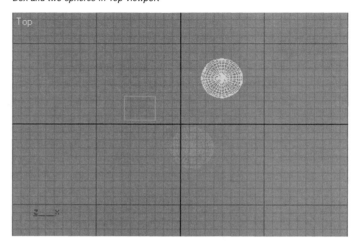

FIGURE 19
Three objects selected

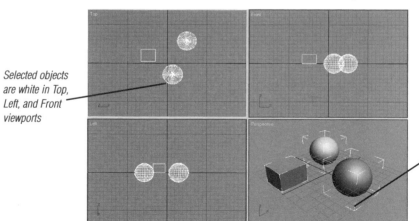

Selected objects are white in Top, Left, and Front viewports

Selected objects have white brackets in Perspective viewport

2-16 AUTODESK 3D STUDIO MAX

Building and Modifying Objects

FIGURE 20
First segment of fence selection region

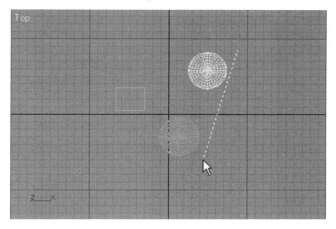

FIGURE 21
Completed fence selection region

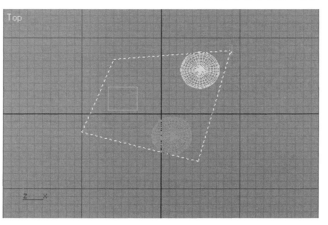

Select multiple objects using a selection region

1. Click the **Selection Region flyout**, hold down the mouse button, point to the **Fence Selection Region tool**, then release the mouse button.

2. In the Top viewport, click just above and right of the upper sphere, hold down the mouse button and drag to just below and to the right of the lower sphere, then release the mouse button.

   A dotted line appears to indicate the fence selection region you are creating, as shown in Figure 20.

3. Drag the mouse below and to the left of the box, click, drag the mouse to a point above the box, click, drag the mouse back to where you started the selection region near the upper sphere, then click one more time.

   You created a fence selection region made up of dotted lines running around all three of the objects, as shown in Figure 21. After the final click, the dotted lines disappear and all three objects within the region are selected.

4. Click away from the objects to deselect them, then save the file.

You selected three objects using a fence selection region, then deselected the objects.

Select objects by name

1. Click the **Select by Name tool** on the Main toolbar.

   The Select Objects dialog box opens.

2. In the object list, click **Sphere01**, press **[Ctrl]** and click **Sphere02**, then click **Select**.

   The Select Objects dialog box closes. Both spheres are now selected in the viewports.

3. Click the **Select by Name tool** again to open the Select Objects dialog box.

   Both spheres are highlighted in the objects list, indicating that they are selected.

4. Click **Invert** underneath the objects list.

   Box01 becomes highlighted and Sphere01 and Sphere02 are no longer highlighted, as shown in Figure 22.

5. Click **Select**.

   Only the box is now selected in the viewports.

6. Click away from the box to deselect it.

You used the Select by Name tool to select two spheres, and used the Invert button in the Select Objects dialog box to deselect the spheres and select the box.

FIGURE 22
Inverting a selection

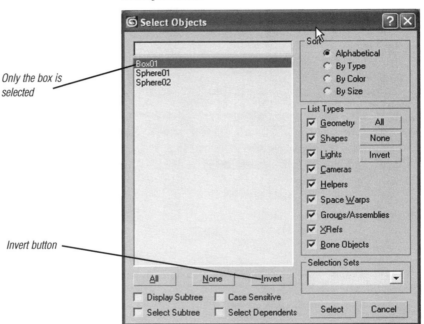

Only the box is selected

Invert button

2-18 AUTODESK 3D STUDIO MAX

Building and Modifying Objects

FIGURE 23
Working with Selection Sets

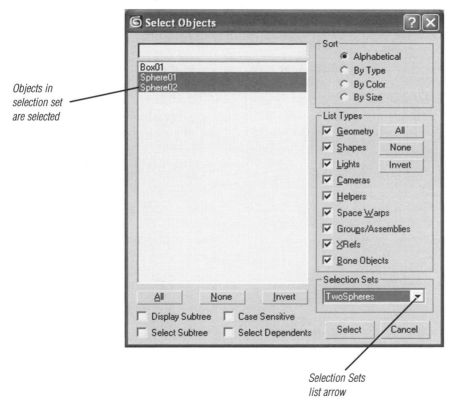

Objects in selection set are selected

Selection Sets list arrow

Create and use a selection set

1. Click the **Selection Region flyout** on the Main toolbar, then click the **Rectangular Selection Region tool**.
2. Click and drag the selection region around the two spheres to select them.
3. Click in the Named Selection Sets text box, type **TwoSpheres**, then press **[Enter]**.

   The two spheres now make up a selection set called TwoSpheres.
4. Click away from the spheres to deselect them, then click the **Select by Name tool** on the Main toolbar.

   The Select Objects dialog box opens.
5. Click the **Selection Sets list arrow**, then click **TwoSpheres**.

   Sphere01 and Sphere02 are now highlighted in the objects list, as shown in Figure 23.
6. Click **Select**.

   The Select Objects dialog box closes and the two spheres are selected in the viewports.
7. Save the file as **Two Spheres**, then reset 3ds Max.

You created a selection set containing two spheres, then selected the selection set using the Select by Name tool.

LESSON 3

MOVE, ROTATE, AND SCALE OBJECTS

What You'll Do

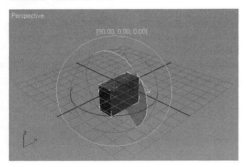

▶ *In this lesson, you will learn how to move, rotate, and scale an object using the Move, Rotate, and Scale tools on the Main toolbar. You will also learn about transform gizmos and how to use them effectively when moving, rotating, and scaling.*

There are three selection tools on the Main toolbar that you will use frequently as you work in 3ds Max. Technically, they are called the Select and Move tool (for selecting an object and changing its position), the Select and Rotate tool (for selecting an object and rotating it in relation to an axis or axes), and the Select and Scale tool (for selecting an object and changing its size). However, each of these tools is used so frequently that they'll be referred to as the Move, Rotate, and Scale tools.

Understanding Axes and Transform Gizmos

When you create an object, that object is created based on x-, y-, and z-axes known as the **axis tripod**. **Axes** measure points in space. If you are looking at the axis tripod from the front, the x-axis runs from the origination point to the right, the z-axis runs from the origination point upward, and the y-axis runs from the origination point away from you. All three axes of a selected object are shown in each viewport; however, only in the Perspective viewport can you see all three axes represented by lines. For example, in the Top viewport, you see an object's x- and y-axes as lines; but because you are looking at the z-axis head on (as though looking straight at the top of a needle), you only see the letter "z," not a line. See Figure 24.

QUICKTIP

Note that in 3ds Max, the z-axis is perpendicular to the home grid in the Perspective viewport. If you have used other graphics programs, you might be more familiar with the y-axis appearing in this position.

When you click the Move, Rotate, or Scale tools on the Main toolbar and then click an object, that object becomes selected and a transform gizmo appears within the object. A **gizmo** is geometry that appears on-screen within an object to help you manipulate the object. The gizmo that appears in an object to help you move, rotate, or scale the object is called a **transform gizmo**.

QUICKTIP

You can change the size of a gizmo by clicking it, holding down the mouse button, and then pressing + (the plus key) to increase the size or − (the minus key) to decrease the size.

Each transform gizmo is based on the axis tripod of the object. When you use the transform gizmo to transform the object, you can limit the transformation you make to the object to just one axis or two axes, or affect all three.

QUICKTIP

If you click the Move, Rotate, or Scale tool and then select an object and you don't see a transform gizmo, it might be turned off. To show the transform gizmo, click Views on the menu bar, and then click Show Transform Gizmo (a check mark appears next to the words when the gizmo is showing).

Using the Move Tool

After you create an object, you might decide that you want it to appear in a different place within a scene. If so, you can use the Move tool to change the position of an object relative to its axes. To move an object,

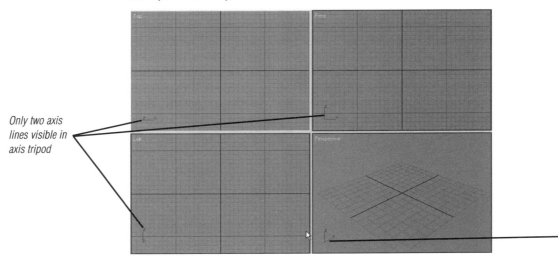

FIGURE 24
Axis tripod in each viewport

Only two axis lines visible in axis tripod

All three axis lines visible

Lesson 3   *Move, Rotate, and Scale Objects*

AUTODESK 3D STUDIO MAX 2-21

click the Select and Move tool on the Main toolbar (or press [w]), and then click the object you want to move. The Move gizmo appears in the object, as shown in Figure 25. Each arrow in the gizmo is colored according to the axis it affects; the x-axis arrow is red, the y-axis arrow is green, and the z-axis arrow is blue (a simple way to remember this is RGB = XYZ). If you want to move the object in relation to the x-axis, click the red arrow in the transform gizmo (the arrow line is yellow when selected), then drag. The movement of the object is constrained to the x-axis when moving the object this way; note that in the Top and Front viewports, the object moves only left or right. Clicking the arrow for the y-axis, or the z-axis and then dragging similarly constrains the movement of the object to those axes.

You can also use the transform gizmo to constrain the movement of an object along the plane between two axes. In the Move gizmo, select the square between the axes that you would like to move the object between, then drag to move the object. For instance, if you would like to move an object within the plane created by the x- and y-axes, select the square between the axes, as shown in Figure 25, then drag to move the object. Note that in the Top viewport the object moves in any direction you drag; in the Front and Left viewports the object only moves back and forth between right and left; you aren't able to move it along the z-axis (up and down).

Using the Rotate Tool

Just like the Move tool, the Rotate tool enables you to transform an object you have created; in this case, you can rotate the object in relation to one or more of its axes.

FIGURE 25
Move gizmo

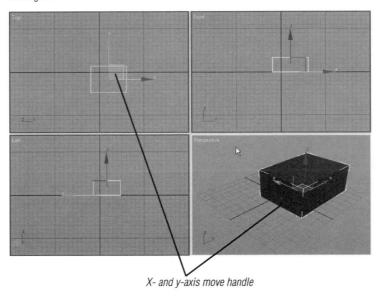

X- and y-axis move handle

To rotate an object, click the Rotate tool on the Main toolbar (or press [e]), then select an object. The Rotate gizmo appears, as shown in Figure 26. This gizmo is set up like a trackball, with circles around the ball representing the rotation handles for each axis. The red circle lets you rotate the object along the x-axis; the green circle enables rotation around the y-axis; and the blue circle enables rotation around the z-axis (RGB = XYZ). Click a circle to select it, and drag up or down to rotate the object along the axis it represents.

As you drag one of the axis handles in the Rotate gizmo, a set of three numbers appears above it. These numbers tell you how many degrees the object has rotated along the x-, y-, or z-axis as you drag. For example, as shown in Figure 26, when you rotate an object around the x-axis, the first number tells you how many degrees the object has rotated from its original position. The y and z rotation numbers are zero because the object is not rotating along those axes.

QUICKTIP

As you drag, if the pointer goes off the edge of the screen, it reappears on the opposite edge of the screen so you can continue dragging.

To rotate the object freely, as though you were actually using the Rotate gizmo as a trackball, click between the axis handles in the Rotate gizmo, then drag in the direction you want to rotate the object.

The outermost circle in the Rotate gizmo is called the Screen handle. When you click this handle and drag, you can rotate the object on a plane parallel to the viewport you are in.

Using the Scale Tool

If you want to change the size of an object, you use the Scale tool. There are three different versions of this tool available from

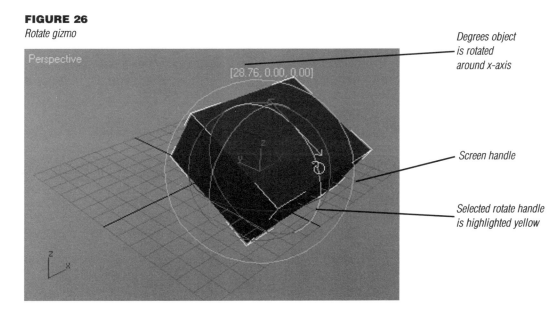

FIGURE 26
Rotate gizmo

Degrees object is rotated around x-axis

Screen handle

Selected rotate handle is highlighted yellow

Lesson 3 Move, Rotate, and Scale Objects

the Select and Scale flyout, as shown in Figure 27: the Select and Uniform Scale tool, the Select and Non-Uniform Scale tool, and the Select and Squash tool. Select and Uniform Scale enables you to change the size of an object by the same amount along all three axes. Select and Non-Uniform Scale lets you change the size of an object according to the axis to which you choose to constrain the change. Lastly, Select and Squash enables you to change the size of an object along one axis constraint and have the object change along its other axes in order to maintain its visual volume (for instance, if you shorten an object along the x-axis, it will get taller along the y-axis).

To change an object's size, click and hold the Scale tool, click the tool you want to use to change the object's size (or press [r] until the tool you want is active), and then click the object. The Scale gizmo appears in the object, as shown in Figure 28. Click and drag the red dot to scale an object along the x-axis; click and drag the green dot to scale an object along the y-axis; click and drag the blue dot to scale an object along the z-axis (RGB = XYZ). To scale an object uniformly along all three axes, click the center of the Scale gizmo, then drag. To scale an object uniformly between two axes, click the plane handle between the two axes.

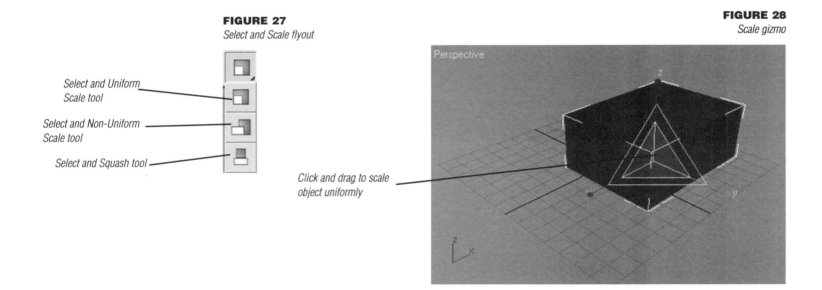

FIGURE 27
Select and Scale flyout

FIGURE 28
Scale gizmo

Using Transform Type-In Boxes

In addition to using transform gizmos, you can use Transform Type-In boxes to move, rotate, and scale objects. As shown in Figure 29, Transform Type-In boxes are available at the bottom of the screen in the status bar, or can be accessed by right-clicking the active Move, Rotate, or Scale tool on the Main toolbar.

The Transform Type-In boxes have two modes: Absolute and Offset. **Absolute** shows the exact position, rotation, or scale of an object along each axis; to change the object's absolute values, type in the box next to the X, Y, and/or Z axes to change the existing numbers. **Offset** enables you to enter a value to offset the object relative to its absolute position. For instance, if you want to rotate a sphere an additional 15 degrees along the x-axis from its current position, you would type 15 in the the X text box, and then press [Enter]. Transform Type-In boxes that appear when you right-click a tool on the Main toolbar show the Absolute and Offset settings at the same time. The Transform Type-In boxes on the status bar show only one mode at a time; click the Absolute/Offset Mode Transform Type-In button on the status bar to toggle between modes.

It is interesting that whether you select the Uniform or Non-Uniform Scale tool, the Scale gizmo that appears in your selected object enables you to make uniform or nonuniform changes, no matter which tool you chose. You will, however, see a difference between the Uniform and Non-Uniform tools in the Transform Type-in box for each. In the Uniform tool type-in box, the Offset area contains only one box where you can enter a percentage to increase the object's entire size. In the Non-Uniform tool Transform Type-In box, you can enter a percentage for each of the X, Y, and Z axes in the Offset area.

FIGURE 29
Transform Type-In boxes

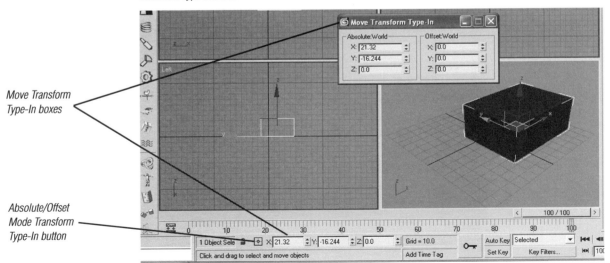

Move Transform Type-In boxes

Absolute/Offset Mode Transform Type-In button

Lesson 3 Move, Rotate, and Scale Objects

Move an object

1. Create a box like that shown in Figure 30, then click the **Select and Move tool** on the Main toolbar.

    The transform gizmo for the Move tool appears in the object in each of the viewports.

2. Click in the Top viewport, hold the mouse pointer over the red arrow until the pointer becomes a , then click and drag about four grid squares to the right.

    You can count the grid squares in the Perspective viewport as you drag in the Top viewport.

    The box moves to the right along the x-axis. You can view its movement in every viewport except the Left viewport, which looks at the x-axis head on.

    (continued)

FIGURE 30
Box in Perspective viewport

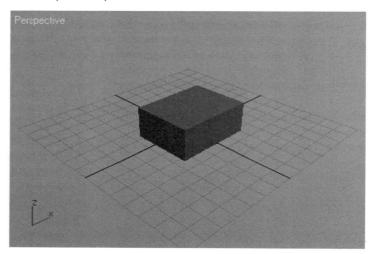

FIGURE 31
Move gizmo

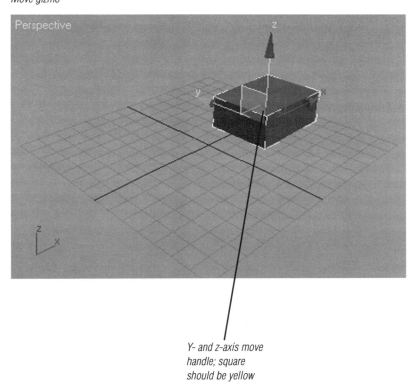

Y- and z-axis move handle; square should be yellow

3. Click in the Perspective viewport to activate it, click the **box** to select it, hold the mouse pointer over the square between the y- and z-axes to make it yellow, as shown in Figure 31, then click the square and drag the box up and down in the viewport.

    The box moves up and down along the z-axis in the Front and Left viewports (the Top viewport does not have a z-axis).

4. With the mouse pointer still over the square between the y- and z-axes to make it yellow, as shown in Figure 31, click the square and drag the box back and forth in the direction of the y-axis.

    The box moves along the y-axis in the Top and Left viewports. The Front viewport does not have a y-axis. If you see any movement in the Front viewport, it's because you are not dragging the box in a straight line, and therefore there is movement along the z-axis as well.

You used the Select and Move tool to move a box along one axis and then move the box along two axes.

Lesson 3 Move, Rotate, and Scale Objects

Rotate an object

1. Click the **Select and Rotate tool** ↻ on the Main toolbar, then select the **box** (if necessary).

   The Rotate gizmo appears around the box.

2. In the Perspective viewport, click the **red axis handle** in the Rotate gizmo so that it is yellow (selected), then drag down until the left number in the numerical data above the gizmo is around 90, as shown in Figure 32.

   The box is now rotated 90 degrees along the x-axis from its original orientation.

   TIP As you rotate, the circle within the axis fills with color. The darker the color, the more rotations have taken place.

3. Click the **green axis handle** in the Rotate gizmo so that it is yellow (selected), then drag up until the middle number in the numerical data above the gizmo is around 90, as shown in Figure 33.

   The box has now rotated 90 degrees along its y-axis. Notice that the numerical data above the gizmo reflects only the current change in orientation, so the x-axis number in the data is 0 even though the box was rotated along the x-axis in a previous step.

4. Click the **blue axis handle** in the Rotate gizmo so that it is yellow (selected), then drag to the right until the right number in the numerical data is around 45.

   The box has now rotated 45 degrees along its z-axis.

5. Save the file as **Rotate Object**, then reset 3ds Max.

You used the Rotate gizmo to rotate a box along its x-, y-, and z-axes.

2-28 AUTODESK 3D STUDIO MAX

FIGURE 32
Box rotated around x-axis

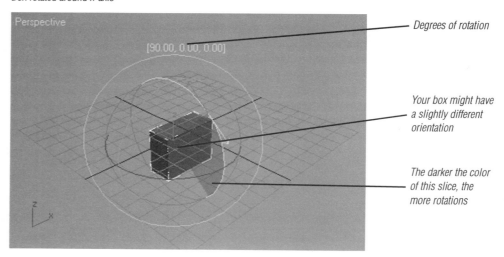

Degrees of rotation

Your box might have a slightly different orientation

The darker the color of this slice, the more rotations

FIGURE 33
Box rotated around y-axis

Only current rotation data are reflected

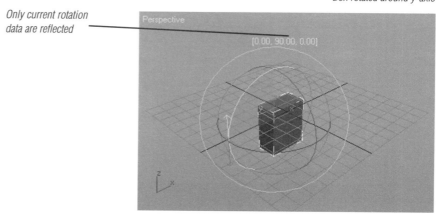

Building and Modifying Objects

FIGURE 34

Teapot with scale increased along x- and y-axes

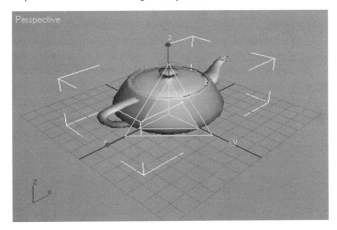

Scale an object

1. Create a teapot whose body is about four grid squares in diameter.
2. Click the **Select and Uniform Scale tool** on the Main toolbar, then click the **teapot** (if necessary) in the Perspective viewport.

   The Scale gizmo appears in the teapot.
3. Click the **handle** between the x- and y-axes, then drag down about one inch.

   The scale of the teapot increases along both its x- and y-axes, as shown in Figure 34.
4. Click the **handle** at the center of the Scale gizmo, then drag up about one-half inch.

   The scale of the object increases uniformly along all three axes.
5. Click the **Select and Scale flyout**, then click the **Select and Squash tool**.

   (continued)

Lesson 3   Move, Rotate, and Scale Objects

AUTODESK 3D STUDIO MAX 2-29

6. Click the **blue dot** in the Scale gizmo and drag down about one-half inch.

   Because the Select and Squash tool is being used, the teapot decreases in length along the z-axis, but maintains about the same volume by increasing in length along its x- and y-axes. See Figure 35.

7. Save the file as **Scale Object**.

You increased the scale of the teapot along two axes, increased the scale uniformly along all axes using the Select and Uniform Scale tool, then used the Select and Squash tool to increase the teapot's length along one axis while maintaining its volume.

Use the Transform Type-In to transform an object

1. Right-click the **Select and Squash tool** on the Main toolbar.

   The Scale Transform Type-In dialog box opens, with boxes for both Absolute and Offset values.

2. In the Absolute: Local rollout, type **100** in each of the X, Y, and Z boxes.

   The teapot returns to the size it was before you made any scaling changes to it.

3. Click the **Scale Transform Type-In dialog box Close button**, then right-click the **Select and Rotate tool** to open the Rotate Transform Type-In dialog box.

4. In the Absolute: World rollout, click the **X spinner** and drag up until the value in the X text box is approximately 30.

(continued)

FIGURE 35
Squashed teapot

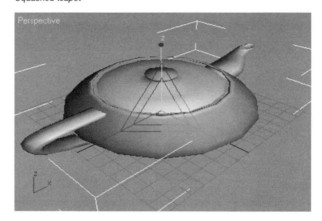

FIGURE 36
Rotate Transform Type-In dialog box

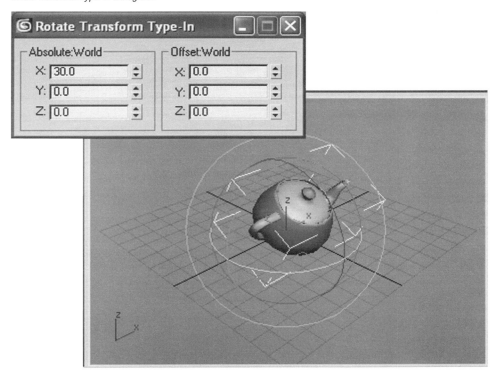

The teapot is now rotated 30 degrees from its original orientation, as shown in Figure 36.

5. Click the **Rotate Transform Type-In Close button** ⊠, then click the **Select and Move tool** ⊕.

   At the bottom of the screen, the Transform Type-In boxes in the status bar show the absolute location of the box relative to the center of the home grid.

6. At the bottom of the window, click the **Absolute Mode Transform Type-In button** to the left of the Transform Type-In boxes to toggle to offset mode, type **10** in the X box, press **[Enter]**, type **10** in the Y box, press **[Enter]**, type **10** in the Z box, then press **[Enter]**.

   The teapot moves 10 spaces along each of its axes in the viewports.

7. Click the **Offset Mode Transform Type-In button**.

   Notice that the absolute X, Y, and Z values for the teapot have each increased by 10.

8. Save the file, then reset 3ds Max.

You used Transform Type-In boxes to scale an object back to its original size, to rotate an object along one of its axes, and to offset an object from its current position.

Lesson 3   Move, Rotate, and Scale Objects

AUTODESK 3D STUDIO MAX 2-31

LESSON 4

MODIFY
A POLYGON OBJECT

What You'll Do

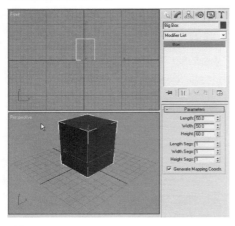

In this lesson, you will learn how to use the Modify panel to rename, recolor, and change the physical parameters of an object.

After you create an object, you can modify its many aspects using the Modify panel. You can make very basic modifications such as renaming the object, or you can make complex changes to the object. After you create an object, select the object and then click the Modify tab on the Command panel to open the Modify panel.

QUICKTIP

If you do not have an object selected, no information appears on the Modify panel when opened.

Renaming and Recoloring an Object

After you have selected an object and opened the Modify panel, the text box at the top of the panel displays the default name for the object, as shown in Figure 37. This is the name that appears for the object in the Select by Name list or in a selection set. If you want to give the object a name other than the default, simply select the text in the text box, type the name you want to give the object, and then press [Enter].

To the right of the name text box is a color box. This box shows the current display color of the object, automatically assigned to the object when created. In 3ds Max, the display color of the object isn't as significant as the colors and materials applied to the object using the Material Editor (covered in Chapter 4). However, as you work you might want to use color to classify objects within a scene or to help you distinguish between wireframe objects in a complicated scene. To modify an object's color, click the color box on the Modify panel, click a color in the Object Color dialog box, and then click OK.

Changing the Parameters of an Object

All objects have physical settings, or **parameters**. You can modify the parameters of an object using the Parameters section of the Modify panel. To change the parameters of an object, select the object, then change the appropriate parameter in the Parameters section by either typing in a number or using the spinner to adjust a number up or down.

The parameters that an object has depend on the type of object it is, although for all objects you can adjust the number of segments on an object's faces (and/or the number of sides the object has) using the Parameters section. See Lesson 5 for more about segments and sides. For a box, you can adjust the length, height, and width parameters; for a plane, you can adjust the length and width parameters; for a pyramid, the height, width, and depth are adjustable parameters.

You can adjust the radius of a sphere or geosphere, the height of a cylinder or cone and the radii of its surfaces, and the radii of the inner and outer circumferences of a torus and a tube in the Parameters section. You can also change the radius of a teapot's body and deselect check boxes to make any of its four parts (body, handle, spout, or lid) disappear from the screen.

QUICKTIP

When you first create an object, you can manually adjust the parameters of the object by typing into the Parameters section of the Create panel before deselecting the object. You can also create an object with specific parameters by clicking the button for the object on the Create panel, then entering the parameters in the Keyboard Entry section of the Create panel instead of clicking and dragging in a viewport.

Setting Smooth, Slice, and Hemisphere Parameters

Objects with rounded surfaces (sphere, geosphere, cylinder, cone, tube, and torus) are by default smooth in appearance—this means that the software has made the edges between the segments appear to be rounded. To turn off the smoothing effect for an object, deselect the Smooth check box in the Parameters section of the Create panel.

You can greatly affect the appearance of an object in this same group by using the slice function available in the Parameters section. When you turn on slice for an object, you

FIGURE 37
Modify panel

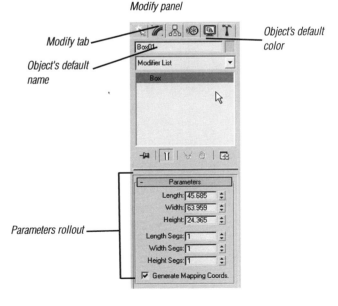

Lesson 4   Modify a Polygon Object

AUTODESK 3D STUDIO MAX 2-33

are showing only a slice of the object from one point to another around the vertical axis, as defined in the Parameters section. For instance, the sphere in Figure 38 shows a slice of the sphere from 90 to 180 degrees. To turn on slice, click the Slice On check box to select it, and then type the desired settings in the Slice From and Slice To boxes (or click the spinner buttons to adjust the numbers in the boxes).

QUICKTIP

You can slice a geosphere only if you first convert it to a polygon. See Chapter 3, "Modeling," for more information on converting objects to polygons.

For a sphere, you can change the parameters of the sphere so that only part of it appears. A sphere can have a hemisphere value from 0.0 to 1.0, where 0 is a full sphere, .5 is a hemisphere, and 1 is nothing. Click the Chop option button if you want the number of segments in the hemisphere to go down as the sphere is reduced in size; click the Squash check box if you want the number of segments to remain the same. A geosphere can also be changed into a hemisphere from a full sphere; click the Hemisphere check box in a geosphere's Parameters section to make this happen.

QUICKTIP

You can click a spinner button and drag to the top of the interface to adjust a parameter. If you drag to the top of the interface, notice how the cursor reappears at the bottom of the screen. You can drag a spinner button up or down forever!

FIGURE 38
Sphere sliced from 90 to 180 degrees

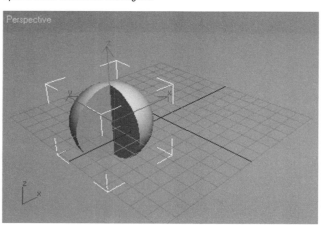

FIGURE 39
Object Color dialog box and renamed and recolored box

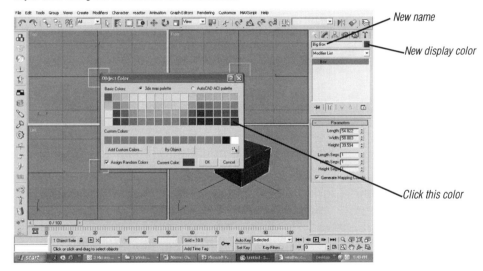

Rename and recolor an object

1. Create a box in the Top viewport, then click the **Modify** tab on the Command panel.

   The Modify panel opens in the Command panel.

2. Select the text **Box01** in the text box at the top of the panel, type **Big Box**, then press **[Enter]**.

3. Click the **color box** to the right of the name text box.

   The Object Color dialog box opens, as shown in Figure 39.

4. Click the **red box** at the far right of the bottom row under Basic Colors, then click **OK**.

   The color of the box on-screen changes to the color you just chose, as shown in Figure 39.

You used the Modify panel to give an object a new name and change its display color.

Modify the parameters of a box

1. Make sure the box is selected.

2. In the Parameters rollout in the Modify panel, select the value in the Length text box, type **50**, then press **[Enter]**.

   The length of the box changes to 50 in the viewports.

3. Select the value in the Width text box, type **50**, select the value in the Height text box, type **60**, then press **[Enter]**.

(continued)

Lesson 4   Modify a Polygon Object

AUTODESK 3D STUDIO MAX 2-35

The Width and Height parameters of the box change to those you typed, as shown in Figure 40.

4. Save the file as **Box Param**, then reset 3ds Max.

You used the Modify panel to change the Length, Width, and Height parameters of a box.

Modify the parameters of a sphere

1. Create a sphere in the Top viewport, then click the **Modify tab** on the Command panel.

   The Modify panel opens, showing the parameters of the sphere.

2. In the Parameters rollout of the Modify panel, increase the value in the Radius text box by approximately 5.

   The sphere's size increases in the viewports.

3. Select the value in the Hemisphere text box, type **.5**, then press **[Enter]**.

   Half of the sphere disappears, as shown in Figure 41.

4. Select the value in the Hemisphere text box, type **.8**, then press **[Enter]**.

   Only about 20% of the original sphere is still visible in the viewport.

5. Select the value in the Hemisphere text box, type **0**, then press **[Enter]**.

   The sphere returns to a full sphere.

(continued)

FIGURE 40
Box with modified parameters

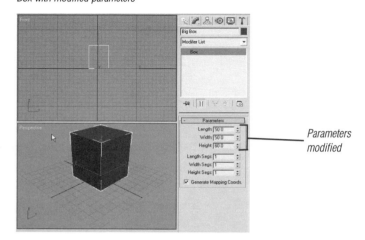

Parameters modified

FIGURE 41
Sphere with hemisphere parameter at .5

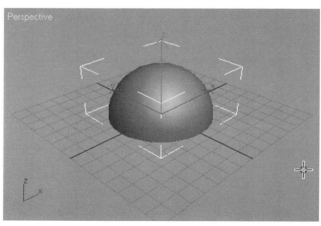

FIGURE 42
Cone in Perspective viewport

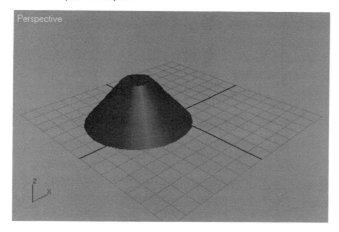

FIGURE 43
Sliced cone

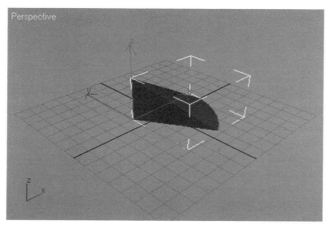

6. Save the file as **Sphere Param**, then reset 3ds Max.

You increased the radius of a sphere, then used the Hemisphere parameter to show only 50% and 20% of the sphere, before returning the sphere to its full size on-screen.

Modify the parameters of a cone

1. Create a cone similar to the one shown in Figure 42.
2. Click the **Modify tab** on the Command panel to open the Modify panel.
3. In the Parameters rollout, use the spinner buttons to increase Radius 1 by 20 and to decrease Radius 2 to 0.

   The cone now has a wider base and comes to a point (with a radius of 0) at the top.
4. Click the **Slice On check box** to select it, select the value in the Slice From box, type **350**, select the value in the Slice To box, type **300**, then press **[Enter]**.

   Only a slice of the cone is showing. The slice is the part of the cone between the points 350 and 300 degrees from the x-axis. The cone should now look similar to Figure 43.
5. Save the file as **Cone Slice**, then reset 3ds Max.

You created a cone, modified its base and top radius parameters, and sliced the cone using the Modify panel.

AUTODESK 3D STUDIO MAX 2-37

LESSON 5

WORK WITH SEGMENTS

What You'll Do

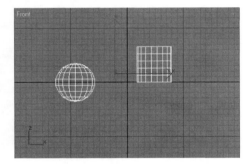

In this lesson, you will learn about the importance of segments on an object and how to use the Modify panel to adjust the number of segments used in an object.

Understanding Segments

When you create an object, the surfaces of the object are made up of segments. **Segments** are straight lines that visually divide an area of an object. Segments don't actually divide an object into pieces; they simply break down an object's surface into smaller parts, so that the object might appear to be smoother or more flexible as the modifications to the object become more complex.

As you add segments to the surface of an object, that surface becomes more flexible and, if deformed, more rounded. Think of a flexi-straw you might get at a fast-food restaurant. The straw has creases so it bends easily where the creases exist; a straw without such creases could only bend sharply at one point. Segments on an object's surface are like the creases in the straw—they enable an object to deform more gradually and naturally. In Figure 44, two boxes with the same dimensions have each been bent 100 degrees. The height of the box on the left contains seven segments, whereas the height of the box on the right contains only two. Thus, like the flexi-straw, the box on the left bends more gradually and looks more rounded.

Segments might run left to right or up and down on a flat surface. On a round surface, such as the height of a cylinder or height of a cone, the segments appear around the circumference of the surface rather than from one end of the surface to the other, as shown in Figure 45. However, you can adjust the roundedness of the cylinder by adjusting the number of **sides** it has. The more sides it has, the more rounded its surface.

Adjusting the Segments on an Object

You can adjust the number of segments on an object, and the number of sides in a round object, in the Parameters section of the Modify panel. Select the object, and then click the Modify tab on the Command panel. Type numbers or use the slider buttons in the appropriate object area to adjust the number of segments on the selected object. For instance, you can change the number of segments on the length, height, or width

2-38 AUTODESK 3D STUDIO MAX

Building and Modifying Objects

areas of a box, or on the cap (top surface) and height of a tube. For rounded objects, change the number of sides to increase or decrease the smoothness of the round area of the object.

Note that the number shown in a segments box isn't necessarily the number of segments you will see; rather, it shows the number of sections the surface is divided into by segments. If you change the number of segments in the length of a box to four, you'll see the length of the box divided into four sections by the addition of three segments, rather than seeing four segment lines added.

Although adding segments to an object that doesn't have many adds flexibility and/or smoothness to an object, it is possible to have too many segments. There is a point beyond which more segments don't add more smoothness or more flexibility. In addition, using too many segments can mean the file size of your scene is increased unnecessarily. However, there is no magic formula for knowing the right number of segments to use in an object; as you work with 3ds Max over time, you will get a feel for what works best in the different situations you encounter.

QUICKTIP

As a modeler you will have to decide how many segments are necessary to get the shape you need. If you use too few segments, your shape might be deformed. If you use too many segments, 3ds Max takes too long to render the scene.

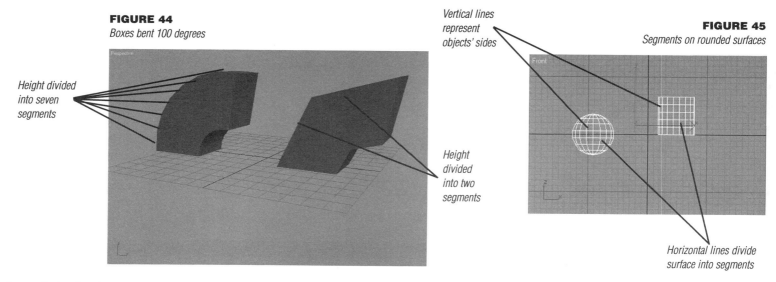

FIGURE 44
Boxes bent 100 degrees

Height divided into seven segments

Vertical lines represent objects' sides

Height divided into two segments

FIGURE 45
Segments on rounded surfaces

Horizontal lines divide surface into segments

Lesson 5 Work with Segments

AUTODESK 3D STUDIO MAX 2-39

Adjust the segments on an object

1. Create a box and a cylinder similar to those shown in Figure 46, then save the file as **Segments**.
2. Select the **box**, then click the **Modify tab** to open the Modify panel.
3. In the Parameters rollout in the Modify panel, click the **top spinner button** next to the Length Segs box and drag it up until the value in the box is 4.

   The length of the box is now divided by segments into four sections, which you can see in the Top viewport and the Left viewport.

4. Click the **top spinner button** next to the Width Segs until the Width Segs value is 4.

   The width of the box is now divided by segments into four sections, viewable from the Top and the Front viewports.

5. Select the **cylinder**, then in the Parameters rollout of the Modify panel, click the **spinner button** next to Height Segments and increase the Height Segments value to 7.

   The cylinder is now divided into seven sections by segments that run around its circumference.

6. Click the **top spinner button** next to the Cap Segments box until the Cap Segments value is 4.

(continued)

FIGURE 46
Box and cylinder

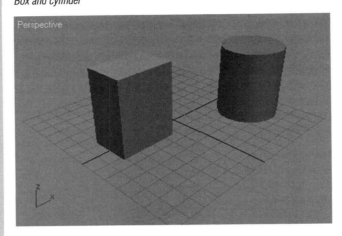

FIGURE 47
Box and cylinder with segments modified

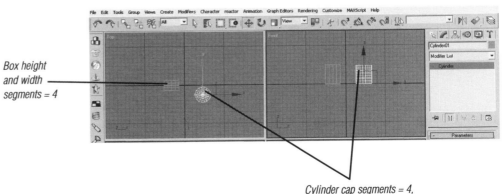

Box height and width segments = 4

Cylinder cap segments = 4, height segments = 7

The top surface of the cylinder is now divided into four circular sections, as shown in Figure 47. Notice that the cylinder is also divided into sections according to the number of sides it has, which is 18.

You used the Modify panel to increase the number of segments on the surfaces of a box and a cylinder.

Adjust the sides on an object

1. Make sure the cylinder is selected.
2. In the Parameters rollout of the Modify panel, click the **lower spinner button** next to the Sides box until the Sides value is 8.

   The cylinder goes from being round to having an octagonal shape, as shown in Figure 48. Even though 3ds Max is smoothing the corners between sides, the cylinder does not have enough sides to maintain a round shape.

3. Click the **top spinner button** next to the Sides box to increase the Sides value to 15.

   Increasing the number of sides to 15 greatly increases the rounded appearance of the cylinder, although some faint corners between sides are still visible.

4. Click the **top spinner button** next to the Sides box to return the Sides value to 18.

   The cylinder is once again as round as it was when it was created.

5. Save the file, then reset 3ds Max.

You lowered the number of sides in a cylinder to see the effect on the cylinder's roundness, then increased the number of sides to increase the cylinder's roundness.

FIGURE 48
Cylinder with eight sides

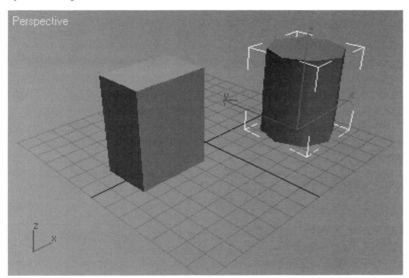

AUTODESK 3D STUDIO MAX 2-41

LESSON 6

APPLY MODIFIERS

What You'll Do

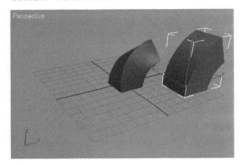

In this lesson, you will learn how to use the Modify panel to apply modifiers to an object.

Modifiers are a key part of creating scenes in 3ds Max. **Modifiers** are specific methods of changing an object's appearance and structure or the appearance and structure of its subcomponents. For example, you can use the Bend modifier to bend an object, or you can use the Twist modifier to twist an object.

Understanding the Modifier Stack

There are over a hundred modifiers available for use in 3ds Max, but we won't try to cover each one in detail. However, it is important to know how to apply modifiers to an object so that you can experiment with different modifiers and become more familiar with the modifiers available for your use in creating scenes.

It's also important to note that modifiers are applied to an object in a "stack." The **modifier stack** has an object at its base, and modifiers applied to that object appear above the object in the stack, in the order that the modifiers were applied. For instance, the box in Figure 49 first had a Bend modifier applied to it, then a Twist modifier. You can apply as many modifiers as you want to an object, and you can apply the same modifier to one object multiple times. To apply a modifier to an object, select the object, click the Modify tab on the Command panel to open the Modify panel, click the Modifier List list arrow, then select a modifier from the list. The modifier appears at the top of the modifier stack in the Modify panel; change the parameters of the modifier in the Parameters rollout to modify the object.

One of the most important things to know about the modifier stack is that you can come back to an existing modifier and adjust it. You can also always go back down to your base object and adjust that. This process is referred to as "moving up and down the stack." To do this, find a modifier in the stack and click it. Notice that the parameters listed in the Modify panel now refer to the particular modifier you have selected. As you continue to work with an object, you can adjust the parameters of any modifier by clicking the modifier in the modifier stack, and then adjusting the parameters as needed. Click the object at the base of the modifier stack if you want to adjust the parameters of the original object.

FIGURE 49
Box with Bend and Twist modifiers applied

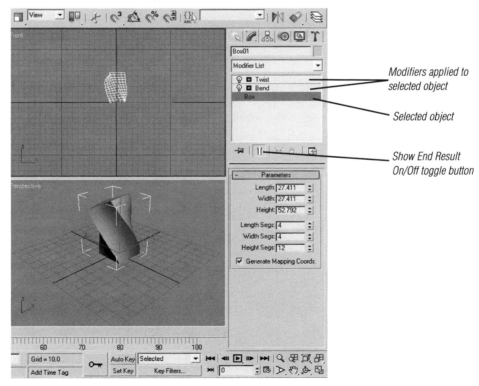

Lesson 6 Apply Modifiers

Working with the Modifier Stack

The order that you place modifiers onto an object is important. As shown in Figure 50, if you bend and then twist an object, you will get a different result than if you twist and then bend the same object, with all of the same parameters. You can rearrange modifiers in the stack simply by clicking, dragging, and dropping modifiers into a new location in the stack.

If you no longer want or need a modifier, you can delete the modifier by selecting it and then clicking the Remove modifier from the stack button under the modifier stack, as shown in Figure 51. An alternative way to delete a modifier is to right-click the modifier and choose Delete from the right-click menu. In addition, if you want to temporarily see what an object looks like without a modifier applied, yet you don't want to delete the modifier, click the Lightbulb icon to the left of the modifier name in the modifier stack. The object will be shown on-screen without the modifier applied. Click the icon again to reapply the modifier.

Sometimes you might be working on a modifier but need to select another object in the scene. To continue to view the modifier you are working on, you can "pin the stack."

Pinning the stack allows you to keep your current modifier active in the Modify panel no matter which object is selected. To pin the stack, make sure you have the modifier you want to pin selected, and then click the Pin Stack button under the modifier stack in the Modify panel.

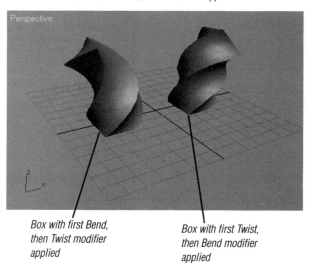

FIGURE 50
Boxes with Bend/Twist and Twist/Bend modifiers applied

Box with first Bend, then Twist modifier applied

Box with first Twist, then Bend modifier applied

You can control what version of the object you see on-screen by using the Show end result on/off toggle button. When this button is selected ("on"), the selected object appears on-screen with all active (light bulbs on) modifiers applied, no matter which modifier is selected in the modify panel. When you choose a modifier from the stack, an orange outline known as the modifier's gizmo appears on-screen for adjusting the parameters of the modifier, but the object still appears with all modifiers applied. When the Show end result on/off toggle button is not selected ("off"), when you click a modifer the object appears on-screen with only that modifier applied, as shown in Figure 51.

You can create your own set of modifiers to appear in the Modifier List if you want to have quick access to a standard set of modifiers you use frequently. To create your own set of modifiers, click the Configure Modifier Sets button, and then click Configure Modifier Sets on the menu that appears. Adjust the number in the Total Buttons box to the number of modifiers you want to have in your set. Then drag and drop modifiers from the list on the left to the empty buttons on the right (and, similarly, drag and drop modifiers you don't need from the buttons on the right to clear space for new modifiers). After you have the set of modifiers you want, enter a name for the set into the Sets text box, click Save, and then click OK. In the Modify panel, click the Modify List list arrow; your newly configured set should appear at the top of the list.

Applying Modifiers to Multiple Objects

There are several ways to apply the same modifier to multiple objects. Most simply, of course, you can apply a modifier to one object with a specific set of parameters and then apply that same modifier to another object and manually enter the same set of parameters. There will be no connection between the modifiers, even though they are the same.

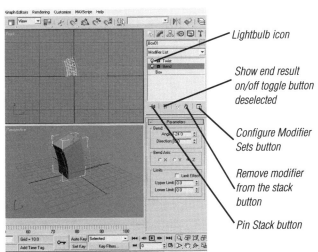

FIGURE 51
Show End Result on/off toggle button turned off

You can also drag and drop a modifier from one object to another. To do this, select an object, click the modifier you want to apply to the second object, and then drag the modifier to the object on-screen. This applies the modifier's original parameters to the new object without you having to enter the parameters manually; then the modifiers can still be edited independently of one another.

You can also select several different objects and apply a modifier to all of them at once. As with applying a modifier to a single object, simply select all of the objects you would like to modify, click a modifier on the Modifier List, and then adjust the parameters of the modifier until the objects appear as you desire. For instance, Figure 52 shows four boxes that have had a single Bend modifier applied to them.

If you apply a single modifier to multiple objects, you'll notice that in the modifier stack for any of the objects, the modifier is in italics, as shown in Figure 52. If you deselect all of the objects, and then select just one of them and adjust the modifier parameters, all of the objects are still affected. However, it is possible to change the modifier parameters for one object in a group without affecting the other objects. To do this, select the object, click the Make Unique button under the modifier stack, and then adjust the parameters of the modifier as needed. Only the selected object is affected by changes you make to the modifier's parameters; the modifier in the modifier stack for the selected object is no longer italicized.

FIGURE 52
Bend modifier applied to four boxes

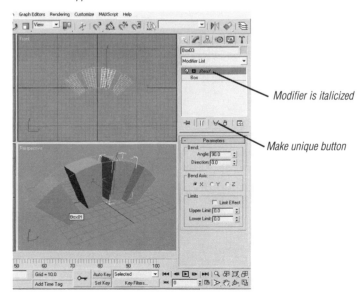

2-46 AUTODESK 3D STUDIO MAX

Building and Modifying Objects

FIGURE 53
Box with modifiers applied

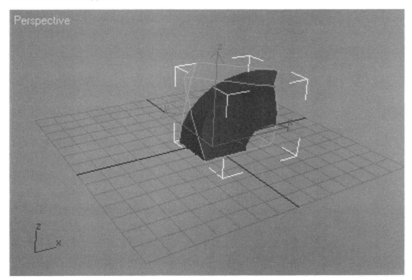

Apply modifiers to an object

1. Create a box with a Length of **25**, a Width of **25**, and a Height of **45**.
2. Click the **Modify tab**, then in the Parameters rollout on the Modify panel, increase the number in the Height segs box to **8**.
3. Click the **Modifier List list arrow** on the Modify panel, then click **Bend** in the modifier list.

   TIP Bend appears under OBJECT-SPACE MODIFIERS.

   The Bend modifier is applied to the box; because you have not adjusted the modifier's parameters, it does not bend the box yet. On your screen an orange outline appears around the box representing the modifier.
4. In the Parameters rollout, click the **Angle spinner button** until the Angle number reaches 90.

   TIP The box bends to the right.
5. Click the **Modifier List list arrow**, then click **Twist** in the modifier list.

   TIP You might need to scroll the list to see Twist.

   A Twist modifier appears above the Bend modifier in the modifier stack.
6. In the Parameters rollout, click the **Angle spinner button** until the Angle number reaches 45.
7. Save the file as **Modifiers**.

   The box twists 45 degrees around its z-axis, as shown in Figure 53.

You created a box and applied Bend and Twist modifiers to the box.

Work with the modifier stack

1. Click the **Lightbulb icon** next to the Bend modifier in the modifier stack.

   The Bend modifier becomes inactive, and the box is now twisted, but not bent.

2. Click the darkened **Lightbulb icon** next to the Bend modifier to reactivate it.

3. Click the **Bend modifier**, then drag the **Bend modifier** so that it is located above the Twist modifier in the modifier stack.

   The order in which the modifiers are applied (bend, then twist) changes (twist, then bend), and the box appears as shown in Figure 54.

4. Click the **Show end result on/off toggle button** to deselect it, then click the **Twist modifier** in the modifier stack.

   The box shows only the selected Twist modifier applied to it.

5. Click the **Show end result on/off toggle button** again.

   The box now has all active modifiers applied.

6. Click the **Create tab**, create a second box (Box02) in the Top viewport with the dimensions **30 × 30 × 50**, click the **Modify tab**, then adjust the box's Length segments to **8**.

   (continued)

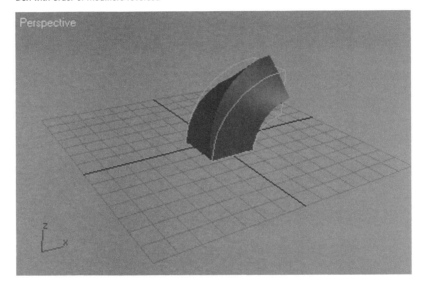

FIGURE 54
Box with order of modifiers reversed

FIGURE 55
Box with pinned modifier stack

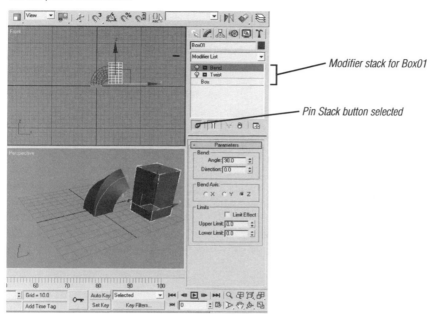

Modifier stack for Box01

Pin Stack button selected

7. Click the **original box** to select it, click the **Pin Stack button** under the modifier stack, then click the **new box**.

    The Modify panel continues to show the modifier stack for the first box, even though the second box is selected, as shown in Figure 55.

8. Click the **Pin Stack button** again to deselect it.

You made a modifier temporarily inactive, moved a modifier up in the modifier stack, toggled the Show end result button on and off, and pinned the modifier stack for one object while selecting another.

Lesson 6 Apply Modifiers

Copy a modifier to another object

1. Select the **first box (Box01)**, click the **Bend modifier** in the modifier stack, then drag the **Bend modifier** to Box02.

   The Bend modifier from Box01 is applied, with the same parameters, to Box02.

2. Click the **Angle spinner button**, then adjust the Angle number down until it reaches **60**.

   The bend angle of Box02 changes as its Bend modifier's parameters change, as shown in Figure 56. Notice Box01 and its modifiers are unaffected.

   You copied the modifier from one object to another, then adjusted the modifier's parameters.

FIGURE 56
Bend modifier copied to second object and changed

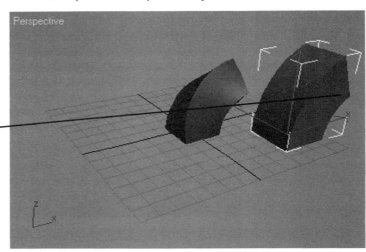

Bend angle changed to 60 degrees

FIGURE 57
Taper modifier applied to two boxes

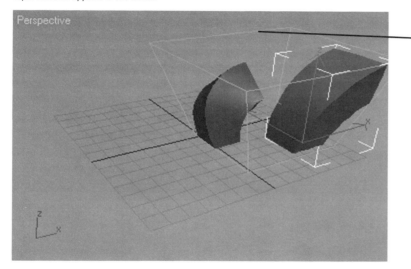

Orange outline encompasses both boxes

Apply modifiers to a group of objects

1. Select both **Box01** and **Box02**, click the **Modifier List list arrow**, then click **Taper**.

   TIP You might need to scroll to see Taper on the list.

   The Taper modifier is now applied to both objects at once, as indicated by the orange outline appearing around both boxes.

2. In the Parameters rollout, adjust the Amount number until it is **.5**.

   Both objects are tapered as though they are one object, as shown in Figure 57.

3. Click **Box01** to select it, then click **Box02** to select it.

   The Taper modifier appears, in italics, at the top of each object's modifier stack.

4. With Box02 selected, click the **Make unique button** under the modifier stack, then adjust the Amount number in the Parameters rollout to **1**.

   The Taper modifier now only applies to Box02. Box02 changes, while Box01 remains unaffected.

5. Save the file, then reset 3ds Max.

You applied one modifier to multiple objects, then made one object unique and adjusted its modifier without affecting the other object.

Lesson 6   Apply Modifiers

AUTODESK 3D STUDIO MAX 2-51

LESSON 7

CLONE OBJECTS

What You'll Do

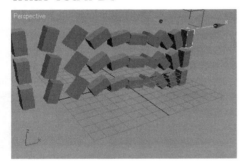

▶ *In this lesson, you will learn how to clone objects by creating a copy, instance, or reference of an object. You will also learn how to create an array of objects.*

As you work in 3ds Max, you often need to duplicate, or **clone**, objects that you have already created in order to save time and enhance your creative options. There are several different kinds of object clones that you can make, each with its own advantages.

Cloning an Object

To create a clone of an object, select the object, click Edit on the menu bar, and then click Clone. The Clone Options dialog box appears, as shown in Figure 58, giving you several options from which to choose.

If you want to create a **copy** of the object only, with no subsequent effect on the copy if you apply modifiers to the original, click the Copy option button in the Clone Options dialog box, type a name for the copy in the Name text box, and then click OK. A copy of the object will appear in the same location as the original object.

You can also use the Clone Options dialog box to create an instance of an object. An **instance** is a clone of an object that is affected by any modifiers applied to the original, and vice versa. Whatever you do to one is done to the other. If you apply a bend modifier to the original, the instance bends in exactly the same way. If you apply a twist modifier to the instance, the original twists exactly the same way. To create an instance, click the Instance option button in the Clone Options dialog box, type a name for the instance in the Name text box if you want another name for it besides the default, and then click OK. An instance of the object will appear in exactly the same location as the original object.

A third type of clone you can create is a reference. A **reference** is a copy of an object that changes according to the changes made to the original, but changes to the reference won't affect the original. In other words, what you do to the original is done to the reference, but not vice versa. If you apply a modifier to the original, it is applied to the reference copy, but if you apply a modifer to the reference copy, it does not affect the original. To create a reference, click the Reference option button in the Clone Options dialog box, type a name for the reference in the Name text box, and then click OK. A reference of the object will appear in exactly the same location as the original object.

QUICKTIP

If you change the position, rotation, or scale of an object, an object's instance, or an object's reference, those changes are not reflected elsewhere. However, if you apply a modifier to an instance, its original, or its reference, those changes are reflected elsewhere.

Creating a Transformational Clone

You can also clone objects while using the Move, Rotate or Scale tools. As you transform an object using one of these tools, hold down the [Shift] key. When you do this, you automatically create a clone of the object with the new transformational parameters (such as a clone in a new position, with a different rotation, or a different scale). When you complete the transformation and let go of the mouse button, the Clone Options dialog box appears containing the Copy, Instance, and Reference options. Click the option button for the type of clone you want to create. There is one additional option in this dialog box that you don't get when you choose Edit/Clone to open the dialog box; in this instance of the dialog box, you can also choose the number of clones. This is particularly useful for creating numerous clones with the Move tool because each copy will be offset the exact distance that you move it. This means that as you move the clone, for instance, five units to the right, all of the copies will be five units to the right of each other. See Figure 59 for an example of two copies of a cone made by using the Move gizmo and holding down [Shift].

Creating an Array

When you want to clone and transform multiple objects and position them in relation to each other, your best bet for doing this is the Array tool. The array tool enables you to combine transformations (moving, rotating,

FIGURE 58
Clone Options dialog box

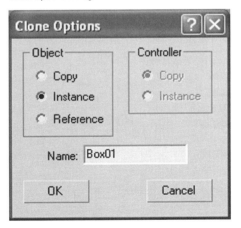

FIGURE 59
Two cone copies created by transformational cloning

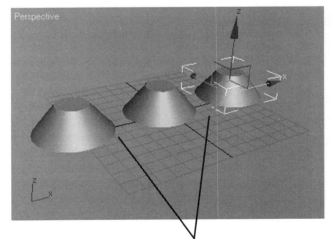

Distance first clone moved duplicated with second copy

Lesson 7   Clone Objects

AUTODESK 3D STUDIO MAX 2-53

scaling) when cloning and create an **array**, or a series of objects arranged along one or more axes. See Figure 60.

To create an array, select an object, click Tools on the menu bar, and then click Array. The Array dialog box appears, as shown in Figure 61. The first thing you want to do in this dialog box is to click the Preview button; this enables you to view the array in the viewports as you create and adjust it.

QUICKTIP

The ability to preview arrays was new in version 7 of 3ds Max and is incredibly handy. In earlier versions of 3ds Max, you had to set up the parameters, apply the array, and then if it was not right, you had to undo it and try again.

The other sections of the Array dialog box appear complicated, but they are pretty straightforward. The default number of objects in an array is 10, as shown in the Total in Array text box. You can adjust the object count as necessary in the Array Dimensions rollout. You can also click an option button in the Type of Object rollout to designate the objects in the array as copies, instances, or references of the original.

The Array Transformation rollout in the Array dialog box enables you to adjust the position, rotation, and scale of the array objects along the x-, y-, and/or z-axes. The Incremental coordinates are the units between objects; enter 20 in the x-axis box

FIGURE 60
Array of boxes

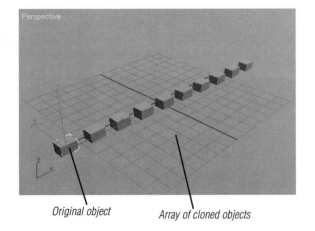

Original object   Array of cloned objects

FIGURE 61
Array dialog box

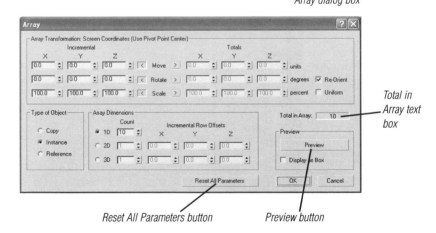

Total in Array text box

Reset All Parameters button   Preview button

in the Incremental Move section, and the 10 objects in the array will be arranged along the x-axis, 20 units apart from each other, as shown in Figure 62. In the Totals section, which shows the coordinates from the beginning to the end of the array, the X total is 200 units (10 objects offset 20 units each). Enter 20 in the x-axis box in the Incremental Rotate section, and each object in the array is rotated 20 degrees further around the x-axis than the object before it. In the Totals section, the x-axis box will show 200 (10 objects rotated a total of 200 degrees around the x-axis). Enter 75 in the x-axis box in the Incremental Scale section, and each object in the array will be 75% of the size of the previous object along the x-axis. In the Totals section, the x-axis box shows 5.631, meaning length along the x-axis of the last object in the array is 5.631% of the length of the original object. Spend some time playing with the Array tool to get familiar with how each adjustment is reflected in an array.

The Array Dimensions area of the Array dialog box allows you to create clones of your array. By default the 1D option is selected. To create arrays in two dimensions, click the 2D option button, adjust the number in the Count box as needed, and then adjust the coordinates in the X, Y, and Z boxes as desired to position the cloned arrays, as shown in Figure 63. Click the 3D option button to clone all of the arrays created in two dimensions and adjust their coordinates.

As you are working on an array, if you want to start over, click the Reset All Parameters button in the Array dialog box and all of the coordinates will return to their default values. When you have finished creating an array or arrays based on an object, click OK to apply the array, or Cancel to return to the workspace with no changes.

FIGURE 62
Cone array

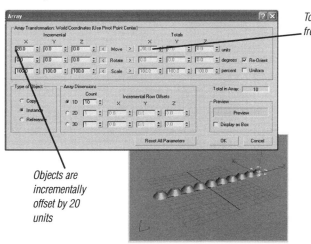

FIGURE 63
Two-dimensional array

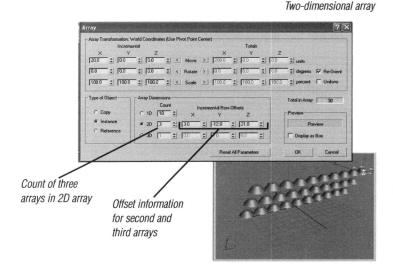

Lesson 7 Clone Objects

AUTODESK 3D STUDIO MAX 2-55

Clone an object

1. Create a box in the Top viewport with the dimensions **25 × 25 × 50**, select the **box**, click **Edit** on the menu bar, then click **Clone**.

    The Clone Options dialog box appears.

2. Click the **Copy option button**, type **Copy** in the Name text box, click **OK**, click the **Select and Move tool**, then click and drag the **box** in the Top viewport to move the copy to the right and up from the original.

3. Click **Box01** (the original box) again, click **Edit** on the menu bar, click **Clone**, click the **Instance option button**, type **Instance** in the Name text box, click **OK**, click the **Select and Move tool** (if necessary), then click and drag the **box** to move the instance to the right of the original, as shown in Figure 64.

4. Select **Box01** again, click **Edit** on the menu bar, click **Clone**, select the **Reference option button**, type **Reference** in the Name text box, click **OK**, click the **Select and Move tool**, then click and drag the **box** to move the reference to the right and down from the original.

5. In the Perspective viewport, select the **original box**, click the **Modify tab**, click the **Modifier List list arrow**, then click **TurboSmooth** on the modifier list.

    The TurboSmooth modifier is applied to the original box, its instance (Instance), and its reference (Reference), as shown in Figure 65. The copy is unaffected.

(continued)

FIGURE 64
Box cloned as an instance

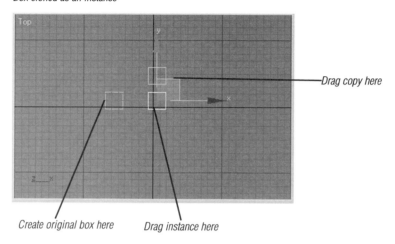

FIGURE 65
Modifier applied to original, instance, and reference

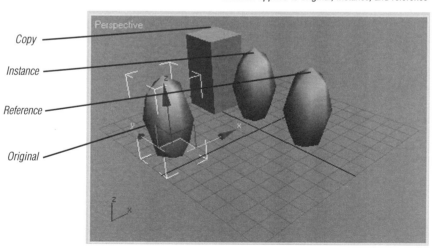

2-56 AUTODESK 3D STUDIO MAX

Building and Modifying Objects

FIGURE 66
Modifier applied to reference only

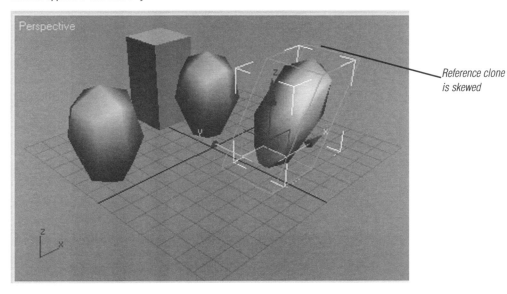

Reference clone is skewed

6. Select the **Instance box**, click the **Modifier List list arrow**, click **Taper**, then change the Amount number in the Parameters rollout to **.5**.

   As the Taper modifier is applied to the Instance, it is applied to the original box in the exact same way. As the modifier is applied to the original box, it is applied in the exact same way to the original box's reference. The copy is still unaffected.

7. Select the **Reference box**, click the **Modifier List list arrow**, click **Skew**, then change the Amount number in the Parameters rollout to **30**.

   The Skew modifier is applied to the reference but not to the original, as shown in Figure 66.

8. Save the file as **Clones**, then reset 3ds Max.

You made a copy, instance, and reference of an object, then applied modifiers to the object and its instance and reference.

Create a transformational clone

1. Create a sphere in the Top viewport with a radius of **15**.

2. Click the **Select and Move tool**, click the **sphere**, press **[Shift]**, then drag the **red arrow** of the transform gizmo to the right until a copy of the sphere appears to the right of the original sphere.

   The Clone Options dialog box opens.

3. Click the **Instance option button**, change the Number of Copies number to **3**, then click **OK**.

(continued)

Three instances of the sphere appear to the right of the original sphere, each offset from the copy next to it by the same amount.

4. Click the original **sphere**, click the **Modify tab** (if necessary), click the **Modifier List list arrow**, click **Taper**, then adjust the Amount number in the Parameters rollout to **.4**.

   Each instance of the sphere has the Taper modifier applied to it, as shown in Figure 67.

5. Save the file as **Tapered Spheres**, then reset 3ds Max.

You cloned a sphere three times by using the Select and Move tool while pressing the Shift key, then applied a modifier to the original.

Create an array

1. Create a box with the dimensions **10 x 10 × 20** in the Top viewport.

2. Select the **box** (if necessary), click **Tools** on the menu bar, then click **Array**.

   The Array dialog box opens.

3. Click the **Reset All Parameters button**, click the **Copy option button** in the Type of Object rollout, click the **Preview button** on the right side of the dialog box, then move the dialog box so that you can see the Perspective viewport.

   The objects in the array are copies of the original object. With the Preview button selected, you can see the effect in the viewports as you change the values and options in the Array dialog box.

(continued)

FIGURE 67
Modifier applied to sphere and its instances

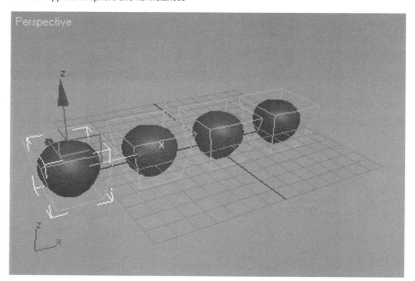

2-58 AUTODESK 3D STUDIO MAX

Building and Modifying Objects

FIGURE 68
Array moved and rotated incrementally

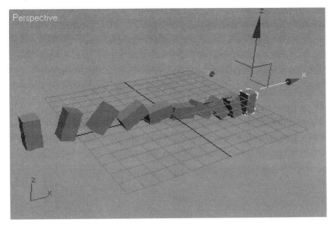

FIGURE 69
Two-dimensional array

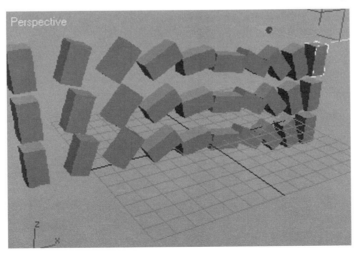

4. In the Move section of the Array Transformation rollout, change the Incremental X value to **20**.

   An array with 10 objects is created along the x-axis, separated by increments of 20.

5. In the Rotate section of the Array Transformation: Screen Coordinates rollout, change the Incremental Y value to **20**.

   Each object in the array is rotated 20 degrees around the y-axis from the orientation of the previous object, as shown in Figure 68.

6. In the Array Dimensions rollout, click the **2D option button**, adjust the 2D Count to **3**, type **25** in the Incremental Row Offsets Z box, press **[Enter]**, then click **OK**.

   As shown in Figure 70, two copies of the array appear, each offset 25 units from the previous array along the z-axis.

7. Save the file as **Array**, then reset 3ds Max.

You created an array, offset the position and rotation of the objects in the array incrementally, and then created a two-dimensional array.

LESSON 8

LINK AND GROUP OBJECTS

What You'll Do

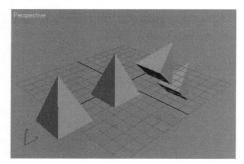

▶ In this lesson, you will learn how to create links between objects so that changes to one object affect another. In addition, you'll explore grouping and ungrouping objects.

Linking Objects

Linking two objects is also known as creating a **parent-child relationship** between the objects. What this means is that one object is the child and one is the parent; the child object can act independently of the parent object, but when the parent object is transformed (moves, rotates, or is scaled) its child is, too. Think of the child object like a dog on a long leash; the dog can walk around and sniff things while on the leash; however, if the owner crosses the street or goes inside, the dog goes with her. Note that an object that is the parent of one object can be the child of another.

Linking objects is an effective way to deal with complicated movement and is an essential tool for character animators. When building a character, you might have bones that make the character move and those bones can be linked together to make the character easier to animate. For instance, in an animation of a character's arm like that shown in Figure 70, the bicep might be the parent object of the forearm, the forearm

FIGURE 70
Animation of an arm

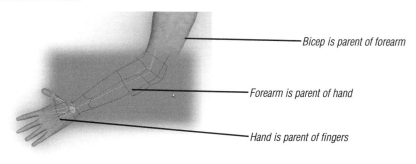

might be the parent object of the hand, and the hand might be the parent object of the fingers. When the bicep is moved, the children (forearm, hand, and fingers) would then follow. This set of parent-child relationships between objects is also known as a **hierarchy**. Because transforming a parent object transforms any child objects linked to it, consider carefully how your objects should be linked before creating relationships between objects. If objects are not linked in the correct order, they do not perform correctly.

Having a good strategy for linking objects in a scene takes some time; actually linking and unlinking objects is quite simple. To link two objects, click the Select and Link tool on the Main toolbar, click the object that will be the child object first, hold the mouse button down and drag to the object that will be the parent (a dotted line appears as you drag, as shown in Figure 71), then release the mouse button. The parent object should blink once. If you are not sure the link was created, simply move the parent object around and you should notice the parent affect the child. If not, try again. To break a link between objects, select the objects, and then click the Unlink Selection tool on the Main toolbar.

QUICKTIP

The best way to remember how to link is to remember the phrase "I am holding the child and looking for the parent." After clicking the Select and Link tool, you are holding (selecting/starting with) the child object and are finding (linking to) the parent object.

On occasion you might find that your scene gets crowded with objects and it might be hard to find the object to which you want to link as the parent object. When this happens, click the Select and Link tool on the Main toolbar, select the child object, and then press the [h] key to open the Select Parent dialog box. In

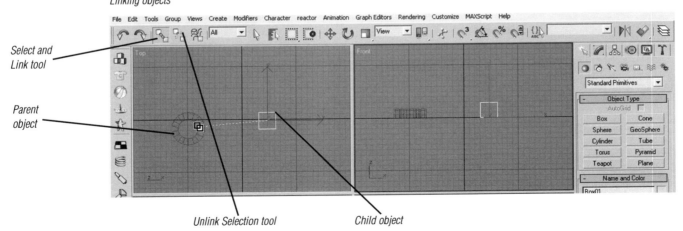

FIGURE 71
Linking objects

Select and Link tool

Parent object

Unlink Selection tool

Child object

Lesson 8 Link and Group Objects

the dialog box, click the name of the object you would like to be the parent object, and then click the Link button to create the link.

Grouping Objects

As you work with objects in a scene, you can **group** a set of objects together in order to move them or otherwise transform the whole set of objects at the same time. Unlike linked objects, grouped objects have no hierarchy—they are either in the group, or not in the group. To group a set of objects, select all of the objects you want to be in the group, click Group on the menu bar, and then click Group. The Group dialog box appears, as shown in Figure 72; type a name for the group in the Group name text box, and then click OK. The objects you selected will now all be in a group; when you click one of the objects, all of the objects in the group are selected. When you move, rotate, or scale the group of objects, you'll use just one transform gizmo to affect all of the objects, as shown in Figure 73.

> **QUICK**TIP
> When grouping objects, it is a good idea to give the group a unique name that provides an accurate description of what is in the group. The name of the group appears in brackets in the Select by Name dialog box; as you work on more complicated scenes, being able to select a group in this way becomes extremely helpful.

Even when objects are in a group, you can still edit a single object in that group by **opening** the group. To open a group, select

FIGURE 72
Group dialog box

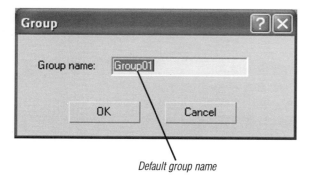

Default group name

FIGURE 73
Move gizmo for grouped objects

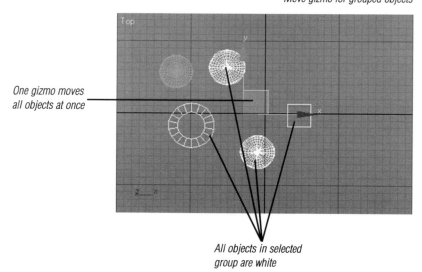

One gizmo moves all objects at once

All objects in selected group are white

2-62 AUTODESK 3D STUDIO MAX

Building and Modifying Objects

the group, click Group on the menu bar, and then click Open. Pink brackets appear around the group of objects indicating it is open, as shown in Figure 74; you'll be able to select a single object in the group and transform it independently of the other objects. When you are finished making changes to objects in the open group, close the group by selecting the group, clicking Group on the menu bar, and then clicking Close.

You can add, or **attach**, an object to a group after a group has been created. To do so, select the object you'd like to attach to a group, click Group on the menu bar, click Attach, then click the group to which you want to attach the object. The object becomes part of the group. To **detach** an object from a group, first open the group (select the group, click Group on the menu bar, and then click Open), select the object you want to detach, click Group on the menu bar, and then click Detach.

QUICKTIP
Don't forget to close the group again after detaching the object.

When one group of objects is part of another, larger group of objects, that group is known as a **nested** group. If you ungroup a group that has a group nested within it, the nested group remains intact. However, you can ungroup all of the objects in a group that has groups nested within it by **exploding** the group. To explode a group, select the group, click Group on the menu bar, and then click Explode.

QUICKTIP
If you animate a group of objects and then ungroup the objects, you lose the animation.

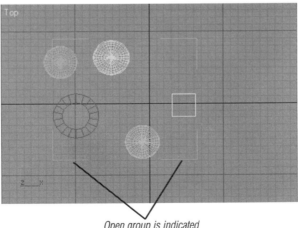

FIGURE 74
Open group

Open group is indicated by (pink) brackets

Lesson 8   Link and Group Objects

AUTODESK 3D STUDIO MAX 2-63

Link and unlink objects

1. Create a pyramid in the Top viewport with the dimensions **30 × 30 × 40**.

2. Click the **Select and Move tool**, press **[Shift]**, then move the pyramid's transform gizmo in order to create three copies of the pyramid, as shown in Figure 75.

3. Click the **Select and Link tool**, click the **pyramid on the far right**, then drag to and click the **pyramid second from the right**.

   The pyramid second from the right blinks once, and the two pyramids are now linked. The pyramid on the far right is the child, and the pyramid second from the right is the parent.

4. Click the **Select and Rotate tool**, click the **pyramid second from the right**, then rotate the pyramid 45 degrees along its y-axis (using the yellow gizmo).

   As the pyramid rotates, its child pyramid rotates with it, as shown in Figure 76.

5. Click the **pyramid on the far right**, then rotate the pyramid approximately 45 degrees along its z-axis (using the blue gizmo).

   The child pyramid rotates independently of the parent.

6. Save the file as **Link Pyramids**.

You created four pyramids, linked two of the pyramids in a parent-child relationship, rotated the parent and the child objects by rotating the parent, and rotated the child independently of the parent.

FIGURE 75
Four pyramids

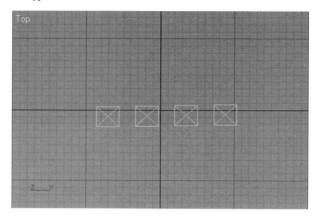

FIGURE 76
Rotated parent and child pyramids

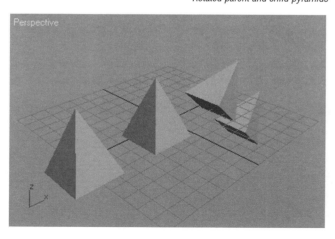

FIGURE 77
Moved pyramid hierarchy

Children move with the parent

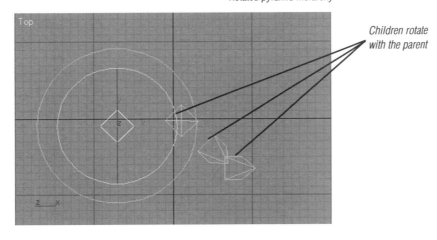

FIGURE 78
Rotated pyramid hierarchy

Children rotate with the parent

Create a link hierarchy

1. Deselect the pyramids, click the **Select and Link tool**, click the **pyramid second from the right** in the Top viewport, then drag to and click the **pyramid second from the left**.

2. Click the **pyramid second from the left**, then drag to and click the **pyramid on the far left**.

   There is now a hierarchy of relationships between the pyramids. The far-left pyramid is the parent to the pyramid on its right, which is the parent to the pyramid on its right, which is the parent to the pyramid on its right.

3. Click the **Select and Move tool**, click the **pyramid second from the left**, click the **green arrow** on its transform gizmo, then move it up about one inch, as shown in Figure 77.

   The pyramid and all of its children move at the same time.

4. Click the **Select and Rotate tool**, click the **pyramid on the far left**, then rotate the pyramid –45 degrees along its z-axis.

   The pyramid and all of its children rotate at the same time, as shown in Figure 78.

5. Click **Edit** on the menu bar, click **Select All**, then click the **Unlink Selection tool** to break all of the links between objects.

You created a link hierarchy by linking objects to other objects as both parent and child, moved one parent object and all its children, rotated another parent object and all of its children, then unlinked all of the objects.

Group and ungroup objects

1. Click the **Select Object tool**, select the two pyramids on the left, click **Group** on the menu bar, then click **Group** to open the Group dialog box.

2. Type **Two Pyramids** in the Group name text box, then click **OK**.

3. With the Two Pyramids group selected, click the **Select and Uniform Scale tool**, then in the Top viewport drag the **red dot** to the right about one-half inch to increase the scale of the grouped objects along the x-axis.

4. Click **Group** on the menu bar, then click **Open**.

   The group is now open, with pink brackets around it, and you can edit objects within the group individually. See Figure 79.

5. Click the **Select and Move tool**, click the **pyramid second from the left** in the Top viewport, then click the **green arrow** and move it up about one-half inch.

   The pyramid moves independently of the other pyramid in the group.

6. Click **Group** on the menu bar, then click **Close** to close the group.

7. Click the **pyramid on the far right**, click **Group** on the menu bar, click **Attach**, then click the **Two Pyramids group**.

   The far-right pyramid becomes part of the Two Pyramids group and is now selected.

8. Click **Group** on the menu bar, then click **Ungroup**.

You grouped objects, opened the group and edited one object, and attached an object to a group.

FIGURE 79
Open Two Pyramids group

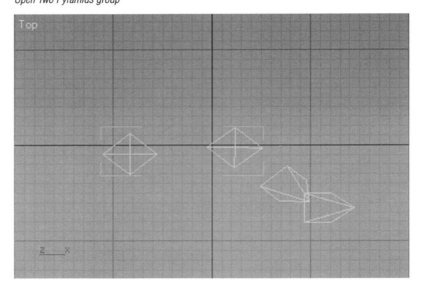

2-66 AUTODESK 3D STUDIO MAX

Building and Modifying Objects

FIGURE 80
Right group selected

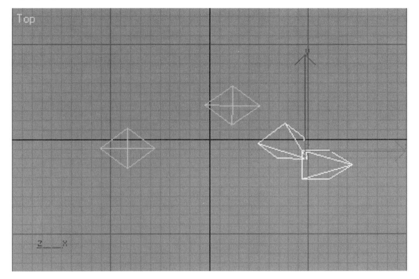

Create and explode a nested group

1. Select the **two pyramids** on the right of the viewport, click **Group** on the menu bar, click **Group**, name the group **Right**, then click **OK**.

2. Select all four pyramids, click **Group** on the menu bar, click **Group**, name the group **All**, then click **OK**.

   The Right group is now a nested group within the All group.

3. Click **Group** on the menu bar, click **Ungroup**, then click one of the pyramids in the Right group.

   Even though you ungrouped the All group, the Right group remains intact. When you select one pyramid in the Right group, the group is selected, as shown in Figure 80.

4. Select all four pyramids again, click **Group** on the menu bar, click **Group**, name the group **All**, then click **OK**.

5. With the All group selected, click **Group** on the menu bar, click **Explode**, then click one of the pyramids in the Right group.

   Exploding the All group ungrouped its nested groups, and now clicking one of the pyramids on the right selects only that pyramid.

6. Save the file, then reset 3ds Max.

You grouped two objects, nested that group within a larger group, ungrouped the larger group while keeping the nested group intact, then exploded the larger group and ungrouped all objects.

LESSON 9

WORK WITH PIVOT POINTS

What You'll Do

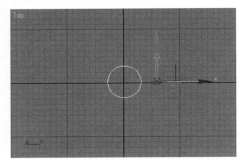

▶ *In this lesson you will learn about the pivot points of objects, and how to change the location of a pivot point either by moving the pivot point or by moving the object in relation to the pivot point. You will also explore how to use the Affect Hierarchy Only button to move or rotate the links between objects.*

Understanding Pivot Points

As you work with objects in 3ds Max, moving them around, rotating and modifying them, often without thinking about it you are making changes to objects via their pivot points. A **pivot point** is essentially the point around which an object rotates and from which it is scaled. If you are applying modifiers to an object, it is also the default location of the center of a modifier (such as the point around which a Twist modifier twists the object to which it is applied). All objects have pivot points; you can see where the pivot point is on an object by looking at the transform gizmo. The point where all of the axes in the transform gizmo intersect is the pivot point.

As you work with an object, you might want to reposition or rotate its pivot point. By doing this, you change the point around which the object rotates. For instance, in Figure 81 the box on the left rotates around its center, where its pivot point is located; the box on the right rotates around a point outside itself, where its pivot point has been moved. When you move a pivot point, you also change where the center of a modifier is located when applied. For instance, you might create an object and use the Symmetry modifier to mirror the object; the position of the pivot point when the modifier is applied affects where the mirror image starts.

You can change the location of an object's pivot point either by moving the pivot point without moving the object, or by moving the object without moving the pivot point. All of the options for affecting the location of the pivot point in relation to an object are located on the Hierarchy panel.

Repositioning a Pivot Point in Relation to Its Object

To move a pivot point without moving the object, first click the Hierarchy tab on the Command panel to open the Hierarchy panel, and then click the Pivot button at the top of the panel, if it is not already selected. The Adjust Pivot rollout appears in the

Hierarchy panel, as shown in Figure 82. Select the object whose pivot point you want to affect, click either the Move or the Rotate tool, and then click the Affect Pivot Only button in the Adjust Pivot rollout. You'll see an additional outline appear around the transform gizmo, indicating that you are editing the pivot point and not the actual object.

With the Move or Rotate tool selected, click the transform gizmo and drag it to change the pivot point's location. Notice that the pivot point moves, but the object stays in place. You can even move the pivot point outside the object.

With the Affect Pivot Only button selected, three buttons become active in the Alignment group box on the Adjust Pivot rollout. These buttons enable you to quickly change the pivot point's location. To move the pivot point to the center of the object, click the Center to Object button. If the pivot point has been rotated away from its original location, click Align to Object to reorient the pivot point to the object's local coordinate system. Click Align to World to reorient the pivot point in relation to the home grid.

Remember to be careful, because it is easy to forget to turn off Affect Pivot Only when you have finished adjusting the position of the pivot point. Make sure that you turn it off by clicking the Affect Pivot Only button again to deselect it. When you next click the object to move, rotate, or scale it, you'll see the pivot point in its new location.

QUICKTIP

You can move or rotate a pivot point to change its position or orientation, but if you try to scale the pivot point, you will just scale the object.

FIGURE 81
Boxes with different pivot point locations

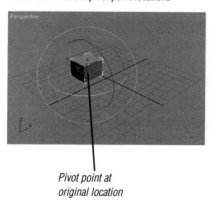
Pivot point at original location

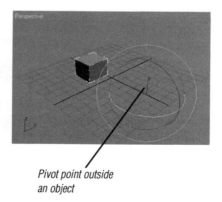
Pivot point outside an object

FIGURE 82
Hierarchy panel

Lesson 9 Work With Pivot Points

Repositioning an Object in Relation to Its Pivot Point

Moving or rotating a pivot point isn't always the best way to adjust the object's relationship to its pivot point. In some cases, it might be easier to move the object around while the pivot point remains in place. To do this, click the Affect Object Only button in the Adjust Pivot rollout on the Hierarchy panel. With this button selected, you can use the Move and Rotate tools to select and transform the object, and the pivot point will stay in place. Click the Affect Object Only button again to deselect it when you have finished moving the object.

As with the Affect Pivot Only button, when you select the Affect Object Only button, three buttons become active in the Alignment group box on the Adjust Pivot rollout. To move the object's center to the location of the pivot point, click the Center to Pivot button. If the object has been rotated away from its original location, click Align to Pivot to reorient the object to the pivot point's axes, as shown in Figure 84. Click Align to World to reorient the object to the home grid.

Whether you have moved a pivot point or moved the object in relation to its pivot point, you can reset the pivot point's location to where it was when the object was first created by simply clicking the Reset Pivot button in the Adjust Pivot rollout.

FIGURE 83
Box before and after being aligned to its pivot

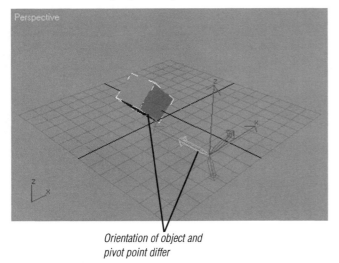
Orientation of object and pivot point differ

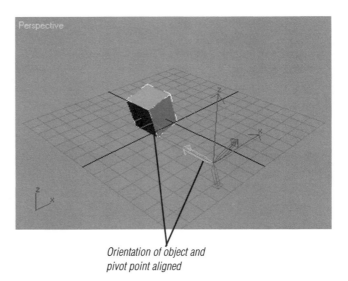
Orientation of object and pivot point aligned

Using the Affect Hierarchy Only Button

In addition to the Affect Pivot Only and Affect Object Only buttons, you'll also find the Affect Hierarchy Only button in the Adjust Pivot rollout. This button enables you to change the rotation or scale of the *links* between parent and child objects, rather than changing the rotation or scale of the objects themselves. For instance, the large box in Figure 84 is the parent object of the two small boxes. If you select the large box, click the Adjust Hierarchy Only button in the Adjust Pivot rollout, click the Rotate tool, and then adjust the rotation transform gizmo, the red boxes rotate around the purple box without changing their individual orientations. Similarly, if you click the Scale tool and adjust the scale transform gizmo, you increase the scale of the space between the boxes without changing the dimensions of the boxes, as shown in Figure 85.

FIGURE 84
Parent box and two child boxes

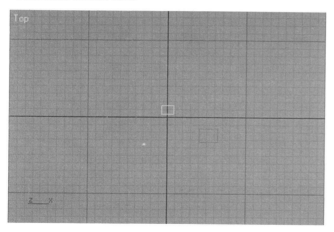

FIGURE 85
Scaled links between objects

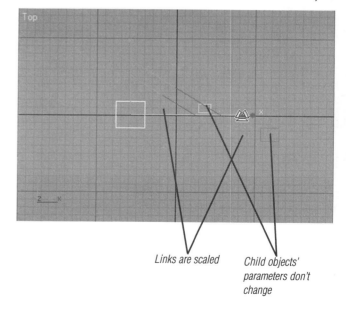

Links are scaled

Child objects' parameters don't change

Lesson 9   Work With Pivot Points

AUTODESK 3D STUDIO MAX 2-71

Reposition an object's pivot point

1. In the center of the Top viewport, create a cylinder with a Radius of **30** and a Height of **40**.

   The pivot point is at the bottom center of the object, where the axes intersect.

2. Click the **Hierarchy tab**, make sure the Pivot button at the top of the Hierarchy panel is selected, then click the **Affect Pivot Only button**.

   Red, green, and blue arrow outlines appear around the pivot point, indicating that any change that you make now only affects the pivot point.

3. Click the **Select and Move tool**, click the **red arrow** in the Top viewport, then drag the **pivot point** to the right outside of the cylinder, as shown in Figure 86.

4. Click the **Affect Pivot Only button** to deselect it.

   Any changes you make to an object now affect both the object and the pivot point.

5. Click the **Select and Rotate tool**, then select the **cylinder**.

   Notice that the Rotate gizmo appears around the pivot point in its new location.

(continued)

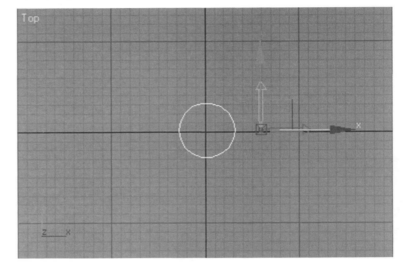

FIGURE 86
Moved pivot point

FIGURE 87
Object rotated away from pivot point

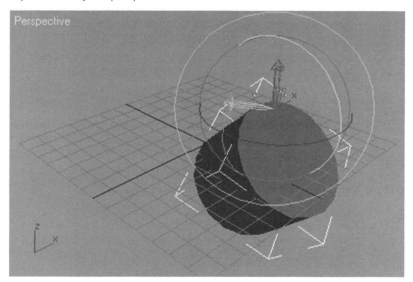

6. Click the **blue handle** on the Rotate gizmo and rotate the cylinder 30 degrees around the z-axis.

   The cylinder rotates around the pivot point in its new location.

7. Save the file as **Cylinder Pivot**.

You moved an object's pivot point to a location outside the object, then rotated the object around the pivot point's new location.

Reorient an object in relation to its pivot point

1. Make sure the cylinder is selected, click the **Hierarchy tab** (if necessary), then click the **Affect Object Only button**.

2. Click the **Select and Rotate tool**, click the **red handle** on the Rotate gizmo, then rotate the object 45 degrees around the x-axis.

   The object rotates, but its pivot point stays in place, as shown in Figure 87. Notice that the Rotate gizmo continues to be centered around the pivot point.

3. Click the **Select and Move tool**, click the **red arrow** in the Top viewport, then drag to the left to move the object away from the pivot point.

4. Click the **Center to Pivot button**.

(continued)

The object moves to the pivot point's location, with the pivot point at the object's center, as shown in Figure 88.

5. Click the **Affect Object Only button** to deselect it.

6. Save the file, then reset 3ds Max.

You rotated and moved an object without affecting its pivot point, then centered the object around the pivot point.

Rotate the links between objects in a hierarchy

1. Create a pyramid with the dimensions **20 × 20 × 40** in the Top viewport, click the **Select and Move tool**, press **[Shift]**, then select and move the pyramid to create two copies of the pyramid.

2. Click the **Select and Link tool**, then, starting with the pyramid on the far right, link each pyramid to the pyramid on its left as its child.

3. Click the **Select and Rotate tool**, select the **pyramid on the far left**, then click the **blue handle** and rotate the pyramid approximately 45 degrees around its z-axis.

   As the pyramid rotates, all of its children rotate with it while remaining in line with it, as shown in Figure 89.

(continued)

FIGURE 88
Object centered to pivot

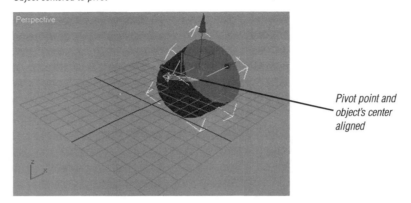

Pivot point and object's center aligned

FIGURE 89
Rotated objects in hierarchy

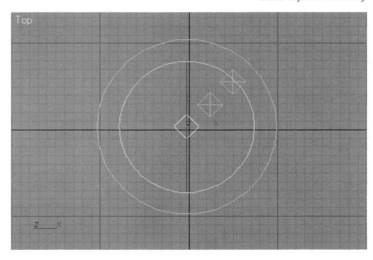

FIGURE 90
Rotated links in hierarchy

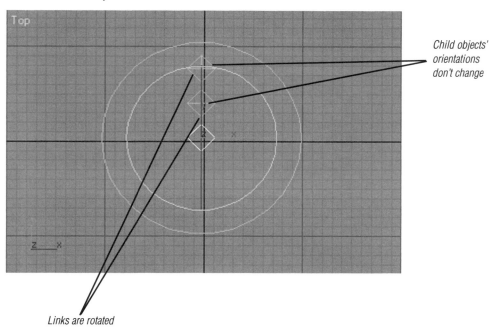

Child objects' orientations don't change

Links are rotated

4. Click the **Hierarchy tab**, click **Affect Hierarchy Only**, then click the **blue handle** and rotate it approximately another 45 degrees around the z-axis.

   Because the Affect Hierarchy Only button is selected, only the positions of the parent pyramid's children are rotated around the parent; the orientations of the children pyramids do not change, as shown in Figure 90.

5. Click the **Affect Hierarchy Only button** to deselect it, save the file as **Rotate Links**, then reset 3ds Max.

You created a hierarchy and rotated the links between the parent object and its children without rotating the child objects themselves.

LESSON 10

USE SNAPPING TOOLS

What You'll Do

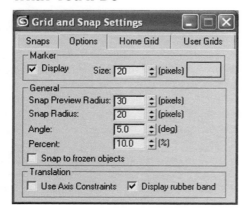

In this lesson, you will learn how to use snapping tools to have better control over the adjustments you make to objects.

In 3ds Max, when you need to have more control over the incremental changes made when you create or adjust an object, you use snapping. **Snapping** is the adjustment of an object's parameters, position, rotation, or scale using predefined increments (such as moving an object five units at a time, or rotating an object five degrees at a time). There are four basic snap tools on the Main toolbar, and each of them has specific settings and controls that you can fine-tune.

| QUICKTIP
| These tools are also referred to as Transform tools.

Using 3D Snap

As you create an object by dragging, it can sometimes be difficult to create it with the exact dimensions you want it to have. In addition, when you adjust an object's position by dragging, you might find it hard to drag it exactly where you want it to be on the grid. You can use the Snaps Toggle button on the Main toolbar to help you with this. When you activate 3D Snap, the parameters of objects that you create by dragging in the viewports are limited to predefined incremental values. For instance, if you create a box, its sides will "snap" to the gridlines in the home grid, and its length, width, and height increase or decrease by increments of 10 as you drag to create it. If you then move that box using the Move tool, the box's sides will "snap" to the gridlines as the box moves, moving in increments of 10 (one grid square) in any direction as you adjust it.

To turn on 3D Snap, click the Snaps Toggle button to select it (or press [s]), as shown in Figure 91. After the Snaps Toggle is selected, you'll notice that an illuminated blue box appears with the cursor, indicating that snapping is on. When you move an object, a blue line will appear leading from where you started to move the object's Move gizmo to the blue cursor box in whatever location to which the object was moved. This can be helpful if you want to move an object a certain number of increments down and over, for example. When you no longer want snapping to occur, click the Snaps Toggle button (or press [s]) to deselect it and turn off snapping.

QUICKTIP

The Snaps Toggle flyout enables you to choose between 2D, 2.5D, and 3D Snap, with 3D Snap on by default. 2D and 2.5D Snap are useful if you are working with construction planes, which are not covered in this book; so just leave 3D Snap on.

You can adjust the increments used in 3D Snap, as well as what parts of an object are snapped, in the Grid and Snap Settings dialog box, shown in Figure 92. Right-click the Snaps Toggle button to open the Snaps rollout in this dialog box, where you can choose from parts of the geometry you can use to snap objects. For instance, you can click the check box next to Pivot, and objects that you move to be next to another object will snap so that their pivot points are in the same place. As you get further into modeling in later chapters, the options in the list other than the default Grid Points become more useful. Click the Home Grid tab to adjust the Grid Spacing in the home grid, thereby changing the increments represented by each grid square.

FIGURE 91
Main toolbar

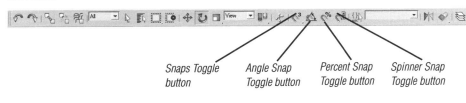

FIGURE 92
Snaps rollout in the Grid and Snap Settings dialog box

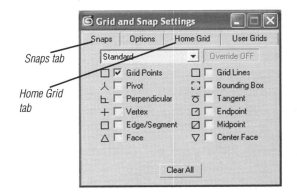

Using Angle Snap

Similar to 3D Snap, Angle Snap enables you to adjust the angle of rotation of an object by incremental values rather than trying to reach an exact angle value as you manually drag. To turn on Angle Snap, click the Angle Snap Toggle button on the Main toolbar (or press [a]). With Angle Snap active, any rotation that you make to an object occurs a set number of increments at a time. By default, the increment used in Angle Snap is five degrees at a time. For instance, if you want to rotate an object 90 degrees, you simply click the axis along which you want the object to rotate in the transform gizmo, then drag until the rotation degrees shown reaches 90.

To adjust the increments used in Angle Snap, right-click the Angle Snap button to open the Options rollout of the Grid and Snap Settings dialog box, as shown in Figure 93. Change the number in the Angle text box up or down to adjust the number of degrees in each increment.

Using Percent Snap

Snapping is also useful when scaling an object. As you scale something, it can sometimes be difficult to control exact values, such as increasing the size of an object by 50% rather than by 49.52%. As with 3D Snap and Angle Snap, Percent Snap lets you scale an object by predefined increments; by default, Percent Snap is set to scale objects 10% at a time. To use Percent Snap, click the Percent Snap Toggle button on the Main toolbar (or press [Shift][Ctrl][P]), click the Scale tool, and then select and scale an object. As you scale the object, notice that the values in the Transform Type-In boxes at the bottom of the screen (representing the scale of the object) increase or decrease by increments of 10.

To adjust the increments used in Percent Snap, right-click the Percent Snap button to open the Options rollout of the Grid and Snap Settings dialog box. Change the number in the Percent text box up or down to adjust the number of percentage points used in each increment.

FIGURE 93
Options rollout in the Grid and Snap Settings dialog box

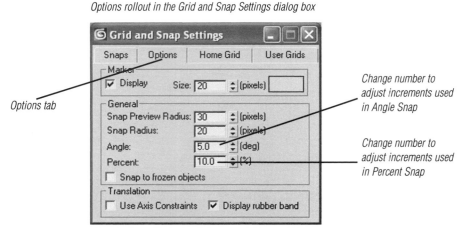

Using Spinner Snap

There are spinners all over 3ds Max. Almost everywhere there is a value, you will find a spinner. The Spinner Snap tool makes using a spinner a snap! Often when you use a spinner to adjust a number, the number increases or decreases by minute amounts, giving you values that can go to several decimal places. If you turn on Spinner Snap, however, you can limit the change to a number in a spinner box to be an increase or decrease of 1 at a time. This gives you much greater control over how fast and precisely you can get to a particular value.

To turn on Spinner Snap, click the Spinner Snap Toggle button on the Main toolbar to select it. After selected, any spinner you use adjusts according to Spinner Snap's predefined increments. Click the Spinner Snap Toggle button again to deselect it and turn off Spinner Snap.

To adjust the increments used in Spinner Snap, right-click the Spinner Snap Toggle button to open the Preference Settings dialog box (*not* the Grid and Snap Settings dialog box). In the Spinners rollout, as shown in Figure 94, adjust the number in the Snap text box up or down to change the increments used in Spinner Snap.

FIGURE 94
Preference Settings dialog box

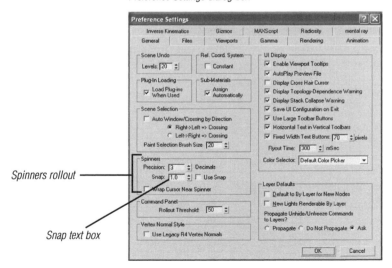

Lesson 10   Use Snapping Tools

AUTODESK 3D STUDIO MAX 2-79

Use 3D Snap to create and position an object

1. Click the **Snaps Toggle button** on the Main toolbar.

   3D Snap is turned on.

2. Click the **Cone button** on the Create panel, click in the center of the Top viewport, drag down four grid squares, and then release the mouse button.

   Notice that a light blue box appears behind the pointer as you move it. As you place the pointer in the center of the viewport, the blue box snaps into place on the four boxes surrounding the center. As you drag down, the blue box snaps from one grid square to the next.

3. Drag up four grid squares to create the height of the cone, click, drag down two grid squares, then click to create the radius of the top of the cone, as shown in Figure 95.

   Using snap, you've created a cone with a Radius 1 of precisely 40, a Radius 2 of precisely 20, and a height of precisely 40.

4. Click the **Select and Move tool**, in the Top viewport, click the **handle** on the Move gizmo between the x- and y-axes, then drag up five grid squares and to the right five grid squares.

5. Click the **Snaps Toggle button** on the Main toolbar to deselect it and turn off 3D Snap.

You turned on 3D Snap, created a cone using increments of 10 in its radii and height, moved the cone in increments of 10 along the x- and y-axes, then turned off 3D Snap.

FIGURE 95
Object created using increments of 10

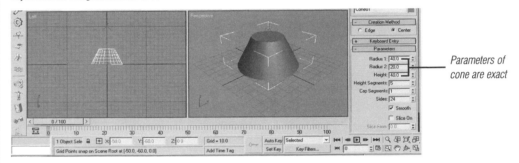

Parameters of cone are exact

2-80 AUTODESK 3D STUDIO MAX

Building and Modifying Objects

FIGURE 96
Object rotated by increments of 10 degrees

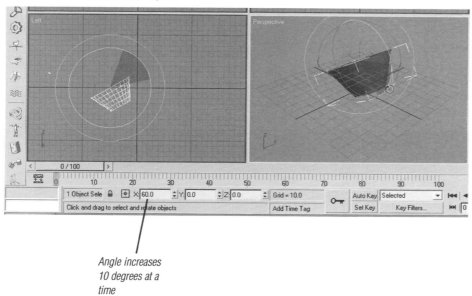

Angle increases
10 degrees at a
time

Use Angle Snap to rotate an object

1. Click the **Angle Snap Toggle button**.
2. Click the **Select and Rotate tool**, click the **cone** (if necessary), then click the **red handle** on the Rotate gizmo and rotate the cone 90 degrees along its x-axis.

   Notice that as you rotate the cone, the angle changes in the Transform Type-In X box in the status bar in increments of five.

3. Right-click the **Angle Snap Toggle button** to open the Grid and Snap Settings dialog box.
4. In the General rollout, click the **upper spinner button** on the Angle box until the number changes to 10, then click the Grid and Snap Settings dialog box **Close button**.
5. Click the **red handle** on the Rotate gizmo again, then rotate the cone another 90 degrees around its x-axis.

   As you drag the handle, the degree count changes in increments of 10 based on the change you made in the Grid and Snap Settings dialog box. See Figure 96.

6. Right-click the **Angle Snap Toggle button**, change the Angle box value back to **5**, then close the Grid and Snap Settings dialog box.
7. Click the **Angle Snap Toggle button** to deselect it and turn off Angle Snap.

You turned on Angle Snap, rotated an object along its x-axis in increments of five degrees, changed the snap settings, rotated an object along its x-axis in increments of 10 degrees, then turned off Angle Snap.

Lesson 10 Use Snapping Tools

AUTODESK 3D STUDIO MAX 2-81

Use Percent Snap to scale an object

1. Click the **Percent Snap Toggle button**, click the **Select and Uniform Scale tool**, then click the **cone** (if necessary) in the Perspective viewport to select it.

2. Click the **green dot** on the Scale gizmo and drag to the right to increase the scale of the object on its y-axis to 150%.

   The status bar's Transform Type-In Y box changes from 100 to 150.

3. Click the **triangle** at the center of the Scale gizmo, then drag down to scale the cone to 70% of its original size.

   The Transform Type-In X, Y, and Z boxes in the status bar each change from 100 to 70 in increments of 10. See Figure 97.

4. Click the **Percent Snap Toggle button** to deselect it and turn off Percent Snap.

You turned on Percent Snap, increased the scale of an object along its y-axis in increments of 10%, decreased the scale of the object to 70% in increments of 10%, then turned off Percent Snap

FIGURE 97
Object scaled down by increments of 10%

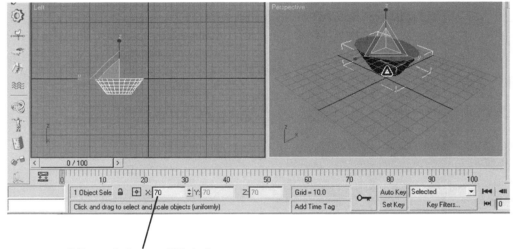

Uniform scale decreases 10% at a time

FIGURE 98
Height of object increased using Spinner Snap

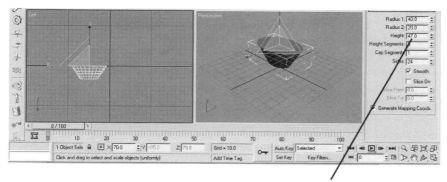

Height increased to exactly 47

Use Spinner Snap to change an object's parameters

1. With the cone selected, click the **Modify tab**, then click the **top spinner button** next to the Height box in the Parameters rollout three times.

   The Height box value changes to 41.212.

2. Click the **bottom spinner button** next to the Height box three times.

   The Height box value changes to 39.988.

3. Select the number in the Height box, type **40**, then click the **Spinner Snap Toggle button**.

4. Click the **top spinner button** next to the Height box three times.

   The value changes to 43, 1 unit per click.

5. Right-click the **Spinner Snap Toggle tool**, in the Spinners rollout of the Preferences dialog box, type **2** in the Snap text box, then click **OK**.

6. Click the **top spinner button** next to the Height box two times.

   As shown in Figure 98, the Height increases to 47, two units per spinner button click.

7. Right-click the **Spinner Snap Toggle button** again, change the value in the Snap box back to **1**, click **OK**, then click the **Spinner Snap Toggle button** to deselect it.

8. Save the file as **Snapping Cone**, then reset 3ds Max.

You used Spinner Snap to increase the height of an object in increments of one and changed the increment amount used in Spinner Snap.

LESSON 11

ALIGN OBJECTS

What You'll Do

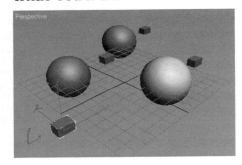

In this lesson, you will learn how to align objects with each other and how to align clones at the same time they are created.

Aligning Objects with the Align Tool

As you work in 3ds Max, you will find myriad reasons to align objects with each other in space. You might want an object to appear in exactly the same place as another object, or you might want an object to be offset from another object by a certain amount of space. To precisely align objects with each other in the most effective way, you can use the Align tool. To align one object with another, first select the object you want to align with another, called the **current object**. Then, click the Align tool on the Main toolbar (or press [Alt][A]); the cursor will look like an outline of the Align tool icon. Next, position the cursor over the object with which you want the object to align, called the **target object** (at this point, the cursor looks like crosshairs), and then click. This opens the Align Selection dialog box, shown in Figure 99, where you can choose the method of alignment you want to use.

To align an object with another's x-axis location, y-axis location, z-axis location, or any combination of the three, click the appropriate check box(es) next to the axis in the Align Position rollout. If you align an object with all three axes, you move the selected object to the location of the target object. Also in the Align Position rollout, you can choose which parts of the current object and target object should be aligned with each other: the Minimum, Center, Pivot Point, or Maximum. (The minimum of an object is the point on the object's bounding box that has the lowest X, Y, and Z values; the maximum of an object is the point on the bounding box that has the highest

X, Y, and Z values.) To have the current object inherit the target object's orientation or scale along any or all of the x-, y-, and z-axes, click the appropriate check box(es) in the Align Orientation and/or Match Scale rollouts. As you choose different options in the dialog box, you should be able to see the changes in alignment, as shown in Figure 100; reposition the dialog box (if necessary) to get the best view. When you are satisfied with the alignment options chosen, click the Apply button in the Align Selection dialog box to apply the options. To cancel the alignment instead of applying it, click the Cancel button.

Using the Quick Align Tool

As you work in 3ds Max, you will often want to align objects center to center. Because this is a frequently needed option, in version 7, 3ds Max introduced the Quick Align tool. This tool aligns objects by their centers in one quick step and avoids the Align Selection

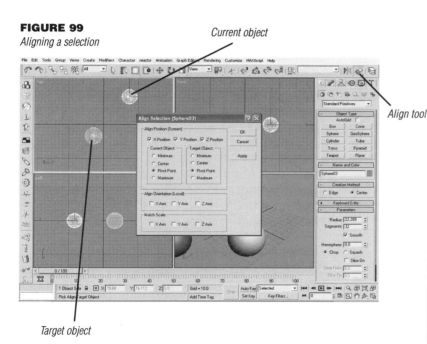

FIGURE 99
Aligning a selection

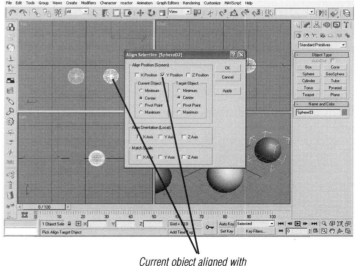

FIGURE 100
Alignment changes

Lesson 11 Align Objects

AUTODESK 3D STUDIO MAX 2-85

dialog box altogether. To use the Quick Align tool, simply select one object as the current object, click the Align tool flyout on the Main toolbar, as shown in Figure 101, click the Quick Align tool (or press [Shift][A]), and then click a target object. The current object quickly moves to the center of the target object. Notice that this tool does not inherit rotation or scale settings.

Using the Clone and Align tool

You can clone an object and have its clones be aligned with other objects by using the Clone and Align tool. To do this, select an object, click Tools on the menu bar, and then click Clone and Align. The Clone and Align dialog box opens, as shown in Figure 102. To create clones of the object that are aligned with other objects in the workspace (called **destination objects**), click the Pick button to select it. With the Pick button selected, click the object or objects with which you want the clones to be aligned (a clone will be created for each object clicked). If you want to pick destination objects by name, click the Pick List button; in the Pick Destination Objects dialog box, click the

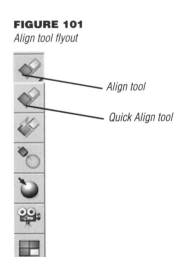

FIGURE 101
Align tool flyout

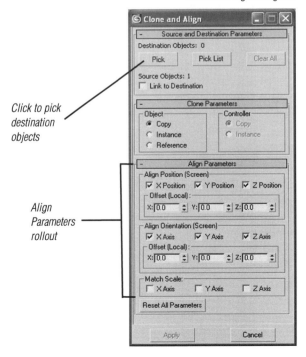

FIGURE 102
Clone and Align dialog box

2-86 AUTODESK 3D STUDIO MAX

name or names of the destination objects, and then click Pick. If you want to clear all of the selections you have made and start again, click the Clear All button.

In the Clone and Align dialog box, you can choose whether the clones will be copies, instances, or references by choosing the appropriate option in the Clone Parameters rollout. In the Align Parameters rollout, you can also adjust how the clones are positioned or rotated in relation to their destination objects. To do this, change the coordinates in the Align Position and/or the Align Orientation sections under Align Parameters. See Figure 103 for an example of clones that are aligned with objects and positioned 50 units along the x-axis from those objects. To match the scale of a clone with the scale of its destination object, in the Match Scale rollout click the check box for the axis or axes scale you want the object to match. Note that if a destination object has not been scaled, clicking any of the check boxes in this rollout has no effect on the clone. If you want to reset all of the parameters in the Align Parameters rollout to zero, click the Reset All Parameters button.

As you work in the Clone and Align dialog box, you can see the clones on-screen. When you are satisfied with the clones you have created and their alignments with the destination objects, click Apply. Click Cancel to cancel the creation of the clones.

FIGURE 103
Box cloned and aligned with spheres

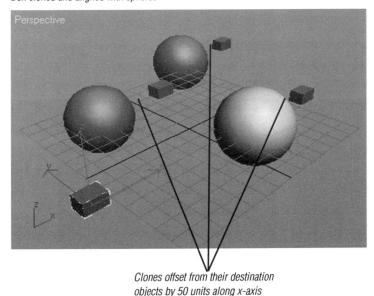

Clones offset from their destination objects by 50 units along x-axis

Lesson 11   Align Objects

Align objects by position

1. Create a box and a pyramid in the Top viewport, similar to those shown in Figure 104.
2. Select the **box**, click the **Align tool**, then click the **pyramid**.

   The Align Selection dialog box opens.
3. Drag the title bar of the dialog box and move it so that you can see objects in the Top viewport (if necessary).
4. In the Current Object and Target Object rollouts, click the **Center option buttons** if they are not already selected.
5. In the Align Position rollout, click the **X position check box** to select it. Deselect the Y and Z Position check boxes (if necessary).

   The box is aligned with the pyramid's position on the x-axis.
6. Deselect the **X position check box**, then click the **Y Position check box** to select it.

   The box is aligned with the pyramid's position on the y-axis, as shown in Figure 105.
7. Click **OK** to accept the new alignment of the box with the sphere, then save the file as **Align Objects**.

You used the Align tool to center two objects along the x-axis.

FIGURE 104
Box and pyramid

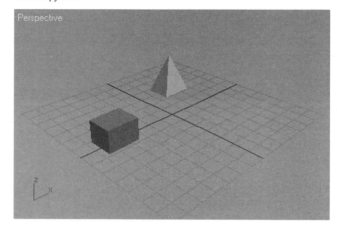

FIGURE 105
Objects with y-axis position aligned

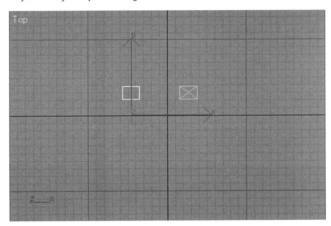

Align objects by orientation and scale

1. Use the **Select and Move tool** to move the box back to its original position.

2. Click the **Angle Snap Toggle button** on the Main toolbar, click the **Select and Rotate tool**, click the **pyramid**, then click the **red handle** on the Rotate gizmo and rotate the pyramid 45 degrees around its x-axis.

3. Click the **Select and Uniform Scale tool**, click the **triangle** at the center of the Scale gizmo, and drag up until the scale of the pyramid increases to 130 along all three axes.

4. Click the **Select Object tool**, select the **box**, click the **Align tool**, then click the **pyramid**.

   The Align Selection dialog box opens.

5. Deselect the **X, Y**, and **Z Position check boxes** in the Align Position section if they are selected.

6. In the Align Orientation section, click the **Y Axis check box** to select it.

   The box rotates 45 degrees around its x-axis to match the orientation of the pyramid.

   (continued)

Lesson 11 *Align Objects*

AUTODESK 3D STUDIO MAX 2-89

7. In the Match Scale rollout, click **the X Axis check box** and the **Z Axis check box** to select them, then click **OK**.

   The scale of the box along its x-axis and z-axis increases from 100% to 130%, as shown in Figure 106. The scale of the box along its y-axis remains the same.

You scaled and rotated a pyramid, then used the Align tool to match another object's orientation and scale along two axes to that of the pyramid.

Use the Quick Align tool

1. Select the **box** if necessary, click and hold the **Align flyout**, then drag to and click the **Quick Align tool** on the Main toolbar.
2. Click the **pyramid**.

   As shown in Figure 107, the Quick Align tool aligns the centers of the box and pyramid without opening the Align Selection dialog box.

You aligned the centers of the pyramid and the box automatically using the Quick Align tool.

FIGURE 106
Box with orientation and scale matched to target object

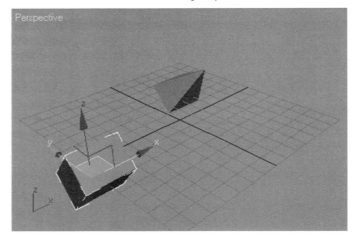

FIGURE 107
Box and pyramid with centers aligned

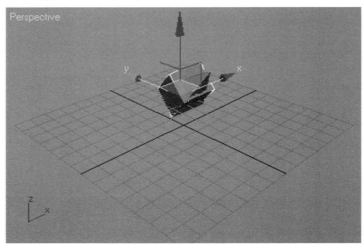

FIGURE 108
Box and three pyramids

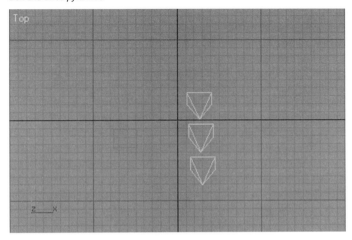

FIGURE 109
Clones offset from destination objects

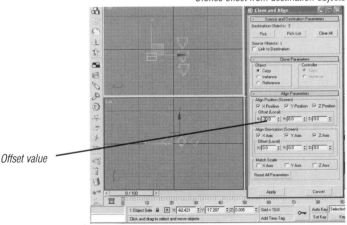

Offset value

Clone and align objects

1. Use the **Select and Move tool** to move the box back to its original position, then select the **pyramid** and move it while holding down **[Shift]** in order to create and position two copies of the pyramid, as shown in Figure 108.

2. Select the **box**, click **Tools** on the menu bar, then click **Clone and Align**.

3. Move the Clone and Align dialog box so that you can see the Top viewport, click **Pick**, then click each of the three pyramids.

   As you pick each pyramid, a clone of the box appears aligned with the each pyramid's location and orientation. Although the box was matched to the orientation of the pyramid in a previous objective, the orientations are matched once again and the box clones are rotated further around the x-axis.

4. In the Align Position rollout of the Align Parameters rollout under Offset (Local), click the **bottom spinner button** next to the X box and drag down until the number becomes –30.

   Each clone is now offset 30 units to the left along the x-axis from its destination pyramid, as shown in Figure 109.

5. Click **Apply** to accept the clones and their alignment to the pyramids, then click the Clone and Align dialog box **Close button**.

6. Save the file, reset 3ds Max, then exit.

You used the Clone and Align tool to create copies of an object aligned with three destination objects.

AUTODESK 3D STUDIO MAX 2-91

Lesson 11   Align Objects

CHAPTER SUMMARY

In this chapter, you learned the different methods for creating and working with standard polygon primitives. You explored the selection tools that let you select objects in different ways, including selecting the individual object, selecting an object by name, or creating a selection set to simplify the process of selecting a group of related objects. You also learned to move, rotate, and scale the objects you create and learned how to use the different transform gizmos available in 3ds Max. You learned how to modify polygons by changing their parameters. You also learned the important role that segments play in 3ds Max, and how to apply modifiers to an object and work with the modi-fier stack. The chapter also covered cloning, linking, and grouping objects, as well as creating arrays of objects. You learned how to adjust and work with pivot points, how to use the snapping tools, and how to align objects in a scene.

What You Have Learned

- How to create planes and spheres
- How to create boxes, cylinders, and pyramids
- How to create cones, tubes, and toruses
- How to select objects and create selection sets
- How to move, rotate and scale objects and work with transform gizmos
- How to modify the parameters of an object
- How to work with segments and apply modifiers
- How to reorder modifiers in a stack to get a different result
- How to clone, link, and group objects
- How to work with pivot points
- How to align objects

Key Terms

Standard polygon primitives Called standard primitives in 3ds Max, they are the building blocks for most of the things you will create.

Parameters Settings applied to objects in 3ds Max.

Modeling The process of creating realistic-looking objects.

Polygons In 3ds Max, closed sequences of 3 or more edges connected by a surface.

Selection region A shape with a dashed-line border that appears as you click and drag over an area with the Select Object tool active.

Selection set A predefined group of selected objects, to make it easier to select the objects you need.

Axis tripod Three axes that orient an object in space.

Gizmo Geometry that appears on-screen within an object to help you manipulate the object (for example, move, size, or rotate it).

Modifiers Specific methods for changing an object's appearance and structure.

chapter 3
MODELING

1. Understand editable polygons.
2. Apply modifiers to subobjects.
3. Understand normals.
4. Chamfer, extrude, and bevel objects.
5. Use Paint Deformation and Soft Selection.
6. Create and connect vertices, edges, and polygons.
7. Model efficiently.
8. Model a character.
9. Understand splines.
10. Edit splines.
11. Model with splines.

chapter 3 MODELING

There are multiple ways to model objects using 3ds Max. You can work with an object as an editable mesh, which enables you to work with the surfaces of an object composed of polygons. You can also model an object as an editable patch or as a NURBS object, both of which allow you to control curves and the behavior of curves in an object. However, this chapter, and this book overall, focuses on modeling with objects as editable polygons (polys) and editable splines. This is because modeling with editable polys and splines enables you to create a wide range of objects, from very simple to quite complex, using a relatively small set of easily understandable tools.

You will explore many of the most important tools for modeling with editable polygon objects in this chapter. First you'll learn about editable polys, their subobjects, and modeling the subobjects with modifiers. Then you'll begin to learn about easy ways to dramatically modify objects with just a few clicks by chamfering, extruding, and beveling, or by using paint deformation to create hills and troughs on a previously flat surface. You'll also learn about soft selecting multiple vertices to transform an entire surface area by working with only one selected vertex. This chapter also includes tips for modeling as efficiently aspossible—for instance, by creating a well-formed, complicated object with the least effort by using the MeshSmooth or Symmetry modifiers, or limiting the amount of time spent working on a project by working with object references or including an updatable object in a collaborator's scene. And lastly, understanding splines and editable splines will give you another way to think about how simple, mostly two-dimensional shapes can be used to great effect when modeling three-dimensional objects.

Tools You'll Use

LESSON 1

UNDERSTAND EDITABLE
POLYGONS

What You'll Do

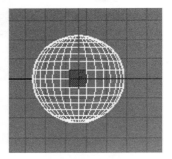

▶ *In this lesson, you will gain an understanding of editable polygons, learn how to convert standard primitives into editable polygons, and explore the subobjects that make up editable polygons.*

Understanding Editable Polygons

In Chapter 2, you worked with standard primitive objects and learned how you could modify parameters and apply modifiers to change the appearance of a standard primitive. Even though animations might start as standard primitives, through the process of **modeling**, or sculpting objects in a 3D animation program, those primitives become unrecognizable. This chapter focuses on **polygon modeling**, which begins when a primitive object is converted into an editable polygon, or editable poly. An **editable poly** is an object broken down into **polygons**, renderable surfaces enclosed by sequences of three or more connected edges. The polygons that make up an object's surface are also known as the object's **faces**, and are formed by the segments and sides in an object. If a box has one segment for each of its length, width, and height dimensions, each surface of the box is a polygon. If a box is divided into three segments on each of its sides, each surface will be divided into nine rectangular polygons, as shown in Figure 1.

Converting an Object into an Editable Poly

There are several ways that you can convert an object into an editable poly. The fastest way to do this is to select the object in a viewport, right-click the object, point to Convert To on the Transform menu, and then click Convert to Editable Poly, as shown in Figure 2. You can also convert an object into an editable poly using the Modify panel, but only if the object has no modifiers applied to it yet. Click the Modify tab to open the Modify panel, select the object, right-click the name of the object in the modifier stack display, and then click Editable Poly in the Convert To list on the right-click menu.

In addition to right-clicking, you can apply the Turn to Poly modifier to an object to convert it into an editable poly. To do this, select the object, click the Modify tab, click the Modifier List list arrow, and then select Turn to Poly to apply it. Next, click the Utilities tab, click the Collapse button, make sure the Modifier Stack Result

3-4 AUTODESK 3D STUDIO MAX   *Modeling*

option button is selected in the Output Type rollout, and then click the Collapse Selected button.

After an object has been converted into an editable poly, the name of the object changes in the modifier stack display (from, for instance, Box) to Editable Poly with a plus sign next to it.

When an object is converted into an editable poly, you can no longer edit the parameters of the object, such as height, length, or radius, number of segments or sides, or slice parameters. If you have applied modifiers to the original object, they are blended into the object when it is converted into an editable poly, so only one object, Editable Poly, appears in the modifier stack after conversion. The only exception to this rule is the Edit Poly modifier. The Edit Poly modifier, when applied to an object, makes that object into an editable poly that can be edited when the modifier is selected, while maintaining the primitive and its parameters at the bottom

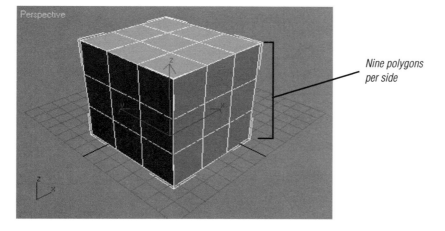

FIGURE 1
Editable poly

Nine polygons per side

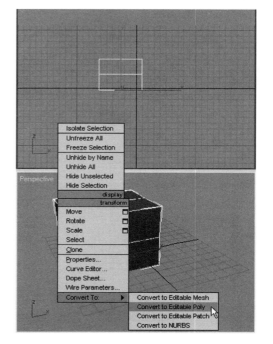

FIGURE 2
Convert To submenu

of the modifier stack. One of the plusses of using this modifier, besides not losing the parameters of the original object, is that changes to the subobjects in this modifier can be animated. However, there are a couple of downsides to using this modifier to work with an object as an editable poly: If you want to change the parameters of the primitive, those changes will affect any editing you've done to the object as an editable poly. In addition, using the Edit Poly modifier uses more computer space than if you simply converted an object into an editable poly object.

Accessing Subobject Levels

When working with primitives, you are able to select an object only in its entirety. With editable polys, you can select specific parts of the object known as subobjects. A **subobject** is a subset of an object's geometry. Editable polys are not the only objects in 3ds Max with subobject levels. Modifiers and other types of objects, such as editable mesh objects, have subobject levels.

To select one or more subobjects, you need to be in the appropriate subobject level. To view the subobject levels for an object, click the Modify tab if necessary, and then click the plus sign next to the object's name in the modifier stack display. The available list of subobject levels, known as the **hierarchy**, appears beneath the object's name, and the plus sign turns into a minus sign. Click the appropriate subobject level in the list to select it.

QUICKTIP
An additional way to access a subobject level is to right-click the selected object in the viewport to open the Quad menu, as shown in Figure 3, and then select the subobject level from the Tools 1 menu on the upper left.

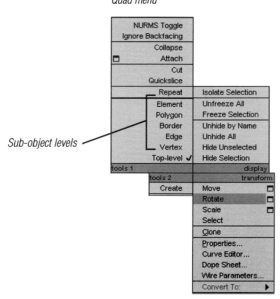

FIGURE 3
Quad menu

Sub-object levels

3-6 AUTODESK 3D STUDIO MAX

Modeling

When a subobject level is selected, the subobject level in the modifier stack display is highlighted in yellow. If the object's hierarchy is closed in the modifier stack display but a subobject level is selected, the object itself (for example, "Editable Poly") is highlighted yellow in the display. If no subobject level is selected, the object is not highlighted. If no subobject level is selected and you double-click the object in the modifier stack display, the first level in the hierarchy is selected automatically and the object is highlighted yellow.

Selecting Editable Poly Subobjects

An editable poly has five subobject types: vertices, edges, borders, polygons, and elements. Each subobject can be selected, moved, rotated, scaled, and/or have modifiers applied to it. A **vertex** is a point in space that defines the structure of an object or a polygon. A vertex can be the corner of a polygon or the point at which several polygons meet (for instance, a corner of a plane is a vertex; the tip of a pyramid, where four triangles meet, is a vertex). Vertices appear as blue dots when you are in the Vertex subobject level; when selected, vertices appears as red dots. An **edge** is a line that is both the side of a polygon and connects two vertices. When selected, an edge appears as a red line in the viewport. A **border** is a sequence of edges that border a hole in the object. When selected, a border appears red in the viewport. A **polygon**, as shown on the left side of Figure 4, is a multiple-edged surface. When selected, a polygon is colored red in the viewport. An **element** is all of an

FIGURE 4
Editable poly subobjects

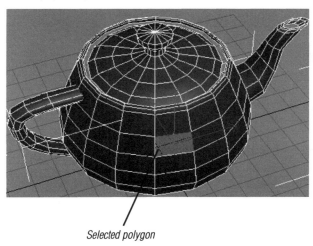

Selected polygon

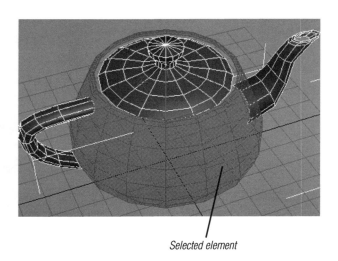

Selected element

object's polygons. A teapot is actually made up of four elements, the body, lid, spout, and handle. On the right side of Figure 4, the body element is selected.

To select one or more editable poly subobjects, you need to be in the right subobject level in the hierarchy. To view the subobject levels for an editable poly, click the Modify tab if necessary, and then click the plus sign next to Editable Poly in the modifier stack display. 3ds Max displays the five subobject levels. Click a subobject level, and then click or use a selection region to select the subobjects with which you want to work. For instance, if you want to work with the top point of a pyramid, click the Vertex subobject level, and then click or drag a selection region around the point of the pyramid in a viewport to select the vertex.

As shown in Figure 5, you can also use buttons available in the Selection rollout of the Modify panel to select a subobject level without clicking the plus sign next to Editable Poly in the modifier stack display. Click either the Vertex, Edge, Border, Polygon, or Element button to open its respective subobject level.

FIGURE 5
Modify panel for an editable poly

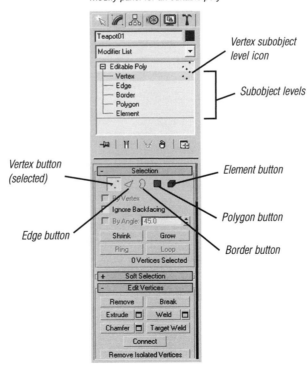

3-8 AUTODESK 3D STUDIO MAX

Modeling

When an editable poly subobject level is selected, the icon from the level's button appears next to the level, and "Editable Poly" appears in the modifier stack display, as shown in Figure 5. When the hierarchy is closed, the icon for the selected subobject level continues to appear next to "Editable Poly" in the modifier stack.

Using Other Options in the Selection Rollout

The Selection rollout offers some different options for selecting within a subobject level. If you click the By Vertex check box, when you select a vertex you select all subobjects (except vertices) connected to that vertex. If you click the Ignore Backfacing check box, you can select only those subobjects that are facing you. In the Polygon subobject level, click the By Angle check box to select all polygons that connect to the selected polygon at an angle less than that shown in the By Angle text box.

Four buttons in the selection rollout enable selection or deselection of several subobjects at once. Click the Shrink button to deselect in all directions the outermost subobjects in a selection. For instance, if all of the edges on the lid of a teapot were selected, clicking the Shrink button once would deselect the edges of the polygons on the outer rim of the lid. Click the Grow button to increase the size of the subobject selection area in all directions. When in the Edge or Border subobject levels, click the Ring button to select all edges that are parallel to the selected edge, as shown in Figure 6. When in the Edge subobject level, click the Loop button to select all of the edges aligned with a selected edge. For example, if you selected one edge on the outside edge of a cylinder's cap, clicking the Loop button would select all of the edges around the outside edge of the cap.

FIGURE 6
Edges selected using Ring button

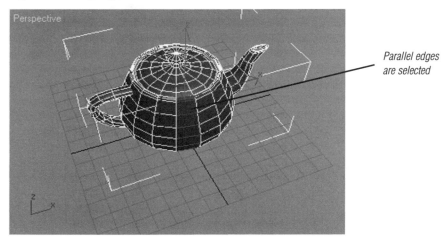

Parallel edges are selected

Lesson 1   Understand Editable Polygons

DISCREET 3D STUDIO MAX 3-9

Convert primitives into editable polys

1. Create a **sphere** and a **box** in the Top viewport, then click the **Modify tab** to open the Modify panel.

2. Select the **sphere**, right-click it, point to **Convert To** on the Transform quadrant of the Quad menu, then click **Convert To Editable Poly**.

   The sphere becomes an editable poly, and the text "Sphere" in the modifier stack display on the Modify panel becomes "Editable Poly" with a plus sign next to it.

3. Select the **box**, click the **Modifier List list arrow**, then click **Turn to Poly** on the modifier list.

4. Click the **Utilities tab**, click the **Collapse button** on the Utilities panel to select it, then click the **Modifier Stack Result option button** in the Output Type group to select it (if necessary), as shown in Figure 7.

5. Click the **Collapse Selected button** above the Output Type group.

   The box flashes once, indicating its stack has been collapsed.

6. Click the **Collapse button** to deselect it, then click the **Modify tab**.

   The box has been converted into an editable poly, and the modifier stack display now shows "Editable Poly" with a plus sign next to it.

7. Save the file as **Editpoly**.

You created a sphere and a box, then converted them into editable polys using two different conversion methods.

FIGURE 7
Utilities panel

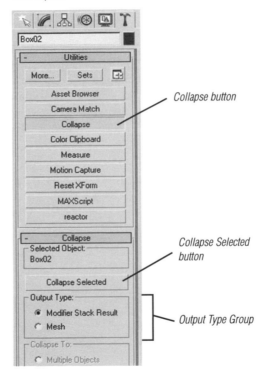

FIGURE 8
Taper modifier gizmo selected

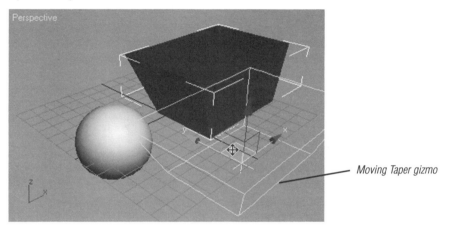

Moving Taper gizmo

Review subobject levels

1. With the box is selected, click the **Modifier List list arrow**, click **Taper**, then change the Taper Amount to **.5**.

2. In the modifier stack display, click **Editable Poly**, click the **plus sign** next to Editable Poly, then click the **Vertex subobject level**.

   The selected Vertex subobject level turns yellow, and Vertex icons appear to the right of Vertex, Editable Poly, and Taper.

   > TIP While a subobject level is selected, the effect of the Taper modifier doesn't show. It shows if you select the Taper modifier or if you select the Editable Poly when no subobject level is selected and the Show End Result button is selected.

3. Right-click the **box**, then click **Edge** on the Tools 1 quadrant of the Quad menu.

   In the modifier stack display, the Edge subobject level is now selected and yellow.

4. Click **Editable Poly** in the modifier stack display, click the **minus sign** next to Editable Poly to close the subobject list, click **Taper**, then click the **plus sign** next to Taper.

   The Taper modifier has two subobjects, Gizmo and Center.

5. Click **Gizmo** on the Taper subobject list, click the **Select and Move tool** (if necessary), click in the Perspective viewport, click the **XY axis handle** (the yellow square) in the Move gizmo, then move the gizmo away from the box, as shown in Figure 8.

(continued)

The location of the gizmo affects the tapering applied to the box.

6. Click the **minus sign** next to Taper, click **Taper**, then click the **Remove modifier from the stack button** 🖱.

You applied a modifier to the box, accessed the Vertex subobject level via the modifier stack display, then accessed the Edge subobject level using the Quad menu. You also viewed the Taper modifier's subobjects and accessed its Gizmo subobject.

Select single and multiple editable poly subobjects

1. Select the **sphere** in the Perspective viewport, then click the **Vertex button** in the Selection rollout on the Modify panel.

   All of the vertices on the sphere appear, as shown in Figure 9. Each vertex is blue on-screen.

2. Click the **vertex** at the top of the sphere to select it.

   The vertex is red when selected.

   (continued)

FIGURE 9
Sphere showing all vertices

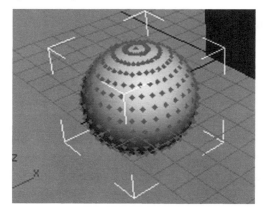

3-12 AUTODESK 3D STUDIO MAX

Modeling

FIGURE 10
Box with polygon selected

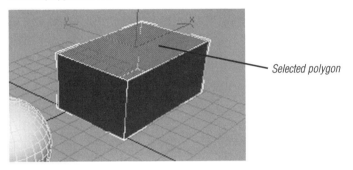

Selected polygon

3. Click the **Edge button** on the Modify panel, press **[F4]** (if necessary) to show the gridlines in the Perspective viewport, click one of the **edges** on the sphere to select it, then click another **edge** on the sphere to select it.

4. Click the **Edge button** to deselect it, select the **box**, click the **Polygon button**, then click the **polygon** on top of the box, as shown in Figure 10.

5. Press **[Delete]**.

   The polygon is deleted, and now there is a hole in the top of the box.

6. Click the **Border button**, then click one of the **edges** around the hole in the box.

   The border around the hole is selected and red.

7. Click the **Element button**, then click anywhere on the box to select the entire box.

8. Click the **Element button** again to deselect it.

You selected a single vertex and a single edge on a sphere, selected a polygon on a box and deleted it, selected a border on the box, and selected the box as an element.

Lesson 1   Understand Editable Polygons

Select multiple subobjects

1. Select the **sphere**, click the **Vertex button**, click in the Front viewport, then click and drag to select the **vertices** on the top half of the sphere, as shown in Figure 11.

   All of the vertices within the selection region are now selected. In the Top viewport, you can see that all of the vertices on the entire top half of the sphere are selected, even those not visible in the Front viewport.

2. Click the **Edge button**, click the **By Vertex check box** in the Selection rollout to select it, then click the **vertex** in the center of the sphere in the Front viewport.

   The four edges connected to the vertex are selected.

3. Click the **Polygon button**, then click the **vertex** in the center of the sphere again.

   All four polygons around the vertex are selected, as shown in Figure 12.

4. Click the **By Vertex check box** to deselect it.

You selected multiple vertices on a sphere by dragging a selection region, then selected multiple edges on the sphere by selecting one edge and clicking the By Vertex check box. You also selected four polygons by vertex.

FIGURE 11
Selection of vertices on sphere

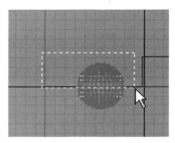

FIGURE 12
Sphere with polygons selected by vertex

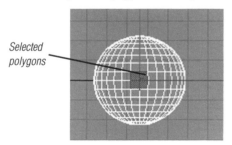

Selected polygons

FIGURE 13
Edges selected with Grow button

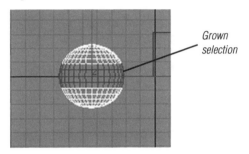

Grown selection

Grow and shrink a selection area

1. With the sphere selected, click the **Edge button** again, click one of the **horizontal edges** in the center of the sphere in the Front viewport, then click the **Loop button** in the Selection rollout.

   All of the edges aligned with the selected edge are now selected, forming a complete circle of selected edges around the sphere.

2. Click the **Grow button** in the Selection rollout once.

   All of the edges connected directly to the selected edges become selected.

3. Click the **Grow button** again to grow the selection of edges by another level, as shown in Figure 13.

4. Click the **Shrink button** in the Selection rollout two times.

   The selection is now back to where it was after you clicked the Loop button.

5. Click the **Edge button** to deselect it.

You selected a single edge, used the Loop button to select multiple edges around the center of a sphere, used the Grow button to grow the selection twice, then used the Shrink button to shrink the selection twice.

Transform subobjects

1. Click in the Perspective viewport, select the **box**, click the **Polygon button** ■, click the **By Vertex check box** (if necessary) to deselect it, then click the **polygon** on the left side of the box to select it.

2. Click the **Select and Move tool** ✥ (if necessary), then use the **Y handle** on the Move gizmo to move the polygon toward the back of the grid, as shown in Figure 14.

   As the polygon is moved, the shape of the box changes and the shape of the polygons connected to the moved polygon changes.

3. Click the **Edge button** ◁, click the **Select and Rotate tool** ↻, click the **top edge** of the polygon you just moved, click the

   (continued)

FIGURE 14
Box with moved polygon

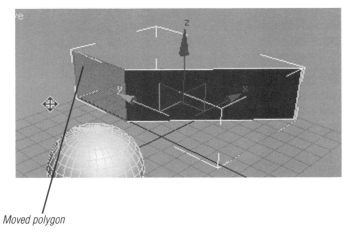

Moved polygon

FIGURE 15
Box with rotated edge   Rotated edge

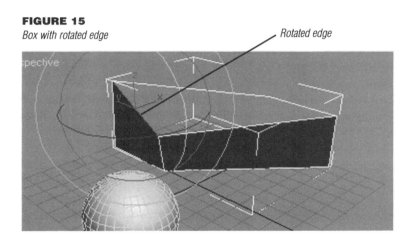

X handle in the Rotate gizmo, then rotate the edge by 30 degrees around the x-axis.

The box now looks similar to that shown in Figure 15.

4. Click the **Edge button** to deselect it, click the **Select Object tool**, click the **sphere**, click the **Polygon button**, then click a **polygon** in the center of the sphere.

5. Click the **Select and Uniform Scale tool**, drag the **Z handle** of the Scale gizmo up about one inch, then click the **Select Object tool**.

    The size of the polygon increases along the z-axis. The polygons connected to the scaled polygon change shape because of the changes to the scaled polygon.

6. Click the **Polygon button** to deselect it, save the file, then reset 3ds Max.

You moved a polygon and rotated an edge on a box, then increased the scale of a polygon in the center of a sphere.

LESSON 2

APPLY MODIFIERS TO SUBOBJECTS

What You'll Do

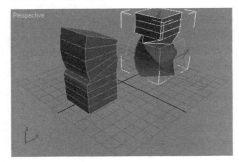

In this lesson, you will learn how to apply modifiers to the subobjects of an editable poly.

Applying Modifiers to Editable Poly Subobjects

In Chapter 2, you learned how to apply modifiers to objects to affect the appearance or behavior of the object. Using subobjects, you can apply modifiers to part of an object to change that part of the object's appearance or behavior. This enables the modifications you make to an object to be more specific and sophisticated than if you were only able to work with the object as a whole.

To apply a modifier to a subobject, click the Modify tab if necessary, select the appropriate subobject level, select the subobjects that you want to modify in the viewport, click the Modifier List list arrow, click the name of the modifier you want to apply, and then adjust the modifier's parameters as necessary. When a modifier is applied to a particular subobject level, the icon for the subobject level appears to the right of the modifier name in the modifier stack, as shown in Figure 16.

FIGURE 16
Modifier stack display

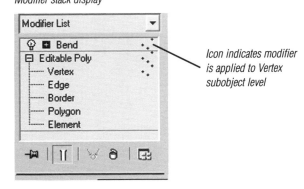

Icon indicates modifier is applied to Vertex subobject level

3-18 AUTODESK 3D STUDIO MAX   *Modeling*

QUICKTIP

Only some modifiers can be applied to just subobjects; others, such as MeshSmooth and TurboSmooth, are applied to the whole object no matter which subobjects are selected when the modifier is applied. Explore the modifier list to find out which modifiers can affect subobjects.

You might need to adjust the subobjects in a modifier to get the look that you want in your object. For instance, the Bend modifier has been applied to the vertices at the top of the box shown on the left in Figure 17. However, the center of the modifier is located at the center of the selected vertices, causing an awkward bend away from the rest of the object. By moving the center of the modifier to the bottom of the subobject selection, the bent part of the box on the right in Figure 17 appears more smoothly connected to the rest of the editable poly.

QUICKTIP

The ability or need to adjust a modifier's subobjects is not limited to when you are working with editable polys; you can adjust a modifier's subobjects whenever you are using a modifier.

Using the Mesh Select Modifier

You might want to apply modifiers separately to more than one type of subobject in the same editable poly. You can do this by using the Mesh Select modifier. The Mesh Select modifier enables you to select subobjects in the editable poly and apply subsequent modifiers to that selection only, even if a different subobject level is selected lower down in

FIGURE 17
Vertices with Bend modifier applied

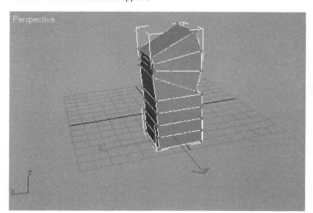
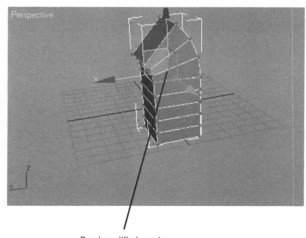

Bend modifier's center moved lower

Lesson 2 Apply Modifiers to Subobjects

the modifier stack. For example, in Figure 18, the Twist modifier has been applied to the edges on the lower half of the box, and the Bend modifier has been applied to the vertices on the upper half of the box. The Mesh Select modifier is used in the modifier stack to designate the selected edges as the selection to which the Twist modifier should be applied.

To use the Mesh Select modifier in this way, apply the Mesh Select modifier to the editable poly, select a subobject level in the Mesh Select Parameters rollout in the Modify panel, select the appropriate subobjects if they are not already selected, and then apply a modifier or modifiers to the selection. Or, you can insert the Mesh Select modifier underneath an already applied modifier and then select a different subobject level to which the modifier should be applied. The icon for the selected subobject level will appear next to Mesh Select and the modifiers applied to the selection will appear in the modifier stack, as shown in Figure 18. If you want to apply a modifier to the entire object after applying modifiers to its subobjects, make sure that no subobjects are selected when you apply the Mesh Select modifier. Subsequent modifiers will be applied to the object as a whole.

QUICKTIP

Remember that the Mesh Select modifier is only for selection; you cannot move, rotate, or scale the subobjects you select using it.

FIGURE 18
Mesh Select modifier applied

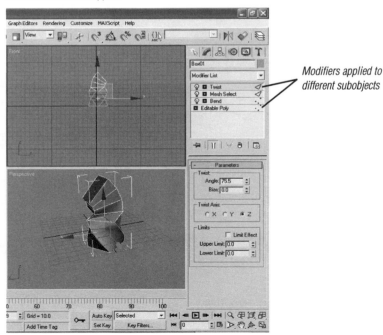

Modifiers applied to different subobjects

FIGURE 19
Box01 with Bend modifier applied to vertices

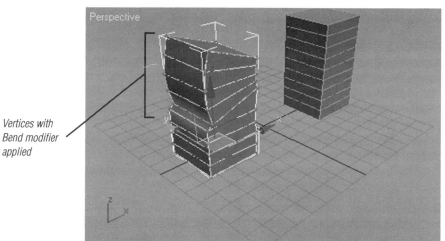

Vertices with Bend modifier applied

Apply and adjust subobject modifiers

1. On the left side of the Top viewport, create a **box** with the dimensions **30** × **30** × **60** and **9** Height segments, then create a copy of the box located to the right of the first box.

   TIP You can set dimensions and height segments in the Parameters rollout when you create the box.

2. Right-click the **first box** (**Box01**), point to **Convert To** on the Transform quadrant of the Quad menu, click **Convert To Editable Poly**, then repeat the right-clicking to convert the second box (**Box02**) to an editable poly.

3. Select **Box01**, click the **Modify tab**, click the **plus sign** next to Editable Poly in the modifier stack display, then click the **Vertex subobject level**.

4. Click in the Front viewport, click and drag to select the **vertices** in the top half of the box, click the **Modifier List list arrow**, then click **Bend**.

   The Bend modifier is applied to the selected vertices. The Vertex icon appears to the right of Bend in the modifier stack display.

5. Change the Angle number on the Bend modifier's Parameters rollout to **40**.

   In the Perspective viewport, Box01 should look like Figure 19.

   (continued)

6. Select **Box02**, click the **Edge button**, click and drag in the Front viewport to select the **edges** on the bottom half of Box02, click the **Modifier List list arrow**, then click **Twist** to apply the modifier to the selected vertices.

7. Change the Angle number on the Twist modifier's Parameters rollout to **40**.

   The Twist modifier is applied to the selected edges and looks like Box02, as shown in the Perspective viewport in Figure 20. The Edge icon appears to the right of Twist in the modifier stack display.

You selected the vertices in the top half of a box editable poly, applied the Bend modifier to the vertices, selected the edges on the bottom half of the second box editable poly, and applied the Twist modifier to the edges.

Use the Mesh Select modifier

1. Select **Box02**, click the **Modifier List list arrow**, click **Taper** on the modifier list, then change the Amount number in the Taper modifier's Parameters rollout to **−.5**.

   The Taper gizmo appears around the selected edges of the editable poly, and the gizmo and Box02 change shape when you adjust the Amount number, as shown in Figure 21. The Edge icon appears next to Taper in the modifier stack display.

(continued)

FIGURE 20
Box02 with Twist modifier applied to edges

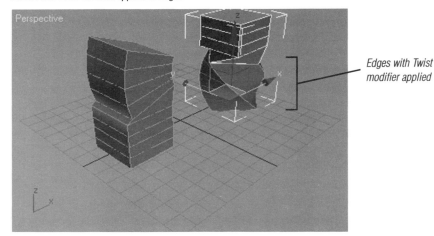

Edges with Twist modifier applied

FIGURE 21
Edges with Taper modifier applied

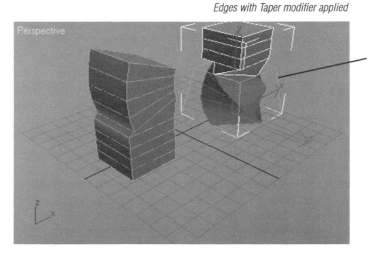

Taper gizmo around selected edges

FIGURE 22
Box02 with Mesh Select modifier applied

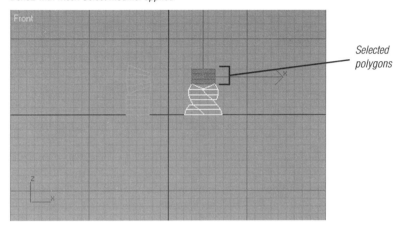

Selected polygons

FIGURE 23
Box02 with Taper modifier applied to polygons

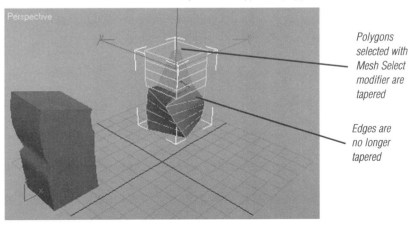

Polygons selected with Mesh Select modifier are tapered

Edges are no longer tapered

2. Click the **Modifier List list arrow**, then click **Mesh Select** on the modifier list.

   The Mesh Select modifier is applied to the object, appearing above the Taper modifier in the modifier stack display. No icon appears next to Mesh Select because no subobjects have been selected with it.

3. With the **Mesh Select modifier** selected, click the **Polygon button** ■ , then in the Front viewport select the **polygons** at the top of Box02 that have not been twisted and tapered, as shown in Figure 22.

   The Polygon icon now appears next to Mesh Select in the modifier stack display.

4. Click and drag the **Mesh Select modifier** from its place above the Taper modifier to a new location between the Taper and Twist modifiers in the modifier stack display, then click the **Show end result on/off toggle button** � .

   The Taper modifier is now applied only to the polygons selected in the Mesh Select modifier. As shown in Figure 23, the top of the box is now tapered, and the Polygon icon appears next to the Taper modifier in the modifier stack display.

5. Click the **Polygon button** ■ to deselect it, save the file as **Modifypoly**, then reset 3ds Max.

You applied a second modifier to selected edges in a box, applied the Mesh Select modifier to the box, selected polygons within the Mesh Select modifier, then moved the Mesh Select modifier between the first and second modifier so that the second modifier was applied to the selected polygons.

DISCREET 3D STUDIO MAX 3-23

Lesson 2   Apply Modifiers to Subobjects

LESSON 3

UNDERSTAND NORMALS

What You'll Do

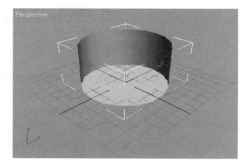

In this lesson, you will learn what normals are, how they affect what you see on-screen, and how to change the direction of normals.

Understanding Normals

As you've learned, the surface of an editable poly is made up of polygons. Each polygon in an object has a **normal**, or direction that the polygon surface faces. The surface on which the normal is based is the outer surface, or front, of the polygon and is the side of the polygon that you see displayed on-screen.

The inner surface of a polygon is not displayed on-screen. For instance, if you create a plane, and then rotate the plane in the Perspective home grid so that you can see it from the bottom, you'll see that it is not visible from underneath, as shown in Figure 24. The reason for this is that modeling objects takes computer space and computer time, and most objects animated in 3ds Max are shown from the outside only; no rendering is needed for the inside surface. Thus the inside surface of polygons in 3ds Max is invisible and uneditable, making the work of modeling in the software more efficient.

Because the inside surface of a polygon is invisible, you might run into some situations where an object you create looks

3-24 AUTODESK 3D STUDIO MAX   *Modeling*

strange because the inside surfaces of the object are displayed on-screen. For example, if you cut a sphere in half, you could see the front of the half sphere, as shown in Figure 25, but the back would not show. There is a way to make such an invisible surface visible using the Materials Editor; this process will be covered in Chapter 4, "Materials and Maps."

Flipping Normals

Because normals appear on only one side of a polygon, you can create some interesting effects in the appearance of an object by flipping its normals. Some modifiers, such

FIGURE 24
Outer and inner surface of plane

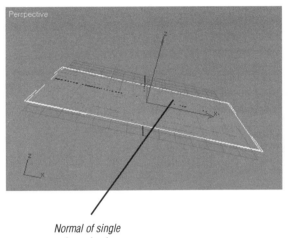

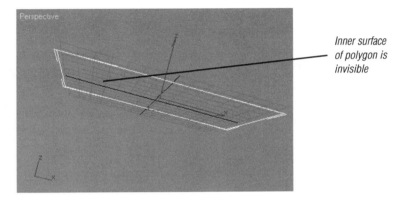

Inner surface of polygon is invisible

Normal of single polygon in plane

FIGURE 25
Sphere cut in half

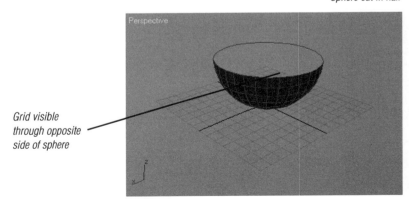

Grid visible through opposite side of sphere

Lesson 3   Understand Normals

DISCREET 3D STUDIO MAX 3-25

as the Lathe modifier, might when first applied, have the normals faced in the wrong direction, as shown in Figure 26, which is supposed to show a wine glass. This modifier has in its parameters, however, a Flip Normals check box. When this check box is selected, the normals flip to the opposite surface and show the object as intended.

Another way to flip normals is to apply the Normal modifier. Applying the Normal modifier automatically flips the normals of an object. Click the Flip Normals check box in the Parameters rollout for the modifier to flip them back. The teapot shown in Figure 27 has the Normal modifier applied to it. The reason you can see the inside of the teapot is that polygons on the outside of the teapot closest to you are seen from the back, so are they invisible. If an object has normals that are facing in opposite directions, click the Unify Normals check box in the Normal modifier to make them all face the same direction.

FIGURE 26
Lathe modifier applied

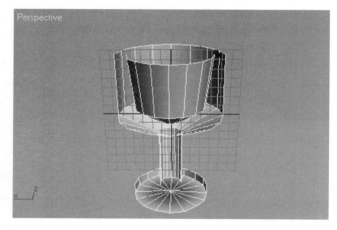

FIGURE 27
Teapot with Normal modifier applied

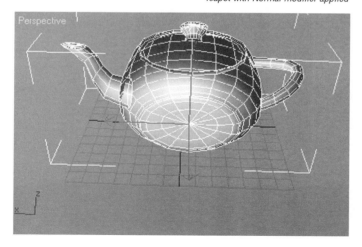

FIGURE 28
Plane and sphere in Perspective viewport

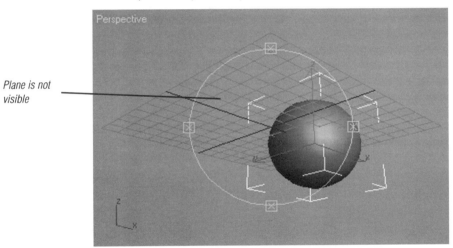

Plane is not visible

View normals

1. Create a **plane** with dimensions of **80 × 60** on the left side of the center gridline in the Top viewport and a **sphere** with a radius of **30** on the right side of the center gridline.

2. Click the **Perspective viewport**, click the **Arc Rotate button**, click the **bottom handle** on the view rotation trackball, and drag up until you are looking at the plane and sphere from underneath the grid, as shown in Figure 28.

   The plane is not visible from underneath. Its normal is the direction its top surface faces. The back surface is uneditable.

3. Click the **top handle** on the view rotation trackball and drag down until you can see both the plane and sphere again.

4. Click the **Select Object tool**, click the **sphere**, right-click the **sphere**, point to **Convert To**, click **Convert to Editable Poly**, then click the **Edge button** on the Modify panel.

(continued)

Lesson 3   Understand Normals

DISCREET 3D STUDIO MAX 3-27

5. In the Front viewport, select all of the **edges** in the top half of the sphere, then press **[Delete]**.

   The sphere in the Perspective viewport appears as shown in Figure 29. The normals of the side of the halved sphere that is farthest from you face away from you, and thus are invisible.

6. Click in the Perspective viewport, click the **Arc Rotate button**, click the **right handle** on the view rotation trackball, then drag to the right until the plane is on the right side of the screen.

   As your view of the halved sphere rotates, the normals of the other side of the halved sphere continue to face away from you and be invisible.

7. Save the file as **Viewnormal**, then reset 3ds Max.

You created a plane and looked at it from underneath, deleted all of the vertices in the top half of a sphere, and viewed the normals effect on what you see on-screen.

FIGURE 29
Plane and halved sphere

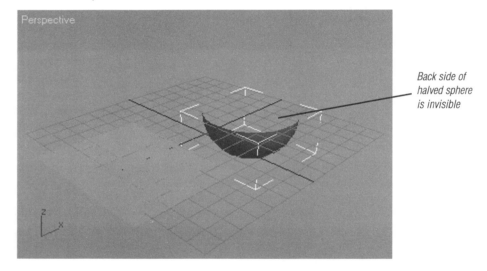

Back side of halved sphere is invisible

3-28 AUTODESK 3D STUDIO MAX   *Modeling*

FIGURE 30
Cylinder with Normal modifier applied

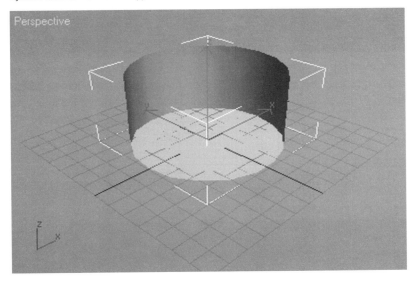

Flip normals

1. In the Top viewport, create a **cylinder** with a radius of **40** and a height of **40**.

2. Click the **Modify tab**, click the **Modifier List list arrow**, then click **Normal** on the modifier list.

   With the Normal modifier applied, the cylinder's normals are reversed, and it looks inside out, as shown in Figure 30.

3. In the Parameters rollout on the Modify panel, click the **Flip Normals check box** to deselect it.

   The cylinder's normals are flipped back, and it appears again as it did when it was created.

4. Reset 3ds Max without saving the file.

You created a cylinder, applied the Normal modifier to the cylinder, then flipped the normals of the cylinder from within the Normal modifier.

LESSON 4

CHAMFER, EXTRUDE, AND BEVEL OBJECTS

What You'll Do

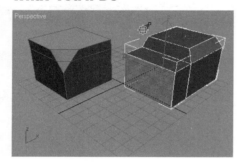

In this lesson, you will learn how to use chamfering, extruding, and beveling of subobjects to model an object.

Each of an editable poly's subobject levels has several Edit options available in the Modify panel. The three most popular of these options used in modeling are Chamfer, Extrude, and Bevel. With these three options, you can model extensively and creatively using 3ds Max.

Chamfering an Object

When you **chamfer** an object, you cut off a corner or edge of the object to make the corner or edge more rounded. The top corners of the box in Figure 31 have been chamfered, and the edges around the top cap of the cylinder in the figure have also been chamfered. In both cases, you can see that the objects appear more rounded where they have been chamfered. When you are working with an editable poly, you can chamfer its vertices, edges, or borders. You cannot chamfer a polygon or element.

When you chamfer a vertex, the effect of the chamfer depends on the number of edges connected to that vertex. If a vertex connects three edges, as in the corner of a box, the chamfered vertex is split into three vertices, each of which moves along an edge connected to the original vertex, creating a new polygon, as shown in Figure 32. Each vertex moves the same distance from the original vertex. If one or more of the vertices reaches another vertex in the object as you are creating the chamfer, it won't move farther.

Remember that an edge is the line that connects two vertices. When you chamfer an edge in an editable poly, the edge splits into two

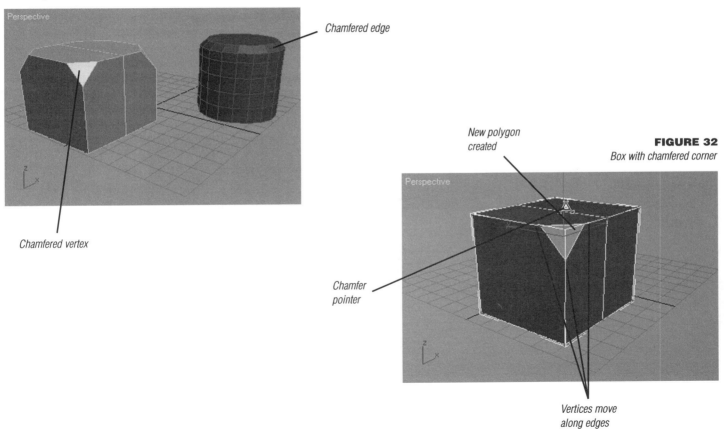

FIGURE 31
Box and cylinder

FIGURE 32
Box with chamfered corner

edges that move away from each other along the edges that are connected to the original edge's two vertices. For instance, in Figure 33, the left image shows an edge selected in a cylinder. That edge has two vertices, and each of its vertices connects to two other edges. When the edge is chamfered, as shown in the right image of Figure 33, the edge and its vertices split and the vertices move the same distance along the other edges to which they are connected. If one of the edges reaches another parallel edge as you are creating the chamfer, it won't move farther. The result is a new polygon with new edges and new vertices.

To chamfer a border, you follow the same process as if you were chamfering a vertex or an edge, but the result is different. When a border is chamfered, the object does not become more rounded. What happens is that a second border is created parallel to the original border and moved away from the original by the chamfer amount. While this doesn't affect the outward appearance of the object right away, what it does create is a new polygon or polygons between the new and original borders that can be edited. This can be particularly useful if you want the area near the outer edges of an object to appear different from the rest of the object.

To chamfer a vertex, edge, or border in an editable poly, make sure you are in the appropriate subobject level, select the vertex, edge, or border, and then click the Chamfer button in the Edit Vertices (or Edit Edges, or Edit Borders) rollout on the Modify panel. Next, click and then drag the selected vertex, edge, or border up or down until the chamfer appears as desired. An alternative method that enables you to more precisely control the distance of the chamfer is to click the

FIGURE 33
Cylinder with chamfered edge

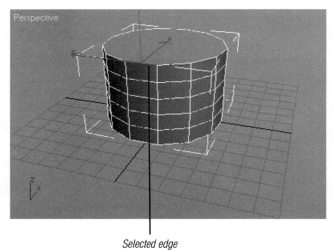

Selected edge

Selected edge chamfered

Chamfer vertices stop when another vertex is reached

3-32 AUTODESK 3D STUDIO MAX

Modeling

Settings button next to the Chamfer button instead of the Chamfer button itself. When you click the Settings button, the Chamfer Edges dialog box opens, as shown in Figure 34. In addition, the selected vertex, edge, or border is immediately chamfered the amount shown in the Chamfer Amount box in the dialog box. Type in or use the spinner buttons to enter a new Chamfer Amount, if necessary. If you click Apply in the Chamfer Settings dialog box, each selected vertex, edge, or border created by the first chamfer is chamfered again.

QUICKTIP
The Edit rollout on the Modify panel might not show completely when you first open the Modify panel for an object. To show more of the panel, move the mouse pointer to the bottom edge of the panel until it becomes a hand, and then click and drag up or down to move, or "pan" the panel up or down.

Extruding an Object

A modeling technique that comes in handy over and over again while modeling is extrusion. To **extrude** something is to push it out, or make it project away from its original location. With editable polys in 3ds Max, extruding enables you to expand an object in a controllable way. The most commonly extruded subobject is a polygon, but you can extrude vertices, edges, and borders, too.

When you extrude a polygon, you move it away from its original location while keeping it connected to its original location. In Figure 35, one side of the box has been extruded, creating four additional polygons

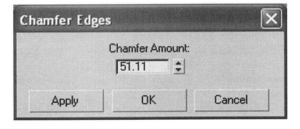

FIGURE 34
Chamfer Edges dialog box

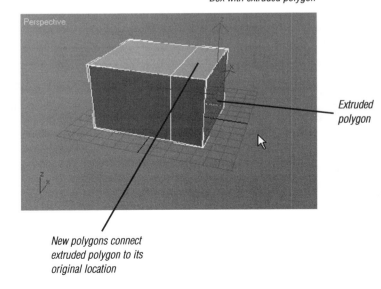

FIGURE 35
Box with extruded polygon

Extruded polygon

New polygons connect extruded polygon to its original location

Lesson 4   Chamfer, Extrude, and Bevel Objects

that connect the extruded polygon to its original location. The size of the original polygon is the same, and the normal of the polygon still faces the same way as it did in its original location.

To extrude a polygon, make sure you are in the Polygon subobject level, select a polygon, click the Extrude button in the Edit Polygons rollout on the Modify panel, and then click the polygon and drag up to adjust the amount the polygon is extruded. Instead of clicking the Extrude button, you can also click the Settings button next to the Extrude button to open the Extrude Polygons dialog box, as shown in Figure 36. This immediately extrudes the selected polygon by the Extrusion Height shown in the dialog box; use the spinners or type the numbers a new Extrusion Height, if necessary.

QUICKTIP

Using a negative Extrusion Height pushes the polygon back into the object rather than projecting it out.

Three other options are available in the Extrude Polygons dialog box for extruding multiple polygons at once. If you have multiple polygons selected, click the Group option to extrude them together in the same direction, as shown in the first image in Figure 37. The direction of extrusion is an average of the normals of the selected polygons—in other words, an average of the directions all of the polygon surfaces face. Click the Local Normal option button to extrude each polygon in the direction of its own normal, as shown in the second image in Figure 37.

FIGURE 36
Extrude Polygons dialog box

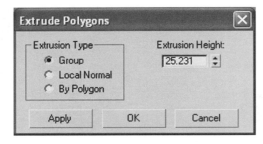

FIGURE 37
Multiple polygon Extrusion Type options

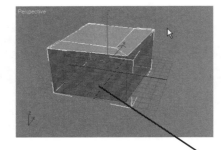

Polygons extruded as a group

Polygons extruded separately

Polygons extruded according to their local normals

3-34 AUTODESK 3D STUDIO MAX

Modeling

Because the polygons remain connected, the direction of each polygon's normal is at a slight angle to its original normal. Click the By Polygon option button to extrude each selected polygon separately from the other selected polygon, as shown in the third image in Figure 37. Click the OK button to accept the extrusion, click Cancel to cancel it, or click Apply to apply the extrusion again to the selected polygons.

As you do with a polygon, when you extrude a vertex, you push it away from its original location while connecting it back to that location. However, as a vertex is extruded, its original location is also chamfered; this creates an extrusion with volume rather than just a straight line from the vertex's original location to its new location. Similarly, when you extrude an edge, the edge is pushed away from its original location while chamfering that edge to create volume in the edge's extrusion. When you extrude a border, the height of the extrusion is the distance you push out the border in all directions, as shown in Figure 38. The extruded border is connected back to its original location by a new polygon or polygons.

To extrude a vertex, edge, or border, make sure you are in the appropriate subobject level, select the vertex, edge, or border, and then click the Extrude button in the Edit Vertices (or Edit Edges or Edit Borders) rollout on the Modify panel. Next, click and then drag the selected vertex, edge, or border up until the extrusion height is as desired, and then drag to the left or right to increase the base width of the extrusion. You can also click the Settings button next to the Extrude button to open the Extrude Vertices or Extrude Edges dialog box (for both edges and borders), as shown in Figure 39. Change the Extrusion Height in the dialog box to adjust the distance the vertex, edge, or border is pushed out. Change the Extrusion Base Width

FIGURE 38
Box with extruded border

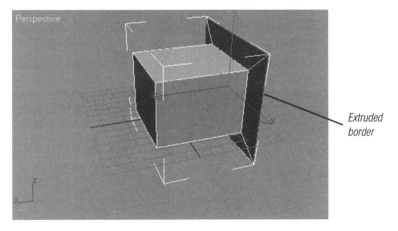

Extruded border

FIGURE 39
Extrude Edges dialog box

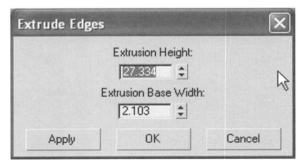

Lesson 4   Chamfer, Extrude, and Bevel Objects

in the dialog box to adjust the distance the original vertex or edge location is chamfered, or the distance the original border moves away from its original location. Click OK to accept the extrusion, click Cancel to cancel the extrusion, or click Apply to apply the extrusion again to the selected subobjects.

Beveling an Object

Beveling an object enables you to extrude a polygon and adjust its size uniformly, creating angled surfaces between the polygon and its original location, as shown in Figure 40. You can use beveling to quickly model a fairly complex object that you can then modify in more detail. It is possible to bevel only a polygon; you can't bevel a vertex, edge, border, or element.

When you **bevel** a polygon, you first extrude the polygon, and then adjust the size of the outer border of the polygon to create the bevel angle that you are seeking. To bevel a polygon, make sure you are in the Polygon subobject level, select a polygon, click the Bevel button in the Edit Polygons rollout on the Modify panel, click the polygon, hold down the mouse button, drag up to set the extrusion height, release the mouse button, and then drag up or down to set the size of the polygon. Or, click the Settings button next to the Bevel button to open the Bevel Polygons dialog box, and then adjust the Height number to set the extrusion height and the Outline Amount to set the size of the selected polygon.

You can also bevel multiple polygons at once, using the same options in the Bevel Polygons dialog box as are available in the Extrude Polygons dialog box. With multiple polygons selected, click the Group option to extrude polygons together in the same direction and change their sizes by the same amount. Click the Local Normal option button to extrude and bevel each polygon in the direction of its own normal. Click the By Polygon option button to extrude and bevel each selected polygon separately from the other selected polygons. Click the OK button to accept the bevel, click Cancel to cancel it, or click Apply to apply the bevel again to the selected polygons.

FIGURE 40
Box with beveled polygon

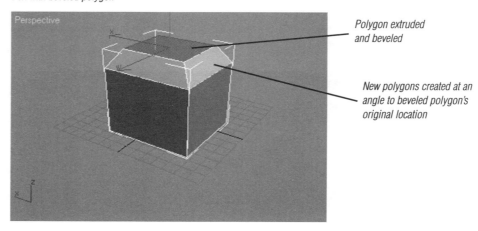

Polygon extruded and beveled

New polygons created at an angle to beveled polygon's original location

FIGURE 41
Box with chamfered vertex

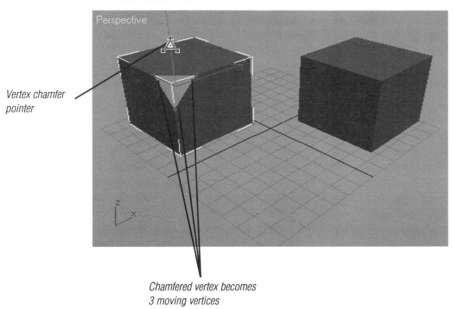

Vertex chamfer pointer

Chamfered vertex becomes 3 moving vertices

Chamfer a vertex and two edges

1. In the Top viewport, create a **box** with the dimensions **50 × 50 × 40**, create a copy of the box, then move the boxes so that both are entirely visible in the Perspective viewport.
2. Convert both boxes into editable polys.
3. Select **Box01**, click the **Vertex button** on the Modify panel, then click the **vertex** on the box that is the intersection of the box's three visible polygons.
4. In the Edit Vertices rollout on the Modify panel, click the **Chamfer button**, hold the mouse pointer over the selected vertex until it becomes , then click and drag up about one-half inch, as shown in Figure 41.

   The vertex breaks into three vertices that move along the edges the original vertices connected. A new polygon is formed, and the polygons that were connected by the original vertex change shape.
5. Click the **Chamfer button** to deselect it, then click the **Vertex button** to deselect it.
6. Select **Box02**, click the **Edge button**, then select the two **edges** at the front of the box's top polygon.
7. Click the **Settings button** next to the Chamfer button, change the Chamfer

(continued)

Lesson 4 Chamfer, Extrude, and Bevel Objects

DISCREET 3D STUDIO MAX 3-37

Amount in the Chamfer Edges dialog box to **10**, then click **OK**.

The selected edges are chamfered, as shown in Figure 42.

You selected and chamfered a vertex on a box, then selected and chamfered two edges on the box at the same time.

Chamfer a border

1. Click the **Edges button** to deselect it, select **Box01** in the Perspective viewport, click the **Polygon button** ■, click the **polygon** on top of the box to select it, then press **[Delete]**.

    Box01 now has a hole in its top.

2. Press **[F4]** to show Edged Faces in the Perspective viewport, click the **Border button** ⟩, then click one of the **edges** around the hole on top of the box to select the border.

3. Click the **Chamfer button** in the Edit Borders rollout on the Modify panel, place the mouse pointer over one of the edges in the border until the pointer becomes ⇌, then click and drag down about one-quarter inch, as shown in Figure 43.

    When the border is chamfered, its edges and vertices don't move, but they are duplicated and moved as you drag the mouse. New polygons are created between the original and duplicate border.

4. Click the **Chamfer button** to deselect it.

You selected a border on a box, then chamfered it.

FIGURE 42
Box with chamfered edges

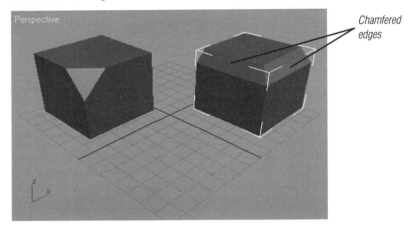

FIGURE 43
Box with chamfered border

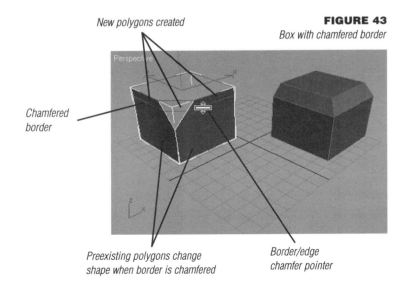

FIGURE 44
Box with extruded polygon

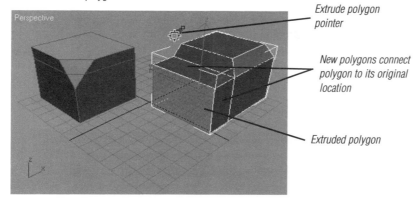

Extrude polygon pointer

New polygons connect polygon to its original location

Extruded polygon

FIGURE 45
Box with multiple extruded polygons

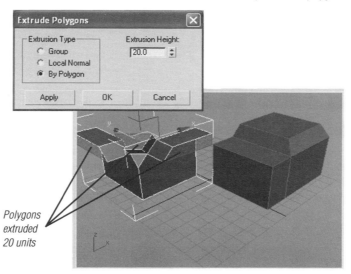

Polygons extruded 20 units

Extrude polygons

1. Click the **Border button** to deselect it, select **Box02**, click the **Polygon button** ■, then click the **polygon** beneath the left chamfered edge to select it.

2. In the Edit Polygons rollout on the Modify panel, click the **Extrude button** to select it.

3. Hold the mouse pointer over the polygon so that the pointer becomes ⬘, click and drag up about one inch, as shown in Figure 44, then click once.

   The polygon is extruded in the direction of its normal, and new polygons connect the extruded polygon back to its original location.

4. Click the **Polygon button** ■ to deselect it, select **Box01**, click the **Polygon button** ■, select the **three polygons** on the front of Box01 that are between the box's border and chamfered border, then click the **Settings button** ☐ next to the Extrude button.

   The three selected polygons are immediately extruded in a single direction by the amount shown in the Extrusion Height box in the Extrude Polygons dialog box. The direction (normal) of the polygons' extrusion is the average of their normals.

5. In the Extrude Polygons dialog box, click the **By Polygon** option button to select it, then change the Extrusion Height amount to **20**.

   Each of the three selected polygons is extruded separately from the others in the direction of its own normal, as shown in Figure 45.

(continued)

6. Click the **Polygon button** ■ to deselect it, save the file as **Extrudepoly**, then reset 3ds Max.

You selected a polygon on a box, extruded the polygon, then selected and extruded three polygons at the same time, each according to its own normal.

Extrude vertices and edges

1. Create a **box** in the Top viewport with 2 Height segments and the dimensions **40 × 50 × 40**, then convert it into an editable poly.

2. Click in the Perspective viewport (if necessary), press **[F4]** to show the edged faces (if necessary), click the **Vertex button** on the Modify panel, then select the **vertex** on the right side of the polygon on top of the box.

3. In the Edit Vertices rollout on the Modify panel, click the **Settings button** □ next to the Extrude button, then, in the Extrude Vertices dialog box, change the Extrusion Height to **20** and the Extrusion Base Width to **10**, as shown in Figure 46.

   The vertex is extruded, creating new polygons between it and its (now chamfered) original location.

4. Click the **Edge button**, then select the **edge** in the center of the left front side of the box.

(continued)

FIGURE 46
Box with extruded vertex

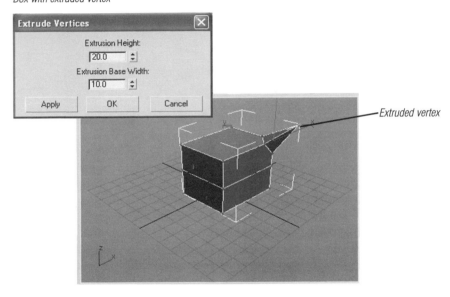

Extruded vertex

FIGURE 47
Box with extruded vertex and edge

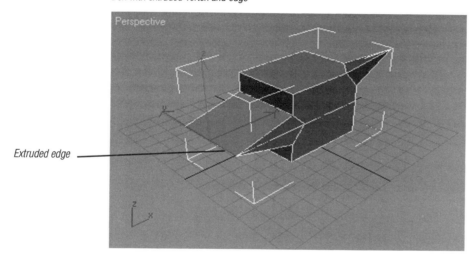

Extruded edge

5. In the Edit Edges rollout on the Modify panel, click the **Extrude button** to select it.
6. Hold the mouse pointer over the selected edge so that it becomes , click and drag up about one inch to extrude the edge, drag to the left about one-quarter inch to increase the base width of the extrusion, then release the mouse button.

   The box should now resemble that in Figure 47.
7. Save the file as **Extrudevert**, then reset 3ds Max.

You extruded a vertex on a box and adjusted the height and base width of the extrusion using the Settings button, extruded an edge on the box, and adjusted the base width of the extrusion by dragging the mouse.

Lesson 4   Chamfer, Extrude, and Bevel Objects

Bevel polygons

1. In the Top viewport, create a **cylinder** with a radius of **25** and a height of **10**, then convert it into an editable poly.

2. Click the **Polygon button** ■, click in the Perspective viewport, then click the **circle** on top of the cylinder to select it.

3. Click the **Bevel button** to select it, hold the mouse pointer over the polygon so that the pointer becomes ⬚, click and drag up about one-quarter inch, then release the mouse button and drag down about one-half inch.

   The circle top of the cylinder is first extruded, then beveled, as shown in Figure 48.

4. With the Bevel button still selected, click and drag the **top polygon** up about one inch, then release the mouse button and drag up about one-half inch.

5. Click and drag the **top polygon** down about one-quarter inch, then release the mouse button and drag down about one-half inch.

   When you drag down, you create a negative extrusion height for the polygon, and it sinks downward instead of rising upward. Subsequently shrinking the selected polygon creates a bowl-like effect in the resulting object.

   (continued)

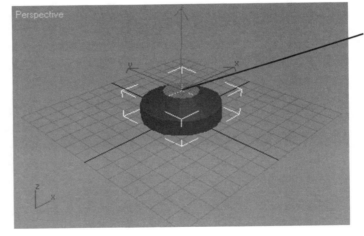

FIGURE 48
Cylinder with top polygon beveled

Polygon extruded and beveled

3-42 AUTODESK 3D STUDIO MAX

Modeling

6. Click the **Settings button** next to the Bevel button to open the Bevel Polygons dialog box, change the Height number to **20** and the Outline Amount to **–9**, then click **OK**.

   The cylinder should now resemble the object in Figure 49.

7. Save the file as **Bevelpoly**, then reset 3ds Max.

You created a cylinder, extruded it, beveled the top polygon on the cylinder three times using the mouse, and beveled the top polygon once using the Settings button.

FIGURE 49
Cylinder with beveling complete

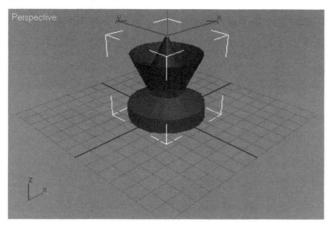

LESSON 5

USE PAINT DEFORMATION AND
SOFT SELECTION

What You'll Do

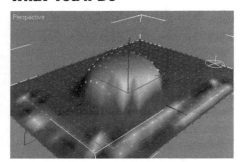

▶ In this lesson, you will use the Paint Deformation and Soft Selection effects to model organic surfaces.

Using Paint Deformation

New in version 7 of 3ds Max was the ability to use Paint Deformation to create organic-looking surfaces, such as the ground surface shown in Figure 50. The **Paint Deformation** options enable you to "push" and "pull" the vertices of a surface up or down as you move the mouse pointer over an object. Pulling the vertices of an object pulls them upward, away from their original location on the object, according to the direction of their normals. Pushing the vertices of an object pushes them downward. In Figure 50, the hills were created by pulling the vertices of the plane, and the troughs were created by pushing the vertices of the plane. You control which vertices are pushed or pulled by moving the mouse pointer over an object's surface—"painting"—the area you would like to affect.

Note: If you are using an earlier version of 3ds Max with this book, the steps in this section will not work for you.

The vertices affected by Paint Deformation are determined by the subobject level selected.

If no subobject level is selected, or if a level is selected but no subobjects are selected, all of the vertices on the object can be affected. If subobjects are selected, only the vertices in those subobjects (such as all of the vertices in a border, or in several selected polygons) can be affected.

> **QUICK**TIP
>
> To create the most organic-looking surfaces, objects on which you use Paint Deformation should have a relatively large number of segments subdividing them, resulting in a large number of vertices fairly close together.

The Paint Deformation options are all available on the Paint Deformation rollout on the Modify panel, as shown in Figure 51 (you might need to drag up the Modify panel from the bottom until you see the Paint Deformation rollout). To push or pull vertices, click the Push/Pull button in the rollout to select it. With this button selected, you'll see that the mouse pointer has a circular paintbrush attached to it, as shown in Figure 52. As you move the pointer over the object or selected subobjects with the mouse button held down, the vertices that the brush touches are pushed or pulled, depending on the value in the Push/Pull Value box in the rollout. Vertices are pulled when this value is positive and pushed when the value is negative. Or, as you are painting, you can press [Alt] to apply the reverse value (for example, push instead of pull).

Before or while you paint, you can adjust the radius of the brush by adjusting the number in the Brush Size box, or by pressing [Shift][Ctrl] and dragging the mouse. You

FIGURE 50
Plane with pushed and pulled vertices

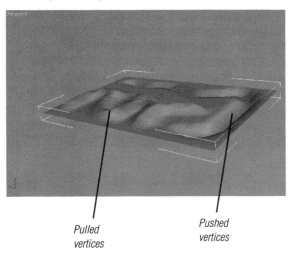

Pulled vertices

Pushed vertices

FIGURE 51
Paint Deformation rollout on Modify panel

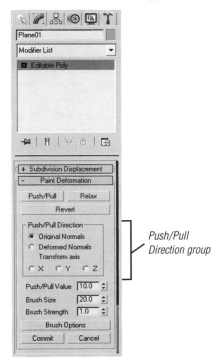

Push/Pull Direction group

FIGURE 52
Paint Deformation paintbrush

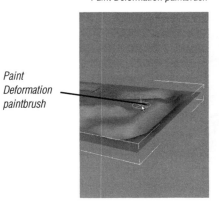

Paint Deformation paintbrush

Lesson 5 *Use Paint Deformation and Soft Selection*

DISCREET 3D STUDIO MAX 3-45

can manually adjust the number in the Brush Strength box (from 0 to 1) or press [Shift][Alt] and drag the mouse to affect the speed at which the Push/Pull value is applied to the vertices. A strength of 0 means there will be no deformation, and a strength of 1 means the deformation will happen at the Push/Pull value.

As you paint, the default direction the vertices move is in the direction of their original normals, even if painted multiple times. Click the Deformed Normals option button in the Push/Pull Direction group if you want painted vertices to deform in the direction of their normals after deformation. Click the Transform Axis X, Y, or Z option button if you want painted vertices to move along a specific axis.

After you've pushed and/or pulled the surface of an object, you can use the Relax button to smooth the deformations you've created, as shown in Figure 53. Relaxing vertices repositions them according to the average of the positions of their neighbors. If a vertex is very high or very low relative to its neighbors, relaxing the vertex will bring it closer to them, making the angles between vertices less sharp and making the surface more smooth. To relax a surface, click the Relax button to select it, and then paint the area you want to affect. If you want to reverse the effects that you have painted onto a surface rather than smoothing them, click the Revert button and then paint the area you want to affect. Vertices thus painted will gradually return to their original locations.

When you have completed the deformations you want to make to the object, click the Commit button to permanently save the deformations as part of the object. Keep in mind that after you click the Commit button, you can only use Revert to return vertices to their previous locations when the Commit button was last clicked. To cancel the deformations you have made to the object since the Commit button was last clicked, click the Cancel button.

FIGURE 53
Plane with pulled vertices

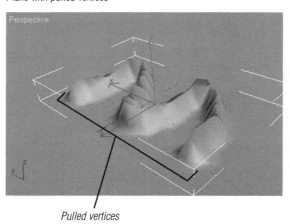
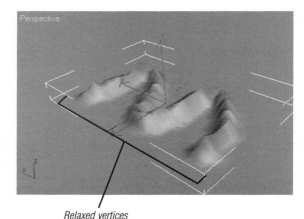

Pulled vertices

Relaxed vertices

Deforming an Object Using Soft Selection

The Soft Selection rollout on the Modify panel makes it easy to create and/or manipulate a contoured area on an object's surface, without having to transform each vertex in the area individually. For example, if you select and move a single vertex on a plane upward, you create a pyramid-like extrusion from the vertex to its surrounding edges, as shown in the left image of Figure 54. However, with soft selection, selecting a single vertex actually partially selects the vertices surrounding it; moving the single vertex also moves the surrounding soft-selected vertices, as shown on the right in Figure 54.

QUICKTIP
You will most often use soft selection when working with vertices, but you can also use Soft Selection in the Edge, Border, and Polygon subobject levels.

To turn on Soft Selection, click the Use Soft Selection check box in the Soft Selection rollout on the Modify panel before selecting a subobject. Adjust the number in the Falloff box to increase or decrease the distance around the subobject that is soft-selected. When an area is soft-selected, the fully selected vertex is red, and the vertices in the soft-selected area change in color from red to orange, then yellow, green, and finally blue the farther from the selected vertex the

FIGURE 54
Planes with a selected vertex moved

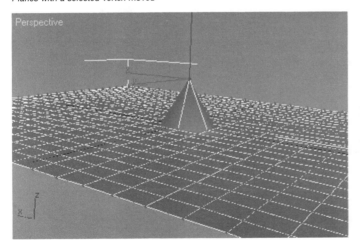
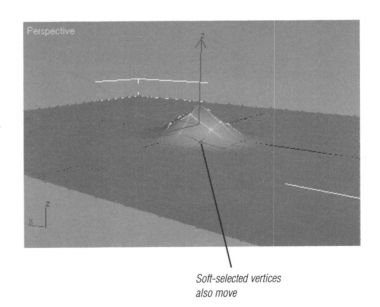

Soft-selected vertices also move

Lesson 5 Use Paint Deformation and Soft Selection

DISCREET 3D STUDIO MAX 3-47

areas are. As the selection color transitions from red to blue, the amount the subobject is affected by the transformation lessens (the closer to red in color, the more it is affected; the closer to blue, the less it is affected). Click the Shaded Face Toggle button in the Soft Selection rollout to make the soft-selected area shaded in color rather than limiting the color to vertices, as shown in Figure 55.

Keep in mind that Soft Selection is a selection tool only; the object won't change until you transform a selected vertex or vertices, and that transformation affects the soft-selected vertices surrounding it. You can change the relationship of the soft-selected vertices relative to the selected vertex they surround by adjusting the numbers in the Pinch and Bubble boxes in the Soft Selection rollout. A graph beneath these two boxes illustrates the effect of such adjustments from one edge of the soft selection to the other, with the center of the graph representing the selected vertex. As the Pinch and Bubble numbers are adjusted, this graph changes. Increasing the Pinch number causes the center to sharpen during transformation or, if negative, to become the bottom of a pointed crater, as shown in Figure 56. Increasing the Bubble number makes the curves on

FIGURE 55
Shaded soft selection

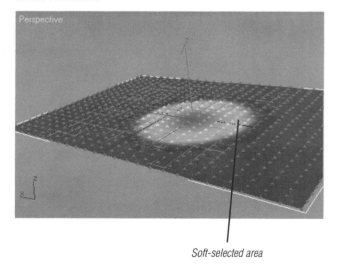

Soft-selected area

FIGURE 56
Moved vertex with pinched soft selection

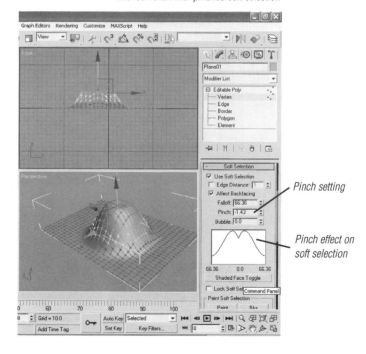

Pinch setting

Pinch effect on soft selection

either side of the center rounder and fuller, or, if negative, makes the curves concave toward the curve's bottom center.

Rather than selecting a single subobject and activating Soft Selection to soft-select the area around the subobject, you can paint an area on an object to which Soft Selection is applied. To do this, click the Paint button in the Paint Soft Selection group, and then click and paint the object with the mouse pointer to soft-select the desired areas. As with Paint Deformation, you can adjust the numbers in the Brush Size and Brush Strength boxes if appropriate. You can also adjust the Selection Value, which determines the "strength" of the selection you are painting—for instance, a value of 1 paints fully selected (red) vertices at the center of the paintbrush to lightly selected vertices on its outer edges; a value of .1 paints only lightly selected vertices from the paintbrush's center outward. If vertices in a painted soft-selected area are closer to red than you would like them to be, you can click the Blur button and paint those vertices to reduce their selection value and soften the effect of transformations on them. Click the Revert button and paint soft-selected areas to reduce their selection value and/or deselect them entirely.

If an area is soft-selected, you can lock the soft selection in place by clicking the Lock Soft Selection check box to select it. After the soft selection is locked, you can select other vertices in the object at the same time and transform both selected areas, but only the locked soft selection is soft selected. See Figure 57 for an example. When you click the Paint, Blur, or Revert buttons, the Lock Soft Selection check box is automatically checked.

FIGURE 57
Locked soft selection

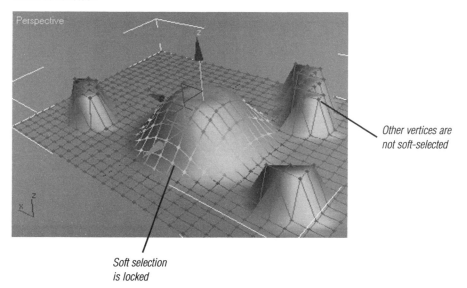

Other vertices are not soft-selected

Soft selection is locked

Lesson 5   Use Paint Deformation and Soft Selection

Push and pull vertices

1. In the Top viewport, create a **plane** with the dimensions **140 × 180**, with **25** Length segments and **25** Width segments, then convert the plane into an editable poly.

2. Pan the Modify panel up until you see the Paint Deformation rollout, click the **plus sign** next to Paint Deformation to open the rollout (if necessary), then click the **Push/Pull button** to select it.

   Because no subobject level is selected, all vertices on the plane can be painted.

3. Make sure that the Push/Pull Value is **10**, the Brush Size is **20**, and the Brush Strength is **1** (if necessary).

4. Click in the Perspective viewport, hold the mouse over the corner of the plane closest to you, then click and drag to pull vertices on the plane, as shown in Figure 58.

   When the pointer is over the plane, the paintbrush attached to it is light blue; as you click and drag, the paintbrush is red.

5. In the Paint Deformation rollout, change the Push/Pull Value to **–20** and the Brush Size to **10**.

(continued)

FIGURE 58
Plane with pulled vertices

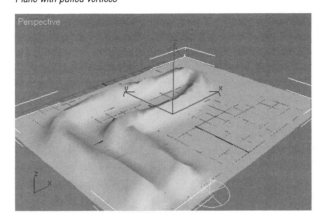

FIGURE 59
Plane with pushed and pulled vertices

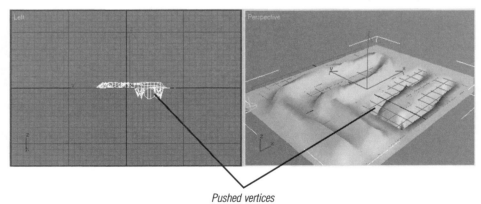

Pushed vertices

FIGURE 60
Plane with relaxed vertices

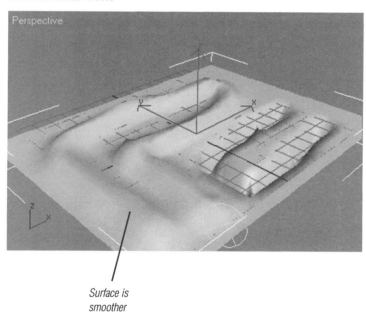

Surface is smoother

6. Hold the mouse pointer over the corner of the plane closest to the viewport's right edge, then click and drag to push the vertices, as shown in Figure 59.

   In the Front and Left viewports, you can see the pushed vertices visible beneath the plane.

7. Click the **Push/Pull button** to deselect it, change the Push/Pull Value back to **10**, change the Brush Size back to **20**, then save the file as **Paintdef**.

You deformed a plane by pulling vertices on the plane, adjusted the Paint Deformation brush options, then pushed vertices on the plane.

Relax pulled vertices

1. In the Paint Deformation rollout, click the **Relax button** to select it.

2. Hold the mouse over the start of the path of pulled vertices you created earlier, then click and drag the **paintbrush** down the length of the path, along its ridge.

   As you paint, the height of the ridge decreases, and the appearance of the pulled vertices becomes smoother, as shown in Figure 60.

   (continued)

3. Click the **Revert button**, then click the **quadrant** of the plane closest to you in the viewport, until it looks like Figure 61.

   As you paint the plane, the pulled vertices return to where they were located when the plane was created. When you are done, the top of the plane in the reverted area should look flat in the Left viewport.

4. Click the **Revert button** to deselect it, then click the **Commit button**.

5. Save the file, then reset 3ds Max.

You relaxed pulled vertices into a smoother shape, then reverted pulled vertices back to their original positions.

Use soft selection when moving a vertex

1. In the Top viewport, create a **plane** with dimensions of 150 × 200, **25** Length segments, and **25** Width segments, then convert it into an editable poly.

2. In the Perspective viewport, select the **plane**, click the **Vertex button** on the Modify panel (you need to pan up to see it), click the **plus sign** next to the Soft Selection rollout (if necessary), click the **Use Soft Selection check box**, then click the **Shaded Face Toggle button**.

(continued)

FIGURE 61
Plane with reverted vertices

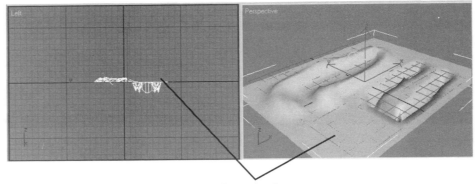

Reverted vertices

3-52 AUTODESK 3D STUDIO MAX

Modeling

FIGURE 62
Plane with moved soft selection

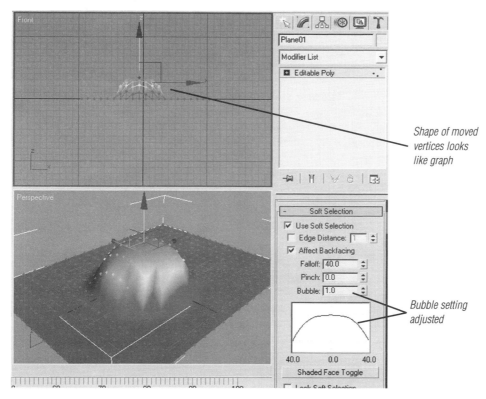

Shape of moved vertices looks like graph

Bubble setting adjusted

3. Change the number in the Falloff box in the Soft Selection rollout to **40**, then click a **vertex** near the center of the plane to select it.

   When the vertex is selected, the vertices within 40 units of it are soft-selected. The degree of selection is indicated by the color of the vertices and the shading of the selection (from red to blue).

4. Change the number in the Bubble box in the Soft Selection rollout to **1**.

   The deformation graph changes, showing that soft-selected vertices closer to the center of the selection are more affected by transformations to the selection. On-screen, the amount of orange shading on the soft selection increases, and the amount of greenish blue shading decreases.

5. Click the **Select and Move tool**, click the **blue (Z) axis arrow** on the Move gizmo, then drag up about one inch.

   As shown in Figure 62, the soft-selected vertices move up along with the selected vertex, each according to the degree of its soft selection. The shape of the deformation looks like the shape on the deformation graph.

6. Save the file as **Softselect**.

You soft-selected a vertex on a plane, adjusted the Falloff and Bubble settings of the soft selection, then deformed the plane by moving the soft-selected vertex.

Lesson 5   Use Paint Deformation and Soft Selection

DISCREET 3D STUDIO MAX 3-53

Paint soft selection

1. Pan the Modify panel up so that the Paint Soft Selection group is visible on the Soft Selection rollout (if necessary), then click the **Paint button** to select it.

   The Lock Soft Selection check box is automatically checked when you click the Paint button

2. Hold the mouse pointer over the left corner of the plane, then click and drag along the front two edges of the plane to paint a soft selection onto it, as shown in Figure 63.

3. Click the **Blur button** in the Paint Soft Selection group to select it, then click and drag along the painted soft selection next to the right edge of the plane, stopping when you get to the front corner.

   As you blur the painted soft selection, on-screen the vertices in the selection change color indicating that they will be less affected by any transformation to the selected vertex.

4. Click the **Blur button** to deselect it, press **[Ctrl]**, then click **two vertices** on the plane that are outside the original and painted soft selections.

   (continued)

FIGURE 63
Plane with painted soft selection

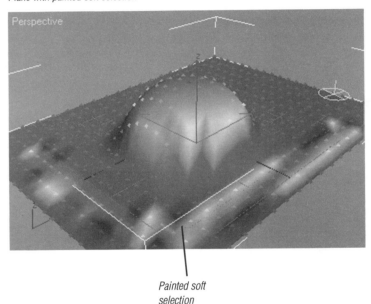

Painted soft selection

3-54 AUTODESK 3D STUDIO MAX

Modeling

FIGURE 64
Plane with moved vertices

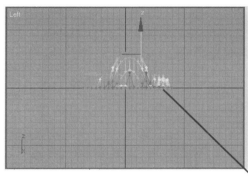
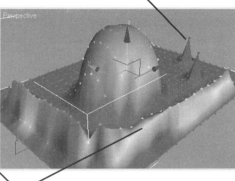

Vertices outside soft selection move individually

Blurred area moves less

5. Click the **blue axis arrow** on the Move gizmo, then drag up about one inch.

   The painted soft selection vertices move according to their selection levels. The blurred area does not move as much, as shown in Figure 64. The vertices you selected outside the soft selection move as single vertices.

6. Save the file, then reset 3ds Max.

You painted a soft selection onto a plane, blurred an area of the painted soft selection, selected two vertices individually, then moved the selected and soft-selected vertices.

Lesson 5   Use Paint Deformation and Soft Selection

DISCREET 3D STUDIO MAX 3-55

LESSON 6

CREATE AND CONNECT VERTICES,
EDGES, AND POLYGONS

What You'll Do

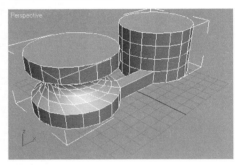

In this lesson, you will learn how to create new vertices, edges, and polygons by connecting and welding subobjects, slicing and cutting existing polygons, and bridging borders and polygons.

As you model an object, you might find it useful to create new polygons or reshape existing ones on an object in order to edit an object according to your specific needs. In 3ds Max, there are several tools available to enable you to create polygons where none exist, change the shape of existing polygons, or divide existing polygons into smaller pieces that can be edited individually.

Creating New Vertices, Edges, and Polygons

There are two primary ways to quickly create new vertices in an object. The first is to use the Insert Vertex button in the Edit Edges, Edit Borders, Edit Polygons, or Edit Elements rollouts in the Modify panel. In the Edge or Border subobject level, click the Insert Vertex button, and then click anywhere on an edge or border to insert a vertex in that location. In Polygon or Element subobject level, click the Insert Vertex button, and then click anywhere on a polygon to insert a vertex in that location. When a vertex is inserted this way, the new vertex is automatically connected to each of the vertices of its polygon by an edge, resulting in the subdivision of the polygon, as shown in Figure 65. When you are done inserting vertices in any subobject level, click the Insert Vertex button to deselect it.

You can also use the Create button on the Edit Geometry rollout when you are in the Vertex subobject level to create new vertices. Click the Create button to select it, and then simply click in space to create isolated vertices in the viewport that are considered part of the editable poly, but are not connected by edges. Click the Create button again to deselect it.

You can create new edges with the Create button when you are in Edge or Border subobject level. Click the Create button, click one of the vertices in the object, and then click another vertex located in the same polygon as the first vertex but not already connected to it (the pointer becomes a cross when you are over a vertex to which you can connect). As you move from the first vertex to the second, a dotted line appears from the vertex to your mouse pointer's location, as

3-56 AUTODESK 3D STUDIO MAX   *Modeling*

shown in Figure 66. When you click the second vertex, a new edge appears that connects the vertices and subdivides the polygon the vertices were originally on. When you are done creating new edges, click the Create button to deselect it.

If you have an object with isolated vertices or a border with vertices, you can create a polygon where one does not already exist. To do this, click the Create button while in the Polygon or Element subobject level, click one of the isolated or border vertices, click the other vertices you need to create the edges of the polygon, and then return to the first vertex and click it. As you move between vertices, a dotted line extends from the first vertex clicked, through the vertices clicked so far, back to the first vertex. After you click the first vertex again, a polygon is created whose edges connect the clicked vertices.

Connecting Vertices and Edges

The Connect button on the Edit Vertices, Edit Edges, or Edit Borders rollout on the Modify panel provides another tool for creating new edges and subdividing existing polygons.

In the Vertex subobject level, create a new edge by clicking the Connect button to select it, clicking a vertex on a polygon, and then clicking a second vertex on the polygon (to which the first vertex is not already connected). An edge appears connecting the two vertices and subdividing the polygon they were originally in.

In the Edge and Border subobject levels, the Connect button offers a way to create a new edge that connects two edges on the same polygon. To do this, select the edges that you

FIGURE 65
Box with vertex inserted

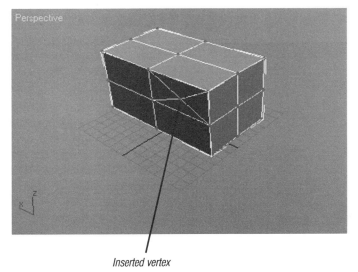

Inserted vertex

FIGURE 66
Creation of a new edge

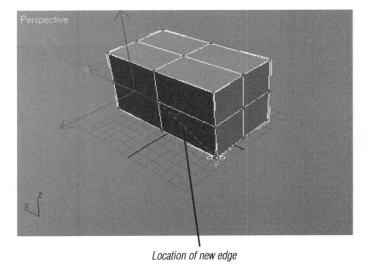

Location of new edge

Lesson 6   Create and Connect Vertices, Edges, and Polygons

DISCREET 3D STUDIO MAX 3-57

would like to connect, and then click the Connect button. A new edge appears connecting the midpoints of the two selected edges, as shown in Figure 67. Note that you can select more than two edges at a time, but only edges on the same polygon are connected when you click the Connect button. To connect two edges by more than one edge at a time, select the edges to be connected, and then click the Settings button next to the Connect button to open the Connect Edges dialog box. Adjust the number in the Connect Edge Segments box to the amount you want to appear between the selected edges, and then click OK. The selected edges are connected by that number of evenly spaced edges, as shown in Figure 67.

Welding vertices

Welding is most useful when you have an object with multiple vertices close together that you'd like to close like a seam. In the Vertex subobject level, there are two buttons in the Edit Vertices rollout that enable you to weld vertices: the Weld button and the Target Weld button. When you click the Weld button with two vertices selected, each selected vertex moves toward the other and the two are welded at the midpoint between their locations. If the vertices are on polygons, the polygons change shape because of the movement of the vertices, as shown

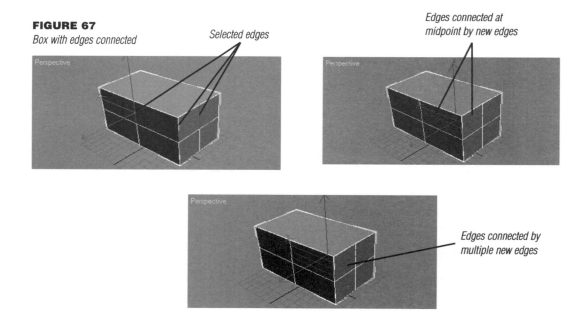

FIGURE 67
Box with edges connected

Selected edges

Edges connected at midpoint by new edges

Edges connected by multiple new edges

in Figure 68. If you click the Weld button with two vertices selected and nothing happens, click the Settings button to open the Weld Vertices dialog box. The distance between the selected vertices needs to be less than the number in the Weld Threshold box for the vertices to be welded. Adjust the number in the Weld Threshold box upward until the selected vertices come together, and then click Apply to retain the welding before changing the threshold again.

The Target Weld button enables you to move an existing vertex to a second vertex's location and weld them together. To do this, click the Target Weld button to select it, click the vertex you want to move, and then click the vertex to which you want to weld the first vertex. As you move the mouse pointer to the second vertex, a dashed line appears from the selected vertex to the mouse pointer. When the vertices are welded, the polygon that the first vertex is located on changes shape, as shown in Figure 68.

> **QUICK**TIP
> You can also weld or target weld edges together. Only an edge attached to one polygon (that is, an edge on a border) can be welded to another.

Slicing and Cutting Polygons

Besides connecting vertices or connecting edges, you can create new edges on an editable poly by using the slicing and cutting features of 3ds Max. **Slicing** cuts an object as though a saw were run straight through the whole object in one direction. This doesn't actually break the object into pieces that aren't connected anymore; it simply inserts edges where the slicing takes place.

To slice an object, click the Slice Plane button in the Edit Geometry rollout on the Modify panel to select it. A yellow slice plane

FIGURE 68
Box with welded vertices

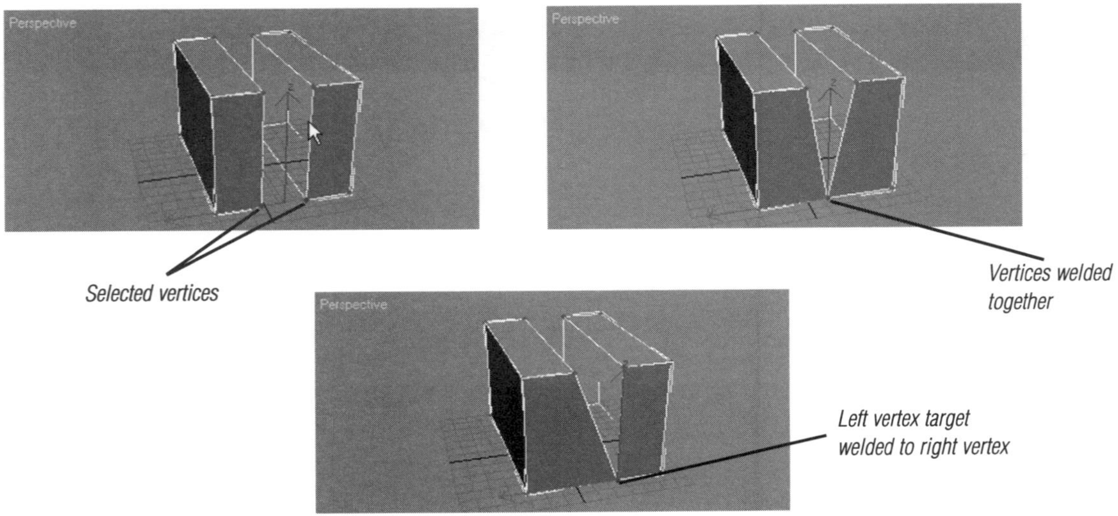

Selected vertices

Vertices welded together

Left vertex target welded to right vertex

Lesson 6 *Create and Connect Vertices, Edges, and Polygons*

DISCREET 3D STUDIO MAX 3-59

gizmo appears in the viewports, as shown in Figure 69. Move, rotate, or scale the plane so that it is located where you want the object to be sliced, click the Slice button, and then click the Slice Plane button again to deselect it. The object now has edges where the plane sliced it, and any polygons that the plane sliced through are now subdivided, as shown in Figure 70. To slice an object without working with the plane gizmo, click the QuickSlice button in the Edit Geometry rollout, click on one side of the object, and then click on the other side of the object.

A straight line appears on the object as you move between clicks, to show you the location of the slice. After your second click, the object is sliced along the line. When you finish slicing, click the QuickSlice button to deselect it.

QUICKTIP

In the Polygon and Element subobject levels, slicing works only on selected polygons or elements. In the Vertex, Edge, or Border subobject level, the entire object is sliced.

Cutting is similar to slicing, except that rather than having the saw effect, it has the effect of running a knife across the surface of the object, resulting in new edges and polygons subdivided into smaller polygons. To cut a surface, when in any (or no) subobject level, click the Cut button in the Edit Geometry rollout on the Modify panel, and click at a point on the object's surface where you would like to start a cut. As you move the mouse pointer after the first click, an edge appears leading from the location of your first

FIGURE 69
Box to be sliced

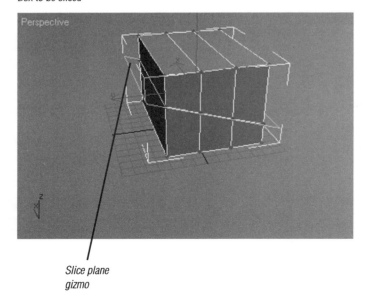

Slice plane gizmo

FIGURE 70
Sliced box

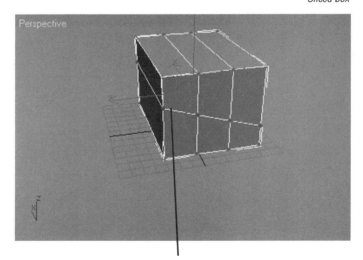

New edges created at plane's location when sliced

click to the mouse pointer's location, and a second line appears leading from the mouse pointer's location to the corner of the polygon you are over, as shown in Figure 71. Click again to create an edge between clicks, and move the pointer and click again until you have cut the surface as desired. When the pointer is over a vertex or edge, it changes to an icon picturing a vertex or edge and a knife; if you click when the pointer is in one of these states, the edge created is connected to the vertex or edge. To complete the cut, right-click. If you have created an edge ending in the middle of a polygon when you right-click, an edge is added leading to the corner of the polygon to complete the cut. Similarly, if you click in the middle of a polygon to start a cut, an edge is automatically added leading from the first click to the corner of the polygon.

Bridging Borders and Polygons

You can bridge the distance between two borders or two polygons in an editable poly to create interesting new forms (and, possibly, multiple new polygons) as you model. Creating a **bridge** between two borders or two polygons connects the two subobjects using polygons. In Figure 72, the box on the left has two borders in its center; the image on the top right shows those two

FIGURE 71
Box with cut

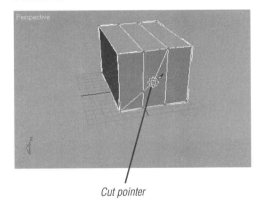

Cut pointer

FIGURE 72
Box with bridged borders and polygons

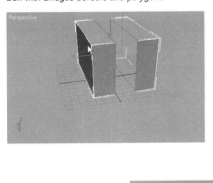

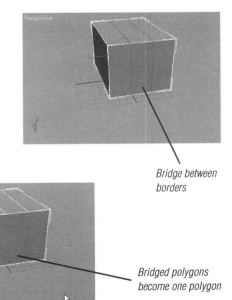

Bridge between borders

Bridged polygons become one polygon

Lesson 6   *Create and Connect Vertices, Edges, and Polygons*

DISCREET 3D STUDIO MAX 3-61

borders connected by a polygon bridge. In the image on the bottom, the two polygons on the front side of the polygon have been connected by a bridge, and now form one large polygon that stretches along the whole side of the box.

To form a bridge between two borders, you use the Bridge button in the Edit Borders rollout in the Modify panel. There are two ways to use the Bridge button to connect two borders. You can select two borders that you want to connect, and then click the Bridge button. The selected borders connect automatically. Or, with no borders selected, you can click the Bridge button, click one border, and then click a second border, and the two are connected. As you move the mouse between the first and second border, a dotted line appears indicating that you will create a bridge with your next click.

When you click the Settings button next to the Bridge button, you open the Bridge dialog box, as shown in Figure 73. This dialog box enables you to create a bridge as well, but also provides several ways to modify the bridge itself. To create a bridge using the Settings button, you can select two borders, click the Settings button, make sure the Use Border Selection option button is selected, and then click OK. Or, you can click the Settings button, click the Use Specific Borders option button, click the Pick Edge 1 button, click one of the borders you want to create a bridge with, click the Pick Edge 2 button, click the second border to be bridged, and then click OK.

FIGURE 73
Box with bridged borders

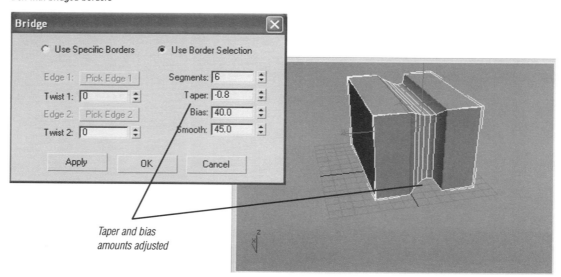

Taper and bias amounts adjusted

3-62 AUTODESK 3D STUDIO MAX

Modeling

Before clicking OK to accept the bridge, you can adjust the settings for the bridge to modify its appearance. Increase the number of segments in the bridge by increasing the number in the Segments box. To twist the bridge, adjust the numbers in the Twist 1 box or the Twist 2 box after you have picked the borders to be bridged. To curve the edges of the bridge inward or outward, adjust the number in the Taper box, which affects the size of the center of the bridge. Change the number in the Bias box to adjust the location of the greatest taper amount to be closer to one border than the other, as shown in Figure 73. The Smooth box enables you to enter the maximum angle between polygons in the bridge across which smoothing can occur.

To create a bridge between two polygons, you use the same methods used to bridge borders (Bridge button and Settings button in the Edit Polygons rollout). You can twist, taper, bias, smooth, and add segments to the polygon bridge using the Bridge Polygons dialog box that appears when you click the Settings button. By bridging two borders or polygons on the same object, you can create an internal bridge between them. An internal bridge is more like a tunnel, with the normals of the bridge polygons facing inward, as shown in Figure 74. To bridge polygons that are in two different objects, select one object, click the Attach button in the Edit Geometry rollout, click the object you want to attach the first object to, and then click the Attach button to deselect it. After the objects are attached to each other, you can bridge polygons from one object to another.

FIGURE 74
Box with bridged polygons

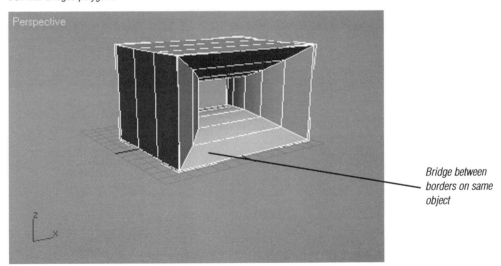

Bridge between borders on same object

Create a vertex, edge, and polygon

1. In the center of the Top viewport, create a **pyramid** with the dimensions **80 × 80 × 40**, then convert it into an editable poly.

2. Click the **Polygon button** on the Modify panel, click in the Perspective viewport, click the visible right side of the **pyramid** to select it, then press **[Delete]** to delete the polygon.

3. Press **[F4]** to make edged faces visible in the viewport, click the **Edge button** on the Modify panel, click the **Insert Vertex button** in the Edit Edges rollout, click in the **center** of the left edge of the visible polygon, then click in the **center** of the bottom edge of the visible polygon.

   Vertices are inserted on the edges at the location of your clicks.

4. Click the **Insert Vertex button** to deselect it, pan the Modify panel up (if necessary), then click the **Create button** on the Edit Geometry rollout to select it.

5. Click the **first vertex** you inserted, move the mouse, then click the **second vertex** you inserted.

   As you move the mouse, a dashed line appears from the vertex clicked to the pointer. After you click the second vertex, a new edge appears.

   (continued)

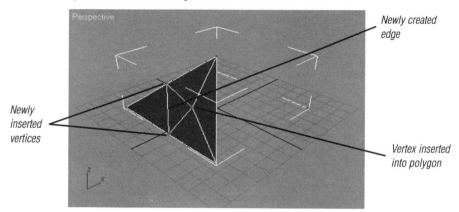

FIGURE 75
Pyramid with vertices and edges inserted

FIGURE 76
Creating a polygon

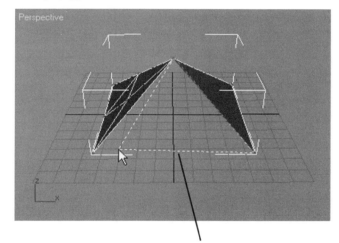

Dashed line shows edges of polygon being created

6. Click the **Polygon button** ■, move the Modify panel up, click the **Insert Vertex button**, then click in the **center** of the polygon to the right of the edge you just created.

   The vertex is inserted, with new edges connecting it to each corner of the polygon, as shown in Figure 75.

7. Click the **Insert Vertex button** to deselect it, click the **Arc Rotate button**, click the right viewport **rotation handle** on the trackball, then drag to the left until you can see polygons on either side of the deleted polygon.

8. Pan the Modify panel up (if necessary), click the **Create button** on the Edit Geometry rollout to select it, click the **top vertex** in the pyramid, click the **bottom-right vertex**, click the **bottom-left vertex**, then click the **top vertex** again.

9. Save the file as **Createconnect**.

   As you click and move the mouse, a dashed line appears between each vertex in the polygon you are creating, as shown in Figure 76. When you click the top vertex for the second time, the new polygon appears between the vertices you just clicked.

You inserted two vertices onto edges, created a new edge between the vertices, inserted a new vertex into a polygon, and created a new polygon by connecting vertices.

Connect vertices and edges

1. Click the **plus sign** next to Editable Poly in the modifier stack display (if necessary), click the **Edge subobject level**, click the **Insert Vertex button** in the Edit Edges rollout on the Modify panel, then click in the **center** of the bottom edge of the polygon you just created to insert a vertex there.

2. Click the **Vertex subobject level**, click the **vertex** at the top of the pyramid, press **[Ctrl]** and click the **vertex** you just inserted, click the **Connect button** on the Edit Vertices rollout on the Modify panel, then click outside the pyramid.

   The new vertices are connected and an edge divides the polygon into two polygons, as shown in Figure 77.

3. Click the **Edge subobject level**, click the **edge** just created, press **[Ctrl]**, click the **edge** to the left of the new edge's bottom vertex, then click the **Connect button** in the Edit Edges rollout.

   The two edges are connected at their centers by a new edge.

4. Click the **edge** just created, press **[Ctrl]**, click the **edge** between the pyramid's top vertex and lower-left vertex, then click the **Settings button** ☐ next to the **Connect button** in the Edit Edges rollout.

   The Connect Edges dialog box opens.

   (continued)

FIGURE 77
Pyramid with connected vertices

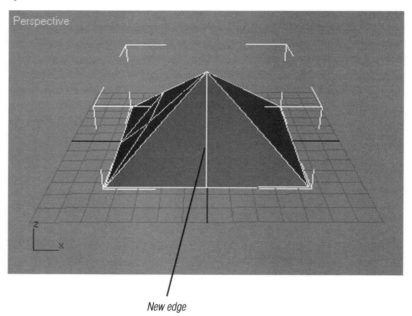

New edge

3-66 AUTODESK 3D STUDIO MAX

FIGURE 78
Pyramid with connected edges

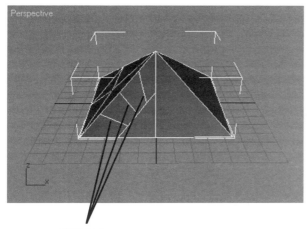

Three new edges created

FIGURE 79
Vertices welded with Target Weld

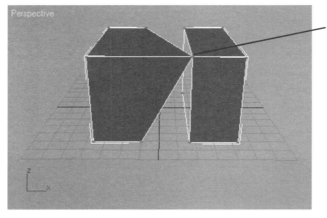

First vertex moves here and is welded

5. Change the number in the Connect Edge Segments box to **3**, click **OK**, then click outside the pyramid.

   Three new edges are created, as shown in Figure 78.

6. Save the file, then reset 3ds Max.

You inserted a vertex onto an edge, created an edge between the new vertex and another vertex, connected the new edge to another edge, and connected two edges with multiple new edges.

Weld vertices

1. Create a **box** in the Top viewport with dimensions **80 × 80 × 50** and **3** Width segments, then convert the box into an editable poly.

2. Click the **Edge button**, drag in the Top viewport to select the **edges** at the top and bottom of box top's center polygon, then press **[Delete]**.

   The polygons in the center of the box are deleted.

3. Click in the Perspective viewport, press **[F4]** to show edged faces, and rotate your view of the box until you can see all the way through the center of the box.

4. Click the **Vertex button**, click the **Target Weld button** in the Edit Vertices rollout to select it, click the **upper-right vertex** of the left polygon facing you, then click the **upper-left vertex** of the right polygon facing you.

   The first vertex you clicked moves to the location of the second vertex clicked and is welded to it, as shown in Figure 79.

(continued)

Lesson 6   Create and Connect Vertices, Edges, and Polygons

DISCREET 3D STUDIO MAX 3-67

5. Click the **Target Weld button** to deselect it, click the **vertex** on the bottom-right of the left polygon facing you, press **[Ctrl]**, then click the **vertex** on the bottom-left of the right polygon facing you.
6. Click the **Settings button** ☐ next to the Weld button in the Edit Vertices rollout to open the Weld Vertices dialog box.
7. Click and drag the **top spinner button** in the Weld Threshold box upward until the two selected vertices move toward each other and are welded together, as shown in Figure 80, then click **OK**.
8. Save the file as **Weldvert**.

You deleted polygons from a box, welded one vertex to another with TargetWeld, then welded two vertices together by adjusting the Weld Threshold in the Weld Vertices dialog box.

Slice and cut an object

1. Pan the Modify panel up (if necessary), then click the **Slice Plane button** in the Edit Geometry rollout.

   The slice plane gizmo appears, slicing the box horizontally through its center.

2. Click the **Select and Rotate tool** ↺ , click the **green rotate handle**, then drag down until the plane has rotated to the position shown in Figure 81.

(continued)

FIGURE 80
Weld Vertices dialog box

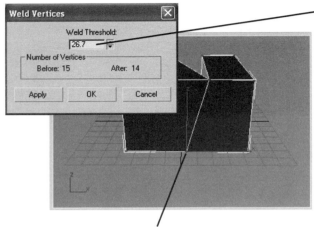

Only vertices closer than this distance apart can be welded

Vertices are welded at the midpoint of the distance between them

FIGURE 81
Rotated slice plane gizmo

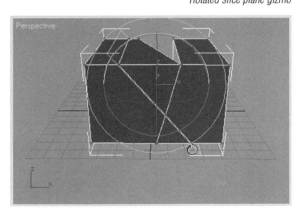

FIGURE 82
Sliced and cut box

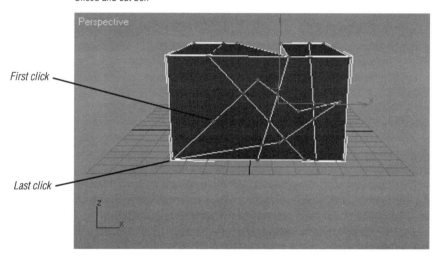

3. Click the **Slice button**, then click the **Slice Plane button** to deselect it.

   Edges now appear in all polygons that the plane gizmo sliced.

4. Click the **QuickSlice button** in the Edit Geometry rollout, click above the box on its right side, move the mouse below the box on its right side, then click again.

   New edges are created in all polygons through which you sliced.

5. Click the **Cut button** in the Edit Geometry rollout, click once in the **center** of each polygon on the side of the box facing you, click the box's **lower-left corner vertex**, then right-click.

   Your first click creates an edge between your click location and one of the polygon's corners; your remaining clicks create edges between click locations. An example cut is shown in Figure 82.

6. Click the **Cut button** to deselect it, save the file, then reset 3ds Max.

You created new edges and polygons on a box by slicing the box with a rotated slice plane gizmo, by slicing the box using QuickSlice, and by cutting the box.

Bridge borders and polygons

1. In the Top viewport, create a **cylinder** (Cylinder01) with a radius of **35**, a height of **50**, and **4** Height segments, convert it into an editable poly, then make a copy of the cylinder (Cylinder02) and move the copy to Cylinder01's right in the viewport.

2. Click **Cylinder01**, click the **Polygon button**, drag in the Front viewport to select the **polygons** on one side of the central height segment, press **[Delete]**, drag to select the **polygons** on the other side, press **[Delete]**, then click the **Polygon button** to deselect it.

3. Select **Cylinder01** in the Perspective viewport, click the **Border button**, then click and drag to select the **two borders** around the holes in Cylinder01.

4. Click the **Settings button** next to the Bridge button in the Edit Borders rollout.

   The selected borders are bridged by polygons, and the Bridge dialog box opens.

5. In the Bridge dialog box, increase the Segments number to **6**, change the Taper number to **–1**, change the Bias number to **–50**, then increase the Twist 1 number to **4**.

   The bridge between the borders changes as you adjust the numbers, with the final result as shown in Figure 83.

6. Click **OK**, then click the **Border button** to deselect it.

(continued)

FIGURE 83
Cylinder with bridged borders

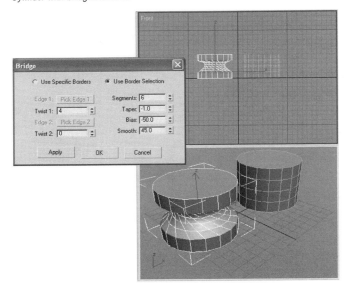

FIGURE 84
Cylinders with bridged polygons

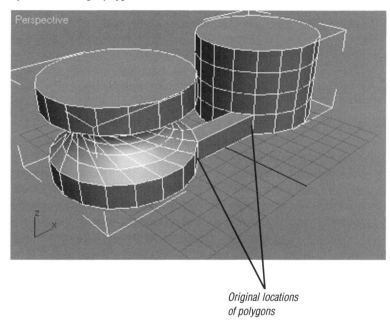

Original locations of polygons

7. On the Edit Geometry rollout, click the **Attach button**, then click **Cylinder02** to make Cylinder01 and Cylinder02 one object.

8. Click the **Polygon button** ■, in the Front viewport select a single **polygon** on the far-right side of Cylinder01's bottom level of polygons, press **[Ctrl]** and select a single **polygon** on the far-left side of Cylinder02's bottom level of polygons, click the **Bridge button** in the Edit Polygons rollout, then click outside the objects in the viewport.

   A bridge is created between the two polygons, connecting Cylinder01 to Cylinder 02. The cylinders appear in the Perspective viewport, as shown in Figure 84.

9. Save the file as **Bridgepoly**, then reset 3ds Max.

You created a tapered, biased, and twisted bridge between two borders in a cylinder, attached the cylinder to another cylinder, then created a bridge between polygons on each of the cylinders.

LESSON 7

MODEL EFFICIENTLY

What You'll Do

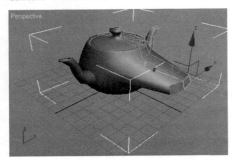

▶ *In this lesson, you will explore methods of modeling that take advantage of tools available in 3ds Max to simplify the modeling process.*

Now that you have explored many of the techniques you can use while modeling, it is time to take a look at different methods you can use while modeling to create organic, creative models as easily as possible.

Applying the MeshSmooth Modifier

When standard primitives were introduced in Chapter 2, you learned that they are often just the starting point for much more complex models that are modified so heavily that you can't tell what kind of primitive the modeler might have started with. Using the MeshSmooth modifier enables you to take a very basic object, such as a box, and quickly modify and model it into something entirely different.

Applying the MeshSmooth modifier to a low-resolution object such as a box smoothes the object as though it has many more segments and vertices than it actually does. For instance, if you created a box with two segments on its width, length, and height, as shown on the left in Figure 85, converted it to an editable poly, and then applied the MeshSmooth modifier, the box would appear as shown on the right in Figure 85. Not using the modifier, and transforming the vertices and edges of a box to create an object with the same appearance would take a huge amount of time. In this case, with the Show End Result button selected, the outline of the original box appears around the smoothed end result. Working with the small amount of polygons in the original box outline and modeling the object by, for example, extruding and beveling it several times, you can quickly create a complex and interesting object with only a few clicks and drags of a few polygons. See Figure 86 for an example of a model created by applying the MeshSmooth modifier to a box and then extruding and beveling several times.

Modeling with a Reference

In Chapter 2, you learned what a reference of an object is; now you'll see how handy references are for modeling. A reference is affected by modifications to the object it was created from, but can be modified itself without affecting the original. Similar to applying the MeshSmooth modifier, using reference copies makes it possible to change the appearance of a complicated object by

FIGURE 85
Box with MeshSmooth modifier applied

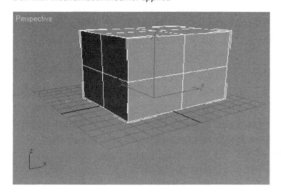
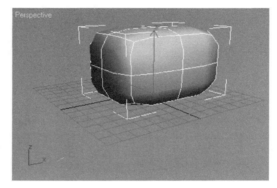

FIGURE 86
Beveled box

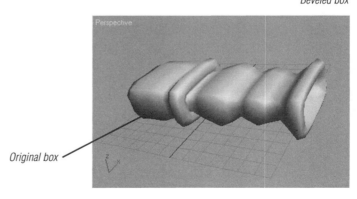

Original box

actually modifying or transforming a much simpler object. For example, in Figure 87, the object on the left is the original object and the object on the right is a reference copy to which the TurboSmooth modifier has been applied. As you can see, the reference copy has many more segments and vertices than the original object because of the application of the modifier. However, by working with the smaller group of segments and vertices in the original object, you can make changes to the reference copy and save yourself both effort and time. In addition, working with a reference gives you an opportunity to try things out on the reference object while maintaining the simple original object in the Modifier stack until you are happy with your changes.

Applying the Symmetry Modifier

When you are modeling an object that is symmetrical, the Symmetry modifier enables you to model half of the object and then create a mirror image of it. This means you need to build only half of the model, and you also will be able to produce a perfectly symmetrical end result. This is particularly helpful when modeling a character, because you can model half of a character and then use the Symmetry modifier to mirror the half of a character into a whole character. In addition to creating a mirror image of the original half of the object, changes that you make to the original half after the Symmetry modifier is applied are mirrored in the mirrored half of the model, as though the mirrored half were an instance. See Figure 88 for an example.

FIGURE 87
Box and reference with TurboSmooth modifier applied

FIGURE 88
Object with Symmetry modifier applied

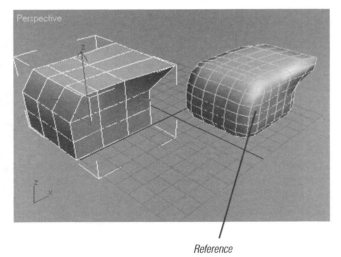

Reference

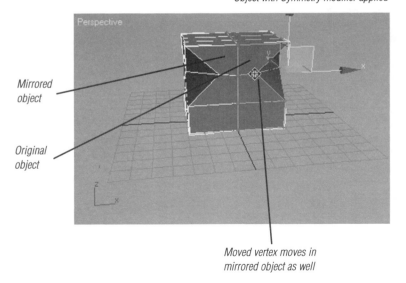

Mirrored object

Original object

Moved vertex moves in mirrored object as well

You can change how the Symmetry modifier is applied using the modifier's Parameters rollout, as shown in Figure 89. Click the X, Y, or Z option button in the Mirror Axis group to choose the axis along which the object is mirrored. Click the Flip check box to flip the original half to the opposite side of the mirrored axis. By default, the Slice Along Mirror check box is selected, and when you mirror the object, a slice is made where the objects meet, creating edges around the center of the symmetrical object if they do not already exist. Also by default, the Weld Seam check box is selected, which means that where edges and vertices of the welded object meet they are welded together, as long as the distance between them is less than the number in the Threshold box. If the Weld Seam check box is unchecked, moving vertices or edges away from the center of the symmetrical object creates a gap in the object.

Using XRef Objects

Externally referenced objects, or **XRef objects**, are objects that you can use in a scene that exist in another scene. This makes it easier for multiple people to work simultaneously on models that will ultimately appear in the same scene. If, for instance, one person in a studio is creating a character and another is creating an environment for the character in a different scene, the character in its early stages could be used as an XRef in the environment scene. The environment modeler would have the character's scale and could create the environment accordingly even though not all of the character's detail is complete. As the character modeler updates the character, the XRef object in the environment scene is updated as well.

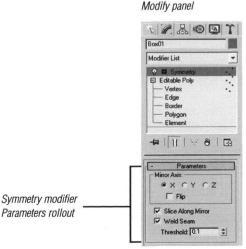

FIGURE 89
Modify panel

Symmetry modifier Parameters rollout

To add an XRef object to a scene, click File on the menu bar, and then click XRef Objects to open the XRef Objects dialog box, as shown in Figure 90. Click the Create XRef Record from File button, navigate to the file from which you want to access the XRef object, click the file name, and then click Open to open the XRef Merge dialog box. Click the name of the object you want to XRef, and then click OK. The name of the file that is the source of the XRef object appears in the XRef Files list box in the XRef Objects dialog box, and the name of the XRef object appears in the XRef Objects list box. Click the Automatic Update check box to make sure any changes to the source file are reflected in the XRef object in your scene, and then close the dialog box.

QUICKTIP

To add an XRef object to a scene in earlier versions of 3ds Max, click the Add button in the XRef Objects dialog box, open the file from which you want to access the XRef object, then click the name of the object you want to Xref in the XRef Merge dialog box and click OK. Click Automatic under Update File and then click the Close button.

You can transform or apply modifiers to an XRef object in your scene, and they do not affect the source file. If the XRef Object option button or Ignore option button is selected in the Modifiers group of the XRef Objects dialog box when you add an XRef object, you will not have access to the modifiers applied to the object at its source. Click the Merge option button in the Modifiers group when adding an XRef object to your scene to be able to access and work with the modifiers (this does not affect the modifiers in the source file).

FIGURE 90
XRef Objects dialog box

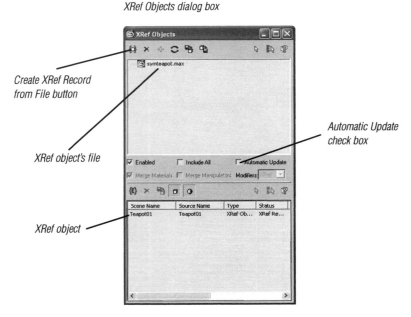

Create XRef Record from File button

Automatic Update check box

XRef object's file

XRef object

FIGURE 91
Box with MeshSmooth modifier applied

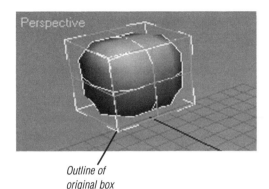

Outline of original box

FIGURE 92
Example of box beveled 4 times

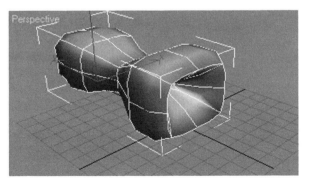

Apply the MeshSmooth modifier

1. In the top center of the Top viewport, create a **box** with dimensions of **40** × **50** × **40**, with **2** Width segments and **2** Height segments, then convert the box into an editable poly.

2. Apply the **MeshSmooth modifier** to the box, click **Editable Poly** in the modifier stack display, click the **Polygon button** ■, then click the **Show end result on/off toggle button** to select it.

   The box appears with the MeshSmooth modifier applied, and an outline of the original box appears around the smoothed box, as shown in Figure 91.

3. Select the **four polygons** on the side of the box outline closest to you in the viewport.

   You click the four boxes on the orange outline to select the polygons, but the polygons on the smoothed object are highlighted in red (selected).

4. Click the **Bevel button** in the Edit Polygons rollout, extrude and bevel the selected polygons four times, click the **Bevel button** to deselect it, then click the **Polygon button** ■ to deselect it.

   An example of what your smoothed box could look like after being beveled four times is shown in Figure 92.

5. Save the file as **Meshsmooth**, then reset 3ds Max.

You applied the MeshSmooth modifier to an editable poly, and extruded and beveled four polygons on the box.

Model using a reference

1. Create a box (**Box01**) on the left of the Top viewport with the dimensions **40 × 40 × 40** and **3** Length, Width, and Height segments, then convert the box into an editable poly.

2. Click the **Select and Move tool**, press **[Shift]**, click and drag the **box** to the right in the viewport to clone it (creating Box02), release the mouse and **[Shift]**, click the **Reference option button** in the Clone Options dialog box, then click **OK**.

3. Select **Box02**, click the **Modifier List list arrow**, then click **TurboSmooth** to apply the modifier, as shown in Figure 93.

   The reference with the modifier applied has many more segments and vertices than Box01.

4. Select **Box01**, click the **Vertex button**, select the **vertices** on the back corners of Box01's top surface, click the **Select and Move tool** (if necessary), then click the **YZ axis handle** on the Move gizmo and drag up and slightly back about two inches.

   As Box01 changes, so does Box02, with different and smoother results.

5. Click the **Polygon button**, select the bottom **six polygons** on the side of Box01 closest to you, then click the **Y axis handle** on the Move gizmo and drag down until the polygons look similar to Figure 94.

(continued)

FIGURE 93
Reference with TurboSmooth modifier applied

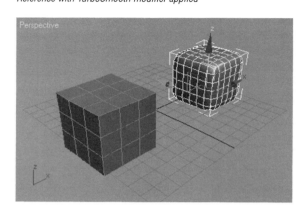

FIGURE 94
Box and reference with moved polygons

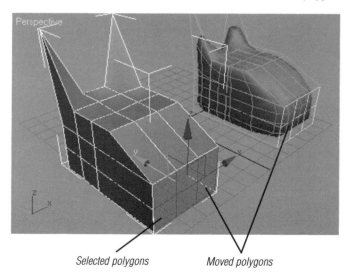

Selected polygons   Moved polygons

FIGURE 95
Teapot with Symmetry modifier applied

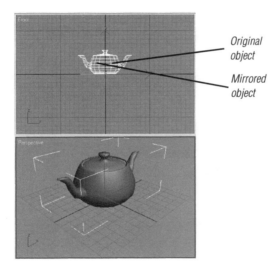

Original object

Mirrored object

6. Click the **Polygon button**, then click **Box02**.

   Your changes to six polygons in Box01 result in changes to even more polygons in Box02.

7. Save the file as **Modelref**, then reset 3ds Max.

You created a box and a reference copy of the box, applied a modifier to the reference, then transformed the original box to see the results on the reference.

Apply the Symmetry modifier

1. In the Top viewport, create a **teapot** with a radius of **35** whose center is in the center of the viewport, then convert it into an editable poly.

2. Click the **Edge button**, click in the Front viewport, select all of the **edges** on the left half of the teapot, then press **[Delete]**.

3. Apply the Symmetry modifier to the teapot.

   The teapot is now symmetrical, with two spouts and no handles, as shown in Figure 95.

4. Click in the Perspective viewport, click **Editable Poly** in the modifier stack, click the **Polygon button**, then select a **polygon** about halfway down the teapot's body and on its border.

5. Click the **Select and Move tool** (if necessary), click and drag the **green arrow handle** on the Move gizmo to the right about one inch, then click the **Show end result on/off toggle button**.

(continued)

As you moved the polygon, the mirroring polygon created by the symmetry modifier moved as well, as shown in Figure 96.

6. Save the file as **Symteapot**, then reset 3ds Max.

You created a teapot, deleted half of the teapot, then used the Symmetry modifier to make a mirror image of the half teapot. You also moved a polygon on the teapot and saw the same transformation applied to the polygon's mirror image.

Add an XRef object to a scene

1. Click **File** on the menu bar, then click **XRef Objects**.

2. Click **Create XRef Record from File button** in the XRef Objects dialog box, navigate to the folder containing the Symteapot file, click the **Symteapot file**, then click **Open**.

3. In the XRef Merge dialog box, click **Teapot01**, then click **OK**.

   The XRef Merge dialog box closes, and the XRef Objects dialog box now looks like Figure 97. The name of the file appears in the list near the top of the dialog box, and the name of the teapot object appears in the list in the bottom part of the dialog box under Scene Name. The teapot appears in the viewports in the new scene.

4. Click the **Automatic Update check box**, then close the dialog box.

   (continued)

FIGURE 96
Teapot with moved polygons

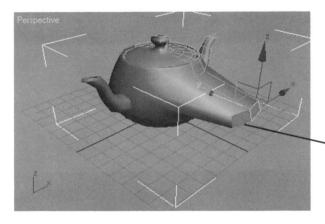

Mirrored polygon is selected and moved, too

FIGURE 97
XRef Objects dialog box

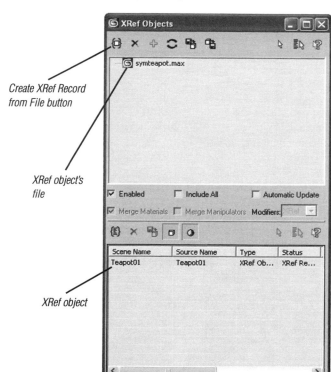

Create XRef Record from File button

XRef object's file

XRef object

5. Click **File** on the menu bar, click **Open**, click **Yes** to save the changes to your current scene, save the file as **XRefscene**, click **Symteapot** in the Open File dialog box, then click **Open**.

6. Select the **teapot**, click **Editable Poly** on the Modifier list (if necessary), click the **Element button**, select the **spout** on the right side of the teapot, then press **[Delete]**.

7. Click **File** on the menu bar, click **Open**, click **Yes** to save the changes to Symteapot, click **XRefscene** in the Open File dialog box, then click **Open**.

   Because the teapot in XRefscene is an XRef object, the modifications you made to the teapot in Symteapot are reflected in XRefscene, where the teapot now also has no spouts.

8. Reset 3ds Max.

You added an XRef object to a new scene, modified the XRef object in its original scene, then viewed the updated XRef object in the new scene.

Lesson 7 Model Efficiently

DISCREET 3D STUDIO MAX 3-81

LESSON 8

MODEL A
CHARACTER

What You'll Do

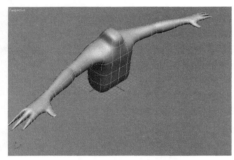

▶ *In this lesson, you will learn how to use the modeling tools in 3ds Max to build a model of a character.*

Modeling a Character

Believe it or not, at this point in the book you know enough to model a character—although you'll find it takes time and great attention to detail. You can start with a simple geometric shape and, by using the techniques learned in this chapter's earlier lessons, you can turn that geometric form into something that resembles a human form.

FIGURE 98
Symmetry modifier applied

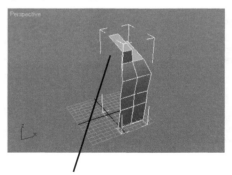

Half of object's polygons deleted

The basic outline of a process for modeling a character using these techniques is as follows: Create an editable polygon box with multiple segments and vertices, and then edit its vertices and polygons until it resembles a torso trunk with a neck. Delete half of the object, and then re-create the deleted half of the object by applying the Symmetry modifier to the remaining half, as shown in Figure 98. Doing this means that as you edit

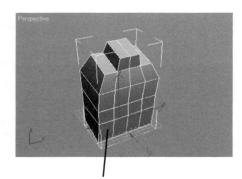

Polygons regenerated by applying Symmetry modifier

3-82 AUTODESK 3D STUDIO MAX

Modeling

one half of the object, the other half receives the same changes. After the Symmetry modifier is applied, apply the MeshSmooth modifier to the model to change it from a boxy form to a curvy, smooth one. Then, bevel and extrude polygons in the box to create arms, legs, a head, hands and feet, and facial features. As you bevel and extrude, you'll move individual vertices and edges, and even create new ones, to make the appendages and produce as much realism as possible, as shown in Figure 99. The result is a character that, when you're finished working through this book, you'll be able to animate, move using internal bone systems, give a head of hair, and plunk down into exciting scenes containing cool special effects!

FIGURE 99
Beginnings of a character

Create character torso

1. Open **MAX03-01.max**, then save the scene as **Character**.

    The scene contains a box with 1 Length segment, 4 Width segments, and 4 Height segments.

2. Convert the box into an editable poly, then click the **Polygon button** ▪ in the Selection rollout on the Modify panel to enter Polygon subobject level.

3. Select the **center two polygons** on top of the box, click the **Bevel button** in the Edit Polygons rollout on the Modify panel, then extrude and bevel both polygons so that they resemble Figure 100.

4. Click the **Vertex button** ∴ in the Selection rollout to enter Vertex subobject level, then with the **Select and Move tool** ✥, select and move **vertices** in the box until the object resembles Figure 100.

    When you have finished moving the vertices, the object will resemble a boxy version of a torso.

    | TIP Don't worry if your vertices don't match the figure exactly.

5. Click the **Polygon button** ▪, then in the Front viewport, select all of the **polygons** on the left half of the object.

6. Press **[Delete]**.

    The polygons are deleted and only half of the original object remains.

    (continued)

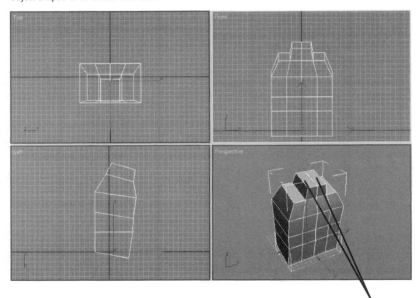

FIGURE 100
Object shaped to be a neck and torso

Extruded and beveled polygons

3-84 AUTODESK 3D STUDIO MAX   *Modeling*

FIGURE 101
Smoothed object

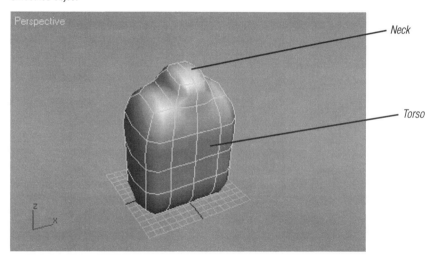

Neck

Torso

7. On the Modify panel, click the **Modifier List list arrow**, then click **Symmetry** to apply the Symmetry modifier.

   The deleted polygons reappear. Any changes made to the polygons on the right side of the object will be mirrored on the left side of the object.

8. Click the **Modifier List list arrow**, then click **MeshSmooth** to apply the MeshSmooth modifier.

   The entire object becomes smooth and curved and it looks like the neck and torso of a person, as shown in Figure 101.

9. Save the file.

You converted an object into an editable poly, extruded and beveled two polygons on the object, selected and moved several vertices in the object, deleted half of the object's polygons, then applied the Symmetry and MeshSmooth modifiers.

Create arms and hands

1. Select the **object**, click **Editable Poly** in the modifier stack on the Modify panel, then click the **Polygon button** ■ (if necessary) to enter Polygon subobject level.

   In the viewports, only half of the object is shown, with no smoothing.

2. Click the **Show end result on/off toggle button** under the modifier stack, maximize and arc rotate the **Perspective viewport** until you have a good view of both the front and right side of the object, click the **Select Object tool**, then select the **polygon** at the top of the object's right side, as shown in Figure 102.

   After you click the toggle button, the complete smoothed object is visible again, and an orange outline of the object before smoothing appears around half of the object.

3. On the Modify panel, click the **Bevel button** in the Edit Polygons rollout, extrude and bevel the **polygon** once, click the **Select and Rotate tool**, then rotate the **polygon** after the first bevel so that it is vertical.

   Rotating the polygon at this point ensures that the arm as it is created extends horizontally from the shoulder rather than diagonally up from the shoulder.

(continued)

FIGURE 102
Object with polygon selected

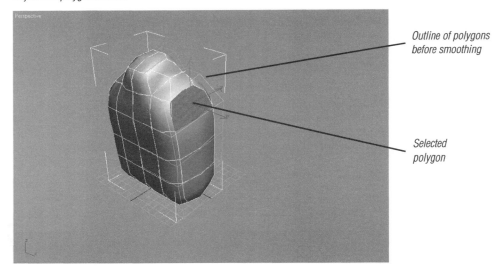

Outline of polygons before smoothing

Selected polygon

FIGURE 103
Creating the arms

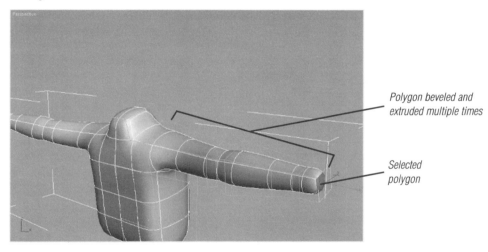

Polygon beveled and extruded multiple times

Selected polygon

4. Click the **Bevel button** again, then extrude and bevel the **polygon** multiple times, shrinking and expanding it to create the curves in the arm, as shown in Figure 103.

   TIP Again, don't worry if your arms don't match the figure exactly. The point is to practice creating something that looks like an arm.

   As you create the arm, an arm is also created on the other side of the object. Notice the appearance of the orange outline as you bevel. This is the geometry you're creating with your bevels, and the MeshSmooth modifier is smoothing it.

5. With the selected polygon at about the wrist point of the arm, click the **Select and Uniform Scale tool**, decrease the polygon's scale along its z-axis, then slightly increase the size of the polygon along its y-axis.

   (continued)

Lesson 8   Model a character

DISCREET 3D STUDIO MAX 3-87

6. Click the **Bevel button** again, then extrude and bevel the **polygon** again so that it looks like Figure 104.

   The bevel just created will serve as the central part of the character's hand.

7. Save the file.

You selected a polygon in the object, extruded, beveled, and rotated it, then extruded and beveled it multiple times to create an arm for the character. You also changed the polygon's scale and extruded and beveled it again to create the basis for a hand.

Create fingers

1. Select the **polygon** on the front side of the beveled hand section.

2. Click the **Bevel button**, extrude and bevel the **polygon** once so that the polygon is about half its size, click the **Select and Uniform Scale tool**, then scale the polygon down to the size of the base of a thumb relative to the central hand section.

3. Extrude and bevel, move, rotate, and scale the **polygon** until you the extrusion is generally shaped and positioned as a thumb.

4. Click the **Vertex button** to enter the sub-object level, then move and rotate **vertices** and **edges** as necessary to shape the thumb as realistically as possible.

(continued)

FIGURE 104
Creating the hand

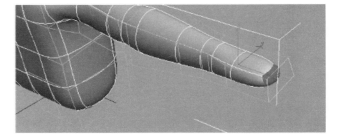

3-88 AUTODESK 3D STUDIO MAX

Modeling

FIGURE 105
Character thumb

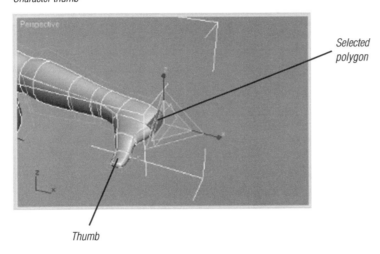

Selected polygon

Thumb

5. Click the Polygon button ■, click the **Select and Uniform Scale tool** □, select the **polygon** at the end of the hand section, as shown in Figure 105, then slightly increase the scale of the polygon along its y-axis, the way a hand is wider where it connects to the fingers.

6. Extrude and bevel the **polygon** once, a small distance, click the **Slice Plane button** in the Edit Geometry rollout on the Modify panel, then move and rotate the **plane** so that it is vertical and positioned about a third of the way from the left side of the polygon.

   | TIP It might help to switch to the Right viewport and zoom in to get a clearer view of where the plane hits the polygon.

7. Click the **Slice button** in the Edit Geometry rollout, move the **plane** another third of the way down the polygon, then click the **Slice button** again.

   Edges are created in the polygon where the plane is positioned when the Slice button is clicked. The original polygon is now three selected polygons.

   | TIP If you want to create four fingers on the hand, slice the polygon three times instead of twice to make four selected polygons.

   (continued)

8. Click the **Settings button** □ to the right of the Bevel button to open the Bevel Polygons dialog box, click the **By Polygon option button**, click **OK**, then extrude and bevel the **polygons** three or four times to create fingers on the hand, as shown in Figure 106.

   Because you selected the By Polygon option button, each polygon is extruded and beveled separately from the others, rather than as a group.

9. Save the file.

You extruded and beveled and scaled a polygon to create a base for the thumb, then manipulated polygons and vertices in multiple ways to produce a thumb. You also extruded and beveled another polygon, sliced it, then extruded and beveled the resulting new polygons to create fingers on the character's hand.

FIGURE 106
Creating the fingers

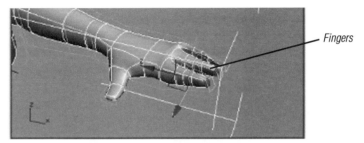

Fingers

FIGURE 107
Character so far

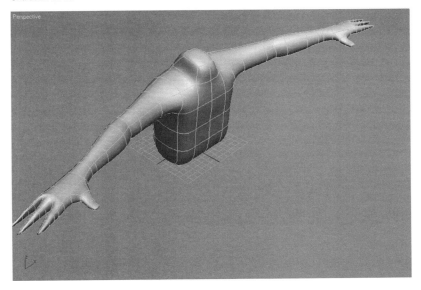

Add finishing touches

1. Extrude and bevel the **polygon** at the end of the central finger to make it slightly longer than the others.

2. Select, move, and rotate **vertices** and **edges** in the fingers and hand to create the appearance of knuckles, and to position the fingers more realistically in relation to each other, such as spreading them out a bit.

3. Select and move **vertices** so that the forearm is slightly forward of the upper arm, then make any other changes you think necessary to the arms, hands, and fingers to improve the object's appearance.

   At this point, your object might resemble that shown in Figure 107.

4. Now that you have practiced using several different tools to model the torso, neck, arms, hands, and fingers of a character, use the same tools to continue to model the object into a complete character, with legs, feet, and even a head.

5. Save the file, then reset 3ds Max.

You added finishing touches to the object to make it more realistic, then used the modeling tools to complete the character as desired.

LESSON 9

UNDERSTAND SPLINES

What You'll Do

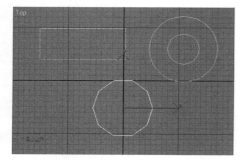

▶ In this lesson, you will learn what splines are and how to create them using different creation methods.

Up to now you have worked with standard primitives as objects and editable poly objects. Now you'll explore another set of objects called splines. A **spline** is an object that is basically a line composed of at least two vertices connected by a straight or curved segment. As you'll see, most splines contain many vertices and many segments.

There are several kinds of splines available in 3ds Max. To create splines, click the Create tab, click the Shapes button, and then, if necessary, click the list arrow in the list box under the Shapes button, and choose Splines. There are 11 types of splines you can create using the buttons on the Splines panel, as shown in Figure 108: Line,

Rectangle, Circle, Ellipse, Arc, Donut, NGon, Star, Text, Helix, and Section. An example of each of these, except for Section (which will be covered in a later chapter), is shown in Figure 109. Unlike primitives, most splines are two-dimensional when created, which might make them seem pretty unexciting. However, they are quite useful in modeling, as you'll see in Lesson 11.

A spline can be open or closed. An **open** spline has a starting vertex and ending vertex that don't meet and is also called a **path**. An example of an open spline is an arc. A **closed** spline's starting and ending vertex do meet to create a **shape**; for instance, a rectangle is a closed spline.

Creating Paths

The most basic spline is a line. To create a line that is a path, click the Line button in the Object Type rollout on the Create panel, click in a viewport, click where you want the line to start, move the mouse, click again to add another vertex to the line, and then continue to move the mouse and click until you have created a line with the vertices and segments needed. When you have created the last segment in the line, right-click to complete the line.

An arc is another type of open spline. An arc is a curved line connecting four vertices; you might also think of it as a segment of a circle. To create an arc, click the Arc button on the Create panel, click in a viewport, hold the mouse button down, and drag to the location of the second (endpoint) vertex, release the mouse button, and then drag up or down to increase or decrease the radius of the arc between the two vertices.

When you create a helix, you create a more complex type of path than a line or an arc—one with two radii and a height dimension as well. If you are familiar with the double helix form of DNA, think of a helix as a "single helix," or just one of the two lines to

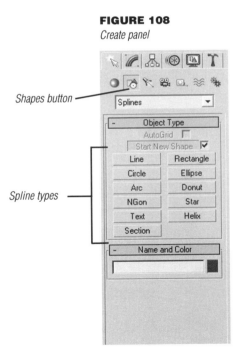

FIGURE 108
Create panel

Shapes button
Spline types

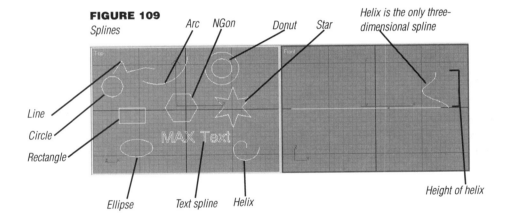

FIGURE 109
Splines

Arc NGon Donut Star Helix is the only three-dimensional spline

Line
Circle
Rectangle
Ellipse Text spline Helix Height of helix

Lesson 9 *Understand Splines*

DISCREET 3D STUDIO MAX 3-93

which DNA is connected. To create a helix, click the Helix button, click and drag to create the radius of the bottom of the helix, click and drag up to create the height of the helix, and then click and drag to create the radius of the top of the helix.

Creating Shapes

In addition to creating a line that is a path, you can create a line that is a free-form shape, as shown in Figure 110. To do this, click the Line button, click and move the mouse to create the line in the shape you need, and then click the line's starting vertex as the location of the last vertex. A small Spline dialog box opens, asking "Close spline?" Click Yes and your free-form shape is complete.

> **QUICK**TIP
> You can also close an arc spline by clicking the starting vertex with the endpoint vertex and clicking Yes in the Spline dialog box. The arc created will be a circle.

The processes for creating a circle, rectangle, and ellipse spline are the same as for creating a sphere or the first part of a box primitive. To create a circle, click the Circle button, click in the Top viewport at the location of the circle's center, hold the mouse button down and drag to set the radius of the circle, and then release the mouse button to complete the circle. To create a rectangle, click the Rectangle button, click in the Top viewport at the location of one corner of the rectangle, hold the mouse button down and drag to the location of the rectangle's opposite corner, and then release the mouse button to complete the rectangle. An ellipse is like a circle, except that it has a length and a width rather than a radius. To create an ellipse, click the Ellipse button,

FIGURE 110
Free-form shape created with line spline

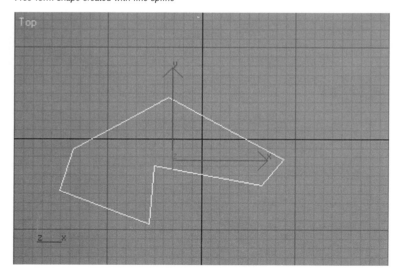

and then click and drag in the Top viewport as you would to create a rectangle.

Creating a donut spline is just like creating a torus primitive, but with a two-dimensional result. Click the Donut button, click in the Top viewport at the location of the donut's center, hold down the mouse button, and drag to create the donut's outer radius, release the mouse button, and drag to determine the donut's inner radius, and then click again to complete the donut. You might be surprised that this is the same method you use to create a star spline after clicking the Star button, only the outer radius and inner radius are the distance from the center of the star to the star's outer and inner points, as shown in Figure 111.

An NGon is a polygon with "N" number of sides of the same length, "N" being an amount that you can adjust. To create an NGon, click the NGon button, click in the Top viewport at the location of the NGon's center, hold down the mouse button and drag to create the radius of the NGon, and then release the mouse button. To adjust the number of sides in the NGon, adjust the number in the Sides box on the Parameters rollout for the NGon before or after you create it.

A text spline is a shape containing letters (and numbers and punctuation) that are themselves composed of splines. To add text to a scene, click the Text button, and then click in a viewport where you want the center of the text to be. Alternatively, you can click and drag in the viewport to drag the text to a chosen location. By default, the text is "MAX text," but you can edit the text (and font and formatting) in the Parameters rollout for the spline.

FIGURE 111
Setting the inner radius of a star's points

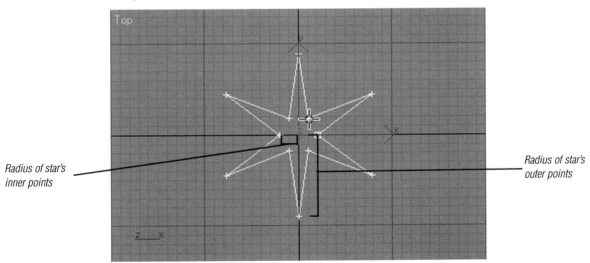

Lesson 9   Understand Splines

DISCREET 3D STUDIO MAX 3-95

Using the Creation Method Rollout

As with primitives, you can adjust the method used when creating splines by changing the options in the Creation Method rollout on the Create panel. For most splines (circle, rectangle, ellipse, donut, NGon, and helix), the Creation Method options are Edge, which creates the spline from edge to edge as you click and drag the mouse, or Center, which creates the spline from the center out as you click and drag. The default creation method for rectangle and ellipse splines is Edge, and for the circle, donut, NGon, and helix, the default method is Center. Click the option button for Edge or Center in the Creation Method rollout for the spline you are creating if you want to change it from the default.

QUICKTIP

Text splines and star splines do not have a Creation Method rollout.

Line splines and arc splines have unique creation methods. There are two groups of options in the line spline Creation Method rollout, as shown in Figure 112: Initial Type group and Drag Type group. The Initial Type group contains options for the type of vertex created when you click a location. Click the Corner option before creating a line for the vertices to connect segments with corners; click the Smooth option for the vertices to connect segments with curves, as shown in Figure 113. The Drag Type group contains options for the type of vertex created when you click to create a first vertex, and then drag while holding down the mouse button to get to the next vertex location. Click the Corner or Smooth option button to create

FIGURE 112
Create panel interface for a line spline

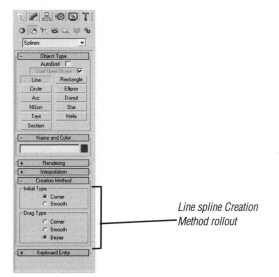

Line spline Creation Method rollout

FIGURE 113
Lines with smooth and Bezier vertices

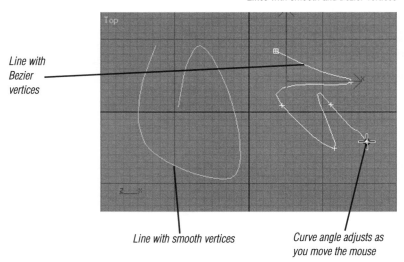

Line with Bezier vertices

Line with smooth vertices

Curve angle adjusts as you move the mouse

3-96 AUTODESK 3D STUDIO MAX

Modeling

vertices with corners or curves when you drag while creating the first vertex. Click the Bezier option button to adjust as you drag the angle of the curves that run through each new vertex, as shown in Figure 113. As you drag, the curve of the segment leading to the vertex you just created is adjusted; when you release the mouse button, the curve of the new segment you are creating is adjusted.

QUICKTIP
If you plan for your line to have both cornered and curved vertices, it is often easier to create the line with all cornered vertices, and then modify the vertices at the subobject level after converting the line into an editable spline, as shown in Lesson 10.

The creation method options for an arc are End-End-Middle or Center-End-End. By default, the End-End-Middle option button is selected, and the arc is created as described earlier in this lesson. If you click the Center-End-End option button, your first click in a viewport to create an arc is the center of the circle of which the arc is a segment. Hold down the mouse button, drag, and then release the mouse button at the location of one of the arc's endpoints. Move the mouse again to create the arc, as shown in Figure 114, and then, to complete it, click when the arc is the length you want.

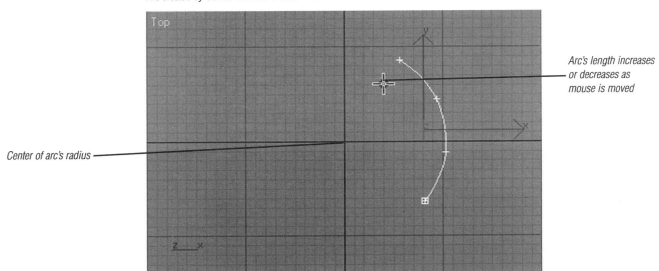

FIGURE 114
Arc created by Center-End-End creation method

Center of arc's radius

Arc's length increases or decreases as mouse is moved

Lesson 9 Understand Splines

DISCREET 3D STUDIO MAX 3-97

Create a line, arc, and helix

1. Click the **Create tab** (if necessary), click the **Shapes button** at the top of the Create panel, click the **list arrow** under the Shapes button (if necessary), then click **Splines**.

2. Click in the Top viewport, click the **Line button** on the Create panel, click on the left of the Top viewport, move the **mouse** up and to the right, click, move the **mouse** down and to the right, click, move the **mouse** up and to the right, click, then right-click.

   You created a line spline that is an open path, with cornered vertices.

3. Click the **Arc button** on the Create panel, click on the far-right side of the Top viewport, hold the **mouse button** down and drag up and to the left, release the **mouse button** and drag down about one inch, as shown in Figure 115, then click.

   You created an arc spline.

4. Click the **Helix button** on the Create panel, click in the bottom center of the Top viewport, hold the **mouse button** down and drag until Radius 1 in the Parameters rollout for the helix is about **40**, click and drag up until the Height of the helix is about **50**, click, then drag down until Radius 2 of the helix is about **4**.

   The height of the helix should appear in the Front viewport, as shown in Figure 116. The line and arc have no height.

5. Reset 3ds Max without saving the scene.

You created a line spline, an arc spline, and a helix spline.

FIGURE 115
Creating an arc spline

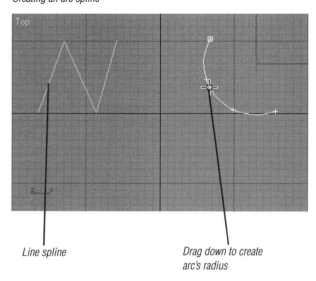

Line spline

Drag down to create arc's radius

FIGURE 116
Helix in Top and Front viewports

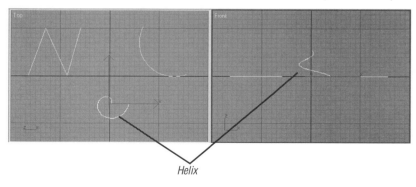

Helix

3-98 AUTODESK 3D STUDIO MAX

Modeling

FIGURE 117
NGon spline with 10 sides

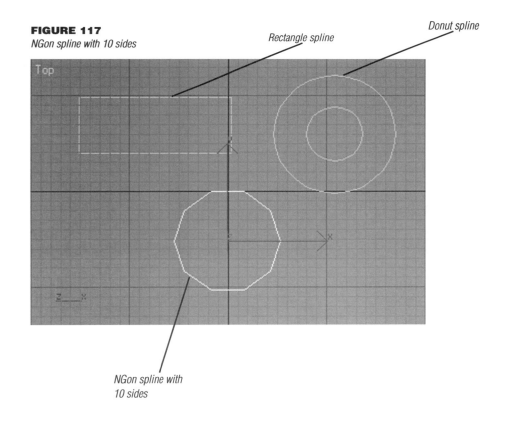

Rectangle spline

Donut spline

NGon spline with 10 sides

Lesson 9 Understand Splines

Create a rectangle, donut, and NGon

1. Click the **Shapes button** on the Create panel, then click the **Rectangle button**.
2. Click in the upper-left of the Top viewport, hold the **mouse button** down, and drag down about one inch and to the right about three inches, then release the **mouse button** to complete the rectangle.
3. Click the **Donut button** on the Create panel, click in the upper-right area of the Top viewport, hold the **mouse button** down and drag down about one inch to create the outer radius of the donut, release the **mouse button** and drag up about one-half inch to create the donut's inner radius, then click to complete the donut.
4. Click the **NGon button** on the Create panel, click in the bottom-center area of the Top viewport, hold the **mouse button** down and drag down about one inch, then release the **mouse button** to complete the NGon.
5. In the Parameters rollout for the NGon, change the number in the Sides box to **10**.

    The NGon now has 10 sides, as shown in Figure 117.
6. Reset 3ds Max without saving the scene.

You created a rectangle spline and a donut spline. You also created an NGon spline and increased the number of sides in the NGon using the Parameters rollout.

DISCREET 3D STUDIO MAX 3-99

Create a text spline

1. Click the **Shapes button** on the Create panel, then click the **Text button**.
2. Click in the center of the Top viewport.

   A text spline is inserted, the center of which is the location of your click.

3. In the Parameters rollout for the text spline, select the **text** in the Text box, then type **Spline** in its place.

   The text spline content changes, as shown in Figure 118.

4. Reset 3ds Max without saving the file.

You added a text spline to a scene and changed the text content of the spline.

FIGURE 118
Modified text spline

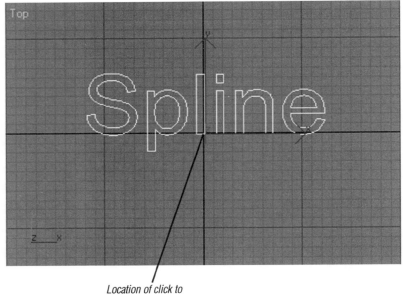

Location of click to insert text spline

FIGURE 119
Line spline with smooth vertices

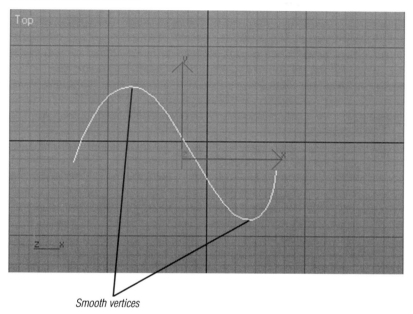

Smooth vertices

Create a line with smooth vertices

1. Click the **Shapes button** on the Create panel, then click the **Line button**.
2. In the Initial Type group on the Creation Method rollout for the line spline, click the **Smooth option button** to select it.
3. Click on the left side of the Top viewport, move the **mouse** up and to the right about two inches, click, move the **mouse** down and to the right about three inches, click, move the **mouse** up and to the right about one inch, click, then right-click.

    Because you chose the Smooth creation method for the line spline, the line running through the vertices you create is curved instead of cornered, as shown in Figure 119.
4. Reset 3ds Max without saving the scene.

You chose the Smooth creation method for a line spline, then created a line with smooth vertices.

Lesson 9   Understand Splines

DISCREET 3D STUDIO MAX 3-101

LESSON 10

EDIT SPLINES

What You'll Do

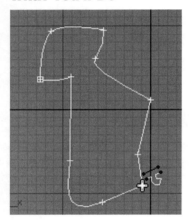

In this lesson, you will learn how to change the parameters of a spline and how to convert it into an editable spline with subobjects. You will also learn how to convert cornered vertices and straight segments into smooth or Bezier vertices and curved segments (and vice versa). Lastly, you'll practice inserting new vertices into a spline.

After you have created a spline, you can modify it in several ways. Like primitives, splines can be moved, rotated, and scaled using the Select and Move, Select and Rotate, and Select and Scale tools on the main toolbar. They can also be cloned, linked, grouped, and aligned in the same way as primitives. Nearly all splines also have parameters that can be changed to alter their appearances. And what is most important, splines can be converted into objects called editable splines that have editable subobjects.

Modifying Spline Parameters

You can modify a spline's parameters in the Parameters rollout on the Create panel (before or just after you create a spline), or on the Modify panel with the created spline selected. Line splines do not have parameters. Circle and donut parameters are simply the values of their radii. The parameters for an ellipse are its length and width, and the parameters for a rectangle are length and width, plus a Corner Radius value for the radius of the rectangle's corners if they are curved, as shown in Figure 120.

An arc's parameters are its radius, as well as the From value (the start point's location as an angle from local x-axis) and the To value (the endpoint's location from local x-axis). Click the Pie Slice check box if you want straight lines to connect the center of the arc to the endpoints, forming a closed shape that looks like a pie piece or a pie with a piece missing, as shown in Figure 120. Click the Reverse check box to switch the locations of the start and endpoint vertices.

As mentioned earlier, you can adjust the number of sides in an NGon in its Parameters rollout. In addition, you can change its radius and its corner radius value. You can also click the Inscribed or

Circumscribed option button to determine whether the NGon's radius is the distance from its corners to the center (inscribed) or from its sides to its center (circumscribed). Click the Circular check box to make the NGon a circle.

In the Parameters rollout for a star, you can change the number of points it has, the radii of its inner and outer points, and the distortion of its inner points away from their original location, as shown in Figure 120. You can also adjust the radii of the star's inner and outer points if you want them to be curved (called the Fillet Radius).

As the only three-dimensional spline, a helix has a height parameter in addition to its outer and inner radii. You can also vary the number of curves in a helix, and adjust the Bias parameter to make its curves gather more toward one end of the helix than another, as shown in Figure 120. Lastly, if the CW option button is clicked, the helix turns clockwise, and if the CCW option button is clicked, the helix turns counterclockwise.

The parameters of a text spline focus on the text content, font and formatting. Type the text you want to appear in the spline in the Text box in the Parameters rollout. Changes to the text in the Text box appear in the viewport automatically unless you click the Manual Update check box at the bottom of the rollout. If this check box is selected, changes you make to the text in the Text box won't be reflected in the spline until you click the Update button. You can also choose the font face and size, adjust the kerning (distance between letters) and leading (distance between lines), italicize, underline, and change the text alignment.

FIGURE 120
Splines with parameters adjusted

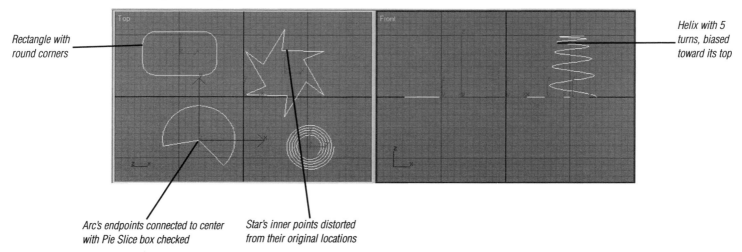

Rectangle with round corners

Arc's endpoints connected to center with Pie Slice box checked

Star's inner points distorted from their original locations

Helix with 5 turns, biased toward its top

Converting a Spline into an Editable Spline

After you create a spline and its parameters are as desired, you can convert the spline into an editable spline to edit its subobjects. There are several ways to convert a spline into an editable spline. You can right-click the spline, point to Convert To on the Transform menu, and then click Convert to Editable Spline. You can right-click the name of the object (such as Line) in the modifier stack display on the Modify panel, and then click Convert to Editable Spline in the Convert To list on the right-click menu.

> **QUICK**TIP
> Because a line has no dimension parameters to appear on the Modify panel, clicking the Modify tab with a line selected automatically converts the line into an editable spline.

The Edit Spline modifier can also be applied to a spline, and its modifier stack collapsed to make it an editable spline. To do this, select the object, click the Modify tab if necessary, click the Modifier List list arrow, and then select Edit Spline to apply it. Next, click the Utilities tab, click the Collapse button, make sure the Modifier Stack Result option button is selected in the Output Type rollout, and then click the Collapse Selected button. If you do not collapse the stack, the spline can be edited as an editable spline when the Edit Spline modifier is selected, while maintaining its parameters at the bottom of the modifier stack. This is useful when you might need to be able to adjust the spline's original parameters as you work with it, or if you want to edit the spline's subobjects before committing to its conversion to an editable spline. However, it can result in larger file sizes and unwanted effects on modifications made to the editable spline when you alter the spline's parameters.

After an object has been fully converted into an editable spline, you can no longer edit the parameters of the spline, and the name of the object changes in the modifier stack display (from, for instance, Line) to Editable Spline with a plus sign next to it. When you click the plus sign, the Vertex, Segment, and Spline subobject levels appear underneath "Editable Spline," as shown in Figure 121. In the Vertex subobject level, you can edit the spline's vertices; in the Segment subobject level, you can edit the spline's segments, and in the Spline subobject level, you can edit the whole spline or the splines within it if it contains more than one. Click one of the subobject levels to work within it. You can also click the Vertex button, Segment button, or Spline button in the Selection rollout of the Modify panel to go to a subobject level.

Converting Vertices, Segments, and Splines

Editable spline subobjects can be moved, rotated, and scaled just like editable poly subobjects. One important difference between an editable spline and an editable poly is that you can convert and adjust the curve (or lack thereof) of the segments that pass through vertices in an editable spline.

To convert a vertex from a corner vertex into a smooth or Bezier vertex, click the Vertex subobject level, select a vertex or vertices, right-click a selected vertex, and then click Smooth, Bezier, or Bezier Corner on the

Tools 1 quadrant of the Quad menu. As mentioned in the last lesson, the easiest approach to creating a line with different curves and corners is to create a spline with all cornered vertices, convert it to an

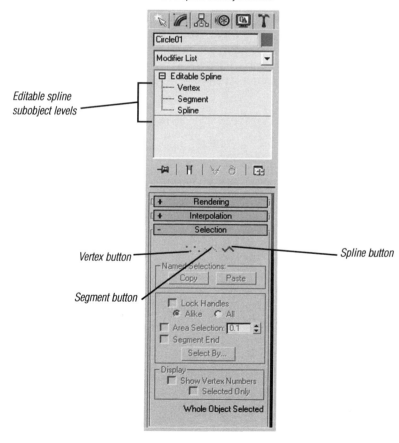

FIGURE 121
Editable spline subobject levels

Lesson 10   Edit Splines

DISCREET 3D STUDIO MAX 3-105

editable spline, and then convert the vertices and segments desired into smooth or Bezier vertices and segments. One of the reasons for this is that in editable splines, a Bezier vertex has a visible tangent handle that you can use to adjust the curve of the line as it passes through the vertex, as shown on the left in Figure 122. A Bezier Corner vertex has a tangent handle for each of the segments to which the vertex is connected; when you adjust each handle, you affect the curve of the segment as it arrives at the vertex, as shown on the right in Figure 123. If you are converting a vertex into a corner vertex from smooth, Bezier, or Bezier Corner, click Corner on the Tools 1 quadrant of the Quad menu.

You can also change a segment between two vertices from a curve into a straight line, or vice versa. To do this, click the Segment subobject level, select a segment or segments, right-click a selected segment, and then, on the Tools 1 quadrant of the Quad menu, click Line to convert a curve into a straight segment, or click Curve to convert a line segment into a curve segment. The success of this conversion depends on the type of vertices that the segment connects. Corner vertices can only support line segments, so segments between them cannot be changed to curves. Smooth, Bezier, and Bezier Corner vertices can support either line or curve segments. Bezier vertices' handles do not affect line segments, but can still be adjusted, as shown in Figure 124. A tangent handle supporting a line segment appears as an "X." If the line segment is then converted into a curve, the adjusted handle affects the resulting curve segment.

At the Spline subobject level, converting the object from Line to Curve or from Curve to

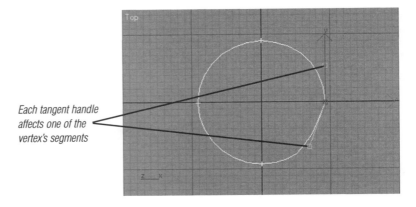

FIGURE 123
Bezier Corner vertex

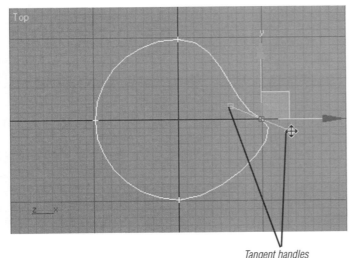

FIGURE 122
Adjustment of a Bezier vertex's segments

3-106 AUTODESK 3D STUDIO MAX

Modeling

Line on the Tools 1 quadrant of the Quad menu converts all of the spline's vertices and segments accordingly. If you convert a spline to Line, all of its vertices become corner vertices. Converting a spline to Curve makes all of its vertices Bezier vertices.

Inserting Vertices

You can insert new vertices into an editable spline at any time to modify its appearance. Inserting new vertices in an editable spline works somewhat as though you were creating a new line spline within the editable spline. For an example, see Figure 125. To insert new vertices, click the Insert button in the Geometry rollout on the Modify panel (you might need to drag the bottom of the panel up to see the Insert button). Clicked, the Insert button becomes yellow (selected). Click the editable spline in the location on the spline you want the first vertex to be, click again to place a vertex there, or move the mouse and click again to place the first vertex elsewhere in the viewport, move to where you want the second vertex, click, continue clicking and moving the mouse until you have added the vertices and segments desired, and then right-click when you are done. If you want a new vertex to be cornered, release the mouse button just after clicking the vertex's location. If you want a new vertex to be smooth, click and drag at the new vertex's location, and the new vertex becomes a Bezier vertex. As you drag, the curve of the segment leading to the vertex you just created is adjusted; when you release the mouse button, the curve of the new segment you are creating is adjusted. When you are done inserting new vertices, click the Insert button to deselect it.

You follow the same process to insert new vertices whether you are in the Vertex, Segment, or Spline subobject level. Once inserted, new vertices and segments can be converted between corner, smooth, and Bezier just like vertices and segments that were in the original spline.

FIGURE 124
Bezier Corner vertex connected to a straight segment

FIGURE 125
Circle with new vertices inserted

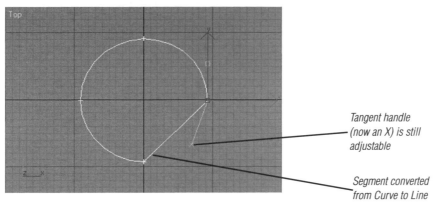
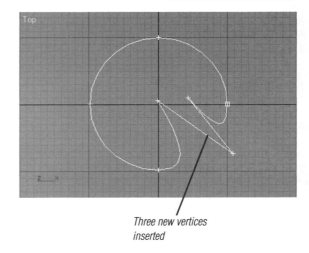

Tangent handle (now an X) is still adjustable

Segment converted from Curve to Line

Three new vertices inserted

Lesson 10   Edit Splines

DISCREET 3D STUDIO MAX 3-107

Modify parameters of an arc and star

1. Click the **Shapes button** on the Create panel, click the **Arc button**, then create an arc in the left half of the Top viewport similar to the one in Figure 126.

2. Click the **Modify tab**, select the value in the Radius box in the Parameters rollout for the arc, then change the value to **60**.

   If the radius of the arc you initially created was smaller than 60, the arc increases in size; if the radius was greater than 60, the arc decreases in size.

3. Click the **Pie Slice check box** in the arc's Parameters rollout to select it.

   Straight lines connect the endpoints of the arc to the center of its radius, making it look like a portion of a pie.

4. Click the **Create tab**, click the **Star button**, then create a star in the right half of the Top viewport.

5. Click the **Modify tab**, change the Radius 1 number in the Parameters rollout for the star to **80**, change the Radius 2 number to **25**, change the Points number to **10**, and change the Fillet Radius 1 number to **30**.

   The star should now look like the star in Figure 126, with 10 rounded outer points.

You created an arc and modified its parameters on the Modify panel, then created a star and modified its parameters on the Modify panel.

FIGURE 126
Star with parameters modified

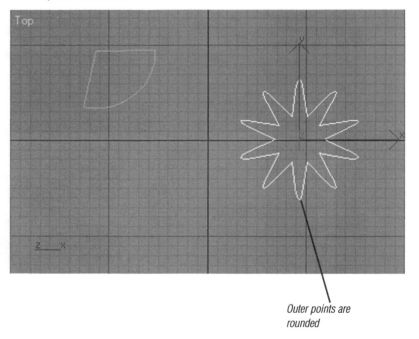

Outer points are rounded

3-108 AUTODESK 3D STUDIO MAX

Modeling

FIGURE 127
Modify panel

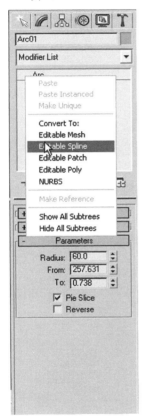

FIGURE 128
Arc spline

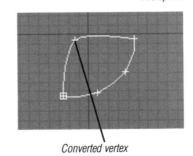

Converted vertex

Lesson 10   Edit Splines

Convert splines to editable splines

1. Right-click the **star**, point to **Convert To** on the Transform menu, then click **Convert To Editable Spline**.

   The object changes from "Star" in the modifier stack display to "Editable Spline" with a plus sign next to it. The Selection rollout contains the Vertex button, Segment button, and Spline button for the editable spline's subobjects.

2. Select the **arc**, right-click **Arc** in the modifier stack display, then click **Editable Spline** under Convert To on the right-click menu, as shown in Figure 127.

   The arc is converted to an editable spline.

You converted splines into editable splines using two different conversion methods.

Convert vertices and segments

1. Select the **arc**, then click the **Vertex button** in the Selection rollout.

2. Select the **vertex** at the center of the arc's radius, right-click the **vertex**, then click **Smooth** on the Tools 1 quadrant of the Quad menu.

   The vertex is converted from a corner vertex to a smooth vertex, and the line running through the vertex is now curved, as shown in Figure 128.

(continued)

DISCREET 3D STUDIO MAX 3-109

3. Click the **Segment button** to select it, select the **segment** at the center of the arc's curve, right-click the **segment**, then click **Line** on the Tools 1 quadrant of the Quad menu.

   The segment is now a straight line between vertices instead of a curved line.

4. Click the **Segment button** to deselect it, select the **star**, then click the **Spline button** to select it.

5. Right-click the **star**, click **Line** on the Tools 1 quadrant of the Quad menu, then click the **Spline button** to deselect it.

   All of the segments in the star become straight line segments between the star's vertices, as shown in Figure 129.

6. Click the **Vertex button**, right-click any vertex on the star, then click **Bezier Corner** on the Tools 1 quadrant of the Quad menu.

   The vertex becomes a Bezier Corner vertex. Because the segments to which it is connected are straight rather than curved lines, the Bezier handles for the vertex appear as green "X"s instead of green squares.

7. Click the **Vertex button** to deselect it.

You converted a corner vertex into a smooth vertex, converted a curved segment into a straight line segment, and converted an entire spline into a spline with only straight line segments. You also converted a corner vertex into a Bezier corner vertex and viewed the Bezier handles for the vertex.

FIGURE 129
Star spline converted to straight line segments only

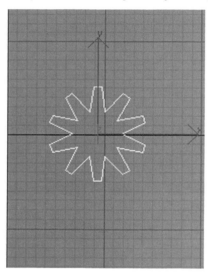

3-110 AUTODESK 3D STUDIO MAX

Modeling

FIGURE 130
Vertices inserted into arc spline

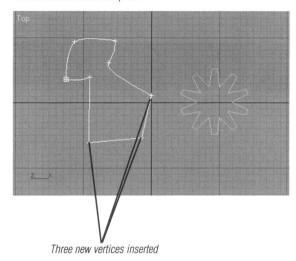

Three new vertices inserted

FIGURE 131
Arc spline with Bezier vertex inserted

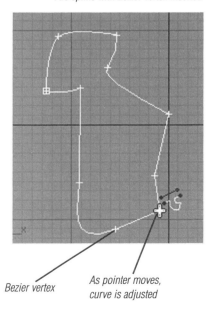

Bezier vertex   As pointer moves, curve is adjusted

Insert vertices

1. Select the **arc**, click the **Vertex button**, move the Modify panel up (if necessary) so that you can see the Geometry rollout, then click the **Insert button**.

2. Click the **segment** in the arc previously converted into a straight line segment, move the **mouse** down below the arc, click, move the **mouse** to the right, click, move the **mouse** up, click, then right-click.

   Your first click inserted a vertex, your second click determined the location of the inserted vertex, subsequent clicks inserted new vertices in the locations clicked, and the right-click completed the insertion of vertices. An example of what the new vertices might look like is shown in Figure 130.

3. Click on the **segment** between the first and second new vertices you inserted, move the **mouse** down about one-half inch, click and drag to create a Bezier curve through a newly inserted vertex, as shown in Figure 131, then right-click when the curve looks like you want it to.

4. Click the **Vertex button** to deselect it, then reset 3ds Max without saving the file.

You inserted three cornered vertices and three new segments into an editable spline, then inserted a Bezier vertex onto one of the new segments.

LESSON 11

MODEL WITH SPLINES

What You'll Do

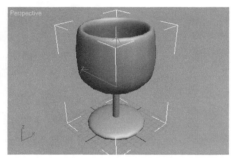

▶ *In this lesson, you will explore the different ways splines are useful in modeling. You'll learn how to extrude splines, how to apply the Lathe modifier to a two-dimensional line to create a 3D object, and how to create a loft compound object using shapes and a path.*

Modeling with splines is not just moving lines around a scene—in fact, using splines can enable you to create some pretty complicated objects rather easily. Not only can the lines in a two-dimensional spline be extruded to create a three-dimensional object, they can also serve as the outline for an object that is symmetrical all around its axis. This is what is called a **lathe**.

Extruding Splines

The most basic modeling technique you can use with splines is extruding them. You can extrude all kinds of splines, whether or not they are closed shapes. Keep in mind, though, that an extruded open spline, such as a line or helix, will be visible only on the side that its normals face, so its usefulness might be limited. If you extrude a closed spline, however, it is visible on all sides of the extrusion. In addition, you can choose whether or not the start or end of the extruded spline is covered by a flat surface, as shown in Figure 132.

To extrude a spline, select the spline, and then apply the Extrude modifier to the spline. In the Parameters rollout for the modifier, change the number in the Amount box to extrude the spline by that amount. The number in the Segments box can be adjusted to increase the number of segments in the extruded spline. To have the start of the extruded spline covered with a flat surface, make sure the Cap Start check box is selected. Make sure the Cap End check box is selected to have the end of the extruded spline covered with a flat surface.

Applying the Lathe Modifier

When you want to create an object that is symmetrical at all points around a central axis, such as a wine glass or a barrel, you can use the Lathe modifier applied to a spline to create the object. To understand how this works, think of a pottery wheel with a piece of clay spinning on it. As the clay spins, pressing in one location on the clay makes the same indentation all the way around its surface. Similarly, applying the Lathe modifier to a spline rotates the spline around a central axis; the shape of the spline is replicated all the way around the resulting three-dimensional object, as shown in Figure 133.

To create an object with a spline and the Lathe modifier, start by working in the Front viewport. Pan the view so that the dark lines that cross at the center of its grid are in the lower-left corner. These dark lines serve as your reference point as you draw the profile of the object you want to create with a line spline. The vertical line is the central axis for the object, and the horizontal line is where the bottom of the object is located. On the Create Panel, click the Line button, and then, to start drawing the profile, click at the point where the dark lines of the grid intersect in the Front viewport. Move the mouse and click as needed to create the profile of the object. Remember that you are drawing a profile of *half* of the object and that the line spline should be open, with the starting vertex and ending vertex both touching the vertical dark gridline, as shown in Figure 133. After you have drawn the profile, edit and insert vertices as necessary to refine the profile and add new features, if necessary. After you are satisfied with the profile you have drawn, select the line and apply the Lathe modifier to it.

QUICKTIP
When you click the Modify tab to go to the Modify panel for the line spline, the line automatically becomes an editable spline.

FIGURE 132
Extruded splines

FIGURE 133
Lathe modifier applied to line spline

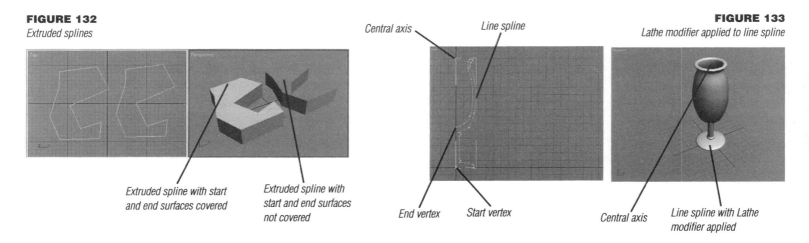

Extruded spline with start and end surfaces covered

Extruded spline with start and end surfaces not covered

Central axis

Line spline

End vertex Start vertex

Central axis

Line spline with Lathe modifier applied

Lesson 11 Model with Splines

DISCREET 3D STUDIO MAX 3-113

When first applied, the Lathe modifier does not automatically "know" the location of the axis around which the object should be rotated. Click the plus sign next to the Lathe modifier in the modifier stack, and then click the Axis subobject. Select and move the axis so that it is aligned with the vertical dark gridline, which is the axis location on which you based your profile drawing. If you are using a central axis different from the one described above, you can click the X, Y, or Z button in the Direction group on the Lathe modifier's Parameters rollout to rotate the spline around one of its axes. Alternatively, you can click the Min, Center, or Max button in the Align group to rotate the object around its minimum, center, or maximum.

If the normals in the object are facing the wrong way, as shown in Figure 134, click the Flip Normals check box to flip the normals and make the object appear as you intended. If you want to make further adjustments to the object's appearance, click Line in the modifier stack, and then move, convert, or insert new vertices as needed. To improve the roundness of the lathed object, you can increase the number of segments in the resulting object by increasing the number in the Segments box in the Lathe modifier's parameters. If your start or end vertex does not touch the central axis and you have a hole at one or both ends of the lathed object, make sure that the Cap Start and/or Cap End check box is selected to create a flat surface covering the top or bottom of the object.

Creating Loft Objects

A **compound object** is produced when two or more objects are combined, with one object as the result. A **loft** compound object

FIGURE 134
Object with normals facing the wrong direction

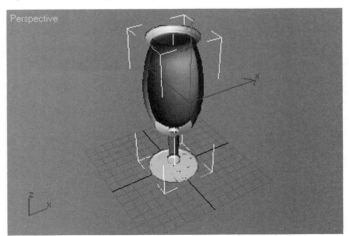

is the result of combining one or more shapes with a path; the shapes are located along the path as cross-sections, and 3ds Max generates a surface between them. In other words, the shapes are extruded along the path to create an object whose outer surface is formed by the shapes. For example, in Figure 135, the line in the left image is the path used in the right image. The circle in the left image has been extruded along the first 75 percent of the path, gradually changing into a full-sized star extruded along the last 25 percent of the path. The start and end of the path in a lofted object are shaped like the shape applied to that part of the path.

To create a loft object, you need to have at least two splines in a scene. You can either start by selecting the shape or the path object. If you select the path object, click the Geometry button on the Create panel, click the list arrow on the list box at the top of the Create panel, click Compound Objects, and then click the Loft button in the Object Type rollout. In the Creation Method rollout that appears on the Create panel, as shown in Figure 136, click the Get Shape button, and then click the Move option button to move the shape to the path's location, click the Copy option button to place a copy of the shape at the path's location, or click the Instance option button to place an instance of the shape at the path's location. Click the object you want to be the shape, and the selected path and clicked shape are then combined into a loft object. The shape moves to the path's start vertex and is extruded from the start vertex to the end vertex.

To create a loft object starting with a shape, follow the same process, but click the Get Path button instead of the Get Shape button. Click the object you want to be the path, and the selected shape and clicked path are combined into a loft object. The path's starting vertex is located at the shape's pivot point, and the path is aligned with the shape's local

FIGURE 135
Loft compound object containing two shapes

FIGURE 136
Create panel interface for loft object

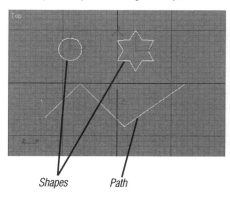
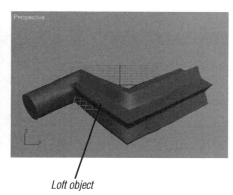
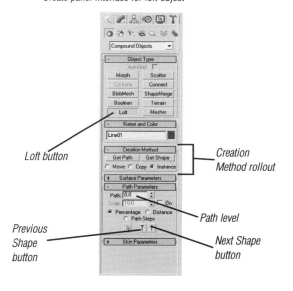

Lesson 11 Model with Splines

DISCREET 3D STUDIO MAX 3-115

z-axis. To change the path, with the shape selected, click the Get Path button again, and then click a different object.

To add a shape to a path, adjust the path level by adjusting the number in the Path box on the Path Parameters rollout. Click the Percentage option button if you want the Path number to be a percentage of the distance along the path, or click the Distance option button if you want the Path number to be the distance along the path in units. As you adjust the Path number, the loft object disappears and a yellow X appears on the path to show your current path location. With the Get Shape button selected, click another shape in the scene. That shape then becomes the shape of the loft object from your current path location to the end vertex of the path. Rather than changing abruptly, the loft object gradually transforms from the previous shape to become the newly added shape at the location the new shape was added. You can insert shapes at any location along the path. Click the Previous Shape button or the Next Shape button to move to the location of the previous or next shape on the path.

Deforming Loft Objects

After a loft object has been created, the object appears in the modifier stack as "Loft" with Shape and Path subobjects. You can adjust the object's parameters as you could on the Create panel when the object was first created, but you have two additional options. First, there is a Pick Shape button on the Path Parameters rollout that isn't available on the Create panel. Click the Pick Shape button, and then click a shape's starting path location to set that as the current path location.

What is more important, the Modify panel contains a Deformations rollout that enables you to deform the loft object you have created. The two deformations that you might use most frequently are Scale and Twist. To deform a loft object using Scale, select Loft in the modifier stack, and then click the Scale button. The Scale Deformation dialog box appears, as shown in Figure 137. A red line called the **deformation curve** goes from the

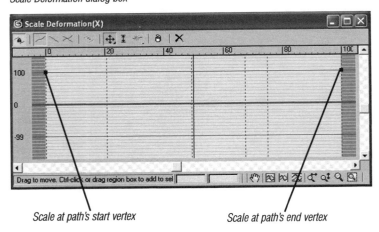

FIGURE 137
Scale Deformation dialog box

Scale at path's start vertex *Scale at path's end vertex*

left to the right side of the **deformation grid** in the dialog box, connected by control points, showing the scale of the shapes used on the path from its start to end vertex. Move a **control point** up or down to increase or decrease the scale of the shape at that location on the path. In Figure 138, the scale of the object goes from 0 percent at the start of the path to 100 percent at its end; 75 percent of the distance along the path, an outline of the shape appears at 100% scale.

To deform a loft object by twisting it, click the Twist button with the object selected to open the Twist Deformation dialog box. To twist the loft object one revolution counterclockwise from start to end vertex, set the first control point to 0 and the end control point to 100 (or, to produce a clockwise twist, set the end control point to –100). To twist the object two revolutions counterclockwise, set the end control point to 200.

You can insert control points along the path in the Deformation dialog box to alter the level of deformation at different points on the path. To insert a control point, click the Insert Control Point flyout on the Deformation dialog box toolbar, click the Insert Corner Point or Insert Bezier Point button, and then click the red line to insert a control point in that location. A corner control point creates a sharp corner where it is inserted; a Bezier control point creates a smooth curve with adjustable tangent handles where it is inserted. See Figure 139. You can convert existing control points by right-clicking a control point and clicking Corner on the right-click menu to convert it to a corner point, clicking Bezier-Smooth to convert it to a Bezier point, or clicking Bezier-Corner to convert it to a Bezier corner point.

FIGURE 138
Scaled loft object

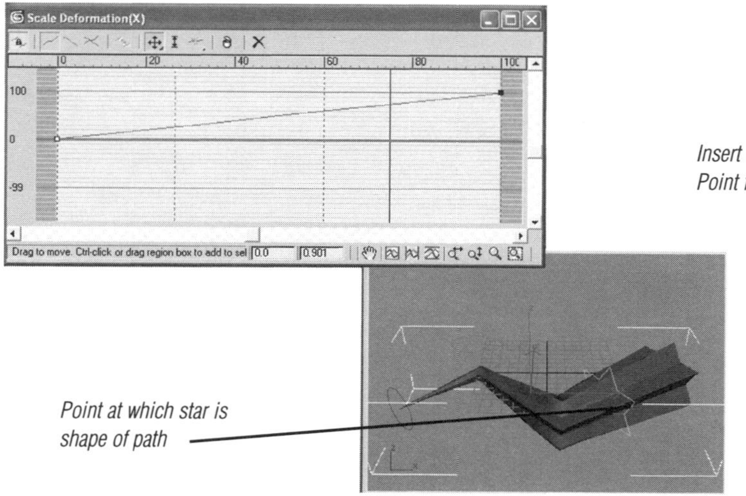

FIGURE 139
Deformation grid with new control points

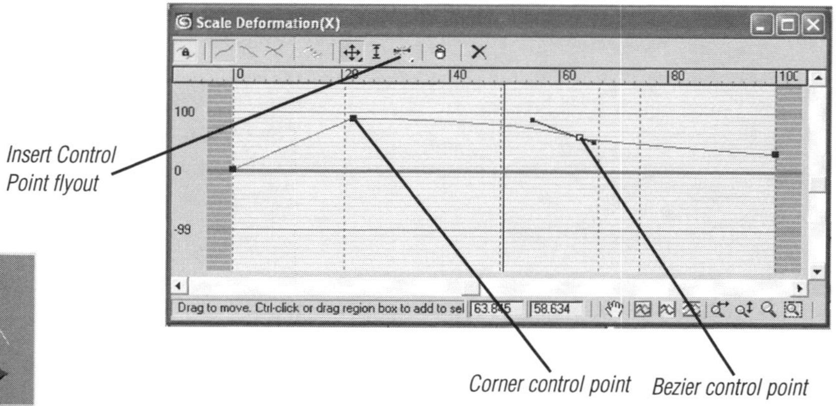

Lesson 11   Model with Splines

DISCREET 3D STUDIO MAX 3-117

Extrude splines

1. Click the **Shapes button** on the Create panel (if necessary), click the **Line button**, click on the left side of the Top viewport, move the **mouse** down and to the right, click, move the **mouse** up and to the right, click, move the **mouse** up and to the right again, click, move the **mouse** to the left so it is over the start vertex, click the **start vertex**, then click **Yes** to close the spline.

2. Click the **Donut button**, create a **donut** on the right side of the Top viewport, then convert the donut into an editable spline.

3. Click the **Modifier List list arrow** on the Modify panel, click **Extrude**, then change the number in the Amount box on the Parameters rollout to **20**.

   The donut is extruded 20 units, as shown in Figure 140. The Cap Start and Cap End check boxes are checked, so the extruded spline has a top and bottom surface.

   (continued)

FIGURE 140
Extruded donut spline

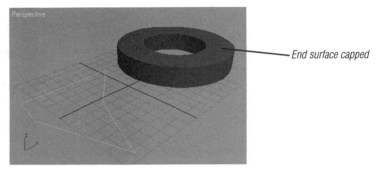

End surface capped

FIGURE 141
Extruded line spline

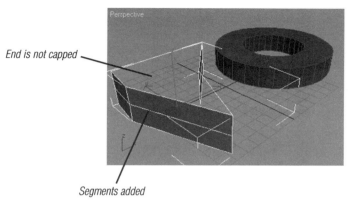

End is not capped

Segments added

FIGURE 142
Open line spline

Convert to smooth vertices

Line's start and end points are on vertical dark gridline

Intersection of dark gridlines

4. In the Perspective viewport, select the **line**, press **[F4]** to show edged faces in the viewport, apply the **Extrude modifier** to the line, change the Amount number to **30** in the Parameters rollout, change the Segments number to **2**, then click the **Cap End check box** to deselect it.

   The line is extruded, has two segments, and has no top surface, as shown in Figure 141.

5. Save the file as **Extrudespline**, then reset 3ds Max.

You created a closed line spline and a donut, converted both to editable splines, and extruded the donut with both a top and bottom surface. You also extruded the line without a top surface and increased its segment number.

Apply the Lathe modifier to a spline

1. Click in the **Top viewport**, click the **Pan view button**, then click and drag in the Top viewport until the intersection of the dark lines in its center is moved to the lower-left of the viewport.

2. Click the **Shapes button**, click the **Line button**, click the **intersection** of the dark lines, move the **mouse pointer** and click until you have created a line resembling that in Figure 142, then right-click to complete the line.

3. Click the **Modify tab**, click the **Vertex button**, then convert all of the vertices indicated in Figure 142 into smooth vertices.

(continued)

DISCREET 3D STUDIO MAX 3-119

4. Apply the **Lathe modifier** to the spline, click the **plus sign** next to Lathe in the modifier stack display, click the **Axis subobject**, click the **red arrow handle** on the Move gizmo in the Front viewport, then move the **handle** to the left until the axis lines up with the vertical dark line on the left side of the viewport.

   In the Front viewport, the line now looks like a wine glass. However, because the normals are facing inward, the object looks inside out in the Perspective viewport.

5. Pan and zoom as necessary in the Perspective viewport until you can see the entire lathed object in the viewport, then click the **Flip Normals check box** in the Lathe modifier's Parameters rollout to select it.

   The normals in the object flip and the object looks like a wine glass in the Perspective viewport, as shown in Figure 143.

6. Save the files as **Lathespline**, then reset 3ds Max.

You created a line spline, applied the Lathe modifier to the line spline, moved the axis of the Lathe modifier, and flipped the object's normals.

FIGURE 143
Lathed object with normals flipped

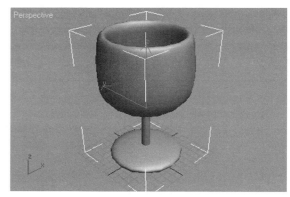

FIGURE 144
Two ellipse shapes and line path

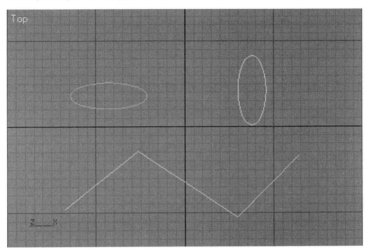

Create a loft object

1. Click the **Shapes button** on the Create panel, create **two ellipses** and a **line** in the Top viewport like those shown in Figure 144, then convert both ellipses into editable splines.

2. Select the **line**, click the **Create tab**, click the **Geometry button**, click the **list arrow** under the Geometry button, click **Compound Objects**, then click the **Loft button** to select it.

3. Click the **Copy option button** in the Creation Method rollout on the Create panel, click the **Get Shape button** to select it, then click the **ellipse** on the left of the Top viewport.

   The ellipse shape is extruded along the length of the path. The original ellipse remains visible in the Top and Perspective viewports because the loft object uses a copy of the ellipse, not the ellipse itself.

   (continued)

Lesson 11   Model with Splines

DISCREET 3D STUDIO MAX 3-121

4. Enter **60** in the Path box in the Path Parameters rollout on the Create panel.

   In the Top, Front, and Left viewports, a small yellow "X" is now visible at a point 60 percent along the distance of the path.

5. Click the **Get Shape button** again, then click the **ellipse** on the right of the Top viewport.

   The ellipse shape used at the start of the path evolves into the second ellipse shape as it gets to the 60 percent point on the path.

6. Click in the **Perspective viewport**, then pan, zoom, and/or arc rotate in the viewport as necessary until the entire loft object is visible in the viewport, as shown in Figure 145.

7. Save the file as **Loftdeform**.

You created two ellipses and a line, created a loft object with the line as a path and one ellipse as a shape, then added the second ellipse as a shape to the loft object at a point 60 percent down the path.

Deform a loft object

1. With the **loft object** selected in the Perspective viewport, click the **Modify tab**, click the **plus sign** next to Deformations to open the Deformations rollout, then click the **Scale button** on the Deformations rollout to select it.

   The Scale Deformation dialog box opens, showing the loft object at 100 percent of scale from the start to end of the path.

(continued)

FIGURE 145
Loft object with two shapes included

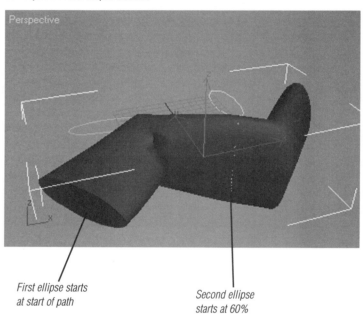

First ellipse starts at start of path

Second ellipse starts at 60%

3-122 AUTODESK 3D STUDIO MAX

Modeling

FIGURE 146
Deformed loft object

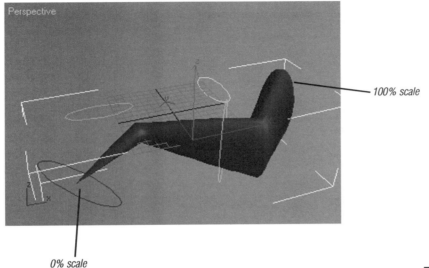

100% scale

0% scale

FIGURE 147
Inserted and moved control point

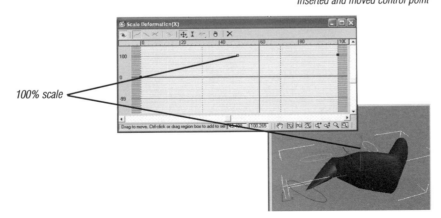

100% scale

2. Click and drag the **left control point** from 100 to 0.

   The shape at the start of the path is reduced to a point, increasing in scale along the length of the path; the shape at the end of the path is full-sized, as shown in Figure 146.

3. Click the **Insert Corner Point button** on the Scale Deformation toolbar, then click the **line** on the deformation grid at about the 50 percent point.

4. Click the **Move Control Point button** on the Scale Deformation toolbar, then click and drag the **control point** up to move it to 100.

   The loft object now reaches 100 percent scale at a point 50 percent along the path, as shown in Figure 147.

5. Save the file, then reset 3ds Max.

6. Close 3ds Max.

You deformed a loft object by changing its scale to 0 at the start of the path, added a control point to the object's deformation grid, then moved the control point to change the scale of the object to 100 percent at its halfway point.

CHAPTER SUMMARY

This chapter focused on modeling with objects as editable polygons (polys) and editable splines. You learned how to convert an object into an editable poly so that you could work with it more efficiently. You learned how to select the subobject levels of an editable poly, and to apply modifiers to those subobjects to affect just part of the object's appearance or behavior. You learned how to weld, slice, and cut objects while modeling. You also learned about normals, and how they work in 3ds Max. You learned how to model with a reference, so that a change to the original object results in a change to the reference. You also learned how to create, edit, and model with splines, essential tools for many of the tasks you perform as you work in a scene. What is most important, you learned how to use your knowledge thus far to create a character.

What You Have Learned

- How to convert an object into an editable poly
- How to select subobject levels
- How to apply modifiers to subobjects
- How to work with normals
- How to chamfer, extrude, and bevel an object to model it
- How to use Paint Deformation to push and pull the vertices of a surface
- How to weld two polygons, and how to slice and cut polygons
- How to apply and work with the MeshSmooth modifier
- How to model with a reference
- How to model a character
- How to work with and edit splines
- How to model with splines

Key Terms

Bevel   To extrude and angle a polygon border.

Border   A sequence of edges that border a hole in the object.

Chamfer   To cut off a corner or edge of an object.

Edge   A line that is the side of a polygon and that also connects two vertices.

Editable poly   An object broken down into polygons.

Element   In an editable poly, all of an object's polygons.

Extrude   To push out.

Polygon modeling   Converting an object into an editable poly and then working with it to create a model.

Spline   A line composed of at least two vertices connected by a straight or curved segment. Most splines contain many vertices and many segments.

Vertex   The corner of a polygon or the point at which several polygons meet.

Weld   To permanently combine two vertices into one vertex.

chapter 4
MATERIALS AND MAPS

1. Understand materials.
2. Apply materials.
3. Edit materials.
4. Understand and assign maps.
5. Navigate materials and maps.
6. Map basic shader components.
7. Map other Standard material components.

chapter 4 MATERIALS AND MAPS

In Chapters 1, 2, and 3, you learned how to create and work with primitives, splines, and editable polys and how to model to create diverse, interesting objects and complex scenes. However, you have not yet created scenes in which the objects respond to light in a real way; this conveys realistic depth, distance, texture, color, and shadow. This chapter covers the most essential tools for creating objects that look real—materials and maps.

Materials are what you apply to objects in to control how those objects appear in response to light. Maps are what you apply to a material to make its appearance even more intricate without having to model those intricacies. In this chapter, you'll explore what materials are, what shaders are and how they control the response of materials to light, and what the visual components of a material are. You'll learn how to use the Material Editor to adjust the parameters of material components and apply materials to objects in a scene. You'll then explore maps and how you can use them to further control the appearance of a material's components. You'll learn the best ways to move between maps and materials as you work on a scene, and you'll practice assigning maps to material components to produce different responses to the surrounding environment.

Tools You'll Use

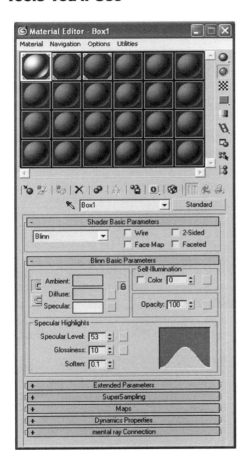
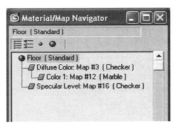
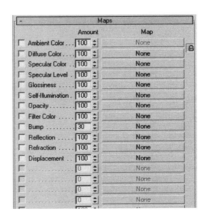

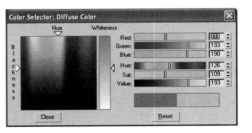

LESSON 1

UNDERSTAND MATERIALS

What You'll Do

▶ *In this lesson, you will gain an understanding of materials and shaders and how the different components of a material affect its appearance. You will also learn the basic steps used to apply a material.*

Understanding Materials

In Chapter 2, you learned how to change the display color of an object to distinguish the object from (or associate it with) other objects in a scene. The display color might help you keep track of objects as you create a scene, but it is not used to control the actual color and appearance of an object in a scene. To control the color of an object and its actual appearance in a scene—in other words, how the object responds to light—you apply a material to an object.

Materials are what make it possible for an object to look nearly photo-realistic. You can put lights, geometry, and an environment in a scene, but if you do not have materials assigned to anything, then you will have a hard time making things look the way they should.

Applying materials comes down to understanding a material's components and adjusting those components to get the surface appearance that looks the best. The first three material attributes you will look at are the ambient, diffuse, and specular colors. Consider a sphere that is the same color of grey all over, but in an environment containing a light source, as shown in the rendered scene in Figure 1. The color of the sphere where it is in shadow is its **ambient color**. The color of the sphere where it is reflecting the light source (that is, highlighted) is its **specular color**. The color of the sphere in general lighting, neither in shadow nor direct light, is its **diffuse color**. When you refer to the color of an object in general conversation, you are usually referring to its diffuse color.

Other components of a material enable you to further control its response to light. The **specular level** of an object refers to the strength or intensity of the highlights on the object; the object's **glossiness** (that is, shininess) determines the size of its highlights. The first sphere in Figure 2 has high specular level and glossiness. You can adjust the **self-illumination** of a material to make an object appear to glow from within by replacing its ambient color with diffuse color. The second sphere in Figure 2 is fully self-illuminated. And lastly, you can adjust the **opacity** of a material, which determines the amount of transparency of the material. A material can be **opaque**, with no light passing through it, **translucent**, with some light passing through it, or relatively **transparent** (like glass). The third sphere in Figure 2 is translucent.

FIGURE 1
Material color components

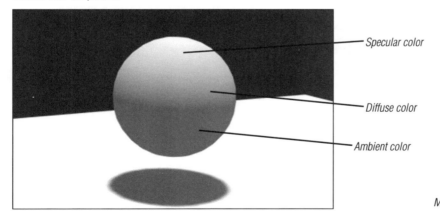

FIGURE 2
Shiny, illuminated, and translucent material

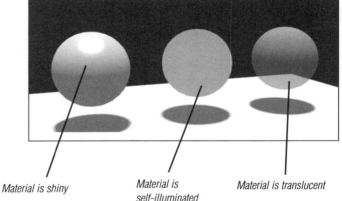

Lesson 1 Understand Materials

AUTODESK 3D STUDIO MAX 4-5

Understanding Material Types

There are several material types available in 3ds Max, but the default material, and the one most commonly used, is the Standard material. Standard material can be adjusted in a variety of ways and works well in several different situations, so this chapter will focus on it. An object with **Standard material** applied appears to have a single color applied to it, with standard reflective properties.

Although the focus is on Standard material, you might want to separately explore the other materials available, because some are particularly fun, interesting, or useful for specific tasks. Also, as your skills with 3ds Max advance, there will certainly be times that materials other than Standard material will be a better option for your needs, so it is good to be familiar with all of them. For example, you might want to use Raytrace material when creating a reflective object because it produces more accurate reflections and refractions than Standard material. For a completely different look from Standard material, you can apply the Ink 'n Paint material, which makes objects appear to be drawn like cartoons, as shown in Figure 3. Applying the Matte/Shadow material to an object creates an invisible surface onto which you can cast a shadow or behind which you can move objects, as shown in Figure 3. There are also

FIGURE 3
Ink 'n Paint and Matte/Shadow materials

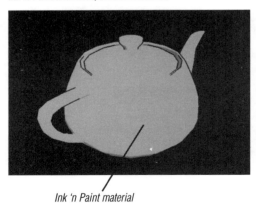

Ink 'n Paint material applied to teapot

Matte/Shadow applied to shape in front of background window

4-6 AUTODESK 3D STUDIO MAX

Materials and Maps

compound materials, such as Shellac and Multi/Sub-Object, which enable you to work with more than one material at a time on an object.

Understanding Shaders

The appearance of Standard material as you adjust its components depends on the shader that is associated with the material. A **shader** primarily controls how the highlights on an object look. As you adjust the settings for the Standard material's specularity, diffuse color, glossiness, and so on, the material's attributes change and the shader applied to the material determines the ultimate appearance of the object. There are several shaders that can be used with Standard material, but the most commonly used shader in 3ds Max is the Blinn shader. The Blinn shader is pretty versatile; it can be used on many different types of objects to generate a wide variety of textures. You can find the Blinn shader in many other 3D animation programs as well. This shader produces soft, round highlights, as shown in Figure 4. Examples of two other shaders are also shown in the figure: the **anisotropic shader**, whose highlights are elliptical, and the **metal shader**, whose highlights produce the appearance of a metallic surface.

FIGURE 4
Standard material with different shaders applied

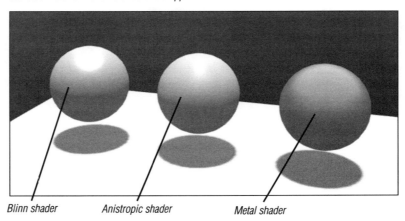

Blinn shader   Anistropic shader   Metal shader

Lesson 1 Understand Materials

AUTODESK 3D STUDIO MAX 4-7

Understanding Rendering

As you work with materials on objects in the viewports, you can see how objects actually appear in a scene by rendering the scene. In other words, rendering in 3ds Max is the equivalent of taking a picture with a digital camera in the real world. In reality, a camera absorbs the light from the environment and generates an image. Rendering is essentially the same process, except that you have to manually generate the content of the image in 3ds Max. When you render a viewport, that viewport is essentially the "digital camera." You can render single images, or you can render a sequence of images to create an animation.

This book will take an in-depth look at rendering in Chapter 7, because there are many render settings that you can adjust, but to quickly render a scene without adjusting the render settings, you can click the Quick Render (Production) tool on the main toolbar.

FIGURE 5
Rendered scene

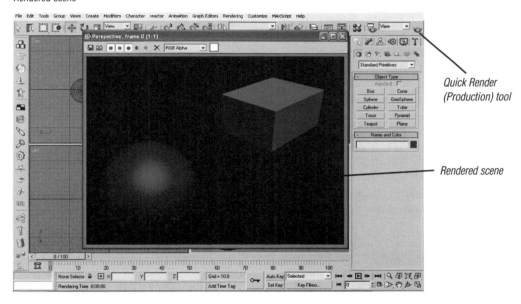

Quick Render (Production) tool

Rendered scene

Render a scene

1. Start 3ds Max, create a sphere on the left side of the Top viewport, then create a box to its right.
2. Click the **Perspective viewport**.
   When you render a scene, you render the selected viewport.
3. Place the mouse pointer all the way to the right on the main toolbar (if necessary) until it becomes a small hand, then click and drag the **toolbar** to the left until the Quick Render (Production) tool on the main toolbar appears on the far right.
4. Click the **Quick Render (Production) tool** on the main toolbar.
   The scene is rendered in a new window, as shown in Figure 5.
5. Click the rendered scene window **Close button**, then save the file as **Materials**.

You created two objects, then rendered the scene containing the two objects.

Lesson 1 Understand Materials

AUTODESK 3D STUDIO MAX 4-9

LESSON 2

APPLY MATERIALS

What You'll Do

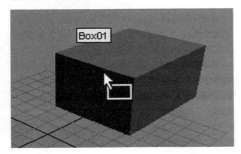

▶ In this lesson, you will learn how to open the Material Editor, how to view and edit materials in sample slots, and how to apply materials to objects in a scene.

Using the Material Editor

The Material Editor is to materials as a paint palette is to paint: it provides you with a place to build materials, modify them, and then apply them to objects in a scene. If you apply a material to an object and then modify the material in the Material Editor, the material is updated with your changes on all of the objects to which it is applied. You can save materials from the Material Editor in a library for use with other objects and scenes at a later time. You can also import materials into the Material Editor from an existing materials library, either your own or a third party's. To open the Material Editor, click the Material Editor tool on the main toolbar, press [M], or click Rendering on the menu bar, and then click Material Editor.

Viewing Materials in Sample Slots

As you work with materials, the Material Editor displays each material inside a sample slot, as shown in Figure 6. **Sample slots** are squares in the top of the Material Editor, each of which shows a material as it would appear when applied to a sample object (by default, a sphere), with sample lighting. The shape of the sample object and the lighting you see on it have no relation at all to the objects to which the material is applied in the scene; it simply provides an example of what the material would look like on an object. For instance, if you apply a material shown on a sphere in a sample slot to a teapot in your scene, the teapot will not change into a sphere, nor will it be lit the same way you see in the sample slot—it will just have the material shown in the sample slot applied to it.

Also by default, when the Material Editor is first opened, 3ds Max displays six sample slots out of the 24 available. If you leave this setup as is, you access the remaining 18 slots using the scroll bars below and to the right of the sample slots. However, we recommend that you change the Material Editor options to make all 24 sample slots available at once.

You can change the number of slots that are visible by right-clicking a selected slot to open the right-click menu, and then clicking 5 × 3 Sample Windows to show 15 windows, or 6 × 4 Sample Windows to show all 24 sample slots. Although showing all 24 sample slots means each is rather small, you can double-click a sample slot to open a sample slot in its own resizable window, as shown in Figure 7. This window is easier to work with than the slots in the 3 × 2 Sample Windows configuration.

Applying Material to a Sample Slot

To select a sample slot in which to work, click it. When a sample slot is selected ("active"), a thick white line appears around its border. Information about the material applied to the selected sample slot appears below the sample slot display. By default, when the Material Editor is first opened, the sample object shown in each slot is a sphere, and the Standard material is applied to each slot. To change the shape used in a sample slot

FIGURE 6
Material Editor

FIGURE 7
Single sample slot window

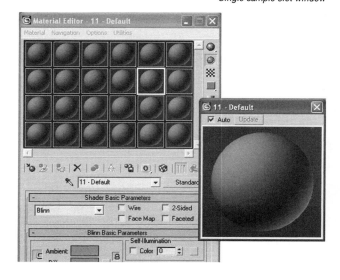

Lesson 2 Apply Materials

AUTODESK 3D STUDIO MAX 4-11

(to a shape that might be more like an object or objects in your scene), click the Sample Type button at the top of the column of buttons to the right to open the Sample Type flyout. Click either the sphere, cylinder, or box button to change the sample slot to that shape.

Below the sample slots is a set of buttons, and below the buttons are the material Name field and the material Type button, as shown earlier in Figure 6. The material Name field contains the name of the material in the currently selected sample slot (for example, "01 – Default"). Every material must have a unique name, different from the other materials used in a scene. To change the name of the material, select the text in the material Name field and then type the new name in the field. To stay organized, it can be a good idea to name materials by the objects to which they are applied. This makes it both easier to find in the Material Editor and easier to understand immediately where it is applied when you see it listed somewhere.

Next to the material Name field, the material Type button shows the name of the material applied to the selected sample slot, which by default is Standard. To change the material used in the active sample slot, click the material Type button to open the Material/Map Browser, as shown in Figure 8, and then double-click a material in the list. The Material/Map Browser closes, the material Type button has the name of the newly selected material on it, and the new material is shown in the sample slot, replacing any previously applied material.

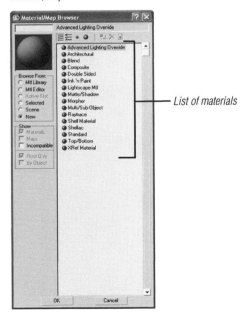

FIGURE 8
Material/Map Browser

List of materials

4-12 AUTODESK 3D STUDIO MAX

Materials and Maps

You can also apply a new material to a sample slot by clicking the Get Material button on the far left of the row of buttons under the sample slot display. Clicking this button also opens the Material/Map Browser; however, when opened this way, the Material/Map Browser also lists maps (materials have blue circles next to them, and maps have green parallelograms next to them). To apply a material to a sample slot, you can click and drag the material from the browser to the sample slot, or to the material Type button, and the material is applied to the active sample slot (replacing any previously applied material).

QUICKTIP

Be careful to pick only from the list of materials and not from the list of maps if you are changing the material in a sample slot.

Below the material Name field and material Type field in the Material Editor are a series of rollouts that change depending upon the material and shader applied to the selected sample slot. Later in this chapter, you will use these rollouts to edit the material in sample slots.

Applying Material to an Object

There are two different options you can use to apply a material to an object in a scene. In the Material Editor, click the sample slot showing the material you want to apply, drag the slot until it is over the object in the viewport (a tooltip with the object's name in it appears as the pointer passes over each object), and then release the mouse button. The material is applied to the object whether the object is selected or not.

QUICKTIP

If there is already a material applied to the object, the newly applied material replaces the previous material.

An alternative method is to make sure the object (or objects) to which you want to apply the material is selected, select the appropriate sample slot to make it active, and then click the Assign Material to Selection button below the sample slot display, as shown in Figure 6. The material is applied to all selected objects.

If you have multiple objects in a scene selected, and you drag a material over one of the objects in the selection, a dialog box opens with two available options: Assign to Object or Assign to Selection. Click the Assign to Object option button to assign the

Lesson 2 Apply Materials

material to only the object to which you dragged the material, or click the Assign to Selection option button to assign the material to all objects in the selection, and then click OK.

When the material in a sample slot is applied to an object or objects in a scene, that material becomes "hot." A **hot material** is in use in the scene, and any changes made to it in the sample slot are reflected in the objects in the scene to which it is applied. When a material is hot and is used on the currently selected object, solid white triangles appear in the sample slot's corners, as shown in Figure 9. When a material is used in a scene but not in the currently selected object, hollow white triangles appear in the slot's corners. When a material in the Material Editor is not used in the scene, no triangles appear in its corners—this is known as a "cool" material.

QUICKTIP

If you double-click a sample slot to open a single sample slot window, the new window does not show whether a material is hot or cool.

When a material is applied to an object, you see the material applied in the Perspective viewport but not the orthographic (Top, Left, or Bottom) viewports, where the object appears in a wireframe. This is where the display color of an object comes in handy (rather than its diffuse color), because the wireframes are shown in the assigned display color. Note, however, that some aspects of a material are not visible in any viewport, and can only be seen once a scene is rendered.

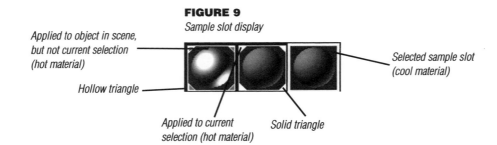

FIGURE 9
Sample slot display

Applied to object in scene, but not current selection (hot material)

Hollow triangle

Applied to current selection (hot material)

Solid triangle

Selected sample slot (cool material)

FIGURE 10
Material Editor with 24 sample slots displayed

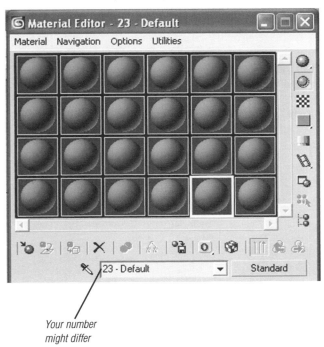

Your number might differ

View materials in sample slots

1. Open **Materials** (if necessary), click **Rendering** on the menu bar, then click **Material Editor**.

   The Material Editor opens, showing six shots in the sample slot display.

   TIP If you have previously changed the sample slot display, the number of slots displayed might differ.

2. Click the **scroll box** to the right of the sample slot display, drag it down as far as it can go, click the **scroll box** under the sample slot display, then drag it to the right as far as it can go.

   As you scroll, you can view each of the 18 sample slots not visible when the Material Editor opened.

   TIP If you already have all 24 slots displayed, no scroll bars are available.

3. Click a **sample slot** to select it, right-click the **sample slot** to open a right-click menu, then click **6 × 4 Sample Windows** on the right-click menu.

   All 24 sample slots are now visible in the sample slot display, as shown in Figure 10.

4. Double-click a **sample slot** to open it in a separate single sample slot window.

5. Click the **Close button** on the single sample slot window.

You opened the Material Editor, scrolled through the available sample slots, changed the number of slots in the sample slot display, then viewed a sample slot in a single window.

Apply material to sample slots

1. Click the **sample slot** in the upper-left corner of the sample slot display to make it active.

2. Click and hold the **Sample Type button**, to the right of the sample slot display to open the Sample Type flyout, as shown in Figure 11, then click the **Box button**.

   The shape in the sample slot changes from a sphere to a box.

3. Select the **text** in the material Name field, type **Box**, then press **[Enter]**.

4. Click the **sample slot** to the right of the active sample slot, select the **text** in the material Name field, type **Sphere**, then press **[Enter]**.

   The materials in the first and second sample slots are now named for the objects to which they will be applied.

5. With the Sphere material sample slot still selected, click the **material Type button** (it should say Standard) to open the Material/Map Browser, then double-click the **Ink 'n Paint material** in the Material/Map Browser.

   The Material/Map Browser closes and the sample sphere now appears light blue, with no shadow. The rollouts underneath the Name field and Type button change to those appropriate for the Ink 'n Paint material.

(continued)

FIGURE 11
Sample Type flyout

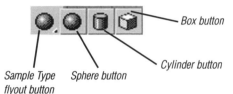

FIGURE 12
Material Editor and Material/Map Browser

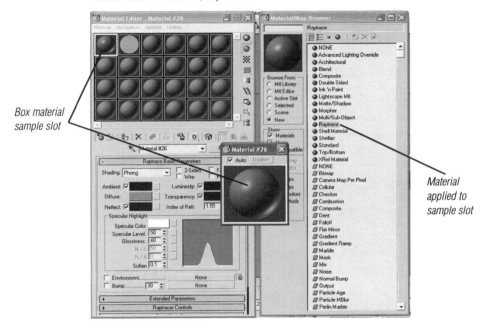

Box material sample slot

Material applied to sample slot

6. Double-click the **Box material sample slot** to open it in a single window, click the **Get Material button** under the sample slot display, then double-click **Raytrace** in the Material/Map Browser.

   The Material Editor and Material/Map Browser now look as shown in Figure 12. Notice that applying a new material returns the sample shape to a sphere.

   TIP When it is opened with the Get Material button, the Material/Map Browser does not automatically close after a material is chosen.

7. Double-click **Standard** in the Material/Map Browser to return the Box material sample slot to Standard material, click the **Close button** on the single sample slot window, then click the **Close button** on the Material/Map Browser.

You selected a sample slot, changed its sample shape, and named the material in two sample slots. You also changed the material in each sample slot using two different methods, then changed the material in one sample slot back to standard material.

Lesson 2 Apply Materials

AUTODESK 3D STUDIO MAX 4-17

Apply material to objects in a scene

1. Make sure that the **Box material sample slot** is selected, click and drag the **sample slot** until the mouse pointer is over the box in the Perspective viewport and a Box01 tooltip appears, as shown in Figure 13, then release the mouse button.

   The box turns gray, the color of the default Standard material.

2. Click the **sphere** in the Perspective viewport to select it, click the **Sphere material** in the sample slot display, then click the **Assign Material to Selection button** under the sample slot display.

   The sphere turns the color of the default Ink 'n Paint material. Your screen should look similar to Figure 14. Notice that only the Perspective viewport shows the objects with the material applied. In addition, there are hollow triangles in the corner of the Box material sample slot (in use in the scene, but not in the selected object) and solid triangles in the corners of the Sphere material sample slot (in use in the selected object).

   (continued)

FIGURE 13
Applying material by dragging and dropping

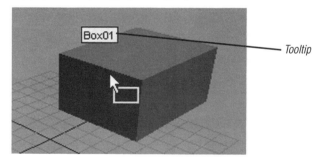

4-18 AUTODESK 3D STUDIO MAX

FIGURE 14
Scene with two materials applied to two objects

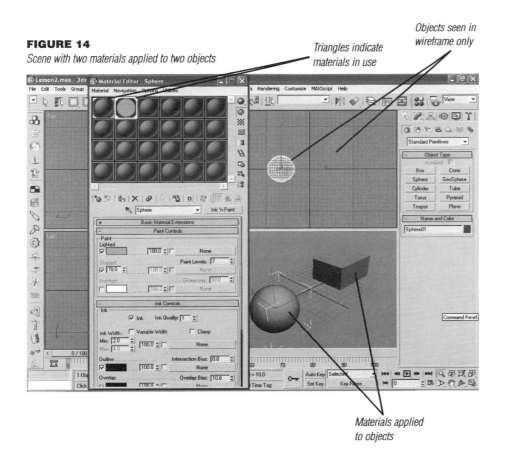

3. Click the **Quick Render (Production) tool** on the main toolbar to render the scene.
4. Click the **Close button** on the rendered scene window.
5. With the Sphere material still selected in the Material Editor, click the **material Type button**, then double-click **Standard** in the Material/Map Browser.

   The Sphere material becomes Standard material in the sample slot and on the sphere to which it is applied.
6. Save the file, then reset 3ds Max.

You applied two materials from the Material Editor to objects in a scene using drag and drop and the Assign Material to Selection button, then rendered the scene. Next, you changed the Sphere material back into Standard material, altering the object in the scene to which the Sphere material was applied.

LESSON 3

EDIT MATERIALS

What You'll Do

In this lesson, you will explore how to modify the parameters of a material to control its appearance. Specifically, you will learn how to edit the shader parameters and the material's colors, specularity, self-illumination, and opacity.

Editing Basic Shader Parameters

Below the material Name field and material Type button in the Material Editor are a series of rollouts; which rollouts appear depends on the material and shader selected. When the Material Editor is opened, by default the Blinn shader is applied to the standard material in each sample slot. With a default sample slot selected, the Shader Basic Parameters rollout appears under the material Name field and Type button, and the Blinn Basic Parameters rollout appears underneath it, as shown in Figure 15. To change the shader to one other than Blinn, click the Shading list arrow in the Shader Basic Parameters rollout, and then click the name of the shader you want to apply. The rollout underneath the Shader Basic Parameters rollout changes to reflect the parameters for the shader you have chosen.

FIGURE 15
Default shader parameters rollouts

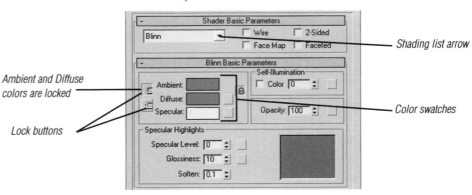

Next to the Shading drop-down list in the Shader Basic Parameters rollout are four check boxes that enable you to further affect the appearance of the material. Click the Wire check box to apply the material to the object as a wireframe object, as opposed to one with continuous surfaces, as shown on the left in Figure 16. Click the 2-Sided check box to apply the material to both sides of the faces in the object. For instance, if an object has been sliced in half, exposing the interior of the object, usually you would not be able to see the interior because only one side of a face is shown in 3ds Max. With a 2-sided material applied to the object, the material is visible on each side of the surfaces to which it is applied. Click the Faceted check box to be able to see the polygons in the geometry of the objects to which the material is applied, as shown on the right in Figure 16. You use the Face Map check box when you are working with a material that has a map or maps attached to it. When the Face Map check box is selected, the maps are applied to the face of each polygon in the objects to which the material is applied. (Maps are covered later in this chapter.)

Editing Material Color

With the Blinn shader selected, the Blinn Basic Parameters rollout enables you to adjust the components of the Standard material that were discussed in Lesson 1: ambient, diffuse, and specular color; specular highlight data; self-illumination; and opacity.

FIGURE 16
Basic shader parameters applied

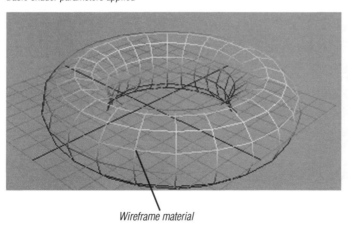
Wireframe material

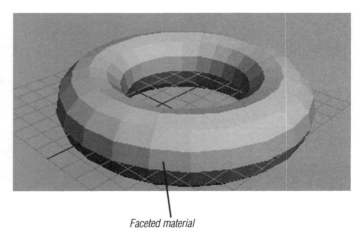
Faceted material

Lesson 3 Edit Materials

AUTODESK 3D STUDIO MAX 4-21

To change the ambient, diffuse, or specular color, in the upper-left section of the rollout, click the color swatch next to the name of the color component that you want to change. The Color Selector dialog box opens, as shown in Figure 17. In this dialog box, you can define the color to be used in three different ways. The Hue/Blackness/Whiteness (HBW) model is shown on the left side of the dialog box. Click in the boxes to adjust the color or click and move the sliders alongside the boxes to adjust the color. As you change the color in the HBW model, the color values in the Red/Green/Blue (RGB) model and the Hue/Saturation/Value (HSV) model adjust accordingly. Similarly, you can type new values or move the sliders in either the RGB or HSV models to select a color, and the other models will change at the same time. The color you select will appear in the right half of the rectangle in the lower-right of the dialog box; the original color will appear in the rectangle's left half. It will also show in the color swatch next to the component in the Material Editor, in the selected sample slot, and on any objects to which the material is applied in the scene. If you want to return the component to its original color, click the Reset button. Click the Close button to close the Color Selector dialog box.

You can lock two color components together so that changing the color of one component changes the color of the other as well.

It is typically a good idea to lock the Ambient and Diffuse colors, because they are usually based on the same color. When a color is in shadow, it is the same color, just a darker version. For example, it wouldn't usually make sense for a material with a yellow diffuse color to be blue where the material is in shadow. In fact, Ambient and Diffuse colors are locked by default. However, you do not usually want to lock diffuse color and specular color together, because a specular highlight that is a version of the diffuse color implies that the light source is the same color as the object. (A blue highlight on a blue sphere makes it seem like the sphere is being lit by a blue light; a white highlight implies

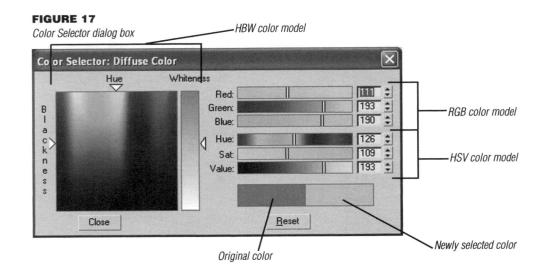

FIGURE 17
Color Selector dialog box

a white light.) To lock two color components, click the lock button to the left and between the two components to select it. The higher color changes to the lower color—for instance, the Ambient color changes to the selected Diffuse color when the two are locked. To unlock two components, click the lock button to deselect it.

Editing the Specular Level of a Material

Below the color components in the Blinn Basic Parameters rollout, you'll find the Specular Highlights group, where you can adjust the strength and size of the highlights on a material. The number in the Specular Level box indicates the intensity of the specular highlight on the material. As the specular level in a material increases, the specular highlight becomes brighter, and the material appears to shine. The number in the Glossiness box indicates the size of the highlight, which further affects how sharp the shininess of the object is. A shiny object reflects light more directly than an object that is less shiny, resulting in a smaller, sharper highlight. To adjust the glossiness of a material, increase the number in the Glossiness box to increase shininess, or decrease the number to decrease shininess. To the right of the Specular Level and Glossiness boxes is the highlight graph, which shows the intensity of the highlight by its height, and the size of the highlight by its width, as shown in Figure 18. The sample sphere also shows the changes to specular level and glossiness of the material as you adjust these parameters.

By default, the sample sphere is lit from both the front and the back in the sample slot to demonstrate how the applied material looks when lit from different directions. To turn off the backlighting, click the Backlight button.

QUICKTIP

Remember that specular highlight information only determines how a material responds to light; it does not actually add light to a scene.

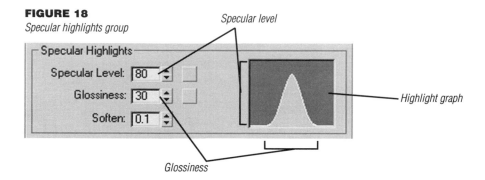

FIGURE 18
Specular highlights group

Lesson 3 Edit Materials

AUTODESK 3D STUDIO MAX 4-23

Editing the Self-Illumination and Opacity of a Material

You can adjust the self-illumination of Standard material and its opacity above the highlight graph to the right of the Specular Highlights group in the Blinn Basic Parameters rollout. A self-illuminated material appears to be lit from within because its ambient color is replaced by its diffuse color, reducing shadow on the material (or eliminating it entirely). There are two ways to adjust self-illumination on material. You can click the Color check box in the Self-Illumination area, and then click the color swatch that appears to the right of the check box to open the Color Selector and choose a self-illumination color. The greater the number in the Value box in the HSV color model in the Color Selector, the greater the material's self-illumination. You can also choose not to click the color box and can instead adjust the number in the Self-Illumination spinner box. The diffuse color is used as the self-illumination color. When the spinner is at 0, there is no self-illumination, and when it is at 100, the diffuse color completely replaces the ambient color in the material, as shown in the self-illuminated torus rendered in Figure 19.

> **QUICK**TIP
>
> When an object is self-illuminated, it appears to glow but does not actually give off light. In Chapter 5, "Cameras and Lighting," you'll learn more about incorporating light into scenes.

As discussed earlier, the opacity of a material refers to the degree to which light can or can't pass through the object. Below the Self-Illumination controls you can adjust the opacity of a material by adjusting the number in the Opacity spinner box. At 100, the material is opaque and no light can pass through it; at 0, the material is completely transparent, except for specular highlights. Sometimes it can be difficult to understand exactly how transparent your material is, because the sphere in the sample slot showing the material is against a black background by default. To address this, click the Background button to the right of the sample slot display, the third button from the top. This adds a sample multicolored background behind the sample shape and more clearly shows how light passes through your material, as shown in Figure 20.

FIGURE 19
Self-illuminated torus

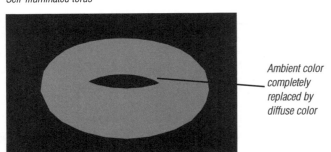

Ambient color completely replaced by diffuse color

FIGURE 20
Translucent material

Background button selected

Background shows translucence of material

4-24 AUTODESK 3D STUDIO MAX

FIGURE 21
Wireframe, 2-sided material applied to teapot

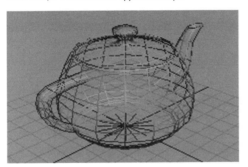

Edit basic shader parameters

1. In the Top viewport, create a **teapot** with a radius of **35**, then click in the **Perspective viewport**.

2. Place the mouse pointer on the far right of the main toolbar until it becomes a hand, click and drag the **toolbar** to the left until you can see the Quick Render (Production) button, then click the **Material Editor tool** on the main toolbar to open the Material Editor.

3. Click and drag the **upper-left sample slot** until the pointer is over the teapot, then release the mouse button.

   The default sample slot material, Standard material with Blinn shader, is applied to the teapot.

4. In the Shader Basic Parameters rollout, click the **Shading list arrow**, then click **Anisotropic**.

   The rollout underneath the Shader Basic Parameters rollout changes to the Anisotropic Basic Parameters rollout. Notice the highlight graph in this shader's parameters is different from the Blinn highlight graph.

5. Click the **Shading list arrow** again, click **Blinn**, click the **Wire check box** to select it, then click the **2-Sided check box** to select it.

   In the Perspective viewport, the material of the teapot now appears in wireframe, and you can see the wireframe of the back of the teapot because the material is 2-sided, as shown in Figure 21.

   (continued)

AUTODESK 3D STUDIO MAX 4-25

6. Click the **Wire check box** and the **2-Sided check box** to deselect each, then click the **Faceted check box** to select it.

   The material on the teapot now shows the angled edges between the teapot's polygons, as shown in Figure 22.

7. Click the **Faceted check box** again to deselect it.

You created a teapot and applied the default material to it, then changed the shader of the teapot's material from Blinn to Anisotropic and back again. You also modified the shader's parameters so that the material was applied in 2-sided wireframe, changed the parameters again so that the material was faceted, then returned to the shader's default parameters.

Edit material color

1. Click the **color swatch** to the right of Diffuse in the Blinn Basic Parameters rollout to open the Color Selector dialog box, click in the center of the **HBW model Hue/Blackness box**, then slide the **HBW Whiteness slider** until it is approximately halfway between the top and bottom.

   The diffuse and ambient colors of the material, which are locked together, change to the selected color.

2. Click the **Lock button** to the left of Ambient and Diffuse to deselect it, click the **Ambient color swatch** In the HSV model in the Color Selector dialog box, type **0** in the Hue box, **0** in the Sat box, and **0** in the Value box, then press **[Enter]**.

   (continued)

FIGURE 22
Faceted material applied to teapot

4-26 AUTODESK 3D STUDIO MAX

Materials and Maps

FIGURE 23
Ambient color in Color Selector and Material Editor

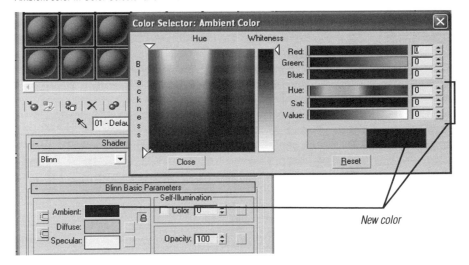

FIGURE 24
Shiny sample sphere and teapot

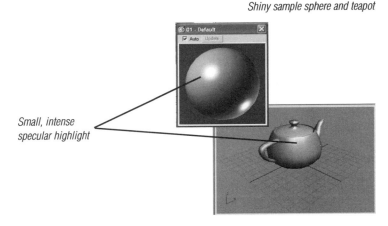

The material's ambient color changes to black, but the diffuse color of the material remains the same as the color chosen in Step 1, as shown in Figure 23. This difference in color is not noticeable in the viewport or when rendered because the scene has no light source at this time.

3. Click the **Close button** in the Color Selector dialog box, click the **Lock button** to the left of Ambient and Diffuse to select it again, then click **Yes** in the Lock Colors dialog box that appears.

The Ambient color swatch changes from black back to the same color as the Diffuse color swatch.

You changed the ambient and diffuse colors of a material using the HBW model, unlocked the colors from each other, chose a new ambient color using the HSV model, then relocked the ambient and diffuse colors so that they would be the same.

Edit specular level and glossiness of a material

1. Double-click the **selected sample slot** to open it in its own window.

2. In the Specular Highlights group in the Blinn Basic Parameters rollout, adjust the number in the Specular Level box to **100** and the Glossiness number to **40**.

As the numbers are adjusted, the curve in the highlight graph gets taller and thinner. The sample sphere and the teapot take on a shiny appearance, as shown in Figure 24.

(continued)

AUTODESK 3D STUDIO MAX 4-27

3. Use the spinner to adjust the Glossiness number down to **10**.

   The highlight graph stays the same height but gets wider; simultaneously, the highlights on the sample sphere and teapot grow bigger.

4. Use the spinner to adjust the Specular Level number down to **50**.

   The height of the highlight graph is reduced, as is the intensity of the specular highlight on the sample sphere and teapot, as shown in Figure 25.

You increased the Specular Level and Glossiness of a material to make it shinier, reduced the Glossiness, then reduced the Specular Level. You saw the effects of these changes on the material and on the highlight graph in the Blinn Basic Parameters rollout.

Edit self-illumination and opacity

1. In the Top viewport, create a box so that it appears behind the teapot when viewed in the Perspective viewport.

   | TIP You might need to move the Material Editor to view the Top viewport.

2. Click in the **Perspective viewport**, then in the Blinn Basic Parameters rollout, adjust the number in the Self-Illumination box to **100**.

   In the sample sphere and on the teapot, the material's ambient color is replaced by the diffuse color so that it is totally self-illuminated. The only colors visible on the material are the diffuse color and the specular color.

   (continued)

FIGURE 25
Sample sphere and teapot with less shininess

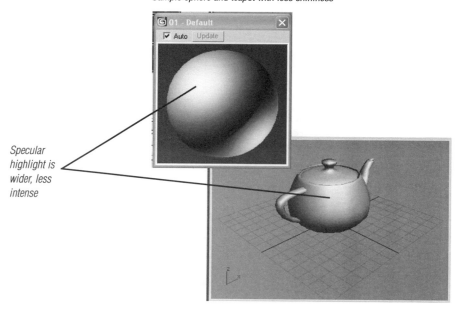

Specular highlight is wider, less intense

4-28 AUTODESK 3D STUDIO MAX

Materials and Maps

FIGURE 26
Teapot and box in rendered scene

Teapot's interior contours visible

3. Reduce the number in the Opacity box to **50**.

   The teapot becomes translucent, and you can see the box through the teapot in the Perspective viewport.

4. Click the **Quick Render (Production) tool** on the main toolbar to render the scene, then click the **title bar** on the Material Editor.

5. In the Shader Basic Parameters rollout, click the **2-Sided check box** to select it, then click the **Quick Render (Production) tool** again.

   When you render the scene again, you can see the interior contours of the teapot because the material is 2-sided, as shown in Figure 26. This increases the realism of the teapot in the scene.

6. Close the rendered scene window, close the single sample slot window, close the Material Editor, save the file as **ShinyMaterial**, then reset 3ds Max.

You changed the self-illumination and opacity of an object to see the effect in a rendered scene. You also displayed both sides of a two-sided material to add realism.

LESSON 4

UNDERSTAND AND
ASSIGN MAPS

What You'll Do

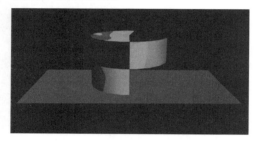

▶ *In this lesson, you will examine what maps are and how to assign maps to Standard material components. You will also learn how to deactivate and remove maps from components, and copy or swap maps between components.*

Understanding Maps

With materials, you can add realism to objects in a scene by controlling how they respond to light. Maps enable you to make objects and scenes even more realistic. A **map** is an image that is applied to a material. Maps can make material have a particular pattern, arrangement of colors, and/or appearance of texture, and maps can make a material show a photographic image or even a movie. In addition, they can literally "map" how different parts of a material are going to respond to light.

Maps are an extremely important part of designing 3D graphics for video games. Because video games have to limit the amount of an object's geometry to make a game play more smoothly, the appearance of detail in objects can be greatly enhanced with maps.

It is essential to remember that a map is not applied to an object; rather, a map is applied to material, and the material is applied to the object. Even more specifically, maps are applied to components of a material, and not just the overall material itself. The sphere on the left in Figure 27, for example, has a Checker map applied to its material's diffuse color component. Thus the sphere is black and white checkered in appearance instead of reflecting a diffuse color chosen from the Color Selector or the Standard material's default color. The sphere on the right in Figure 27 also has a Checker map applied to its material, but in this case the map is applied only to the material's opacity component, which uses a map's color *values* rather than its colors to determine the map's effect. Where the map color value is white, the material is fully opaque and its diffuse color is the Standard material's default diffuse color; where the map color value is black, the material is transparent.

3ds Max contains several maps that are produced by a mathematical algorithm; these are called **procedural maps**. Procedural maps generate a certain look or pattern on material, such as Checker or Marble, and have adjustable controls inside 3ds Max. Maps that are static images (rather than calculated) are known as **bitmaps**, even though .bmp is only one of many file formats you can use as a bitmap (other examples are .jpg, .psd, .tif, and even .avi or .mpg for animated material). You can obtain a bitmap from outside the software, or use one provided in 3ds Max.

QUICKTIP

To assign a bitmap from outside 3ds Max, double-click the Bitmap map in the Material/Map Browser to open the Select Bitmap Image File dialog box, browse to the location of the file you want to use as the map, select the file, and then click the Open button. The Select Bitmap Image File dialog box will close and the bitmap will be applied to the selected material.

Assigning Maps to Material Components

Because the focus is on Standard material in this book, our discussion of maps concentrates on those that can be assigned to Standard material components. There are two ways to apply a map to a Standard material component. The first option is the Maps rollout in the Material Editor, below the Blinn Basic Shader Parameters, Extended Parameters, and SuperSampling rollouts. Click the plus sign next to the rollout title to open the rollout if it is closed. The Maps rollout contains all of the visual components of Standard material that can have maps assigned to them, as shown in Figure 28. This includes the color, specularity, and opacity components, but you can also assign maps for reflection and refraction, bumpiness, filter color, and displacement.

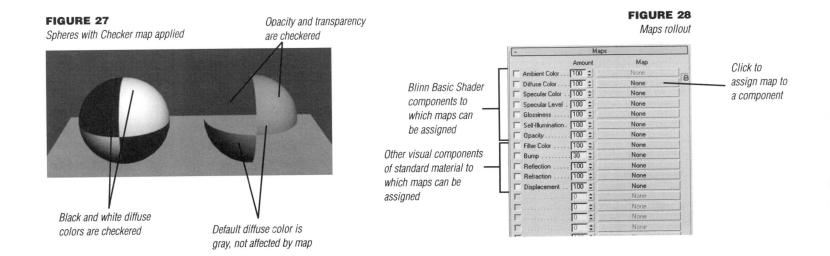

FIGURE 27
Spheres with Checker map applied

Opacity and transparency are checkered

Black and white diffuse colors are checkered

Default diffuse color is gray, not affected by map

FIGURE 28
Maps rollout

Blinn Basic Shader components to which maps can be assigned

Other visual components of standard material to which maps can be assigned

Click to assign map to a component

Lesson 4 Understand and Assign Maps

AUTODESK 3D STUDIO MAX 4-31

To assign a map to one of these components, click the wide map button to the right of the component's Amount spinner box in the Maps rollout. The **Material/Map Browser** opens, showing all of the maps available for assignment, as shown in Figure 29 (each has a green icon to its left). To assign a map to the component, double-click the name of the map, or click the map name once, and then click the OK button.

The Amount spinner box in the Maps rollout enables you to adjust the intensity with which the map is applied. When the amount is 100, the map is applied at full intensity—meaning that its effect covers the entire material, and the colors or effects applied to the material without mapping are not visible. For example, the maps applied to the materials on the spheres on the left in Figure 30 are applied at 50 percent intensity, whereas the maps applied to the materials on the spheres on the right are at 100 percent intensity. In the case of diffuse color as well as of opacity, a setting less than 100 makes the component settings of the unmapped material "show through". The selected diffuse color appears in the material where the map is white, and the opacity of the material is increased because it blends with the material's unmapped opacity.

QUICKTIP

Remember that adjusting the colors or color values in a map is what enables you to best control the appearance of a material's components; changing the Amount for a component's map only changes the strength at which the map is applied to the whole material.

The second option for assigning a map is only available for those components that are adjustable in the Blinn Basic Parameters rollout. In this rollout, to the right of each

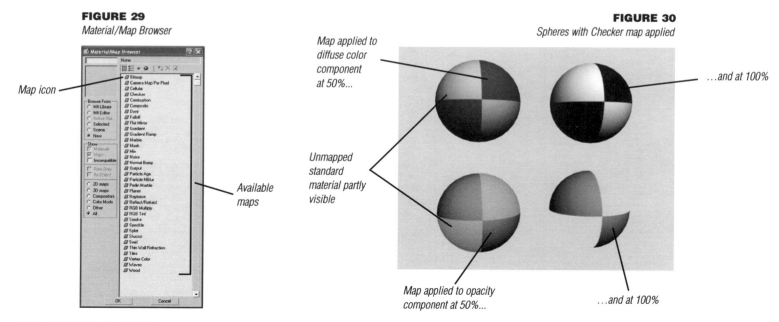

FIGURE 29
Material/Map Browser

Map icon

Available maps

FIGURE 30
Spheres with Checker map applied

Map applied to diffuse color component at 50%...

...and at 100%

Unmapped standard material partly visible

Map applied to opacity component at 50%...

...and at 100%

4-32 AUTODESK 3D STUDIO MAX

Materials and Maps

color swatch for the Ambient, Diffuse, and Specular color components, and to the right of each spinner box for the Specular Highlights, Self-Illumination, and Opacity components, you'll see a small gray square button. To assign a map to one of these components, click this square button. (Note that if the Ambient and Diffuse color components are locked, as they are by default, no gray square appears next to the Ambient color swatch.) When you click one of the gray squares, the Material/Map Browser opens, and you can double-click a map or click a map and then click OK. The Material/Map Browser closes, the map is applied to the sample slot, and the area underneath the sample slot display shows the information about the map, including its parameters, as shown in Figure 31. When you next return to the Blinn Basic Parameters rollout, the gray square next to the component to which you assigned the map will have an "M" on it.

QUICKTIP

The Self-Illumination and Opacity spinners in the Blinn Basic Parameters rollout control the self-illumination and opacity of unmapped Standard material. To adjust the intensity with which an Opacity or Self-illumination map is applied, change the Amount number for the map on the Maps rollout.

When a map is assigned to a material, and the material is in use in an object in a scene, the map won't be shown in the Perspective viewport. Showing a map in the viewport decreases performance, which is why 3ds Max doesn't do this automatically. However, you can show the map in the viewport by clicking the Show Map in Viewport button, the button fourth from the right under the sample slot display. If the map can be shown in viewports (not all maps can), it is. To see a map in full effect, however, the best approach is to render the scene.

FIGURE 31
Material Editor

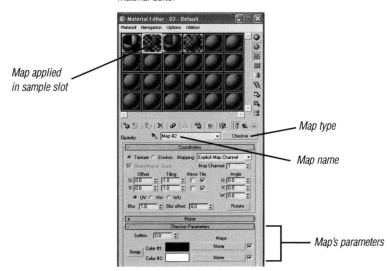

Lesson 4   Understand and Assign Maps

Deactivating or Removing a Map

To deactivate a map while keeping it assigned to a component, click the check box to the left of the component on the Maps rollout to deselect it. Click the check box again to reactivate the map. To remove a map altogether from a component, click the component's map button in the Maps rollout, or click the gray square next to the component in the Blinn Basic Parameters rollout. Next, click the map Type button under the sample slot display, click the NONE map type in the Material/Map Browser and then click OK, or simply double-click the NONE map type. The Material/Map Browser closes, and there is no longer a map assigned to the material component.

Instancing, Copying, and Swapping a Map

If you have assigned a map to a component in the Maps rollout and would like to assign the same map to a different component of the material, you have two options. You can click the map Type button next to the second component and assign the map using the Material/Map Browser. Or you can simply click and drag from the map button next to the first component to the map button next to the second component. When you do this, the Copy (Instance) Map dialog box appears, containing three option buttons, as shown in Figure 32. Click the Instance option button to copy the map to the second component and have any changes to the map in either component be reflected in both components. Click the Copy option button to copy the map but be able to make changes to it that don't affect the other component's map. Or click the Swap option button to swap the second component's map with the first component's (even if one component's map button says "None").

FIGURE 32
Copy (Instance) Map dialog box

FIGURE 33
Cylinder and plane in Perspective viewport

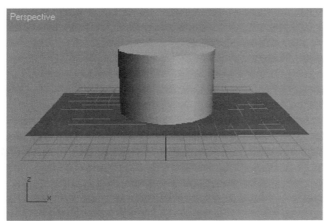

Assign maps to material components

1. Create a cylinder (**Cylinder01**) centered on top of a plane in the Top viewport, click in the **Perspective viewport**, click the **Arc Rotate button**, then adjust the view in the viewport until it resembles that shown in Figure 33.

2. Click the **Material Editor tool** on the main toolbar, double-click the **sample slot** in the upper-left corner of the Material Editor to open it in a single window, then name its material **Cylinder01**.

3. Click the **Diffuse color swatch** in the Blinn Basic Parameters rollout, select a **light blue color** in the Color Selector, click the **Close button**, then click and drag the **sample slot** to Cylinder01.

   The material in the sample slot is applied to Cylinder01.

4. In the Material Editor, click the **plus sign** next to Maps to open the Maps rollout, click the **wide map button** next to the Diffuse Color component (it should say None), then double-click the **Marble map** in the Material/Map Browser.

   The Material/Map Browser closes and the Marble map is applied to the sample slot, completely replacing the appearance of the light blue color with the default colors and pattern of the Marble map. The cylinder does not change in appearance in the viewport.

   (continued)

5. Click the **map Name field list arrow**, then click **Cylinder01** to return to the material's information in the Material Editor.

6. Click the **Background button** to the right of the sample slot display, click the **small gray square button** to the right of the Opacity spinner box in the Blinn Basic Parameters rollout, then double-click **Checker** in the Material/Map Browser to assign it to the material's opacity component.

   > TIP To see the Blinn Basic Parameters rollout, position the pointer under the Maps rollout heading so that it looks like a hand, then drag down.

   The map is assigned to the sample slot. The sphere has a checkered opacity and transparency. Its opaque sections show the Marble map. The cylinder in the viewport does not change.

7. Close the **single sample slot window**, click the **map Name field list arrow**, click **Cylinder01**, then click the **Show Map in Viewport button** below the sample slot display.

   In the viewport, the material on Cylinder01 now shows the maps assigned to it.

8. Render the scene, as shown in Figure 34.

9. In the Maps rollout, change the Amount for the Opacity map to **50**, then render the scene.

   With the intensity of the Checker map reduced, areas of Cylinder01's material previously transparent are less so, and some of the Marble map pattern is visible in those areas.

(continued)

FIGURE 34
Rendered cylinder with maps assigned

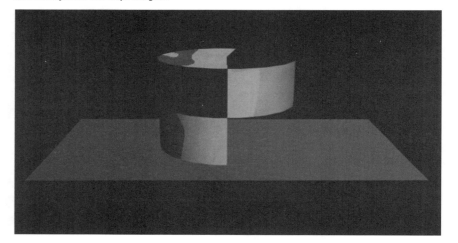

FIGURE 35
Maps rollout and Perspective viewport

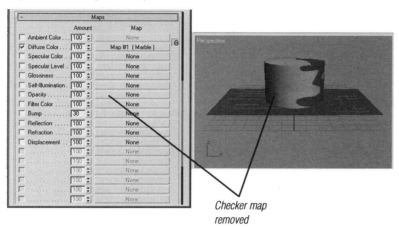

Checker map removed

10. Close the rendered scene window, in the Maps rollout, change the Opacity map Amount back to **100**, then save the file as **AssignMap**.

You named a material and assigned it to a cylinder, and assigned maps to the material's Diffuse and Opacity components. You also showed the maps on material in the Perspective viewport and reduced the intensity of one of the maps.

Deactivate and remove a map

1. In the Maps rollout, deselect the **check box** next to the Diffuse component, then deselect the **check box next to the Opacity component**.

    The maps are deactivated, although still assigned to the material, and now Cylinder01's material shows no maps in the sample slot or on the cylinder itself.

2. Click the **Diffuse and Opacity check boxes** to select each and reactivate the maps.

3. Click the **Opacity map button**, click the **map Type button** on the Material Editor to open the Material/Map Browser, then double-click **NONE** in the Material/Map browser.

    The Checker map is removed from the material's Opacity component, as shown in Figure 35.

You deactivated both maps assigned to a material, reactivated the maps, then removed one of the maps from the material.

Copy maps between components

1. In the Maps rollout, click and drag the **Diffuse map button** to the Opacity map button, then release the mouse button.

   The Copy (Instance) Map dialog box opens.

2. Click the **Copy option button** (if necessary), then click **OK**.

   The Marble map is now also assigned to the Opacity component of the material, and the sample slot looks like Figure 36. This means that the material's opacity varies according to the color values in the Marble map, with darker values more transparent and lighter values more opaque. Because you made a copy (rather than an instance) of the map, changes to the map for either component do not affect the other map.

   (continued)

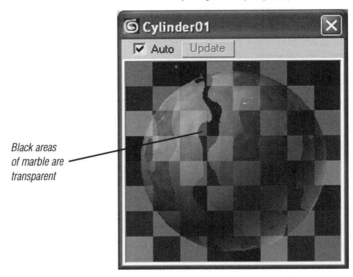

FIGURE 36
Marble map assigned to Opacity component

Black areas of marble are transparent

FIGURE 37

Marble map assigned to Self-Illumination component

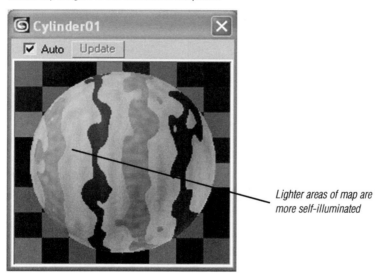

Lighter areas of map are more self-illuminated

3. Click and drag the **Opacity map button** to the Self-Illumination map button, release the mouse button, click **Swap** in the Copy (Instance) Map dialog box, then click **OK**.

   The Opacity map is swapped with the Self-Illumination map, and the sample slot now looks like Figure 37; thus the Opacity component no longer has a map assigned, and the Self-Illumination component has the Marble map assigned.

4. Save the file, then reset 3ds Max.

You copied a map from one material component to another, then swapped a map between components.

LESSON 5

NAVIGATE MATERIALS
AND MAPS

What You'll Do

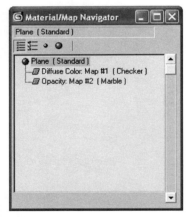

In this lesson, you will learn how to move between materials and maps using the Material/Map Navigator and tools within the Material Editor.

Navigating with the Material/Map Navigator

It is important to understand how to navigate between the different maps and materials used in each sample slot and in the Material Editor. A visual way to do this is by using the Material/Map Navigator, as shown in Figure 38. Unlike the Material/Map Browser, the Navigator is specifically for helping you move between the materials and maps in use in the Material Editor.

Materials and maps have a hierarchical relationship, and maps assigned to other maps are part of that hierarchy as well. In a material with a map assigned to it, the material is the parent and the map is the child; if a map is assigned to another map, it is a child of the map to which it is assigned. Maps assigned to the same material are siblings. These relationships are shown in the Material/Map Navigator. To open the Material/Map Navigator, click the Material/Map Navigator button at the bottom of the column of buttons to the right of the sample slot display, as shown in Figure 38. The material applied to the active sample slot is listed at the top of

FIGURE 38
Material/Map Navigator

Selected material
Child map assigned to parent map
Map siblings assigned to same parent material
Material/Map Navigator button

4-40 AUTODESK 3D STUDIO MAX   *Materials and Maps*

the window, with each map assigned to the material listed below it and indented. If a map is assigned to another map, that map is listed below the map to which it is assigned, and indented further. Figure 38 shows an example material hierarchy.

When you click a material or map in the Navigator to select it, the selection is highlighted turns yellow and the controls for that material or map are displayed on the lower part of the Material Editor. You can adjust these controls as necessary and then click another material or map in the Navigator to view or adjust its controls. For this reason, keeping the Material/Map Navigator open can improve your efficiency.

Navigating Within the Material Editor

You can also use the material Name field to switch between the maps and material in a sample slot. When you first assign a map to a material component, the material Name field becomes a map Name field, as shown on the left in Figure 39; the material Type button becomes the map Type button; and the controls for the map appear in the lower part of the Material Editor. To select the material to which the map is assigned, click the map Name field list arrow, and then click the material name. As shown on the right in Figure 39, the controls appearing in the Material Editor change to those for the selected material (and if the Material/Map Navigator is open, the material is selected, and the map is deselected). Note that once you have switched

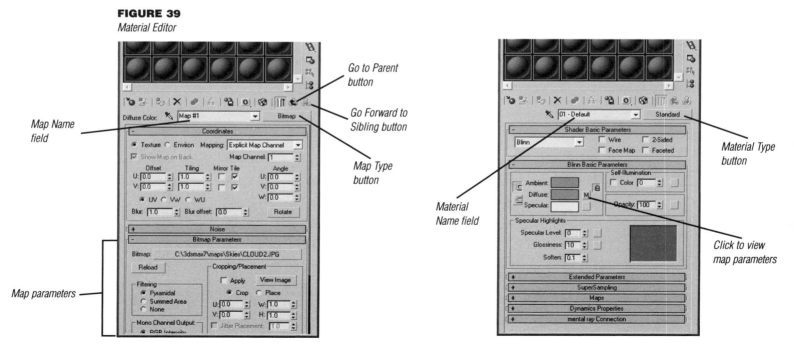

FIGURE 39
Material Editor

Lesson 5   Navigate Materials and Maps

AUTODESK 3D STUDIO MAX 4-41

to the material from the selected map, clicking the material Name field list arrow does not give you the map names on the drop-down list. To select a map and open its parameters in the Material Editor, either click the name of the map on a map button in the Maps rollout or in the Material/Map Navigator.

Lastly, there are two buttons in the Material Editor that further enable navigation between materials and maps. If you have a map selected and would like to go to the map's parent (either material or map), click the Go to Parent button, the second button from the left in the row of buttons under the sample slot display. The parent map or material name, type, and controls appear in the Material Editor. If you have a map selected and would like to go to another map assigned to the same parent material or map, click the Go Forward to Sibling button until the name, type, and controls for the map you seek appear in the Material Editor. If the Material/Map Navigator is open as you use these buttons, each map or material is highlighted in the Navigator as they are selected in the Material Editor.

FIGURE 40
Plane material is parent to the map

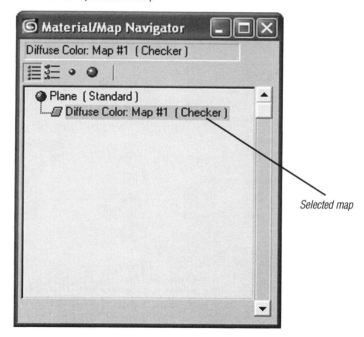

Selected map

Navigate with the Material/Map Navigator

1. Create a plane in the center of the Top viewport, click the **Perspective viewport**, then click the **Material Editor tool** on the main toolbar.

2. Name the first material **Plane**, then apply it to the plane.

3. In the Material Editor, click the **Diffuse map button** in the Blinn Basic Parameters rollout, then double-click **Checker** in the Material/Map Browser.

    The Checker map is assigned to the Diffuse component of the Plane material, and the parameters for the map are shown in the Material Editor.

4. Click the **Material/Map Navigator button** to the right of the sample slot display.

    The Material/Map Navigator opens, as shown in Figure 40. The map is currently selected and highlighted in yellow. Its parent is the Plane material.

5. In the Material/Map Navigator, click **Plane (Standard)** to select it.

    The information in the Material Editor changes to that of the material. The material Name field says "Plane," the material Type button says "Standard," and the parameters and other information in the lower part of the material editor pertain to the selected material.

(continued)

Lesson 5   Navigate Materials and Maps

AUTODESK 3D STUDIO MAX 4-43

6. Click the **Opacity map button** in the Blinn Basic Parameters rollout, then double-click **Marble** in the Material/Map Browser.

   The Marble map is now assigned to the Plane material, and appears in the Material/Map Navigator, as shown in Figure 41.

7. Click the **Diffuse color map** in the Material/Map Navigator to select it and show its information in the Material Editor.

8. Click and drag the **sample slot** to the plane to apply it, then render the scene.

   The material and maps are applied to the plane.

9. Close the **rendered scene window**, then save the file as **NavigateMap**.

You created a plane, applied a material to it, assigned a map to the material, then opened the Material/Map Navigator and used it to select the material in the Material Editor. You assigned a second map to the material, then selected the first map using the Material/Map Navigator. Finally, you applied the modified material to the plane and rendered it.

FIGURE 41
Second child map assigned to parent material

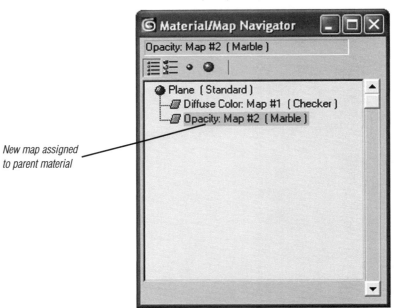

New map assigned to parent material

FIGURE 42
Material Editor and Material/Map Navigator

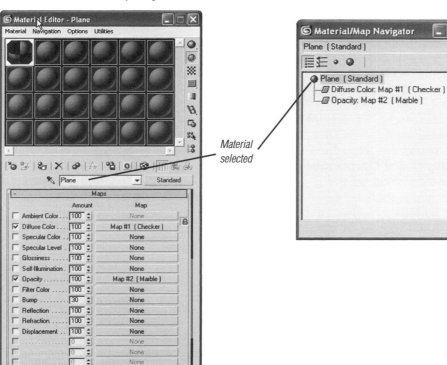

Material selected

Navigate with the Material Editor

1. With the Diffuse color map selected in the Material Editor, click the **map Name field list arrow**, then click **Plane**.

   The information for the Plane material appears in the Material Editor.

2. Click the **Opacity map button** M in the Blinn Basic Parameters rollout to open the Opacity map information in the Material Editor.

3. Click the **map Name field list arrow**, then click **Plane**.

4. Open the **Maps rollout**, then click the **Diffuse map button** to open the Diffuse map information in the Material Editor.

5. Click the **Go Forward to Sibling button** on the far right of the row of buttons under the sample slot display.

   The information for the Opacity map, the sibling of the Diffuse map, opens in the Material Editor.

6. Click the **Go to Parent button** second from the right on the row of buttons under the sample slot display.

   The information for the Plane material, parent to the Diffuse and Opacity maps, opens in the Material Editor. The Material Editor and Material/Map Navigator should now look like Figure 42.

7. Save the file, then reset 3ds Max.

In the Material Editor, you used the map Name field list arrow, map buttons, the Go Forward to Sibling button, and the Go to Parent button to navigate among maps and a material.

AUTODESK 3D STUDIO MAX 4-45

LESSON 6

MAP BASIC SHADER
COMPONENTS

What You'll Do

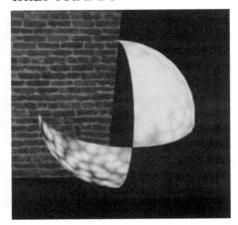

In this lesson, you will learn how maps assigned to basic shader components of a material (color, specularity, self-illumination, and opacity) affect the appearance of the material. You'll also learn about map parameters and how to edit map parameters to enhance the look of a material.

Now that you have learned how to assign maps to components and how to navigate between materials and maps, you'll take a closer look at how assigning a map to a component actually affects the look of a material.

Mapping Color Components of Standard Material

Maps can be assigned to the diffuse, ambient, and specular color components of Standard material. Assigning a map to one of these color components replaces whatever color might be selected for the component with the colors, pattern, and/or textures depicted in the map. Diffuse color is the most frequently mapped component. Just as the diffuse color is the main "color" of an object, a map assigned to the diffuse color component becomes the basic appearance of an object to which the component's material is applied, whether a picture, texture, or pattern. For example, Figure 43 shows three vertical planes, each with a material applied to it whose diffuse color is mapped. As you can see, the map makes a big difference in what

FIGURE 43
Diffuse maps

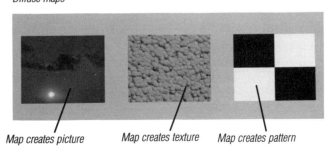

Map creates picture   Map creates texture   Map creates pattern

4-46 AUTODESK 3D STUDIO MAX   *Materials and Maps*

you would say each plane looks like. You can also map the ambient color component of a material—that is, the areas of an object that appear in shadow—but usually this isn't necessary. As long as the Diffuse and Ambient components are locked together, the map applied to the Diffuse component is applied in a complementary way to the Ambient component as well.

When you map the specular color component of Standard material, you assign a map to appear wherever the specular highlights appear on the material. This isn't that useful if you are showing a standard object reflecting light in a normal way, because you would usually want specular color to be white. But imagine a specular highlight on an object made to look like glass; if a map containing the image of a person is assigned to it, it could look like a person's reflection.

Mapping Specular Highlight Components

In addition to the color components, you can map the specular highlight components of a material by assigning maps to a material's Specular Level and Glossiness components. Unlike color components, Specular Level and Glossiness maps affect the material based on the color values used in the map. The value of a color is its Value (V) number on the HSV color model, as shown in Figure 44. Black has a color value of 0, white has a color value of 255, and all colors between have number values between 0 and 255. If you apply a Checker map to the Specular Level component of a sphere, the black portions of the map will have no specular highlights (no intensity) and the white portions of the map

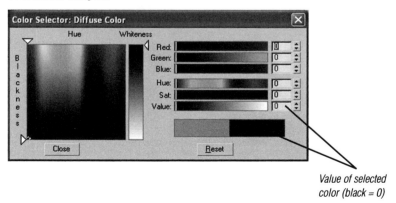

FIGURE 44
Color Selector dialog box

Value of selected color (black = 0)

will show specular highlights at full intensity, as shown in Figure 45. Using a map in this case enables the animator to use only one material to make a sphere appear to have two or more kinds of material applied to it, each with a different response to light.

A map applied to the Glossiness component operates the same way. Remember that glossiness affects the size of the highlight—the glossier a material is, the smaller its highlight. Black color value (0) in a glossiness map produces full glossiness and a small highlight, while white produces a larger highlight, creating a dull appearance.

QUICKTIP

For the most realistic appearance of a material, use the same map for Glossiness and Specular Level.

Mapping Self-Illumination and Opacity

Color values come into play again when you are mapping Self-Illumination or Opacity components of a material. White areas of a self-illumination map applied to a material are fully self-illuminated, while black areas of the map have no self-illumination, as shown in Figure 45. Colors with values between white and black have a corresponding amount of self-illumination.

In an Opacity map, areas on the map that are white are fully opaque, and black areas are transparent (except for specular highlights); colors with values between black and white have a corresponding amount of opacity (or transparency).

Editing Map Parameters

When you first assign a map to a material component, or when you select a map in the Material Editor or in the Material/Map Navigator, the map's parameters appear on the lower part of the Material Editor. You can transform the look of a material easily by assigning a map to it, but adjusting the map's parameters gives you even more options for controlling the look of the material to which the map is assigned. In this chapter, you'll look at the parameters for a few simple maps. You can explore the parameters for all of the maps, many of which are quite complex, on your own using the 3ds Max Help system.

When the Checker map is assigned to a Standard material component and selected, its parameters appear as shown in Figure 46

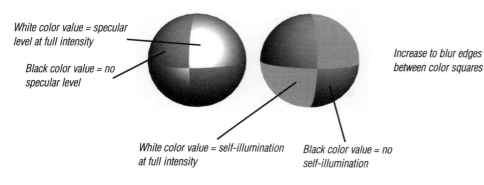

FIGURE 45
Materials with specular level and self-illumination mapped

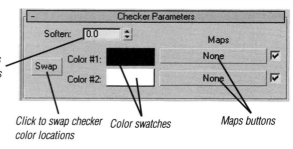

FIGURE 46
Checker Parameters rollout

4-48 AUTODESK 3D STUDIO MAX

Materials and Maps

in the Material Editor in the Checker Parameters rollout. To blur the transition between the two colors and color values in the map, increase the number in the Soften box by one one-hundredth at a time. You can click the Swap button on the left of the rollout to swap the locations of the checker colors in the map. You can change the colors in the map entirely by clicking the color swatch next to Color #1 or Color #2 to open the Color Selector, and then selecting different colors (or color values) to be used in the map. Lastly, you can actually assign maps to be used with the Checker map in place of where a color would appear. For instance, you could assign a Wood map to appear in place of Color #1 in a Checker map. Figure 47 shows such a Checker map applied to the Diffuse color component on the left, and the same map applied to the Opacity component on the right. A map assigned to another map is called a **submap**. Submaps appear, indented, under their parent maps in the Material/Map Navigator. In the Checker Parameters rollout, click the map button next to the Color #1 or Color #2 color swatch, and then double-click a map in the Material/Map browser (or locate and assign a Bitmap map) to assign the map as a submap. Click the check box next to the map button to turn off the map and revert Color #1 or Color #2 to the color shown in the color swatch.

Several maps other than Checker, such as Marble, Speckle, and Dent, also have color choices, submap options, and a Swap button for switching around the color values in the map. These maps also have unique parameters. For example, the Marble map has Size and Vein width parameters you can adjust to change the space between the marble's veins and the width of the veins. You can change the size of the speckles in the Speckle map by increasing or decreasing its Size parameter. You can adjust the size and number of dents in a Dent map by adjusting its Size and Strength parameters. In addition, the Dent map has an Iterations parameter, which you can change to control the number of times the Size and Strength parameters are calculated and applied to the mapped material. Each iteration adds more dents to the surface, as shown in Figure 48.

FIGURE 47
Checker map with submap assigned

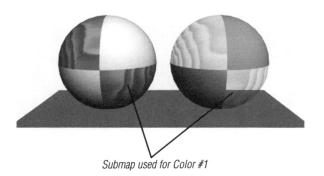

Submap used for Color #1

FIGURE 48
Dent map assigned to material

Dent map at one iteration   Dent map at three iterations

Lesson 6   Map Basic Shader Components

Map diffuse color

1. Create a plane in the Front viewport, create three spheres below the plane in the Top viewport, then click the **Arc Rotate tool** and use it so that your scene resembles Figure 49.

   Because you created the plane in the Front viewport, it is vertical in the Perspective viewport, like a wall, and the three spheres are in front of it.

   TIP Adjust the view in the Perspective viewport as necessary to see all three spheres completely.

2. Click the **Perspective viewport**, click the **Material Editor tool** to open the Material Editor, then click the **Material/Map Navigator button** to open the Material/Map Navigator.

3. Click the **first sample slot**, name its material **Wall**, click the **Diffuse map button** in the Blinn Basic Parameters rollout, then double-click **Bitmap** in the Material/Map Browser.

   The Select Bitmap Image File dialog box opens.

4. Navigate to the maps/Brick subdirectory in 3ds Max, click **BrickWall.jpg**, then click **Open**.

   BrickWall.jpg is mapped to the diffuse component of the Wall material.

   TIP If BrickWall.jpg is unavailable, choose another brick JPG file.

   (continued)

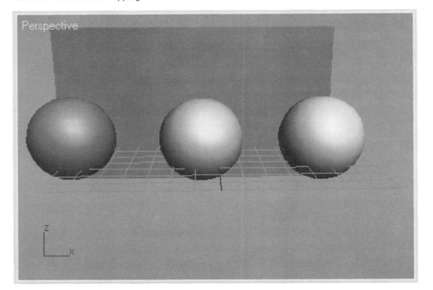

FIGURE 49
Scene for diffuse color mapping

FIGURE 50
Material with Speckle map assigned

FIGURE 51
Rendered scene

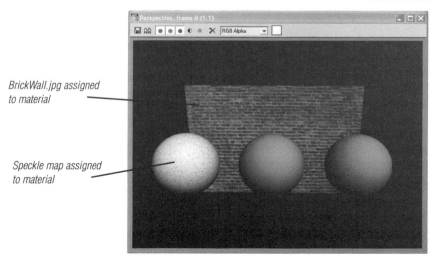

BrickWall.jpg assigned to material

Speckle map assigned to material

5. Click the **second sample slot**, open it in a single sample slot window, name its material **Ball1**, click the **Diffuse map button** in the Blinn Basic Parameters rollout, then double-click **Speckle** in the Material/Map Browser.

 The sample slot should look like Figure 50.

6. Apply the **Ball1 material** to the sphere on the far left in the Perspective viewport, then apply the Wall material to the plane.

7. Click the **Quick Render (Production) tool** on the main toolbar to render the scene, as shown in Figure 51.

8. Close the **rendered scene window** and the **single sample slot window**.

You created a plane and three spheres, created and named two materials and assigned maps to the Diffuse color components of the materials, and applied the materials to objects in a scene.

Lesson 6   Map Basic Shader Components

AUTODESK 3D STUDIO MAX 4-51

Map specular highlight components

1. Click the **third sample slot**, open it in a single sample slot window, then name its material **Ball2**.

2. Click the **Specular Level map button** in the Blinn Basic Parameters rollout, then double-click **Dent** in the Material/Map Browser.

   The Dent map is assigned to the Ball2 material's Specular Level component.

3. Click the **Go to Parent button** below the sample slot display, adjust the Specular Level of the Ball2 material to **50**, apply the **Ball2 material** to the middle of the three spheres in the Perspective viewport, then render the scene.

   As shown in the rendered sphere in Figure 52, where the Dent map has white color values, the specular level is at full intensity; where it has black color values, there is zero intensity.

4. Click the **Glossiness map button** in the Blinn Basic Parameters rollout, then double-click **Dent** in the Material/Map Browser.

   (continued)

FIGURE 52
Specular level map assigned to material

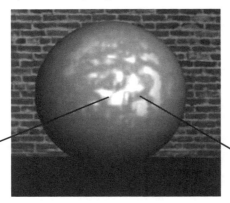

Specular level at full intensity

Specular level at zero intensity

FIGURE 53
Glossiness map assigned to material

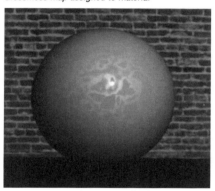

5. Click the **Go to Parent button**, adjust the Glossiness of the Ball2 material to **20**, then render the scene.

   With the Dent map applied to Ball2's specular level and glossiness components, the shininess of the material is at its greatest in the light areas of the map, and at its weakest (or nonexistent) in the map's dark areas. See Figure 53.

6. Close the rendered scene window, then close the Ball2 sample slot window.

You created and named a new material, assigned a map to its Specular Level component, adjusted its specular level, and applied it to an object. You also assigned a map to the material's Glossiness component and adjusted the material's glossiness.

Map self-illumination and opacity

1. Select the **fourth sample slot**, open it in a single window, then name its material **Ball3**.

2. Click the **Diffuse color swatch** in the Blinn Basic Parameters rollout, select a **bright yellow color** in the Color Selector, then click **Close**.

3. Open the **Maps rollout**, click the **Self-Illumination map button**, then double-click **Cellular** in the Material/Map Browser.

   The Cellular map is assigned to Ball3's Self-Illumination component. The black color values in the map have no self-illumination, and the white areas are fully self-illuminated.

4. Click the **Go to Parent button**, apply the **Ball3 material** to the sphere on the far-right in the Perspective viewport, then render the scene.

   The rendered sphere should resemble Figure 54.

5. In the Material Editor, click the **Opacity map button** in the Maps rollout, double-click **Checker** in the Material/Map Browser, then render the scene.

   (continued)

FIGURE 54
Self-illumination map assigned to material

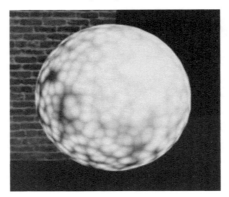

FIGURE 55
Opacity map assigned to material

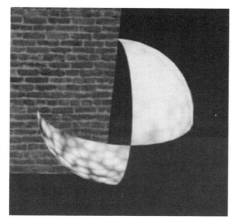

FIGURE 56
Opacity map Amount adjusted

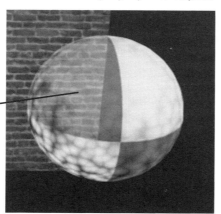

Self-illumination map visible when semitransparent

The Cellular map controls the material's self-illumination, but the Checker map controls its opacity. Where the Checker map has black color values, the sphere is completely transparent, as shown in Figure 55.

6. Click **Ball3 (Standard)** in the Material/Map Navigator, adjust the Opacity map Amount in the Maps rollout from 100 to **50**, then click the **Quick Render (Production) tool** on the main toolbar.

   The sphere now looks like that in Figure 56.

7. Close the **rendered scene window**, then close the **single sample slot window**.

You created and named a new material, changed its diffuse color, assigned a map to its Self-Illumination component, and applied the material to an object in a scene. You also assigned a map to the material's Opacity component and adjusted the map's Amount setting.

Edit map parameters

1. Double-click the **Ball1 material sample slot**.

   Because the last thing you did with this material was assign a map to it, the Speckle map's parameters open in the Material Editor.

2. In the Speckle Parameters rollout, click the **Swap button**.

   The black and white colors in the Speckle map swap places, making the sample sphere black with white speckles.

(continued)

Lesson 6   Map Basic Shader Components

3. Click the **Swap button** again, click the Color #2 color swatch, select a **red color** in the Color Selector, click **Close**, then render the scene.

    The sphere now appears red with black speckles, as shown in Figure 57.

4. Close the **single sample slot window**, click the **Ball3 material sample slot** in the Material Editor, open the **Opacity Checker map** in the Material Editor, increase the Soften number in the Checker Parameters rollout to **.04**, then render the scene.

    In the sphere on the far-right, the lines between the checkers in the map are blurred, as shown in Figure 58.

5. Close the **rendered scene window**.

6. Save the file as **Mapparam**.

You edited the parameters of a Diffuse map to swap its colors' locations and change one of its colors. You also edited the parameters of an Opacity map to soften the edges between color values in the map.

FIGURE 57
Map with edited color parameter

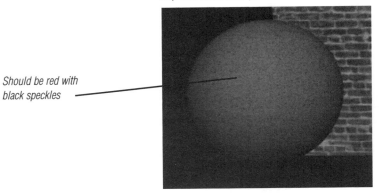

Should be red with black speckles

FIGURE 58
Map with edges softened

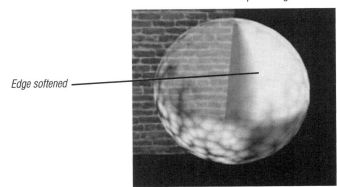

Edge softened

FIGURE 59
Material with map and submap

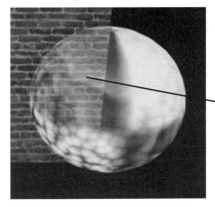

Wood map replaces black color in Checker opacity map

FIGURE 60
Material/Map Navigator

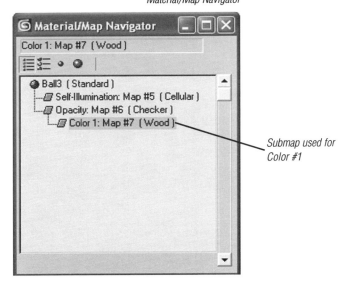

Submap used for Color #1

Assign a map to another map

1. Open the **Ball3 material** in the Material Editor, open the **Maps rollout**, adjust the Opacity map Amount in the Maps rollout from 50 to **100**, then render the scene.

   The black color values on the Checker map are now completely transparent.

2. Open the **Opacity Checker map** in the Material Editor, click the **Color #1 map button** in the Checker Parameters rollout, double-click **Wood** in the Material/Map Browser, then render the scene.

   With the Wood map appearing where just the single color black appeared previously in the Checker map, the transparency is no longer absolute. Instead, the material's opacity depends on the color values in the Wood map, making more of the Cellular Self-Illumination map visible, as shown in Figure 59.

3. Close the **rendered scene window**.

   The Material/Map Navigator should look like Figure 60.

4. Save the file, then reset 3ds Max.

You replaced one of the colors in an assigned map with a submap.

LESSON 7

MAP OTHER STANDARD
MATERIAL COMPONENTS

What You'll Do

In this lesson, you will learn more about other Standard material components available for mapping in the Maps rollout, including Reflection, Refraction, Bump, Filter Color, and Displacement.

In addition to the Color, Specular, Self-Illumination, and Opacity components, there are five other mappable material components available on the Maps rollout: Reflection, Refraction, Bump, Filter Color, and Displacement.

Understanding Map Reflection

To create a realistically reflective material, you can use reflection mapping. There are three approaches to creating a reflective material. You can assign to a material a map whose image you want to be reflected by the material. You can assign a map to a material to make the material automatically reflect the objects and environment that surround it. And you can assign a map to material that appears on a flat object to specifically make it reflect like a mirror. When you have an image that you would like to be reflected by the surface of a material, click the map button next to Reflection in the Maps rollout, double-click the Bitmap map to open the Select Bitmap Image File dialog box, browse to the location of the file you want reflected, select the file, and then click Open. The sample slot will show the map reflected by the material, and any objects to which the material is applied will also reflect the map. In Figure 61, the two spheres on the left have the same cloud bitmap reflected by their materials.

To create an automatic reflection on material, click the Reflection component's map button in the Maps rollout, and then double-click the Reflect/Refract map in the Material/Map Browser. In Figure 61, the sphere on the far-right has a Reflect/Refract map assigned to its material and is reflecting its environment.

In the Maps rollout, adjust the Amount number to reduce the intensity of the reflection as needed. Unless you want objects to which your material is applied to clearly reflect everything around them, adjust the Amount downward to add more realism. For instance, shiny objects such as a clean tabletop or a dark TV screen should reflect their surroundings, but not at 100% intensity. In reality, the surfaces of these objects would still look like wood or glass, but with a reflection visible on their surfaces.

The Reflect/Refract map doesn't produce an accurate effect if you are trying to create a mirror on a flat surface. Instead, the Flat Mirror map should be used, because it enables the faces of the object to which its material is applied to realistically reflect large portions of the environment, as a real mirror would. To apply the Flat Mirror map, click the Reflection component's map button in the Maps rollout, double-click the Flat Mirror map in the Material/Map browser to assign it to the component, and then apply the mapped material to a flat surface in the scene. In Figure 61, the plane beneath the spheres has a Flat Mirror map assigned to its material.

Understanding Map Refraction

Refraction is the redirection of light as it passes through a substance. For instance, if you look through a glass of water at the objects behind the glass, the objects appear distorted; this is because as the light from the objects passes through the water and the glass to your eye, it is refracted. As with reflection mapping, you can assign a map to a material's Refraction component to create an automatic refraction, where the material refracts the light that passes through it. To create an automatic refraction, click the Refraction component's map button in the Maps rollout, and

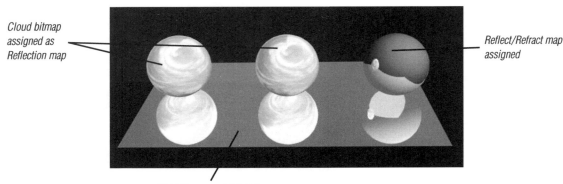

FIGURE 61
Reflection mapped three ways

Cloud bitmap assigned as Reflection map

Reflect/Refract map assigned

Flat Mirror map assigned

Lesson 7   Map Other Standard Material Components

then double-click the Reflect/Refract map in the Material/Map Browser. In Figure 62, the left and right spheres are automatically refracting their environments.

In the physical world, substances that refract light do so at a calculable rate, known as the **index of refraction (IOR)**. In 3ds Max, to make the behavior of your refractive material as realistic as possible, you can adjust the IOR of a material to equal that of a real substance, such as water, glass, or ice. To adjust the IOR of a material, open the Extended Parameters rollout for the material in the Material Editor, and then adjust the number in the Index of Refraction box in the Advanced Transparency group to the number desired. The default IOR of a material is that of glass, which is 1.5. 3ds Max lists the actual IORs for several substances in Help, under Refraction Mapping. For instance, water has an IOR of 1.333, ice an IOR of 1.309, and crystal an IOR of 2.0.

You can also assign a bitmap image to Refraction so that the image appears on the material's surface as though it is being seen through a refracting substance. In this case, as the object moves, the refracted image on the material's surface remains fixed. To assign a Bitmap map to Refraction, click the Refraction component map button in the Maps rollout, double-click the Bitmap map to open the Select Bitmap Image File dialog box, browse to the location of the file you want refracted, select the file, and then click Open. The sample slot will show the map refracted by the material, and any objects to which the material is applied will also show the refracted map. In Figure 62, the center sphere is refracting an assigned bitmap of a sky.

Understanding Map Bumpiness

With bump mapping, you can assign a map to a material so that its surface looks uneven or bumpy. Bump maps distort the material's surface according to the intensity of the colors in a map. White areas of the map appear to protrude, while black areas appear in shadow. Shades between white and black are at corresponding levels between the two colors. Bump maps can be particularly helpful in creating an engraved or embossed look or in making a surface look naturally bumpy, like pores in skin seen close up. To apply a bump map, click the Map button next to Bump in the Maps rollout, and then assign the map that you want to use to give the material its

FIGURE 62
Refraction mapped two ways

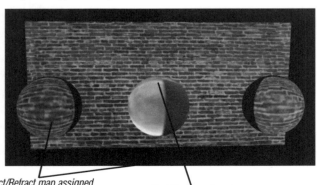

Reflect/Refract map assigned

Sky bitmap assigned as Refraction map

bumpy look. Note that for Bump, increasing or decreasing the Amount in the Maps rollout affects the degree of bumpiness; higher numbers make higher bumps, lower numbers the opposite. In Figure 63, the Cellular map has been assigned to the material's Bump component. The white areas of the cellular map appear raised, the black areas appear to be in shadow. Keep in mind that because of the way they are rendered, the bumps on a material are not shown in silhouette when viewed from the side, as on the edge of an object. The edge appears smooth instead.

QUICKTIP

Bump maps do not show in viewports; to see the effect, render the scene.

Mapping the Filter Color

The **filter color** of an object is the color that is able to pass through the object; for instance, if you look through a stained glass window, objects that you see on the other side of the window are tinted the color of the glass through which you are looking, also known as the glass's filter color. In a scene, the objects behind a semitransparent object with a blue filter color are tinted blue when seen through the object. In addition, when light in a scene passes through a semitransparent object, the shadow cast is tinted the filter color. To choose a single filter color for an object, open the Extended Parameters rollout in the Material Editor, click the color swatch to the right of the Filter option button in the rollout, and then select a color using the Color Selector. Using a map, you can assign an image or pattern to a material to give the object multiple filter colors, such as a geometric design for a stained glass window. To assign a map to a material's filter color, click the map button next to Filter in the Extended Parameters box, or click the map button next to Filter Color in the Maps rollout, and then select the map desired using the Material/Map Browser. Once the map is assigned to the material, objects behind the object to which the material is applied are tinted according to the colors in the map, and light passing through the object casts a shadow containing the design and its colors. In Figure 64, the Cellular map has been assigned as the filter color to the small plane.

FIGURE 63
Material with Bump map

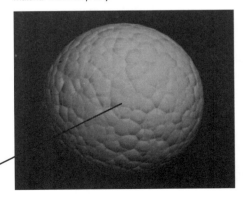

Cellular map assigned

FIGURE 64
Material with Filter Color map

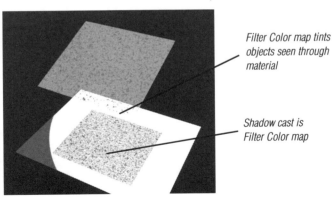

Filter Color map tints objects seen through material

Shadow cast is Filter Color map

Lesson 7   Map Other Standard Material Components

AUTODESK 3D STUDIO MAX 4-61

Map reflection

1. In the Top viewport, create a plane, create two spheres above the plane in the Front viewport, then click in the **Perspective viewport**.

2. Click the **Material Editor tool** on the main toolbar, double-click the **first sample slot** to open it in a single window, name the material **Sphere1**, then apply it to the sphere on the left.

3. Open the **Maps rollout** for the Sphere1 material, click the **Reflection map button** in the Maps rollout, double-click **Bitmap** in the Material/Map Browser, navigate to the maps/Skies subdirectory in 3ds Max, click **SKYSUN2.jpg**, then click **Open**.

   SKYSUN2 is assigned to the Sphere1 material as a reflection map.

   | TIP If you don't see SKYSUN2, select another file from the Skies directory.

4. Close the **single slot sample window**, double-click the **second sample slot** to open it in a single window, name the material **Sphere2**, then apply it to the sphere on the right in the scene.

(continued)

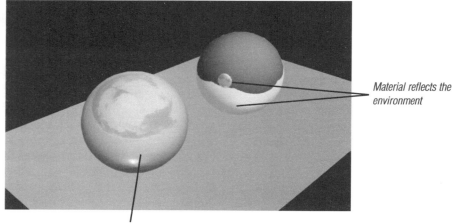

FIGURE 65
Materials with Reflection mapping

Material reflects the environment

Material reflects SKYSUN2.jpg

Using map displacement

Unlike bump mapping, displacement mapping actually changes the geometry of an object by displacing its surfaces according to the light (displaced greatly) and dark (displaced less) areas of the map assigned. How far surfaces are displaced is determined by the Amount number in the Maps rollout, which indicates the percentage of the size of the object's bounding box that the displacement will be. If you assign a map to the Displacement component of a material, the sample sphere shows the map displaced, but when the material is applied to an object in the viewport and rendered as a scene the displacement does not happen. To make the displacement take effect, select the object(s) to which the material will be or is applied, and then apply the Displace Mesh modifier.

If you want to displace surfaces of an object, it is recommended that you not use Displacement mapping, because it can be clunky and uses a lot of memory. Instead, use the Displace modifier to displace the surfaces of an object. Using the modifier's gizmo gives you more control over the displacement.

FIGURE 66
Material with Flat Mirror map assigned

Material reflects environment

5. Open the **Maps rollout** for the Sphere2 material, click the **Reflection map button** in the Maps rollout, double-click **Reflect/Refract** in the Material/Map Browser, then render the scene.

   As shown in Figure 65, the sphere on the left shows SKYSUN2 reflected on its surface. The sphere on the right reflects its environment, including Sphere1 and the plane.

6. Close the single slot sample window, double-click the **third sample slot** to open it in a single window, name the material **Plane**, then apply it to the plane.

7. Open the **Maps rollout** for the Plane material, click the **Reflection map button** in the Maps rollout, double-click **Flat Mirror** in the Material/Map Browser, then render the scene.

   The rendered scene should look like Figure 66.

8. Close the **rendered scene window**, then close the **single sample slot window**.

You created two spheres and a plane, and applied Standard material to each. You also applied a Bitmap map to one sphere's material as a Reflection map, assigned a Reflect/Refract map as a Reflection map to the other sphere's material, and assigned the Flat Mirror map to the material applied to the plane.

Map refraction

1. Click the **Sphere1 material sample slot**, click the **map Name field list arrow**, click **Sphere1**, open the **Maps rollout** (if necessary), click and drag the **Reflection map button** to the Refraction map button, release the mouse button, click the **Swap option button** in the Copy (Instance) Map dialog box (if necessary), then click **OK**.

   SKYSUN2.jpg is reassigned to the material as its refraction map.

2. Click the **Refraction map button**, click the **map Type button**, double-click **Bitmap** in the Material/Map Browser, navigate to the maps/Skies subdirectory, then double-click **DUSKCLD1** to assign it to the Sphere1 material's Refraction component.

   | TIP If you don't see DUSKCLD1, choose a different file.

3. Click the **Sphere2 material sample slot**, click the **Name field list arrow**, click **Sphere2**, then in the Maps rollout, drag the **Reflection map button** to the Refraction map button, release the mouse button, click the **Swap option button** in the Copy (Instance) Map dialog box (if necessary), then click **OK**.

   With the Reflect/Refract map now assigned to the material's Refraction component, the material refracts its environment.

4. With the Perspective viewport selected, render the scene.

   The rendered scene should resemble Figure 67.

   (continued)

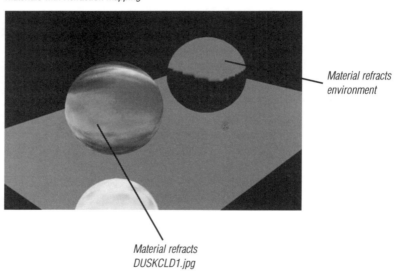

FIGURE 67
Materials with Refraction mapping

Material refracts environment

Material refracts DUSKCLD1.jpg

4-64 AUTODESK 3D STUDIO MAX

Materials and Maps

FIGURE 68
Material with Bump mapping

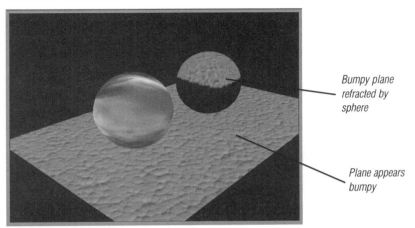

Bumpy plane refracted by sphere

Plane appears bumpy

5. Close the **rendered scene window**.

You swapped the Sphere1 material's Reflection map with its Refraction map, replaced the bitmap assigned to Refraction with a new bitmap, swapped the Sphere2 material's Reflection map with its Refraction map, then rendered the scene.

Map bumpiness

1. Click the **Plane material sample slot**, click the **Name field list arrow**, click **Plane**, click the **Reflection map button** in the Maps rollout, click the **map Type button** (Flat Mirror), then double-click **None** in the Material/Map Browser to remove the Plane material's Reflection map.

2. Click the **Bump map button**, double-click **Cellular** in the Material/Map Browser, then render the scene.

   As shown in Figure 68, the plane now has a textured, bumpy appearance. The sphere on the left does not change in appearance, and the sphere on the right is now refracting a bumpy plane instead of a mirrored plane.

3. In the Cellular Parameters rollout in the Material Editor, click the **Chips option button** in the Cell Characteristics group.

   | TIP You might need to scroll the rollout up to make the Cell Characteristics group visible.

(continued)

4. Render the scene.

   The plane appears in the scene as shown in Figure 69, with its bumps having straight edges. Notice that the edges of the plane do not show any texture or silhouettes of bumps.

5. Close the **rendered scene window**, save the file as **Bumpymap**, then reset 3ds Max.

You deleted the Plane material's reflection map, assigned the Cellular map to its Bump component, rendered the scene, changed one of the Bump map's parameters, then rendered the scene again.

Map filter color

1. Create a plane in the Front viewport, create a box in front of the plane in the Top viewport, click the **Perspective viewport**, then click the **Material Editor tool** on the main toolbar.

2. Create a material called **Plane** and apply it to the plane, then create a material called **Box** and apply it to the box.

3. With the Box material selected in the Material Editor, open the **Extended Parameters rollout**, click the **Filter color swatch** in the Advanced Transparency group, click a **red color**, then adjust the Opacity in the Blinn Basic Parameters rollout to **70** from 100.

4. Render the scene.

   With the Box material semitransparent, the color of the plane behind the box—as seen through the box (the box's filter color)—is tinted red.

(continued)

FIGURE 69
Bump map with parameters edited

Bump edges are straight

FIGURE 70
Material with Filter Color map

Marble map tints objects seen through material

5. Close the **rendered scene window**, open the **Maps rollout** for the Box material, click the **Filter Color map button**, then double-click **Marble** in the Material/Map Browser.

6. Render the scene.

   As shown in Figure 70, the red filter color is replaced by the Marble map as the box's filter color. Notice that the only parts of the box that show the Marble map are those in front of the plane— where light is passing through the box.

7. Close the **rendered scene window**, save the file as **Filter**, reset 3ds Max, then close 3ds Max.

You created a plane and a box and applied Standard material to each, changed the filter color for the Box's material using the Extended Parameters rollout, rendered the scene, assigned a map to the Box material's Filter Color component, then rendered the scene.

CHAPTER SUMMARY

In this chapter, you learned how to apply materials to objects so that they respond to light in a realistic way, conveying realistic depth, distance, texture, color, and shadow. You also learned how to edit materials using the Material Editor to get the effect you want. You learned about the most commonly used shaders in 3D animation, and worked extensively with the Blinn shader. The chapter also covered the use of maps in 3ds Max. Using maps, you were able to further control the appearance of a material's components. You also learned the best ways to move between maps and materials as you work on a scene by using the Material/Map Navigator.

What You Have Learned
- How to work with maps and shaders
- How to work with sample slots in the Material Editor in order to have a variety of materials at your fingertips as you work on a scene
- How to edit basic shader parameters
- How to assign and remove a map from an object
- How to instance, copy, and swap a map
- How to navigate within the Material Editor
- How to map Specular Highlight and other components
- How to edit map parameters
- How to work with map reflection, refraction, and bumpiness
- How to map a filter color
- How to use displacement mapping to change the geometry of an object

Key Terms

Materials   Make it possible for an object to look nearly photo-realistic.

Ambient color   The color of an object where it is in shadow.

Specular color   The color of an object where it is reflecting the light source (that is, highlighted).

Diffuse color   The color of an object in general lighting, neither in shadow nor direct light. When you refer to the color of an object in general conversation, you are usually referring to its diffuse color.

Standard material   When you apply this material, an object appears to have a single color applied to it, with standard reflective properties.

Shader   Controls how the highlights on an object look.

Render   When you render a scene, the scene you have created is converted into a two-dimensional image or animation, using the materials, lighting, background, and environment settings you have put in place.

Submap   A map assigned to another map.

chapter 5
CAMERAS AND LIGHTING

1. Add cameras to a scene.

2. Position cameras.

3. Add lights to a scene.

4. Adjust light parameters.

5. Work with shadows.

6. Use lights.

chapter 5 CAMERAS AND LIGHTING

Now that you have learned how to work with objects and apply materials to those objects to control their appearance and responses to light, it is time to address two other aspects of 3ds Max scenes: cameras and lighting.

When creating scenes and animations, think of yourself as a designer and cinematographer rather than an animator. As you create, you should always consider what's going on design-wise in a scene, instead of simply trying to get across a single idea on the screen. To effectively design scenes and animations, you need to have control over how a scene is viewed, but you also need flexibility so that there are a variety of ways to approach the same scene and execute your design vision. As they are for film and television directors, cameras and lighting are essential tools that enable you to carefully design your shots and plan for motion.

Tools You'll Use

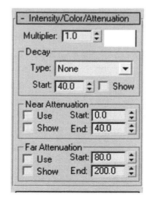

LESSON 1

ADD CAMERAS TO A SCENE

What You'll Do

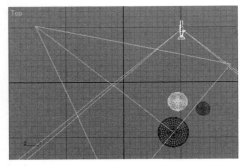

In this lesson, you will learn what camera objects are and how they are used to render scenes from different viewpoints. You will also learn about the two camera types, how to insert each into a scene, and how to adjust camera parameters.

Understanding Cameras

A camera in a scene creates a **viewpoint** (or point of view) of a scene that is fixed in space. For instance, a camera might provide a close-up of objects in a scene, an overhead view, or a perspective from a set distance away from the objects in the scene, as shown in Figure 1. To see this viewpoint, you use a Camera viewport.

You might wonder what the value of cameras is when you already have many different ways to control how a scene is seen through a viewport, and thus how it looks when rendered. The answer is multifaceted. First of all, the view of a scene through any viewport provides you with a distinct perspective on a scene and can be moved, rotated, and zoomed in or out. However, with a Camera viewport, you can save a camera's perspective and return to it again and again, change it if you like, and save it after it has been changed. In addition, you can have multiple cameras in a scene, enabling you to look at the same scene, or same moment in a scene, from different fixed viewpoints. This is a great advantage to creating still scenes and animations with a certain style or overall feel.

This ability to keep a fixed perspective on a scene also comes in handy as you work with a scene. No matter where you move in a non-Camera viewport to look at, adjust, insert, or modify objects, you do not lose the perspective of a camera that is fixed in place. Another advantage cameras have is that they can be animated. For instance, if you are creating an animation of a person walking down the street, and you want the person to be at the center of the scene as she walks, and you also want the angle of the camera shot to change as the person is walking, you can use a camera to change the perspective as the scene progresses.

Lastly, although this book won't provide great detail about them, cameras in 3ds Max have adjustable parameters that can be to conform with stock lenses that ship with traditional cameras. If there is a particular view on a scene or camera setting that you want to use that is based on a real-world camera lens and its settings, you can adjust a camera's parameters to match the shot you would get using that particular lens.

Although camera objects can be seen in viewports, they do not show when the scene is rendered; camera object icons are simply for positioning and reference purposes.

Creating Cameras

There are two kinds of cameras: target cameras and free cameras. A **target camera** is a camera that always focuses on a target object and the area around it. Such a camera can be rotated or moved, but not in a direction that causes it to face away from its target object. When a target object is animated, the camera's focus always remains on that target object. To add a target camera to a scene, click the Cameras button on the Create panel, as shown in Figure 2, and then click the Target button on the Object Type rollout. Click in the Top viewport in the

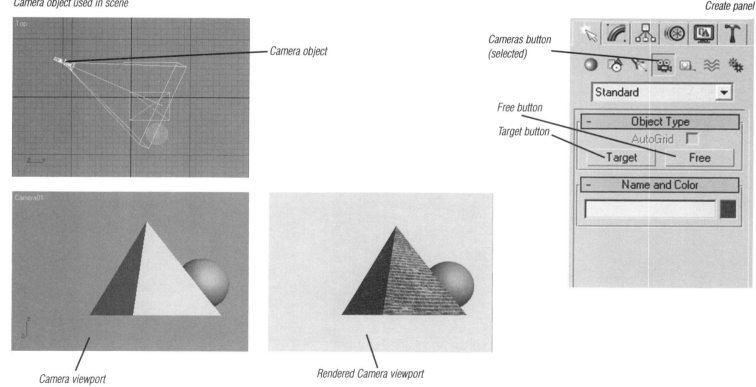

FIGURE 1
Camera object used in scene

FIGURE 2
Create panel

Lesson 1   Add Cameras to a Scene

location you want the camera to be, drag to the location of the target object, and then release the mouse button. As you drag to insert the target object, a light-blue triangle appears between the camera and the mouse pointer, with the target object centered at the bottom of the triangle, as shown in Figure 3. The target camera and target object are two separate objects and can be manipulated independently of each other, although the camera always remains pointed at the object.

A **free camera** simply takes in the scene that appears in the direction the camera is aimed, without sticking to a particular target, as shown in Figure 3. A free camera can be rotated or moved in any direction, because it is not restricted by a target object's location. To add a free camera to a scene, click the Cameras button on the Create panel, and then click the Free button on the Object Type rollout. Click in the Top viewport in the location you want the camera to be. When you insert a free camera into a scene, the camera will point away from you (as it would if you were holding it in the real world). In the viewport in which you insert the camera, a rectangle appears around the camera. As you'll see in other viewports, this rectangle is simply the top end of a pyramid shape leading from the camera and ending a specified distance from it.

It is recommended that you add cameras to a scene using the Top viewport, because it is easy to understand where in a scene the camera appears by inserting it while looking down at the scene. You can adjust the height and horizontal location of the camera in the scene using the Front viewport. When you insert a free camera in the Top viewport, the camera will face away from you, and thus point down. You can use the Select and Rotate tool to adjust its position.

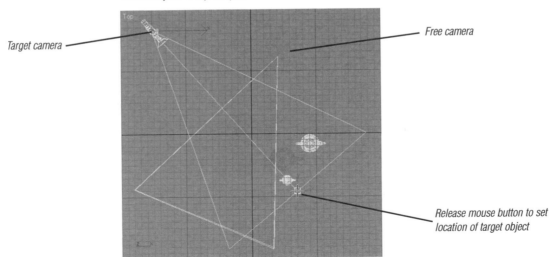

FIGURE 3
Camera objects in Top viewport

Adjusting Camera Parameters

Every camera object has parameters, and the parameters of a target camera and free camera are almost identical. You can change a camera's name and icon color using the Name and Color rollout on the Create Cameras panel. To rename the camera, select the text in the Name text box, and then type a name for the camera to replace the default. To choose a color for the camera icon, click the color swatch next to the Name text box, select a color in the Object Color dialog box, and then click OK. Remember that camera icons do not appear in a rendered scene, so choosing a color for a camera icon simply colors the icon in the viewport.

When you first insert a camera, the Parameters rollout for the camera appears under the Name and Color rollout on the Create panel. After you have deselected the camera and then reselected the camera, you need to click the Modify tab and go to the Modify panel to regain access to the camera's Parameters rollout, as shown in Figure 4.

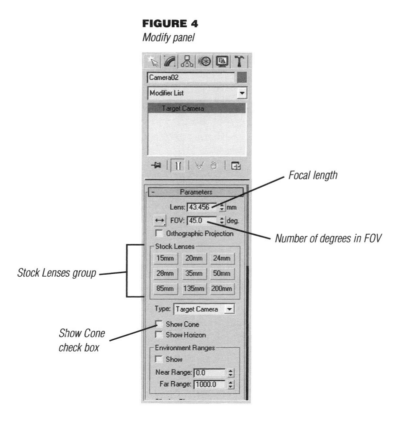

FIGURE 4
Modify panel

Lesson 1   Add Cameras to a Scene

AUTODESK 3D STUDIO MAX 5-7

A camera has two key parameters that you can adjust to change how a camera views a scene: field of view and focal length. The light-blue pyramid shape that appears when a camera is inserted is the camera's **field-of-view cone**. A camera's **field of view (FOV)** is the amount of the scene that is visible through the camera and is measured in degrees of the horizon. The rectangle at the end of a camera's field-of-view cone encompasses the camera's field of view, that is, what appears in the scene from that camera's point of view.

The field of view of a camera depends on the camera's **focal length**, which is the distance between a camera's lens and the surface onto which a scene is captured (such as film in a camera). Focal length is measured in millimeters (mm); a 35 mm camera has a focal length of 35 mm. The greater the focal length, the smaller the field of view of the camera, and the smaller the focal length, the greater the field of view.

In 3ds Max, cameras have the same parameters as cameras in the real world. At the top of the Parameters rollout in the Create panel, as shown in Figure 4 on the previous page, you can adjust the focal length of a camera by adjusting the number in the Lens box. You can also adjust the number of degrees in the FOV by changing the number in the FOV box. Adjusting the focal length changes the FOV number, and vice versa. You can also choose a focal length based on that of a commonly used stock camera lens. To do so, click the corresponding button in the Stock Lenses group on the Parameters rollout, such as the 35 mm button.

QUICKTIP

A camera's field-of-view cone appears on-screen when the camera is selected. To always show a camera's FOV cone whether or not it is selected, select the camera, click the Modify tab on the Create panel, and then select the Show Cone check box in the Parameters.

The distance between a target camera and its target appears at the bottom of the Parameters rollout in the Target Distance box. For a free camera, the Target Distance is the distance between the camera and a point at the center of the plane at the end of its FOV cone, an invisible target that serves as a reference point but is not a separate object.

FIGURE 5
Top and Front viewports

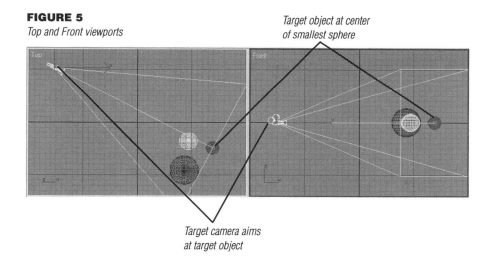

Target object at center of smallest sphere

Target camera aims at target object

Create cameras in a scene

1. Start 3ds Max, then using Figure 5 as a guide, create three spheres of differing sizes in the lower right of the Top viewport.
2. Click the **Create tab** (if necessary), click the **Cameras button**, then click the **Target button** in the Object Type rollout.
3. Click in the upper-left corner of the Top viewport to insert a target camera object, hold down the mouse button and drag until the pointer is in the center of the smallest sphere, then release the mouse button.

   The target object is located at the center of the smallest sphere, as shown in Figure 5, and the target camera is aimed at the target object.
4. Click the **Select and Move tool**, click the **target object**, then move the target object to the center of the largest sphere.

   As you move the target object, the target camera rotates so that it continues to aim at the target object.
5. Click the **Free button** in the Object Type rollout on the Create panel, then click once in the upper-right of the Top viewport, above the spheres.

   A free camera is inserted, pointing straight down.
6. Click the **Select and Rotate tool**, click the **red axis handle** on the Rotate gizmo, drag down until the free camera is aiming directly away from the spheres, click the **blue axis handle**, drag down until the camera is aiming at the spheres, then release the mouse button.

(continued)

AUTODESK 3D STUDIO MAX 5-9

Lesson 1 Add Cameras to a Scene

The location and orientation of the cameras should match those in Figure 6.

7. Save the file as **Camerascene01**.

   TIP Because you will be saving the same file multiple times with different numbers, click File, click Save As, type Camerascene in the File name text box, then click the plus sign so that 3ds Max appends an 01 to the file name.

You created three spheres, inserted a target camera and a target object, set the location of the target object at the center of the smallest sphere, then moved its location to the center of the largest sphere. You also inserted a free camera into the scene and aimed it at the spheres.

Adjust camera parameters

1. Click the **Select Object tool**, select the **target camera**, then click the **Modify tab** to open the Parameters rollout for the camera.

2. Select the **Show Cone check box**, then click away from the camera in the Top viewport.

   The FOV cone for the target camera continues to appear even though the camera is no longer selected.

3. Select the **target camera** again, then click the **35 mm button** in the Stock Lenses group on the Parameters rollout.

   The number in the Lens box on the Parameters rollout changes to 35 mm, and the number in the FOV box changes to from 45 to 54.432, the degrees of the horizon that are captured by the FOV of a 35 mm camera lens. In the viewports, the FOV cone widens.

   (continued)

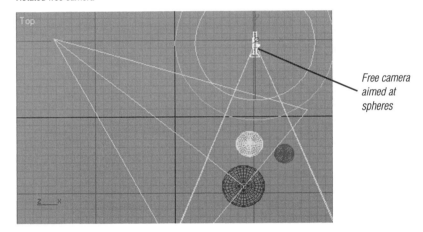

FIGURE 6
Rotated free camera

Free camera aimed at spheres

FIGURE 7
Free camera at 15 mm focal length

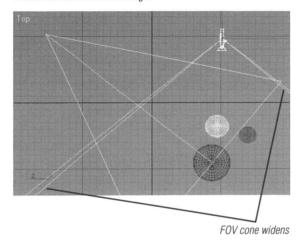

FOV cone widens

FIGURE 8
Target camera with modified target distance

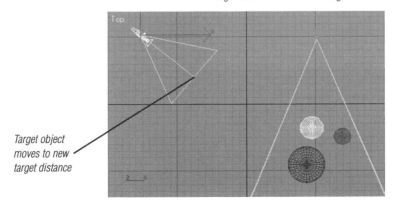

Target object moves to new target distance

4. Select the **free camera**, then change the number in the FOV box on the Parameters rollout from 45 to **60**.

   As you change the FOV, the number in the Lens box (the focal length of the camera) changes to 31.177, and the FOV cone in the viewports widens.

5. Select the number in the Lens box on the Parameters rollout, change it to **15**, then press **[Enter]**.

   The FOV number changes to 100.389, and the FOV cone for the free camera looks like that shown in Figure 7. Your screen might look different based on exactly where you placed the camera.

6. Change the FOV number for the free camera to **45**, press **[Enter]**, then click the **Show Cone check box** to select it.

7. Select the **target camera** again, pan down the Parameters rollout until the Target Distance box is visible, then change the number in the Target Distance box to **100**, as shown in Figure 8.

8. Click the **Select and Move tool**, then move the **target object** back to the center of the largest sphere.

9. Click **File** on the menu bar, click **Save As**, then click the **plus sign** to save the scene as **Camerascene02**.

You modified the parameters of a target camera to always show its FOV cone, match its settings to a 35 mm stock camera lens, and change its target distance. You also manually adjusted the FOV and focal length parameters of the free camera, and elected to show its FOV cone when not selected.

AUTODESK 3D STUDIO MAX 5-11

LESSON 2

POSITION CAMERAS

What You'll Do

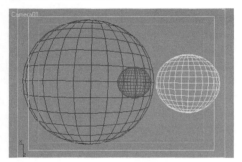

▶ *In this lesson, you will learn how to change a viewport into a Camera viewport, how to position a camera using the main toolbar tools, and how to adjust the scene as shown in a Camera viewport using the camera viewport controls. You will also gain an understanding of how to use Safe Frames to design your scene appropriately for TV monitors.*

Changing a Viewport into a Camera Viewport

After you have inserted a camera or cameras into a scene, you can change the viewport into a Camera viewport, which shows the scene from the selected camera's point of view. You render a scene from a camera's point of view by rendering a Camera viewport based on that camera. To change a viewport into a Camera viewport, click in the viewport you want to change to make it active, right-click the viewport label, point to Views on the right-click menu that appears, and then click the name of the desired camera on the submenu, as shown on the left in Figure 9. As shown on the right in Figure 9, the viewport then shows the scene from the camera's viewpoint, and the name of the viewport becomes the name of the camera (for example, Camera01 instead of Top). Another way to change an active viewport into a Camera viewport is to press [C] on the keyboard. If there is only one camera in the scene, or only one camera currently selected, the viewport changes to a Camera viewport for that camera. If there are multiple cameras in the scene and/or multiple cameras currently selected, a Select Camera dialog box opens, listing the cameras in the scene. Click the name of the camera you want to be used for the viewport, and then click OK.

Positioning a Camera

Although camera objects in a scene are not themselves rendered, you can control their locations in the same way you control other types of objects. As mentioned earlier, you can move and rotate a camera with the Select and Move and Select and Rotate tools, with target camera rotation limited by the location of the target object. The Select and Uniform Scale tool has no effect on a target camera, but you can use it to change the Target Distance for a free camera. Similarly, using the Select and Non-Uniform Scale and Select and Squash tools enables you to change the shape and size of the FOV cone for a free camera, but for a target camera these tools affect only the camera icon and not its FOV.

After you have positioned a camera and have it active as a Camera viewport, you have even more specific tools available for adjusting its location. With a Camera viewport active, the viewport controls in the bottom-right of

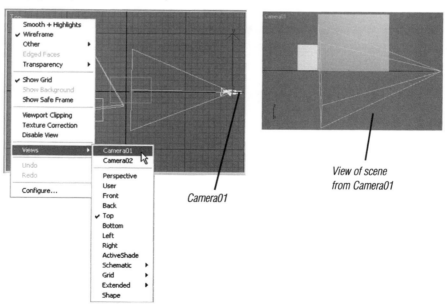

FIGURE 9
Changing a viewport into a Camera viewport

the screen become the Camera viewport controls, as shown in Figure 10. These buttons enable you to change the position of the camera (or target object) in order to get the desired perspective on your scene. Instead of a User viewport's Zoom button, for instance, for a Camera viewport you have the Dolly Camera flyout. Dollying a camera or target moves it along its primary axis, either away from or toward its target object or camera:

- To dolly the camera only, click the Dolly Camera button on the Dolly Camera flyout, and then drag up or down in the Camera viewport to adjust the camera's position. The target stays in place while the camera moves.
- To dolly the target only, click the Dolly Target button and then drag up or down in the viewport to adjust its position toward or away from the camera.
- To dolly both the camera and target at the same time, click the Dolly Camera + Target button, and then drag up or down in the Camera viewport. If a Camera viewport's camera is a free camera, only the Dolly Camera button is available.
- Click the Perspective button and drag up or down in the Camera viewport to dolly the camera toward or away from the objects in a scene and increase or decrease the distortion of the objects due to perspective changes. The objects aren't actually deformed; the camera is simulating the perspective effect of a round camera lens, which distorts the image.
- To rotate the camera around its axis while keeping it aimed in the same direction, click the Roll Camera button, and then drag horizontally in the viewport.
- Click the Field-of-View button, and then drag up or down in the Camera viewport to increase or decrease the size of the camera's field of view (thereby adjusting its focal length as well).
- Click the Truck Camera flyout button, click the Truck Camera button, and then click and drag in the Camera viewport to move the camera's position parallel to the Camera viewport's view.
- Click the Truck Camera flyout button, click the Walk Through button, and then use the arrow keys to move the

FIGURE 10
Camera viewport controls

5-14 AUTODESK 3D STUDIO MAX   *Cameras and Lighting*

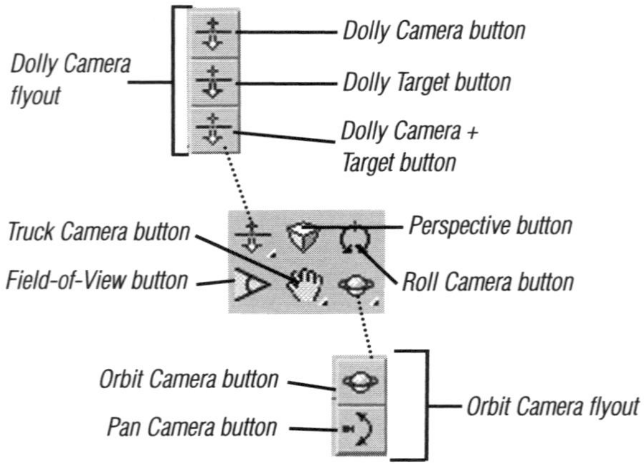

camera through the scene as though you were walking through the scene holding the camera.

- Click the Orbit Camera button on the Orbit Camera flyout to rotate a target camera around its target or to rotate a free camera around the plane at the end of its FOV cone.
- Click the Pan Camera button on the Orbit Camera flyout to rotate a target around its target camera or to rotate a free camera around its own axes.

Using Safe Frames

If you are creating a 3D animation using 3ds Max, chances are that you are creating something that will ultimately be shown on a TV monitor. The Safe Frames feature of 3ds Max provides a way for you to know what elements of a scene in an active viewport, especially a resized one, will be rendered. Safe Frames are frames that you can activate that appear on a scene in a viewport. There are three types of Safe Frames, as shown in Figure 11–the outer yellow frame is the **live area** frame, which encompasses all parts of the scene that will be rendered. What appears in the live area frame is what will appear in the rendered scene. When designing a camera shot, it is essential to work with the live area frame in mind so that you know where the rendered scene will be clipped. The smaller green frame is the **action safe** frame. This encloses the area of the screen in which important objects and activity should be enclosed; if outside this frame, objects might be cut off when shown on a TV monitor. Last is the **title safe** frame, within which titles (or other wording) should remain to prevent distortion by the slant of a monitor near its edges.

To turn on Safe Frames, right-click the active viewport name, and then click Show Safe Frame on the right-click menu to select it. The Safe Frames will appear in the viewport, and then you can adjust the view of the scene as needed to fit the scene appropriately within the frames. Safe Frames can be used in any viewport, not just Camera viewports, to help you understand the boundaries of a scene you plan to render.

FIGURE 11
Resized viewport with Safe Frames activated

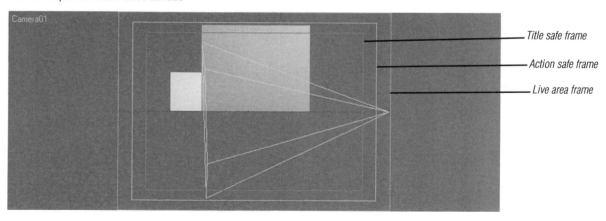

Change viewports into Camera viewports

1. With **Camerascene02** open in the viewports, click in the Perspective viewport to activate it, right-click the **viewport title**, point to **Views**, then click **Camera01** on the submenu.

    The Perspective viewport becomes the Camera01 viewport, as shown in Figure 12. Camera01's target object is at the center of the viewport, but is not visible.

2. Right-click the **title** of the Camera01 viewport, point to **Views**, then click **Camera02** on the submenu to change the viewport into the Camera02 viewport.

3. Click in the Left viewport to activate it, then press **[C]**.

    The Select Camera dialog box opens, as shown in Figure 13.

4. Click **Camera01** in the Select Camera dialog box, then click **OK** to close the dialog box and change the Left viewport into the Camera01 viewport.

5. Save the file as **Camerascene03**.

You changed the Perspective viewport into a Camera viewport first from Camera01's perspective, then from Camera02's perspective. You then selected the Left viewport and changed it into a Camera viewport from Camera01's perspective.

FIGURE 12
Camera01 viewport

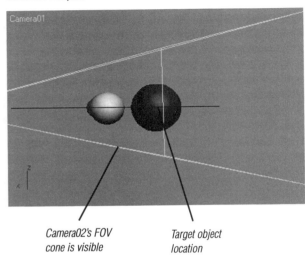

Camera02's FOV cone is visible — Target object location

FIGURE 13
Select Camera dialog box

List of cameras in scene

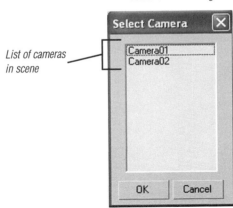

FIGURE 14
Camera01 viewport after Camera01 is rolled

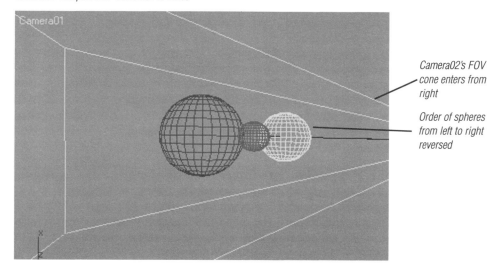

Camera02's FOV cone enters from right

Order of spheres from left to right reversed

Position cameras

1. Click the **Select and Move tool**, then in the Top viewport, select and move **Camera01** so that it is in the lower-left corner of the Top viewport.

   > TIP Your viewports might differ slightly from the figures, but the relative positions of the objects and cameras you place should be similar.

   Because it is a target camera, Camera01 can be moved but always remains aimed at its target object. Notice that the scene shown in the Camera01 viewport changes as the camera is moved.

2. Click in the Camera01 viewport, click the **Dolly Camera flyout button** in the lower-right of the screen, click the **Dolly Target button** to select it, then click and drag in the Camera01 viewport until Camera01's FOV cone is no longer visible in the Camera02 viewport.

   As you drag down, the target object moves closer to the target camera. The scene in Camera01's viewport does not change, however, because the camera is still pointed in the same direction and has the same FOV.

3. Click the **Roll Camera button**, then click and drag in the Camera01 viewport until the scene is upside down.

   The FOV cone for Camera02 should enter the Camera01 viewport from the right side of the screen when it is upside down, as shown in Figure 14.

   (continued)

AUTODESK 3D STUDIO MAX 5-17

4. Click in the Camera02 viewport, click the **Truck Camera flyout button**, click the **Truck Camera button**, then click in the Camera02 viewport and drag to the left until you can see only part of one sphere.

   The camera has moved parallel to its view in the Camera02 viewport.

5. Click in the Camera01 viewport, click the **Dolly Camera flyout button**, click the **Dolly Camera + Target button**, then click and drag up in the Camera01 viewport until Camera01's FOV cone fully encompasses one of the spheres.

6. Click the **Select Object tool**, in the Top viewport, select **Camera01's target object**, then right-click in the **Camera01 viewport** to select it and keep the target object selected.

7. Click the **Orbit Camera flyout button**, click the **Pan Camera button**, and drag in the Camera01 viewport to rotate the target object around the camera until it is between Camera01 and Camera02, as shown in the Top viewport in Figure 15.

8. Click the **Select and Move tool**, in the Top viewport move **Camera01's target object** to the center of the smallest sphere, click **File** on the menu bar, then save the file as **Camerascene04**.

You used the Select and Move tool to move Camera01, then used the Camera viewport controls to dolly its target object and roll the camera. You moved Camera02

(continued)

FIGURE 15
Top viewport after target object is rotated

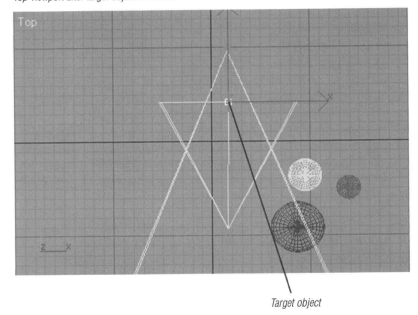

Target object

5-18 AUTODESK 3D STUDIO MAX   *Cameras and Lighting*

FIGURE 16
Camera01 viewport scene within live area frame

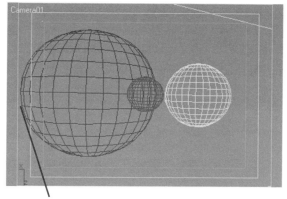

Spheres do not go beyond live area frame

FIGURE 17
Camera01 viewport object within action safe frame

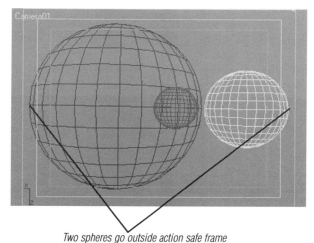

Two spheres go outside action safe frame

using the Truck Camera button, then dollied both Camera01 and its target closer to the objects in the scene. You used the Pan Camera button to rotate Camera01's target object around it to a new position, then moved the target object to the center of a sphere.

Use Safe Frames

1. Click in the Camera01 viewport to activate it, right-click the **viewport title**, then click **Show Safe Frame** on the right-click menu.

   Three colored frames appear in the viewport.

2. Click the **Dolly Camera flyout button**, click the **Dolly Camera button**, then drag down until all three spheres are fully visible within the live area frame, as shown in Figure 16.

3. Use the Dolly Camera button and the Truck Camera button to adjust the view so that all three spheres are within the title safe frame.

4. Use the Camera viewport controls to adjust the view so that only one sphere is fully encompassed within the action safe frame, as shown in Figure 17.

5. Save the file as **Camerascene05**, then reset 3ds Max.

You activated Safe Frames within a Camera viewport, then adjusted the camera to fit scene objects within the live area frame, the title safe frame, and the action safe frame.

LESSON 3

ADD LIGHTS TO A SCENE

What You'll Do

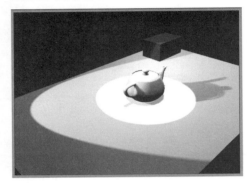

In this lesson, you will look at the three main types of standard light objects available in 3ds Max. You will learn how to insert a light into a scene, give it a name and display color, adjust its target distance manually, change a light into a different light, and make a light cast shadows.

Lights are objects in a scene that reproduce the look of indoor and outdoor light sources such as lamps, streetlights, and sunlight. The simplest kind of light object you can use is a **standard** light. A more complex option is a **photometric** light, whose parameters are based on the actual physical characteristics of light in the real world, including those of actual commercial lighting products. Because photometric lights are more complicated than standard lights, this chapter focuses on standard lights.

Exploring Standard Light Types

There are three main types of standard lights, as shown in Figure 18: spotlight, directional light, and omni light. A **spotlight** emits light rays from a source as a single beam. A **direct light** emits light rays parallel to each other in one direction. An **omni light** emits rays in all directions.

Spotlights, directional lights, and omni lights have just about the same parameters—what differentiates them is the way that they radiate—as a cone (spotlight), as a cylinder (directional), or in all directions (omni). As illustrated in Figure 18, if you have two different objects lit by the same spotlight, chances are that the shadows for each object would fall in a different direction from the other, because the light rays hitting them are traveling at an angle to each other. Light rays in a directional light are parallel to each other, and thus produce shadows that fall in the same direction. Although you could think of the sun as an omni light, it is so far from Earth that the rays we get from it are basically parallel and produce shadows in the same direction. Because this is true, directional lights are best for outdoor light sources, and spotlights are best used for indoor light sources. Omni lights are particularly useful if you want to accentuate an area of a scene that might be too dark, such as the corner of a room.

Because omni lights cast light in all directions, moving an omni light simply changes the location of the center of the light being emitted. Such is not the case for spotlights and directional lights, which, like cameras, fall into one of two categories: target or free. Target spotlights and target directional lights radiate from the light object onto a target object. As is true of camera target objects, light target objects can be moved, and the light object moves accordingly to continue being aimed at the target. Free spotlights and free directional lights do not have a target; you can change the direction a free light is aimed only by moving the light object itself. It is often most useful to use a target light (spotlight or directional) when lighting any scene, simply because it gives you more control over exactly where a light is aimed. A target light can also be particularly helpful when you are lighting a moving target in an animation.

Adding Lights to a Scene

Scenes containing no light objects have default lighting consisting of two unseen lights, one below and to the right of the scene, one above and to its left. This is why, up to this point, you have been able to see the ways light affects material in rendered scenes even though you have not added any lights to those scenes. As soon as a light object is added to a scene, the default lighting is turned off. To add a light to a scene, first click the Lights button on the Create panel. By default, the drop-down list under the Lights button is set to Standard, and a set of standard light buttons appears in an

FIGURE 18
Standard light types

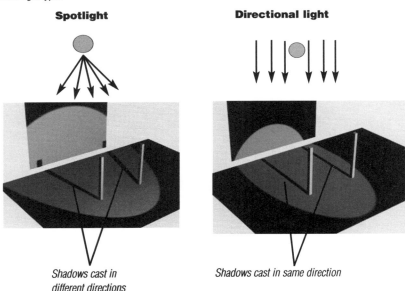
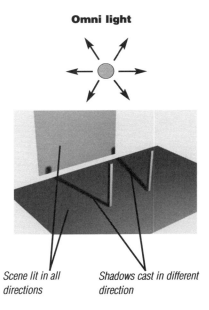

Lesson 3   Add Lights to a Scene

Object Type rollout beneath the drop-down list, as shown in Figure 19.

To create a target spotlight or a target directional light, click the Target Spot or Target Direct button on the Object Type rollout, click in the Top viewport in the location you want the light to appear, drag to another location in the viewport, as shown in Figure 20, and then release the mouse button to set the location of the target.

To create a free spotlight, free directional, or omni light in a scene, click the Free Spot, Free Direct, or Omni button on the Object Type rollout, and then click in the Top viewport in the location you want the light to appear. When you click in a viewport to insert the light, it is inserted facing away from you.

Use the Select and Move and Select and Rotate tools to change its location and/or direction.

QUICKTIP

Remember that when you add a light object to a scene, rendering the scene shows the effect of the light, but not the light object itself.

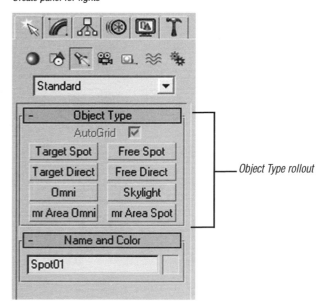

FIGURE 19
Create panel for lights

— Object Type rollout

5-22 AUTODESK 3D STUDIO MAX   *Cameras and Lighting*

After you have inserted a light, several rollouts appear on the Create panel that you can use to adjust the light object's parameters. In the Name and Color rollout, type a name for the light in the box to replace the default, click the color swatch to the right of the Name box, click a color in the Object Color dialog box, and then click OK to change the display color of the light object. After the light is deselected, return to the Modify panel to change the name or display color.

In the General Parameters rollout on the Create panel, when a light is first created, the On check box is checked, meaning that the light is on. In addition, the Targ. Dist. box lists the distance between the light source and its target or the end of the light's cone or cylinder. For a free light, this distance is 300 by default. Adjust the Targ. Dist. box number to change the target distance. Omni lights have no target distance.

After the light has been created and deselected, the General Parameters rollout is accessible only on the Modify panel for the

FIGURE 20
Inserting a target spotlight

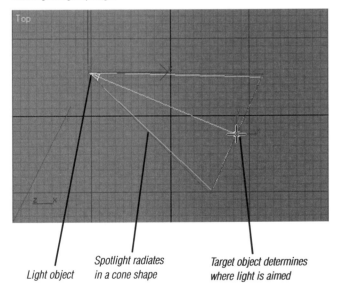

Light object   Spotlight radiates in a cone shape   Target object determines where light is aimed

Lesson 3   Add Lights to a Scene

AUTODESK 3D STUDIO MAX 5-23

light. As shown in Figure 21, in place of the Targ. Dist. parameter is a Light Type list box. Click the Light Type list arrow, and then click Spot, Directional, or Omni to change the light to a different type. Under the On check box is the Targeted check box. To change a free light into a targeted light, select this check box. To change a targeted light to a free light, deselect the check box. To the right of the Targeted check box, the target distance is shown. If the light is targeted, you can't change the target distance in the rollout, but if it is not targeted, you can.

> **QUICK**TIP
>
> Keep in mind that the cone and cylinder target distances are for reference; the light rays they indicate shine into infinity past the point where the cone or cylinder ends, until they hit a surface along the way.

In the Shadows group in the General Parameters rollout, click the Shadows check box to have the light cast shadows. The default method for generating shadows is Shadow Map, as shown in the Shadow Type drop-down list under the Shadows On check box. Shadow maps produce soft shadows quickly and are usually the best choice for shadow generation. However, shadow maps do not account for transparency or translucency in an object. Raytrace shadows are the next best choice; they support transparency and translucency and produce highly accurate shadows quickly, but do not produce soft shadows.

> **QUICK**TIP
>
> Soft shadows are generally more realistic in a scene. Hard-edged shadows have a distinct computer-generated look.

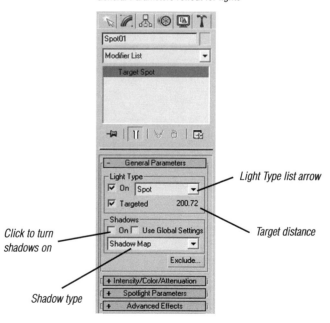

FIGURE 21
General Parameters rollout for lights

5-24 AUTODESK 3D STUDIO MAX   *Cameras and Lighting*

FIGURE 22
Moved target spotlight

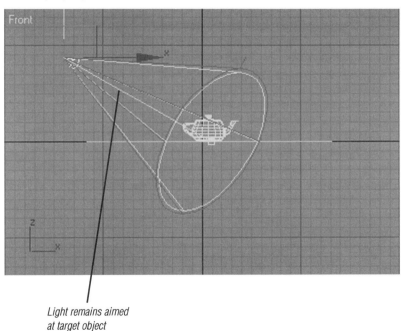

Light remains aimed at target object

Lesson 3   Add Lights to a Scene

Insert spotlights

1. Create a **plane** in the center of the Top viewport, then create a **teapot** in the center of the plane.

2. Click the **Lights button** on the Create panel, click the **Target Spot button** in the Object Type rollout, click in the Top viewport above and to the left of the upper-left corner of the plane, drag to the center of the teapot, then release the mouse button.

   A target spotlight is inserted, with its target at the center of the teapot. Notice that in the Perspective viewport, the teapot is not properly lit. Because the default lighting is off, you need to move the light to adjust the way it hits the teapot.

3. Click the **Select and Move tool**, click in the Front viewport, select the **light object** (if necessary), grab the **green move handle** on the move gizmo, then move it up about two inches.

   The light moves higher than the plane and teapot in the viewport, but remains aimed at the target object at the center of the teapot, as shown in Figure 22. Notice the difference in the lighting in the Perspective viewport.

4. Click the **Modify tab**, then click the **On check box** in the Shadows group on the General Parameters rollout to have the light cast shadows.

   (continued)

AUTODESK 3D STUDIO MAX 5-25

5. Click in the Perspective viewport, then click the **Quick Render (Production) tool** on the main toolbar.

   Your scene should look similar to Figure 23. Although you cannot see the location of the light in the scene, you can see the light's effect on the scene.

6. Close the rendered scene window, select the **light** in the Front viewport (if necessary), click the **Modify tab**, then deselect the **On check box** in the Light Type group of the General Parameters rollout.

   The target spotlight is turned off.

7. Save the file as **Lightscene01**.

   TIP Type Lightscene in the dialog box and click + (plus sign) instead of the Save button to add the 01 to the name. Click + each subsequent time you save to increase the filename value by 1.

You created a scene, inserted a target spotlight and target object, moved the spotlight up, turned on its shadows, rendered the scene, then turned off the light.

FIGURE 23
Spotlight in rendered scene

FIGURE 24
Directional light in Front viewport

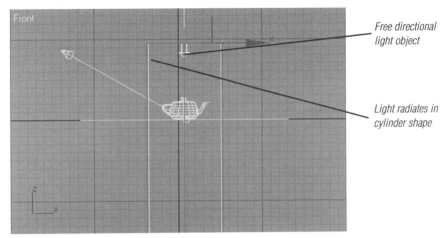

Free directional light object

Light radiates in cylinder shape

FIGURE 25
Directional light rendered in scene

Insert a directional light

1. Click the **Create tab**, click the **Free Spot button**, then click the **center of the teapot** in the Top viewport.

   A free spotlight is inserted where you click in the Top viewport. As you can see in the Front viewport, it is actually below the teapot and the plane.

2. Click the **Select and Move tool**, click in the Front viewport, select the **light object** (if necessary), then move the **green handle** on the move gizmo up about two inches.

   The light now shines onto the teapot and the plane.

3. Click the **Modify tab**, click the **Light Type list arrow** in the Light Type group on the General Parameters rollout, then click **Directional**.

   The light changes from a free spotlight to a free directional light, as shown in the Front viewport in Figure 24.

4. Right-click in the Perspective viewport, deselect the **On check box** in the Shadows group of the General Parameters rollout (if necessary), then render the scene.

   The rendered scene looks like Figure 25. The target spotlight inserted earlier is off and casts no light or shadows.

5. Close the rendered scene window, then save the file as **Lightscene02**.

You inserted a free spotlight, moved it up, changed it from a spotlight to a directional light, turned on its shadows, then rendered the scene.

Insert an omni light

1. Click the **Create tab**, click the **Shapes button**, click the **Box button** in the Object Type rollout, then create a **box** on the upper-right corner of the plane in the Top viewport.

2. Click the **Select Object tool**, select the **target spotlight (Spot01)** in the Top viewport, click the **Modify tab**, then click the **On check box** in the Light Type group on the General Parameters rollout to turn on the target spotlight.

3. Click in the Perspective viewport, then render the scene.

   As shown in Figure 26, the effect of the target spotlight and the free directional light are both shown in the rendered scene. The teapot has two shadows, one from each light. The box you created is either partially lit or not lit at all.

4. Minimize the **rendered scene window**, click the **Create tab**, click the **Lights button**, click the **Omni button** in the Object Type rollout, then click the **box** in the Top viewport.

   An omni light is inserted where you click in the Top viewport, but as you can see in the Front viewport, the light is even with the plane and the bottom of the box and isn't lighting the scene from above.

   (continued)

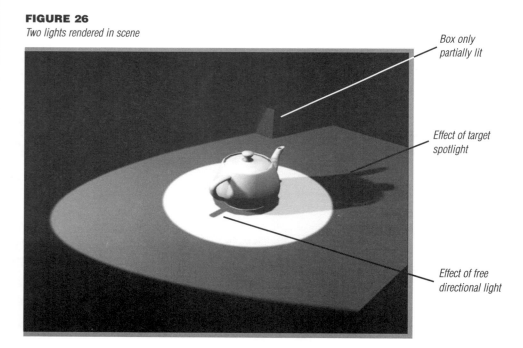

FIGURE 26
Two lights rendered in scene

Box only partially lit

Effect of target spotlight

Effect of free directional light

5-28 AUTODESK 3D STUDIO MAX   *Cameras and Lighting*

FIGURE 27
Omni light rendered in scene

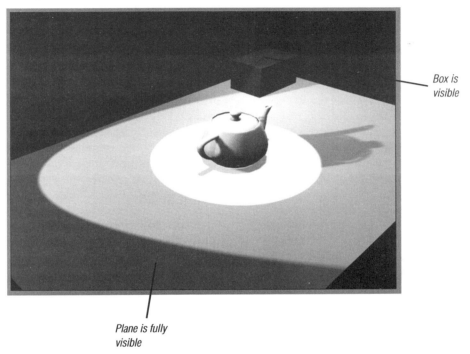

Box is visible

Plane is fully visible

5. Click the **Select and Move tool**, select the **omni light** in the Front viewport, and move the **green handle** on the move gizmo up about two inches.

6. Click in the Perspective viewport, then render the scene.

   The rendered scene looks like Figure 27. The target spotlight and free directional lights light the teapot, part of the plane, and part of the box. The omni light lights all of the objects in the scene, making the box visible and lighting previously unlit parts of the plane.

7. Close the **rendered scene window**, save the file as **Lightscene03**, then reset 3ds Max.

You inserted a box in the scene, turned back on the target spotlight, rendered and reviewed the scene, added an omni light to the scene, moved the omni light, and rendered the scene again.

LESSON 4

ADJUST LIGHT
PARAMETERS

What You'll Do

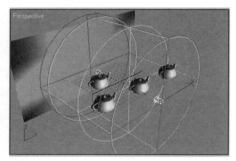

▶ In this lesson, you will learn how to change the parameters of a light to fit your needs in a scene. You will explore how to alter light intensity and color, how to control the size of the light as it hits surfaces, how to make a light reduce in intensity as it travels from its source, and how to clone lights so that changing parameters for one changes the parameters of several lights.

There is a wide range of information available about lighting concepts and how to think about lighting a scene, either in a TV studio or on a computer screen. As you work with lights in 3ds Max, you might want some guidance on how to establish a certain mood or accentuate a particular object in a scene or animation; you might also want to know more about the how and why of positioning a light to its best effect. This book includes an online bibliography you can use to further your understanding of how to think about lighting design. To see the bibliography, go to *www.courseptr.com/downloads* and enter the ISBN for this book. In this lesson, you'll look at the tools 3ds Max provides to adjust each light to maximum effect.

Changing Light Intensity and Color

A light's **multiplier** is its intensity, or brightness. The intensity of a standard light has a baseline value of 1; changes to the intensity are controlled by its multiplier, which is 1 by default (baseline of 1 multiplied by 1 = 1).

Increasing the multiplier multiplies the intensity accordingly–for instance, as shown in Figure 28, increase the multiplier to 2 and the light is twice as intense (2 × 1). Reduce the multiplier to .5 and the light is half as intense (.5 × 1). You can adjust the intensity of a light on the Intensity/Color/Attenuation rollout on the Modify panel for a selected light, as shown in Figure 29. Increase or decrease the number in the Multiplier box in the Intensity/Color/Attenuation rollout to control the intensity of a light.

You can also choose the color of the light emitted by a light object. Often you'll keep this color at white to reflect the color of most light sources, but you can change it to whatever color you need–such as red, green, or yellow if you are creating light emitted by a stoplight in a scene set at night, for example. To change a light's color, click the color swatch to the right of the Multiplier box in the Intensity/Color/Attenuation rollout, choose a color in the Color Selector dialog box, and then click Close.

Adjusting Cone and Cylinder Parameters

The cones and cylinders of spot and directional light objects help you see where light hits an object and the size and shape of the light cast. You can use the Light Cone group in the Spotlight Parameters or Directional Parameters rollout, as shown in Figure 30, to make additional changes to the cone and ultimately the light's effect on the scene.

If you want to see the cone for a light at all times, whether or not it is selected, click the Show Cone check box in the Light Cone group to turn on the cone.

Beneath the Show Cone check box are the Hotspot/Beam and Falloff/Field boxes. A light's **hotspot** is the area of the light that is at its brightest, or full intensity. The **falloff** is the transition between the hot spot to the unlit area, or in other words, from full

FIGURE 28
Lights with different intensity multipliers

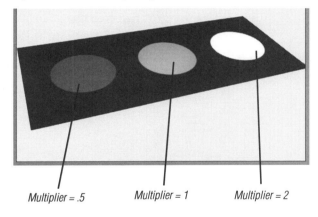

FIGURE 29
Intensity/Color/Attenuation rollout

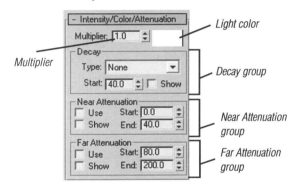

FIGURE 30
Directional Parameters rollout

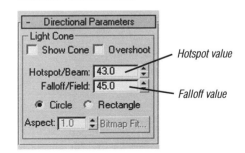

Lesson 4 Adjust Light Parameters

AUTODESK 3D STUDIO MAX 5-31

intensity to no intensity, as shown in Figure 31. By default, the hotspot size is 43 and the falloff size is 45. For a spotlight, this means that light rays opposite each other on the outer circumference of the hotspot circle is 43 degrees, and the rays opposite each other on the outer circumference of the falloff circle are at a 45 degree angle to each other. For a directional light, this means the diameter of the light's hotspot is 43 units, and the falloff's diameter is 45 units. By default then, the size of the transition between the hotspot and unlit area is 2 degrees for a spotlight and 2 units for a directional light. Because the falloff cannot start inside the hotspot, the hotspot number will always be less than or equal to the falloff. The falloff will increase accordingly if you increase the hotspot past the falloff's original value. If the falloff is large relative to the hotspot, the transition from lit to unlit happens across a larger distance and will be feathered and blurred. If the falloff is small, the transition occurs over a small distance, and the edge of the hotspot is sharper.

QUICKTIP

The hotspot and falloff values for a spotlight cannot increase past 180 degrees, but the same values for a directional light can go into the millions of units (not recommended!).

To engulf an entire scene in bright light, you can increase the hotspot size dramatically. You'll often want to do this with a directional light, because its default hotspot size produces a spotlight effect if you don't increase its size. An alternative way to do this is to click and select the Overshoot check box to the right of the Show Cone check box in the Light Cone group. This causes the light to be cast in all directions, lighting everything in the scene. One important thing to remember about the Overshoot feature is that even though light is cast in all directions, if shadows are on for the light they are only visible in the

FIGURE 31
Hotspot and falloff of a light on a surface

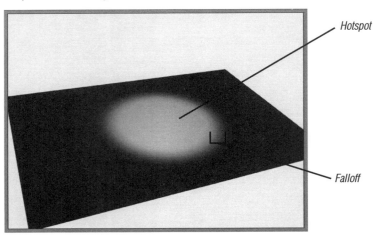

hotspot. You need to increase the hotspot accordingly when using Overshoot if you want to produce realistic shadows.

At the bottom of the Light Cone group are two option buttons, Circle and Rectangle. With the Circle option button selected, the light's shape is circular. Click the Rectangle option button to change the light's shape to rectangular, as shown in Figure 32, which you might use to create a light shining through a window onto the floor of a room. When the Rectangle button is selected, the Aspect Ratio box becomes active. The aspect ratio is the ratio of the width of the rectangle to its height–for instance, a rectangle with an Aspect Ratio of 2 is twice as wide as it is high. This parameter should come into play for you only if you are using the Projector Map advanced lighting effect to project a bitmap as the light. See Lesson 6 for more on this topic.

Using Decay and Attenuation

The intensity of a light from its source to its target or the end of its cone is based on its multiplier and color. How that light affects objects is based only on the intensity of the light and the angle at which the light hits a surface (its **angle of incidence**). In other words, the light does not automatically decrease in intensity as it travels farther from the light source, as it would in the natural world. Think of the headlights on a car; they light the street in front of you, but because light intensity decreases over distance, they won't light the person crossing the street five blocks ahead. Decay and attenuation are two processes you can use to control how light decreases over distance.

FIGURE 32
Rectangular light cone in viewport and rendered

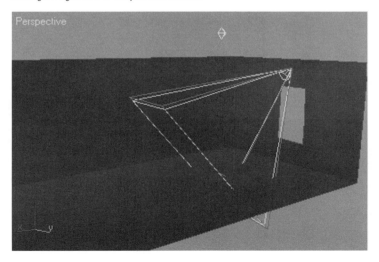 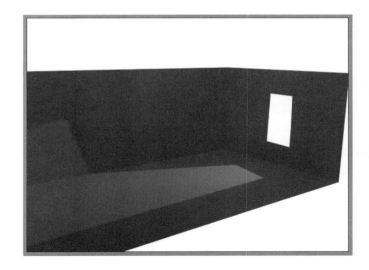

The settings for both decay and attenuation are in the Intensity/Color/Attenuation rollout.

With attenuation, you control where a light starts relative to its source, where it reaches full intensity, how far it maintains its full intensity, and where its full intensity starts to fade back to zero (if so desired). **Near attenuation** is the setting for where the light starts at zero and goes to full intensity. **Far attenuation** is the setting for where the light goes from full intensity to zero. To use near attenuation, select the light, select the Use check box in the Near Attenuation group on the Intensity/Color/Attenuation rollout (see Figure 29), adjust the number in the Start box to indicate the distance from the source the light should start, and adjust the number in the End box to indicate the distance from the source the light should shine at full intensity. Between the Start and End points, the light changes from zero to full intensity, as shown in Figure 33. From the End point, the light continues at full intensity into infinity, or until it reaches a far attenuation Start point. To use far attenuation, select the Use check box in the Far Attenuation group on the Intensity/Color/Attenuation rollout, adjust the Start number to indicate the distance from its source the light will start diminishing, and adjust the End number to indicate the distance from its source that the light's intensity reaches zero.

> **QUICK**TIP
>
> Near and far attenuation can be used together, or separately. It depends what you want your light to do.

FIGURE 33
Light with near and far attenuation

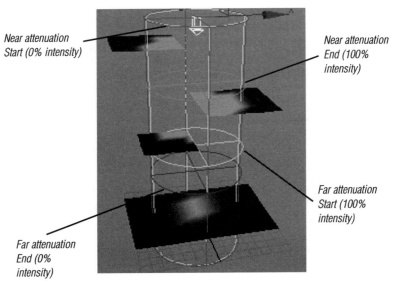

Near attenuation Start (0% intensity)
Near attenuation End (100% intensity)
Far attenuation Start (100% intensity)
Far attenuation End (0% intensity)

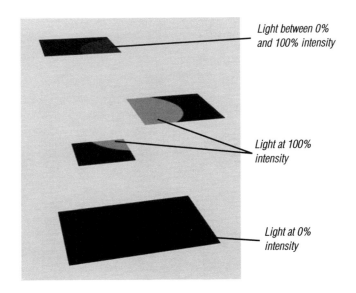

Light between 0% and 100% intensity
Light at 100% intensity
Light at 0% intensity

As you adjust the Start and End numbers for either near or far attenuation, in the viewports the Start and End locations are shown by circles in directional lights, as shown in Figure 33, lens-shaped sections for spotlights, and spheres for omni lights. Whatever shape the indicator, each moves as you make adjustments to the Start and End numbers. Click the Show check box in the Near Attenuation group to have the attenuation indicators show in the viewports whether or not a light is selected. Render the scene to see the effect of attenuation on your light.

Unlike attenuation, decay uses a formula rather than manual settings to determine how the light weakens as its distance from its source increases. By default, there is no decay and None appears in the Type list box in the Decay group on the Intensity/Color/Attenuation rollout. Click the Type list arrow, and choose Inverse to set the light to decay according to a formula based on the distance of a lit surface from either the light source or, if attenuation is used, the near attenuation End point. Decay starts at the light source or the near attenuation End point, if used, and continues according to its formula until the light's far attenuation End point, if used, or into infinity. To set the decay according to the formula for actual, real-world light decay, click the Type list arrow, and then click Inverse Square on the list. Although this formula is equivalent to what you would experience in the real world, in the reality of computer graphics it can be too dim. Inverse is your best choice when decaying standard lights.

To manually set the decay start point, adjust the number in the Start box to the start location you want to use. As with attenuation, you'll see an indicator in the viewports for the decay start location. Click the Show check box if you want this indicator to appear in the cone whether or not the light is selected.

Instancing Lights

Just as you can with objects, you also can create instances of lights. This is an excellent tool because it enables you to control multiple lights at once. When you are doing indoor lighting you'll find that many rooms have several lights that all have the same intensity–like, for example, in a classroom with twenty fluorescent lights on its ceiling. Because the lights all have the same parameters, instancing one light to create the lighting for that scene enables you to adjust all of them at once. To instance a light, the process is the same as instancing objects. Select a light, click Edit on the menu bar, and then click Clone to open the Clone Options dialog box. Click the Instance option in the dialog box, and then click OK. You can also select the light with the Select and Move tool, and then press Shift while moving the light to create a clone and open the Clone Options dialog box, click the Instance option button, adjust the number of instances of the light you want in the Number of Copies box, and then click OK. After you have instanced the lights, adjusting the parameters for one instance changes the parameters of all of the instances.

Change light intensity

1. In the Front viewport, create a **plane** that fills much of the viewport, then in the Top viewport, create a **teapot** below the plane and make two copies of the teapot to the right of the original.

   > TIP To make your screen match the results in this lesson, spread out the teapots evenly so that one appears in the center of the viewport, and the other two appear halfway to the left and right edges of the viewport, respectively.

2. Click the **Lights button**, click the **Target Direct button** in the Object Type rollout, click in the Top viewport beneath the center teapot, drag up until the mouse pointer is above the plane in the viewport, then release the mouse button.

3. Click the **Modify tab**, click the **On check box** in the Shadows group of the General Parameters rollout, click in the Perspective viewport, then use the viewport controls to make all three teapots fully visible in the viewport (if necessary).

4. Select the **directional light object** (**Direct01**), open the **Intensity/Color/Attenuation rollout** on the Modify panel, change the number in the Multiplier box to **.5**, then render the scene.

   The intensity of the light is reduced by half from its original intensity, and should look similar to Figure 34.

   (continued)

FIGURE 34
Light intensity reduced by 50%

5-36 AUTODESK 3D STUDIO MAX   *Cameras and Lighting*

FIGURE 35
Light intensity increased to 50% more than original

5. Minimize the **rendered scene window**, change the number in the Multiplier box to **1.5**, then render the scene.

   The intensity of the light increases to 50% more than the original intensity (whose multiplier value was 1), as shown in Figure 35.

6. Close the **rendered scene window**, then change the number in the Multiplier box to **1**.

7. Save the file as **Lightadjust01**.

You created a scene containing three teapots and a plane, inserted a free directional light aimed at one of the teapots and the plane, turned on the light's shadows, decreased the light's intensity, rendered the scene, increased the light's intensity, then rendered the scene again.

Adjust hotspot and falloff

1. With the **light object** selected, pan down the Modify panel until you see the Directional Parameters rollout, open the **Directional Parameters rollout**, then click the **Show Cone check box** to always show the light's cone.

2. Increase the number in the Hotspot/Beam box on the Directional Parameters rollout to **87**, then render the scene.

   The size of the hotspot increases so that it is large enough to cast light on all three teapots. In the viewports, this is shown as the increased circumference of the cylinder that is the light's cone. The Falloff increases to 89 automatically.

   (continued)

3. Minimize the **rendered scene window**, increase the number in the Falloff/Field box on the Directional Parameters rollout to **125**, then render the scene.

   The size of the falloff increases, and the area between the hotspot and unlit surfaces becomes wider and blurrier, as shown in Figure 36. The larger falloff also means that more of the outer teapots' surfaces are lit. In the viewports, a second cylinder that serves as an indicator for the falloff value increases in size.

4. Minimize the **rendered scene window**, reduce the number in the Hotspot/Beam box on the Directional Parameters to **50**, then render the scene.

   The hotspot is reduced in size, further widening and blurring the area between the hotspot and falloff values.

5. Close the **rendered scene window**, then save the file as **Lightadjust02**.

You increased the size of a light object's hotspot, rendered the scene, increased the size of the light's falloff, rendered the scene, reduced the size of the light's hotspot, then rendered the scene again.

Use Overshoot to light a scene

1. With the **light** selected, change the Hotspot/Beam number in the Directional Parameters rollout to **43** and the Falloff/Field number to **45**.

(continued)

FIGURE 36
Light with falloff increased to 125

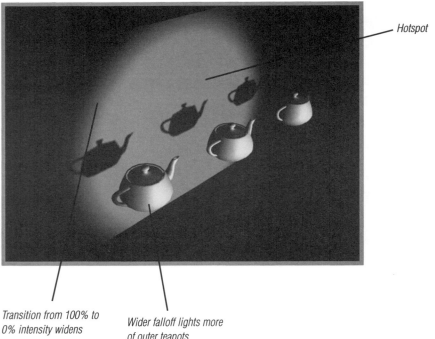

Hotspot

Transition from 100% to 0% intensity widens

Wider falloff lights more of outer teapots

FIGURE 37
Scene with Overshoot turned on

FIGURE 38
Falloff indicator in Front viewport

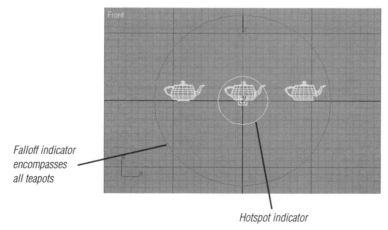

Falloff indicator encompasses all teapots

Hotspot indicator

2. Click the **Overshoot check box** in the Light Cone group on the Directional Parameters rollout, then render the scene.

   The entire scene is lit. However, only the teapot in the center of the row casts a shadow, as shown in Figure 37, because it is the only teapot within the hotspot/falloff of the light.

3. Minimize the **rendered scene window**, then change the Falloff/Field number in the Directional Parameters rollout to **125**.

   All three teapots now fall within the hotspot and falloff of the light, as the Front viewport shows in Figure 38.

4. Render the scene.

   All three teapots cast shadows on the plane.

5. Minimize the **rendered scene window**, then save the file as **Lightadjust03**.

You adjusted the hotspot and falloff size for a light in a scene, used Overshoot to light the whole scene, then increased the light's falloff size to have all objects in the scene cast shadows.

Use attenuation

1. Click the **Select and Move tool**, click in the Top viewport, move the **plane** from the center of the viewport to the top of the viewport, select the **center teapot**, press **[Shift]** and move the **teapot** to create a copy of the teapot, then position the **copy of the teapot** above and between the left and center teapots in the row of three.

   (continued)

2. Click in the Perspective viewport, select the **light object** (if necessary), click the **Modify tab**, open the **Directional Parameters rollout** (if necessary), click the **Overshoot check box** to deselect it, then change the Hotspot/Beam number to **125**.

All of the teapots should fall within the hotspot of the light and be lit at full intensity.

3. Open the **Intensity/Color/Attenuation rollout** (if necessary), then click the **Use check box** in the Near Attenuation group to use near attenuation for the light.

Near attenuation is turned on, with its Start point at the light object and its End point at 40. The End point is indicated as a blue circle in the light's cylindrical light cone.

4. Adjust the number in the End box in the Near Attenuation group until the End attenuation point is just below all of the teapots in the Top viewport, click in the Perspective viewport (if necessary), then render the scene.

The light reaches 100% intensity before it hits the teapots, and all are fully lit, as is the plane.

5. Minimize the **rendered scene window**, click the **Use check box** in the Far Attenuation group on the Intensity/Color/Attenuation rollout, then adjust the numbers in the Start and End boxes in the Far Attenuation group so that the Start indicator is between the front row of teapots and the back teapot, and the End indicator is between the back teapot and the plane, as shown in Figure 39.

(continued)

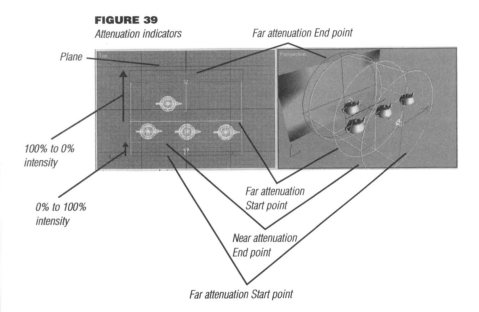

FIGURE 39
Attenuation indicators

5-40 AUTODESK 3D STUDIO MAX

Cameras and Lighting

FIGURE 40
Scene with near and far attenuation turned on

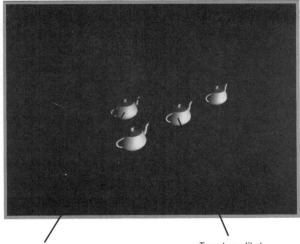

Teapot lit at slightly less than full intensity

Teapot row lit at full intensity

6. Click in the Perspective viewport (if necessary), then render the scene.

   As shown in Figure 40, the light is at full intensity when it hits the row of teapots, it starts waning in intensity as it hits the back teapot, and is at 0% intensity before it gets to the plane, leaving the plane unlit.

7. Minimize the **rendered scene window**, then save the file as **Lightadjust04**.

You moved the plane in the scene and made a copy of a teapot, turned off the Overshoot feature for the light in the scene, turned on near attenuation and adjusted its End point, then rendered the scene. You then turned on far attenuation, adjusted its Start and End points, then rendered the scene again.

Use decay

1. Deselect the **Use check box** in the Far Attenuation group on the Intensity/Color/Attenuation rollout.

   Far attenuation is turned off. The light reaches full intensity at the near attenuation End point and continues at full intensity thereafter.

2. Click the **Type list arrow** in the Decay group on the Intensity/Color/Attenuation rollout, then click **Inverse**.

   Because near attenuation is in use, at the near attenuation End point, the light starts to decay according to the Inverse formula.

(continued)

3. Render the scene.

   As shown in Figure 41, the back teapot and the plane are lit at less than full intensity because the light decays after it hits the row of teapots.

4. Minimize the **rendered scene window**, click the **Type list arrow** in the Decay group, then click **None** to turn off Decay.

5. Save the file as **Lightadjust05**.

You turned off far attenuation for a light, turned on decay using the Inverse formula, rendered the scene, then turned off decay.

Instance lights

1. Delete the **back teapot** from the scene, then reduce the hotspot and falloff of the light object so that only the center teapot in the row of teapots is lit at full intensity.

2. Scroll up on the Modify panel (if necessary), then deselect the **Targeted check box** in the Light Type group of the General Parameters rollout.

   The light becomes a free directional light instead of a target directional light.

3. Click in the Top viewport (if necessary), click the **Select and Move tool** on the main toolbar, select the **light object**, press **[Shift]**, move the light to the left until it points at the left teapot in the row of teapots, then release the mouse button.

(continued)

FIGURE 41
Scene with decay turned on

Teapot and plane lit by decayed light

FIGURE 42
Three light instances

FIGURE 43
Three light instances with far attenuation turned on

4. In the Clone Options dialog box, click the **Instance option button**, change the number in the Number of Copies box to **2**, then click **OK**.

   Two instances of the light have been created, one pointing at the left teapot in the row of teapots, and one further to the left of that one.

5. Select the **far left light object**, then use the **red axis handle** on the move gizmo to move the light until it is pointing at the teapot on the far-right in the row of teapots.

6. Click in the Perspective viewport, then render the scene.

   Your scene should look similar to Figure 42.

7. Minimize the **rendered scene window**, select the **center light object**, click the **Use check box** in the Far Attenuation group on the Intensity/Color/Attenuation rollout to turn on far attenuation, then render the scene.

   Because the lights are instanced, far attenuation is turned on for all three lights at the same settings. The light is at full intensity when it hits the teapots and reaches zero intensity before the plane, as shown in Figure 43.

8. Close the **rendered scene window**, save the file as **Lightadjust06**, then reset 3ds Max.

You reduced the hotspot and falloff size of a light, changed the light from a targeted light to a directional, created two instances of the light, moved one instance, rendered the scene, turned on far attenuation for one instance, then rendered the scene again.

LESSON 5

WORK WITH SHADOWS

What You'll Do

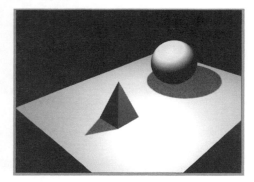

▶ In this lesson, you will learn how to adjust the parameters of a shadow to change its color and increase or decrease its darkness. You will also learn how to assign a map to a shadow.

Modifying Shadow Parameters

After you have set a light to cast shadows, you can actually change the shadow's appearance using the Shadow Parameters rollout, as shown in Figure 44. Usually you want shadow color to be black, but if you want to change the shadow color for a light, open the Shadow Parameters rollout with the light selected, click the Color color swatch in the Object Shadows group to open the Color Selector dialog box, choose a color for the shadow, and then click Close.

The **density** of a shadow is its darkness, and you can modify this as well. The default density of a shadow is 1. To increase or decrease the density of a light's shadows, adjust the number in the Dens. box to the right of the Color color swatch in the Shadow Parameters rollout. Decreasing

FIGURE 44
Shadow Parameters rollout

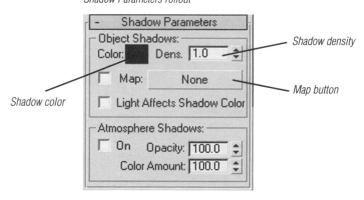

the density makes the shadow lighter, and increasing it makes the shadow darker.

If you want the color of the light to have an impact on the color of the shadow, click the Light Affects Shadow Color check box at the bottom of the Object Shadows group to select it. When selected, the color of the light's shadows are a blend of the light's color and of the shadow color selected in the Object Shadows group.

Mapping a Shadow

You can also control a shadow's appearance by mapping it; this is useful if, for example, you want shadows on a brightly lit surface to reveal detail about the surface that isn't visible in the lit areas. When you assign a map to shadows, the color of each shadow is a blend of its original color and the colors in the map. To use a shadow map, click the Map check box in the Object Shadows group, and then click the map button next to the Map check box, click the name of the map you want to use in the Material/Map Browser, and then click OK. After the shadow is mapped, as shown in Figure 45, you can click the Map check box to deselect it if you don't want the map to be assigned.

FIGURE 45
Light with mapped shadows

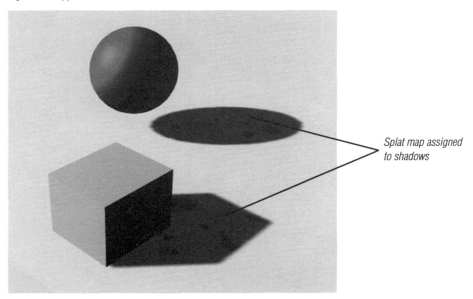

Splat map assigned to shadows

Lesson 5   Work with Shadows

Modify shadow parameters

1. In the Top viewport, create a **plane**, create a **pyramid** on top of the left side of the plane and a **sphere** on the right side of the plane near its center, then use the **Select and Move tool** to move the sphere above the plane in the Perspective viewport.

2. Click the **Create tab**, click the **Lights button** on the Create panel, click the **Omni button**, then click in the top center of the Front viewport to insert an omni light above the sphere, pyramid, and plane.

3. Click the **Modify tab**, click the **On check box** in the Shadows group of the General Parameters rollout, click in the Perspective viewport, then render the scene, as shown in Figure 46.

4. Minimize the **rendered scene window**, select the **light object** (if necessary), open the **Shadow Parameters rollout** on the Modify panel, click the **Color color swatch** in the Object Shadows group, click a **red color** in the Color Selector dialog box, click **Close**, click in the Perspective viewport, then render the scene.

   The shadows are a dark red color now, rather than pure black.

5. In the Shadow Parameters rollout, change the number in the Dens. box in the Object Shadows group to **.25**, then render the scene.

(continued)

FIGURE 46
Omni light casts shadows in scene

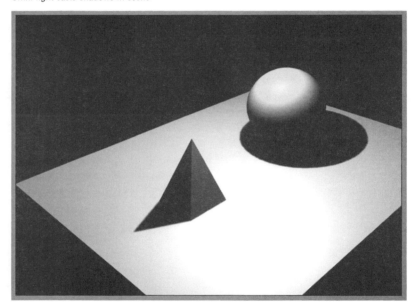

5-46 AUTODESK 3D STUDIO MAX

Cameras and Lighting

FIGURE 47
Light with low-density shadows

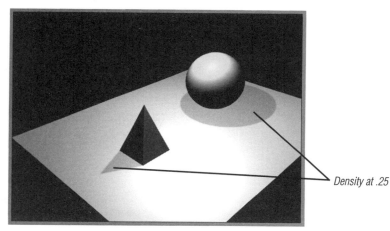

Density at .25

FIGURE 48
Light with Speckled mapped shadows

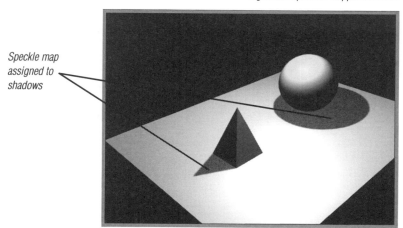

Speckle map assigned to shadows

The shadows decrease in density, as shown in Figure 47.

6. Minimize the **rendered scene window**, then save the file as **Shadowscene01**.

You created a scene, inserted an omni light, set the light to cast shadows, adjusted the color of its shadows, rendered the scene, adjusted the density of the light's shadows, then rendered the scene again.

Map a shadow

1. With the **omni light** selected, click the **Color color swatch** in the Shadow Parameters rollout, select **black** in the Color Selector dialog box, click **Close**, then change the number in the Dens. box in the Shadow Parameters rollout to **1**.

2. Click the **map button** to the right of the Map check box in the Object Shadows group of the Shadow Parameters rollout.

   The Material/Map Browser opens.

3. Double-click **Speckle** in the Material/Map Browser to assign it to the light's shadows, then render the scene.

   The shadows now look like those shown in Figure 48.

4. Close the **rendered scene window**, save the file as **Shadowscene02**, then reset 3ds Max.

You changed the color and density parameters of a light's shadows, assigned a map to the light's shadows, then rendered the scene.

LESSON 6

USE LIGHTS

What You'll Do

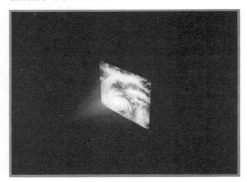

In this lesson, you will learn how to control how light affects the color components of the surfaces it hits, and how to project an image using a light. You will also discover some quick ways to add interesting effects to a light, such as adding volume to light and adding effects that make a light appear as seen through a camera lens.

Controlling How Light Affects Surfaces

Options in the Modify panel's Advanced Effects rollout, shown in Figure 49, enable you to make a light object light only one or two of a surface's ambient, diffuse, or specular color components. You might want to do this if you are using multiple lights but want one light to affect just the specular component, and another light to affect a surface's diffuse and ambient components. Click the Diffuse check box to deselect it and light only the specular (if checked) and ambient components of a surface, as shown on the left in Figure 50. Click the Specular check box to deselect it and light only the diffuse

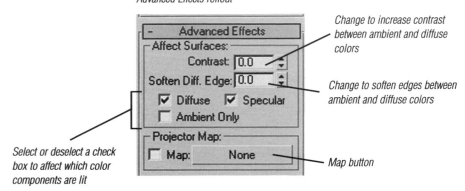

FIGURE 49
Advanced Effects rollout

5-48 AUTODESK 3D STUDIO MAX

Cameras and Lighting

(if checked) and ambient components of a surface, as shown on the right in Figure 50. Click the Ambient Only check box to select it and light only the ambient component of a surface, as well as to deactivate Contrast, Soften Diffuse Edge, Diffuse, and Specular.

Projecting a Map with a Light

Say you want to create a scene in which a movie is showing on a screen or an image is projected onto a wall. You can handle the task of creating the projection easily by projecting a map using a light. To do this, select the light you want to use to project the map, select the Map check box in the Projector Map group on the Advanced Effects rollout, click the map button to the right of the Map check box, click Bitmap in the Material/Map Browser, in the Select Bitmap Image File

FIGURE 50
Lights affecting different color components

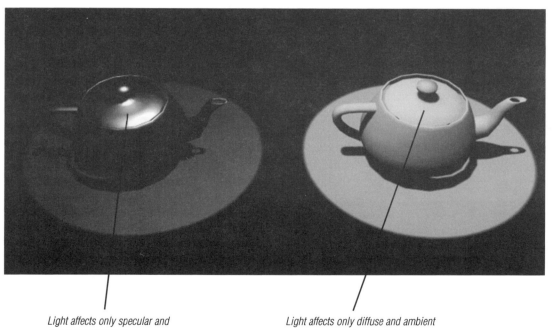

Light affects only specular and ambient components

Light affects only diffuse and ambient colors (no specular highlight)

Lesson 6   Use Lights

AUTODESK 3D STUDIO MAX 5-49

dialog box navigate to the file you would like to project, click the file, and then click Open. The name of the file appears on the Projector Map map button, and when you render the scene the image appears on any surface that the light hits, as shown on the left in Figure 51.

If you have a circular light cone and the bitmap image you choose is rectangular, or if you have a rectangular light cone that has a different aspect ratio than the image you choose, you can adjust the size and shape of the cone to fit the image. To fit the cone to the aspect ratio and shape of the bitmap

FIGURE 51
Projecting a map with a light

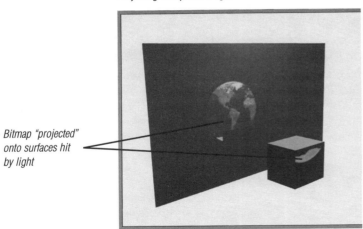
Bitmap "projected" onto surfaces hit by light

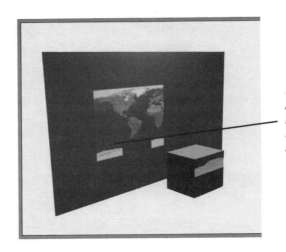
Cone shape adjusted to fit bitmap image shape and aspect ratio

image you have chosen, go to the Directional Parameters or Spotlight Parameters rollout, and then click the Rectangle option button in the Light Cone group to shape the cone for a rectangular image. Next, click the

Bitmap Fit button to the right of the Aspect box in the Light Cone group. Navigate to the bitmap file that is assigned as the projector map, click it, and then click Open. The next

time you render the scene, you see that the rectangle's height and width (its aspect ratio) now fit the projected bitmap, as shown on the right in Figure 51.

Exploring advanced lighting

In older versions of 3ds Max, to get realistic, nuanced outdoor lighting and shadows you had to create multiple spotlights in a dome shape over a scene, or use a third-party script to help create realistic lighting. Fortunately, in the current version of 3ds Max you can much more quickly and easily create such natural-looking shadows by creating a Skylight. **Skylight** is a photometric light that lights a scene as though it is a dome around the scene. To use Skylight, you also need to use an advanced lighting tool called the Light Tracer to render the scene. To render a scene lit by skylight, click Rendering on the menu bar, point to Advanced Lighting, and then click Light Tracer on the submenu to open the Advanced Lighting tab in the Render Scene: Default Scanline Renderer dialog box. At the top of the tab, Light Tracer is selected in the Select Advanced Lighting dialog box. Click the Render button at the bottom of the dialog box to close the dialog box and render the scene. The shadows in the newly rendered scene are natural, soft, and not overpowering.

Lesson 6 Use Lights

AUTODESK 3D STUDIO MAX 5-51

Control how light affects surfaces

1. In the Top viewport, create a **plane**, then create a **cone** on top of the center of the plane with a Radius 1 of **35**, Radius 2 of **10**, and Height of **45**.

2. Click the **Lights button** on the Create panel, click the **Target Spot button**, click in the upper-left corner of the Top viewport, drag to the center of the cone object, release the mouse button, then use the **Select and Move tool** in the Front viewport to move the **light object** to the upper-left corner of the Front viewport.

3. Click the **Modify tab**, click the **On check box** in the Shadows group on the General Parameters rollout, click in the Perspective viewport, then render the scene.

   The rendered scene should look similar to Figure 52.

4. Minimize the **rendered scene window**, select the **light object** (if necessary), open the **Advanced Effects rollout** on the Modify panel, increase the number in the Contrast box in the Affect Surfaces group to **30**, then render the scene.

   When the scene is rendered again, the lit side of the cone appears brighter in contrast to the side in shadow, and the line between the diffuse and ambient colors is more defined.

   (continued)

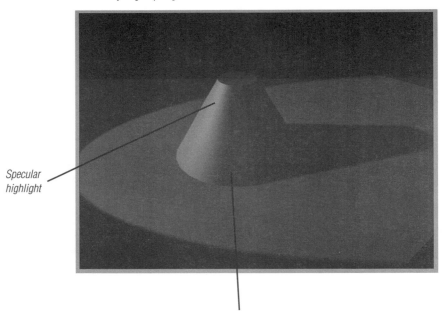

FIGURE 52
Scene lit by target spotlight

Specular highlight

Gradual change from diffuse to ambient color

FIGURE 53
Light affects surfaces differently

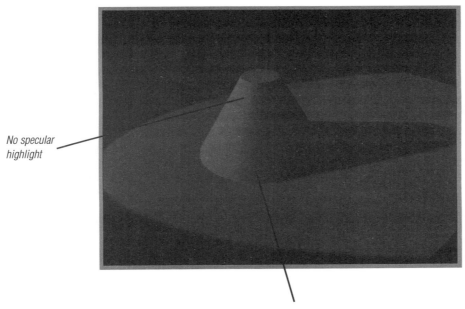

No specular highlight

Transition from diffuse to ambient is sharper

5. Click to deselect the **Specular check box** in the Affect Surfaces group on the Advanced Effects rollout, then render the scene.

   As shown in Figure 53, the light no longer affects the specular component of surfaces, and the cone no longer has a specular highlight.

6. Minimize the **rendered scene window**, then save the file as **Advancedlight01**.

You created a scene, inserted a light into the scene, rendered the scene, adjusted the contrast between diffuse and ambient colors created by the light on the surfaces, rendered the scene, changed the light to have it affect only diffuse and ambient color components of surfaces, then rendered the scene again.

Project a map with a light

1. Select the **cone**, delete it, click the **Select and Rotate tool** on the main toolbar, select the **plane** in the Perspective viewport, then click and drag down on the **green axis handle** of the Rotate gizmo until the plane has rotated approximately 90 degrees.

2. Use the **Select and Move tool** and the necessary viewports to move the **light object** so that the line connecting the light object and its target object is perpendicular to the plane in both the Top and Front viewports, as shown in Figure 54.

3. Click in the Perspective viewport, select the **light object** (if necessary), click the **Modify tab** (if necessary), open the **Advanced Effects rollout**, and click the **map button** next to the Map check box in the Projector Map group to open the Material/Map browser.

4. Double-click **Bitmap** in the Material/Map Browser, navigate to the **3dsMax8/maps/Space folder**, click **CloudMap**, click **Open**, click in the Perspective viewport, then render the scene.

   | TIP Click a different map if CloudMap isn't available.

The map is projected onto the plane by the light in the shape of its light cone. The map might not be colored the same as its unprojected version, because its color is blended with that of the surface it hits in the scene.

(continued)

FIGURE 54
Light aimed at plane

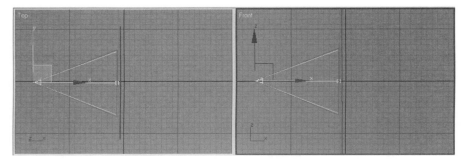

FIGURE 55
Projector map with correct shape and aspect ratio

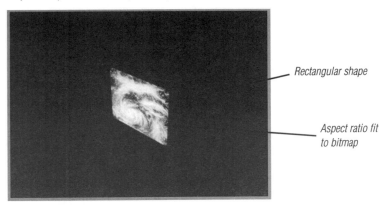

Rectangular shape

Aspect ratio fit to bitmap

Generating radiosity in a scene

Another advanced lighting tool available in 3ds Max can help you produce photorealistic indoor lighting by calculating the radiosity of the lights in a scene. **Radiosity** is a calculation of the way light moves around a scene, from its first contact with a surface to its effect on other surfaces when it bounces in a different direction. For instance, imagine that you are walking into a room with bright white walls, bright red carpet, and a lot of natural light spilling into the room. As light pours into the room, it bounces off the carpet and hits the walls, turning the walls a bit pink. Even the ceiling will turn different hues as the light bounces around the room. Without radiosity, when a scene is rendered the lights in that scene originate at their source and hit surfaces with no bounce, producing no indirect light on other objects in the scene. This feature is primarily used by architects working with 3ds Max to create visualizations of interiors (buildings and how sunlight affects interiors). Character animators might be less inclined to use radiosity because photorealism is usually less important than an artistic look in a scene.

To use radiosity, click Rendering on the menu bar, point to Advanced Lighting, and then click Radiosity on the submenu to open the Advanced Lighting tab in the Render Scene: Default Scanline Renderer dialog box. In the Radiosity Processing Parameters rollout, click the Start button. Click Yes in the Radiosity dialog box that appears (if necessary), and then click Start again.

5. Minimize the **rendered scene window**, select the **plane**, then change its display color to **white**.

6. Select the **light object** again, open the **Spotlight Parameters rollout** on the Modify panel, click the **Rectangle option button** in the Light Cone group to select it, then change the shape of the light cone.

7. Click the **Bitmap Fit button** beneath the Rectangle option button, navigate to **3dsmax8/maps/Space**, click **CloudMap** (if available), click **Open**, click in the Perspective viewport, then render the scene.

   The plane is now white, and the bitmap looks more like its unprojected image. And as shown in Figure 55, the shape of the light's cone is rectangular, and its aspect ratio fits that of the bitmap.

8. Minimize the **rendered scene window**, save the file as **Advancedlight02**, then reset and close 3ds Max.

You deleted a cone, rotated a plane, and moved a light object in the scene. You then assigned a projector map to the light, rendered the scene, changed the display color of the plane, changed the light cone shape and aspect ratio, and rendered the scene again.

CHAPTER SUMMARY

In this chapter, you learned how to work with cameras and lights in a scene. You learned what camera objects are and how they're used to render scenes from different viewports. You also learned about the two camera types, target and free, and how to insert each into a scene. Later in the chapter, you learned how to change a viewport into a Camera viewport, and how to work with a camera using the tools on the Main toolbar. You worked with Safe Frames, which help you design your scene for TV monitors so that nothing gets cut from the image. You also learned how to add lights to a scene, change one kind of light into a different kind of light, and how to make a light cast shadow. You adjusted light parameters, including size, intensity, and color. You also worked with shadows, and assigned a map to a shadow.

What You Have Learned

- How to add cameras to a scene and adjust camera parameters
- How to target an object with a camera
- How to dolly a camera
- How to use a Camera viewport
- How to use Safe Frames to determine which elements in a scene will be rendered, based on the size of a TV screen
- How to work with spotlights, omni lights, and direct lights
- How to change light intensity and color
- How to use lighting decay and attenuation
- How to create instances of lights
- How to apply shadows and work with shadow parameters
- How to map a shadow

Key Terms

Target camera   A camera that always focuses on a target object and the area around it.

Free camera   Takes in the scene that appears in the direction the camera is aimed, with no target.

Field-of-view cone   The light-blue pyramid shape that appears when a camera is inserted.

Field of view (FOV)   The amount of the scene that is visible through the camera measured in degrees of the horizon.

Spotlight   Emits light rays from a source as a single beam.

Direct light   Emits light rays parallel to each other.

Omni light   Emits rays in all directions.

Multiplier   A light's intensity, or brightness.

Hotspot   Where light is at its brightest, or full intensity.

Falloff   The transition between a light's hotspot to the unlit area.

Near attenuation   The setting for where the light starts at zero and goes to full intensity.

Far attenuation   The setting for where the light goes from full intensity to zero.

chapter 6
ANIMATION

1. Animate with Auto Key.
2. Animate with Set Key.
3. Configure animation timing.
4. Edit keys.
5. Use the Dope Sheet.
6. Use the Curve Editor.
7. Assign animation controllers.
8. Assign animation constraints.

chapter 6 ANIMATION

Animation is all about bringing life to inanimate objects. 3ds Max offers a robust toolset for doing this. In this chapter, you will learn the principles behind animation and take an in-depth look at the many tools that 3ds Max offers for animating scenes.

When you animate an object, you change something about the object over time, such as its position, rotation, materials, or some other feature. In this chapter, you'll animate objects in a scene that shows a plane on an airstrip. You'll animate the plane as it moves down the runway and takes off. You'll animate the lights along the runway so that they power on as the plane passes, and you'll animate a flag to make it wave in the breeze. You'll also animate the propeller so that it spins, and you'll animate the pilot's eyes so

that they blink and move from side to side. One of the main tools you'll use as you work with animation is the key or keyframe, which is what you use to tell 3ds Max how an object's parameters change over time. You set keys at different frames, and 3ds Max does the work of changing an object gradually—or quite suddenly, if you say so—between the keys you set.

3ds Max provides many tools for manipulating keys after you set them, including the Dope Sheet and Curve Editor. You can work with animation controllers and constraints to add to and edit existing animations. By the end of this chapter, you'll know how to use these tools and you will have a strong foundation for exploring additional animation features on your own. Remember—when you animate in 3ds Max, the sky's the limit.

Tools You'll Use

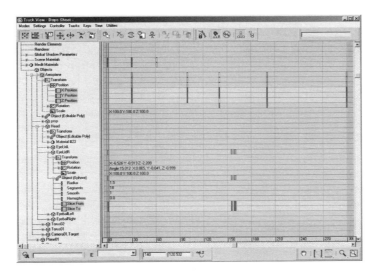
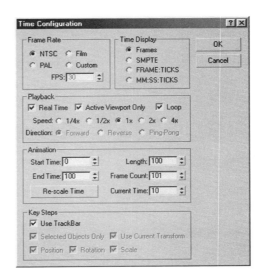
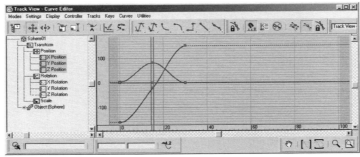

LESSON 1

ANIMATE WITH AUTO KEY

What You'll Do

In this lesson, you will learn the basic elements of animation in 3ds Max, how to animate a scene using Auto Key, and how to play an animation. You'll also practice animating different kinds of objects and parameters.

Understanding Animation

There are several key terms that you need to know to understand animation, and how to animate scenes within 3ds Max. Basically, an **animation** is a sequence of still images that changes slightly from one image to the next; when viewed quickly and in order by the human eye, the images depict an object or objects moving or changing. A movie on film is such a collection of photographic images; a 3ds Max animation is a collection of still images of a scene.

Each single image in an animation is called a **frame**. With movie cameras, frames are created when successive pictures are taken of a moving object. With old-style animation, such as was used for Looney Tunes cartoons or early Disney movies, each frame in an animation would be drawn and colored by hand to create the appearance of motion. Using 3ds Max, you get to skip all of this work and let the computer do most of the animating for you. Your job is to create **keyframes**, or frames that capture change values for an object or objects (also known as **keys**). For instance, as shown in Figure 1,

if an animation shows a sphere moving from the left of a scene to the right of a scene, the sphere's original location would be a starting keyframe, and its final location after moving to the right would be a second keyframe. The sphere's horizontal position would have one value in the first keyframe, and a different value in the second keyframe. 3ds Max calculates the intermediate values of the sphere's horizontal position and creates all of the frames in between. This process of generating intermediate values between known values is called **interpolation**. If the sphere animation is 50 frames in length, you create keyframes at 1 and 50, and the software creates, or **interpolates**, the values from frame 2 through frame 49.

> **QUICK**TIP
> Animators also refer to this process as **tweening** (short for in-betweening).

The track bar, time slider, and frame and key navigation buttons in the 3ds Max interface, including how to play an animation and move between frames on the track bar, are

6-4 AUTODESK 3D STUDIO MAX   *Animation* covered in Chapter 1. Please review this material to refamiliarize yourself with these tools and actions.

Setting Keyframes with Auto Key

The simplest way to animate a scene is by using the Auto Key function. With Auto Key, changes that you make to objects in a scene are automatically captured as keyframes; the software then creates the frames between keyframes to create the animation.

To turn on Auto Key, click the Toggle Auto Key Mode button on the status bar at the bottom of the screen, as shown in Figure 2.

After it is selected, the Toggle Auto Key Mode button turns red, the area above the track bar and surrounding the time slider becomes red, and a red outline appears around the active viewport. This bright red color in many parts of the screen lets you know that what you do in the scene now will be animated, so pay attention! To animate an object in the scene, first move the time slider on the track bar from the 0 frame to a later frame, such as 50. Next, select and change an object in the scene. When you complete the change to the object, two keyframes appear on the track bar. The first keyframe appears at 0 on the track bar; this keyframe contains the original key value of the object before it was changed. The second keyframe will appear at 50 on the track bar; this keyframe contains the key value of the object after it was changed.

Transformation keys (position, rotation, scale) are color coded. If the value changed was position, the key on the timeline will be red; if the rotation value was changed, the key will be green; and if the scale value changed, the key will be yellow. If a combination of the three was changed, the key will be multi-colored.

Remember that every item in a scene has its own timeline. To view the timeline and keyframes for an object, select the object in the scene. If you select more than one object, the keyframes for all of the objects appear on the timeline.

FIGURE 1
Animated sphere

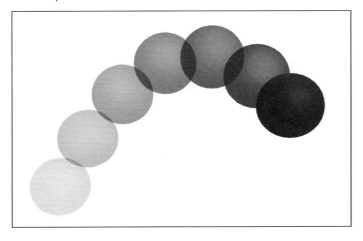

FIGURE 2
Toggle Auto Key Mode button on the status bar

Toggle Auto Key Mode button

Lesson 1 Animate with Auto Key

Displaying Trajectories

If you are animating the movement of an object, you can display the object's trajectory to track its movement in detail. As shown in Figure 3, an object's **trajectory** is a line that starts where the object starts and follows the path of the object as it moves. The trajectory line is a reference that gives you more control over movement of an object. It will not appear in a scene when the scene is rendered. To display an object's trajectory, right-click an animated object, and then click Properties on the right-click menu that appears to open the Object Properties dialog box. In the Display Properties section in the dialog box, click the Trajectory check box to select it, and then click the OK button.

Squares appear on the trajectory where keyframes are set for the object's position. Along the length of the trajectory between the squares, white dots appear spaced apart from each other. Each dot represents a frame in the object's animation, as shown in Figure 3. By default, the dots are closer together near a keyframe and farther apart as they move away from a keyframe. This is because by default 3ds Max does its best to simulate natural motion in animation. From one position, an object starts slowly (the object moves only a little between frames), speeds up and reaches a consistent speed (the object moves further between frames), and then slows down again as it approaches a change in direction (the next keyframe). Later in this chapter, you'll learn how to adjust the timing of an object's animation; if the timing for an object's movement is adjusted, the arrangement of the white dots along the trajectory changes.

QUICKTIP
When Auto Key is off, moving an object will move its entire trajectory along with it.

FIGURE 3
Animation trajectory

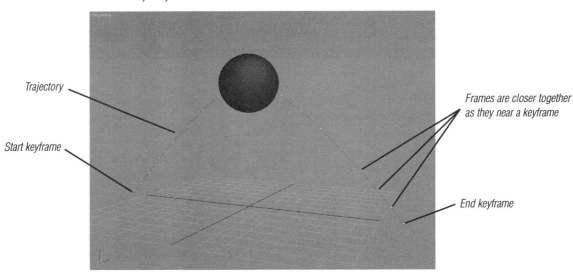

Trajectory

Start keyframe

Frames are closer together as they near a keyframe

End keyframe

Animation

Playing an Animation

After you have set at least two keyframes, you can view the animation in two ways. You can manually move the time slider from left to right (or right to left to see the animation in reverse). Moving the time slider manually can be helpful if you are trying to get to a particular frame, but it does not show the animation at the correct frame rate. To view the animation with accurate timing, click the Play Animation button in the frame navigation tools area of the status bar, as shown in Figure 4. All animated objects in the scene in the active viewport will be animated and, by default, play continuously. The time slider will travel from left to right on the track bar, the length of the active time segment–by default, from 0 to 100. If objects in the scene change only between 0 and 50, then as the animation moves from 51 to 100 nothing will happen on the screen. You can click a different viewport while the animation is playing to make it active and to see the objects within it animated.

If you click the Play Animation button when the time slider is in the middle of the track bar, the animation will start at the currently selected frame. To stop the animation, click the Stop button. To view a particular frame in the animation, move the slider to the frame's number on the track bar, or enter the frame's number into the Current Frame (Go To Frame) box under the frame navigation buttons.

What Can Be Animated?

After you understand how keyframes work, and understand that changes between keyframes are what drive animation, you have an unlimited number of options to use in designing and creating animated scenes. Almost any parameter or change you make to an object can be animated, including moving, rotating, scaling, adjusting object parameters, applying modifiers, and applying materials. You can animate all kinds of objects, including cameras and lights. Keep in mind that every object in a scene has its own timeline, which can have keyframes applied to it.

The easiest way to find out whether something can be animated, in fact, is to just give it a try–chances are it can be. This lesson provides several chances to practice animating many different types of objects and parameters.

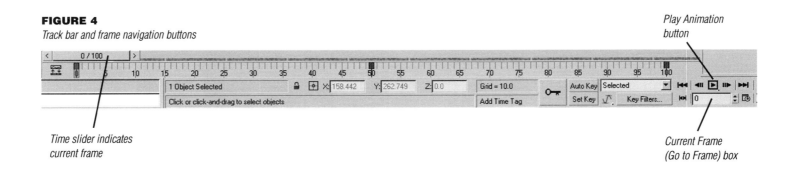

FIGURE 4
Track bar and frame navigation buttons

Set keyframes with Auto Key

1. Open **MAX06-01.max**, then save it as **Toy Plane**.

   This is a scene of an airstrip with a toy plane that's ready for take off. There is a camera that has a target linked to the plane, so that the camera will track with the plane as it moves. In the current viewport configuration, the lower-right viewport is the viewport for this camera.

2. Press **[H]** to display the Select Objects dialog box, then select the object called **Aeroplane**.

3. Drag the **time slider** to frame **200**, then click the **Toggle Auto Key Mode button** to activate it.

   The track bar is now red to indicate that Auto Key is turned on.

4. In the Front viewport, move the **plane** along the x-axis so that it sits just outside the wall at the other end of the runway, as shown in Figure 5.

   TIP As you move the object in the Front viewport, keep an eye on the Camera01 viewport to see the plane close up.

5. In the Front viewport, move the **plane** up along the y-axis, so that it sits a little above the camera.

6. Drag the **time slider** back to frame **100**.

7. Right-click in the **Left viewport**, then press **[Alt][W]** to maximize the view.

   (continued)

FIGURE 5
Moving the plane

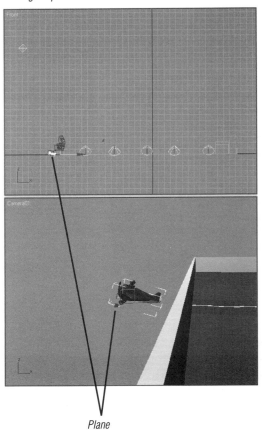

Plane

FIGURE 6
Plane on the ground

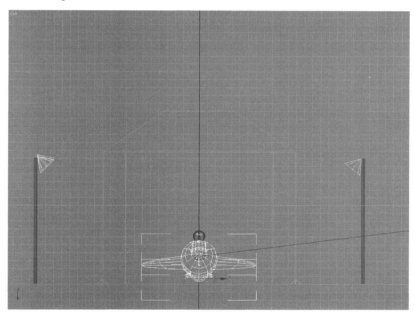

8. Zoom in to see the plane better, then drag the **plane** down along the y-axis so its wheels sit on the runway, as shown in Figure 6.

   Because you went back to frame 100 and dragged the plane down with Auto Key on, a key is automatically placed there. Now the plane won't leave the ground until frame 100.

9. Click the **Toggle Auto Key Mode button** to turn off Auto Key, press **[Alt][W]** to see all of the viewports, then click in the **Camera viewport**.

   Turning off Auto Key ensures that you don't accidentally make keyframes.

10. Drag the **time slider** back to frame **0**, then click the **Play Animation button** ▶.

    The plane travels down the runway and lifts off at frame 100; it then continues to climb until frame 200, where it stops.

11. Stop the animation, then save the file.

You selected an object, turned on Auto Key mode, animated the movement of the object's position, turned off Auto Key mode, then played the animation.

Animate a camera

1. Maximize the **current viewport**, switch to the **Top viewport**, then select the **camera**.

   TIP You might need to zoom out to see the camera.

2. Drag the **time slider** to frame **300**, then turn on **Auto Key**.

3. Move the **camera** along the y-axis to the other corner of the airfield, as shown in Figure 7.

4. Switch to the **Front viewport**, then drag the **camera** up along the y-axis, so it sits a little above the plane.

5. Switch back to the **Camera viewport**, then drag the **time slider** back to frame **0**.

6. Make sure the **camera** is selected, then in the Parameters rollout of the Modify Panel, click the **200mm Stock Lens button** to zoom into the plane.

7. Drag the **time slider** to frame **40**, then click the **50mm Stock Lens button**.

   By choosing two different lens settings with Auto Key on, you have created two keyframes. The camera lens will now perform a zoom out during the first 40 frames of the animation.

8. Turn off Auto Key mode by clicking the **Toggle Auto Key Mode button**.

9. Drag the **time slider** back to frame **0**, then click the **Play animation button** ▶.

   Now the camera zooms out and moves from its keyframed position at frame 0 to a higher

(continued)

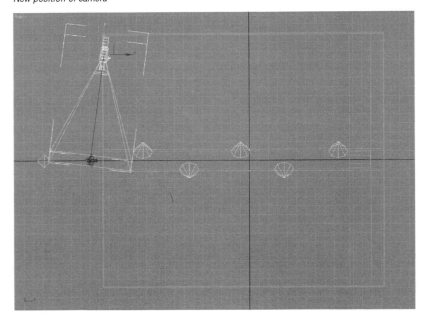

FIGURE 7
New position of camera

FIGURE 8
Animated Camera viewport

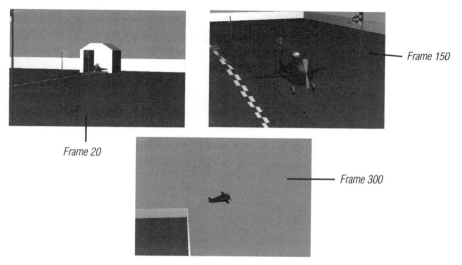

Frame 150

Frame 20

Frame 300

FIGURE 9
Selecting flag vertices

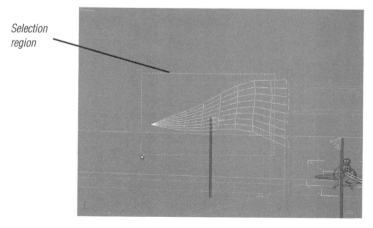

Selection region

position on the other side of the airfield by frame 300. Figure 8 shows the animation at frame 20, frame 150, and frame 300. The camera always looks at the plane because the camera target is linked to it.

10. Stop the animation, then save the file.

You selected a camera, animated its movement in a scene, animated the zooming of the Camera viewport, then played the animation.

Animate a modifier

1. Maximize the **Camera viewport** (if necessary), right-click the viewport **label**, point to **Views**, then click **Perspective** to switch to the Perspective viewport.

2. Make sure the **time slider** is at frame **0**, then press **[H]** to open the Select Objects dialog box.

3. Double-click **Flag** to select it, then press **[Z]** to zoom in on the flag.

> TIP Make sure to select the flag, not the flagpole.

4. Press **[F3]** to enter wireframe view.

5. Press **[1]** to enter vertex sub object mode, then drag a selection region around all vertices in the flag except the row inside the flagpole, as shown in Figure 9.

All the vertices within the region turn red to indicate they have been selected.

(continued)

6. On the Modify panel, click the **Modifier list list arrow**, then click **Wave**.

   The Wave modifier is added to the selected vertices in the Flag, and it appears in the modifier stack.

7. In the Wave modifier Parameters rollout, change the Amplitude 1 and Amplitude 2 settings both to **8**, then change the Wave Length to **30**.

   The orange Wave gizmo now appears to be wavy, as shown in Figure 10.

8. Click the **Toggle Auto Key Mode button**, then drag the **time slider** to frame **300**.

9. Change the value of the Phase parameter in the Parameters rollout to **50**.

   This parameter animates the phase of the waves in the flag, giving it a waving motion.

10. Turn off **Auto Key**, drag the **time slider** back to frame 0, then click away from the flag to deselect it.

11. Press **[C]** to return to the camera view, press **[F3]** to enable Smooth + Highlights in the view, then play the animation.

    The flag now waves as the camera trucks by it. You might notice that the propeller on the plane is not spinning. You'll change that later in the chapter.

12. Stop the animation and save the file.

You selected the vertices of an object, applied a modifier to the vertices, adjusted the parameters of the modifier, animated a change in the parameters of the modifier, then played the animation.

FIGURE 10
Wave gizmo

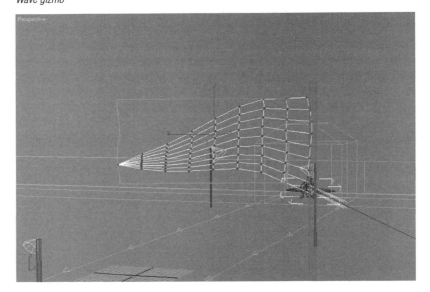

FIGURE 11
Red value of 255

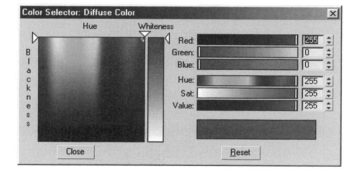

Animate a material

1. Drag the **time slider** to **0**, then press **[M]** to open the Material Editor.

2. Click the **black sample slot** called RunwayLights in the lower-right corner (if necessary).

3. Turn on **Auto Key**, then drag the **time slider** to frame **30**.

4. Click the Diffuse color swatch to open the Color Selector, then select a **red** color in the Color Selector, as shown in Figure 11.

   The Red value in the RGB area of the Color Selector reads 255. Notice that the Ambient and Diffuse color swatches now have red brackets around them, indicating that those values have a keyframe at the current frame.

5. Drag the **time slider** to frame **60**, then change the color in the Color Selector back to **black**.

   You just set another keyframe at frame 60, defining the diffuse color as black again.

   (continued)

6. Turn off **Auto Key**, then drag the **time slider** back and forth between frames **0** and **60**.

   The color of the runway lights is animated from black to red and back again over the course of 60 frames. Also, you can see the color being animated in the sample slot in the Material Editor. Figure 12 shows the animation at frame 45, when the lights are red on-screen, and at frame 60, when they are black again.

7. Close the **Color Selector**, close the **Material Editor**, then save the file.

You turned on Auto Key, selected a material, animated the diffuse color of the material, turned off Auto Key, then played the animation.

Animate object parameters

1. Maximize the **Camera viewport** (if necessary), then drag the **time slider** to frame **150**.

2. Press **[H]** to open the Select Objects dialog box, then select the object called **EyeLidR**.

3. Press **[P]** to switch to a perspective view, then press **[Z]** to zoom in on the eyes.

4. Click the **Toggle Auto Key Mode button**.

(continued)

FIGURE 12
Animated runway lights

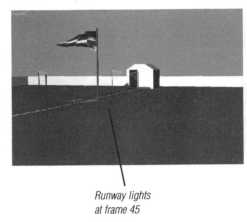

Runway lights at frame 45

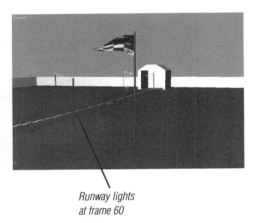

Runway lights at frame 60

6-14 AUTODESK 3D STUDIO MAX

Animation

FIGURE 13
Right eye blinking

5. On the Modify panel, change the Slice From setting to **90** and the Slice To setting to **–270**.

   The eye appears to close, as shown in Figure 13. The parameters you set are now keyframed at frame 160.

6. Drag the **time slider** back to frame **140**, then press **[Z]** to zoom in to the eye again.

7. Change the Slice From setting back to **68** and the Slice To setting back to **–240**.

8. Drag the **time slider** to frame **160**, then press **[Z]** to zoom in to the eye again.

9. Change the Slice From setting back to **68** again and the Slice To setting back to **–240**.

10. Turn off **Auto Key**, then zoom out a little and drag the **time slider** back and forth between frames **140** and **160**.

    The right eye now appears to blink over the course of 21 frames.

11. Repeat the above steps on the left eye, **EyeLidL**.

    TIP Don't forget to turn on Auto Key to make the changes, and to turn off Auto Key when finished.

12. Play the animation back in the Camera viewport, then save your scene.

You animated the slice of the eyelid spheres so that it looks like the pilot blinks.

Animate lights

1. Press **[Alt][W]** to see all four viewports, switch to the **Front viewport**, then zoom out (if necessary) to see all of the lights (there are five).

2. Select the spotlight (**Fspot01**) closest to the plane.

3. Drag the **time slider** to frame **10**, turn on **Auto Key**, then in the light's Intensity/Color/Attenuation rollout on the Modify panel, change the Multiplier value to **1**.

   This animates the brightness of the light, causing it to ramp up over the first 10 frames.

4. Select the next spotlight to the left (**Fspot02**), click its Multiplier value **up spinner** once, then click the **down spinner** once to change the Multiplier value back to **0**.

   By changing the Multiplier value with Auto Key on, then changing it back to 0, you have performed a little trick that forces 3ds Max to create a key at that frame, yet keep the Multiplier value at 0.

5. Drag the **time slider** to frame **20**, then change the Multiplier value to **1**.

   The selected light will ramp up from frame 10 to 20. The keys on the track bar for Fspot02 should look like those shown in Figure 14.

   (continued)

FIGURE 14
Keys for Fspot02

FIGURE 15
Rendered frame 140

6. Select the next spotlight to the left (**Fspot03**), then again, click the Multiplier value **up spinner once**, then click the **down spinner** once to change the value back to **0**.
7. Drag the **time slider** to frame **30**, then set the Multiplier value to **1**.
8. Perform the same actions for the remaining two spotlights, having each light sequentially ramp up its Multiplier value over 10 frames.
9. Turn off **Auto Key**, maximize the **camera view**, move the **time slider** to frame **0**, then play the animation back in the camera view.
10. Stop the animation, move the **time slider** to frame **140**, then render the scene.

    As shown in Figure 15, the lights have all powered up and light the runway as the plane takes off.
11. Close the **rendered scene window**, save the file, then reset 3ds Max.

You animated the spotlights in the scene so that they appeared to turn on in sequence.

LESSON 2

ANIMATE WITH SET KEY

What You'll Do

▶ *In this lesson, you will learn how to animate objects using Set Key mode, and how to filter the parameters for which keyframes are set using the Key Filters button.*

Setting Keyframes with Set Key

When you animate with Auto Key, 3ds Max keeps track of all of the changes that you make to an object and sets keyframes accordingly. When you change an object, a keyframe is set. Set Key animation mode gives you more control over when a keyframe is set; you can try out things, and then not capture a change as a keyframe until you are ready to do so. It's also an easy way to set keys for the beginning and end of a period where the object's values don't change. For instance, when something is at rest for a while, you need to set a key that marks the beginning of a time period when the object doesn't move. You also need to set a keyframe later in the timeline at the end of the object's rest period. Both keys will have the same position values.

To use Set Key mode, click the Toggle Set Key Mode button on the status bar, as shown in Figure 16. Just like in Auto Key mode, in Set Key mode the Toggle Set Key Mode button turns red, the area around the time slider turns red, and the active viewport is outlined in red. Move the time slider to the appropriate frame, and then modify the object as desired. Unlike in Auto Key mode, the software will not automatically create a keyframe at 0 and another at the current frame based on the changes you make. Instead, after you are satisfied with the changes you've made to the object, click the Set Keys button (the large button that looks like a key) to create a keyframe of the object. One keyframe will appear on the timeline at the current frame. Move the slider to another frame, make changes, and then click the Set Keys button again to create a keyframe at the second frame location.

If you are in Set Key mode and you move the time slider to a new frame, and make changes to an object, do NOT click the Set Keys button, and then move to another frame, the changes you made at the previous frame are not saved. The object will revert to the settings it had at the previously set keyframe.

Filtering Keys

In Auto Key mode, when a keyframe is created, it contains only the information about the object that changed from the previous keyframe. One of the most important differences between Auto Key and Set Key is that the keyframes you create in Set Key contain all of the item's information. By default, each keyframe contains the position, rotation, scale, and IK parameters information for the object, even if that information didn't change from the previously set keyframe. You can change the parameters that are captured in a keyframe by filtering it.

To filter a keyframe in Set Key mode, move the time slider to the appropriate frame on the timeline, and then click the Key Filters button on the status bar to open the Set Key Filters dialog box, as shown in Figure 17. This dialog box contains a list of the values for the object for which you can create keyframes (that are **keyable**). Each item on the list has a check box next to it. Click a check box to select it and have the parameter's value keyed when you click the Set Keys button. Click a check box to deselect it if you don't plan to change that value in the keyframe. If you want all parameters for the object to be keyed, click the All check box to select it.

After you have confirmed that the appropriate check boxes are selected in the Set Key Filters dialog box, close the dialog box, make appropriate changes to the object, and then click the Set Keys button on the status bar. Only changes to parameters you checked will be recorded in the set keyframe.

FIGURE 16
Toggle Set Key mode button

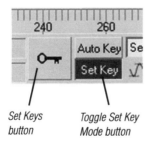

Set Keys button
Toggle Set Key Mode button

FIGURE 17
Set Key Filters dialog box

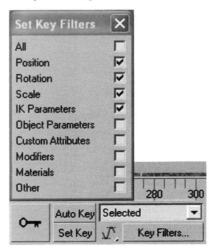

Filter keys

1. Open **MAX06-02.max**, then save it as **Toy Plane02**.
2. Click the **Key Filters button**.
   The Set Key Filters dialog box appears.
3. Deselect the **Scale** and **IK parameters check boxes**, as shown in Figure 18.
   Now when you create keys in Set Key mode, you will create keys only for Position and Rotation.
4. Close the dialog box, then save the file.

You opened the Set Key Filters dialog box, deselected two types of keyframes in the dialog box to keep them from being set during Set Key mode, then closed the dialog box.

Set keyframes with Set Key

1. Maximize the **Camera viewport** (if necessary), select the **plane** (Aeroplane), then click the **Toggle Set Key Mode button**.
   The button turns red.
2. Drag the **time slider** to frame **140**, then click the **Set Keys button** ⊶.
   A keyframe for the plane's position and rotation are created, and they are represented on the track bar by a green and red square at frame 140.
3. Drag the **time slider** to frame **200**.

(continued)

FIGURE 18
Set Key Filters dialog box

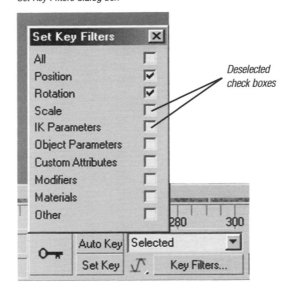

Deselected check boxes

FIGURE 19
Reference Coordinate System list

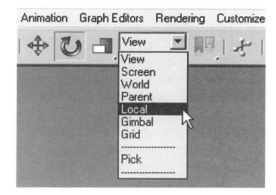

FIGURE 20
Plane moved away from camera

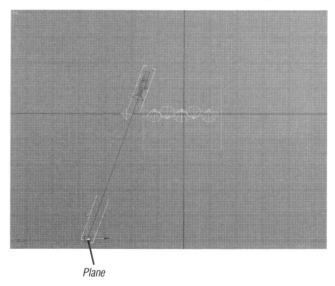

4. Click the **Select and Rotate tool**, click the **Reference Coordinate System list arrow** on the main toolbar, then click **Local**, as shown in Figure 19.

   The Rotate gizmo now aligns its rotational axes to the plane instead of the Viewport.

5. Rotate the **plane** around its local z-axis **−90** degrees, so that the wings are perpendicular to the ground and the bottom of the plane faces the camera, then click the **Set Keys button**.

6. Switch to the **Top viewport**, then drag the **time slider** to frame **300**.

7. Zoom the viewport out (if necessary), then with the **Select and Move tool**, move the **plane** far away from the camera, as seen in Figure 20.

8. Switch to the **Camera viewport**, then move the **plane** up along its z-axis until the airfield is no longer in view.

9. Rotate the **plane** around its local z-axis until the wings level out, then rotate it around its local y-axis so that it points away from the camera.

10. Click the **Set Keys button**, then turn off Set Key mode.

11. Save the file, then go to the start of the animation and play it.

    The plane now takes off and makes a roll to the left, before leveling out.

12. Stop the animation.

Using Set Key mode, you placed the airplane in different poses throughout the timeline and created keys for multiple transforms at once.

LESSON 3

CONFIGURE ANIMATION
TIMING

What You'll Do

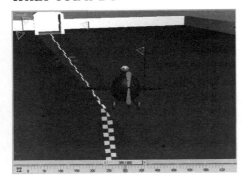

In this lesson, you will explore how to time an animation using its frame rate, how to define the length of your animation, and how to re-scale an animation when its timing has changed. You will also learn what the different options are for displaying time on the timeline, and how to control the way animations are played back.

Setting the Frame Rate

Animation is all about timing. You set the timing of an animation based on its **frame rate**, which is the number of frames displayed per second. The standard frame rate for video in the United States is set by the National Television Standards Committee (NTSC) and is approximately 30 frames per second (FPS). This is the default frame rate used in 3ds Max. At this frame rate, an animation of 100 frames will be 100/30 or $3\frac{1}{3}$ seconds long. If you want to animate an object's position over the first two seconds of the animation, you would set keyframes for it at frames 0 and 60.

You have the ability to change the frame rate because you might need to create an animation for eventual output to film, which runs at 24 FPS, or you might want to create animation for the Web at a lower frame rate of 12 FPS, due to Internet bandwidth limitations.

To change the frame rate, click the Time Configuration button, as shown in Figure 21, to the right of the Current Frame (Go to Frame) box on the status bar. The Time Configuration dialog box opens, as shown in Figure 22. In the Frame Rate group, you can change from the default NTSC frame rate to the European standard frame rate of 25 FPS by clicking the PAL option button, or you can choose the film standard frame rate of 24 FPS by clicking the Film option button. If you want to set your own frame rate, click the Custom option button, and then enter the frame rate you want to use in the FPS box under the Custom option button.

Changing the frame rate does not automatically affect the timing of your animation in 3ds Max. If you create an animation at 30 FPS and then change it to the PAL frame rate of 25 FPS, 3ds Max will reduce the number of frames in the active time segment accordingly while maintaining the timing you originally set. An object that moves in 60 frames at 30 FPS would move in 50 frames at 25 FPS.

Setting the Active Time Segment

You can change the number of frames in your animation by using the options in the Animation group on the Time Configuration dialog box. By default, the track bar for an animation shows frames 0 to 100. This doesn't mean that you can only animate 100 frames of content. What the timeline shows is called the **active time segment**. This is the animation segment that will be played when you click the Play button and that is accessible via the time slider.

In the Animation group, the default Start Time for the active time segment is 0, the End Time is 100, the Length of the animation is 100 (number of frames), and the Number of Frames is 101 (the number of frames is equal to the animation's length + 1), as shown in Figure 22. To change the length of the active time segment, you can either change the number in the Start and/or End Time boxes (the Start Time number does not have to be 0; it can be less than or greater than 0). Alternatively, you can change the number in the Length box, and the number in the End Time box will increase or decrease accordingly. Click OK to save your changes to the active time segment. The start and end frames are always displayed on the timeline; if you have a large number of frames, you might not see a tick on the timeline for each frame, as shown in Figure 23.

The Current Time box in the Animation group shows the number of the frame in which the animation is currently located. To go to a different frame, change the number to the frame number to which you want to go, and then click OK.

QUICKTIP

If you change the frame rate for an animation in the Time Configuration dialog box, you'll see that the numbers in the Animation group of the dialog box change automatically.

FIGURE 21
Time Configuration button

Time Configuration button

FIGURE 22
Time Configuration dialog box

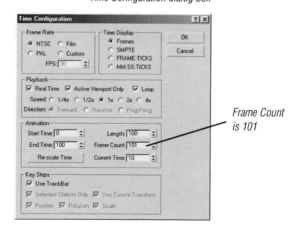

Frame Count is 101

FIGURE 23
Track bar timeline with hundreds of frames

100 frames = 10 ticks

Lesson 3 Configure Animation Timing

DISCREET 3D STUDIO MAX 6-23

Re-Scaling Time

If you have set keyframes for an animation already, at 0 and 60 for example, and then you add several frames to the active time segment, the frames will be added to the segment, but the keyframes you already set will stay in their original locations at 0 and 60. If you want to stretch or shrink an animation over a greater or lesser number of frames, you need to **re-scale** the timing of your animation. To do this, click the Re-scale Time button in the Animation group on the Time Configuration dialog box. The Re-scale Time dialog box opens, showing the current active time segment in the Current group and providing an area for changing the length of the segment in the New group, as shown in Figure 24.

Change the numbers in the appropriate boxes to change the length of the active time segment, and then click OK. The animation will now stretch across the new active time segment, with the keyframes spaced from each other in the same proportions as in the previous time segment. When you play the animation, it will play more slowly if you increased the length of the active time segment, or it will play more quickly if you decreased the length of the active time segment.

Changing the Time Display

By default, the time slider shows the frame number where you are on the timeline and the total number of frames in the timeline (for example, 50/105); the timeline itself shows the range of frame numbers in the active time segment; and the active time segment is defined in the Animation group by frame numbers. You can change how time is displayed in all three areas using the options in the Time Display group in the Time Configuration dialog box. This can be useful if you prefer to work with minutes and seconds, rather than frames, or if you are working with extremely small segments of time called **ticks**. Each second of an animation contains 4800 ticks. At 30 FPS, there are 160 ticks per frame, and if you are working with a time display that shows ticks, you can move between ticks using the navigation buttons the same way you move between frames at the default time display. Using ticks, you can see the minute changes that occur at the intra-frame level.

FIGURE 24
Re-scale Time dialog box

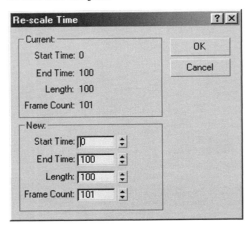

When you open the Time Configuration dialog box, Frames is the time display selected by default. Click the SMPTE option button to change the time display to show you time using SMPTE timecode. SMPTE timecode is a standard that video editors use to number each and every frame in a video clip. The time will display as minutes, seconds, and number of frames past the previous second, separated by colons. For example, 0:3:10 is 3 seconds, 10 frames into the animation.

You also have the option of changing the display to read FRAME:TICKS and MM(minutes):SS(seconds):TICKS. When you change the time display, the time slider, timeline, Current Frame (Go To Frame) box, and Animation group number boxes all reflect the display format, as shown in Figure 25.

Editing Playback Properties

When you click the Play Animation button, by default the animation plays in real time, from beginning to end, and continues to play again and again until you click the Stop button. To change how the animation is played back, you use the options in the Playback group on the Time Configuration dialog box, as shown in Figure 26.

3ds Max plays animation in real time, showing only the frames necessary to have the animation match the designated frame rate. To adjust the speed at which the animation is played, click one of the Speed option buttons under the Real Time check box (selected by default). You can slow the animation to 1/4 or 1/2 of real time (1/4x or 1/2x option buttons) or double or quadruple its speed (2x or 4x option buttons). The 1x option button is selected by default. If you want the animation to play back in all viewports, deselect the Active Viewport Only check box.

Deselecting the Real Time check box causes 3ds Max to show all of the frames (and not skip any) in the animation when it is played back. Note that this might slow the timing of the animation accordingly. With Real Time deselected, the Loop check box and Direction option buttons become available. Click to deselect the Loop check box if you want the animation to play only one time and stop. By default, the animation plays in the Forward direction; click the Reverse option button if you want the animation to play in reverse, or click the Ping-Pong option button if you want the animation to play forward, then in reverse, then forward, then in reverse, and so on until you click the Stop button.

FIGURE 25
Time display locations

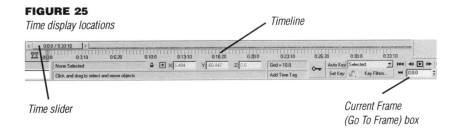

FIGURE 26
Playback group options

Lesson 3 Configure Animation Timing

DISCREET 3D STUDIO MAX 6-25

Set the frame rate

1. Continue working with the scene file from the previous lesson, or open **MAX06-03.max**, then save it as **Toy Plane03**.

2. Click the **Time Configuration button** in the lower-right corner of the screen.

   The Time Configuration dialog box appears.

3. In the Frame Rate group, click the **Custom option button**.

4. In the FPS field, change the value to **15**, as shown in Figure 27, then press **[Enter]**.

   Notice in the timeline at the bottom of the screen that the active time segment has changed to 150 frames.

5. Click **OK** to close the Time Configuration dialog box.

6. Click the **Play animation button**.

   The animation still plays for 10 seconds, but the frame rate has been cut in half, so the animation is slower. By changing the frame rate, you don't affect the duration of the animation, only the number of frames per second of animation that are rendered are affected.

7. Click the **Time Configuration button** again, then change the Frame Rate back to **NTSC**.

You changed the frame rate of an animation, viewed the effect on the active time segment and speed of the animation, then changed the frame rate back to its original frame rate.

FIGURE 27
Frame rate group

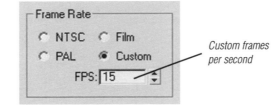

Custom frames per second

FIGURE 28
Animation group

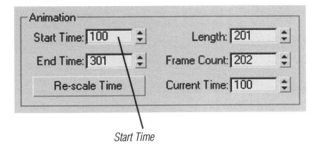

Start Time

FIGURE 29
Shortened active time segment

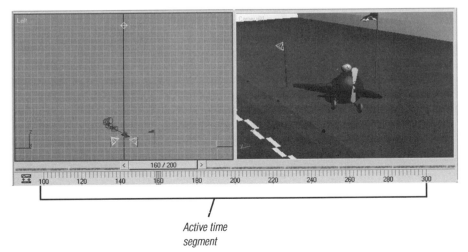

Active time segment

Set the active time segment

1. Click the **Time Configuration button** to open the Time Configuration dialog box (if necessary).
2. In the Animation group, change the Start Time parameter to **100**, as shown in Figure 28, then click **OK**.
3. Play the animation, then stop the animation.

   The animation now begins at frame 100 and the active time segment goes from 100 to 300, as shown in Figure 29.
4. Open the **Time Configuration dialog box**, change the Start Time back to **0**, then press **[Enter]**.

   The track bar is updated to reflect the new active time segment.
5. Change the Length parameter to **600**, then click **OK**.
6. Play the animation, then stop the animation.

   The active time segment has 600 frames, but the animation still exists from frames 0 to 300. The extra 300 frames were merely tacked onto the end of the timeline. You can do this anytime you need to add frames to the timeline.
7. Open the Time Configuration dialog box, change the Length parameter back to **300**, then click **OK** to close the dialog box.

You changed the start frame for an animation, viewed the effect on the active time segment, then changed the start frame back to 0. You also changed the length of an animation and viewed the effect on the animation, then returned the animation to its original length.

DISCREET 3D STUDIO MAX 6-27

Lesson 3   Configure Animation Timing

Re-scale time

1. Open the Time Configuration dialog box, then click the **Re-scale Time button** in the Animation group.

    The Re-scale Time dialog box appears.

2. Change the Length parameter to **600**, then click **OK**.

3. Click **OK** to close the Time Configuration dialog box.

4. Play the animation, then stop the animation.

    Notice that the animation plays at half the speed. By scaling the original 300 frames over 600 frames, we have doubled the time that it takes for the plane to go through its keyframes, thereby making the motions slower. Figure 30 shows the animation at frame 300, halfway through the keyframes.

5. Open the Time Configuration dialog box, then click the **Re-scale Time button** again.

6. Change the Length parameter back to **300**, click **OK** to apply the changes, then click **OK** to close the Time Configuration dialog box.

    The animation has been scaled back down to 300 frames.

7. Play the animation again.

    Notice the animation is back to its original speed and duration.

You re-scaled the time in an animation so that the animation stretched over double the number of frames, viewed the effect on the animation, re-scaled the animation's time back to its original, then viewed the animation again.

FIGURE 30
Re-scaled animation at frame 300

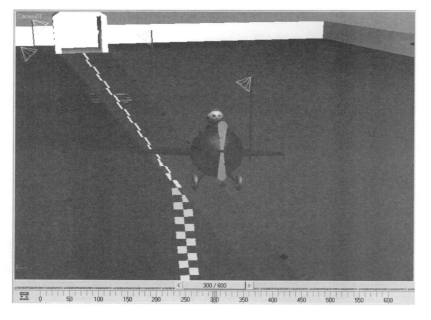

6-28 AUTODESK 3D STUDIO MAX

Animation

FIGURE 31
SMPTE time display

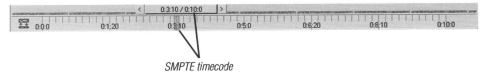

SMPTE timecode

Change the time display

1. Open the Time Configuration dialog box.

2. In the Time Display group, click the **SMPTE option button**, then click **OK**.

   As shown in Figure 31, the track bar now displays SMPTE timecode as minutes: seconds:frames, showing that the duration of the animation is 10 seconds. The time slider also displays the current frame and active time segment information as SMPTE timecode.

   > TIP Changing the time display to SMPTE timecode is useful for seeing how long your animations are without having to perform the frames per second (FPS) calculation in your head. However, as an animator, it's a necessary skill to see a frame count and be able to quickly determine its duration at various FPS rates.

3. Open the Time Configuration dialog box, click the **Frames option button** in the Time Display group, then click **OK** to close the dialog box.

You changed the time display to SMPTE, viewed the time display onscreen, then changed the time display back to Frames.

Edit playback properties

1. Open the Time Configuration dialog box.
2. In the Playback group, click the **1/4x option button**, as shown in Figure 32, then click **OK**.
3. Play the animation.

    The animation plays back at one-quarter the original playback speed.

4. Stop the animation.
5. Open the Time Configuration dialog box, deselect the **Real Time check box**, click the **Ping-Pong option button**, as shown in Figure 33, then click **OK** to close the dialog box and play the animation.

    The animation plays back each frame as fast as your display hardware allows, disregarding any playback rate. After the time slider gets to the end, the sequence plays in reverse, going back and forth between forward and reverse in a continuous loop.

(continued)

FIGURE 32
Playback group

1/4x option button

FIGURE 33
Playback group

6. Open the **Time Configuration dialog box**, click the **Forward option button**, click the **Real Time check box**, then **click the 1x option button** to restore the settings to their defaults.

   By adjusting the Playback options, you didn't affect the frame rate of the animation; you simply adjusted the speed at which it played back in the viewport. This is useful for evaluating the motion qualities of your animation.

7. Close the dialog box, then reset 3ds Max.

   There is no need to save the file, because you haven't made any changes to the scene.

You set the playback rate for an animation to one-quarter speed, played the animation, changed the animation so it had no specific playback rate, played the animation again, then restored the original playback options.

LESSON 4

EDIT KEYS

What You'll Do

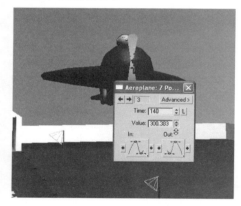

In this lesson you will learn how to select, move, delete, and clone keys on the track bar. You will also discover how to view and edit the properties for single key values.

Selecting and Moving Keys

After setting keyframes for an object or objects in an animation, you can work in multiple ways with the keys for selected objects on the track bar. To select a key, all you need to do is make sure that the object whose key you want to select is selected itself, and then click the key on the track bar. To select multiple keys at once, click and drag on the track bar to create a selection region, and then release the mouse button when the region is around all the keys you want to select. When selected, keys are white.

To move a key, click and drag the key to a new location on the timeline. The key values are thus moved to the new frame location, and the object will be animated to those values either sooner or later in the animation. If you select more than one key at a time, clicking and dragging will move all of the selected keyframes at once. The changes between the moved keyframes in the animation will have the same timing, but will occur earlier or later in the animation overall.

With multiple keys selected, you can display a selection range bar beneath the timeline to help you visualize the key-to-key segment of the animation that you are moving. To display the range bar, right-click the track bar, point to Configure, and then click Show Selection Range. A black line stretching from key to key appears under the selected keys, as shown in Figure 34. This is the selection range bar; when you move the keys, the bar moves, too.

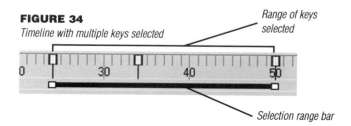

FIGURE 34
Timeline with multiple keys selected

Or, click the bar itself to move the selected keys. You can also use the selection range bar to re-scale the timing of the animation between the selected keyframes. To do this, click and drag one of the squares on the end of the bar, as shown in Figure 35; as you drag, all of the selected keys except the one on the opposite end of the range bar move apart or away from each other in a way proportional to their original arrangement. In this way, the animation between the keyframes will play more quickly or slowly, depending on whether you shortened or lengthened the selection range bar.

Cloning and Deleting Keys

To delete a keyframe, select it and then press [Delete]. Rather than deleting an entire key, you can also delete one or more of the keyed values that a keyframe contains. To delete a keyed value from a keyframe, right-click the key on the track bar, point to Delete Key, and then click the key that you would like to delete. For example, Figure 36 shows the Delete Key submenu for a box whose position changes at the keyframe. Click the Box01: X Position key to delete the X Position key value from the keyframe, click the Box01: Y Position key to delete the Y Position value, or click the Box01: Z Position to delete the Z Position key value. Deleting one of these values does not delete the other two. However, if you clicked the Box01: Position value on the submenu, the entire key would be deleted from the track bar.

If you change an object from one parameter value to another, and then back to the original parameter value, you can clone a keyframe rather than duplicating it by manually setting a new keyframe's values. To clone a key, press and hold [Shift], and then

FIGURE 35
Selection range

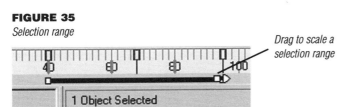

FIGURE 36
Delete Key submenu

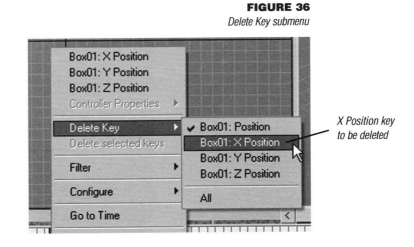

Lesson 4 Edit Keys

DISCREET 3D STUDIO MAX 6-33

click and drag the key or keys you want to clone to a new location. A key with the same keyed values will be placed at the new location.

Editing Key Properties

Each keyed value in a keyframe has properties. To view the properties for a value in a key, right-click the key, and then, on the right-click menu, click the key for which you want to see the properties. A dialog box for the key's properties opens. Figure 37 shows the dialog box for the X Position value in a key.

In the upper-left corner of the dialog box, you can move between keyframes that contain the same key (though not necessarily the same value) by clicking the arrow buttons. The box to the right of the arrows lists the number of the currently selected key. The Time box in the dialog box lists the frame number where the key is located. The value of the key appears in the Value box. For instance, if you are looking at the properties for the X Position key, the Value will be the object's location on the X axis. To change the keyed value, adjust the number in the Value box, and its value will change in the keyframe.

If you want to move just a single keyed value to another location in the timeline, change the number in the Time box on the keyed value's properties dialog box. The value will move to (not be copied to) the new location on the timeline, and if no key exists at the frame number you enter in the Time box, a new key will be created there. The key from which you moved the keyed value will no longer contain that value.

Beneath the Value box or boxes in the dialog box are In and Out tangent type buttons. Tangents will be covered in Lesson 6.

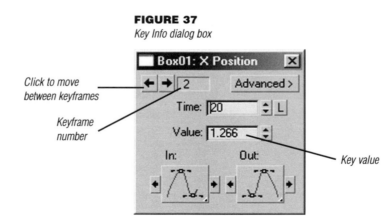

FIGURE 37
Key Info dialog box

FIGURE 38
Moving a key

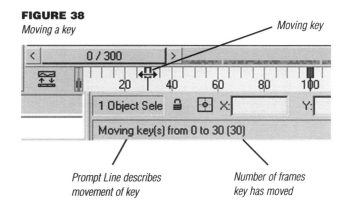

Prompt Line describes movement of key

Number of frames key has moved

Select and move keys

1. Open **MAX06-04.max**, then save it as **Toy Plane04**.
2. Maximize the **Camera viewport** (if necessary).
3. Select the **plane**.

   The keys for the plane appear in the track bar.

4. Click the **key** at frame 0, then drag the **key** to frame **30**.

   Notice that as you drag, as shown in Figure 38, the Prompt Line tells you that you are "Moving key(s) from frame 0 to 30". It also shows you in parentheses how many frames away you are moving it.

5. Save the file, make sure the **time slider** is at frame **0**, then play the animation.

   By sliding the position key that was originally at frame 0 to frame 30, the plane now waits one second before moving. Because it now has a shorter duration between when it begins to move at frame 30 and when it lifts off at frame 100, it travels down the runway faster.

6. Stop the animation.

You selected a key in an animation, moved the key, then played the animation to see the effect.

Clone and delete keys

1. Drag the **time slider** to frame **150**.
2. Open the **Select Objects dialog box**, then double-click the **EyeLidR** object to select it.

   The keys for the eyelid animation are shown in the track bar.
3. Click and drag a selection region to select the **3 keys** between **140** and **160**, as seen in Figure 39.
4. Press and hold **[Shift]**, then place the pointer over the **key** at frame **150**.

   The pointer turns into a double-headed arrow as it rolls over the key.
5. Click and drag the **first key** in the range to frame **117**, as shown in Figure 40.

   By holding down [Shift], you clone the selected keys instead of just moving them.
6. Drag the **time slider** back and forth slowly over the original and cloned clusters of keys.

   The eyelid blinks twice.
7. Click and drag a **selection region** over the three newly created keys.
8. Right-click the **track bar** to display a right-click menu, then click **Delete selected keys**.

You selected an object, selected a range of its keys on the track bar, cloned the keys, then selected the cloned keys and deleted them.

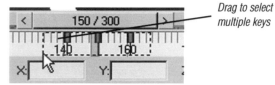

FIGURE 39
Selecting keys

Drag to select multiple keys

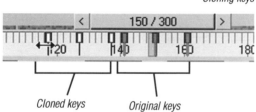

FIGURE 40
Cloning keys

Cloned keys   Original keys

FIGURE 41
Adjusting the Value in the Key Info dialog box

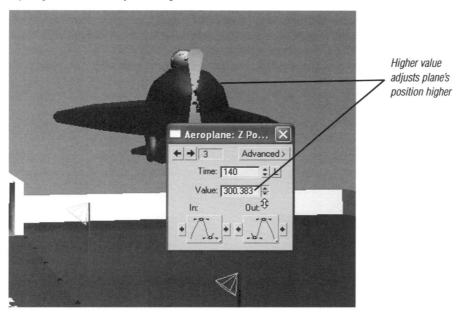

Higher value adjusts plane's position higher

Edit key properties

1. Select the **plane**, drag the **time slider** to frame **150**, then right-click the **key** at frame **140**.
2. Click **Aeroplane: Z position** on the right-click menu.

   The Key Info dialog box for the Aeroplane Z:Position key appears.
3. Click and drag the **Value spinner** up and down.

   As the Z position value changes for the key at frame 140, you can see how it affects the position of the plane at frame 150. See Figure 41 for an example.

   TIP Right-click before releasing the left mouse button to cancel the operation and return to the original Value.
4. Click and drag the **Time spinner** up and down.

   As you change the Time of the keyframe, you see the Z position key slide back and forth on the track bar. You also see the plane's positional changes in the viewport.
5. Close the dialog box, then undo any changes you might have made to the keyframes.
6. Save the file, then reset 3ds Max.

You opened the Key Info dialog box for a key, adjusted its Value and Time values and viewed the effects in the viewport, then undid your changes.

DISCREET 3D STUDIO MAX 6-37

LESSON 5

USE THE
DOPE SHEET

What You'll Do

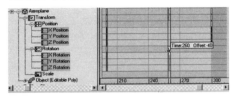

In this lesson, you will learn what Track View is and what the Dope Sheet in Track View shows. You will also explore how to adjust individual keyframes and parent-child keyframes using the Dope Sheet.

So far in this chapter, you have learned how to animate objects by creating keyframes on the timeline. **Track View** provides a way of seeing all the information related to your scene and keyframed animation from a very data-driven point of view, as opposed to the visual representation that the viewports offer. From Track View, you can see and edit the data for all of the objects, materials, keyframes and parameters that make up your scene. Track View can be viewed in two different modes: Dope Sheet and Curve Editor. As shown in Figure 42, on the left side of either of the Track View modes is the **Controller window**, which shows all of the objects in the scene that can be animated, listed in a hierarchy of tracks. A **track** is like a separate timeline for each and every parameter you can animate. Every object has a separate track for each X, Y, and Z Position, each X, Y, and Z Rotation and each X, Y, and Z Scale. And that's just for the transforms. In fact, every object can have many, many animation tracks that correspond to the many parameters that can be animated. The **track hierarchy** is a way of viewing the parent-child relationship between objects and parameters in Track View.

Understanding the Dope Sheet

The **Dope Sheet** provides you with another way to look at the keyframes in your animation and adjust their placement. The Dope Sheet offers a graphical "spreadsheet-like" interface that makes it easy to see the keyframe timing and how keyframes relate to the other objects and keyframes in the scene. As shown in Figure 42, on the right side of the Dope Sheet is the **Key window**. In this window, the keys are arranged on tracks in a horizontal fashion. Each track represents an individual animated parameter.

Adjusting Keys

To adjust a single key in the Dope Sheet, thereby adjusting the frame number or value of the keyframe, you can click and drag it to adjust that key's placement in time. You can also right-click a key to display the Key Info dialog box, and then change the value of the key.

Keys in the Dope Sheet are organized by hierarchy, and tracks that are children of other tracks have keyframes that are children of other keyframes. When you move a parent keyframe on the Dope Sheet, all of its children keyframes move as well. For instance, if you drag the parent Transform key to move it, the keys for the object's Position, Rotation, and Scale will move too, including the individual keys for each axis, as shown in Figure 43.

FIGURE 42
Track View–Dope Sheet window

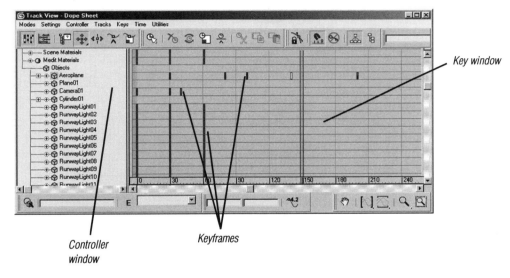

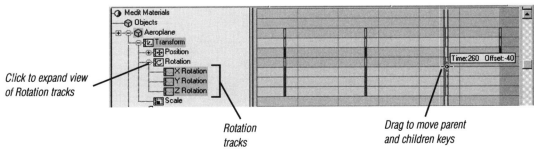

FIGURE 43
Adjusting parent and child keys

Lesson 5 Use the Dope Sheet

DISCREET 3D STUDIO MAX 6-39

Adjust a key in the Dope Sheet

1. Open **MAX06-05.max**, then save it as **Toy Plane05**.
2. Select the **plane**, then drag the **time slider** to frame **100**.
3. Click **Graph Editors** on the menu bar, then click **Track View–Dope Sheet**.

   The Dope Sheet appears and the Aeroplane object is highlighted in the Controller window.
4. Click the **Edit Keys button** (if necessary), pan the Controller window (if necessary) to find the Aeroplane object, expand its track by clicking the **plus sign** next to the word Aeroplane, then expand the Transform and Position tracks by clicking their **plus signs**, as shown in Figure 44.
5. Select the **key** for the plane's Z Position at frame **100**, then drag it to frame **80**, as seen in Figure 45.

   You moved only the Z position key; the X and Y stayed behind.
6. Rewind the animation, then play it in the Camera viewport.

   The plane now lifts off a little earlier, at frame 80.
7. Stop the animation, then save the file.

You opened the Dope Sheet, selected the key for one of an object's tracks, then moved the key. You then viewed the effect of the change in the animation.

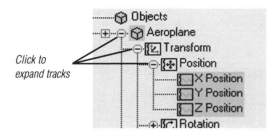

FIGURE 44
Dope Sheet with Aeroplane tracks highlighted

Click to expand tracks

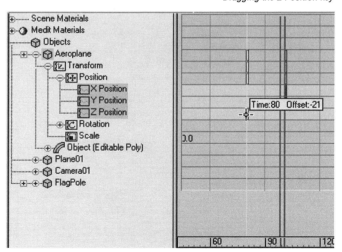

FIGURE 45
Dragging the Z Position key

FIGURE 46
Expanded Rotation track

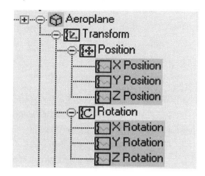

FIGURE 47
Repositioned parent and children keyframes

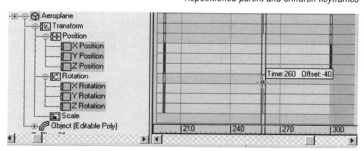

Adjust parent keys and their children

1. Restore the Dope Sheet (if necessary).
2. Click the **plus sign** next to the Aeroplane Rotation track to expand the X, Y, and Z Rotation tracks, as shown in Figure 46.
3. Click the **double-blue line** that represents the time slider, then drag it to frame **260**.

   The Camera view moves to that frame. Notice that the plane is still in a little bit of a roll.
4. Click to select the **parent Rotation key** at frame **300**, then drag it back to frame **260**.

   The parent Rotation key and the three keyframes for each axis (its children) move back to frame 260, as shown in Figure 47.
5. Close the Dope Sheet, then play the animation in the Camera view.

   Because you moved the rotation, the plane now levels out by frame 260.
6. Stop the animation, save the file, then reset the viewports.

You opened the Aeroplane Rotation track and expanded its child tracks, then moved the Rotation key to an earlier frame, thereby moving its children, too. You then played the animation to see the effect.

Lesson 5   *Use the Dope Sheet*

DISCREET 3D STUDIO MAX 6-41

LESSON 6

USE THE
CURVE EDITOR

What You'll Do

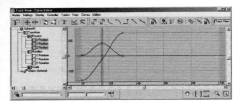

In this lesson, you will learn what the Curve Editor is and how to understand the curves and tangents that appear in it. You will also take a look at the different ways you can use the Curve Editor to modify animation timing, values, and motion, and to add keys to an animation.

Understanding the Curve Editor

Like the Dope Sheet, the Curve Editor enables you to see where keyframes are and manipulate the keyframes as desired. However, the Curve Editor provides much more detail by graphing out all of the animated parameters for an animated object. As shown in Figure 48, in the Key window the Curve Editor shows the keyframes for a selected track and a graph of the value of the track's parameter at each frame–in other words, a visual representation of the interpolation between keyframes.

Figure 48 shows how the position values of an animated object get interpolated between keyframes by default. This object has been animated to move upward on the Z axis and back down again over the course of 20 frames. There are 3 keyframes, one at frame 0 with a position value of 0 on the Z axis, another at frame 15 with a position value of 10, and a third at frame 20 with a position value of 0. Notice that when 3ds Max interpolates these values, by default it produces a smooth curve.

How does this indicate the positioning of the object? Well, take a look at the curve again, but this time look between keyframes. If you look where the curve is plotted at frame 5, you will see that the position value lies between the 2 and the 3, or around 2.5 units on the Z axis. At whatever value the curve lies in a given frame determines the position of the object during that frame of the animation.

There are four ways to access the Curve Editor. You can click Graph Editors on the menu bar, and then click Track View–Curve Editor. You can click the Curve Editor (Open) tool on the main toolbar. You can right-click an object, and then click Curve Editor on the Transform menu. Finally, to open a small version of the Curve Editor called the **Mini Curve Editor**—it's blended into the interface beneath the viewports, as shown in Figure 49—click the Open Mini Curve Editor button to the left of the timeline.

Understanding Tangent Types

A **tangent** refers to the shape of an animation curve as it is plotted from keyframe to keyframe. When you animate an object, 3ds Max will by default produce smooth tangents between keyframes. Smooth tangents produce natural-looking motions as you animate. However, you also have the abilty to change the shape of the animation curve by assigning preset tangent types. Each keyframe has an **In tangent** that defines the shape of the curve as it comes into a keyframe, and an

FIGURE 48
Position keyframe interpolation curve

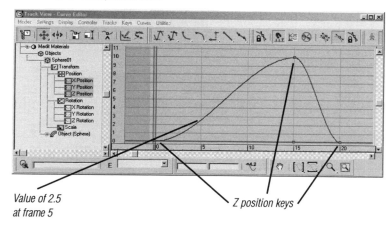

Value of 2.5 at frame 5

Z position keys

FIGURE 49
Mini Curve Editor

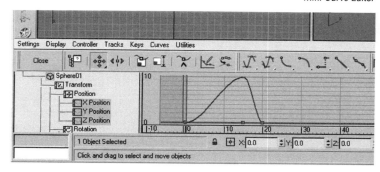

Lesson 6 Use the Curve Editor

DISCREET 3D STUDIO MAX 6-43

Out tangent that defines the shape of the curve as it leaves a keyframe. You can change In tangents and Out tangents to one of the following tangent types:

- **Smooth**: Creates smooth interpolation through the key, as shown in Figure 50.
- **Linear**: Creates linear interpolation at the key, as shown in Figure 50. A linear In tangent will produce a curve that comes into a keyframe in a straight line. To have true linear interpolation from key to key, you must have a linear Out tangent on one key and a linear In tangent on the next.
- **Step**: Holds a value constant from one key to the next, producing an instantaneous switching of the values at the key. In other words, there is really no interpolation at all between keys; a value will simply change when it reaches the next key.
- **Slow**: Slows down the interpolated rate of change at the key, producing a slowing down effect as a curve enters a key, but a speeding up effect as it leaves a key.
- **Fast**: Speeds up the interpolated rate of change at the key, producing a speeding up effect as a curve enters a key, but a slowing down effect as it leaves a key.
- **Custom**: Lets you manually adjust the tangent handles that appear at each key in the Curve Editor.
- **Flat tangent**: Creates a smooth curve that does not produce any overshoot, as does the Smooth type. Curves will take the most direct path to a key value. The Flat tangent is shown in Figure 50.

Changing Tangent Types

You can change the In and Out tangents for a keyframe by right-clicking on a keyframe in the Key window of the Curve Editor to display the Key Info dialog box for that key, as shown

FIGURE 50
Smooth, Flat, and Linear tangents

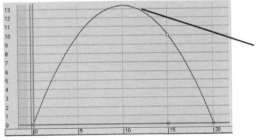

Smooth curves produce an overshoot of the value

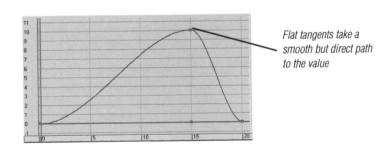

Flat tangents take a smooth but direct path to the value

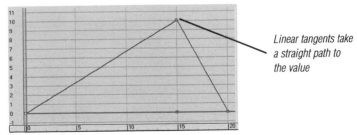

Linear tangents take a straight path to the value

in Figure 51. At the bottom of the dialog box, there are two key tangent flyouts that show the current In and Out tangent types. To change them, simply click the tangent flyout that you want to change, and hold down the mouse button. The whole tangent flyout appears, showing the other tangent type options. Point to the one you want to change, then release the mouse button.

The Key Info dialog box also has buttons that let you copy tangent types to adjacent In and Out tangents. To do this, click the arrows on either side of the key tangent flyouts. If you click the arrow to the right of the In tangent flyout, it will copy that tangent type to the Out tangent. If you click the arrow to the right of the Out tangent, it will copy the type to the In tangent of the next key on the timeline.

Adjusting key timing and values

To adjust the position of a keyframe in the Curve Editor, click the Move Keys button on the Curve Editor toolbar, and then click and drag the keyframe to move it around the graph, as shown in Figure 52. If you move it left or right, you are adjusting the frame location of the key in time. If you move it up or down, you are adjusting the value of the key. You can also click and drag to select a range of keys, and then move them together.

The Slide Keys tool lets you move a selected group of keys to the left or right on the timeline, as shown in Figure 53. Sliding

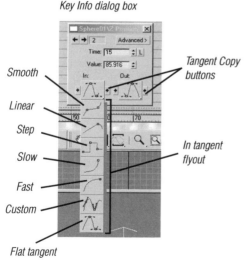

FIGURE 51
Key Info dialog box

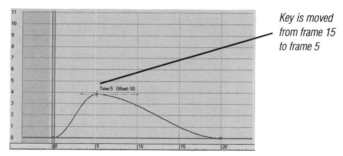

FIGURE 52
Moving a key

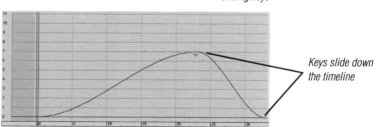

FIGURE 53
Sliding keys

Lesson 6 Use the Curve Editor

DISCREET 3D STUDIO MAX 6-45

to the right moves all of the selected keys, plus all the keys to their right, forward in time. Sliding to the left moves all of the selected keys, plus all the keys to their left, backward in time.

The Scale Keys tool lets you select a range of keys and scale their horizontal relationship to one another, in essence expanding or contracting their placement in time. Figure 54 shows keys being scaled.

You can also scale a key value by using the Scale Values tool. If you click a key and drag up or down with this tool active, it will scale the value up or down. Don't confuse this tool with the Scale Keys tool. Scale Keys adjusts a key's location in time, not its parameter values.

Adding Keys

You can add keys anywhere along the function curve by using the Add Keys tool, also located on the Curve Editor toolbar. Click the Add Keys tool, then, as shown in Figure 55, click anywhere on the curve to create a keyframe at the click point. As you add points to the function curve, keys will also appear in the track bar.

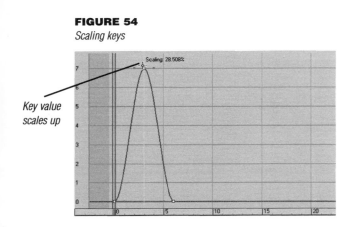

FIGURE 54
Scaling keys

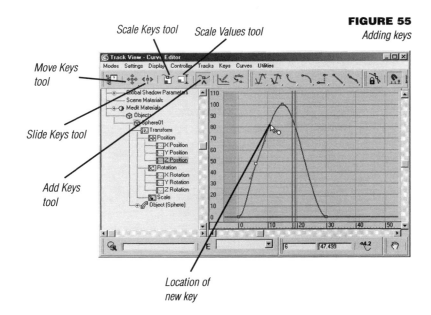

FIGURE 55
Adding keys

FIGURE 56
Sphere with keyframes and trajectory

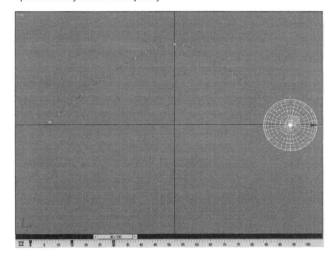

FIGURE 57
Curve Editor

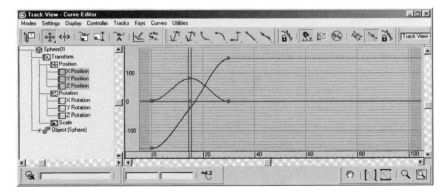

Lesson 6 *Use the Curve Editor*

Examine keys in the Curve Editor

1. Create a **sphere** on the left side of the Front viewport, click the **Toggle Auto Key Mode button** to turn on Auto Key, drag the **time slider** to frame **15**, then drag the **sphere** to the top-center of the Front viewport.

   TIP You can use Figure 56 to help you with the sphere's placement.

2. Drag the **time slider** to frame **30**, then drag the **sphere** down and to the right side of the Front viewport.

3. Right-click the **sphere**, click **Properties** on the Transform menu, click the **Trajectory check box** in the Display Properties area of the Object Properties dialog box, then click **OK**.

   The trajectory of the ball appears in the viewports, as shown in Figure 56.

4. Play the animation, then stop the animation when you have finished viewing it.

   During the animation, the ball follows the curve of the trajectory, and there is a tick mark for each frame in the animation.

5. Click the **Curve Editor (Open) tool** on the main toolbar.

   The Curve Editor opens, showing three curves for each axis position, as shown in Figure 57.

   TIP Your curves might look slightly different due to different magnifications of the curve editor and the size of the window when it opens.

(continued)

DISCREET 3D STUDIO MAX 6-47

6. Click the **X Position track** in the hierarchy on the left side of the Curve Editor window.

   The X Position curve is isolated in the graph on the right side of the window.

7. Click the **Y position track** to isolate it in the graph, then click the **Z position track** to isolate it in the graph.

   The curve for the Y position track appears as a flat line, because the sphere does not change position at all on the y-axis during the animation. The curve for the Z position represents the height that the sphere achieves.

   TIP Whenever 3ds Max shows you a visual representation of the X, Y, and Z axes, it color codes them as follows: X = red, Y = green, and Z = blue (XYZ = RGB).

8. Close the Curve Editor, then maximize the **Perspective viewport** and make sure the **sphere** is selected.

9. Click the **Open Mini-Curve Editor button** located on the left side of the track bar, as shown in Figure 58.

   The track bar disappears and the Mini Curve Editor appears in its place, showing the X, Y, and Z curves.

   TIP Pan down in the Controller window to the Sphere01 object (if necessary), then click the plus sign next to it to open its tracks and show the curves.

10. Make sure **Auto Key** is still on, type **15** in the Current Frame (Go to Frame) box, then in the

(continued)

FIGURE 58
Open Mini Curve Editor button

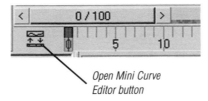

Open Mini Curve Editor button

6-48 AUTODESK 3D STUDIO MAX

Animation

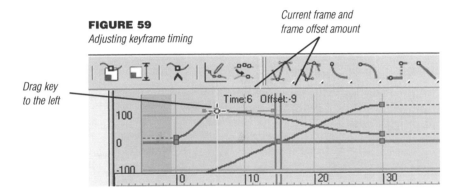

FIGURE 59
Adjusting keyframe timing

Perspective viewport, move the **sphere** up and zdown on the z-axis, then move the **sphere** back and forth on the x-axis.

As you adjust the Z and X values of the objects in the viewport, the values of the Z and X curves at the current frame in the Mini Curve Editor adjust accordingly. Notice how the trajectory remains curved, no matter how you adjust the sphere's position.

11. Undo the changes in the sphere's position, then save the file as **Sphere Animation**.

You manipulated an object and its keyframes in the viewport, then saw how the Curve Editor offers an interactive graphical display of the timing and values of the keyframes. You also used the Mini Curve Editor to save screen real estate while working in both the viewport and the editor.

Adjust timing and values

1. On the **Mini Curve Editor toolbar**, make sure the **Move keys tool** is selected, select the **key** at frame 15 on the blue Z Position curve, then drag it to the left, as shown in Figure 59.

   While you are dragging, a number display shows you the current frame and how many frames you have offset the key.

2. Release the **mouse button** to drop the **key** at the new location.

   The sphere trajectory is updated in the Perspective viewport to show you the new path that the sphere will travel as a result of the change.

(continued)

DISCREET 3D STUDIO MAX 6-49

3. Drag the same **key** up so that it goes up and off the chart.

   The sphere goes higher at frame 15. Notice the two fields in the Mini Curve Editor toolbar that display the current frame and value of the key. You can view these when you move the keys beyond the limits of the graph.

4. Undo the movement of the key so that it appears on the graph again, then save the file.

You moved a key in the Mini Curve Editor to adjust its timing and position values, then moved it again off the Curve Editor and viewed the frame number display for the key when it was off the graph.

Adjust In and Out tangents

1. Right-click on the same **key** in the middle of the Z position curve.

   The Key Info dialog box appears.

2. Click and hold the **In tangent flyout**.

   The flyout appears, showing buttons for the different tangent types.

3. Point to the **Linear tangent type button**, as shown in Figure 60, then release the mouse button.

   The In tangent changes to the Linear type, and the trajectory is updated in the perspective view. The value curve straightens out as it approaches the second key.

   (continued)

FIGURE 60
Change In tangent to Linear

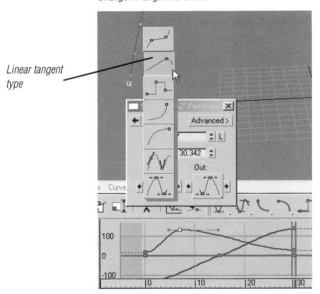

Linear tangent type

FIGURE 61
Adding and moving a key

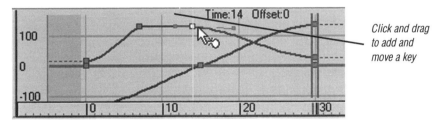

Click and drag to add and move a key

4. In the Key Info dialog box, click the **Tangent Copy button** just to the right of the In tangent flyout.

   The Linear tangent type is copied to the Out tangent, and the trajectory shows a hard angle, indicating an abrupt change in position at the keyframe.

5. Close the Key Info dialog box.
6. Play the animation, then stop the animation.

   | TIP Zoom out (if necessary) to see the complete trajectory.

By changing the In and Out tangent types, you adjusted how the sphere's position values are interpolated between the keyframes.

Add and move a key

1. On the **Mini Curve Editor toolbar**, click the **Add Keys tool** to activate it.
2. Click the **blue Z Position curve** around frame 15, then in one motion drag the new **key** up to flatten off the curve between frames 7 and 15, as shown in figure 61.
3. Turn off **Auto Key**, close the **Mini Curve Editor**, then play and stop the animation.

   The sphere's trajectory shows a new keyframe that causes a leveling-off effect around frame 15.

4. Save the file as **Curve Edits**, then reset 3ds Max.

Using the Add Keys tool, you added a key and moved it in one click-and-drag operation.

LESSON 7

ASSIGN ANIMATION CONTROLLERS

What You'll Do

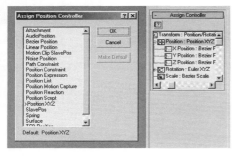

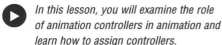

In this lesson, you will examine the role of animation controllers in animation and learn how to assign controllers.

Understanding Animation Controllers

In Track View, the values of a track across the timeline are contained in a controller. A **controller** is a part of 3ds Max that handles all of the tasks associated with animating an object. As soon as you create a keyframe for an object, 3ds Max automatically assigns the default controller for that specific animation track.

So far in in this chapter, you have learned that you can animate objects by creating keyframes on the timeline. As you change the way an object looks at specific keyframes in time, 3ds Max automatically animates the object and determines the way it should look (interpolates it) at each and every frame between the keyframes. How 3ds Max interpolates between keyframe values depends on the type of animation controller that has been assigned to the object.

For example, when you move an object, all of the calculations needed to animate the move are handled by the Position XYZ controller, as shown in Figure 62. In fact, the Position XYZ controller is actually a **compound controller** made up of three separate controllers called Bezier Float controllers, one for each of the X, Y, and Z axes. Bezier controllers produce a curve on any animated parameter. Thus, the Position XYZ controller, by default, produces a smooth curve (as shown in the Curve Editor) when interpolating the values between two keyframes.

> **QUICK**TIP
> Pierre Bezier developed the usage of curves in computer graphics as a tool for designing automobiles for Renault.

There are many different animation controllers, and depending on what type of parameter you animate, 3ds Max will assign the default controller for that parameter. For example, the default controller for position is the Position XYZ controller, and the default controller for scale is the Scale XYZ controller. When you have animated an object parameter and you adjust its keys and tangents in the Curve Editor, or move keyframes around in the Dope Sheet, the resulting interpolated values are dependent on what controller type is applied to that parameter.

You can assign a new controller to a parameter from a list of all the controllers available for that parameter. You would do this when you want the software to interpolate the animation in a specific way, differently from the default controller assigned. For instance, you might want to change the interpolation of an object's movement from a smooth curve to a straight line, and rather than changing each curve tangent manually, you can change the controller that calculates the interpolation.

Assigning Animation Controllers

There are a few different ways to assign controllers to an object. You can use the Animation menu, the Motion panel, or the Curve Editor. If you want to swap a controller for one of the object transforms in a quick and simple manner, then you might want to use the Animation menu. To assign a controller in this way, select the object, click Animation on the menu bar, and choose the transform for which you would like to change the controller. You can choose from a list of applicable controller types, as shown in Figure 63. You can assign controllers only to an object's transforms (Position, Rotation, Scale) using this method.

You can also assign transform controllers using the Motion panel. To assign a controller

FIGURE 62
Controllers in the Motion panel

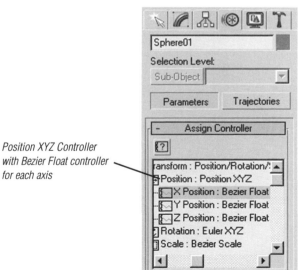

Position XYZ Controller with Bezier Float controller for each axis

FIGURE 63
Animation menu and submenus

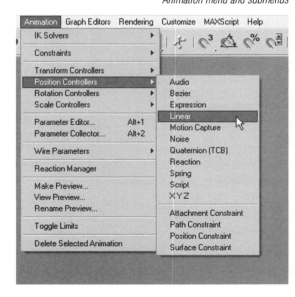

Lesson 7 *Assign Animation Controllers*

DISCREET 3D STUDIO MAX 6-53

using the Motion panel, select the object, click the Motion tab on the Create panel to open the Motion panel, open the Assign Controller rollout, as shown in Figure 64, and then click the desired transform track in the list. After you select the transform, click the Assign Controller button above the list to open the Assign Controller dialog box, select a controller from the list, and then click OK.

You can assign controllers to any of an object's animation tracks using Track View, as shown in Figure 65. To do this, with Track View open, right-click the track to which you want to assign the controller, and select Assign Controller from the Quad menu. A similar list box full of controllers appears, and you can select one from the list.

The combination of animation effects that you can achieve with controllers is pretty much endless. It's important that as you familiarize yourself with 3ds Max, you experiment with different controllers and their capabilities. You can apply many different controllers to the various parameters of an object in the scene. You can even apply controllers to material properties.

FIGURE 64
Assign Controller rollout

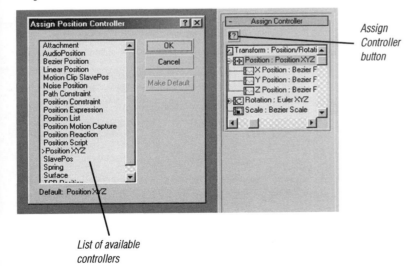

List of available controllers

FIGURE 65
Assigning a controller in Track View

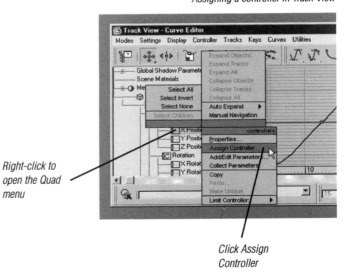

Assign Controller button

Right-click to open the Quad menu

Click Assign Controller

6-54 AUTODESK 3D STUDIO MAX

Animation

FIGURE 66
Plane in perspective view

Create an animation loop

1. Open **MAX06-07.max**, then save it as **Toy Plane07**.
2. Maximize the **Perspective viewport**, then orient it to get a good view of the plane's propeller, as shown in Figure 66.
3. Click the **Toggle Auto Key Mode button** in the status bar, then drag the **time slider** to Frame **10**.
4. Press **[E]** to access the **Select and Rotate tool**, click the **Reference Coordinate System list arrow** on the main toolbar, then click **Local**.
5. Click the **propeller**, rotate it **360 degrees** around its x-axis, then click the **Toggle Auto Key Mode button** to deselect it.
6. Drag the **time Slider** back and forth between frames **0** and **10** to see the animation.

   The propeller completes a full 360-degree rotation over the course of 10 frames.
7. Right-click the **propeller**, then click **Curve Editor** in the Transform section of the Quad menu.

   The Curve Editor appears with the rotation tracks selected, showing the rotation keys and curves in the editor window.

   (continued)

8. Click the **Parameter Curve Out-of-Range Types button** on the Curve Editor toolbar, click to select the **Loop option** in the Param Curve Out-of-Range Types dialog box, as shown in Figure 67, then click **OK**.

   The rotation that occurs between frames 0 and 10 occurs for the duration of the animation, as shown in the Curve Editor in Figure 68.

9. Close the **Curve Editor**, switch to the **Camera viewport**, then play and stop the animation.

   The propeller spins for the full 10 seconds. However, it seems to pause at every revolution because the Euler XYZ controller assigned by default is creating a curve as it animates the rotation from frame 0 to 10. The propeller actually slows down as it reaches a rotational value of 360 degrees. This effect is sometimes referred to as "easing". In this situation, you really need that rotation value to increase in a more linear fashion, with *no* easing as it approaches 360 degrees.

10. Save the file.

You animated the rotation of an object, viewed the rotation curves in the Curve Editor, then looped the rotation so that it would continue throughout the animation. You also observed the easing behavior that occurs when 3ds Max applies a default rotation controller.

FIGURE 67
Param Curve Out-of-Range Types dialog box

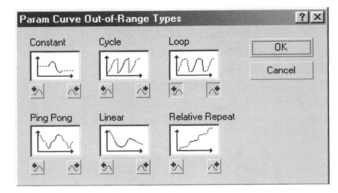

FIGURE 68
Looped rotation in Curve Editor

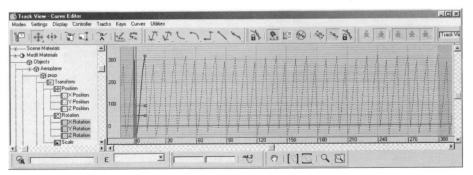

FIGURE 69
Rotation controller in Assign Controller rollout

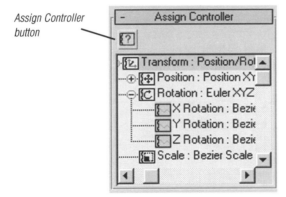

Assign a controller using the Motion panel

1. Make sure the **propeller** is still selected, then click the **Motion tab**.
2. In the Assign Controller rollout, click the **plus sign** next to Rotation to expand the controllers list, as shown in Figure 69.
3. Click the **X Rotation:Bezier Float controller** to highlight it.
4. Click the **Assign Controller button**, then double-click **Linear Float**.

   Linear Float now appears as the X Rotation controller.
5. Play the animation.

   The Linear Float controller causes the rotational value to increase in a linear fashion, and the propeller doesn't pause every time it spins 360 degrees.
6. Stop the animation, then save the file.

You assigned a new controller type to an individual track of animation and viewed its effect on the animation.

Assign a controller using the Curve Editor

1. Zoom out in the Perspective viewport to get a good view of the flag, then play the animation.

   Notice that at the beginning of the animation the waving of the flag ramps up to a faster speed, then slows down toward the end of the animation. This is because the phase parameter of the Wave modifier that you used to animate the ripples in the flag also uses a Bezier controller, which produces smooth curves. You can switch this controller in the Curve Editor.

2. Stop the animation.

3. Select the **flag**, right-click it, then click **Curve Editor** on the Quad menu.

   The Curve Editor appears.

4. In the Controller window, scroll to find the Modified Object item in the Flag hierarchy, as shown in Figure 70.

5. Click the **plus sign** next to Modified Object to expand the list.

   The list expands, showing the Wave modifier.

6. Click the **plus sign** next to Wave to expand it, then scroll down and find the Phase parameter.

7. Right-click **Phase**, then click **Assign Controller** on the Quad menu.

   (continued)

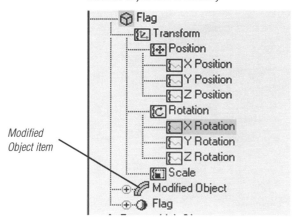

FIGURE 70
Modified Object item in hierarchy

Modified Object item

FIGURE 71
Linear Float controller assigned to Phase parameter

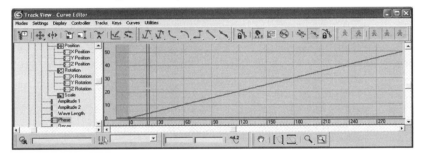

8. Double-click the **Linear Float controller** to assign it to the Phase parameter.

   As shown in Figure 71, you see a straight line in the Curve Editor, which indicates a linear interpolation between keys.

9. Close the Curve Editor, then play the animation.

   The flag now waves in a more linear fashion, without any speed ramp-up.

10. Stop the animation, save the file, then reset 3ds Max.

You used the Curve Editor to access and change the controller that drives an object's individual parameters, something that cannot be done in the Animation menu or Motion panel.

LESSON 8

ASSIGN ANIMATION
CONSTRAINTS

What You'll Do

In this lesson, you will learn how constraints operate, how to assign a constraint, and how to adjust the parameters and options within a constraint using the Motion panel. You will also learn what a List controller is and how to use one to assign multiple controllers at once.

Understanding constraints

Animation constraints are tools that help you automate the animation process. There are several different constraints, each with their own function and usefulness. Constraints are very similar to controllers. The difference between a controller and a constraint is that, typically, you use a constraint to bind the animated transforms of an object to another object in the scene. In other words, a **constraint** causes the behavior of an animated object in a scene to depend on the parameters and/or behavior of a second object in the scene.

One example of a constraint is the LookAt constraint. Using this constraint, you can bind the rotation of an object (such as a character's eyes) to another object so that it always points to the other object, as shown in Figure 72. As the second object moves, the constrained objects move accordingly. Thus, using this constraint, you can animate eyes that always look at a particular object, or you can use a **dummy object** that isn't visible in the scene to control where the eyes are looking during the animation. A dummy object is a kind of helper object that doesn't have any parameters and doesn't render. As you will see later in this book, it is useful for linking to other objects to help you control them. Dummy objects are covered in detail in Chapter 8.

A second, very useful constraint is the Path constraint, which enables you to bind an object's position transform to a two-dimensional shape, or spline. This means you can use the Line tool to draw a shape along which you would like an object to travel throughout an animation, as shown in Figure 73.

Assigning a Constraint

To assign a constraint, select an object, click Animation on the menu bar, point to Constraints, then click the constraint on the submenu that you would like to apply. When you do, a dashed line will appear connected to your cursor. You click the object to which you want the selected object to be constrained. In the case of the LookAt constraint, you'd click the object at which you want the selected object to look. If you are using the Path constraint, you click the path you want the object to follow.

To assign a constraint from the Motion panel, select the object, open the Motion panel, and then, in the Assign Controller rollout, choose the controller to which you want the constraint to be applied.

When you assign the LookAt constraint, the LookAt Constraint rollout on the Motion

FIGURE 72
LookAt constraint assigned

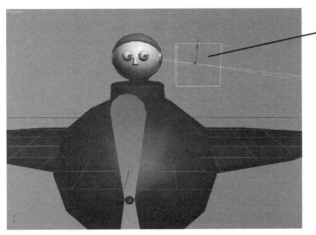

Eyes always look at dummy object

FIGURE 73
Path constraint assigned

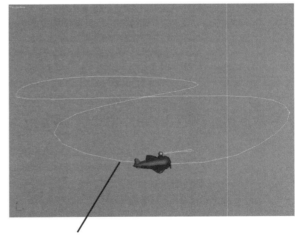

Plane follows spline path

Lesson 8 Assign Animation Constraints

DISCREET 3D STUDIO MAX 6-61

Panel appears, as shown in Figure 74. You choose a target using this rollout. To choose a target for the constraint, click the Add LookAt Target button and then click the object in the viewport where you would like the constrained object to look. You can access this panel at any time by selecting the object with the constraint applied and displaying the Motion panel.

When you assign a Path constraint, the Path Parameters rollout on the Motion panel appears, as shown in Figure 75. When you assign the constraint, 3ds Max automatically creates two keyframes, one at the beginning of the animation and another at the end of the animation. These are keys that drive a parameter of the Path constraint called **Percent Along Path**. The first key tells the plane to be at 0% of the path at the beginning of the animation, while the second key tells the plane to be at 100% of the path by the end of the animation. The plane will appear to fly along the path over the course of the animation.

If you want, you can change the speed at which the object moves around the path by adjusting the value at these keys, or by keyframing the Percent Along Path parameter value throughout the animation. You first need to add a path to be constrained to by clicking the Add Path button in the Path Parameters rollout, and then clicking the spline that you would like to use as a path in the viewport.

Using a List Controller

A List controller gives you the ability to apply multiple controllers to a single object and blend their effects. This is nice if you would like an object to follow a path and

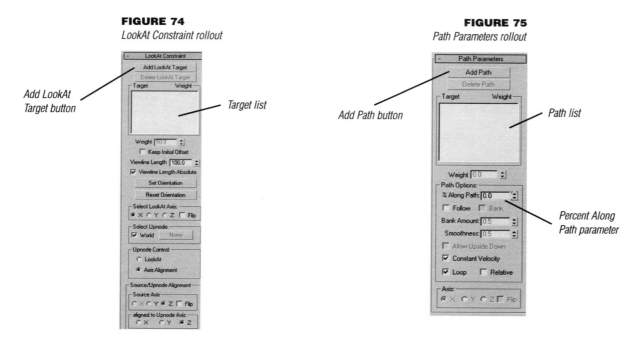

FIGURE 74
LookAt Constraint rollout

FIGURE 75
Path Parameters rollout

do something else as well, such as bounce up and down. For example, with a List controller, both a Path constraint and a Noise controller (which produces varying patterns of random movement, and is good for simulating a bumpy ride) can be assigned to an object at the same time.

You can assign a List controller automatically or manually. If you apply a Path constraint using the Animation menu, it automatically adds a List controller to the Position of the object and adds the Path constraint to the list. After it is assigned in this way, when you look in the Assign Controllers rollout in the Motion Panel, you will see the List controller in the Assign Controller list, with the original Position XYZ Controller and the Path Constraint added to the list. As shown in Figure 76, you will also see a controller called Available in the list—this is an empty controller that you can click to add another controller to the list if needed.

If you add the Path constraint using the Assign Controller button in the Motion Panel, you would not automatically have a List controller assigned. The Plane would simply have the Path controller assigned to its Position track. To assign a List controller manually, simply assign it using the Motion panel Assign Controller rollout as you would another controller. To assign a new controller to the list, select the Available controller in the list to highlight it, and click the Assign Controller button. You can then select any controller that you want from the list.

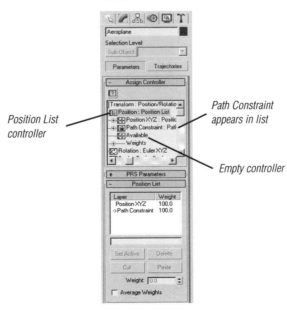

FIGURE 76
List controller

Position List controller

Path Constraint appears in list

Empty controller

Lesson 8 Assign Animation Constraints

Assign the LookAt constraint

1. Open **MAX06-08.max**, then save it as **Toy Plane08**.
2. Click the **Create tab**, click the **Helpers button**, then click the **Dummy button** in the Object Type rollout.
3. In the plane pilot's line of sight, click and drag to create a **dummy object** just above the propeller, as shown in Figure 77.
4. Press **[H]** to open the Select Objects dialog box, then double-click **EyeballLeft** to select it.
5. Click the **Motion tab**, click the **Rotation track** in the Assign Controller list, click the **Assign Controller button**, then double-click the **LookAt Constraint** in the Assign Rotation Controller dialog box to assign it to the Rotation track.
6. In the LookAt Constraint rollout on the Motion panel, click the **Add LookAt Target button**, then click the **Dummy01 object** in the Front viewport to add it to the Target list.
7. Click the **Add LookAt Target button** again to deselect it.

   The dummy object is added to the Target list.

   (continued)

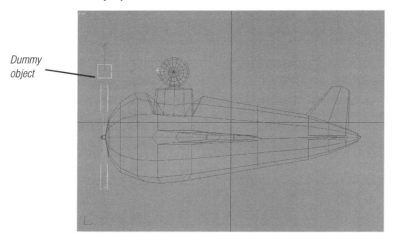

FIGURE 77
Dummy object

Dummy object

FIGURE 78
LookAt constraint applied to eyeball objects

Eyes look at dummy object

8. Repeat Steps 4–7 for EyeballRight.
9. Click the **Select and Link tool** on the main toolbar, click the **dummy object**, then drag it to the plane object.

   This makes the dummy object the child of the plane.

10. In the Perspective viewport, move the **dummy object** around to see how the pilot's eyeballs move with it, then move the **plane** around to see how the dummy object goes where it goes, as shown in Figure 78.

You assigned a LookAt constraint to an object's Rotation track, then targeted the constraint to a dummy object. You also linked the dummy object to the plane so that it would move with it.

Assign the Path constraint

1. Zoom out in the Top viewport so that you have plenty of room to draw a path.
2. Click and drag to create a **closed, curvy spline** in the Top viewport, similar to that shown in Figure 79.

   Each click will place a vertex, and each drag will adjust the Bezier curve at that point.

   > TIP If you would like to tweak the shape that you made, you can do so by entering Vertex sub-object mode, then adjusting the Bezier handles at each vertex.

3. Select the **plane**.
4. Click **Animation** on the menu bar, point to **Constraints**, then click **Path Constraint**.

   A dashed line connects the Aeroplane object to the mouse pointer on-screen, as shown in Figure 80.

5. In the viewport, click the **path** that you just made.

   The toy plane is now constrained to the path, and it moves to the first vertex in the path.

6. Play the animation in the Perspective viewport.

   The plane follows the path over the course of the animation, but it does not continually point in the direction it is traveling.

7. Stop the animation.

You created a closed spline path, then assigned a Path constraint to the plane. You then constrained the plane's movement to the path.

FIGURE 79
Closed spline

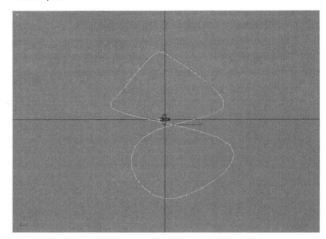

FIGURE 80
Constraining the Aeroplane object to a path

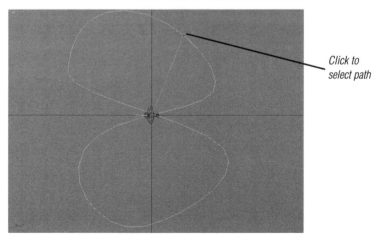

Click to select path

6-66 AUTODESK 3D STUDIO MAX

Animation

FIGURE 81
Aiming the plane

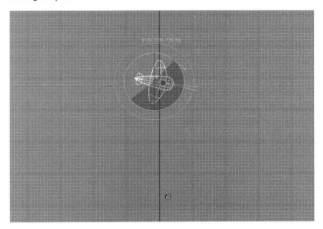

FIGURE 82
Plane's path options adjusted

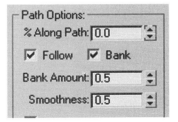

Adjust path options

1. Move the **time slider** back to frame **0**.
2. Pan down the Motion panel until you can see the Path Options group in the Path Parameters rollout, click to select the **Follow check box**, then click to select the **Bank check box**.

   Selecting the Follow check box causes the plane to always point in the direction of the path, relative to its initial rotation. Selecting the Bank check box produces a banking effect as the plane goes around curves.
3. In the Top viewport, rotate the **plane** so that it is pointing in the direction that it travels along the path when animated, as shown in Figure 81.
4. Play the animation in the Perspective viewport.

   Now that you have selected Follow and Bank as shown in Figure 82, the plane flies around the path, pointed in the right direction, and banks its wings as it goes around curves.
5. Stop the animation, click the **Time Configuration button** on the status bar, then click the **Re-scale Time button** in the Animation group of the Time Configuration dialog box.

   (continued)

DISCREET 3D STUDIO MAX 6-67

Lesson 8   Assign Animation Constraints

6. In the Re-scale Time dialog box, change the Length parameter to **200**, click **OK**, then click **OK** in the Time Configuration dialog box.

   Changing the length of the animation from 100 to 200 doubles the length of the animation, which will cause the plane to take twice as long to get around the path.

7. Play the animation.

8. Stop the animation, then save the file.

You changed the parameters of a path constraint to affect how the constrained object followed the path, then viewed the effect in the animation. You also re-scaled the time in the animation by lengthening the active time segment, causing the object to follow the path more slowly.

Use a List controller

1. In the Assign Controller rollout on the Motion panel, click the **plus sign** next to the Position track.

   You see the Position List controller applied to the Position track. Listed below that is a Position XYZ controller, a Path Constraint, and an item that says Available.

2. Click the word **Available**, then click the **Assign Controller button**.

3. Double-click **Noise Position** in the Assign Position Controller dialog box to assign the Noise Position controller to the Position track.

4. The Noise Controller dialog box opens, as shown in Figure 83.

(continued)

FIGURE 83
Noise Controller properties

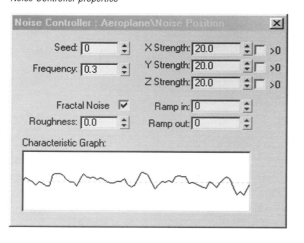

FIGURE 84
Plane bounces with noise

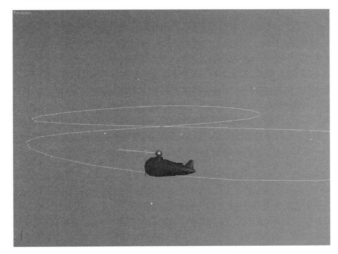

5. Lower the Frequency setting using the **spinner**.

   As you lower the value, the wave in the Characteristic Graph area smooths out, and there are fewer peaks and valleys to the noise.

6. Set the X and Y Strength to **0**, then close the dialog box.

   This will make it so the plane bounces on only the z-axis, or up and down.

7. Play the animation.

   The plane bounces as it travels along the path, as shown in Figure 84.

8. Stop the animation, save the file, then close 3ds Max.

You assigned a controller using a List controller so that you could blend the effects of multiple controllers on the position of an object.

CHAPTER SUMMARY

In this chapter, you learned how to animate a scene using Auto Key, and you practiced animating different kinds of objects and parameters. You also learned how to animate objects using Set Key mode, and how to filter the parameters for which keyframes are set. You explored animation timing and learned how to adjust frame rate, how to define the length and re-scale the timing of an animation, and how to control the way animations are played back. You also learned how to select, move, delete, and clone keys on the track bar and edit the properties for single key values. You examined Track View's Dope Sheet and adjusted individual keyframes and parent-child keyframes using the Dope Sheet. You also gained an understanding of the Curve Editor and looked at the different ways you can use the Curve Editor to modify animation timing, values, and motion, and to add keys to an animation. You learned about the role of animation controllers in 3ds Max animation and learned how to assign controllers to animation tracks. You learned how animation constraints operate, how to assign a constraint, and how to adjust the parameters and options within a constraint. Lastly, you learned how to use a List controller to assign multiple controllers to an animation track at the same time.

What You Have Learned

- How to set keyframes with Auto Key and Set Key
- How to animate object parameters, cameras, lights, materials, and modifiers
- How to filter keys set using Set Key mode
- How to set the frame rate and active time segment for an animation
- How to re-scale the timing of an animation
- How to edit the playback properties of an animation
- How to select, move, clone, and delete keys
- How to edit key properties
- How to adjust keys and their child keys in the Dope Sheet
- How to adjust key values and timing and add keys using the Curve Editor
- How to adjust the In and Out tangents of curves in the Curve Editor
- How to assign a new animation controller to an animation track
- How to assign an animation constraint to an animation track and constrain it to another object in a scene
- How to use a List controller

Key Terms

Active time segment   The segment of an animation that is played when you click the Play button and that is accessible via the time slider on the timeline.

Animation   A sequence of still images that changes slightly from one image to the next, creating the appearance of change over time.

Constraint   Controller that causes the behavior of an animated object in a scene to depend on the parameters and/or behavior of a second object in the scene

Controller   Part of 3ds Max that handles all of the tasks associated with animating an object.

Frame   A single image in an animation.

Frame rate   The number of frames displayed per second in an animation.

Interpolation   In 3ds Max, the process of calculating the intermediate values between keyframes and generating the frames in between.

Keyframe   Frame that captures change values for an object or objects.

Tangent   The shape of an animation curve as it is plotted from keyframe to keyframe.

chapter 7
RENDERING

1. What is rendering?
2. Render with ActiveShade.
3. Understand file output.
4. Create and save renderings.
5. Use the Print Size Wizard.

chapter 7 RENDERING

Rendering is the process you use to cause 3DS Max to generate an image or animation from a scene that you have created. Rendering is typically the last stage of the workflow pipeline, and it is all about giving your scene its final appearance. In this chapter, you will explore many of the concepts involved in this process. You will also get to see how you can use a feature called ActiveShade to see preview-quality renderings of a scene before you commit to the time-intensive process of performing the final render.

As you progress through the chapter, you will step through the process and parameters of setting up scenes to be rendered as image files. Once you understand rendering, you have the final piece of the puzzle needed to take a scene from concept to completion.

Tools You'll Use

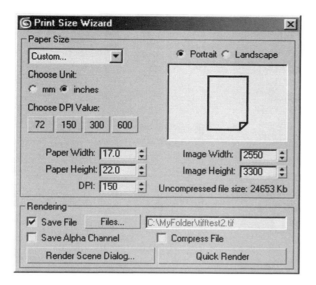
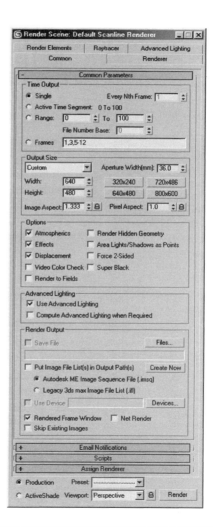

LESSON 1

WHAT IS RENDERING?

What You'll Do

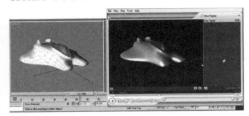

In this lesson you will learn what rendering is, what renderers are, and which renderers are available with 3ds Max.

What Is Rendering?

Rendering is the process of calculating all of the information in a scene, including the geometry, lighting, materials, and so on, and creating an image for display. Generally speaking, with 3D graphics there are two main ways to think of rendering: real-time rendering and prerendered images.

Real-time rendering is what occurs in the viewports in 3ds Max. In other words, a viewport continually updates the color shading, lighting, and scene geometry as they change in a scene, and, when the animation is played, immediately displays the changes at the current frames per second (fps) playback rate. This is the same kind of rendering that occurs in 3D video games, where the 3D models are drawn and shaded immediately, as the user interacts with the scene. The more detail and color that a viewport displays, the more it resembles what the final product will look like.

In an ideal real-time display, there would be no delay in the display of graphics or changes to the scene. 3ds Max does its best to achieve real-time display in the viewports,

Displaying texture correctly

Sometimes mapping appears distorted in the real-time viewport, because 3ds Max doesn't use the extra display memory necessary to display it correctly. If your display card is using an OPEN GL driver, you can right-click the viewport label, and then click Texture Correction to force the real-time view to display your texture correctly. However, keep in mind that this takes away memory from your display card's ability to perform, so turn on this feature only when you need it, and turn it off when you are done.

but factors such as the complexity of the scene and the processing power of your computer affect the playback rate. This means that, as shown in Figure 1, real-time rendering in a viewport shows you much less detail than what will appear in your final rendering (for example, scene background and accurate lighting effects).

Prerendered images are 2D image files, either static images or animations, created from a 3ds Max scene. The software takes as much time as it needs to calculate and display each and every frame in the scene. In this situation, the rendering of the frame usually occurs nowhere near real time, but the final result has a much higher level of detail and sense of realism than real-time rendering. As with real-time rendering, the complexity of the scene and the amount of available computer resources are big factors in how long it takes a scene to render.

When you create prerendered images, you can choose to save them in a wide variety of

FIGURE 1
Scene in viewport and media player

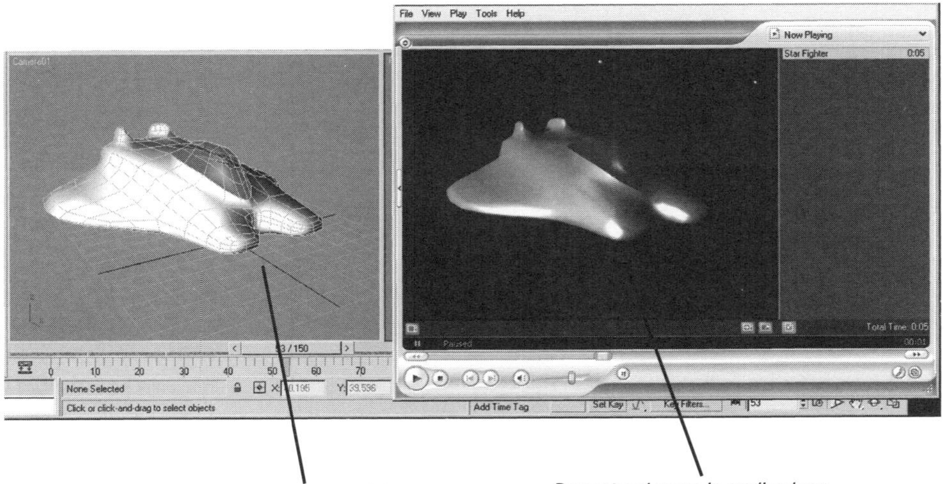

Scene rendered in real time   *Prerendered scene in media player*

image file formats. After the images have completely finished the rendering process, you can further view or manipulate them in any other program that can read the file format. For instance, with still images, you can save your rendering as a single TIFF file, and then open the TIFF file and touch it up in a photo-editing program. In the case of animated scenes, you can render a sequence of multiple JPEG files or a video clip, and then edit the images or video clip in a video-editing program.

Understanding Renderers

For handling the task of rendering image files, 3ds Max comes with two different renderers: the default scanline renderer and the mental ray renderer. As the name suggests, the **scanline renderer** renders an image or frame one line of pixels at a time, pixels being the tiny dots of color that make up a digital picture on a computer monitor. Scanline rendering moves from the top line of pixels to the bottom line of pixels in a scene until the entire image is completed.

The **mental ray renderer** uses a more advanced rendering technique to generate photo-realistic images. It does a great job of producing advanced lighting effects such as raytraced reflections, global illumination (such as radiosity), caustic lighting effects (such as when light gets distorted by passing through water or transparent objects), and other physical properties of light. Because these concepts require an understanding of many advanced parameters, many of the features that the mental ray renderer offers are outside the scope of this text. What you should know, however, is that 3ds Max lets you easily designate which renderer you would like to use, including the integration of third-party rendering plug-ins that you can buy to enhance the rendering capabilities of 3ds max.

To change the renderer from the default scanline renderer to the mental ray renderer, click Rendering on the menu bar, click Render on the menu to open the Render Scene dialog box, pan to the bottom of the Common panel in the dialog box, and then open the Assign Renderer rollout, as shown in Figure 2. Click the Choose Renderer button to the right of Production or ActiveShade, click mental ray Renderer in the Choose Renderer dialog box, and then click the OK button.

QUICKTIP

By default, the renderer used in Material Editor slots is the same as the renderer used for production rendering.

FIGURE 2
Assign Renderer rollout

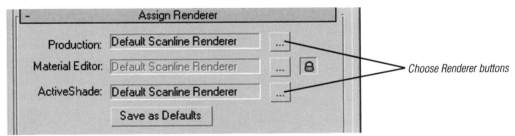

LESSON 2

RENDER WITH ACTIVESHADE

What You'll Do

In this lesson, you will learn what ActiveShade rendering is and how to use it to preview scenes without going through a full rendering process.

Understanding ActiveShade Rendering

3DS Max lets you switch between two different rendering modes: production rendering and ActiveShade rendering. **Production rendering** uses either the scanline renderer or mental ray renderer to produce a high-quality image; this is the method of rendering you used in earlier chapters when clicking the Quick Render (Production) tool on the main toolbar. Production rendering is covered in greater depth in Lessons 4 and 5 of this chapter.

ActiveShade rendering uses the default scanline renderer to display a preview-quality rendering. As you work with the ActiveShade window open, the results of changes that you make to lighting and materials appear in the window, as shown in Figure 3, without having to go through the whole production-rendering process. ActiveShade offers a higher-quality rendering than that which

FIGURE 3
ActiveShade window docked as a viewport

Perspective viewport   ActiveShade viewport

7-8 AUTODESK 3D STUDIO MAX   *Rendering*

appears in the shaded viewport, but is less precise than production rendering. ActiveShade is most useful when you are working with materials and the real-time viewport just isn't showing you the kind of detail that you need.

There are two ways that you can display the ActiveShade window. It can be docked in place of a viewport, or it can exist as a floater that can be freely moved around the desktop. To dock it in place of a viewport, right-click the viewport label, point to Views, and then click ActiveShade on the submenu. To activate it as a floater, simply click and hold the Quick Render (Production) tool on the main toolbar until the Quick Render flyout appears, and then click the Quick Render (ActiveShade) tool on the flyout, as shown in Figure 4.

QUICKTIP

When you already have an ActiveShade window open and try to open another, a warning appears telling you that you can have only one ActiveShade window open. If you click OK in the warning dialog box, the new ActiveShade window opens and the original closes.

FIGURE 4
Quick Render flyout

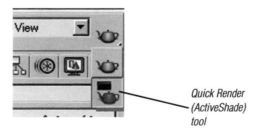

Quick Render (ActiveShade) tool

Initializing the ActiveShade Window

When you first open an ActiveShade window, 3ds Max renders the scene with ActiveShade and holds this data in its memory. This is called initializing. When you make a change to the lighting or materials in the scene, those changes are added to the initial scene data and automatically updated in the window. However, when you transform (move, rotate, or scale) or modify an object in the scene, the changes are not automatically updated in the ActiveShade window, as shown in Figure 5. To update these kinds of modifications in the ActiveShade window, you must reinitialize it. To do this, simply right-click in the ActiveShade window, and then click Initialize on the Tools quadrant of the Quad menu.

If you select an object in a scene before initializing the ActiveShade window, ActiveShade only updates the changes for that selected object. Depending on scene complexity, this can greatly decrease the amount of time it takes to render an update. Another helpful feature of ActiveShade is the ability to draw a region within the window, and then update only that area of the render window. Both of these options save time in calculations when you are concerned only with the way a certain object or portion of the image looks.

FIGURE 5
Effect of transformation on ActiveShade

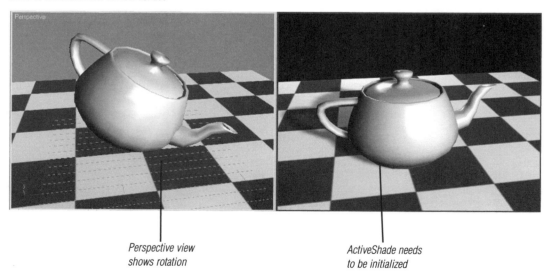

Perspective view shows rotation

ActiveShade needs to be initialized

FIGURE 6
Perspective and ActiveShade viewports

FIGURE 7
ActiveShade viewport being updated

Thin line runs across top and side when updating

Use ActiveShade rendering

1. Open **MAX07-01.max**, then save it as **Table**.
2. Right-click the **Perspective viewport label**, point to **Views** on the right-click menu, then click **ActiveShade**.

   The Perspective viewport is replaced by the ActiveShade viewport.

3. Right-click anywhere in the **Left viewport**, press **[P]** to switch to perspective view, then zoom, pan, and arc-rotate in the view to achieve a similar angle to that in the ActiveShade viewport.

   This gives you a good side-by-side comparison, as shown in Figure 6.

4. Open the **Material Editor**, move it (if necessary) so that the ActiveShade viewport is visible, click the **Checkered Cloth material** in the Material Editor to select it, then in the Blinn Basic Parameters rollout, click the **Diffuse map button** to open the Checker map.

5. In the Checker Parameters rollout on the Material Editor, click the Color #1 swatch, then in the Color Selector, change the color to a bright green color.

   It happens quickly, but when you change the colors, a progress line runs down the right side of the ActiveShade window, as shown in Figure 7. The color of half the checkered squares in the scene is immediately updated from red to green.

   (continued)

6. Close the Color Selector, then close the Material Editor.

You docked the ActiveShade viewport, then updated a material in the scene and viewed its update in the ActiveShade window.

Initialize ActiveShade rendering

1. In the Top viewport, select the **Omni01 light**, then move it to the left side of the teapot.

   The lighting in ActiveShade viewport is updated to reflect the change in the light's position.

2. With the Select and Rotate tool, rotate the **teapot** in the Perspective viewport.

   The ActiveShade viewport shows no change to the teapot's rotation.

3. Right-click anywhere in the ActiveShade viewport, then click **Initialize** on the Tools quadrant of the Quad menu.

   The viewport is updated with the changes, as shown in Figure 8.

You moved a light in the scene, immediately viewed the updated scene in the ActiveShade window, rotated the teapot, then initialized the ActiveShade window in order to view the change in rotation.

FIGURE 8
ActiveShade viewport reinitialized

Rotation is displayed after initializing

FIGURE 9
Region drawn in ActiveShade viewport

—Selected region

FIGURE 10
Region updated in ActiveShade

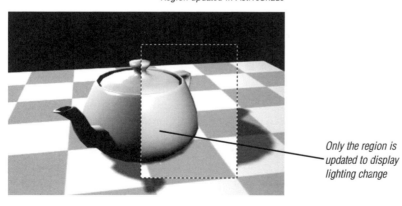

Only the region is updated to display lighting change

Update a region of the ActiveShade viewport

1. Right-click anywhere in the **ActiveShade viewport**, then click **Draw Region** in the Tools quadrant of the Quad menu.

   The mouse pointer turns into a pencil shape.

2. Click and drag to draw a region around half of the teapot, as shown in Figure 9.

3. In the Top viewport, move the **Omni01 light** below the teapot.

   The selected region of the ActiveShade window is the only area that is updated, as shown in Figure 10.

   > TIP If you notice that the quality of the ActiveShade rendering begins to deteriorate after working with it for a while, simply reinitialize the window. This is a normal occurrence.

4. Save the file, then reset 3ds Max.

You drew a region within the ActiveShade viewport, changed the lighting in the scene, then viewed the updated region in the ActiveShade viewport.

Lesson 2   Render with ActiveShade

LESSON 3

UNDERSTANDING FILE OUTPUT

What You'll Do

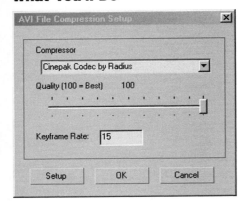

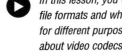
In this lesson, you will learn about rendering file formats and which ones are appropriate for different purposes. You'll also learn about video codecs and about resolution considerations, and how each comes into play as you plan how to render a scene to a file.

Understanding File Formats

In Chapter 4, you learned how to quickly render a scene by clicking the Quick Render (Production) tool on the main toolbar. In upcoming Lessons 4 and 5 of this chapter, you'll take a close look at exactly what is going on when you do production rendering and how to control what is going on when you render. You'll also learn how to save the results of your work on a scene as a digital image file or video clip that can be viewed in a separate format. Taking all of the visual information that you create in a scene and sending it as output to create a new file is really what production rendering is all about. Before you dive in too deeply, though, it is important that you first take a look at the file types to which you can render and the considerations that go into choosing one.

The decision of which file type to use is based on issues external to 3ds Max. In 3ds Max, options are provided, but you need to make the choice. Each file format has its own purpose and its own strengths and weaknesses. The file type to which you choose to render depends on what you plan to do with the resulting image.

If you are doing work for a client, your client will often specify a preferred format. For example, many prepress layout artists who do projects such as magazine cover images are accustomed to working with the TIFF file format. As another example, if your purpose is to render a video clip that you want to put on a DVD and send to potential employers, then you might render an animation to a Quicktime .mov file, or a Video for Windows AVI file, depending on what kind of file formats your DVD authoring software accepts. Table 7-1 contains a list of image file formats and their common uses.

Choosing a Video Codec

Rendering an animation as a video clip can produce extremely large file sizes. A video **codec** is software that reduces the size of video clips by compressing the information contained in the file. Codec stands for "compression/decompression." Typically, the trade-off for reducing the amount of data

TABLE 7-1 Image file formats and uses

Still images

File type	Description	Typical uses
JPG/JPEG	Created by the Joint Photographic Experts Group; provides good-quality images at low file sizes	Web images, video editing
BMP	Microsoft image file format; uses RGB data to display digital pictures	Images
GIF	Graphics Interleaved Format; designed for fewer colors and small file sizes	Web images, Web animation
PNG	Portable Network Graphic; an open source image format	Web images, Web animation
TIFF	Tagged Image File Format; high-quality images that can contain CMYK data and transparency	Images

Animation

File type	Description	Typical uses
MPG/MPEG Type 1	Motion Picture Experts Group; created for full-motion video at very low file sizes	Web downloading, CD-ROM, video
MPG/MPEG Type 2	Motion Picture Experts Group; created for full-motion video at higher-quality levels	DVD
AVI	Microsoft Video for Windows; offers a variety of resolution and quality choices	Video-editing applications, CD-ROM, video
WMV	Microsoft Windows Media; designed for "streaming" media	Web streaming
MOV	Apple's QuickTime format	Web downloading, video editing, CD-ROM

required to play a file (the **data transfer rate**) by compressing it is a loss of image quality. Another issue is that once a certain codec has been used to compress a file, that same codec must be used to decompress the file upon playback. This means that if you make a video clip using a specific codec, that same codec must be present on the end user's computer for him or her to be able to play the video clip.

The good news is that because computer operating systems such as Windows and Mac OSs come with several of the industry standard codecs preinstalled, most users have many of the relevant codecs already. You still have to choose the codec that is right for the purpose of the media files that you are creating. For instance, if you plan on editing your animations using DV video-editing software on Microsoft Windows, then you might want to use the Microsoft DV video encoder. A popular codec among users who produce Quicktime movies is the Sorenson codec, because it does a good job of producing low data rates without sacrificing much image quality. Two video codecs that are good at creating low data rate files, which can be useful for playing clips off a CD-ROM, are the popular Cinepak codec and the Indeo codec.

Once you choose to save your animation into a video clip file format, 3ds Max automatically presents you with a compression settings dialog box that contains a list of all of the video codecs that are installed on your machine, as shown in Figure 11. You should then choose one based on your intended purpose. This dialog box also contains a Quality slider to adjust when choosing how much compression to apply (higher quality = less compression). Many codecs offer additional compression options that you can access by clicking the Setup button in this same dialog box.

FIGURE 11
AVI File Compression Setup dialog box

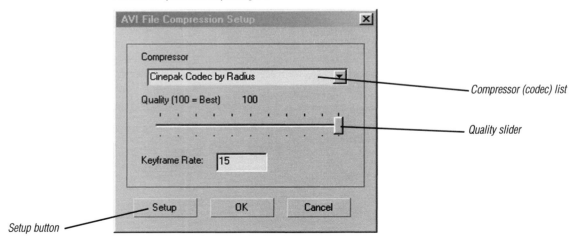

It is outside the scope of this text to include an in-depth discussion of video codecs, but there are many resources in books and on the Web that explain the choices available in video codecs, and why you should use one over the other.

Determining Image Resolution

The physical size of your final image, measured in pixels, is referred to as the **resolution**. This concept sometimes causes confusion because resolution means different things to different people. If you are talking to a graphic designer who is accustomed to designing pictures for printed media, he or she probably thinks of image resolution in terms of "dots per inch" or **DPI**. This is because many printers require a certain DPI to achieve a quality printout. However, a video editor or Web designer thinks of image resolution in terms of the number of pixels in an image's width compared to its height, or what some people refer to as "image size." For instance, the resolution of DV video is 720 × 480 pixels, as shown on the left in Figure 12. If you want to play back your animations on DV, you need to render images that are 720 pixels wide by 480 pixels high.

Although there are a couple of ways to talk about resolution, DPI can be translated into image size in pixels, and vice versa. The most important thing to understand is the resolution requirements of the medium for which you are creating output. The more pixels (or DPI) there are in an image, the higher the quality of its appearance, and the longer it takes to render. So you don't want to waste time rendering lots of pixels for a medium that doesn't require a high resolution. For instance, Web video typically runs at 320 × 240, as shown on the right in Figure 12, so if you are creating an animation for a Web video clip, you wouldn't want to waste time rendering at a resolution higher than that.

FIGURE 12
Two different resolutions

DV video resolution
720 x 480

Web video resolution
320 x 240

LESSON 4

CREATE AND
SAVE RENDERINGS

What You'll Do

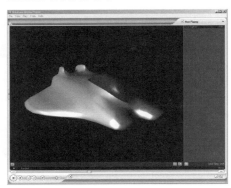

In this lesson, you will explore the Common panel in the Render Scene dialog box, you will learn how to adjust the settings on the Common panel to get the desired file output, and you will also learn how to render a file from the dialog box.

Using the Render Scene Dialog Box

The Render Scene dialog box is where you set up all of the parameters related to rendering the scene in which you are working. There are three easy ways to open the Render Scene dialog box: click the Render Scene Dialog tool on the main toolbar; click Rendering on the menu bar, then click Render on the menu; or press [F10].

As mentioned before, there are two modes for rendering: Production mode and ActiveShade mode. The panels that appear in the Render Scene dialog box change, depending on which mode you are currently in. You can change the mode at the bottom of the dialog box by clicking either the Production or the ActiveShade option button. Because a Production rendering is more precise in its calculations than ActiveShade, you use it when you do most of your test rendering and final renders. The Render Scene dialog box for a Production rendering is shown in Figure 13.

The panels in the dialog box also change depending on which renderer you are currently using. However, there are three panels that are always present: The Common panel, as shown in Figure 13, lets you set options such as which frames of your animation to render, the resolution of the images, the file type to use when saving rendered images, and which renderer to use. The Renderer panel, as shown in Figure 14, contains options specific to the currently assigned renderer. The Render Elements panel lets you assign different aspects of the image into separate image files, so that you can then blend them together in a compositing program for more flexibility. Compositing software such as Discreet Combustion or Adobe After Effects lets you take separate layers of images and blend them together to create a composite image. This is useful because you can then manipulate each of the separate layers independently, as opposed to if these elements were rendered together as a single image.

Adjusting Common Parameters

The Common Parameters rollout on the Common panel of the Render Scene dialog box is the rollout that you access the most often when rendering animations.

The Time Output group in this rollout, as shown in Figure 15, lets you change settings that determine how many and which frames of your animation are rendered. Click the Single option button to

FIGURE 13
Common panel

FIGURE 14
Renderer panel

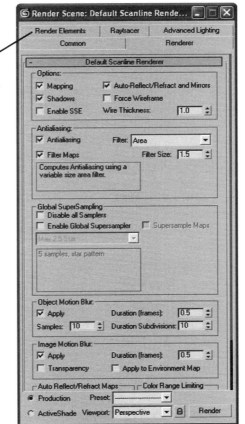

Render Elements tab

Lesson 4   Create and Save Renderings

AUTODESK 3D STUDIO MAX 7-19

render a single frame of an animation; the frame rendered will be the frame at which the time slider is currently located. Click the Active Time Segment option button to render every single frame in your animation. Right next to this option the current range of frames in the active time segment is displayed; by default it reads 0 to 100, but it changes depending on how many frames are in your current animation.

If you want to render a subset of the frames in an animation, click the Range option button., then enter the start frame and end frame in the two fields to the right of the option button. For example, if you only to render only the first 30 frames of an animation, enter 0 in the field on the left and 29 in the field on the right.

> **QUICK**TIP
> Don't forget that frame 0 is counted as a frame, so if you render Frames 0 to 29 you render 30 frames.

Another option in the upper-right corner of this group is the Every Nth Frame box. When the Active Time Segment or Range option is selected, entering a number other than 1 in this box enables you to skip frames while rendering. For example, typing 5 in this field when the Active Time Segment option is selected renders every fifth frame of the active time segment. This can be helpful if you want to render frames from a lengthy animation only at certain intervals. Doing so enables you to see the progression of how the rendering looks before committing to render every frame.

Located just under the Range fields is the File Number Base box. The number in this box is the number used at the end of the first file created when rendering an image file sequence. For example, if you enter 100 in this field and render an animation from Frames 0 to 100, the filename of the first file in the the sequence of images rendered and saved would end with 100. (The sequence files would be Filename0100.jpg, Filename0101.jpg, Filename0102.jpg, and so on.) You might use this option if you render an animation that will get tacked onto the end of a previously rendered sequence of frames. The option is only available when the Active Time Segment or Range option is selected.

You can choose the last option in the Time Output group, Frames, to choose exactly the

FIGURE 15
Time Output group

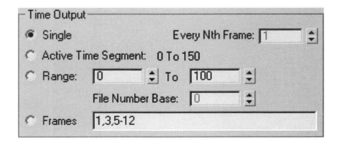

frame numbers that you want to render. To render nonsequential frames, type the frame numbers in the Frames box, separating them by commas. To render a range of frames, separate them by a dash. For instance, 1,3,5–10 renders frames 1, 3, 5, 6, 7, 8, 9, and 10.

Adjusting Output Size

The Output Size group on the Common panel, as shown in Figure 16, is where you determine the resolution of your rendered image files, measured in pixels. At the top of the group is a drop-down list that provides access to preset outputs that reflect common film, video, and print industry standards. For instance, if you want to render an animation that is going to be edited on a DV video-editing system, you can choose NTSC DV (video) from the preset list, and all of the pixel resolution requirements for that format are set up automatically.

After you choose an output, the four resolution buttons to the right of the Width and Height boxes are updated to show common resolution variations for that format. Click a resolution button to choose a new resolution; its values then appear in the Width and Height fields. You can also adjust the output size manually by entering a pixel dimension in the Width or Height fields.

An **aspect ratio** is the relationship of an image's width to its height. For instance, the aspect ratio of a standard television image is 4:3. 3ds Max displays this ratio as a decimal value of 1.333. If you choose any preset option other than Custom, the Image Aspect Ratio field displays the image aspect ratio for that setting, and the field is unavailable to edit. The Pixel Aspect Ratio setting displays the aspect ratio of the individual pixels that make up the image, also expressed as a decimal. A setting of 1.0 means that the width equals the height, and the image is a square. The pixels that are displayed on a standard NTSC television image have a pixel aspect ratio of 0.9, meaning that their width is a little bit smaller than their height. Again, the output resolution that you choose determines this setting for you.

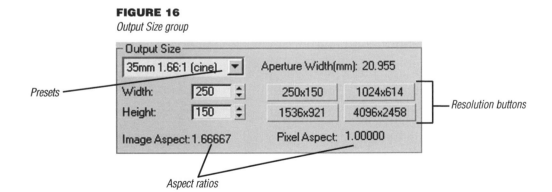

FIGURE 16
Output Size group

QUICKTIP

As you type a value into the Width (or Height) field, the Height (or Width) field value is automatically calculated according to the image aspect ratio.

Designating Render Output

The Render Output group is where you designate locations, names, and file types for the files that 3ds Max renders. To render a scene as a certain file type, click the Files button at the top of this group to open the Render Output File dialog box, as shown in Figure 17. In this dialog box, navigate to a location on your computer to save the rendered file or files, and enter a name for the file. Click the Save as type list arrow, click a file type on the list of available file types to designate the file type of the rendered file, and then click Save. Depending on the file type chosen, you might need to adjust the setting for that particular file type. For instance, when you choose to render a scene to the AVI file type, after you click Save, a dialog box opens in which you can select a video codec for the file, adjust the level of image quality, and adjust the frame rate.

Rendering a Scene

After you finish setting up the Render Scene options, you are ready to render the scene. Click the Render button at the bottom of the dialog box. A window showing the rendered scene appears. If you are rendering an animation, the window is continuously updated to show you the scene as 3ds Max calculates and renders each frame. You'll also see the Rendering progress window during the rendering of an animation; it displays a summary of all the render settings you have chosen. As shown in Figure 18, two blue progress bars at the top of the dialog box show the progress of the Total Animation and the progress of the Current Task. The area above the Current Task progress bar displays a brief description of any special calculations that the default scanline renderer undergoes as it renders the scene. When the progress bars are complete, your animation is finished rendering.

FIGURE 17
Render Output File dialog box

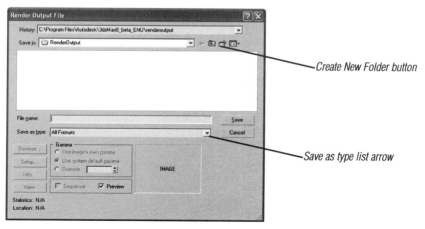

FIGURE 18
Rendering progress window

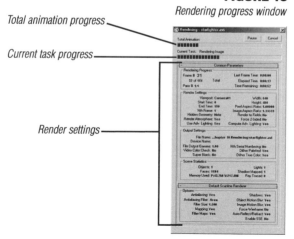

7-22 AUTODESK 3D STUDIO MAX

Rendering

Rendering an Image File Sequence

If you choose to save your animation as a video clip, such as a QuickTime movie, 3ds Max renders a single video clip file. However, you also have the option of rendering an **image file sequence**. When you do this, 3ds Max creates a separate file for each and every frame in your animation, with a number at the end of each file name indicating where it falls in the sequence, as shown in Figure 19. In 3ds Max, an image file sequence is automatically created when you render a range of frames from an animation in one of the still picture file formats. For example, if you render an animation that has one hundred frames into JPEG format, 3ds Max renders one hundred JPEG files, one for each frame.

There are several benefits to creating an image file sequence. One is that if your machine crashes before a rendering is done, you still have all the frames saved up to the point when it crashed. This is not the case with a single video clip file. For example, if you are rendering an AVI file and for some reason your machine crashes after rendering 99% of the file, you lose the entire rendering because it never finished the process of saving that single file. If you render an image file sequence and your machine crashes after 99% of it is rendered, you have to render only the images that it didn't get to before crashing.

Another benefit is that some still picture file formats such as .tga, .tif, and .rpf enable you to embed transparency information and other channels of data into the individual files in a sequence. This information can be utilized in other programs such as

FIGURE 19
Image file sequence

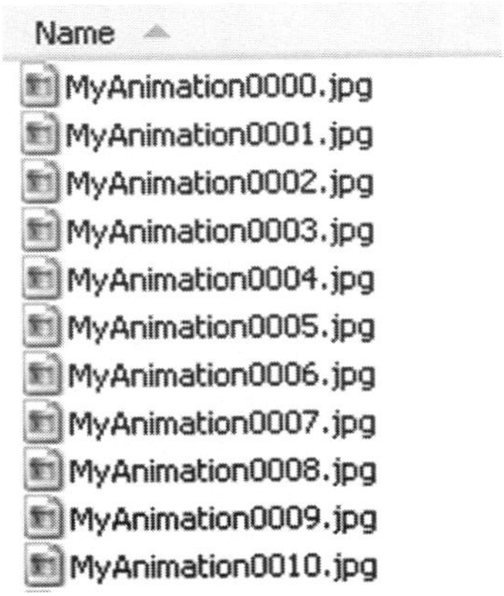

Name
MyAnimation0000.jpg
MyAnimation0001.jpg
MyAnimation0002.jpg
MyAnimation0003.jpg
MyAnimation0004.jpg
MyAnimation0005.jpg
MyAnimation0006.jpg
MyAnimation0007.jpg
MyAnimation0008.jpg
MyAnimation0009.jpg
MyAnimation0010.jpg

compositing programs that can read this information. For instance, if you render an image file sequence of the animation of an object against a transparent background, the object could be superimposed over video content without much fuss, because the information about which pixels should be visible and which should be transparent are rendered into the image files.

After you have rendered an image file sequence, you can then compile the sequence in any image-manipulation or video-editing software. Managing the large amount of files that results from rendering an image file sequence can at first seem unwieldy. A simple 10-second animation running at 30 frames per second produces 300 individual image files. The key to keeping them under control is to make sure that you place a sequence of frames in its own folder. There should be no other files in that folder other than the image file sequence. Any other files mingling with the sequence could result in a break in the sequence and can cause headaches when you want to compile the images together in another program.

FIGURE 20
Output size settings

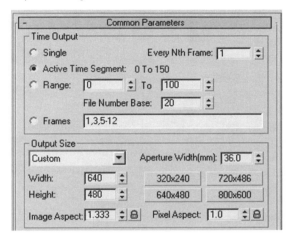

Adjust output options

1. Open **MAX07-02.max**, save it as **Starfighter**, then press the **Play animation button** ▶ to preview the animation in the Camera01 viewport.

   A starfighter model travels past a camera over the course of 150 frames.

2. Stop the animation, click the **Render Scene Dialog tool** to open the Render Scene dialog box, then click the **Common tab** (if necessary) near the top of the dialog box to open the Common panel.

3. In the Time Output group on the Common panel, click the **Active Time Segment option button** to select it.

   The current frame range for the active time segment is 0 to 150.

4. In the Output Size group, make sure that **Custom** is selected in the list box, then click the **640 × 480 button**.

   The Width and the Height fields in the Output Size group are updated to the chosen values, as shown in Figure 20. Setting up these basic options ensures that all 150 frames are rendered at a video resolution of 640 × 480.

5. Save the file.

You opened and viewed an animation, opened the Render Scene Dialog box, then changed its settings to render the active time segment at a resolution of 640 × 480.

Designate an output file type

1. Pan down the Render Scene dialog box, then in the Render Output group, click the **Files button** to the right of the Save File check box.

   The Render Output File dialog box appears.

2. Navigate to the folder where you are saving your Data Files, then in the File name field, type the name **Starfighter**.

3. Click the **Save as type list arrow**, scroll up in the list and click **AVI File**, then click the **Save button**.

   The AVI File Compression Setup dialog box appears.

4. Make sure that **Cinepak codec by Radius** is currently selected in the Compressor list box.

5. Make sure the **Quality slider** is set all the way to the right at **100**, then click the **OK button** to close the dialog box.

6. Click the **Render button** at the bottom of the Render Scene dialog box.

   3ds Max renders the scene frame by frame. A line passes down the window as each frame is rendered, and the Rendering progress window shows the progress of the render, as shown in Figure 21. When rendering is complete, a new AVI file is saved in the folder you designated.

   (continued)

FIGURE 21
Rendering the scene

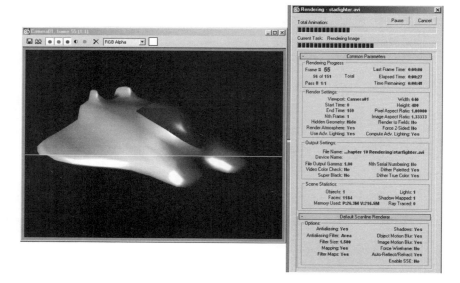

FIGURE 22
AVI file

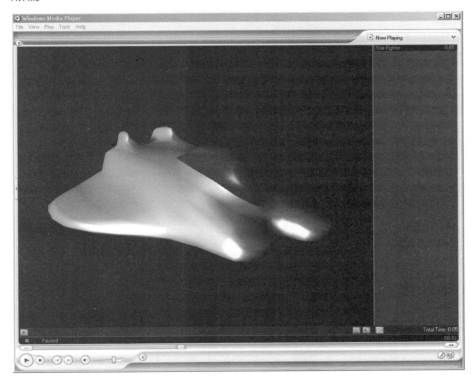

7. When the rendering is done, close the rendered scene window, save the scene, click **File** on the menu bar, click **View Image File**, browse to select in the View File dialog box the **Starfighter AVI file** that you just rendered, then click **Open**.

   Your default media player opens and plays the video clip, as shown in Figure 22.

8. After viewing the AVI file in the media player, close the media player window.

You designated a folder and a file type for the render output, reviewed the settings for the file type, rendered the scene, then opened the newly rendered file.

Render an image file sequence

1. In the Render Output group in the Render Scene dialog box, click the **Files button**, in the Render Output File dialog box, navigate to the folder where you are saving Data Files, click the **Create new folder** button at the top of the dialog box, rename the new folder **sequence**, then press **[Enter]** twice.

   The newly created sequence folder is selected in the Render Output File dialog box. By saving the files in their own folder you ensure that they stay together.

2. In the File name field, type the name **Starfighter** (if necessary), click the **Save as type list arrow**, click **JPEG File**, then click the **Save button**.

   The JPEG Image Control dialog box opens, as shown in Figure 23.

   (continued)

FIGURE 23
JPEG Image Control dialog box

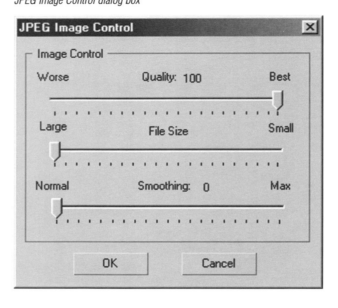

FIGURE 24

Name	Size	Type
Starfighter0000	3 KB	Paint Shop Photo Al...
Starfighter0001	3 KB	Paint Shop Photo Al...
Starfighter0002	3 KB	Paint Shop Photo Al...
Starfighter0003	3 KB	Paint Shop Photo Al...
Starfighter0004	3 KB	Paint Shop Photo Al...
Starfighter0005	3 KB	Paint Shop Photo Al...
Starfighter0006	3 KB	Paint Shop Photo Al...
Starfighter0007	3 KB	Paint Shop Photo Al...
Starfighter0008	3 KB	Paint Shop Photo Al...
Starfighter0009	3 KB	Paint Shop Photo Al...
Starfighter0010	3 KB	Paint Shop Photo Al...
Starfighter0011	3 KB	Paint Shop Photo Al...
Starfighter0012	3 KB	Paint Shop Photo Al...
Starfighter0013	3 KB	Paint Shop Photo Al...
Starfighter0014	3 KB	Paint Shop Photo Al...
Starfighter0015	3 KB	Paint Shop Photo Al...
Starfighter0016	3 KB	Paint Shop Photo Al...
Starfighter0017	3 KB	Paint Shop Photo Al...
Starfighter0018	3 KB	Paint Shop Photo Al...
Starfighter0019	3 KB	Paint Shop Photo Al...
Starfighter0020	4 KB	Paint Shop Photo Al...
Starfighter0021	4 KB	Paint Shop Photo Al...
Starfighter0022	4 KB	Paint Shop Photo Al...
Starfighter0023	4 KB	Paint Shop Photo Al...
Starfighter0024	4 KB	Paint Shop Photo Al...
Starfighter0025	4 KB	Paint Shop Photo Al...
Starfighter0026	4 KB	Paint Shop Photo Al...
Starfighter0027	4 KB	Paint Shop Photo Al...
Starfighter0028	4 KB	Paint Shop Photo Al...
Starfighter0029	4 KB	Paint Shop Photo Al...
Starfighter0030	4 KB	Paint Shop Photo Al...
Starfighter0031	4 KB	Paint Shop Photo Al...
Starfighter0032	4 KB	Paint Shop Photo Al...

3. Drag the **Quality slider** to **Best**, then click **OK**.

   As you drag the Quality slider toward Best, the File Size slider moves toward Large.

4. Click the **Render button** at the bottom of the Render Scene dialog box.

   Once again, the Render window is maximized and 3ds Max renders the scene. This time you have rendered a sequence of 150 JPEG files, numbered in sequence like those shown in Figure 24.

5. When the render is finished, save the file, then reset 3ds Max.

You created a folder, designated an output name and file type, adjusted the file type quality and size settings, then rendered the scene as an image file sequence.

LESSON 5

USE THE PRINT
SIZE WIZARD

What You'll Do

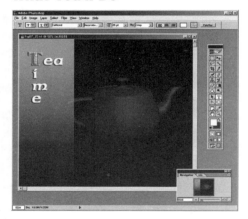

In this lesson, you will learn what the Print Size Wizard is and how to use it to render scenes with the settings necessary to create files appropriate for print media.

Understanding Image Resolution and DPI

As mentioned in Lesson 3, preparing images for print requires different consideration than preparing images to be viewed on a computer monitor or a television. Two questions you have to ask yourself are: what size, in inches, will the image be when it is printed, and what resolution (in DPI) is required in my image? The higher the image resolution, the finer the quality of the print. If you are freelancing for the print industry, you will find that most prepress houses require an image resolution of 300 DPI or greater for printed publications. So, how many pixels does that mean you have to render? If you intend to print an image at a print size of 8.5 × 11 inches and your printer requires a DPI setting of 300 to achieve a nice-quality print, then $300 \times 8.5 = 2550$ and $300 \times 11 = 3300$. Your output resolution (width × height), measured in pixels, is 2550×3300.

Paper Size Settings

It is lucky for those of us who hate or don't have time to do math that 3ds Max includes the Print Size Wizard. The Print Size Wizard is an interface that lets you set up your render settings so that they are optimized for printed mediums. The whole idea behind the wizard is that you typically set the print size that you want, and then choose the required DPI setting. The wizard then calculates the amount of pixels needed in the rendered image's width and height in order to achieve these print settings.

To access the Print Size Wizard, click Rendering on the menu bar, then click Print Size Wizard. As shown in Figure 25, the wizard has a fairly simple interface with only two groups, the Paper Size group and the Rendering group. At the top of the Paper Size group is a drop-down list that features several preset standard print sizes. Click the list arrow, then click the appropriate paper size on the list to choose the print size. The default setting at the top of the preset list is Custom. To manually enter a size not on the list, make sure Custom is selected in the list box, and then enter the paper size settings in the Paper Width and Paper Height boxes or in the Image Width and Image Height boxes. If you choose any other preset option on the Paper Size list, the height and width fields become unavailable for editing.

To use millimeters as the unit of measurement for the paper height and width, click the mm option button; to use inches, click the inches option button. The image width and height are always measured in pixels. Directly below the Choose Unit option buttons, you can choose from four preset DPI setting buttons: 72, 150, 300, and 600. Click the button that matches your needs, or manually enter an exact dots per

inch setting in the DPI box under the Paper Width and Paper Height boxes in the lower part of the Paper Size group. In the upper-right corner of the wizard, click the Portrait or Landscape option button to choose the orientation of the printed image. Choosing one of these options simply flip-flops the Image Width and Height settings.

FIGURE 25
The Print Size Wizard

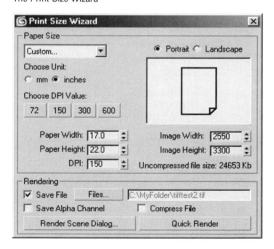

Rendering the Image

After you have adjusted the settings to achieve the print resolution that you require, there are two ways to render your image. In the Rendering group at the bottom of the wizard, the Save File check box is selected by default. To save the scene as a rendered TIFF file, click the Files button to open the Select TIFF File dialog box. After you have selected a location for the rendered TIFF file, clicking the Quick Render button renders the current frame on-screen and saves a TIFF file in the selected location. The reason the Print Size Wizard only renders to the TIFF file format is that this is the industry standard file format that most prepress houses require for digital images. Also, TIFF is one of the only formats that embeds DPI information directly in the file so that it can be read by most printing or image-manipulation software.

If you require a still picture format other than TIFF, click the Render Scene Dialog button at the bottom of the Print Size Wizard after you've chosen your print size settings. The Render Scene dialog box appears, and the print resolution information is automatically transferred to the Output Size group settings. You can then render any file format you need using the options in the Render Output group.

FIGURE 26
New TIFF file

Lesson 5 Use the Print Size Wizard

Render with the Print Size Wizard

1. Create a **teapot** in the Perspective viewport, or open any scene that you would like to work with.
2. Click **Rendering** on the menu bar, then click **Print Size Wizard**.
3. In the Paper Size group, click the **Paper Size list arrow**, then click **A - 11 × 8.5 in**.
   The Paper Width and Height fields dim, and their values show the new settings.
4. Under Choose DPI Value, click the **300 button**.
   The Image Width should now be 3300, and the Image Height should be 2550.
5. In the Rendering group, click the **Files button**, navigate to the folder where you are saving your Data Files, type a name for the new TIFF file in the File name field, then click the **Save button**.
6. Click the **Quick Render button** at the bottom of the Print Size Wizard.
   The Print Size Wizard disappears, and the render window appears. The current frame is rendered and saved to the location you chose as a TIFF file.
7. Save the scene.
8. Click **File** on the menu bar, click **View Image File**, navigate to the folder containing your Data Files, then open the newly created TIFF file, as shown in Figure 26.
9. Close the TIFF file, close the rendered scene window, save the file, then reset 3ds Max.

You created a scene, opened the Print Size Wizard, adjusted the paper size and DPI value settings, designated a location for the rendered file, then rendered the scene. You also opened the newly rendered TIFF file.

AUTODESK 3D STUDIO MAX 7-33

CHAPTER SUMMARY

In this chapter, you learned what rendering is, what renderers are, and which renderers are available with 3ds Max. You also learned about ActiveShade rendering and how to use it to preview scenes in detail without going through a full rendering process. You learned about the file formats that can be produced with rendering and explored their different uses. You found out about video codecs and about resolution considerations and how each can be a factor as you plan how to render a scene to a file. You used the Common panel in the Render Scene dialog box, adjusted the settings on the Common panel to get the desired file output, and rendered files from the dialog box. Last, you investigated what the Print Size Wizard is and how to use it to render scenes with the settings necessary to create files appropriate for print media.

What you have learned

- How to use ActiveShade rendering
- How to initialize ActiveShade rendering
- How to update a region of the ActiveShade viewport
- How to adjust render output options
- How to designate a render output file type
- How to render an image file sequence
- How to use the Print Size Wizard to designate print settings for a file
- How to render a file with the Print Size Wizard

Key terms

ActiveShade rendering Rendering process that uses the scanline renderer to display a preview-quality rendering onscreen in an ActiveShade window, without having to go through the whole production rendering process.

Codec Software that reduces the size of video clips by compressing the information contained in the file.

Image file sequence An animation rendered as a separate file for each and every frame, with a number at the end of each file name indicating where it falls in the sequence.

mental ray renderer 3ds Max renderer that uses a more advanced rendering technique than the scanline renderer to generate photo-realistic images.

Production rendering Rendering process that uses either the scanline renderer or mental ray renderer to produce a high-quality rendered image and/or output file.

Rendering The process you use to cause 3DS Max to take the scene that you have created and generate an image or animation from it.

chapter 8
BONES AND
Inverse Kinematics

1. Create bones.
2. Create bones within a character mesh.
3. Edit bones.
4. Apply inverse kinematics.
5. Use skin.
6. Animate bones.

chapter 8 BONES AND
Inverse Kinematics

Bones are special objects in 3ds Max that you can use to help you animate other objects. You use bones primarily in character animation, but their usage can be applied to other scenarios as well. In many ways, bones in 3ds Max are much like their real-world counterparts. Chains of bones can be linked together to form a skeletal rig that is used to bring life to a character model. This process is known as **rigging**. A **character rig** is a combination of bones and special controls, all set up to make the process of character animation possible. The controls in a character rig can drive the bones to perform specific movements such as waving a hand, making a fist, or performing the strides in a walk cycle. Experienced character animators can rig a character to do pretty much anything they want the character to do. Part of the idea of working with bones is to figure out exactly what you want the character to be able to do, and design the rig to do just that.

At times, character rigging can be quite a daunting task. There are many specialized tools and techniques that go into the process of making a character rig. Some character rigs can have hundreds of specialized controls that allow an animator to breath life into a character model. The purpose of this chapter is to give you a thorough introduction to many of the concepts involved in the process of character rigging and animation.

Once you understand how to create bones, you'll get to see how you can associate bones to certain parts of your character mesh; this process is called **skinning**. After this has been done, you can animate the bones, and the mesh will deform with them. But before you do that, you need to understand how bones work.

Tools You'll Use

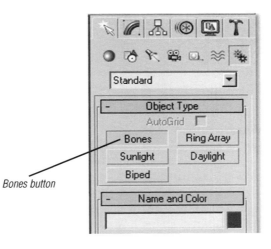

Bones button

Skin modifier

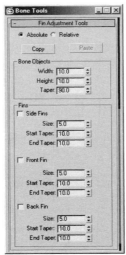

LESSON 1

CREATE BONES

What You'll Do

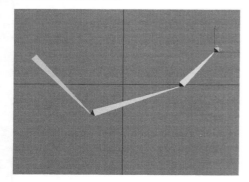

▶ *In this lesson you will learn how bones are used in 3ds Max, and you will learn how to create and manipulate a chain of bones.*

Understanding Bones

Bones are not strictly geometry; they actually function as a **system** in 3ds Max, or as a group of objects that not only have geometry but have a certain behavior as well. A character rig is made up of one or more bone chains, as shown in Figure 1, whose systems work together to create realistic movement in a character. The central important behavior of bones as a system is that they operate with a built-in hierarchy.

In Chapter 2, "Building and Modifying Objects," you learned about linking objects together. When you link objects, you create a relationship between those objects called a **hierarchy**. Objects in a hierarchy have what is commonly referred to as a **parent-child relationship**. This means that the parent object has an influence over the child object. If you move the parent object, the child object moves with it. If you rotate the parent, the child rotates around the parent's pivot point. In fact, all position, rotation, and scale transformations are "inherited" by the child object.

For example, take a look at your arm. There are three major components to it: your upper arm, your forearm, and your hand. When you move your upper arm, your forearm and your hand move with it. When you rotate your forearm at the elbow, your hand also rotates around your elbow. As you create bones in 3ds Max, they are automatically linked together in a hierarchy, with the first bone you create being the parent of the next, and so forth, as shown in Figure 2. Creating bones in 3ds Max is a way to create a structure of objects that have an automatic hierarchy, so you don't have to spend time linking each bone to the next in the chain.

Creating Bones with the Create Panel

To create bones using the Create panel, click the Systems button on the Create panel, as shown in Figure 3, and then click the Bones button in the Object Type rollout to select it. In a viewport, click where you want the bone to begin, and then click once more where you want the bone to end. With each subsequent click, you add more bones to the chain. When you have created the last bone, right-click to complete the process.

You'll notice that an extra little bone appears when you right-click to end the creation process. This bone is referred to as a **nub**, as shown in Figure 4, and it is necessary when you apply inverse kinematics (IK) to a bone hierarchy. You'll learn about IK later in the chapter. When you're not using IK, you can delete this extra nub. To delete the nub, simply make sure the nub is selected, and then press [Delete].

QUICKTIP

To delete a chain of bones, double-click the root parent bone to select the whole chain, and then press [Delete].

FIGURE 1
A character rig

FIGURE 2
Arm and Bones

Third bone (child of second and first)

Second bone (child of first, parent to third)

First bone (parent)

FIGURE 3
Create panel

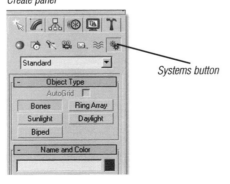

Systems button

FIGURE 4
Chain of bones with a nub at the end

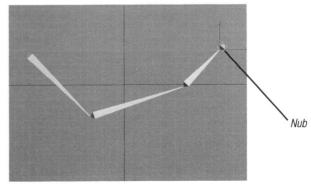

Nub

Lesson 1   Create Bones

AUTODESK 3D STUDIO MAX 8-5

Moving and Rotating Bones

It is important to understand that a bone begins at its own pivot point and ends at the pivot point of its child bone, as shown in Figure 5. The part of the bone that really matters is the pivot point. You are most concerned with the placement of the pivot points when you animate a chain of bones. The actual geometry that makes up the bone is simply a visual aid drawn from pivot point to pivot point.

Another notable thing about bones is that they remain connected. In a regular chain of linked objects, you can move and rotate a child without affecting the parent. However, by default, bone objects behave a little differently. If you move a child bone, the parent bone remains connected to the child and rotates around its own pivot point. You are also able to move that child bone only as far as the parent's length will allow. As shown on the left in Figure 6, when you move a bone with the Select and Move tool, what you are actually doing is rotating that bone, all its children and its parent, around the parent bone's pivot point. However, when you rotate a bone, the bone and all its children will rotate around the bone's own pivot point, as shown on the right in Figure 6.

FIGURE 5
Bone pivot points

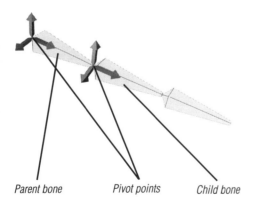

Parent bone   Pivot points   Child bone

FIGURE 6
Moving and rotating a bone

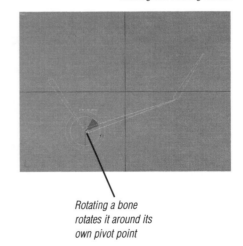

Parent's pivot point

Moving a bone rotates it around its parent's pivot point

Rotating a bone rotates it around its own pivot point

FIGURE 7
Chain of three bones with a nub at the end

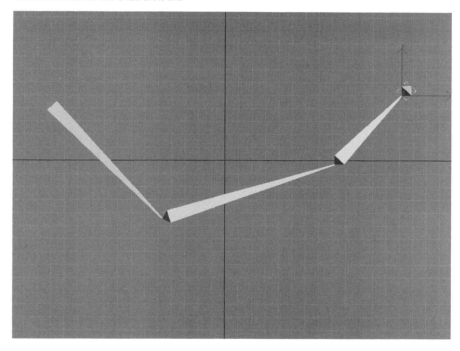

Create bones with the Create panel

1. Start 3ds Max, click in the **Front viewport**, then click the **Maximize Viewport Toggle button** to maximize the Front viewport.
2. Click the **Create tab** on the Command panel (if necessary), then click the **Systems button**.
3. Click the **Bones button** on the Object Type rollout to select it, then click once in the upper-left quadrant of the Front viewport to set the pivot point of the first bone.
4. Move the mouse a short distance away, then click once to set both the end of the first bone and the pivot point of the next bone.
5. Move the mouse a short distance away again, then click once to set both the end of the second bone and the pivot point of the next bone.
6. Move the mouse again, then click once to set the end of the third bone.

   TIP If you make a mistake or something looks awkward, press [Esc] to exit bone-creation mode, then click the Undo button or press [Ctrl]+[Z] a few times until the bones disappear, then try again.

7. Right-click to end the bone-creation process.

   The bones you created should resemble those shown in Figure 7.

(continued)

8. Press **[F3]** so you can see the bones in a shaded view.

The bones are shaded gray and appear to be solid.

You created a series of four bones using the Bones button in the Object Type rollout on the Create panel.

Move and rotate bones

1. Click the **Select and Move tool** on the main toolbar, click the **nub bone**, the last little bone (if necessary), to select it, then press **[Delete]**.
2. Click **Bone03** (the last bone in the chain), then drag the bone around the viewport.

   Bone03 rotates around the pivot point of its parent, Bone02, as shown in Figure 8.

(continued)

FIGURE 8
Moving Bone03

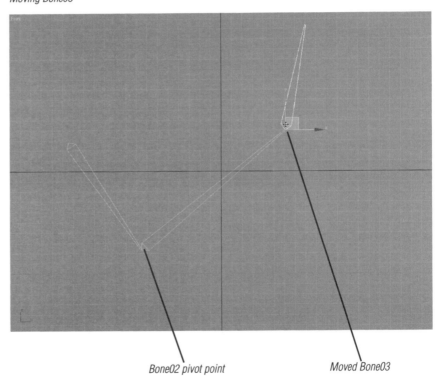

Bone02 pivot point   Moved Bone03

FIGURE 9
Rotating Bone02

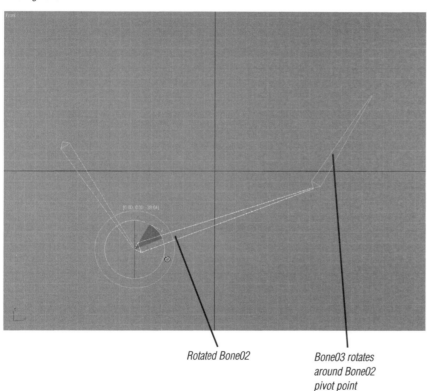

Rotated Bone02

Bone03 rotates around Bone02 pivot point

3. Click **Bone02**, then drag the bone around the viewport.

   Bone02 and Bone03 now rotate around the pivot point of their parent, Bone01.

4. Click the **Select and Rotate tool** on the main toolbar, make sure Bone02 is selected, then click and drag the **blue z-axis handle** on the Rotate gizmo to rotate the bone.

   Bone02 rotates around its own pivot point, as shown in Figure 9. Bone01 does not rotate.

5. Save the file as **Createbone.max**, then reset 3ds Max.

You deleted the nub bone from a chain of bones, moved bones based on their parents' pivot points, then rotated a bone around its own pivot point.

Lesson 1   Create Bones

AUTODESK 3D STUDIO MAX 8-9

LESSON 2

CREATE BONES WITHIN
A CHARACTER MESH

What You'll Do

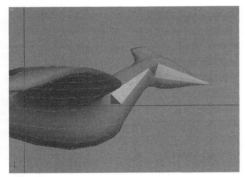

▶ In this lesson, you will learn how to make see-through the mesh in which you plan to create bones, and you will learn how to freeze the mesh. You will also build a bone structure using the Bone Tools floater and name the bones.

Working with the Dragonbird Character

In this lesson and throughout this chapter, you will work with a model of a creature called "dragonbird," a half dragon, half bird-like creature, as shown in Figure 10. You will create a skeletal rig for this model, and then you will animate it. You will use the character's mesh as a guide as you make bones within the mesh and edit the bones' sizes and shapes. When you're initially creating bones, don't worry about being absolutely precise when you place bones within the mesh. You always have the opportunity to tweak bones after they have been made.

Making the Mesh See-Through

Before you create bones, it is a good idea to make your character mesh see-through. This lets you see the bones even though they are inside the character mesh, yet you still are able to use the mesh of the character as a guide. To

FIGURE 10
Dragonbird mesh

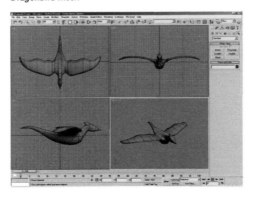

make an object see-through, right-click the object, click Properties on the Transform quadrant of the quad menu to open the Object Properties dialog box, shown in Figure 11, click to select the See-Through check box in the Display Properties group, and then click the OK button to close the dialog box.

QUICKTIP

Another way to make an object see-through is to select the object and then press [Alt]+[X].

Freezing and Unfreezing the Mesh

When you're working with bones, it can be frustrating if you keep accidentally selecting the mesh object, when you are really trying to select the bones. To ensure that this doesn't happen, you can freeze a character mesh. When the mesh is frozen, it can't be selected. To do so, select the mesh, right-click in any viewport, and then select Freeze Selection on the Display quadrant of the Quad menu, shown in Figure 12.

If you need to unfreeze the mesh, simply right-click in any viewport, and then select Unfreeze All on the Display quadrant of the Quad menu.

QUICKTIP

You can find more options for freezing and unfreezing objects by clicking the Display tab on the Command panel, then opening the Freeze rollout.

FIGURE 11
Object Properties dialog box

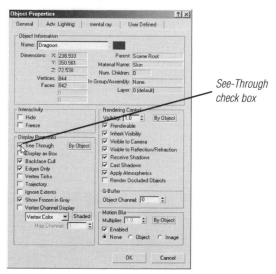

See-Through check box

FIGURE 12
Quad menu

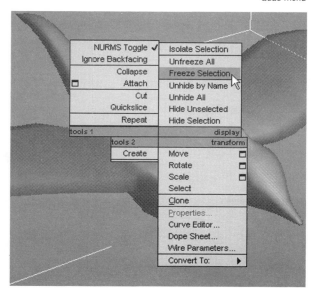

Creating Bones Using the Bone Tools Floater

As an alternative to using the Create panel, you can use the Bone Tools floater to create chains of bones for your character. The Bone Tools floater, shown in Figure 13, contains specific tools for working with bones. The advantage of using the floater is that you can keep it open while you are working in the scene, unlike many dialog boxes that force you to close them before you can resume working. It is also convenient to have many of the tools for working on bones in one place.

To open the Bone Tools floater, click Character on the menu bar, and then click Bone Tools. To create bones, click the Create Bones button in the Bone Tools group on the floater, and then click in the viewport to create the bones you need. When finished, click the Create Bones button to deselect it and exit bone creation mode.

Changing the Names of Bones

When you work with bones, it is a good idea to name them so that the names reflect what the bones represent. This is a very important part of the process, because later on you will rely on the names to ensure that you are animating the correct bones. Because you often need to select multiple bones in order to modify them, consider giving related bones a similar prefix. That way, all bones with that prefix are listed together in the Select by Name dialog box when you use it to select a bone or bones.

To change the name of a bone, first select the bone. 3ds Max displays the bone's default name in the text box at the top of the Modify panel. To change the name, double-click the default name in the text box and replace it by typing a new name, as shown in Figure 14. To change the name of another bone, select the bone and follow the same procedure.

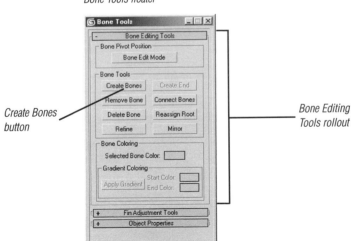

FIGURE 13
Bone Tools floater

Create Bones button

Bone Editing Tools rollout

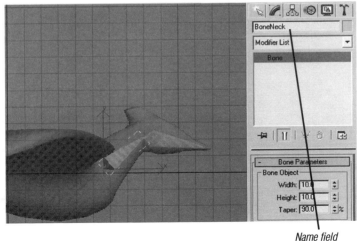

FIGURE 14
Renamed bone

Name field

8-12 AUTODESK 3D STUDIO MAX

Bones and Inverse Kinematics

FIGURE 15
See-through mesh

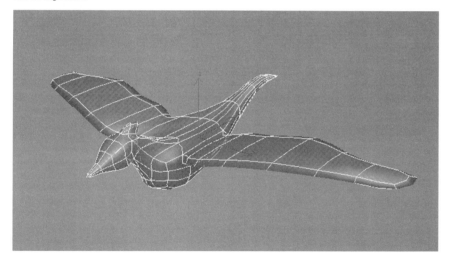

Make the mesh see-through and freeze it

1. Open **max08-01.max** from the drive and folder where your Data Files are stored, then save it as **Dragonbird**.
2. Click the **Select Object tool** on the main toolbar, then click the **Dragonbird object** in the Perspective viewport to select the mesh.
3. Right-click the **object**, then click **Properties** on the Transform quadrant of the Quad Menu to open the Object Properties dialog box.
4. In the Display Properties group in the dialog box, click the **See-Through check box** to select it, then click **OK**.

   The mesh becomes transparent in the viewport, as shown in Figure 15.
5. Right-click in any viewport to display the Quad menu, then click **Freeze Selection** in the Display quadrant of the Quad Menu.

You made the mesh see-through so that you can work more easily with the bones you plan to create. You also froze the mesh so that you won't mistakenly select it while you are working on the skeletal rig.

Lesson 2 Create Bones Within a Character Mesh

AUTODESK 3D STUDIO MAX 8-13

Create bones with the Bone Tools floater

1. Click **Character** on the menu bar, then click **Bone Tools**.

    The Bone Tools floater appears.

    TIP Your Bone Tools floater might look different if the floater has been scrolled by a previous user. Pan up to display the top of the floater (if necessary).

2. In the Bone Editing Tools rollout, click the **Create Bones button** to select it.

3. In the Left viewport, place the pivot point of the first bone by clicking at the base of the neck, as shown in Figure 16.

4. Move the mouse up to where the head joins the neck, as shown in Figure 16, then click again.

5. Move the mouse to the tip of the beak, as shown in Figure 16, and then click once more.

6. Right-click to end the bone-creation process.

    3ds Max automatically creates a nub at the end of the bone chain.

    TIP If you are not happy with the bones you created, feel free to delete them and try again.

(continued)

FIGURE 16
Neck and head bone chain

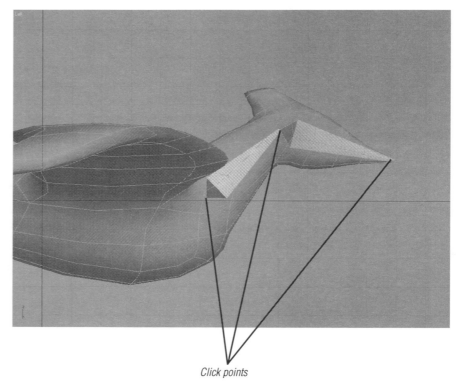

Click points

7. Press **[Esc]** to exit bone-creation mode.
8. With the **nub** (Bone03) still selected, press **[Delete]** to delete the bone.

You used the Bone Tools floater to create a bone chain, and then deleted the nub of the chain.

Change the names of bones

1. Press **[H]** to open the Select by Name dialog box, then double-click **Bone01** (the neck bone) in the list to select it.
2. Click the **Modify tab**, double-click the text in the Name field at the top of the Modify panel to select it, then type **BoneNeck**.

   The new name appears in the Name field in the Modify panel, as shown in Figure 17.
3. Press **[H]** again, select **Bone02** in the Select by Name dialog box, double-click **Bone02** in the Name field to select it, then type **BoneHead**.
4. Save the file.

You selected a bone, changed its name in the Modify panel, selected another bone, changed its name, then saved the file.

FIGURE 17
Neck bone renamed

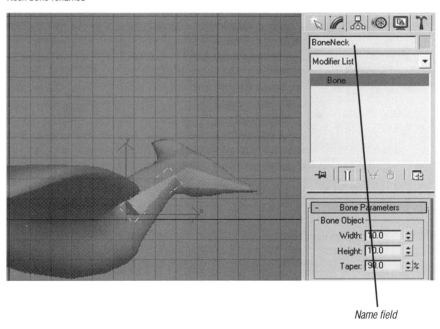

Name field

Lesson 2 Create Bones Within a Character Mesh

AUTODESK 3D STUDIO MAX 8-15

LESSON 3

EDIT BONES

What You'll Do

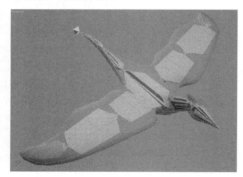

▶ In this lesson, you will create the rest of a skeletal rig for a character mesh. You will learn how to adjust the size of bones in the rig, add fins to the bones, and adjust the size and taper settings of the fins.

Why Edit Bones?

After you create bones, the first thing you want to do is edit them. Usually you want to end up with bones that somewhat resemble the mesh objects that you want to animate. For instance, if you model a character that has two legs, two arms, a torso, and a head, you most likely need to create a skeletal structure that has the same features.

In fact, it works well if the bones themselves represent the size and weight of the character, because proportioning the bones to look like your character helps you visualize what the final animation will look like.

To enable you to achieve this, 3ds Max gives you the ability to change the shape of bones to a certain degree. For instance, if your character has big feet, then the foot bones need to be big. The bones in a character's torso could also be sized to match his big belly, as shown in Figure 18.

The reason for editing bones in this way is that when you animate a character, many times you want to do so with the display of the character mesh turned off (not just see-through, but invisible), so that you actually see only the bones move. This simplifies the process and reduces the memory needed to display the character as you animate it.

Repositioning Pivot Points

After you create bones, you can move and rotate them and they'll move according to their pivot points and those of their parents. However, you might want to move the pivot point of a bone you've created without affecting the other bones in the chain. For instance, it is important to place pivot points at the location of characters' joints, but you might not get it exactly right when you're creating the bones. Using Bone Edit Mode, you can adjust the placement of bones' pivot points after you have already created the bones. To enter Bone Edit Mode, simply click the Bone Edit Mode button at the top of the Bone Tools floater, as shown in Figure 19.

When you reposition a bone's pivot point, it affects the length of both the currently selected bone and its parent. Thus, if you want to alter the length of a bone, you need to reposition the pivot point of its child bone.

You turn off Bone Edit Mode by clicking the Bone Edit Mode button to deselect it. After it is off, you can once again change the position of the bones themselves by moving or rotating them with the Select and Move or Select and Rotate tools. You can always go in and out of Bone Edit Mode as you are editing the placement of bones and their pivot points in a skeletal rig.

Changing a Bone's Size and Shape

After you have created the bones, you usually have to spend some time sizing them to better match the shape of the character mesh. There are several parameters that affect the general shape of bones. You can change the width and height of a bone, and how much a bone tapers along its length. These settings can be changed by adjusting the Width, Height, or Taper settings in the Bone Objects group in the Fin Adjustment Tools

FIGURE 18
Bones sized for character's torso

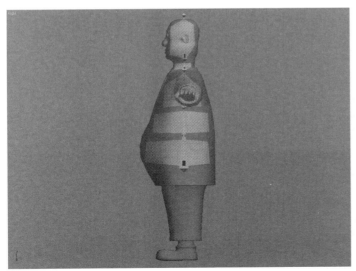

FIGURE 19
Moving a pivot point in Bone Edit Mode

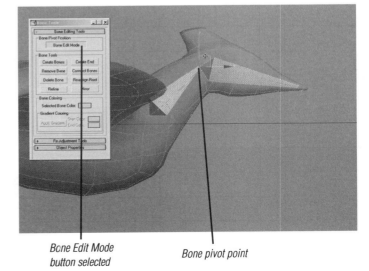

Lesson 3 Edit Bones

rollout on the Bone Tools floater, as shown in Figure 20.

> **QUICK**TIP
>
> You can also adjust the Width, Height, and Taper settings of a selected bone in the Bone Object group in the Bone Parameters rollout on the Modify panel.

How the size and shape of a bone is affected by changes to the Width, Height, and Taper settings is shown in Figure 21. Changing the width or height of a bone changes its thickness. Changing the Taper setting for a bone affects the shape of the end of the bone as it meets the next bone. A Taper setting of 0% puts no tapering on the bone, and the end of the bone will be shaped like a rectangle, whereas a Taper setting of 100% brings the bone to a sharp point where it meets the next bone in the chain.

Adding and Editing Fins

Fins are extra protrusions along the side of a bone that you can create to aid you in simulating the volume of your character. Not only do fins help you to see the way in which a bone is currently oriented, they also give the bone a more defined shaping than if you simply changed the size of a bone's width and height. With fins, you have more options for approximating a character's shape. This is helpful when you are animating and when you get into skinning the character.

You can add side fins, which protrude from both sides of a bone, a front fin, and a back fin. Each fin has its own Size parameter that affects the amount that the fin protrudes from the bone. There is also a Start

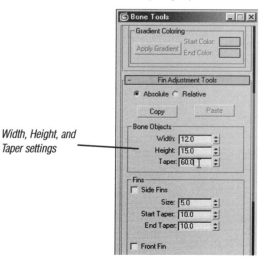

FIGURE 20
Bone Objects group

Width, Height, and Taper settings

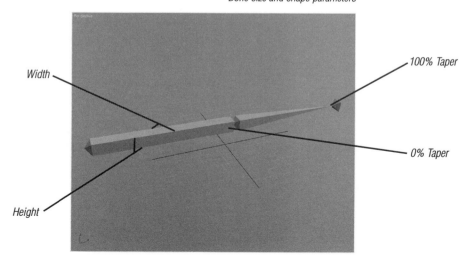

FIGURE 21
Bone size and shape parameters

Width

Height

100% Taper

0% Taper

8-18 AUTODESK 3D STUDIO MAX

Bones and Inverse Kinematics

Taper and an End Taper setting. These taper the shape of the fin at either end of the bone.

There are two methods for adding fins to a bone. One option is to select the bone to which you want to add fins, click the Modify tab, and then in the Bone Fins group on the Bone Parameters rollout, click the Side Fin, Front Fin, or Back Fin check box, and size and taper the new fins as desired. Using the Modify panel you can add fins to a bone one at a time. Alternatively, you can assign fins to multiple bones at once using the Bone Tools floater. To do this, select the bone or bones to which you want to add fins, open the Fin Adjustment Tools rollout in the floater, as shown in Figure 22, and then add, size, and taper fins as desired.

QUICKTIP

While you're working, occasionally look at your model in the Perspective viewport. Reviewing it from various angles helps you see how the bones are taking shape.

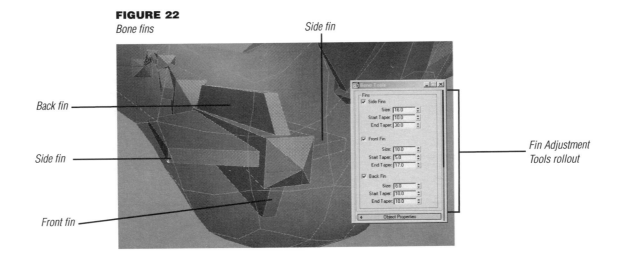

FIGURE 22
Bone fins

Side fin

Back fin

Side fin

Front fin

Fin Adjustment Tools rollout

Lesson 3 Edit Bones

Reposition pivot points

1. Click the **Bone Edit Mode button** at the top of the Bone Editing Tools rollout in the Bone Tools floater.

2. Maximize the Left viewport (if necessary), click the **Select and Move tool**, select **BoneHead**, drag BoneHead around in the viewport to reposition its pivot point, then release the mouse button when the pivot point is located in the center of the dragonbird's head, as shown in Figure 23.

   As BoneHead's pivot point moves, the length of BoneNeck changes as well. With BoneHead's pivot point in the center of the head, the other end of the bone is no longer in the tip of the dragonbird's beak.

3. Move the pivot point of BoneNeck so that the bone runs through the center of the neck.

4. Click the **Bone Edit Mode button** to deselect it and turn off Bone Edit Mode.

   With Bone Edit Mode off, you can rotate the head bone to better position it.

5. Click the **Select and Rotate tool** on the main toolbar, select **BoneHead**, then click and drag up or down on the **blue z-axis handle** to rotate BoneHead until the point of the bone is positioned in the tip of the dragonbird's beak.

Using Bone Edit Mode, you moved the positions of the bones and their pivot points. With Bone Edit Mode off, you then rotated a bone to reposition it.

FIGURE 23
Moved pivot point

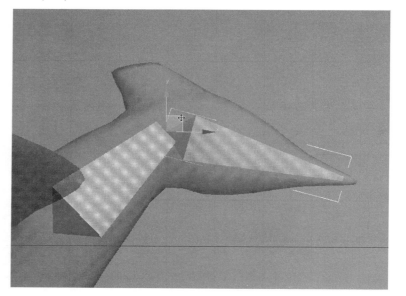

FIGURE 24
Fin Adjustment Tools rollout

FIGURE 25
Body and tail bone chain

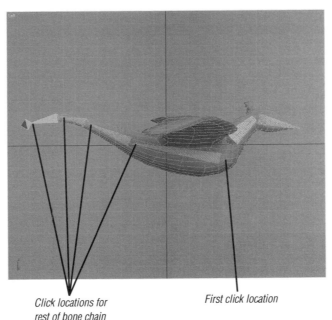

Click locations for rest of bone chain

First click location

Change a bone's size and shape

1. Select **BoneNeck**, then open the Fin Adjustment Tools rollout in the Bone Tools floater.
2. In the Bone Objects group, change the Width setting to **12.0**, change the Height Setting to **15.0**, and change the Taper setting to **60**, as shown in Figure 24.

   The bone now better approximates the shape of the creature's neck.
3. Pan in the Left viewport (if necessary) so you can see the entire dragonbird in the viewport.
4. Click to select the **Create Bones button** in the Bone Tools floater.
5. Click near the chest to place the pivot of the first bone, as shown in Figure 25, then click where the tail meets the body to complete the first bone.
6. Click three more times to make three more bones in the tail, as shown in Figure 25.
7. Right-click to stop making bones.

   A nub bone is created at the end of the tail. Do not delete this bone; you will need it later when you rig the tail for animation.

   (continued)

Lesson 3 Edit Bones

8. Click the **Create Bones button** in the Bone Tools floater to deselect it.

9. Name the first bone you created **BoneBody**, the second bone you created **BoneTail01**, the third bone **BoneTail02**, the fourth bone **BoneTail03**, and the nub **BoneTailNub**.

10. Edit the the Width, Height and Taper settings of each of the bones in the body and tail, so that they fit nicely in the mesh. Don't forget to leave room for fins.

   | TIP Use the Left and Top Viewports to see the bones from above and the side.

You changed the size and shape of a bone, created a new bone chain, renamed each bone in the new bone chain, then edited the size and shape of each bone to correspond with the mesh.

Add and edit fins

1. Select **BoneBody**, then in the Fins group in the Fin Adjustment Tools rollout on the Bone Tools floater, click the **Front Fin check box** to select it.

   In the viewport, a fin appears on the front of the bone.

2. Set the Front Fin Size to **10.0**, the Start Taper to **5.0**, and the End Taper to **17.0**.

   The fins now better match the shape of the body.

(continued)

FIGURE 26
Adding Fins

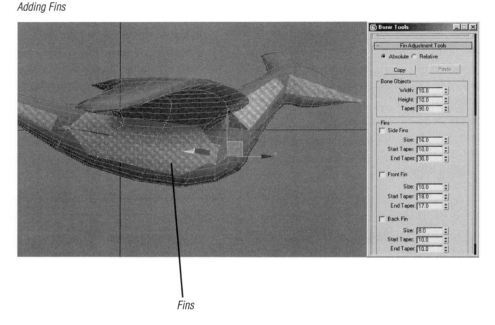

Fins

8-22 AUTODESK 3D STUDIO MAX

Bones and Inverse Kinematics

FIGURE 27
Head, neck, body, and tail bones with fins

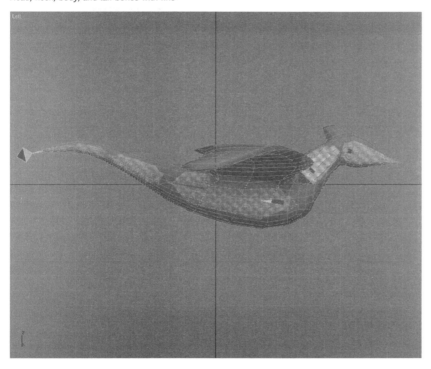

3. In the Fins group in the Fin Adjustment Tools rollout, click the **Back Fin check box** to select it, and then set its Size to **8.0**, leaving the Start and End Taper settings for the fin at 10.0.

4. Press **[Esc]** to exit the Size parameter, then press **[T]** to switch to the Top viewport.

   The top view will let you see the changes in the side fins as you go.

5. Make sure BoneBody is still selected, click the **Side Fins check box** in the Fins group to select it, then set the Size of the side fins to **16.0** and the End Taper to **30.0**, leaving the Start Taper set to 10.0.

   Your body bone should resemble Figure 26. The bone is now complete with fins that form the shape of the creature's torso.

6. Add front, back, and side fins to the remaining bones in the tail, adjusting the Size, Start Taper, and End Taper numbers so that the bones with fins are about three-quarters the size of the actual mesh of the tail, as shown in Figure 27.

7. Add front, back, and side fins to BoneHead and BoneNeck, adjusting the Size, Start Taper, and End Taper numbers, as shown in Figure 27.

You added fins to all of the bones in the head, body, and tail sections of the dragonbird. You also adjusted the size and shape of each fin to best conform the bones and fins to the shape of the character's body.

Complete a skeletal rig

1. Maximize the Front viewport, then right-click and choose **Unhide All** from the Display quadrant of the Quad menu.

   You can now see that the right wing bones have already been created and saved in the character. You will also see some other objects attached to the bones, which you'll learn about in the next lesson.

2. In the Bone Tools floater, click the **Create Bones button** to select it.

3. Click at four points to make three bones in the left wing, as shown in Figure 28, then right-click to end the bone chain.

4. Click the **Create Bones button** in the Bone Tools floater to deselect it, then press **[T]** to switch to the Top viewport.

5. Name the first (parent) bone in the wing **BoneLeftWing01**, name the second bone **BoneLeftWing02**, name the third bone **BoneLeftWing03**, and name the nub **BoneLeftWingNub**.

6. Select **BoneLeftWing01** in the wing and move it to the middle of the wing.

   All of the bones move toward the middle of the wing.

7. Select **BoneLeftWing03** and move it up a little to follow the bend of the wing.

(continued)

FIGURE 28
New wing bones

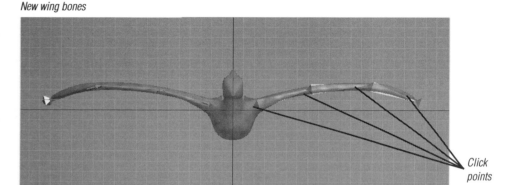

FIGURE 29
Repositioned wing bones

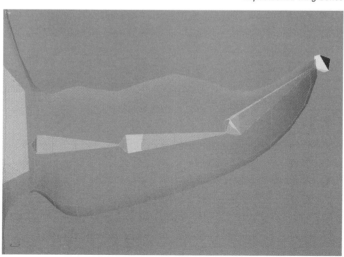

8-24 AUTODESK 3D STUDIO MAX

Bones and Inverse Kinematics

FIGURE 30
Wing bones with Height adjusted

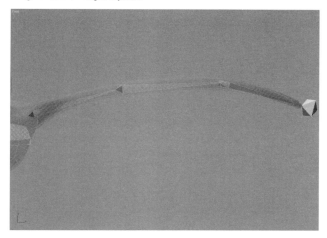

FIGURE 31
Wing bones with fins added

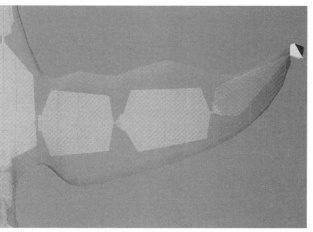

Lesson 3   Edit Bones

8. Click the **Bone Edit Mode button** in the Bone Tools floater, move **BoneLeftWingNub** to the tip of the wing, then click the **Bone Edit Mode button** again to deselect it.

   The wing should look like that shown in Figure 29.

9. Press **[F]** to go to the Front viewport, then adjust the Height of each bone so that it is a little smaller than the mesh itself, as shown in Figure 30.

   TIP Feel free to go into Bone Edit Mode if you have to tweak the placement of the pivot points a little.

10. Press **[T]** to go to the Top viewport, then add side fins to the first three bones in the wing. You don't need to add fins to the nub.

11. Change the fin Size, Start Taper, and End Taper amounts so that the bones with fins are about 75 percent the size of the mesh, as shown in Figure 31.

    TIP When you add fins to the wing bones, be sure that the size of the fins does not make the bone wider than its length; in other words, you want the longest dimension of the bone to be its length. Otherwise, you may run into issues when you skin the character in later lessons.

12. Save the file.

You made a chain of wing bones, moved them so that they follow the curvature of the mesh, then added fins to each bone to better aproximate the shape of the wing.

AUTODESK 3D STUDIO MAX 8-25

LESSON 4

APPLY INVERSE KINEMATICS

What You'll Do

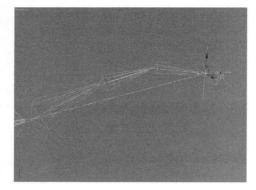

▶ In this lesson you will learn about inverse kinematics and how to use it to affect the normal behavior of a bone hierarchy. You will then utilize dummy objects to add control to the bones.

Understanding Inverse Kinematics (IK) Chains

As discussed earlier, objects in a hierarchy have parent-child relationships in which child objects inherit the transformations of the parent object. In the case of bones, if you rotate or move a parent bone, its child bone (or bones) rotates or moves with it. Rotational and position data are inherited by the child from its parent, down the hierarchy. This idea is referred to as **forward kinematics**, or **FK**.

If you want to animate a character's appendage using FK, it can be quite a tedious process. You first have to rotate the upper arm, then the lower arm, and then finally the hand in order to produce movement that looks natural. However, you have the ability to make the bone chain operate using **inverse kinematics**, or **IK**, and produce the same natural movement much more quickly. With IK, you can move only the hand bone and have the entire arm bone chain move in relation to the hand, even though it is a child bone at the end of the hierarchy. In this situation the hand is called the **end effector**. When you rotate or move the end effector, IK produces the opposite (inverse) effect from FK, and the positional or rotational data are inherited by the end effector's parents, as shown in Figure 32. This makes the process of character animation much easier.

Depending on how you want a particular character's body to move, you might apply IK to some of the bone chains and not others. Character animators come up with different ways to rig their characters, but usually they apply IK to a character's arms and legs. In the case of the dragonbird used in this chapter, you will animate the neck and head using FK, and you will animate the tail and wings using IK.

Applying IK to Bones

To apply IK to bones in 3ds Max, you use a feature called an IK solver. An **IK solver** calculates how all the bones in a chain should move when the end effector moves.

There are different kinds of IK solvers for different purposes. For limbs, a very useful one is the HI (History Independent) Solver. History independent means that, unlike some older solvers, the solver doesn't rely on calculations made in earlier frames of the animation to calculate the IK solution in later frames. This means it works faster.

Before applying IK to bones to create an **IK chain**, you need to decide where you want the IK chain to begin and end. For instance, you might have an IK chain start at the upper arm of a character, and end at the hand. You could then simply animate the position of the hand, and the whole arm would move. If you don't include the shoulder in the IK chain, it will not be affected by the hand's movement.

To apply the HI solver to a bone chain, select the bone where you want the IK chain to begin, click Animation on the menu bar, point to IK Solvers, click HI Solver on the submenu, and then click the bone where you want the IK chain to end. Alternatively, you can click the end effector bone first, click Animation on the menu bar, point to IK Solvers, click HI Solver, and then click the bone where you want the chain to begin. Either way, the bone chain's hierarchy is built in, so the end effector is always the bone at the bottom of the selected bone chain's hierarchy.

After the HI solver is applied to a start and end bone in a bone chain, a crosshair appears at the pivot point of the bone that serves as the end effector, as shown in Figure 33. The crosshair is called the **goal display**, or **goal**. It represents the end of the IK chain and is the object that you select in the viewports to animate the chain.

FIGURE 32
FK and IK chains

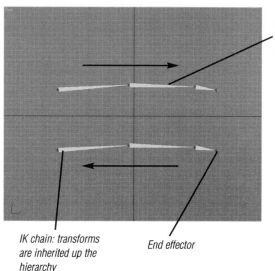

FIGURE 33
Tail bones with an IK chain

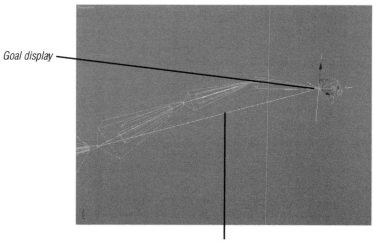

Lesson 4   Apply Inverse Kinematics

AUTODESK 3D STUDIO MAX 8-27

Using the SplineIK Solver

Another kind of IK solver, the SplineIK solver, enables you to have bones conform to the curvature of a spline in the scene. With the bones conforming to the shape of a spline, animating the positions of the vertices that make up the spline causes the bones to follow the curve. You might want to use this to animate something such as a snake, or like the example used in this chapter, the fluid motions of a wing.

To apply the SplineIK solver, select the first bone in the IK chain, click Animation on the menu bar, point to IK Solvers, click SplineIK Solver on the submenu, click the last bone in the bone chain, and then click the spline to which you want the bones to conform.

Once SplineIK has been applied to a chain of bones, you will see boxes called point helpers that appear at each vertex in the spline. **Point helpers** enable you to change the position of the vertices while keyframing to animate the curvature of the spline.

Creating and Linking Dummy Objects

With multiple bones and the different IK chains set up in a character, it might be difficult and tedious to animate each part of the bone structure. To make the process easier, dummy objects can aid you in controlling all the parts. A **dummy** is an object that does not render, but that has coordinates in space and can help you manipulate other objects. For example, if you want to make both of a dragonbird's wings flap at the same time using just one control, you can create a dummy object to help you achieve this. By linking some of the point helpers in the wings to a dummy object, as shown in Figure 35, and then simply animating the position of the dummy object to move up and down, you can make the wings flap much like the wings of a marionette.

FIGURE 34
SplineIK Solver with point helpers

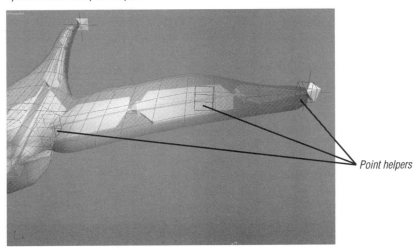

Point helpers

To create a dummy object, click the Helpers button on the Create panel, click the Dummy button in the Object Type rollout, as shown in Figure 36, and then simply click and drag in a viewport to create the dummy. You can use any spline object as a dummy. Some character riggers use rectangles or circles, or even connect different shapes to make custom dummy objects. Once you've created a dummy object, you can then use the Select and Link tool to link the object you want to control to the dummy object.

Dummy objects can help you control certain parts of a character, but they can also enable you to move a character around as a whole. To do this, you create a dummy object that serves as a control that lets you move the entire rig at once. This type of control is known as a **master control**; when you move the master control, the whole rig moves as the master control does. To create a master control, create a rectangle shape as a dummy object in the scene, and then link all the movable components to it. When you move the rectangle, you move the whole rig.

FIGURE 35
Point helpers linked to dummy object

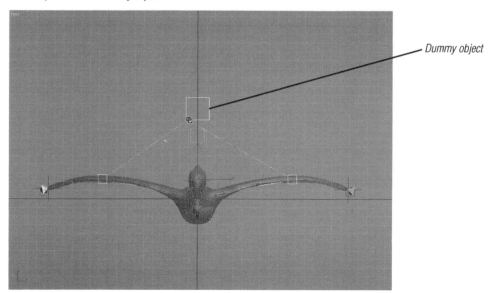

FIGURE 36
Helpers command panel

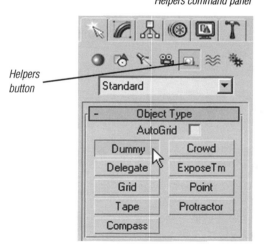

Lesson 4 Apply Inverse Kinematics

AUTODESK 3D STUDIO MAX 8-29

Rotate the wings using forward kinematics

1. Maximize and adjust the the Perspective viewport to get a view of the dragonbird similar to Figure 37.
2. Click the **Select and Rotate tool**, click the **first bone** in the left wing, then click and drag the **green y-axis handle** up and down.

    The other bones rotate with the first bone, as shown in Figure 37.
3. Right-click during rotation, or press **[Ctrl]+[Z]** after the rotation, to return the bones to their original position.
4. Select and rotate the **second bone** in the chain.

    The children of the selected bone inherit its rotation.
5. Return the bones to their original positions.

You selected the first bone in a bone chain and rotated it to see its effect on the other bones in the chain. You then rotated the second bone in the chain to see its effect.

Apply an IK solver to bones

1. Maximize and adjust the Perspective viewport so that you have a good viewing angle on all of the tail bones.
2. Select the **first bone** in the tail (BoneTail01), click **Animation** on the menu bar, point to **IK Solvers**, then click **HI Solver**.

(continued)

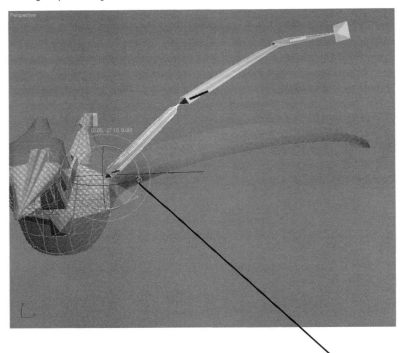

FIGURE 37
Rotating the parent wing bone

Rotate around the y-axis

FIGURE 38
An IK chain in the tail

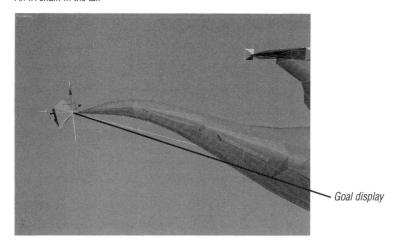

Goal display

FIGURE 39
Line object created in wing

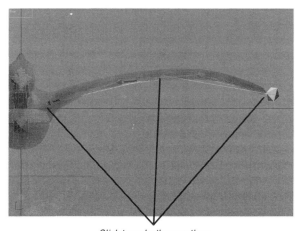

Click to make three vertices

You've selected the HI Solver to apply to this bone chain. As you move the mouse before selecting the end of the bone chain, a dashed line connects the pivot point of the selected bone to the cursor.

3. Click the **last bone** in the tail (BoneTailNub).

   A goal display appears at the pivot point of the BoneTailNub, as shown in Figure 38.

4. In the Perspective viewport, try moving the goal around on different axes.

   As you move the IK goal around, the tail bones automatically rotate to follow. When it comes time to animate later, you simply animate the position of the goal, and it drives the movements of the entire tail.

5. Return the tail bones to their original positions.

You applied the HI Solver to a bone chain to make it an IK chain, moved bones in the chain to see the effect, then moved the bones back to where they started.

Create a spline

1. Maximize the Front viewport, then zoom as necessary so you can see the entire left wing.

2. Activate the **Line tool**, and, as shown in Figure 39, create a line spline by clicking the pivot point of the first bone in the wing, clicking once in the middle of the wing, clicking again at the pivot point of the wing's nub bone, then right-clicking to exit line creation mode.

3. Press **[1]** to enter Vertex subobject level for the line, then click the vertex in the center of the spline.

(continued)

AUTODESK 3D STUDIO MAX 8-31

4. Right-click the **vertex**, then click **Smooth** on the Tools 1 quadrant of the Quad menu to change the vertex type to smooth.

   The line is now a smooth curve.

5. Press **[1]** to exit Vertex subobject level, press **[T]** to switch to the Top viewport, then move the spline down on the y-axis so that it runs down the center of the first bone, as shown in Figure 40.

6. Enter Vertex subobject level again, then move the vertex near the wing tip up so that the line follows the curve of the wing, as shown in Figure 41.

7. Exit Vertex subobject level, then save the file.

You created a spline and moved its vertices so that it conforms to the shape of the bones in the left wing.

FIGURE 40
Spline moved to center of wing

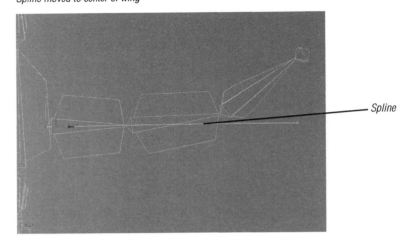

FIGURE 41
Adjusted spline

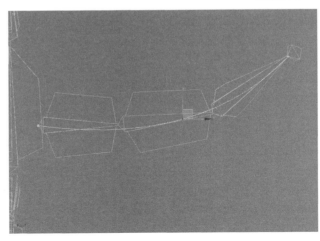

FIGURE 42
Applying the SplineIK Solver

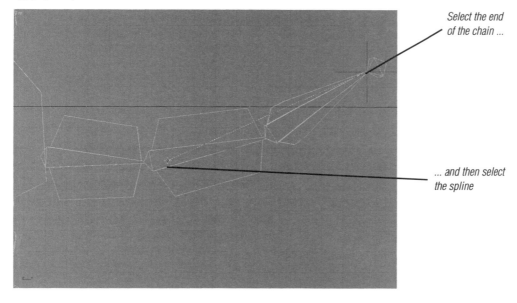

Select the end of the chain ...

... and then select the spline

Use the SplineIK Solver

1. Select the **first bone** in the chain, click **Animation** on the menu bar, point to **IK solvers**, then click **SplineIK Solver** on the submenu.

   As you move the mouse around to select the end of the bone chain, a dashed line connects the pivot point of the selected bone to your cursor.

2. Click the **nub bone**.

   A goal display appears on the nub bone, and a dashed line now connects the goal to the cursor as you move it around, as shown in Figure 42.

3. Click the **spline object** (Line01).

   The wing aligns itself with Line01, and three point helpers appear along the spline.

4. Press **[P]** to switch to the Perspective viewport, click the **Select and Move tool**, select the **point helper** in the middle of the line (Point05), then move it up and down on the z-axis.

   The shape of the spline changes as the vertex is moved, thereby manipulating the rotations of the bones.

   > TIP Remember, you can right-click during the move operation to cancel out of it.

5. If you repositioned the point helper, click the **Undo tool** on the main toolbar to place the point helper back where it was.

(continued)

AUTODESK 3D STUDIO MAX 8-33

6. Move the **point helper** at the tip of the wing (Point06) to review its effect on the bones, then undo the operation after you are done looking at it.

7. Save the file.

You applied the SplineIK solver to a bone chain, selected a spline to which it should align, then moved the point helpers in the spline to review the movement's effect on the bones.

Create and link dummy objects

1. Press **[F]** to switch to the Front viewport, click the **Create tab**, click the **Helpers button**, then click the **Dummy button** in the Object Type rollout.

2. Click and drag above the center of the creature to create a dummy box, then click and drag just under the first dummy box to create another, smaller dummy box, as shown in Figure 43.

3. Click the **Select Object tool**, select the **top dummy box** (Dummy01), click the **Modify tab**, select the text in the Name field at the top of the Modify panel, then type **ControlWingMid** to rename the dummy box.

4. Select **Dummy02**, then change its name to **ControlWingTips**.

(continued)

FIGURE 43
Dummy objects

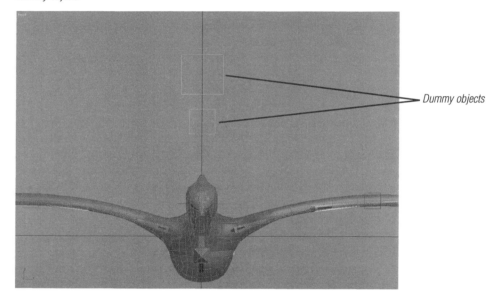

Dummy objects

8-34 AUTODESK 3D STUDIO MAX

Bones and Inverse Kinematics

FIGURE 44
Transform Type-In boxes

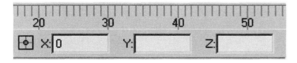

5. Select both dummy boxes at once, then type **0** in the Transform Type-In box for the x-axis, as shown in Figure 44, to center both boxes in world space.
6. Click the **point helper** in the middle of the left wing, press and hold **[Ctrl]**, then click the **point helper** in the middle of the right wing.
7. Click the **Select and Link button**, then click and drag from the selected point helper on the left to the bigger dummy box (ControlWingMid).

   The dummy box flashes to indicate that the objects (both point helpers and ControlWingMid) have been linked.
8. Select both **point helpers** at the tips of the wings, then link them to the smaller dummy box (ControlWingTips).
9. Select and move **ControlWingMid** and **ControlWingTips** up and down.

   By moving the dummy boxes, you cause both wings to flap.
10. Undo any wing position changes you made, then save the file.

You created two dummy boxes, centered them in world space, linked each to point helpers within the wings, then moved the dummies to see the effect on the wings.

Lesson 4 Apply Inverse Kinematics

Create and link a master control

1. In the Top viewport, create a rectangle that surrounds the body of the dragonbird, as shown in Figure 45, then name it **ControlMaster**.
2. Press [F] to switch to the Front viewport and move ControlMaster down so it is underneath the body, as shown in Figure 45.
3. Use the **Select and Link tool** to link BoneNeck to BoneBody.
4. Link the big dummy box (ControlWingMid) to ControlMaster, then link the little dummy box (ControlWingTips) to ControlMaster.

   All of the wing controls now have ControlMaster as their parent object.

(continued)

FIGURE 45
Rectangle dummy object

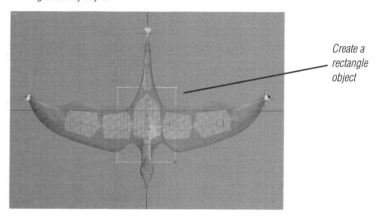

Create a rectangle object

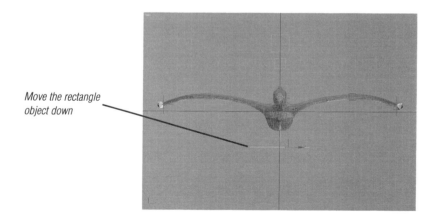

Move the rectangle object down

FIGURE 46
Point helpers linked to master control

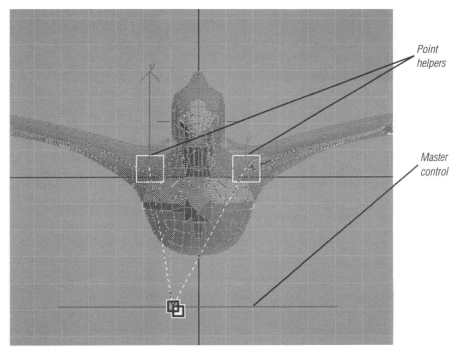

Point helpers

Master control

5. Link BoneBody, the IK goal at the tip of the tail (IK Chain02), and both point helpers at the base of each wing (Point01 and Point04, as shown in Figure 46) to ControlMaster.

6. Click the **Select and Move tool**, then move the ControlMaster up and down.

   The entire rig moves with the body.

7. Cancel or undo any movements you might have made in Step 5, then save the file.

You created a master control object, moved it to a useful positon, linked bone chains and dummy objects to it, then moved the master control to see the effect of its movement.

Lesson 4 Apply Inverse Kinematics

AUTODESK 3D STUDIO MAX 8-37

LESSON 5

USE SKIN

What You'll Do

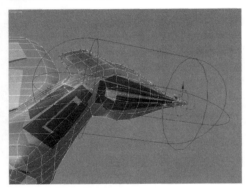

▶ *In this lesson, you will learn what skinning is and why it is important when working with bones and mesh together. You will also learn how to use features in the Skin modifier when skinning to enable bones to control the deformation of the surrounding mesh.*

Understanding Skinning

In previous lessons, you built a character rig that is surrounded by a character mesh. However, just because these two things occupy the same space doesn't mean that the rig has any effect on the mesh. You need a way to connect these two separate entities. That's were skinning comes in. **Skinning** is the process of determining how the movement of the bones within a mesh affects the mesh object itself.

FIGURE 47
Skin deformed by bone movement

— Mesh deforms as bones rotate

Skinning begins with the Skin modifier. When the Skin modifier is applied to a character with a skeletal rig, it enables you to choose the bones that drive the movement, or what 3D artists call the deformation, of the vertices in the mesh. Once the bones are associated with vertices in the mesh object, you can determine the amount of deforming influence each bone has on each vertex in the mesh.

Working with Envelopes

You begin the process of skinning by manipulating envelopes. To work with envelopes, you need to be in Edit Envelopes mode. To enter Edit Envelopes mode, select the mesh to which the Skin modifier has been applied, click the Modify tab, select the Skin modifier in the modifier stack, and then click the Edit Envelopes button on the Parameters rollout.

In Edit Envelopes mode, each bone has two capsule-shaped envelopes surrounding it. The vertices in the mesh that are surrounded by a bone's envelope are influenced by the movement of that bone. Envelopes can overlap where two bones meet at a joint. Vertices around the joint are influenced, to varying degrees, by both bones.

There are two envelopes for each bone, an **inner envelope** and an outer envelope. Vertices that lie within the inner envelope are influenced in a rigid manner, meaning that when a bone rotates, those vertices inherit 100 percent of the movement. Vertices that lie within the **outer envelope** can be influenced less rigidly. When the bone rotates, vertices within the outer envelope can inherit less than 100 percent of the motion, depending on where they lie within the outer envelope. Vertices that lie close to the inner envelope pick up more motion than vertices that lie farther away from the inner envelope. Working with envelopes enables you to simulate skin that slides around at joint areas.

The amount of influence that a bone has over a specific vertex is called the **weight** of the vertex. This is similar to the idea of soft selection, covered in Chapter 3. If a vertex has a weight of 1.0, it means that the currently selected bone has 100 percent control over that vertex. If a bone does not control a specific vertex at all, that vertex has a weight of 0.0 in relationship to that bone. You can change the vertex weighting manually, or by working in Edit Envelopes mode.

When in Edit Envelopes mode, the vertices are shaded to represent their weight in relationship to the currently selected bone (again, similar to soft selection). Red vertices have a weight of 1.0, which means that they deform with that bone 100 percent.

The shading goes from red to orange to yellow to blue, with blue being the color of vertices with the least amount of weight. Grey areas of the mesh are not affected at all by that envelope or the associated bone.

Envelopes have cross-sections with handles that let you adjust their size, as shown in Figure 48. You change the size of the envelopes to either increase, decrease, or eliminate weight from vertices that are associated with the bone.

Testing the Deformation

After applying the Skin modifier and adjusting the weight of vertices in the skin, you can test how the skin performs by keyframing some of the joints going through a motion. It is a good idea to make sure your character remains in its stationary pose at the first keyframe, and then animate the joints to rotate at a later keyframe. You can then scrub the time slider back and forth and see how effectively the skin deforms your mesh. If there are any changes that need to be made, the next step is to go back to the keyframe with the stationary pose, and then adjust the size and position of the envelopes. Inevitably this doesn't fix all the problems either, so the third step is to adjust some of the problem vertex weights manually.

Weighting Vertices Manually

Your main goal in working in Edit Envelopes mode is to deform the mesh the way you want it to deform when you rotate the bones.

FIGURE 48
Envelopes for a selected bone

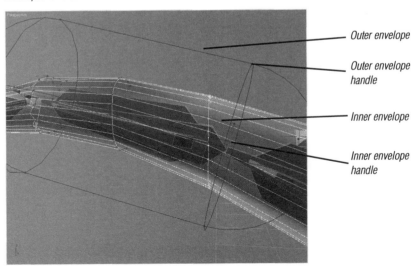

If there are still some rogue vertices after you adjust the envelope sizes, then you can select the problem vertices and set their weights manually. To manually change the weight of a vertex relative to a bone, adjust the number in the Abs. Effect (Absolute Effect) field for the vertex in the Weight Properties group in the Parameters rollout (as shown in Figure 49), while in Edit Envelopes mode for a bone. This field shows the weight of the vertices in relationship to the envelope that is currently being edited. By typing in 1.0 for selected vertices, you make those vertices move 100 percent with the bones.

Two separate bones can both have an influence on a specific vertex. However, the vertex weight for that vertex must always add up to no more than 1.0. For instance, Bone A may influence a vertex with a weight of 0.7, while Bone B influences that same vertex with a weight of 0.3. When you add up both influences it must equal 1.0 or less.

FIGURE 49
Absolute Effect parameter

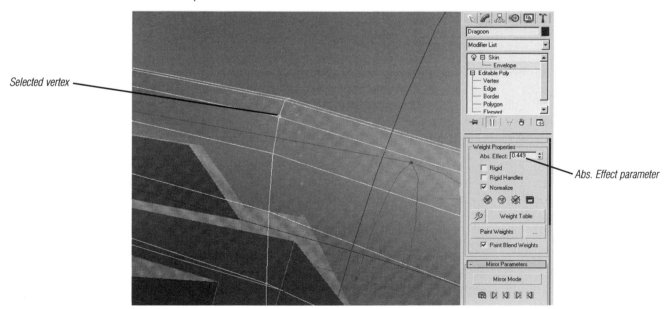

Apply the Skin modifier

1. Right-click in the Perspective viewport, click **Display** on the menu bar, then click **Unfreeze All**.
2. Select the **Dragonbird mesh**, click the **Modify tab**, click the **Modifier List list arrow**, then click the **Skin modifier**.
3. In the Parameters rollout for the Skin modifier on the Modify panel, click the **Add button**.

   The Select Bones dialog box appears.
4. Highlight all of the bone objects (only the bones) in the list, as shown in Figure 50, then click **Select**.

   The bone names now appear in the bone list, below the Add button in the Parameters rollout.
5. Select **BoneHead** from the bone list, then click the **Edit Envelopes button** at the top of the Parameters rollout.
6. Pan and zoom in the Perspective viewport to get a good look at the BoneHead envelopes, as shown in Figure 51.

   TIP Press [F4] to make the vertices in the mesh visible (if necessary).
7. Click the **Edit Envelopes button** again to turn off Edit Envelopes mode.

You applied the Skin modifier to the character mesh, selected the bones to associate with the mesh, entered Edit Envelopes mode, viewed the envelopes for a bone, then exited Edit Envelopes mode.

FIGURE 50
Select Bones dialog box

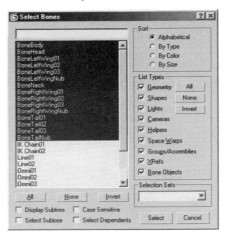

FIGURE 51
BoneHead envelopes

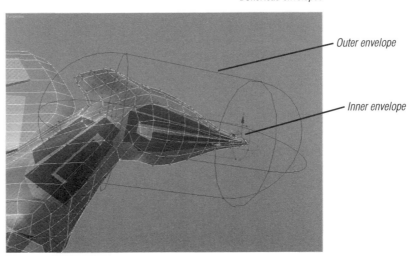

Outer envelope

Inner envelope

8-42 AUTODESK 3D STUDIO MAX

Bones and Inverse Kinematics

FIGURE 52
Head vertices deform with bone rotation

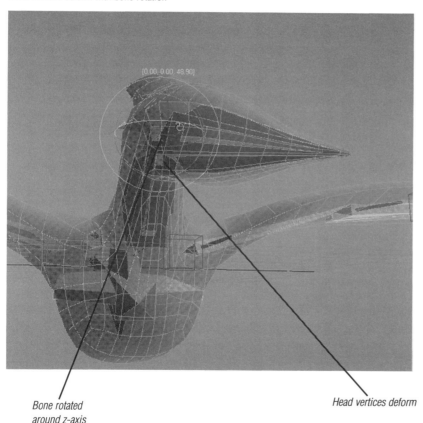

Bone rotated around z-axis

Head vertices deform

Test the skin deformation

1. In the Perspective viewport, select **BoneHead**.
2. Click the **Reference Coordinate System list arrow**, then click **Local**.

   Using the local coordinate system lets you rotate a bone on its own local axis.

3. Click the **Select and Rotate tool** ↻, then click and drag the **blue axis handle** to rotate the head on its z-axis.

   The head vertices move as the head bone moves, as shown in Figure 52.

4. Click and drag the **green y-axis handle** to rotate the bone around its y-axis.
5. Undo any rotation that you might have done.
6. Adjust the view as necessary until you can see the dummy boxes and both wings in the Perspective viewport.
7. Select the dummy box called **ControlWingMid** in the Perspective viewport, then move it up and down along its z-axis to test the deformation of the skin on the wings.

   Observe how the skin deforms the mesh.

8. Undo any position changes you have made.

You selected a bone in the mesh, rotated it twice to see how the mesh deformed, moved the dummy boxes up and down to test the mesh deformation, then undid all position changes.

Adjust skin envelopes

1. Click the **Auto Key button** to select it, then move the **time slider** to Frame 10.

2. In the Front viewport, select **ControlWingMid** and move it down a little to put the wings in a downward position, then click the **Auto Key button** to deselect it.

3. In the Perspective viewport, select the **Dragonbird mesh**, then click the **Edit Envelopes button** at the top of the Parameters rollout on the Modify panel.

4. In the Bone List on the Parameters rollout, click **BoneLeftWing01** to make the envelopes for that bone appear.

   > TIP Make sure the Reference Coordinate System is set to Local.

5. Click one of the handles on the bone's outer envelope cross-section that is closest to the body, then drag it to reduce the size of the envelope at that cross-section, as shown in Figure 53.

   As the envelope gets smaller, the number of vertices weighted by the bone is reduced, and the colors of the weighted vertices change accordingly.

6. Click the **envelope's direction handle**, located in the center of the envelope, as shown in Figure 54.

(continued)

FIGURE 53
Envelope cross-section

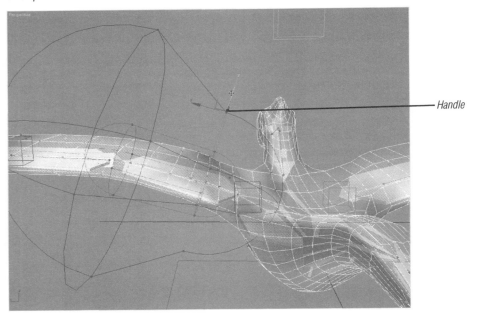

8-44 AUTODESK 3D STUDIO MAX

Bones and Inverse Kinematics

FIGURE 54
Envelope direction handle

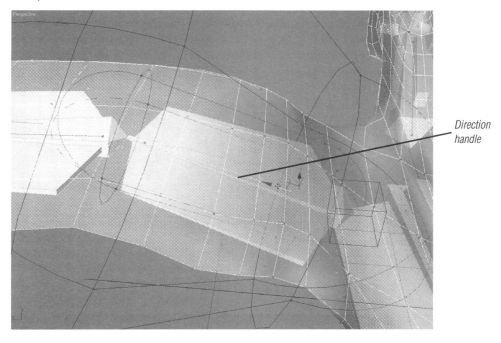

Direction handle

7. Drag the direction handle away from the body along its x-axis to shorten the envelope so that it doesn't overlap too far into the body.

   This reduces the effect that this envelope has on the vertices located where the wing joins the body.

8. Click the **Edit Envelopes button** to turn off Edit Envelopes mode, then drag the **time slider** back and forth between Frames 0 and 10 to see the effect of the changes.

9. Repeat Steps 3 through 8 for the right wing.

10. Drag the **time slider** back and forth between Frames 0 and 10 to see the effect of all the changes you made.

11. When you are done, return the **time slider** to Frame 0 and delete the keyframes at Frames 0 and 10 by selecting them on the track bar and pressing **[Delete]**.

12. Save the file.

You keyframed the left wing position, edited the outer envelope of the selected bone, moved the envelope, then viewed the effect of the changes on the vertices. You then repeated the process with the right wing.

Lesson 5 Use Skin

AUTODESK 3D STUDIO MAX 8-45

Adjust vertex weight manually

1. Turn on **Auto Key mode**, then drag the **time slider** to Frame 10.
2. Use the **Select and Rotate tool** ↻ to select **BoneHead** and rotate it so that the head is looking down, as shown in Figure 55.
3. Turn off **Auto Key mode**, drag the **time slider** back to Frame 0, switch to the Left viewport, then zoom and pan to get a close-up of the head.
4. Select the **Dragonbird mesh**, then click the **Edit Envelopes button** in the Parameters rollout on the Modify panel.
5. In the Select group in the Parameters rollout, click the **Vertices check box**.

   You now have the ability to select individual vertices in the mesh.
6. On the main toolbar, click and hold the **Rectangular Selection Region tool** ▢ until the Selection Region flyout opens, click the **Fence Selection Region tool** ▧ on the Selection Region flyout, then select the vertices that form the crown of the head, as shown in Figure 56, by clicking and dragging to draw a selection region around them.

   | TIP Arc rotate in the Perspective viewport to make sure you have selected the right vertices.
7. In the Weight Properties Group of the Skin Modifier, change the Abs. Effect setting to **1.0** for the selected vertices.

(continued)

FIGURE 55
Rotated head

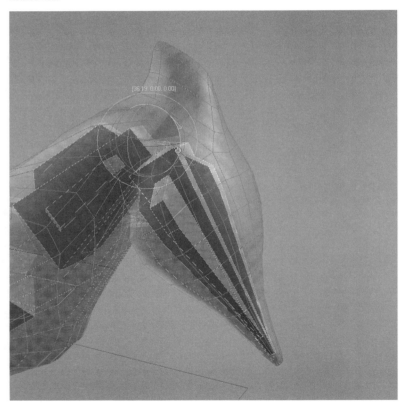

FIGURE 56
Crown of head

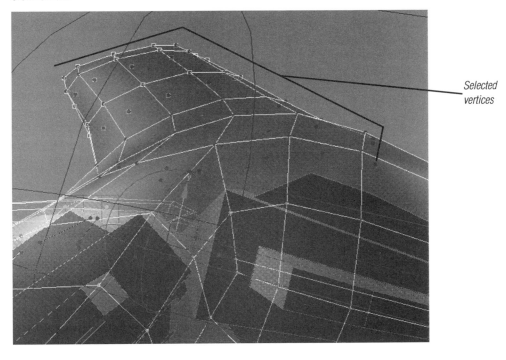

Selected vertices

8. Drag the **time slider** back and forth between Frames 0 and 10 to see the results of the change.
9. When you are done, return the **time slider** to Frame 0 and delete the keyframes at Frames 0 and 10 by selecting them on the track bar and pressing **[Delete]**.
10. Go around the mesh and tweak vertex weighting using the techniques you have just learned, until the mesh deforms the way you want. Make sure you delete any temporary keyframes you made when you are done with this process.
11. Save the scene when you are done.

You animated the rotation of the BoneHead bone and reviewed the result, selected and changed the weight of the vertices that needed adjustment, reviewed the animation again, then adjusted other vertices as necessary in the mesh.

LESSON 6

ANIMATE BONES

What You'll Do

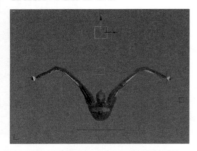

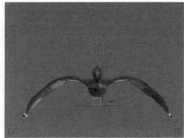

▶ *In this lesson, you will learn how to keyframe the creature created in previous lessons in order to create an animation of it. You will also learn how to loop a cycle of animation, to produce a constant wing-flapping motion.*

Animating the Dragonbird

In this lesson, you get to see all your hard work pay off. Because of the time you have taken to rig the dragonbird character with bones, inverse kinematics, and control objects, as shown in Figure 57, you now have the ability to apply some sophisticated-looking animation.

In Chapter 6, you learned about keyframes and how to apply them to objects. You also learned how to manipulate keyframes for different tracks of animation using the Track View. In this lesson, you will be revisit both of these techniques to make the dragonbird soar through the sky.

Many times animators build their animations by focusing on one track at a time. This idea of building the animated tracks in layers lets you zero in on each specific movement of a character over the duration of the animation. For instance, in this lesson, you will first animate the flapping of the dragonbird's wings as it occurs across the entire animation. Then you will animate the position and rotation of the creature through the duration of the animation.

Next, you will go back and add the motions of the tail and head.

You will also set up a camera and make the dragonbird swoop past it for a nice dramatic effect. Lastly, you will add some head and neck movements by simply animating the rotation of the neck and head bones.

Looping Animation
You can animate an action continuously by creating the motion once and looping the animation, and then copying keyframes. For example, looping enables you to animate the wing flaps three times over a 300-frame animation instead of animating each flap by hand, thus saving a great amount of time.

To loop an animation, select the object whose action you want to loop, open Track View, and then click the Curve Out-of-Range Types button to open the Param Curve Out-of-Range Types dialog box. Click the Loop graph in the dialog box, and then click OK to close the dialog box.

Secondary Motion
In the real world, objects that are flexible tend to produce secondary motion as they move. Imagine holding a photograph in your hand, and moving it back and forth. As you move the top of it one way, the bottom of the picture moves the other way. Paying attention to these subtleties of physics is one way that animators are able to create believable motion and breathe life into their creations.

The rig that you set up gives you the abilty to add some secondary motion to the wing flapping of the dragonbird. To do this, you will animate the up and down positions of the ControlWingTips dummy object separately from the ControlWingMid dummy object.

FIGURE 57
It's alive!

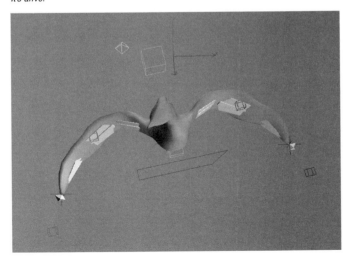

Lesson 6 *Animate Bones*

AUTODESK 3D STUDIO MAX 8-49

Animate the wings

1. Maximize the Front viewport, select the **ControlWingMid dummy box**, then click the **Toggle Set Key Mode button** to enter Set Key mode.

2. Make sure that the time slider is at Frame 0, then click the **Set Keys button**.

   A keyframe appears at Frame 0 on the track bar.

   > TIP Be careful not to confuse the Set Keys button with the Toggle Set Key mode button, which says 'Set Key' on it.

3. Drag the **time slider** to Frame 30, then click the **Set Keys button** again.

   The animation is now keyframed so that from Frames 0 to 30 the wings do not move. This is the period during which the creature is gliding, and doesn't need to flap its wings.

4. Drag **ControlWingMid** up in the viewport so it looks like Figure 58.

5. Drag the **time slider** to Frame 60, click the **Set Keys button** to create a keyframe at Frame 60, drag the **time slider** to Frame 65, then click the **Set Keys button** to create a keyframe at Frame 65.

   Between Frames 30 and 60 in the animation, the wings move to an upstroke position. From Frames 60 to 65, the wings do not move.

   (continued)

FIGURE 58
ControlWingMid moved up

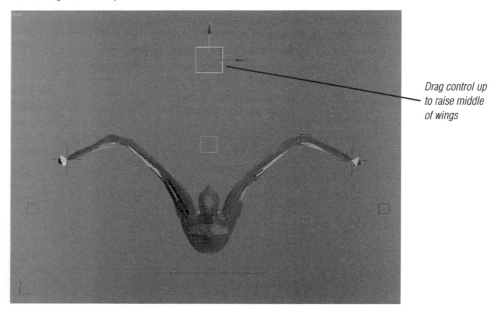

Drag control up to raise middle of wings

FIGURE 59
ControlWingMid moved down

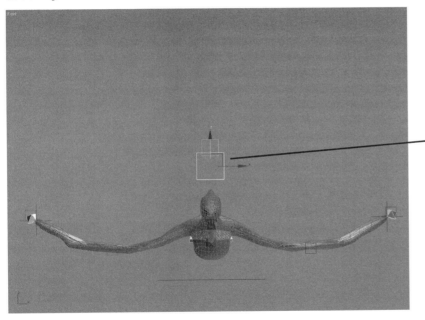

Drag control down to lower-middle of wings

6. Drag **ControlWingMid** down in the viewport so it looks like Figure 59, drag the **time slider** to Frame 80, then click the **Set Keys button** to create a keyframe at Frame 80.

   From Frames 65 to 80 in the animation, the wings move to a downstroke position.

7. Drag **ControlWingMid** up in the viewport so it is positioned a little higher than where it began at Frame 0, drag the **time slider** to Frame 95, then click the **Set Keys button** to create a keyframe at Frame 95.

   From Frames 80 to 95 in the animation, the wings go back up, but they overshoot their original resting place.

8. In the track bar, click to select the **keyframe** at Frame 0, press **[Shift]** and drag a **duplicate key** over to Frame 100.

   From Frames 95 to 100 in the animation, the wings come to a rest.

By creating keyframes for the character in various poses, you animated one cycle of the wing flap. You also copied a keyframe to ensure that the cycle loops seamlessly, without a skip in motion.

Add secondary motion to the wings

1. Select the **ControlWingTips dummy box**, click the **Toggle Set Key Mode button** (if necessary) to turn on Set Key mode, then click the **Set Keys button** to create a keyframe at Frame 0.

2. Drag the **time slider** to Frame 50, click the **Set Keys button** again to create a key at Frame 50, then drag the **time slider** to Frame 70.

3. Move the **ControlWingTips dummy box** so that it sits just above ControlWingMid and the wings straighten out, as shown in Figure 60, then click the **Set Keys button** to create a key at Frame 70.

   Making the wings straighten out 10 frames after the initial upstroke creates a flapping motion.

4. Drag the **time slider** to Frame 85, move the **ControlWingTips dummy box** so that it is positioned just underneath the creature's body, as shown in Figure 61, then click the **Set Keys button** to create a key at Frame 85.

   This now creates some secondary motion for the downstroke.

5. Click the **Toggle Set Key Mode button** to turn off Set Key mode.

(continued)

FIGURE 60
ControlWingTips above ControlWingMid

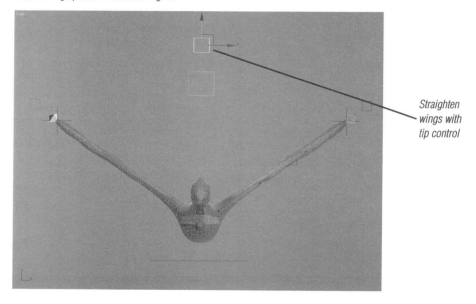

Straighten wings with tip control

FIGURE 61
ControlWingTips under the body

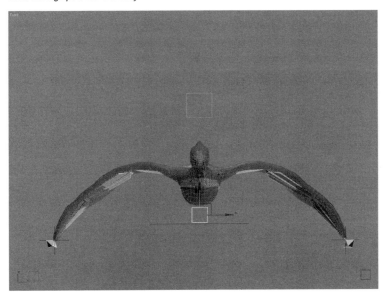

6. Select the keyframe at Frame 0, press [**Shift**], then drag the key to Frame 100 to make a copy of it at Frame 100.

   This seamlessly loops the animation for the wing tips.

   You offset the keyframed poses of the middle of the wing and the tips of the wing to give a nice secondary motion to the entire wing-flapping cycle.

Create a loop cycle

1. Click the **Time Configuration button** on the status bar near the bottom of the screen, to open the Time Configuration dialog box.

2. In the Animation group, change the Length setting to **300**, then click **OK** to close the dialog box.

   The animation now contains 300 frames.

3. Select the **ControlWingMid dummy box**, then click the **Curve Editor (Open) tool** on the main toolbar to open Track View.

   In the Objects list on the left side of the Track View, the ControlWingMid object should be highlighted.

4. Click the **Parameter Curve Out-of-Range Types button** on the Track View toolbar to open the Param Curve Out-of-Range Types dialog box, as shown in Figure 62, click the **Loop graph** in the dialog box to select it, then click the **OK button**.

   This cycles the first 100 frames over the duration of the animation.

   (continued)

AUTODESK 3D STUDIO MAX 8-53

5. In the viewport, select the **ControlWingTips dummy box**.

   This object is now highlighted in Track View.

6. Click the **Parameter Curve Out-of-Range Types button**, click the **Loop graph**, then click **OK** to apply a loop cycle to the ControlWingTips dummy box as well.

7. Close the Track View window.

8. Click the **Play Animation button** to view the animation.

You lengthened the animation, then looped the animation cycle for both of the wing controls to continue through the duration of the animation.

Animate position and rotation

1. Click the **Create tab**, click the **Cameras button**, then click the **Target button** in the Object Type rollout.

2. In the Top viewport, click and drag from in front of the creature's right wing to the center of its body.

   This creates a targeted camera that is looking at the dragonbird.

3. In the Front viewport, select the line that connects the camera to its target and move them both up so that the target is positioned inside the creature, as shown in Figure 63.

4. Select the **camera**, right-click it, then click **Select Camera Target** on the Tools 1 quadrant of the Quad Menu.

(continued)

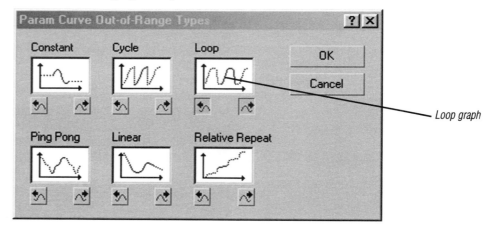

FIGURE 62
Param Curve Out-of-Range Types dialog box

Loop graph

FIGURE 63
Camera and target moved up

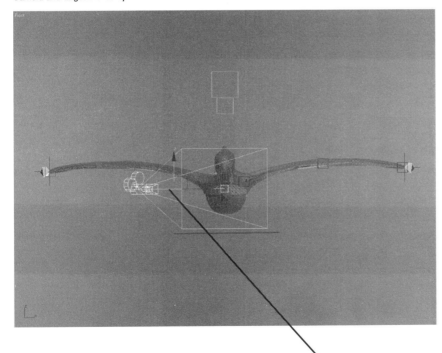

Drag the line that connects camera to its target

> **TIP** This is a good way to select a target if it is hidden by other objects in the scene.

5. Link the target to the ControlMaster rectangle.

   ControlMaster becomes the target's parent object. The camera now points at the creature, no matter where you choose to animate their positions.

6. Make sure the time slider is at Frame 0, turn on **Auto Key mode**, then select the **ControlMaster rectangle**.

7. Zoom out in the Top viewport, then move the ControlMaster back along the viewport's y-axis to move the creature away from the camera.

8. Drag the **time slider** to Frame 300, select the **ControlMaster rectangle** in the Top viewport and move it down on the y-axis past the camera, about as far from the camera as it was at Frame 0, but in the other direction.

9. Drag the **time slider** to Frame 120, then right-click the **time slider** to open the Create Key dialog box.

10. Click to deselect the **Scale check box**, then click **OK**.

    A keyframe for the ControlMaster is placed at Frame 120.

    (continued)

AUTODESK 3D STUDIO MAX 8-55

11. Drag the **time slider** back to Frame 0, make sure **Auto Key mode** is still on, then in the Front viewport rotate the creature a little to give it a dramatic angle, like that shown in Figure 64.

12. Drag the **time slider** to Frame 160, then in the Front viewport, rotate the creature to angle it the other way.

13. Drag the **time slider** to Frame 220, then in the Front Viewport, rotate the creature to level it out.

14. Click the **Auto Key button** to turn off Auto Key mode, maximize any viewport, press **[C]** to switch to a Camera viewport, then play the animation.

You animated the position and rotation of the dragonbird in 3D space, created a camera to track with it, and produced a swooping effect in the animation as the creature flies by the camera.

Complete the animation

1. In the Camera viewport, drag the **time slider** to Frame 80.

2. Click the **Select by Name tool** on the main toolbar (or press **[H]**), select **BoneHead** from the object list in the Select by Name dialog box, then click the **Select button**.

3. Click the **Reference Coordinates System list arrow**, then click **Local** on the list.

4. Right-click the **time slider** to open the Create Key dialog box, click to deselect the **Position** and **Scale check boxes**, then click **OK** to create a keyframe for rotation at Frame 80.

(continued)

8-56 AUTODESK 3D STUDIO MAX

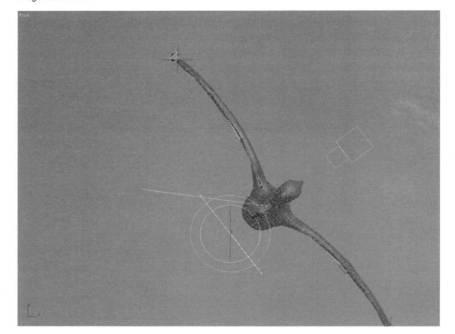

FIGURE 64
Dragonbird rotated

Bones and Inverse Kinematics

FIGURE 65
Dragonbird looking to its right

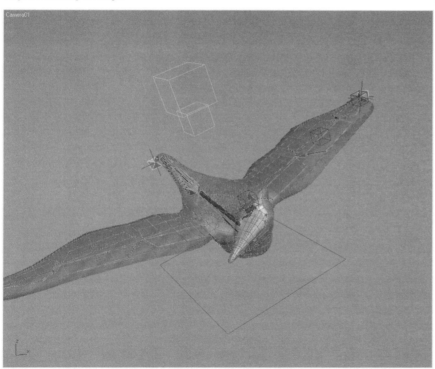

5. Drag the **time slider** to Frame 110, then turn on **Auto Key mode**.
6. Rotate the dragonbird's head around its y-axis to make the creature look to its right, as shown in Figure 65, then rotate the head around its z-axis to make it look down.
7. Drag the **time slider** to Frame 130, then rotate the head to look in another direction.
8. Turn off **Auto Key mode**, then play the animation.
9. Save the file.

   TIP   When you have a chance, try animating the dragonbird flying in other directions around the scene. The sky is the limit, so enjoy!

You animated the creature's head to rotate around its own axes.

CHAPTER SUMMARY

In this chapter, you learned what bones are and how they are used within a character. You created a chain of bones, named the bones, and manipulated bones by manipulating their pivot points. You learned how to make a character mesh see-through and how to freeze the mesh to more easily work with bones. You explored the Bone Tools floater and used it to build a bone structure. You learned how to adjust the size and taper of bones in a character rig, add fins to the bones, and adjust the size and taper settings of the fins. You gained an understanding of inverse kinematics and how it affects the normal behavior of a bone hierarchy. You found out how to use dummy objects to control bones when animating them, and how to use skinning to have bones and character mesh move together. Finally, you created an animation of the bones within a character and looped the animation to produce a continuous motion of the bones.

What you have learned

- How to create bones
- How to move and rotate bones
- How to freeze a character mesh and make it see-through
- How to name bones
- How to reposition bones
- How to change a bone's size and shape
- How to add fins to a bone and edit fins
- How to apply inverse kinematics (IK) to a bone chain
- How to create and link dummy objects
- How to deform mesh with bones
- How to adjust skin envelopes
- How to animate bones with dummy objects

Key Terms

Bones   System of objects that are linked together with a built-in hierarchy. Bone chains work together to create realistic movement in a character.

Character rig   Chains of bones linked together to form a structure used to bring life to a character model.

Dummy   An object that does not render, but that has coordinates in space and can help you manipulate other objects.

End effector   In inverse kinematics, child bone at the end of a hierarchy whose data is inherited by its parents.

Envelope   Capsule-shaped indicator surrounding a bone; vertices in a mesh that are within a bone's envelope will be influenced by the movement of that bone.

Fins   Extra protrusions along the side of a bone that aid in simulating the volume of a character.

Inverse Kinematics (IK)   System of movement in which positional or rotational data of objects in a hierarchy are inherited by the parents from the child object at the end of the hierarchy.

Skinning   Associating bones with certain parts of a character mesh so that the mesh deforms as the bones move.

chapter 9
PARTICLE SYSTEMS

1. Work with particle systems.
2. Use space warps.
3. Create materials for particles.
4. Work with Particle Flow.
5. Use material operators.

chapter 9 PARTICLE SYSTEMS

A **particle system** in 3ds Max is an object that generates clusters of many subobjects called **particles**. Particle systems can have a variety of uses. You can use them to simulate things such as rain, snow, or smoke. However, you can also use particles to create effects such as explosions, pouring water, or schools of fish. You can pretty much use them anytime you want to generate a large number of similar objects.

One of the most important parameters of a particle system is the type of particle used in the system. There are three different particle types that you can have in a particle system. **Standard particles** let you choose from the predefined shapes that appear in the Standard Particles group, such as tetra, sphere, and cube. **Meta particles** generate a type of particle called metaballs. Metaballs blend into blobs when they collide with each other. They are useful for creating flowing water, lava, and other viscous liquid effects, but take much more time to calculate and render than standard particles. **Instanced geometry** are particles that are duplicates of another object or objects in the scene. This is effective for many different applications, especially when you need to make a crowd of something such as swarms of bugs or a school of fish.

In this chapter, you will see the versatility of particle systems firsthand, by using them to make diverse imagery such as a waterfall, missiles with a smoke trail, a fiery explosion, and sparks.

Tools You'll Use

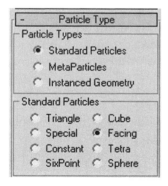
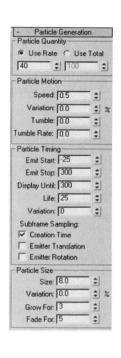
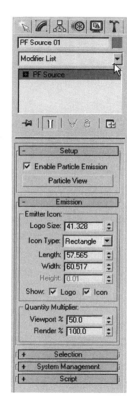
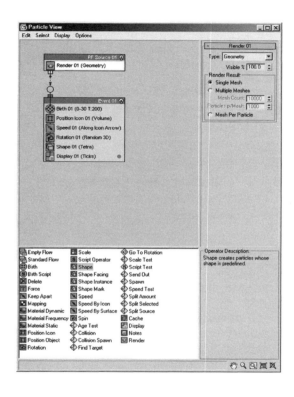

LESSON 1

WORK WITH
PARTICLE SYSTEMS

What You'll Do

▶ *In this lesson, you will learn what a particle system is, how to create a non-event-driven particle system, and how to adjust the parameters of different particle systems.*

What Is a Particle System?

A particle system in 3ds Max is an object that creates particles. The main components of a particle system are the emitter, the particle system parameters, and the particles themselves. The **emitter**, which does not render, is the object that specifies the location from which the particles originate. You set up the particle system parameters to make the particles in the system appear and behave the way you want. Typically, particles emanate from the emitter and move based on the parameters you have set up.

Particles are born and then they die, as shown in Figure 1. During the time the particles exist they can look and behave in a variety of ways depending on how the parameters of the particle system are set up. There are parameters related to timing that control things such as the number of particles that appear in every frame or when particles appear and disappear. There are also parameters that are specific to the type of particles you are using that dictate things such as size and travel speed.

In 3ds Max, particle systems fall into two main categories, non-event-driven particle systems and event-driven particle systems. A **non-event-driven particle system** is a system that operates continuously and is not dependent on a particular event taking place, such as two particles colliding with each other. With non-event-driven particle systems, generally you create an emitter object from which the particles emanate, or you can designate an object in the scene as an emitter. You then change some parameters that affect the amount, appearance, and behavior of the particles. You can also enable outside forces such as wind or gravity to have an effect on the particles.

An **event-driven particle system** enables you to define events that affect particles in many different ways. 3ds Max's event-driven particle system, called Particle Flow, offers you great versatility and control over the particles. It is particularly useful when you must have particles that change their appearance or behavior over time. For example, you might use Particle Flow to design a particle system that simulates a rocket afterburn that eventually turns into a smoke trail. Particle Flow will be covered later in this chapter, so for now you'll look at some of the basics of non-event-driven particle systems.

Creating a Non-Event-Driven Particle System

The six non-event-driven particle systems you can create with 3ds Max are Snow, Blizzard, Spray, Super Spray, PArray, and PCloud, as shown in Figure 2. A **Snow** particle system generates particles from a planar-shaped emitter and has basic parameters to use for creating particle effects such as snow and sand. A **Spray** particle system is good for simulating basic spraying-water effects and uses a planar emitter. A **Blizzard** particle system also uses a planar emitter and is good for snowlike effects, but has many more advanced options than the Snow system. **Super Spray** uses a point-based emitter, meaning that the particles emanate from a single point in space. Like Blizzard, it features many advanced parameters but is geared more toward water-type effects. **PArray** features a parameter set similar to Blizzard and Super Spray but has the added capability of using a designated distribution object as its emitter. This gives you the ability to have particles emanate from an object in the scene or to have particles take the shape of an object. PArray is also useful for creating explosion effects. **PCloud** lets you

FIGURE 1
Spray particle system

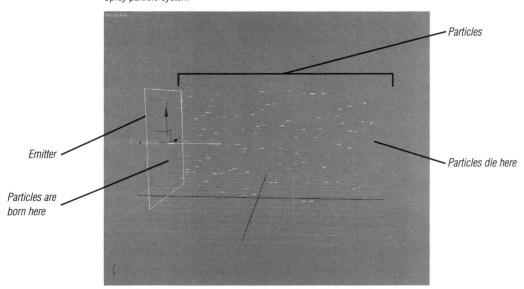

create particles that fill a specific volume. For example, you could model a fish and use PCloud to create a school of that fish that stay together in a certain pattern.

You typically begin working with particles by making a particle emitter in one of the viewports. To create a particle system by creating an emitter, click the Create tab, click the Geometry button, click the list arrow under the Geometry button, and then click Particle Systems to display the Particle Systems command panel, as shown in Figure 3. In the Object Type rollout, click the button for the particle system type you want to create, and then click and drag in one of the viewports to create a rectangular emitter.

QUICKTIP

The PF Source button in the Particle Systems Object Type rollout is used when working with Particle Flow, and will be introduced in Lesson 4.

When you play an animation, 3ds Max sprays out particles from the particle system's emitter object. The Snow, Spray, and Super

FIGURE 2
Six non-event-driven particle systems

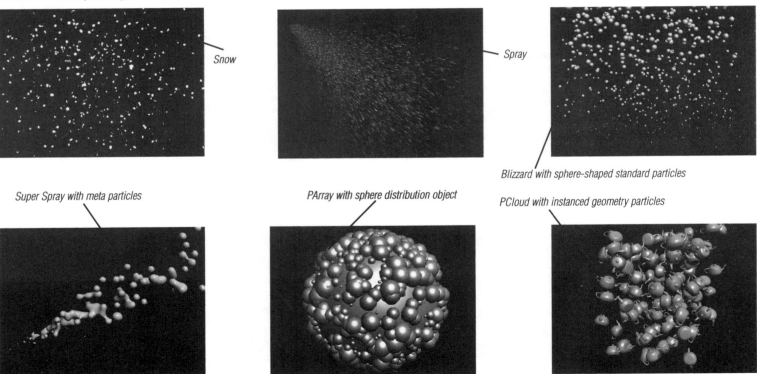

Snow

Spray

Blizzard with sphere-shaped standard particles

Super Spray with meta particles

PArray with sphere distribution object

PCloud with instanced geometry particles

9-6 AUTODESK 3D STUDIO MAX

Particle Systems

Spray particle systems have a line that extends from the center of the emitter plane and represents the direction that the emitter is pointing and the direction that the particles will initially travel.

Particle systems can get very computationally complex and thus heavily tax your system's resources. Like with most concepts in 3D animation, you always need to strike a balance between streamlining a scene's complexity and achieving the effect you want. When you create a particle system, 3ds Max gives you the ability to display a different amount of particles in the viewport than will actually be rendered. Particle systems can be set up to display an enormous amount of particles, which could lead to the slowing down or, worse, the crashing of your computer. Typically, you should set the viewport particle count to be lower than the render count if you find that your computer is having a hard time displaying a large number of particles.

Adjust Spray and Snow Parameters

Once you create a particle emitter, you can manipulate the way the particles behave by adjusting parameters in the rollouts on the Modify panel. With non-event-driven particle systems, this is your primary way of controlling how the particles look and act. Each particle system has a set of default parameters when you create it; to change the parameters, adjust the numbers in the appropriate box on the Modify panel. Once these parameters have been set up, when you play the animation, the emitter shoots out particles based on your settings.

Although they are designed for different purposes and produce differing results, the Spray and Snow particle systems have similar settings. They both have limited parameters and are good for simple particle effects. In addition, both systems have a Parameters rollout containing Particles, Render, Timing, and Emitter groups.

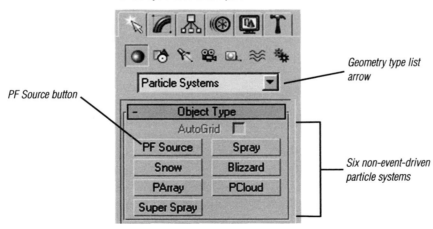

FIGURE 3
Particle Systems command panel

The Parameters rollout for the Spray system is shown in Figure 4. In the Particles group on the Parameters rollout, you can adjust many important settings. To set the the maximum number of particles that can appear in the viewport at any given frame, adjust the number in the Viewport Count box. Once this number of particles has been reached, the system waits for a particle to die before spawning a new one. Similarly, to set the maximum number of particles rendered in any given frame, change the Render Count number. The Drop Size number defines the size of the particle in whatever units of measurement you are currently using. To set the speed at which particles leave the emitter, change the number in the Speed box. The Variation number applies a variation to both the speed and direction that the particles are moving. For instance, a Variation of 5 means particles set to a speed of 20 will have speeds between 15 and 25. Adjust the Variation when you want to give the system a random appearance. To choose how you want the Spray system's particles to appear in the viewport, click the Dots, Drops, or Ticks option button at the bottom of the group. Drops are short lines that resemble drops of rain, dots are dots, and ticks look like plus signs. The shape chosen for particles in viewports does not affect how the particles look when they are rendered.

In the Render group, click the option button for Tetrahedron to render the particles as elongated tetrahedron shapes that are useful for simulating water droplets. Click the Facing option button to render the particles as square faces that always face the viewer. Facing is a very useful feature when you want to apply a material map to each and every face.

FIGURE 4
Spray Parameters rollout

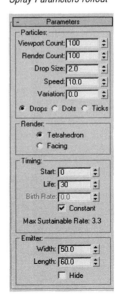

The parameters in the Timing group enable you to control the rates at which particles are born and die. The Start number is the number of the frame at which particles in the system are born. The Life setting is the number of frames that the particle exists. The Birth Rate number determines the number of new particles that are born in every frame. When the Constant check box is checked, the Birth Rate equals the Maximum Sustainable Rate shown at the bottom of the Timing group, and the Birth Rate parameter is unavailable.

The Render Count parameter can have an impact on how these settings function. For instance, at the bottom of the group you see the Max Sustainable Rate. This value is calculated by dividing the Render count by the Life parameter (Max Sustainable Rate = Render Count/Life). If the Birth Rate exceeds the Max Sustainable Rate, the particles are produced in bursts because the system has to wait for some particles to die before producing new particles.

Last but not least, the Emitter group contains the Width and Height dimensions for the emitter, and a Hide check box that hides the emitter in the viewport when checked.

Adjust Super Spray, Blizzard, PArray, and PCloud Parameters

Super Spray, Blizzard, PArray, and PCloud particle systems have more complex capabilities, with a corresponding increase in parameter complexity. The parameters for a single Blizzard system are shown in Figure 5. In fact, these expanded particle systems have a dizzying array of parameters that vary so widely among the four, that providing full detail is beyond the scope of this book. The key to not getting overwhelmed by it all, though, is to understand that these systems' parameters are

FIGURE 5
Parameters for a Blizzard particle system

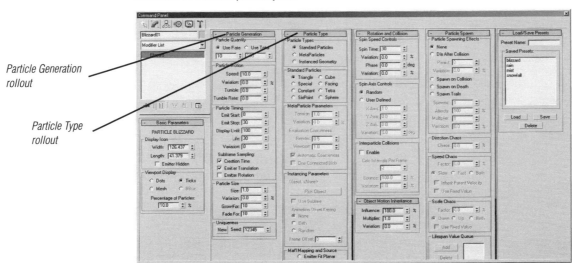

Particle Generation rollout

Particle Type rollout

organized into similar groups within rollouts, and you will almost always find settings related to a certain task grouped together the same way across particle systems, even if the exact settings vary within each group. After you get a handle on remembering which parameters are grouped where, it's not so overwhelming.

For instance, all four systems have a Basic Parameters rollout. In this rollout, you can adjust the initial formation of particles at the emitter and how they are displayed in the viewports. In addition, all four systems have a Particle Generation rollout containing four groups: Particle Quantity, Particle Motion, Particle Timing, and Particle Size and Uniqueness. In the Particle Quantity group you can adjust the creation of particles as a per-frame rate or as a total over their life spans. In the Particle Motion group, there are settings that let you adjust the speed and variation of the particles. Use the Particle Timing group settings to determine the life span and at which frame the particles start and stop, as well the last frame in which they will be displayed. The Particle Size group lets you adjust the size and variation of the particle size, and gives you the ability to set the number of frames by which the particles' size will grow from its birth, and fade to its death. The Uniqueness group lets you apply a random number seed to change the pattern of the particles (see 3ds Max's User Reference for more information on seed value).

Click one of the option buttons in the Particle Types group in the Particle Type rollout to set the particle type used in the system to one of the three mentioned earlier: standard particles, meta particles, or instanced geometry. Parameters for the particle type are available below the Particle Types group.

There are several other rollouts that contain advanced parameters too numerous to mention here, but you should explore them when you feel more comfortable with the basics of creating and editing particle systems.

FIGURE 6
Spray particle system

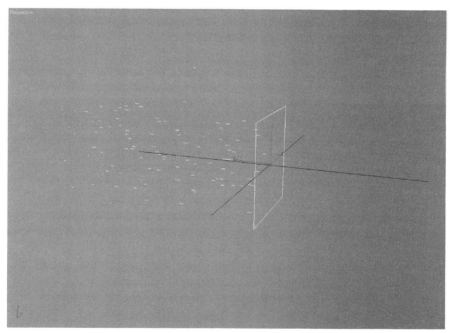

Create a non-event-driven particle system

1. Click the **Create tab** (if necessary), click the **Geometry button** (if necessary), click the **list arrow** underneath the Geometry button, then click **Particle Systems**.
2. Click the **Spray button** in the Object Type rollout to enable it.
3. In the Front viewport, click and drag to make a small rectangular emitter.
4. Click the **Perspective viewport** to activate it, zoom, arc rotate, and pan the viewport to the right a bit, then press the **Play Animation button**.

   Drop-shaped particles spray from the emitter, as shown in Figure 6.
5. Click the **Pause Animation button** to stop the animation.

You created a Spray particle system, then played the animation to see it work.

Adjust Spray parameters

1. Drag the **time slider** to frame **50**.
2. Select the **Spray particle system** (if necessary), click the **Modify tab**, then in the Particles group in the Parameters rollout on the Modify panel, set the Viewport Count number to **500**.

   Many more particles appear in the viewport. The viewport now displays up to 500 particles

   (continued)

AUTODESK 3D STUDIO MAX 9-11

Lesson 1   Work with Particle Systems

for the entire system. However, the Render Count is still set to the default of 100. When you render the animation, the system displays only up to 100 particles.

3. Change the number in the Speed box to **20**.

    Each particle travels 20 units per frame.

4. Change the number in the Variation box to **5**.

    This varies the speeds of the particles by 5 units; each travels at a speed between 15 and 25 units per frame.

5. Press the **Play Animation button**, then stop the animation when you are finished viewing it.

6. Drag the **time slider** to frame **50**, change the Render Count setting to **5000**, then change the Drop Size to **5**.

7. Pan down the Parameters rollout until you see the Emitter group, then change the Width and Length parameters each to **5**, as shown in Figure 7.

8. Click in the **Perspective viewport** (if necessary), then zoom out and pan as necessary so that you can see all of the particles in the viewport, as shown in Figure 8.

    By increasing the Render Count and Drop Size and decreasing the size of the emitter, the particles are packed in tightly as they spray from the emitter. It now looks a little more like a spray of water.

(continued)

FIGURE 7
Emitter group in Parameters rollout

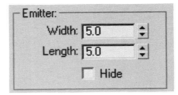

FIGURE 8
Particles in the Perspective viewport

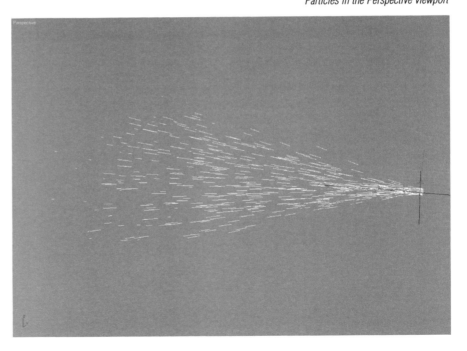

FIGURE 9
Super Spray emitter

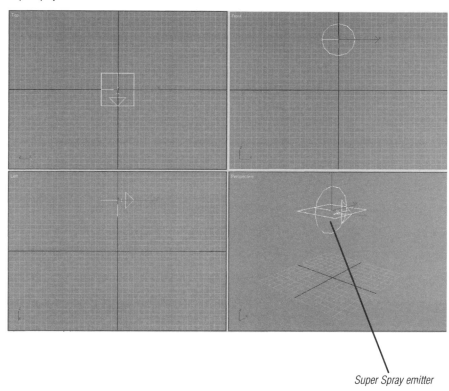

Super Spray emitter

9. Press **[F9]** to render the scene at frame 50.
10. Close the rendered scene window.

You changed the viewport count, speed, and variation parameters for the particles in the Spray system, then viewed the effect on the system when animated. You changed the Render Count and Drop Size of the particles, changed the size of the emitter, viewed the effect on the system when animated, then rendered a frame in the scene.

Create a Super Spray and adjust basic parameters

1. Reset 3ds Max without saving your changes.
2. On the Create panel, click the **list arrow** under the Geometry button, then click **Particle Systems**.
3. Click the **Super Spray button** in the Object Type rollout, click and drag in the Front viewport to create an emitter like that shown in Figure 9, right-click in the Perspective viewport and maximize it, then zoom out until you can see the entire emitter object.
4. Drag the **time slider** to frame 15.

   As you drag, the particles shoot out in a straight line from the emitter.
5. Select the **Super Spray emitter** (if necessary), click the **Modify tab**, then in the Particle Formation group on the Basic Parameters rollout, change the Off Axis setting to **5**.

   This makes the particles deviate from the center of the emitter by 5 degrees.

   (continued)

6. Change the Spread setting underneath Off Plane in the Particles group to **180**.

   The particles now shoot out in a cone-shaped formation.

7. In the Viewport Display group on the Basic Parameters rollout, set the Percentage of Particles to **50**.

   Fifty percent of the particles that are rendered are displayed in the viewport.

8. Play the animation.

   Notice that, as shown in Figure 10, the particles are emitted, but they stop being created after frame 30.

9. Stop the animation.

You reset the viewport, created a Super Spray particle system, changed the particle formation parameters and the system's viewport display parameters, then played the animation.

Adjust particle generation parameters

1. Under the Basic Parameters rollout on the Modify panel, open the **Particle Generation rollout**.

2. In the Particle Quantity group at the top of the rollout, change the number in the box under Use Rate to **50**.

   This generates 50 particles per frame.

   (continued)

FIGURE 10
Particle creation ends

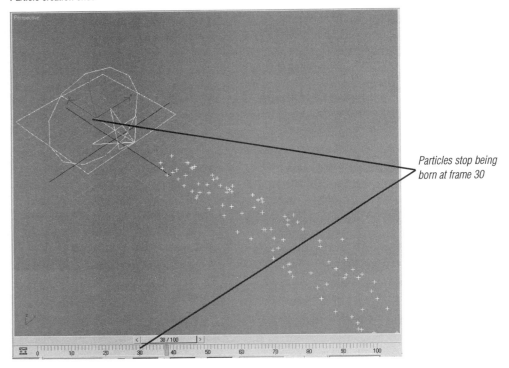

Particles stop being born at frame 30

9-14 AUTODESK 3D STUDIO MAX

Particle Systems

FIGURE 11
Particle Generation rollout

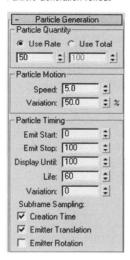

FIGURE 12
Higher concentration of particles

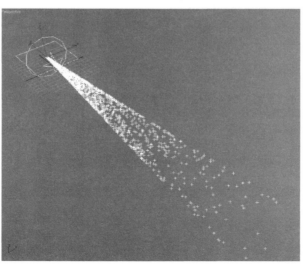

3. In the Particle Motion group on the rollout, change the Speed setting to **5**, then change the Variation setting to **50**.

   The particles are now set to move 5 units per frame, with the speed of particles varying 50 percent from the speed setting, or 2.5 to 7.5 units per frame.

4. In the Particle Timing group on the Particle Generation rollout, set Emit Stop to **100**, then change the Life setting to **60**, as shown in Figure 11.

   Particles will continue to be created up until the last frame in the animation (frame 100), and each particle will exist for 60 frames after its birth.

5. Set the Variation in the Particle Timing group to **30**.

   The life span of each particle now varies 30 frames from the Life setting of 60, or, in other words, it varies between 30 and 90.

6. In the Particle Size group on the Particle Generation rollout, set the Particle Size to **2**, then play the animation.

   The particles are now more concentrated, and they live for a longer period of time, as shown in Figure 12.

7. Save the file as **Particle1**, then reset 3ds Max.

You adjusted the particle quantity, particle motion, particle timing, and particle size parameters for the particles in the Super Spray system, then played the animation to view the system.

Lesson 1 Work with Particle Systems

AUTODESK 3D STUDIO MAX 9-15

LESSON 2

USE SPACE WARPS

What You'll Do

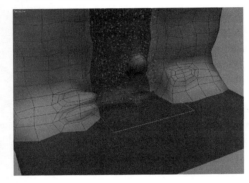

In this lesson, you will learn what space warps are, what they do, and how to bind objects in a scene to a space warp. You will also learn how to create and modify space warps.

Understanding Space Warps

A **space warp** is an object that creates a force field effect that operates on other objects. For example, you can use space warps to create ripples or waves in water, to create wind, gravity, explosions, and much more. For instance, if you wanted to make a ripple in water effect, you first create a plane object that represents the water, and then create a Ripple space warp and bind it to the plane, as shown in Figure 13. Some space warps are designed to work on geometric objects such as primitives and meshes, and some are specifically designed for particles.

To use a space warp, you begin by placing a space warp object in the scene. You then **bind** objects that you want to affect to the space warp object. Only the objects that are bound to the space warp are affected by it. When you bind an object to a space warp, you see the binding listed in that object's modifier stack, as shown in Figure 14.

After you've bound an object to the space warp, you can adjust the space warp's parameters on the Modify panel to achieve several different results. You can also bind multiple objects to a single space warp, and you can also use multiple space warps on a single object. For example, you could have one Wave space warp affect two different flags, or you could assign both the Wind and the Gravity space warps to a particle system.

Creating and Modifying Space Warps

To create a space warp, click the Space Warps button on the Create panel, click the list arrow under the Space Warps button, click the name of the space warp category you want to use, and then click the button for the specific space warp you want in the Object Type rollout, as shown in Figure 15. Click and drag in the viewport to create the space warp icon. You can then bind an object to the space warp by clicking the Bind to Space Warp button, and then clicking and dragging from the object to the space warp icon.

Space warps fall into six categories. **Forces** are used to influence the movement of particle systems. For example, the Gravity force subjects particles to a pulling effect. The Strength setting for the Gravity space warp gives you control over how much gravity is applied. An arrow points out of the Gravity space warp icon that represents the direction that gravity is pulling. If you want, you can point it in any direction, and that is the way in which the particles will be pulled.

Deflectors are also used on particle systems. They give you the ability to create a force field that particles bounce off. There are a variety of deflectors that offer different results.

FIGURE 13
Plane bound to a Ripple space warp

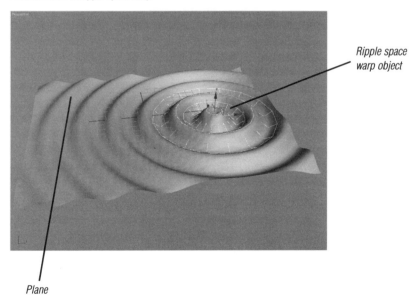

Ripple space warp object

Plane

FIGURE 14
Modifier stack for object bound to space warp

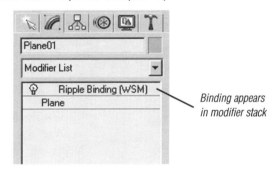

Binding appears in modifier stack

FIGURE 15
Space warp category list

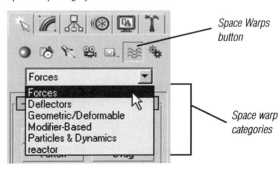

Space Warps button

Space warp categories

Lesson 2   Use Space Warps

AUTODESK 3D STUDIO MAX 9-17

For example, as shown in Figure 16, the Deflector space warp is a planar surface that you can use to block the path of particles. The SDeflector space warp does the same thing, but it deflects in a spherical pattern. There is also a UDeflector space warp that lets you designate an object in the scene as the deflector. Use this one with caution though; the more complex the object, the more 3ds Max has to calculate, possibly resulting in poor system performance and longer render times than if you used several planar deflectors to achieve the same result.

The **Geometric/Deformable** space warp category contains space warps that work mostly on geometric objects, with the exception of Displace, which also works on particles. For instance, Wave applies a linear wave pattern to your objects, and Ripple produces concentric wavelike circle patterns. The Bomb space warp lets you blow apart the faces in an object at a certain frame to help simulate explosions.

QUICKTIP

You can also use the PArray particle system to simulate explosions. It gives you many more options for producing more convincing explosions.

Modifier-based space warps perform the same functions as the modifiers of the same name. However, like all space warps, they work on the world space level instead of the object level. This means that 3ds Max calculates the modification by applying it to the space that the object occupies instead of to the object directly.

The remaining two categories, **Particles & Dynamics** and **reactor**, are for use in dynamics-based simulations.

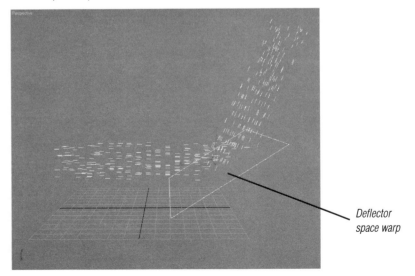

FIGURE 16
Deflector space warp

Deflector space warp

FIGURE 17
Blizzard emitter

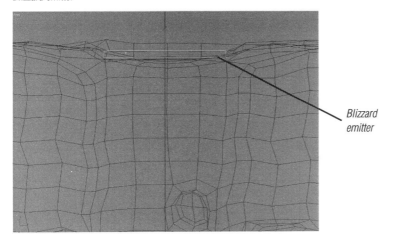

Blizzard emitter

FIGURE 18
Moved emitter

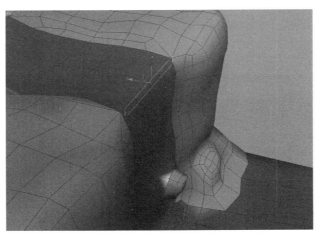

Creating a Blizzard particle system

1. Open **MAX09-01.max**, then save the file as **Waterfall**.
2. In the Front viewport, pan up and zoom in to the top of the waterfall.
3. Click the **list arrow** under the Geometry button on the Create panel, click **Particle Systems**, then click the **Blizzard button** in the Object Type rollout.
4. Click and drag at the top of the waterfall to create a rectangular emitter, as shown in Figure 17.
5. Switch to the Perspective viewport, then rotate the view to get an angle from above and to the side, similar to that shown in Figure 18.
6. With the **Select and Move tool**, move the emitter so that it sits just at the edge of the waterfall, as shown in Figure 18.
7. Click the **Select and Rotate Tool**, then right-click it to open the **Rotate Transform Type-In window**.

(continued)

8. Select the number in the X Axis box under Absolute:World, change the value to **-90**, press **[Enter]**, then close the **Rotate Transform Type-In window**.

   The emitter rotates 180 degrees to face away from the cliff. A line extends from the emitter showing the direction the particles are being emitted.

9. Zoom out a little in the Perspective viewport, then play the animation.

   Some particles shoot straight out of the emitter, and then stop being generated at frame 30, as shown in Figure 19.

10. Stop the animation, then save the file.

You created a Blizzard particle system, moved and rotated its emitter, then viewed the animated particle system.

Adjust the Blizzard parameters

1. Make sure the **Blizzard particle system** is currently selected.

2. Click the **Modify tab**, then in the Basic Parameters rollout, set the Display Icon Width to **76** and the Length to **2**.

3. In the Viewport Display group on the Basic Parameters rollout, change the Percentage of Particles number to **50**.

4. Open the **Particle Generation rollout** on the Modify panel, make sure **Use Rate** in the Particle Quantity group is selected, then set the rate to **40**.

(continued)

FIGURE 19
Animated Blizzard particle system

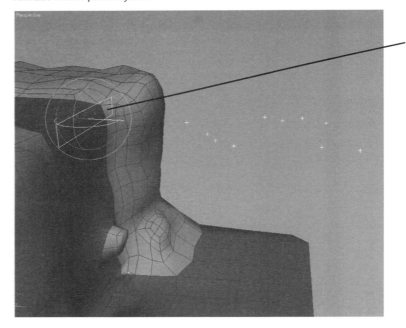

Particles stop after frame 30

FIGURE 20
Particle Size group in Particle Generation rollout

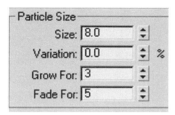

FIGURE 21
Blizzard with adjusted parameters

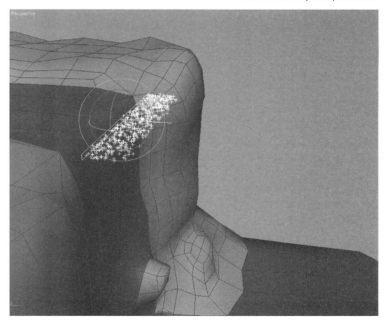

5. In the Particle Motion group, change the Speed to **0.5**.

6. In the Particle Timing group, set the Emit Start to **-25**, then set both Emit Stop and Display Until to **300**.

   The particle system will start before the animation begins and continue to be displayed until the end of the animation at frame 300.

7. Set the Life to **25** and the Variation to **5**.

8. Pan down the rollout, then in the Particle Size group, as shown in Figure 20, change the Size to **8**, set Grow For to **3**, and set Fade For to **5**.

   The particles are set to grow for the first three frames and fade out over the last five frames of their lives.

9. Play the animation.

   It doesn't look much like a waterfall yet, as shown in Figure 21. The particles are still being emitted straight out of the emitter.

10. Stop the animation, then save the file.

You changed the size of the emitter's icon, changed the viewport display, particle generation, particle motion, particle timing, and particle size parameters, then played the animation to view the effect of the changes on the particle system.

Lesson 2   Use Space Warps

Create and modify a Gravity space warp

1. Click the **Create tab**, click the **Space Warps button**, then make sure that **Forces** is chosen in the list box beneath the Space Warps button.
2. Click the **Gravity button** in the Object Type rollout to select it, then in the Top viewport, click and drag in front of the particles to create a Gravity space warp object, as shown in Figure 22.
3. Select the **Blizzard particle system**, then click the **Bind to Space Warp button** on the main toolbar.
4. Roll the mouse pointer over the particle system until you see the Bind to Space Warp icon, click and drag a line from the Blizzard to the Gravity space warp object until you see the Bind to Space Warp icon over the space warp, as shown in Figure 23, then release the mouse button.

   The objects flash to let you know that the binding was successful. The particles are now pulled by the space warp down along the cliff under the waterfall.

5. Switch to the **Perspective viewport**, then zoom out so you can see the entire particle system, then arc rotate (if necessary) to make the space warp object visible.

   The current strength of the Gravity space warp is pulling the particles down too far.

(continued)

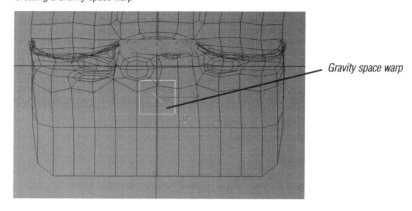

FIGURE 22
Creating a Gravity space warp

Gravity space warp

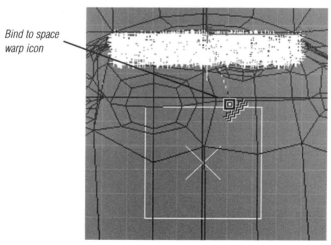

FIGURE 23
Binding an object to a space warp

Bind to space warp icon

FIGURE 24
Gravity space warp in effect

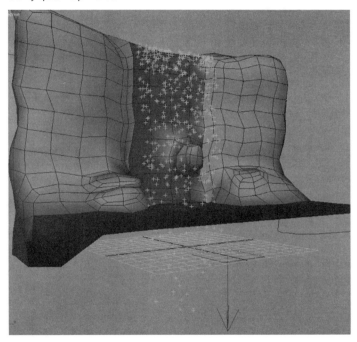

6. Click to select the **Gravity space warp** in the Perspective viewport.
7. Click the **Modify tab**, then in the Force group on the Parameters rollout of the Modify panel, set the Strength to **0.3**.

   The gravity effect is now weaker and the particles don't extend downward as far as they did.
8. Play the animation.

   As shown in Figure 24, the particles continue to extend below the water. Later you will use those extra particles below the water to bubble up at the bottom of the waterfall.
9. Stop the animation, then save the file.

You created a Gravity space warp, bound the particle system to the space warp, adjusted the parameters of the space warp, then viewed the animation.

Create and modify a spherical deflector

1. Switch to the **Front viewport**, then adjust the view until you have a good view of the rock that juts from the cliff.
2. Click the **Create tab**, click the **list arrow** under the Space Warps button, click **Deflectors** in the drop-down list, then click the **SDeflector button** in the Object Type rollout.

(continued)

3. Click and drag from the center of the rock to create a deflector that surrounds it, as shown in Figure 25.

4. Switch to the **Perspective viewport**, zoom to get a good view of the rock again, then move the **deflector** back along the y-axis so it surrounds the rock, as shown in Figure 26.

5. Select the **Blizzard particle system**, click the **Bind to Space Warp button**, click and drag from the particle system to the SDeflector, then release the mouse button to bind them together.

   The particles now appear to bounce off the deflector, but they bounce way too much.

6. Select the **SDeflector**, click the **Modify tab**, then in the Basic Parameters rollout on the Modify panel, change the Bounce setting to **0.1** and the Friction setting to **50**.

   With the Bounce setting reduced, the speed at which the particles bounce off the deflector is reduced. Likewise, lowering the Friction setting to 50 slowed the particles to 50 percent of their speed as they slid along the surface of the Deflector.

7. Play the animation.

   The Particles now slide off the rock smoothly.

8. Stop the animation, then save the file.

You created a spherical deflector, bound the particle system to it, adjusted the bounce and friction settings of the deflector, then played the animation to see the effects on the system.

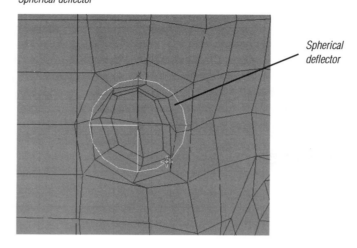

FIGURE 25
Spherical deflector

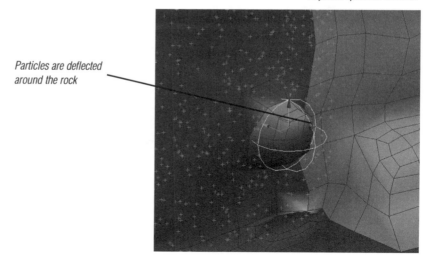

FIGURE 26
Adjusted spherical deflector

9-24 AUTODESK 3D STUDIO MAX

FIGURE 27
Planar deflector

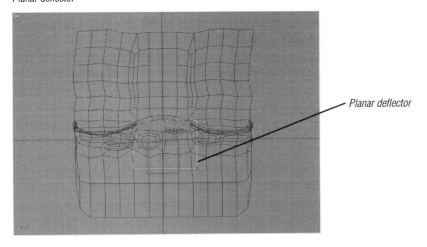

Planar deflector

FIGURE 28
Rotated deflector

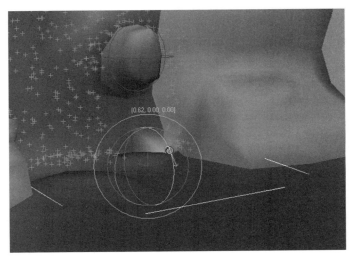

Create and modify a planar deflector

1. Click the **Space Warps button** on the Create panel, click **Deflectors** in the drop-down list, then click the **Deflector button** in the Object Type rollout.
2. In the Top viewport, click and drag to create a deflector that surrounds the base of the falls, as shown in Figure 27.
3. Switch to the **Perspective viewport**, then move the **deflector** up so that it rests at the base of the falls.
4. Use the **Bind to Space Warp button** to bind the particles to the new deflector.
5. Select, then right-click the **deflector**, click **Rotate** on the Transform quadrant of the Quad menu, then rotate the **deflector** around its x-axis a bit, so that it tilts away from the falls a little, as shown in Figure 28.
6. Click the **Modify tab**, then change the Bounce setting in the Parameters rollout to **0.1**.
7. Play the animation.

   The particles seem to hit the water at the bottom of the falls and bubble up.
8. Stop the animation, save the file, then reset 3ds Max.

You created a planar deflector at the base of the waterfall, bound the particle system to it, rotated the deflector a bit and changed its Bounce setting, then viewed the animated system.

AUTODESK 3D STUDIO MAX 9-25

Lesson 2 Use Space Warps

LESSON 3

CREATE MATERIALS
FOR PARTICLES

What You'll Do

In this lesson, you will learn how to build and apply materials to a particle system and how to modify the particle type to optimize the particles' appearance with a material applied.

Building a Material to Apply to Particles

Just like with every other object in 3ds Max, materials have a dramatic effect on how a particle system looks at render time. The process of applying materials to non-event-driven particle systems is no different than for any other object. You can simply drag a material from the Material Editor to any particle or emitter in the scene. The material then appears on each and every particle in the system. What's really nice is that like regular geometry, you can also apply mapped materials to particles, and the maps too can appear on each and every particle. As you learned in Chapter 5, 3ds Max offers many options for creating mapped materials, and you can achieve a wide variety of material effects for particles. For instance, you can create a material that uses a Noise map in the Diffuse color channel. When applied to a particle system, each particle has the color of the Noise map. You can also use maps in the Opacity channel of a material, as shown in Figure 29, to create interesting transparency effects such as smoke and bubbles, or many other creative effects.

Applying a Material to Particles

Until now in this chapter, you have concerned yourself only with how particles are generated and behave in the viewport. The particles in the waterfall particle system created in the previous lessons act like falling water, but if you were to render the scene right now, you would see that the particles look more like falling shards of plastic. This is because the particles' type shape is set to Triangles; in addition, there is no material currently applied to the particles, so each particle looks like a little triangle with the default shading on it.

You can apply a material to any standard particle shape and it will appear on the particles just fine, but the **Facing** shape offers an added dimension to applying materials to particles. The Facing shape makes each particle like a little plane that can be mapped with a material, as shown in Figure 30. Each particle automatically always faces the rendered viewport. This creates the illusion of three-dimensional particles from any point of view, even though they are really just flat planes with a material applied to them, facing toward the viewer.

To change the standard particle shape, select the particle system, click the Modify tab, and then click the option button for the particle shape you want in the Standard Particles group in the Particle Type rollout on the Modify panel, as shown in Figure 31.

When you are using Facing particles, you have to perform an extra step to apply materials onto every face in the particle system. To accomplish this, select the material in the Material Editor, and then click to select the Face Map check box in the Blinn Basic Shader Parameters rollout. You can then use the Material Editor to combine maps to create a material that, when applied to the particle system (and thus to every face in it), creates the look you want.

FIGURE 29
Particles with Opacity mapped

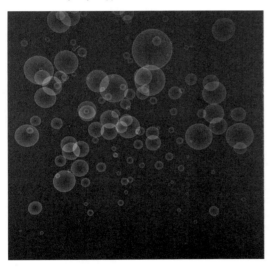

FIGURE 30
Facing particle shape

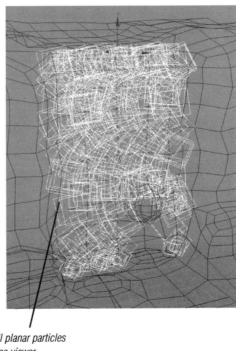

All planar particles face viewer

FIGURE 31
Standard Particles group

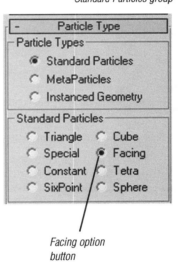

Facing option button

Change the particle type

1. In Waterfall.max, select the **particle system**.
2. Click the **Modify tab**, then select **Blizzard** at the bottom of the modifier stack, as shown in Figure 32.
3. Open the **Particle Type rollout** on the Modify panel, then click the **Facing option button** in the Standard Particles group.
4. Arc rotate the **Perspective viewport** to get a noticeable angle on the waterfall.
5. Click the **Quick Render (Production) tool** on the main toolbar to render the Perspective viewport.

    The particle faces render, but they appear as a solid color, as shown in Figure 33. To look like water, a material needs to be applied.

6. Minimize the rendered scene window, then save the file.

You selected the particle system, selected the Blizzard object in the modifier stack, changed the particle shape, then rendered the scene to view the effect of the shape change.

FIGURE 32
Blizzard modifier stack

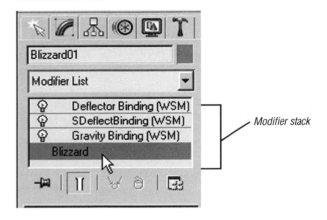

FIGURE 33
Rendered particle system

FIGURE 34
Material Editor

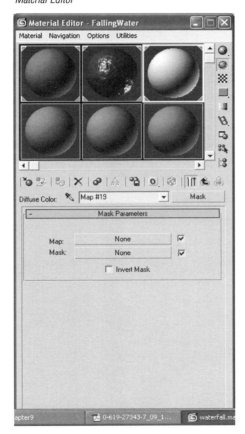

Build and apply a material to particles

1. Open the **Material Editor**, select the slot in the upper-right corner called **03-Default**, highlight the name in the material Name field, then change the material name to **FallingWater**.

2. Click to select the **Face Map check box** in the Shader Basic Parameters rollout, click the **Diffuse color swatch** in the Blinn Basic Parameters rollout, change the color in the Color Selector to a medium grey blue color, then close the **Color Selector**.

3. Click the **Diffuse map button** M, then double-click **Mask** in the Material/Map Browser.

   The Mask map is assigned to the material's diffuse color component, and the map parameters open in the Material Editor, as shown in Figure 34.

4. Click the **Mask map button** in the Mask Parameters rollout, then double-click **Gradient Ramp** in the Material/Map Browser.

   This creates a new Gradient Ramp map and uses it as a mask. A Gradient Ramp map shades from one color to another, and you can designate multiple colors to appear in the gradient.

   (continued)

AUTODESK 3D STUDIO MAX 9-29

Lesson 3   Create Materials for Particles

5. In the Gradient Ramp Parameters rollout in the Material Editor, click the **Gradient Type list arrow**, then click **Radial** to change the mask to a radial gradient.

6. Click the **Go to Parent button** twice to show the material's parameters in the Material Editor, open the **Maps rollout**, click the **Opacity map button**, then double-click **Gradient Ramp** in the Material/Map browser.

7. Set the Gradient Type to **Radial**, double-click the **first gradient color marker**, change the color to **white**, double-click the **far-right gradient color marker**, then change it to black.

   The gradient should now ramp from white on the left to black on the right, as shown in Figure 35.

8. In a viewport, select the **particle system**, click the **Assign Material to Selection button** in the Material Editor, then render the scene.

   With the material applied to the particle system, now the waterfall looks a lot more like water when rendered.

9. Minimize the **rendered scene window**, right-click the **particle system** to open the **Quad Menu**, then click **Properties** on the Transform submenu on the Quad Menu.

(continued)

FIGURE 35
Modified gradient colors

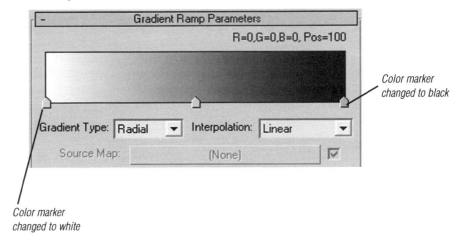

Color marker changed to black

Color marker changed to white

9-30 AUTODESK 3D STUDIO MAX *Particle Systems*

FIGURE 36
Rendered waterfall

10. In the Motion Blur group at the bottom of the Properties dialog box, click the **Image option button**, set the Multiplier to **2**, then click **OK** to close the dialog box.

    With Motion Blur applied, the particle faces now blur as they are moving, the way real water would look to the human eye.

11. Render the scene to view the changes to the waterfall, as shown in Figure 36.

12. Close the rendered scene window, save the file, then reset 3ds Max.

You created and named a new material, clicked its Face Map check box, applied a map to its Diffuse component, applied a map to the Diffuse map, applied a map to its Opacity component, added Motion Blur to the particle system's properties, and viewed the rendered particle system.

LESSON 4

WORK WITH PARTICLE FLOW

What You'll Do

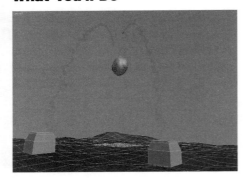

▶ *In this lesson, you will explore 3ds Max's event-driven particle system, Particle Flow. You will learn the components of Particle Flow and how to build flows in Particle View. You will also learn how to add operators and tests to a particle flow to control the behavior of particles through an animation.*

What Is Particle Flow?

With **Particle Flow**, 3ds Max's event-driven particle system, you can design sophisticated particle effects that wouldn't be possible with a non-event-driven particle system. For example, you can have particles collide with something and then spawn, becoming new kinds of particles at the moment of impact.

Particle Flow lets you design custom events that affect the way particles behave. **Events** in Particle Flow are a grouping of parameters or actions that you can perform on the particle system. You can **wire**, or connect, these events together using an interface similar to a flowchart called **Particle View**. This offers you great flexibility in managing how particles act over time.

To better understand Particle Flow, think of the life of a particle. Throughout its life, several things can happen to it. Number one, it is born—that is the first event. It then begins to age, and the age of a particle is a definable event in and of itself. Perhaps the particle travels a certain distance or reaches a certain speed. These are also events. Then, maybe it comes into contact with something; this is yet another event. Particle Flow gives you the ability to test the whether an event has happened or not. If the event has happened, you can then tell the particle to do something else, such as perform some other event. Figure 37 shows a particle system in which the event of a particle reaching an age of 30 frames causes it to change shape.

Creating a Particle Flow System

To create a Particle Flow system, you begin by creating a Particle Flow source (PF source) in the viewport. A PF source object looks somewhat like a regular particle emitter, but it contains a logo in the middle that distinguishes it from other types of emitters, as shown at the bottom of the particle system in Figure 37.

After creating a PF source, you can adjust its shape, size, and other settings in the Emission rollout on the Modify panel, as shown in Figure 38. To change the size of the logo in the center of the PF source object, adjust the Logo Size number in the Emission rollout. To change the geometry of the PF source object (to, say, a sphere or a box), click the Icon Type list arrow, and then click the shape desired on the list. Adjust the size of the PF source object by changing the Width (if active), Length/Diameter, or Height (if active) settings. Click to deselect the Show Logo or Show Icon check boxes to hide or show the logo or object icon in the viewports. In the Quantity Multiplier group, you can adjust the number of particles that are in the Particle Flow system in the viewport or rendered scene by entering a percentage in the Viewport % or Render % boxes. The number of particles changes proportionally throughout the flow, including at each event. If you have 10 particles in a system that, because of an event, spawn and become 20 particles, entering 200 in the Viewport % box adjusts the system so that the viewport contains 20 particles that spawn and become 40.

FIGURE 37
Scene designed with Particle Flow

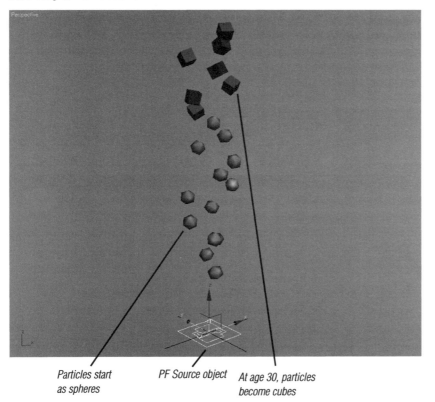

Particles start as spheres
PF Source object
At age 30, particles become cubes

FIGURE 38
Modify panel

Particle View button

Emission rollout

Lesson 4   Work with Particle Flow

AUTODESK 3D STUDIO MAX 9-33

Understand and Use Particle View

Setting the initial values in the Emission rollout is an important step, but the real power to Particle Flow is in Particle View. Particle View enables you to construct and edit your particle system. To open Particle View, click the Particle View button in the Setup rollout on the Modify Panel, or press [6].

Particle View is divided into four areas, as shown in Figure 39. The **event display** is where you build and connect events together to program the behavior of the particles in the Particle Flow; the visual representation of the Particle Flow is called the **particle diagram**. The **parameters panel** lets you change the parameters for the individual operators that make up an event. The **depot** contains all of the **actions** (operators and tests) that are available for building events. The **Description area** describes the function of the action currently selected in the depot.

In Particle View, you drag and drop various actions from the depot into events in the event display. There are three kinds of actions: Initial Flows, Operators, and Tests. An **initial flow** is just that: you can drag one of these out into the event display to get started with building a particle flow. There are two initial flow types: empty flow and standard flow. A **standard flow** starts you out with some basic events. It consists of one global event plus one local event. A **global event** is always the first event in a flow. It is called a global event because the operators that get performed in this event affect every other event in the system. By default, the

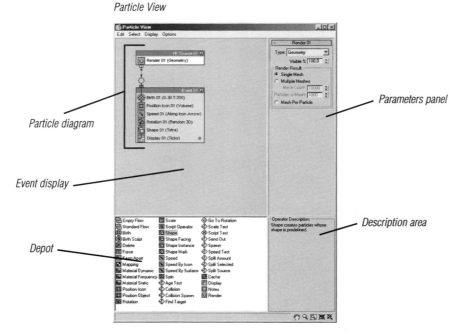

FIGURE 39
Particle View

9-34 AUTODESK 3D STUDIO MAX

global event in a standard flow contains one operator that defines the rendering parameters for the flow. If you want to, you can put other operators in the global event, and they would be valid for the entire flow. However, you usually don't do this, because the power of Particle Flow lies in the ability to place operators in the local events.

A **local event**, on the other hand, contains operators that perform only within that event. The local event in a standard flow, Event 01, contains six default operators: Birth, Position Icon, Speed, Rotation, Shape, and Display. Each of these operators plays a specific role in the look or behavior of the particles. When you create a PF source in the viewport, by default it is a standard flow, and when you open its Particle View you see a basic standard flow in the event display, as shown in Figure 40.

An **empty flow** is also what it's name suggests. It is a flow that contains only the global event and no local events. It simply offers you the option of building your flow from scratch. An empty flow can be inserted into an empty events display to start the creation of a Particle Flow system from scratch. You can then add events and operators to it as you need them. To insert a standard flow or empty flow action into the event display, click the desired action in the depot, drag it to the event display, then release the mouse button.

Add and Define Operators and Tests

You build events by changing and adding operators and tests to them. Each **operator** is responsible for performing a different action in an event, such as changing the speed or rotation of particles, or defining the shape or display qualities of particles.

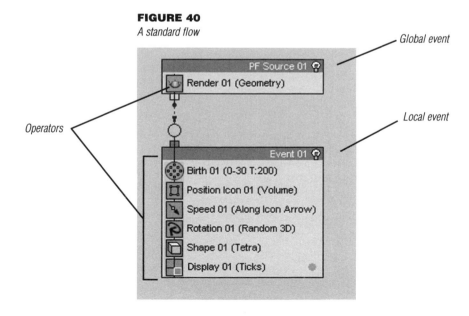

FIGURE 40
A standard flow

Lesson 4   Work with Particle Flow

AUTODESK 3D STUDIO MAX 9-35

After an event is created, you can then add tests to it. **Tests** enable you to test some condition and then, based on the results of the test, perform different actions on a particle and then pass the particle from event to event. For example, you could add a collision test to the end of an event to determine if a particle hits a deflector at some point during the event. If the particle does come in contact with the deflector, the test value equals true. You could have a test parameter set up that says if the test equals "true," then send the particle to a new event that in turn contains a new set of operators that will manipulate the particle. If the test does not equal "true," the particle remains in the event and continues to be subjected to the operators in that event.

There are two ways to add an operator or test to an event. You can drag one out of the depot and drop it anywhere in the event. If you drop it between two operators, you see a blue line, and it inserts the new operator between the existing operators. If you drop it on top of an operator, you see a red line, and the new operator replaces the existing operator. You can also right-click an event, point to Insert or Append on the right-click menu, and then click the desired action on a submenu to insert the action at the click point or append the action to the bottom of the event. Figure 41 shows the Collision test selected to be appended to the end of Event 01 in a standard flow.

To define the parameters for an operator or test, select the operator by clicking it to highlight it, and then adjust its parameters in the parameters panel on the right side of Particle View.

Wiring Events Together

To add an event to an empty flow, or to create a new event in a standard flow, drag an operator or test out of the depot and drop it in the events display. The action becomes a new event in the events display. To actually incorporate the event into the flow, however, you need to wire it to another event. Particle Flow uses **wires** to display the connection

FIGURE 41
Appending a Collision test

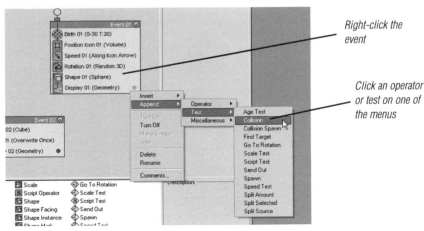

Right-click the event

Click an operator or test on one of the menus

9-36 AUTODESK 3D STUDIO MAX   *Particle Systems*

from one event to another. There are two kinds of wires. The wire that connects a global event to a birth event is a dashed blue line. The particle flow begins with the render operator in the global event; from there the render information travels to the birth operator, which in turn spawns particles. The particle data travels through the birth event and is manipulated by the operators.

For a particle to leave the birth event, or any local event, and enter another event, the particle must meet the conditions of a test, and the events must be wired together. These connections are indicated with a solid blue line. To wire a test to an event, click the test output that protrudes from the left edge of the test, drag it to the input of the new event, as shown in Figure 42, and then release the mouse button. The test in the figure tests whether particles in its event have found a target object. If the test value equals "true," then the particles that have found the target flow to the new event, which spawns new particles.

Splitting Particles Between Events

In some cases you might want to split particles into two separate events. For example, you might be creating a particle system where you want some of the particles that are born to look like fire, and some of them to look like smoke. In this situation, you could add a Split Amount test after the birth operator, and then wire the test to a second event, as shown in Figure 43. This enables you to keep some of the particles in the birth event where certain operators can make them look and behave like fire, while others are split off to the second event to look and behave like smoke.

FIGURE 42
Wiring one event to another

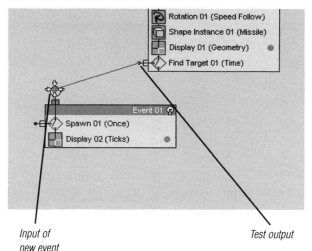

FIGURE 43
Particles split into two events

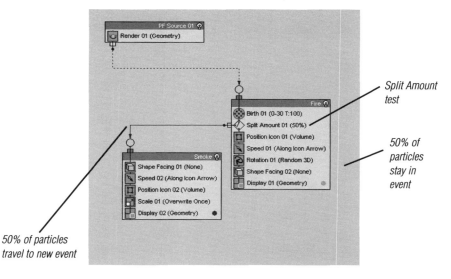

Lesson 4 Work with Particle Flow

Create a Particle Flow

1. Open **MAX09-02.max**, then save the file as **Missiles**.

2. Click the **Geometry button** on the Create panel, click **Particle Systems** on the drop-down list, click the **PF Source button** in the Object Type rollout, then click and drag in the Top viewport to create the PF source object, as shown in Figure 44.

   The size and location of the source is not important, because you will use objects in the scene to emit the particles.

3. In the Quantity Multiplier group in the Emission rollout, change the Viewport % to **100**.

4. Click the **Particle View button** in the Setup group in the Emission rollout.

   The Particle View window opens, showing a Particle Flow containing a standard flow (two events) in the event display.

You created a PF source in the viewport, then opened the system in Particle View.

FIGURE 44
PF Source in Top viewport

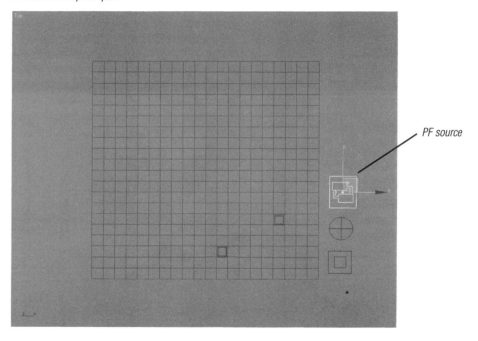

FIGURE 45
Birth operator parameters

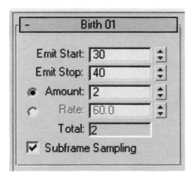

Define the Birth operator

1. At the top of Event01, select the Birth operator by clicking the word **Birth01**.

   TIP Don't click the green Birth icon; this acts as a toggle, turning the operator on and off.

2. In the parameters panel on the right side of Particle View, change the Emit Start to **30** and the Emit Stop to **40**.

   Particles in the system will be born between frames 30 and 40.

3. Make sure the **Amount option button** is selected, then set the Amount number to **2**, as shown in Figure 45.

   The system will emit two particles. Particle Flow spaces the emission of particles evenly between the start and end frames, so one particle will be born at frame 30, and one particle will be born at frame 40.

You selected an operator and edited its parameters in the parameters panel.

Define the Position operator

1. In the depot, click the **Position Object operator**, drag it over the Position Icon operator in Event01, then, when you see a red line going through the Position Icon operator, as shown in Figure 46, release the mouse button.

   The Position icon operator is replaced by the Position Object operator.

2. In Event01, click the new **Position Object 01 operator** to select it, then click the **By List button** in the Emitter Objects group in the parameters panel to open the Select Emitter Objects dialog box.

3. Click the **Ground object** in the list, then click the **Select button**.

   The Position Object operator enables you to use any object as an emitter. In this case, you use the object named Ground.

4. In the Location group on the parameters panel, click the **list arrow**, then click **Selected Faces**.

   Particle Flow lets you select any vertices, edges, or faces to emit particles. The particles in this system will be emitted from the currently selected faces in the Ground object. These faces were previously selected and saved with the scene.

5. Save the file.

You replaced an operator in an event with another operator, then used the operator to designate an object from which particles will be emitted, and to designate specific faces on the object that will emit the particles.

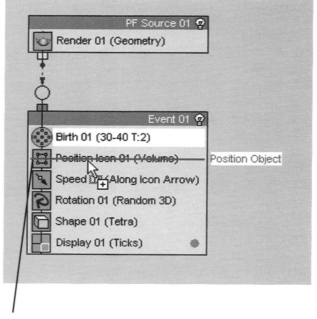

FIGURE 46
Inserting an operator

Position Icon operator is replaced

9-40 AUTODESK 3D STUDIO MAX

Particle Systems

FIGURE 47
Speed operator parameters

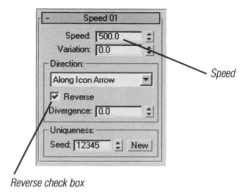

FIGURE 48
Animated particle system

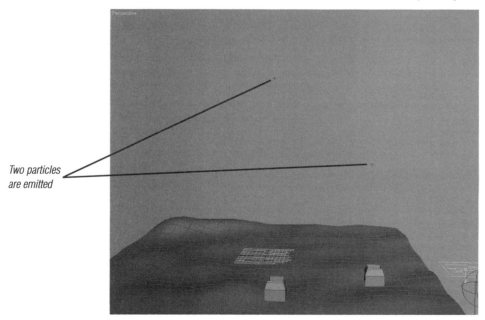

Lesson 4 Work with Particle Flow

Define the Speed and Rotation operators

1. In Event01, select the **Speed01 operator**.
2. In the parameters panel, change the Speed setting to **500**.
3. In the Direction group list box, make sure **Along Icon Arrow** is selected, then click the **Reverse check box** to select it, as shown in Figure 47.

   Along Icon Arrow sends the particles in the direction of the arrow that extends from the PF source. You select Reverse in the Direction group of the Speed operator parameters because you made the PF source object in the Top viewport, so it is facing down. The particles need to be emitted upward.

4. In Event01, select the **Rotation 01 operator**.
5. In the parameters panel, click the **Orientation Matrix list arrow**, click **Speed Space Follow**, then change the Y setting to **90**.

   Selecting Speed Space Follow in the Rotation operator causes the particles to rotate to point in the direction that they travel.

6. Minimize **Particle View**, save the file, then play the animation in the Perspective viewport.

   In the animation, two particles shoot up and out of the objects in the scene (missile silos), as shown in Figure 48.

7. Stop the animation.

You adjusted the parameters of the Speed operator and the Rotation operator in Event 01, then viewed the effect of the parameter changes on the animated particle system.

AUTODESK 3D STUDIO MAX 9-41

Define the Shape operator

1. Press **[6]** to restore the Particle View window, then click and drag the **Shape Instance operator** from the depot over the Shape01 operator in Event 01 to replace it.

2. Select the **Shape Instance operator** (if necessary), then at the top of the parameters panel, click the **Particle Geometry Object button** (it currently says None) to select it.

3. Press **[H]** to open the Pick Object dialog box, click **Missile** in the list, then click the **Pick button**.

    Particle Flow instances, or copies, a missile object previously created and saved in the file, and emits it as particles. The reason to do this, instead of simply animating the missiles, is because it enables you to use the tracking and collision testing features of Particle Flow to tell when the missiles hit the meteor object in the scene.

4. In Event 01, select the **Display01 operator**, click the **Type list arrow** on the parameters panel, then click **Geometry**.

    This displays the actual geometry of the missile shape on-screen, instead of just ticks.

5. Right-click the top of **Event01**, click **Rename** on the right-click menu, then rename the event **Missiles**.

6. Save the file, then play the animation.

    As shown in Figure 49, the two particles are shaped like missiles that shoot straight up and out of the silo objects.

(continued)

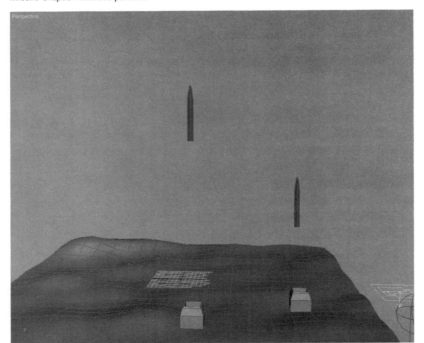

FIGURE 49
Missile-shaped instanced particles

FIGURE 50
Find Target test parameters

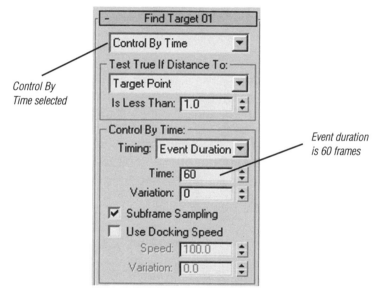

7. Stop the animation.

You replaced an operator with another operator in Event 01, edited the operator's parameters to make the particles be displayed as instanced copies of the missile object, renamed Event 01, and then viewed the animated particle system.

Add and define the Find Target test

1. Click and drag the **Find Target test** from the depot to the bottom of the Missiles event.

   TIP Make sure you do not replace an operator with the Find Target test.

2. Select the **Find Target test** in the Missiles event, click the **list arrow** at the top of the parameters panel, then click **Control By Time**.

   You control the Find by Target test by time so that you can set an exact duration between the time the missiles are born and when they find the target.

3. In the Timing list box in the Control by Time group, make sure **Event Duration** is selected, set the Time to **60**, then set the Variation to **0**, as shown in Figure 50.

   The meteor has previously been animated to become invisible (get hit by the missiles) at frame 90. The missiles launch at frame 30, so with the Event Duration at 60 frames the missiles hit the meteor at frame 90.

   (continued)

4. In the Target group, click the **Mesh Objects option button**, click the **By List button** to open the Select Target Objects dialog box, click **Meteor** in the list, then click the **Select button**.

   This forces the missile particles to find the meteor as a target.

5. Click the **Follow Target Animation check box** to make sure the missiles track with the animation of the meteor; otherwise, they target the original position of the meteor at frame 0.

6. Save the file, then play the animation.

   The missiles now arc after launch to find the meteor, as shown in Figure 51.

7. Stop the animation.

You added a test to the Missiles event, edited the test parameters to cause the particles to find an animated target, then viewed the animated particle system.

Wire events together

1. Click the **title bar** of the PF Source 01 global event, drag it to the middle of the event display, click the **title bar** of the Missiles event, then drag it so it sits just below the global event.

   If you need to increase the size of the event display, click and drag the edges of the Particle View window to enlarge it.

   (continued)

FIGURE 51
Missiles target the meteor

9-44 AUTODESK 3D STUDIO MAX

FIGURE 52
New event in event display

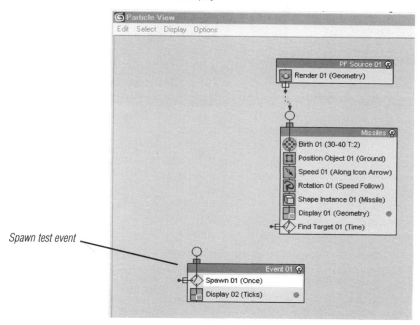

2. Click and drag the **Spawn test** from the depot to a location below and to the left of the Missiles event in the event display, as shown in Figure 52.

   The Spawn test becomes a new event named Event 01 in the event display. The event contains the Spawn test operator and a Display operator.

3. Select the **Spawn test** in the Event 01 event, click the **Delete Parent check box** in the Spawn Rate and Amount group on the parameters panel, then change the Offspring # to **60**.

   The missile particles (the parent of the new particles) are deleted the moment the new particles begin to spawn, and each particle spawns 60 offspring particles.

4. In the Speed group on the parameters panel, click the **In Units check box** to select it, change the In Units setting to **80**, change the Variation to **20%**, then change the Divergence to **180**.

   The spawned particles have a speed between 64 and 96 units per frame (Speed of 80 with a Variation of 20%). Setting the Divergence at 180 causes the spawned particles to scatter in different directions within a 180 degree angle.

5. Roll over the **wire icon** that sticks out from the Find Target01 test in the Missiles event. You see the wire cursor appear.

6. Click the **Find Target test output**, drag to the **Event 01 event input** until the wire cursor appears, then release the mouse button.

   The output of the Find Target test is now wired to the input of the Spawn test event.

   (continued)

7. Right-click the **title bar** of the Event 01 event, click **Rename**, and then rename the event **Explosion**.

8. Save the file, then play the animation.

   In the animation, the missiles disappear when they hit the meteor and spawn 60 particles, as shown in Figure 53.

9. Stop the animation.

You added a Spawn test event to the event display, edited its parameters, wired the output of the Find target test to the input of the Spawn test event, renamed the Spawn test event, and then viewed the animated particle system.

Split particles between events

1. In the Explosion event, right-click between the **Spawn test** and the **Display operator**, point to **Insert** on the right-click menu, point to **Test** on the submenu, then click **Split Amount**.

   The Split Amount test is inserted into the event.

2. Right-click in a **blank area** of the event display, point to **New** on the right-click menu, point to **Operator Event**, then click **Shape**.

(continued)

FIGURE 53
Missiles spawn particles at collision

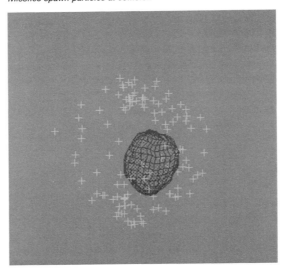

FIGURE 54
Wiring events together

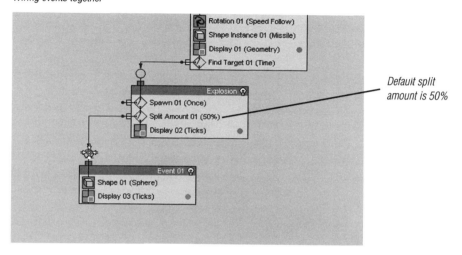

Default split amount is 50%

3. Wire the **output** of the Split Amount test to the **input** of the new event, as shown in Figure 54, then rename the new event **Sparks**.

    Fifty percent of the particles that are spawned in the Explosion event are split by the Split Amount test and sent to the new Sparks event. The other 50 percent stay in the Explosion event.

4. Select the **Shape01 (Tetra) operator** at the top of the new event, click the **Shape list arrow** in the parameters panel, click **Sphere**, then set the Size to **2**.

    The Shape operator defines the particles in the Sparks event as spheres with a size of 2 units.

5. Right-click between the **Shape** and **Display operators** in the Sparks event, point to **Insert** on the right-click menu, point to **Operator** on the submenu, then click **Speed**.

6. Select the new **Speed operator**, then on the parameters panel, change the Speed to **200**, the Variation to **50**, click the **Direction list arrow**, then click **Random 3D**.

    The particles in the Sparks event will shoot out in random 3D directions at speeds varying from 150 to 250.

(continued)

7. Save the file, then play the animation.

   As shown in Figure 55, there are now two sets of explosions in the animation, each containing 50 percent of the spawned particles.

8. Stop the animation.

You inserted a test operator into an event, added a new event to the event display, then wired the new test and the new event together. You also edited the parameters of an operator in the new event, inserted a new operator into the new event, edited its parameters, then viewed the animated particle system.

Apply space warps to event-driven particles

1. Right-click the **Missiles event**, point to **Append**, point to **Test**, then click **Spawn**.
2. Rename the new Spawn test **Spawn Trails**.
3. Click and drag a **Force operator** from the depot to an empty area of the event display to make a new event, then rename the event **Trails**.
4. Wire the **output** of the Spawn Trails test to the Trails event input.
5. Select the **Force operator** at the top of the Trails event, and in the parameters panel, click the **By List** button.
6. Select **Drag01** and **Wind01** on the list in the Force Space Warps dialog box, then click **Select**.

   The space warp forces are applied to the smoke trail. The smoke trails behind the missiles are slowed down by the Drag space warp. The particles also get scattered a little from the Wind space warp.

(continued)

FIGURE 55
Result of Sparks event

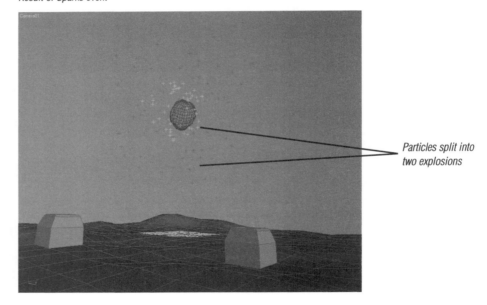

Particles split into two explosions

9-48 AUTODESK 3D STUDIO MAX

Particle Systems

FIGURE 56
Shape Facing operator parameters

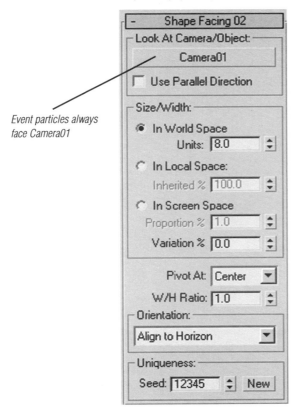

Event particles always face Camera01

7. Beneath the Force01 operator in the Trails event, insert a **Shape Facing operator**, select the **operator**, click the **Look At Camera/Object button** on the parameters panel, press **[H]**, click **Camera01** on the list, then click the **Pick button**.
8. In the Size/Width group on the parameters panel, make sure the **In World Space** option button is selected, then set the Units value to **8**, as shown in Figure 56.

You appended a Spawn test to the Missiles event, renamed it, created a new Force event in the event display, wired the Spawn test to the new event, then edited the operator in the new event. You also inserted a Shape Facing operator in the new event, and edited its parameters.

Define a Scale operator

1. Beneath the Shape Facing operator, insert a **Scale operator**.
2. Select the **Scale operator**, click the **Type list arrow**, then click **Relative First**.

   This setting lets you continually animate the particle scale relative to the size it was when it entered the event.
3. Minimize Particle View (if necessary), drag the **time slider** to frame **200**, then turn on **Auto Key**.
4. In the parameters panel, change the **Scale Factor** of any axis to **500**.

   This creates a keyframe at 200 that increases the scale of the particles' size by 500 percent to create a dissipation effect as the particles grow older.

(continued)

AUTODESK 3D STUDIO MAX 9-49

Lesson 4 Work with Particle Flow

5. Turn off **Auto Key mode**.

   TIP Avoid using Set Key mode with Particle Flow.

6. In the Scale Variation group, change one of the axis values to **50%** to vary the amount of the particles' scale from 250 percent to 750 percent.

7. Beneath the Scale operator, add a **Delete operator**.

8. Select the **Delete operator**, click the **By Particle Age option button** in the Remove group on the parameters panel, then set the **Life Span** to **100** and the Variation to **10** (if necessary), as shown in Figure 57.

9. At the bottom of the Missiles event, select the **Spawn Trails operator**.

10. On the parameters panel, click the **By Travel Distance option button** in the Spawn Rate and Amount group, then make sure the Offspring # is set to **1**.

    New particles will be spawned at regular intervals along the path of the flying missiles.

    TIP If you experiment with these values, be careful not to set the Offspring # too high, because it can be extremely processor intensive.

(continued)

FIGURE 57
Delete operator parameters panel

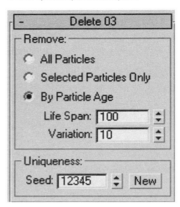

FIGURE 58
Smoke trails

11. In the Speed group, make sure the **Inherited % option button** is selected, set it to **5%** with a Variation of **5%** and a Divergence of **5**.

    The particles inherit a small amount of variable speed from the missiles, and diverge within a 5-degree angle.

12. Save your scene and play the Animation.

    As shown in Figure 58, you now see two realistic smoke trails left behind the missiles in the animation.

You added a Scale operator to the Trails event, animated a change in the particles' scale, then adjusted the parameters of the Delete operator to animate the deletion of particles according to their age. You also adjusted the parameters of the Spawn Trails operator to affect the birth and speed of the particles in the smoke trails.

LESSON 5

USE MATERIAL OPERATORS

What You'll Do

▶ *In this lesson, you will learn how to apply materials that change over time to particles. Specifically, you will use a Particle Age map to change the appearance of particles as they age in an animation.*

Understanding Material Operators

Applying materials to event-driven particles is a little different from simply dragging them to an object in the viewport. As with other concepts in Particle Flow, you use operators in Particle View to assign materials to event-driven particles. Particle Flow offers two different material operators to achieve this. The **Material Static operator** can be added to an event when you want to apply nonanimated materials to particles. After adding the operator to an event, you can select any material that is in the Material Editor, and then directly apply the material to the particles using the operator's parameters panel.

If you want to use animated materials on event-driven particles, then you need to use the **Material Dynamic operator** in the event, as shown in Figure 59. It lets you choose material from the Material Editor in the same manner, but it has the added flexibility of being able to work with a map called Particle Age.

Assigning the Particle Age Map

The **Particle Age map** lets you change the appearance of the material applied to a particle over the life of a particle. For example, by assigning this map to a material, you can determine at what percentage of a particle's age you want a material to look like fire and at what age you want it to look like smoke, as shown in Figure 60. The Particle Age map automatically blends the appearance of the material between the two or three material looks over time.

To use the Particle Age map, simply assign it to a material as you would any map. Next, in the Particle Age Parameters rollout, you will see that there are Color #1, Color #2, and Color #3 map buttons. Also notice that each one has an age percentage. With the default settings as they are, any particle mapped with this material will take on the appearance of the map in the Color #1 slot when it is born. It will then blend to Color #2 by 50 percent of its age. By 100 percent of its life it will look like Color #3.

FIGURE 59
Material Dynamic operator in an event

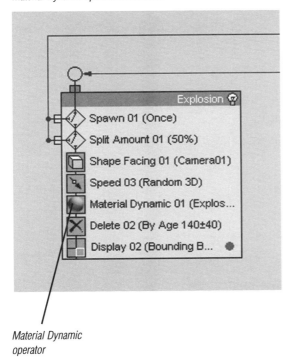

Material Dynamic operator

FIGURE 60
Particles with Particle Age map applied

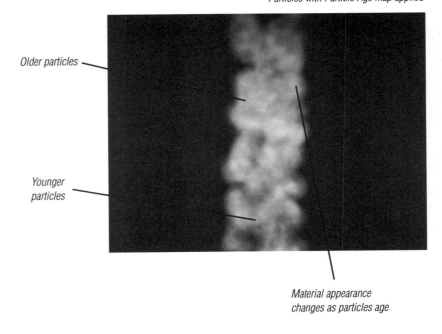

Older particles

Younger particles

Material appearance changes as particles age

Lesson 5   Use Material Operators

AUTODESK 3D STUDIO MAX 9-53

Add and define a Material Static operator

1. In the Sparks event, right-click between the **Speed** and **Display operators**, point to **Insert** on the right-click menu, point to **Operator**, then click **Material Static**.

2. Select the **Material Static operator**, then click the **Assign Material button** at the top of the parameters panel to open the Material/Map Browser.

3. In the Browse From area of the Material/Map Browser, click the **Mtl Editor option button** to open the list of materials in the Material Editor, then double-click the **White Sparks material** to assign it to the particles in the Sparks event.

   The Material Static operator connects the particles in the event to a nonanimated white material from the Material Editor.

4. Right-click anywhere in the **Sparks event**, point to **Append**, point to **Operator**, then click **Delete**.

   A Delete operator is appended to the end of the Sparks event.

5. Select the **Delete operator**, click the **By Particle Age option button** on the parameters panel, set the Life Span to **100**, then set the Variation to **50**.

   The Delete operator will delete the particles at random ages between 50 and 150 frames. The particle diagram in the Particle View event display should now look like Figure 61.

   (continued)

FIGURE 61
Particle diagram

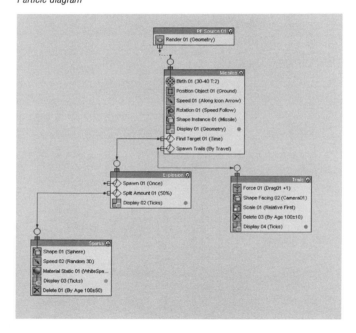

9-54 AUTODESK 3D STUDIO MAX

Particle Systems

FIGURE 62
Speed operator parameters panel

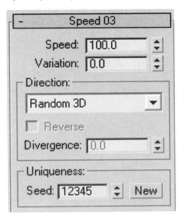

6. Save the file, then play the animation.

   The sparks now have the spark material applied to them.

7. Stop the animation.

You added a Material Static operator to an event, assigned a material to the event's particles using the operator, appended a Delete operator to the event, then edited its parameters to define how the particles disappear.

Setting up particles for material

1. Click and drag a **Shape Facing operator** from the depot to just above the **Display operator** in the Explosion event, then release the mouse button.

2. Select the new **Shape Facing operator**, click the **Look at Camera/Object button** in the parameters panel, then click **Camera01** in the viewport.

   The particles are now set to be faces that always face Camera01.

3. In the Size/Width group in the parameters panel, make sure the **In World Space option button** is selected, then set the Units to **160**.

   This sets a good size for the faces.

4. Below the Shape Facing operator, add a **Speed operator** from the depot, then in the parameters panel for the Speed operator, set the Speed to **100** and the Direction to **Random 3D**, as shown in Figure 62.

   The particles in the Explosion event will disperse in a random 3D fashion.

   (continued)

AUTODESK 3D STUDIO MAX 9-55

5. Below the Speed operator in the Explosion event, add a **Delete operator**.

6. In the parameters panel for the Delete operator, click the **By Particle Age option button**, then set the Life Span to **140** and the Variation to **40**.

   The length of each particle's life will be somewhere between 100 and 180 frames.

7. Select the **Display operator** at the bottom of the Explosion event, click the **Type list arrow** in the parameters panel, then click **Bounding Boxes**.

8. Save the file, then play the animation.

   As shown in Figure 63, when the missiles hit the meteor, the spawned particles are faces shaped like boxes that are ready to be mapped with the particle age material.

You added a Shape Facing operator to the Explosion event, defined the faces to always look at a camera in the scene, and edited the speed, size, and direction parameters of the operator. You also added a Delete operator to the event, edited its parameters, then viewed the animated particle system.

FIGURE 63
Particles spawned as bounding boxes

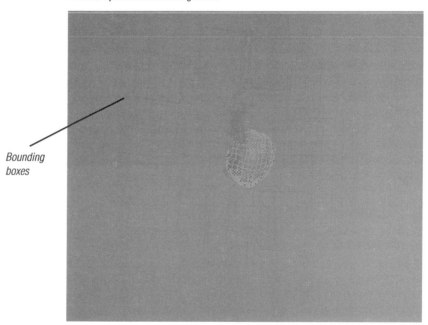

Bounding boxes

FIGURE 64
Particle Age Parameters rollout

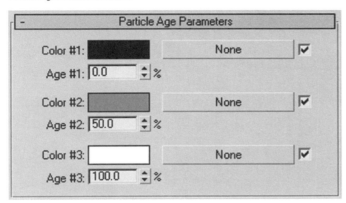

Assign a Particle Age map to a material

1. Open the **Material Editor**, select a blank **sample slot**, then change the name of the material to **Explosion**.
2. In the Shader Basic Parameters rollout, click the **Face Map check box** to select it.
3. In the Blinn Basic Parameters rollout, click the **Diffuse map button**, then double-click the **Particle Age map** in the Material/Map Browser.

   The Particle Age map is assigned to the Diffuse color component of the material, and the Particle Age Parameters rollout appears in the Material Editor, as shown in Figure 64.

You renamed a material in the Material Editor, selected its Face Map shader parameter, and assigned a Particle Age map to the material.

Assign maps to the Particle Age map

1. In the Particle Age Parameters rollout on the Material Editor, click the **Color #1 map button**, then double-click **Noise** in the Material/Map Browser to assign it as the Color #1 map.
2. In the Noise Parameters rollout, click the **Fractal option button** in the Noise Type group, then in the Noise Threshold group, set the High value to **0.7** and the Low value to **0.3**.

   The Fractal option provides a more fiery effect. By adjusting the High and Low values, you

(continued)

AUTODESK 3D STUDIO MAX 9-57

have increased the contrast between the two colors in the Noise map.

3. Click the Color #1 color swatch, select a **bright red color** in the Color Selector, click the Color #2 color swatch, click a **bright yellow color** in the Color selector, then close the **Color Selector**.

   The Noise Parameters rollout should look like Figure 65.

4. Click the **Go to Parent button** to get back to the Particle Age map.

5. Drag the **Noise map button** from Color #1 down to the Color #2 map button, release the mouse button, click the **Copy option button** in the Copy (Instance) Map dialog box, then click **OK**.

   You copied the Noise map in the Color #1 component to the Color #2 component.

6. Click the **Color #2 map button** to open the map, change the Color #1 color swatch to a **medium grey color**, then change the Color #2 swatch to a **white color**.

7. Click the **Go to Parent button** again to get back to the Particle Age map, copy the **Color #2 map button** to the Color #3 map button, click the **Copy option button** (if necessary), then click **OK**.

8. Click the **Color #3 map button** to open the map, change the Color #1 color swatch to a **dark grey**, then change the Color #2 color swatch to a **medium grey**.

(continued)

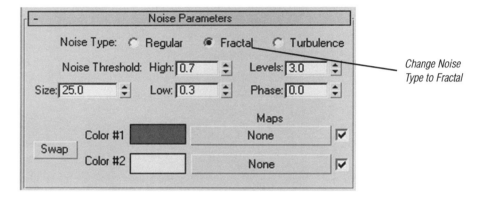

FIGURE 65
Noise Parameters rollout

Change Noise Type to Fractal

9-58 AUTODESK 3D STUDIO MAX

Particle Systems

FIGURE 66
Output rollout

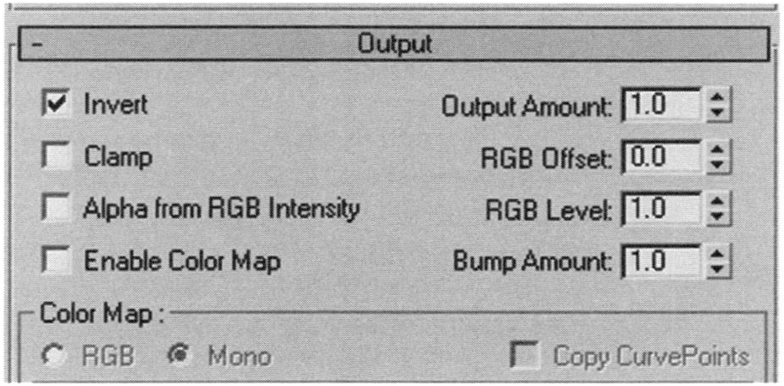

9. Click the **Go to Parent button** twice to get back to the the parent material, click the **Opacity map button** in the Maps rollout, then double-click **Gradient Ramp** in the Material/Map Browser to assign it to the Opacity component of the material.

10. In the Gradient Ramp Parameters rollout, click the **Gradient Type list arrow**, then click **Radial**.

11. Open the **Output rollout** at the bottom of the Material Editor, then click the **Invert check box**, as shown in Figure 66.

    By inverting the output of the map colors, you effectively swap the black and white of the start and end colors.

12. Close the **Material Editor**, then save the file.

You assigned maps to the Particle Age map color components, edited the submap parameters, assigned an Opacity map to the material, then edited the Opacity map's parameters.

Add and define the Material Dynamic operator

1. Open **Particle View**, right-click between the **Speed operator** and the **Delete operator** in the Explosion event, point to **Insert**, point to **Operator**, then click **Material Dynamic**.

    The Material Dynamic operator gets placed between the Speed and the Delete operators.

2. Select the **Material Dynamic operator**, click the **Assign Material button** in the parameters

(continued)

AUTODESK 3D STUDIO MAX 9-59

Lesson 5   Use Material Operators

panel, click the **Mtl Editor option button** in the Browse From area of the Material/Map Browser, then double-click the **Explosion material**.

The newly created material is applied to the event with the particle age map.

3. Play the animation, then stop the animation when you are finished viewing it.

4. Save the file, drag the **time slider** to frame **130**, then render the scene.

   You now have a nice explosion material mapped onto the box-shaped explosion particles, as shown in Figure 67.

5. Close the **rendered scene window**.

You added a Material Dynamic operator to the Explosion event, assigned a material to the operator, played the animation, then rendered the scene.

Create and assign the Smoke material

1. Close **Particle View**, then press **[M]** to open the Material Editor.

2. Drag a copy of the **Explosion material** to the sample slot to its right, then rename the material **Smoke**.

3. In the Maps rollout, click the **Diffuse map button**.

(continued)

FIGURE 67
Explosion material applied to explosion particles

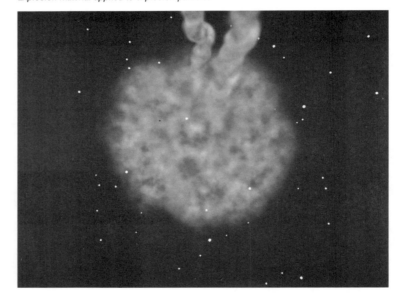

FIGURE 68
Particle Age Parameters rollout

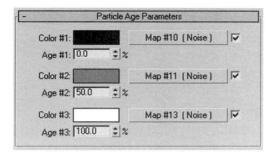

FIGURE 69
Smoke material applied to smoke trails

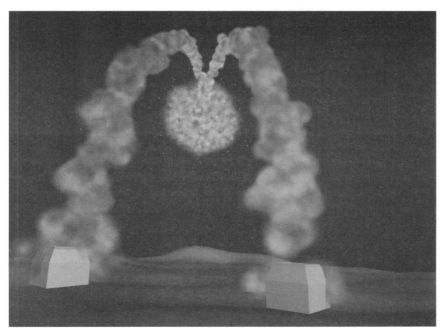

Lesson 5   Use Material Operators

4. In the Particle Age Parameters rollout, drag the **Color #2 map button** to the Color #1 map button, release the mouse button, click the **Copy option button** (if necessary), then click **OK**.

   This replaces the fiery colors in Color #1 with the smoky colors from Color #2. The Particle Age Parameters rollout should now look like Figure 68.

5. Close the **Material Editor**, then press **[6]** to open Particle View.

6. Right-click between the **Scale operator** and the **Delete operator** in the Trails event, point to **Insert**, point to **Operator**, then click **Material Dynamic**.

7. Select the **Material Dynamic operator**, click the **Assign Material button** on the parameters panel, click **Mtl Editor** in the Browse From area of the Material/Map Browser, then double-click the **Smoke material**.

8. Save the file, drag the **time slider** to frame **130,** then render the scene at that frame.

   The rendered scene should look like Figure 69. You have covered a lot of ground in this chapter. Now it's your turn to explore the various tools that you used. Try experimenting with them to create different kinds of particle effects. Have fun!

You copied a material in the Material Editor, renamed the material, opened its Diffuse map, and copied a map from one of its color components to the other. You then added a Material Dynamic operator to an event, assigned a material to the operator, then rendered the scene to see the material applied.

AUTODESK 3D STUDIO MAX 9-61

CHAPTER SUMMARY

In this chapter, you learned what a particle system is and how to create non-event-driven particle systems such as Spray, Super Spray, and Blizzard. You also learned how to adjust the parameters of particle systems. You explored space warps and what they do, learned how to create and modify space warps, and practiced binding objects in a scene to a space warp. You learned how to apply materials to a particle system and how to modify the particle type to optimize the particles' appearance. You also explored, in-depth, 3ds Max's event-driven particle system, Particle Flow, and examined the components of Particle Flow and how to add events in Particle View. You learned how to add operators and tests to a particle flow to control the behavior of particles through an animation, and you learned how to apply materials that change over time to particles.

What You Have Learned

- How to create a non-event-driven particle system
- How to adjust the parameters of a particle system
- How to create and modify a Gravity space warp
- How to bind an object to a space warp
- How to create and modify a deflector
- How to apply materials to a particle system
- How to create a Particle Flow
- How to open Particle View and understand its different sections
- How to add an event to the Particle Flow
- How to add operators and tests in an event
- How to define operators and tests
- How to wire events together
- How to split particles between events
- How set up particles for material by making them Facing particles
- How to use the Particle Age map to change particles' appearances over time

Key Terms

Emitter   Object that specifies the location from which the particles originate.

Event   In Particle Flow, a grouping of parameters or actions that are performed on the particle system.

Operator   In Particle Flow, part of an event that is responsible for performing an action.

Particle Age map   Map with parameters that enable change in the appearance of the material applied to a particle over the life of a particle.

Particle Flow   3ds Max's event-driven particle system that lets you design custom events that affect the way particle behave.

Particle system   An object that generates clusters of many subobjects called particles.

Space warp   An object that creates a force field effect that operates on other objects.

Test   In Particle Flow, part of an event that tests some condition and then, based on the results of the test, performs different actions on a particle, and then passes it from event to event.

chapter 10
EFFECTS

1. Add atmospheric effects.
2. Adjust atmospheric effect parameters.
3. Understand rendering effects.
4. Use lens effects.
5. Apply depth-of-field and blur effects.
6. Apply hair and fur.

chapter 10 EFFECTS

3ds Max offers many ways to add special effects to your final rendered scenes. Two of these methods are to employ **atmospheric effects** and **rendering effects**. You can add both of these effects to your scenes, and edit them, via the Environment and Effects dialog box. This interface is like a combination of two separate panels in one floating window: You access the Environment panel by clicking the Environment tab, and you access the Effects panel by clicking the Effects tab.

In this chapter, you will learn how to add effects that can dramatically enhance the look of your scenes. Adding effects to your scenes is a fun and rewarding process. As you go through the chapter, you will see many of the cool ways in which you can influence the final renderings of your imagery. You will be working with effects such as fire, fog, volumetric lighting (beams of light), glowing objects, hair, and others. After you understand how to apply these effects to your scenes, you'll be able to combine them in an endless number of creative ways to create and animate complicated, realistic, and exciting scenes.

Tools You'll Use

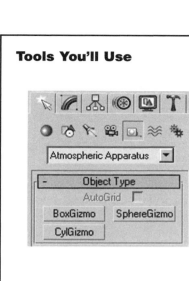
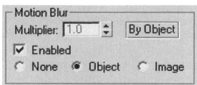
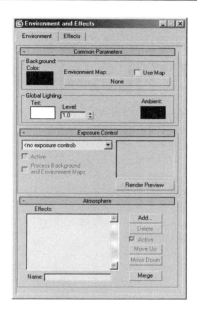
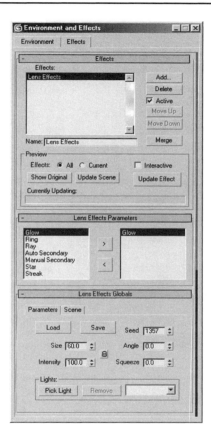

10-3

LESSON 1

ADD ATMOSPHERIC EFFECTS

What You'll Do

In this lesson, you will learn what atmospheric effects are, how to add them to scenes, how to limit some effects to a confined area, and how to apply effects to individual objects in a scene.

Understanding Atmospheric Effects

Atmospheric effects enable you to produce effects that look like things in the real world that don't have easily defined geometry or solid definition. As shown in Figure 1, there are four **atmospheres** that you can apply to any scene: Fire, Fog, Volume Fog, and Volume Light. Generally speaking, **Fire** generates the appearance of flames contained within a specific volume, while **Volume Fog** is fog that you can contain within a specific volume. **Fog** creates a foggy atmosphere that fills your scene. The **Volume Light** effect is used to create the effect of light beams passing through a foggy or dusty environment. It basically adds a colored fog to the area of illumination that extends from a light.

While each atmosphere's name implies a specific effect, the truth is that each has many changeable parameters that make it pretty versatile. For instance, you can use the Fire effect to achieve effects such as a burst of frosty air, or a nebulous cloud. Volume Fog also makes nice clouds or columns of smoke.

To add an atmospheric effect to your scene, click Rendering on the menu bar, and then click Environments on the menu to open the Environment and Effects dialog box with the Environment tab selected, as shown in Figure 2. After you have added an atmosphere to your scene, you can also edit its parameters from this dialog box.

Creating an Atmospheric Apparatus

Two of the atmosphere effects, Fire and Volume Fog, contain the effect within a specific volume called an **atmospheric apparatus**. An apparatus can be created in one of three shapes: a box, sphere, or cylinder. While this might seem limited at first, you do have the ability to change the shape of the apparatus somewhat, by applying a nonuniform scale or squash on it or by altering its parameters to affect its shape. Modifiers, however, cannot be applied to an atmospheric apparatus.

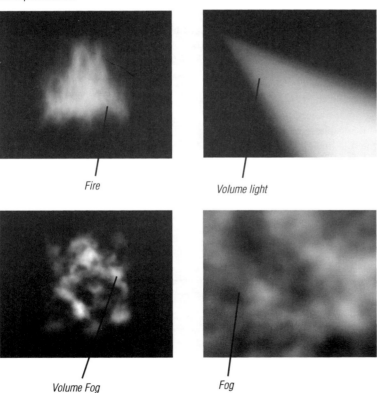

FIGURE 1
Atmospheric effects

Fire
Volume light
Volume Fog
Fog

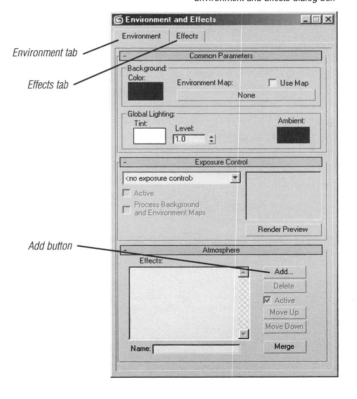

FIGURE 2
Environment and Effects dialog box

Environment tab
Effects tab
Add button

Lesson 1   Add Atmospheric Effects

You can place an apparatus anywhere in the scene and you can even animate its transforms. This means you could, say, contain a ball of fire in a sphere apparatus, and animate it moving, rotating, and scaling across the screen. Or you could use Volume Fog to simulate a puffy cloud and animate it moving across the sky.

To add an effect to a scene using an atmospheric apparatus, click the Helpers button on the Create panel, and then choose Atmospheric Apparatus from the drop-down list. Next, choose the shape that you want by clicking the BoxGizmo, SphereGizmo, or CylGizmo button in the Object Type rollout, as shown in Figure 3. To create the apparatus, click and drag in a viewport the same way that you would to make a box, sphere, or cylinder primitive.

Adding an Effect to an Object

To add an atmosphere to an apparatus or light object, select the apparatus or light, and then click the Add button in the Atmospheres & Effects rollout on the Modify panel for the object, as shown in Figure 4, to open the Add Atmosphere dialog box. Click the effect that you want to add in the Add Atmosphere dialog box, then click OK to add the effect to the list in the Atmospheres & Effects rollout.

Alternatively, you can select an atmosphere, and then pick the apparatus or object to which it should be added. To do this, click Rendering on the menu bar, and then click Environment to open the Environment and Effects dialog box. In the Atmosphere rollout in the dialog box, click the Add button (as shown in Figure 2), and then select the effect in the Add Atmospheric Effect dialog box that you want to add to the scene. After the effect appears selected in the list in the Atmosphere rollout, its parameters rollout should appear just below the Atmosphere rollout. For the Fire effect and the Volume Fog effect, click the Pick Gizmo button in the effect's parameters rollout, and then click the apparatus in the scene to which you want the effect to apply. For the Volume Light effect, click the Pick Light button, then click the light in the scene to which you want the effect to apply. You can pick multiple apparatuses or objects in one scene to which the effect is applied. The names of the affected objects appear in the list to the right of the Remove Gizmo or Remove Light button in the effect's parameters rollout. Click the Remove Gizmo or Remove Light button to remove the effect from the object selected in the list.

FIGURE 3
Helpers panel

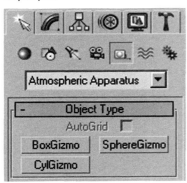

FIGURE 4
Atmospheres & Effects rollout

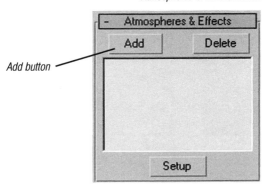

Add button

10-6 AUTODESK 3D STUDIO MAX

Effects

FIGURE 5
Creating an atmospheric apparatus

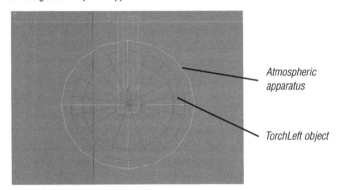

Atmospheric apparatus

TorchLeft object

FIGURE 6
Positioning the apparatus

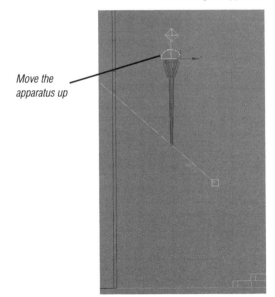

Move the apparatus up

Create an atmospheric apparatus

1. Open the file **MAX10-01.max**, save it as **torchscene**, press **[H]** to open the Select Objects dialog box, click the **[TorchLeft]** object in the list, then click **Select**.

2. Maximize the **Top viewport**, then press **[Z]** to zoom into the selected object.

3. In the Create panel, click the **Helpers button**, click the **list arrow** beneath the Helpers button, then click **Atmospheric Apparatus**.

4. Click the **SphereGizmo button** in the Object Type rollout, then click and drag from the center of the torch to just outside its radius, as shown in Figure 5.

   By creating the apparatus in the Top viewport, you can easily line it up with the torch.

5. Switch to the **Front viewport**, then move the **apparatus** up so the center sits at the top of the torch, as shown in Figure 6.

(continued)

Lesson 1 Add Atmospheric Effects

DISCREET 3D STUDIO MAX 10-7

6. Click the **Modify tab**, then click the **Hemisphere check box** in the Sphere Gizmo Parameters rollout on the Modify panel.

   The sphere gizmo is sliced in half.

7. Click the **Select and Uniform Scale tool**, then scale the apparatus up along the y-axis by about **700 percent**, as shown in Figure 7.

   This creates a more flame-shaped gizmo and ultimately a taller area of flames.

8. Save the file.

You created a sphere atmospheric apparatus and placed it appropriately in the scene, halved it, then increased the scale along its y-axis.

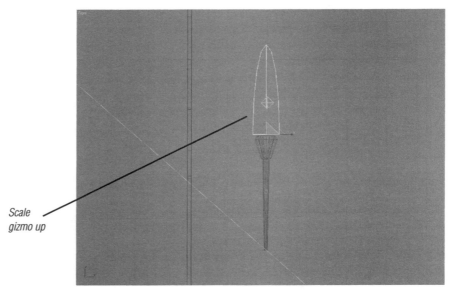

FIGURE 7
Scaling the height of the apparatus

Scale gizmo up

FIGURE 8
Atmospheres & Effects rollout with Fire effect

Add a fire effect

1. Switch to the **Perspective viewport**, make sure the **atmospheric apparatus** is selected, then press **[Z]** to zoom in on the selected apparatus.

   The view zooms into show the apparatus on top of the torch.

2. Click the **Add button** in the Atmospheres & Effects rollout on the Modify panel to open the Add Atmosphere dialog box, click **Fire Effect** in the list, then click **OK**.

   The Fire Effect is now listed in the Atmospheres & Effects rollout, as shown in Figure 8.

3. Render the viewport.

   As shown in Figure 9, the flame appears, but it doesn't look very detailed or torch-like. You'll edit its parameters in the next lesson.

4. Minimize the **rendered scene window**, then save the file.

You added a fire effect to the atmospheric apparatus, then rendered the scene to look at the result.

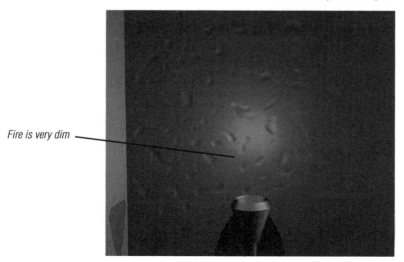

FIGURE 9
Rendered Perspective viewport

Fire is very dim

Lesson 1 Add Atmospheric Effects

DISCREET 3D STUDIO MAX 10-9

Add a volume light

1. In torchscene.max, press **[8]** to open the Environment and Effects dialog box, then click the **Add button** in the Atmosphere rollout.

    The Add Atmospheric Effect dialog box appears.

2. Click **Volume Light**, then click **OK**.

    Volume Light is added to the list of effects in the scene.

    TIP You can also add a Volume Light effect to a light in the scene via the light's Atmospheres & Effects rollout.

3. Switch to the **Top viewport**, then zoom out (if necessary) until the farthest left light (Direct01) is visible.

4. Pan down the Environment and Effects dialog box to the Volume Light Parameters rollout, click the **Pick Light button** in the Lights group, then click the **Direct01 light** in the Top viewport.

    The Direct01 light is now listed in the Lights group list box, as shown in Figure 10.

    (continued)

FIGURE 10
Volume Light Parameters rollout

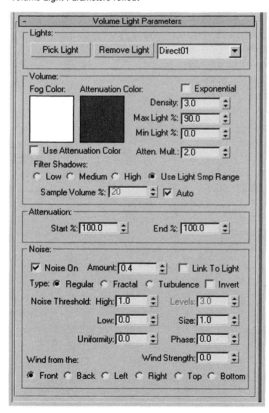

FIGURE 11
Rendered scene with volume light added

5. Switch to the **Camera viewport**, then render the scene.

   Light beams pour through the window in the scene, as shown in Figure 11. The crosses in the window produce a nice break-up pattern in the beams.

6. Minimize the **rendered scene window**, then save the file.

You added a volume light effect to the scene, then picked a light for it to affect.

LESSON 2

ADJUST ATMOSPHERIC
EFFECT PARAMETERS

What You'll Do

▶ *In this lesson, you will learn how to adjust the parameters of different atmospheric effects in a scene.*

Locating an Effect's Parameters

As discussed in the previous lesson, when an atmosphere effect is selected in the Atmospheres rollout list in the Environment and Effects dialog box, the effect's parameters rollout should appear just below the Atmospheres rollout. Similarly, if you add an effect to a selected atmospheric apparatus or light object by selecting the effect in the Atmospheres & Effects rollout list on the Modify panel, click the Setup button underneath the list to open the Environment and Effects dialog box, and then pan down the dialog box to access the effect's parameters under the Atmosphere rollout.

Adjusting Fire Effect Parameters

With the Fire Effect selected in the Atmosphere rollout list, you have a variety of ways to change the appearance of the fire you are adding to a scene. In the Fire Effect Parameters rollout, as shown in Figure 12, the Colors group has three swatches that let you change the Inner Color, Outer Color, and Smoke Color. The Smoke color functions only if the Explosion option is turned on, as discussed later in this lesson. Changing these colors is the key to using this effect to create things other than fire, such as blue and white to make frost, or vivid colors to make nebulae. The colors can also be animated over time, by changing the colors at different frames while the Auto Key button is on.

In the Shape group, you can affect the shape of the flames by choosing the Flame Type. Click the Tendril option button to produce wispy flames, or click the Fireball option button to create a puffier effect.

The Stretch setting scales the flames along the z-axis of the atmospheric apparatus. A value higher than 1.0 stretches the flames, and a value lower than 1.0 compresses the flames. This control is useful for fixing any stretching that occurs from scaling up the height of the gizmo. For example, if you doubled its original height to give it more of a flame shape, the flames themselves also get scaled up, producing a stretching effect. You can counteract this by setting the stretch parameter to 0.5. The Regularity setting determines how the flames fill the gizmo. At a setting of 1, the flames conform to the edges of the gizmo, while lower settings produce more of an irregular shape.

The Characteristics group contains more options that affect the way the fire looks. Many times when you render flames you don't see very much detail. To address this, first adjust the Flame Size. The flame size is related to the size of the gizmo, so if you have a smaller gizmo, you should try reducing the flame size. The Density setting increases or decreases the overall transparency and brightness of the effect. Higher values result in full-bodied, bright flames, while lower values produce a dimmer, transparent effect. Increasing the Flame Detail adds more variation and a higher contrast to the flame colors, but you should raise this value only if it is necessary because it increases the render time. The Samples setting lets you increase or decrease the rate at which the effect gets **sampled**, or calculated. Depending on the rest of the parameters you have chosen, this setting might produce more accurate results, but it also increases the rendering time.

The Motion group has two parameters for animating the flames. If you animate the Phase value, you animate the patterns that appear in the flames, producing a churning effect. The faster the rate of increase in the

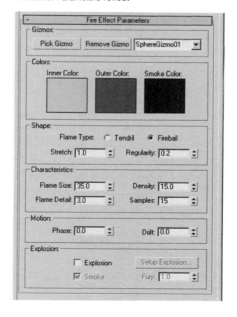

FIGURE 12
Fire Effect Parameters rollout

value, the faster the flames churn. If you animate the Drift value, the flame patterns move along the z-axis of the atomospheric apparatus, giving a rising effect.

The Explosion group has controls that let you simulate the way flames would look during the life of an explosion. Checking the Explosion check box automatically adjusts the settings so that the flames start out small and less dense. Over time, the density and size of the flames grow, and then eventually the inner and outer colors blend into a smoke color (unless you deselect the Smoke check box) as the density shrinks again. Click the Setup Explosion button to open a dialog box that lets you enter the frames in which the effect starts and ends. Adjust the Fury parameter to increase or decrease the speed at which the flame pattern churns during the explosion.

Adjusting Volume Light Parameters

The Volume Light Parameters rollout, shown in Figure 13, also provides a variety of ways to adjust the look of the effect. In the Volume group, you can change settings such as the

FIGURE 13
Volume Light Parameters rollout

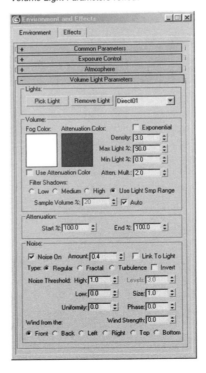

Fog Color and the Density of the fog. There are also settings that give you advanced control over the attenuation and brightness of the fog. The Filter Shadows settings control the quality level of shadows that appear in the light. Increasing these settings increases the render time.

The Attenuation rollout has two settings labeled Start % and End %. Both of these default to 100, which places the start and end attenuation of the volume light effect at the same location as the attenuation parameters of the light itself. At settings less than 100, the effect's attenuation is shortened by the percentage you choose.

The Noise group has settings that let you add and control a noise pattern in the fog. You can use noise to add the illusion of dust in the beams. The settings operate in a similar manner to those that appear in the Noise map settings. To add noise to the volume light, click the Noise On check box to select it. Use the Amount value to control the amount of noise; this value ranges from 0 to 1. At 0 there is no noise in the beam; at 1 you have the full amount. The Type option buttons let you choose between Regular, Fractal, or Turbulence noise. Regular produces a random splotchy pattern, Fractal tends to produce sharper, wispy noise, and Turbulence congeals the noise into a puffy pattern. The Size value affects the size of the splotches that appear in the random pattern. At the bottom of the group, you can add wind to the effect by entering a number in the Wind Strength box. You can also choose the direction from which the wind blows by clicking the Front, Back, Left, Right, Top, or Bottom option button.

Adjusting Fog and Volume Fog Parameters

The Fog Parameters rollout lets you choose between two different fog types, as shown in Figure 14. **Standard fog** adds fog that fills the entire scene. **Layered fog** lets you create effects like fog that collects on the

FIGURE 14
Standard fog and layered fog

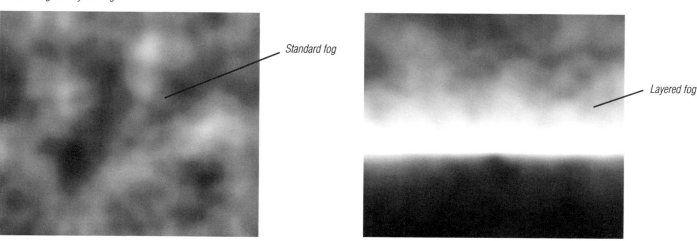

ground, as in a scary graveyard scene. The Fog group also has settings that let you change the Color of the fog or use maps to define the color and opacity of the fog.

If you choose Standard fog, the Standard group of settings becomes available in the Fog Parameters rollout. Here you can adjust how dense the fog is in relation to the distance away from the camera. The Exponential check box increases the density exponentially as the fog gets farther from the camera. Otherwise the fog grows denser in a linear fashion. The Near and Far percentage sets the density of the fog at the near and far ranges of the camera's Environment Range parameter. This setting controls where environment effects begin and end from the camera's point of view.

If you choose Layered fog, then the Layered group becomes available, as shown in Figure 15. This group offers Top and Bottom parameters that enable you to set the location of the top and the bottom of the fog in world units. For example, if you set the bottom to 0 and the top to 100, then the fog exists only between 0 and 100 on the z-axis coordinates. The Falloff option buttons let you determine if the fog dissipates near the Top or the Bottom. Choose None to have no falloff.

If you click the Horizon Noise check box, the fog has a noisy breakup pattern that extends above and below the horizon, the distance of which is based on the angle parameter. A higher angle produces a wider noise area at the horizon, while a lower value thins it out. You also have options for adjusting the Size and Phase of the noise.

The Volume Fog effect can be contained within an atmospheric apparatus gizmo, similar to the Fire effect. Unlike regular Fog, this gives you greater control over exactly where the Volume Fog appears in the scene. It has some basic Fog parameters like the Density and Color of the fog, and also contains standard noise parameters for adding a noisy breakup pattern to the fog.

FIGURE 15
Fog Parameters rollout

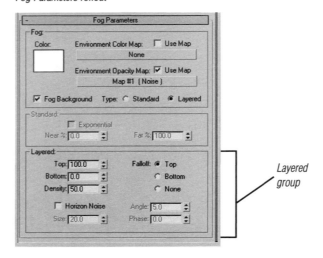

FIGURE 16
Fire Effect Parameters rollout

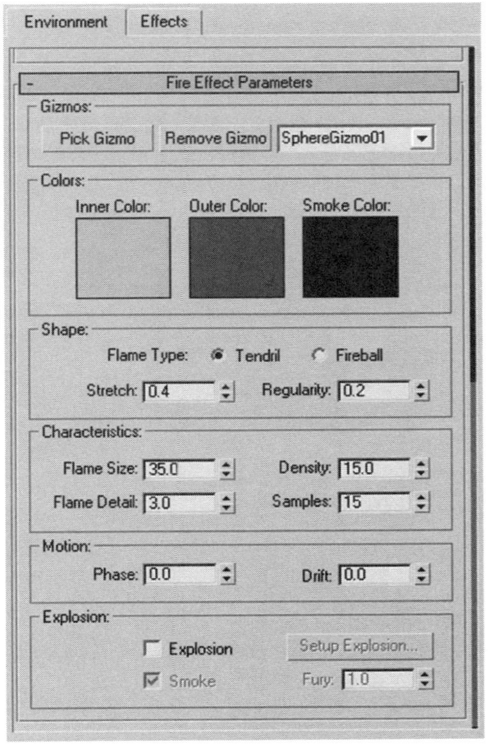

Adjust fire parameters

1. Press **[H]** to open the Select Objects dialog box, then double-click **SphereGizmo01** in the list to select it in the maximized Camera viewport.

2. Click the **Modify tab** (if necessary), click **Fire Effect** in the list on the Atmospheres & Effects rollout, then click the **Setup button** below the list to open the Environment and Effects dialog box.

3. Pan down in the dialog box to the Fire Effect Parameters rollout, then in the Shape group, click the **Tendril option button** and change the Stretch value to **0.4**, as shown in Figure 16.

   Bringing the stretch setting down to a little below half counteracts the stretching that occurred when you scaled up the height of the apparatus in the previous lesson.

4. In the Characteristics group, change the Flame Size to **2** and the Density to **50**, press **[Esc]** to exit the fire parameters, then render the scene.

   The flames look a lot better now because you brought the flame size down and increased the density.

   (continued)

Lesson 2 Adjust Atmospheric Effect Parameters

DISCREET 3D STUDIO MAX 10-17

6. Minimize the **rendered scene window**, switch to the **Front viewport**, click the **Select and Move tool**, press and hold **[Shift]**, drag a copy of the apparatus over to the torch on the right side of the scene, click the **Copy option button** in the Clone Options dialog box (if necessary), then click **OK**.

7. Press **[C]** to switch to the **Camera viewport**, then render the scene.

   You now have two torches on each side of the room, as shown in Figure 17. The ambient orange lighting is coming from an omni light at the top of each torch.

8. Minimize the **rendered scene window**, then save the file.

You adjusted the parameters of the flame, then copied the apparatus to a second location.

FIGURE 17
Rendered camera view

FIGURE 18
Rendered scene with volume light and fire effects

Adjust volume light parameters

1. In the Atmosphere rollout in the Environment and Effects dialog box, select **Volume Light** in the Effects list.
2. Pan down to the Volume Light Parameters rollout, then change the Density parameter in the Volume group to **3**.
3. In the Noise group, select the **Noise On check box**, then change the Amount to **0.4** and the Size to **1**.
4. Render the Camera viewport.

   The light beams have less density, and the new Noise settings produce a dust-like effect in the light beams, as shown in Figure 18.
5. Minimize the **rendered scene window**, then save the scene.

You adjusted the parameters of a Volume Light effect to change its appearance, then rendered the scene.

Add layered fog and adjust its parameters

1. Press **[8]** to open the Environment and Effects dialog box (if necessary), then click the **Add button** in the Atmosphere rollout.

2. Double-click **Fog** in the list in the Add Atmospheric Effect dialog box.

3. Pan down the dialog box to the Fog Parameters rollout, then in the Fog group, deselect the **Fog Background check box** and click the **Layered option button** to the right of Type.

   It's not necessary to add fog to the background; if you did you would see a horizon of fog outside, through the windows.

4. In the Layered group in the Fog Parameters rollout, set the Top parameter to **20** and the Density to **10**, then click the **Top option button** to the right of Falloff.

   The fog will fall off and end at a height of 20 units of World Space, so the fog only appears on the ground. . . . Spooky!

5. In the Fog group, click the **Environment Opacity Map map button** to open the Material/Map browser, then double-click **Noise**.

   As shown in Figure 19, a Noise map is added to break up the opacity of the fog.

   (continued)

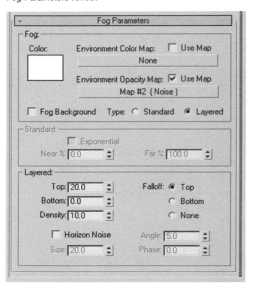

FIGURE 19
Fog Parameters rollout

FIGURE 20
Rendered scene with layered fog

6. Open the **Material Editor**, then click and drag the **Noise map** from the Environment Opacity Map button to a free sample slot in the **Material Editor**.

7. Click the **Instance option button** (if necessary) in the Instance [Copy] Map dialog box, then click **OK**.

   An instance of the Environment Opacity map is placed in the Material Editor. You can now use the Material Editor to edit the default settings of the Noise map, and the changes to its settings will be reflected in the Environment Opacity map.

8. In the Noise Parameters rollout on the Material Editor, click the **Fractal option button**, then change the Size to **10**.

   The Fractal type produced a wispier effect in the fog.

9. Render the Camera viewport.

   As shown in Figure 20, a layer of fog now covers the floor. The opacity is defined by a Noise map, which creates little pockets of fog.

10. Close the rendered scene window, then save the file.

You used the Environment and Effects dialog box to add a layered fog effect, added a Noise map to the opacity of the effect, then rendered the scene.

LESSON 3

UNDERSTAND RENDERING EFFECTS

What You'll Do

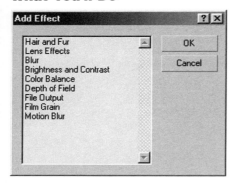

▶ In this lesson, you will learn what rendering effects are, and which ones are available in 3ds Max. You will find out how to add rendering effects to a scene, and how to preview rendering effects in the rendered scene window as you add and adjust the effects.

What Are Rendering Effects?
3ds Max groups together several effects under the single title of rendering effects. **Rendering effects** are effects that you can apply to a scene after it is rendered to process the look of the output image in various ways. The rendering effects that 3ds Max currently offers are as follows:

- **Lens Effects** let you create lensflare-like effects that simulate the distortions of light that can occur through a camera lens. There are six lens effects: Glow, Ring, Ray, Auto secondary, Manual secondary, and Star and Streak.
- **Depth of Field** simulates the depth-of-field effect that can occur in real-world cameras, wherein objects that lie on the focal plane remain in focus while the foreground and background elements are blurred. The effect separates the image into three zones: foreground, focal plane, and background.
- **Motion Blur** reproduces the blurring effect that occurs from fast-moving objects caught on camera. The motion blur effect applies blur to moving objects in a rendered scene, or to the entire rendered frame if the camera itself is a fast moving object.
- **Blur** lets you blur an image using one of three different methods: Uniform, Directional, or Radial. Uniform applies an even blur to the entire image. Directional gives you controls for blurring in a certain direction. Radial lets you define a center point from which the blurring occurs.
- **Hair and Fur** is a plug-in new to 3ds Max 8 that generates hair on mesh or spline objects. This rendering effect works in combination with the Hair and Fur modifier to give you an extensive set of tools that let you grow, style, and design realistic hair effects.

- **Brightness and Contrast** gives you controls for adjusting the brightness and contrast of a rendered image. This feature is a lot like that found in image-manipulation software like Adobe Photoshop.
- **Color Balance** lets you adjust the overall color tint of an image by giving you independent control over the amount of red, green, and blue in the rendered image.
- **File Output**, when added to an object's Render Effects stack in the Effects panel, outputs a rendered image file that contains all of the effects up to that point in the stack.
- **Film Grain** applies a fine grain to the rendered image to reproduce the look of film.

In the following lessons, you'll explore lens effects, depth-of-field effects, blur and motion blur effects, and hair and fur effects. The remaining effects from the list above (with the exception of File Output) tend to be effects that computer graphics artists might typically apply to their rendered images using third-party image-manipulation software. However, you might want to explore these other effects on your own after you have completed this chapter.

Adding a Rendering Effect

You can add a rendering effect to any scene using the Effects panel in the Environment and Effects dialog box. To open the Environment and Effects dialog box with the Effects panel showing, click Rendering on the menu bar, then click Effects. Next, simply click the Add button at the top of the Effects rollout, click the rendering effect you would like to add in the Add Effect dialog box (as shown in Figure 21), and then click OK. After you do this, the effect appears in the Effects list on the Effects panel. The Effects list shows you every effect that has been

FIGURE 21
Add Effect dialog box

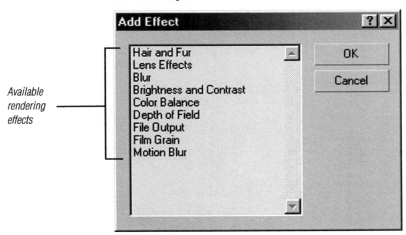

Available rendering effects

Lesson 3 Understand Rendering Effects

DISCREET 3D STUDIO MAX 10-23

applied to the scene, as shown in Figure 22. It is important to note that 3ds Max calculates the effects added to a scene in the order that they appear in this list. In some circumstances this "stacking" order is important. For instance, the Depth of Field effect should always be last, because you want the blurring that it creates to be applied to the other effects in the rendered image.

You can apply multiple types of effects to any scene. You can also apply multiple copies of any specific effect type. This lets you produce an endless number of effects.

For example, you might want to add a lens effect that contains a star effect, and another that creates a streak. Likewise, you might want to create a green glow around one object and a red glow around another object.

QUICKTIP

You can use the Name field in the Effects rollout on the Effects panel to give unique names to every effect that you apply. It's a good idea to take advantage of this, so that you can keep track of how you are using each effect in a scene with lots of effects.

Previewing Effects Interactively

A nice thing about rendering effects is that unlike atmospheric effects, you can work with them interactively in the Render window. For example, if you have a rendered scene that includes a lot of geometry and lighting, you don't have to render the scene again just to see updates you have made to the rendering effect parameters. Changes you make to rendering effect settings can interactively appear in the render window as you make them. This is because 3ds Max calculates rendering effects separately from

FIGURE 22
Effects Panel with effects added

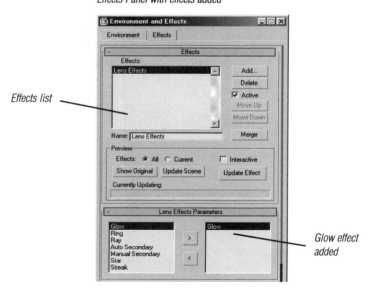

Effects list

Glow effect added

10-24 AUTODESK 3D STUDIO MAX

Effects

the scene data. In fact, when you render a scene that has effects applied to it, the scene is rendered first without the effects, and then the effects appear immediately afterward in a separate pass.

The Effects panel contains a Preview group, shown in Figure 23, that gives you options for managing how and when the render window shows the rendering effects in the Effects list. Make sure the All option button in the Preview group is selected if you want all of the effects to be shown in the rendered scene window. Click the Current option button to preview only the effects highlighted in the Effects list. Select the Interactive check box in the Preview group to have the window display any changes to the effects as soon as you make them. If you don't have this option checked, you can update the render window at any time by clicking the Update Effect button below the Interactive check box. Click the Show Original/Show Effects toggle button to toggle off and on the display of any effects in the render window. You can also update the rendered scene by clicking the Update Scene button. This updates any rendering effects added or removed as well as changes made to the scene being rendered.

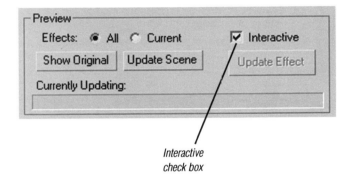

FIGURE 23
Preview group

Interactive check box

Lesson 3 Understand Rendering Effects

DISCREET 3D STUDIO MAX 10-25

LESSON 4

APPLY LENS EFFECTS

What You'll Do

In this lesson, you will learn what lens effects are, how to add them to scenes, how to apply them to lights using the Effects panel, and how to apply them to other objects by using ID numbers common to both the effect and the object or to an object's material.

Understanding Lens Effects

We have all seen the effects of a lens distorting the properties of light, whether it's the fancy lens flares produced by a film camera for a special effect in a movie, or the streaks of light that emanate from a traffic signal, as seen through your car windshield on a rainy day. Our eyes are lenses subject to this phenomenon of light, and we are used to seeing these kinds of effects. Adding these distortions to your 3D scenes can add a sense of realism or create a visually stunning effect.

After you have added the Lens Effect effect to the Effects list in the Environment and Effects dialog box, two rollouts appear below the Preview group on the Effects panel, the Lens Effect Parameters rollout and the Lens Effects Globals rollout. You need to choose from among seven lens effect elements, or types of lens effect, available in the Lens Effects Parameters rollout, to actually create a lens effect in the scene. As shown in Figure 24, the **Glow** lens effect element produces a glowing aura that surrounds the entire object to which the element is applied. This effect is useful in many situations, especially for creating the halo around light bulbs that appear on camera. **Ring** forms a ring of light around a center point. **Ray** causes thin rays of light to radiate outward from a center point. **Star** produces beams of light that emanate from a center point in a star pattern; and **Streak** creates a streaked line of light across the light source. **Auto Secondary Flares** and **Manual Secondary Flares** are ring-shaped lens flares, like those typically produced by shooting into a bright light source. To apply a lens effect element, click the name of the element on the left side of the Lens Effects Parameters rollout, and then click the right arrow button to move the effect or effects to the right side of the rollout.

FIGURE 24
Lens effects

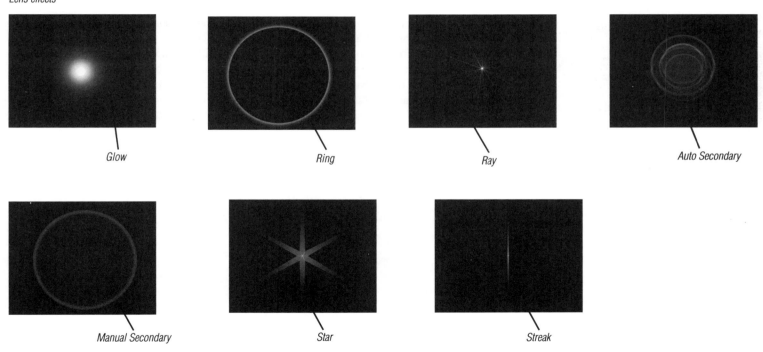

The settings in the Lens Effects Globals rollout, shown in Figure 25, affect all of the elements applied to any given lens effect. For instance, if you have a lens effect that contains a Glow element and a Star element and you adjust the Size parameter in the Global rollout, it affects the size of both the Glow and the Star. However, if you adjust the Size parameter in the Glow Element rollout, it affects only the size of the Glow effect.

When an element is selected on the right side of the Lens Effect Parameters rollout, a parameters rollout specific to the element (for example, Glow Element rollout, Ring Element rollout, etc.) appears below the Lens Effects Globals rollout. If more than one element is selected in the list, the rollout for the element at the top of the stack of selected elements appears. In an element's rollout, you can adjust a variety of parameters. For example, the Glow Element rollout has two groups: Parameters and Options. The Parameters group has many settings that affect the way the element looks. You can also do things like rename the element or adjust the size and intensity of the effect. You also have swatches that let you set the inner and outer colors of the glow, or apply maps that further manipulate the colors. As another example, the Star Element rollout lets you adjust settings like the Size and Intensity of the overall element, or the Width and Taper of the individual beams. The Quantity parameter determines the number of individual beams that make up the star effect, and the Sharp parameter sets the overall sharpness of the beams. Higher Sharp values produce sharper beams, while lower values round them off. The Angle parameter rotates the star's beams around the star's center point, and this can be animated to produce a rotating star effect.

Applying Lens Effect Elements to Objects

A lens effect element or elements can be easily applied to any light in a scene by selecting the element(s) on the right side of the Lens Effects Parameters rollout, clicking the Pick Light button in the Lens Effects Globals rollout of the Effects panel,

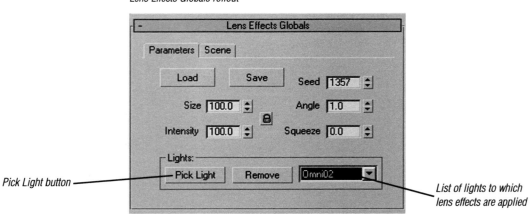

FIGURE 25
Lens Effects Globals rollout

Pick Light button

List of lights to which lens effects are applied

and then clicking a light in the scene. To apply the element to another light, click the Pick Light button again, then click another light in the scene. Any lights to which the effects are applied appear in the list box to the right of the Remove button. Select a light in the list box, and then click the Remove button to remove the element from the light.

If you want to apply a lens effect element to an object other than a light, you must use an Object ID number. You assign an Object ID number in an object's Properties panel. Right-click the object, click Properties on the Transform quadrant of the Quad menu to open the Properties dialog box, then assign a number to the Object ID field, as shown in Figure 26. The number can be any number that you choose. It is simply an identifier so that when you apply a lens effect to the scene with that same Object ID, all objects that have that Object ID number receive the effect.

Alternatively, you can use a Material ID to assign a lens effect to a material. When the material is applied to an object, the object receives the effect applied to the material.

To assign a Material ID to a material, click and hold the Material effects channel button in the Material Editor. A panel of numbers appears, as shown in Figure 27. Point to the number that you want to assign, and then release the mouse button. To set up the lens effect to operate on a certain Object ID or Material ID, use the effect's Options panel, as shown in Figure 28. Click the Object ID or Material ID check box to activate the ID, and then change the number in the Object ID or Material ID box to assign the number you want.

FIGURE 26
Object ID number in Properties panel

FIGURE 27
Material Editor toolbar

FIGURE 28
Lens Effect Element Options panel

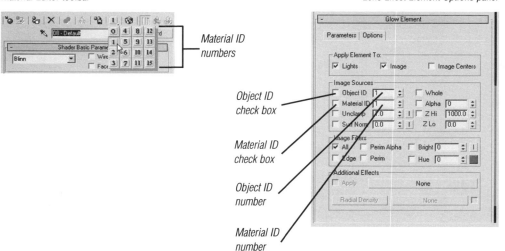

Add a Glow effect

1. Open **torchscene** (if necessary), click **Rendering** on the menu bar, then click **Effects**.

   The Environment and Effects dialog box opens with the Effects panel in front.

2. Click the **Add button** at the top of the Effects rollout, then double-click **Lens Effects** in the Add Effects dialog box.

   Lens Effects appears in the Effects list in the Effects rollout.

3. Click **Glow** at the top of the list on the left side of the Lens Effects Parameters rollout, then click the **right arrow button** >.

   The Glow effect appears in the list on the right, as shown in Figure 29. The effect has been added to the scene, but you still need to designate what you want to glow.

4. In the Glow Element rollout, click the **Options tab**, then in the Image Sources group, click the **Object ID check box** to select it, then make sure the Object ID is set to **1**.

   This is the same Object ID as the Object ID of the Chalice object.

5. Press **[H]** to open the Select Objects dialog box, then double-click **chalice** to select it.

6. Right-click the **chalice** in any viewport, then click **Properties** in the Transform quadrant of the Quad menu.

(continued)

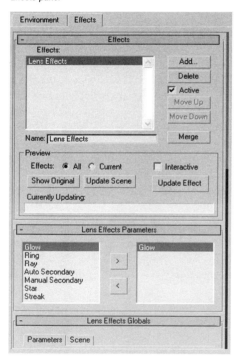

FIGURE 29
Effects panel

FIGURE 30
Rendered scene with glowing chalice

7. In the G-Buffer group in the lower-right of the Object Properties dialog box, set the Object ID to **1** (if necessary), then click **OK**.

   An Object ID of 1 is assigned to the chalice object. Because both the effect and the object share an Object ID of 1, the object will have the glow effect.

8. Press **[C]** to switch to the **Camera viewport** (if necessary), then render the scene.

   As soon as the scene is finished rendering, the Glow effect appears, as shown in Figure 30. It's hard to notice that the effect is actually there, because the glow size is too large and the effect is spread out over a larger area.

9. Minimize the **rendered scene window**, then save the file.

You added the Lens Effect effect to a scene, applied the Glow element, confirmed the element's Object ID, selected an object in the scene and confirmed it had the same Object ID as the Glow element, then rendered the scene to see the element applied to the object.

Preview effects interactively

1. In the Preview group in the Effects rollout on the Effects panel, click the **Interactive check box** to select it.

2. Pan down to the Glow Element rollout, click the **Parameters tab**, then change the Size parameter to **1**.

(continued)

In the render window, the size of the glow is reduced to reflect the change, and the Title bar now says "Effects Preview."

3. In the Glow Element rollout, change the Intensity setting to **60**.

   Again, the render window is updated interactively to show the more subtle effect, as shown in Figure 31.

4. In the Radial Color group in the Glow Element rollout, click the white color swatch, then use the color selector to choose a bright yellow color.

5. In the Name field at the top of the Glow Element rollout, change the name from Glow to **GlowChalice**, as shown in Figure 32.

   It's a good idea to identify specific effects by name, so you can differentiate between them if you add more glow effects to other objects in the scene later.

6. Save the file.

You changed the parameters of the Glow element, previewed the changes interactively in the rendered scene window, then changed the name of the element.

Add a Star effect

1. In the Lens Effects Parameters rollout, double-click **Star** to add the effect to the scene.

   The Star effect appears in the list on the right.

(continued)

FIGURE 31
Rendered scene with updated glow

FIGURE 32
Glow Element rollout

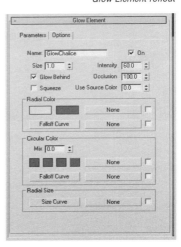

10-32 AUTODESK 3D STUDIO MAX

Effects

FIGURE 33
Rendered scene with star effect

2. In the Lights group in the Lens Effects Globals rollout, click the **Pick Light button** to select it.

3. Press **[H]** to open the Select Objects dialog box, then double-click **Omni02**.

   The render window is updated, showing the Star effect applied to an omni light behind the chalice.

4. Pan down to the Parameters panel in the Star Element rollout, then change the Size to **50**, the Width to **1**, the Qty to **8**, and the Intensity to **10**.

   The Star effect is updated in the rendered scene window, and now it should look like Figure 33.

5. Name the effect **StarChalice**.

6. Pan up to the Preview group in the Effects rollout, then click the **Show Original button**.

   The glow and the star disappear in the rendered scene window to show the original scene without the effects.

7. Click the **Show Effects button** to make the effects reappear, save the file, then reset 3ds Max.

You added the Star effect, applied it to the light behind the chalice, and changed its parameters, previewing the changes in the rendered scene window as they were made. You also renamed the effect, then used the options in the Preview group to see the image with and without the Glow and Star effects.

LESSON 5

APPLY DEPTH-OF-FIELD AND
BLUR EFFECTS

What You'll Do

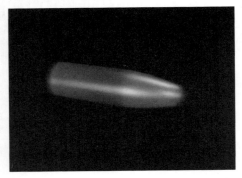

▶ *In this lesson, you will learn what multi-pass rendering effects are and the two multi-pass rendering effects you can use to add realism to a scene. You will also explore several methods for blurring a scene.*

Understanding Multi-Pass Rendering

There are two kinds of rendering effects that are actually applied from the Parameters rollout of a camera rather than the Environment and Effects dialog box. These effects are known as **multi-pass effects**: visual effects created by rendering a scene multiple times, moving the camera's position a bit each time to create a level of blurriness in the scene that matches what you might find in a real-world photograph. In other words, with each rendering pass, the camera is offset a bit in pre-designated areas of the scene.

The two effects that can be generated using multi-pass rendering are **depth-of-field**, in which the main subject of a scene is clearly in focus and the foreground and background are blurred, and **motion blur**, in which the movement of something in an animated scene, such as wings on a bird, is blurred to imply very fast motion. An example of each of these effects is shown in Figure 34.

QUICKTIP

Because these effects require multiple rendering passes, rendering time is dramatically longer than usual when creating them. You need to have a lot of time on your hands if you plan to render an animation with either multi-pass effect.

Generating Depth-of-Field Effects

Multi-pass effects can be generated using either a free or target camera. For a free camera, the focal point of the scene is the center of the plane at the end of its FOV cone. For a target camera, the focal point is the target object. Because you can control the target object as a separate object and move it easily, it's best to use a target camera for depth-of-field effects so that you have as much control as possible over the focal point of the scene.

In a scene for which you plan to use depth-of-field multi-pass rendering, make sure that you have the target object located at the place in the scene you want as the scene's focal point. To activate multi-pass rendering for a camera, select the camera, and then click the Enable check box in the Multi-Pass Effects group on the Parameters rollout for the camera. When this check box is selected, the Preview button next to it becomes active. Click the Preview box to see a preview of the rendered scene in the viewport. Under the check box and Preview button, click the Effect drop-down list arrow to change the effect desired from Depth of Field to Motion Blur, or vice versa; the default is Depth of Field. Under the Effect list box is a Render Effects per Pass check box. Select this check box if you want the rendering effects to be shown at each pass when the scene is rendered, rather than at the end of all of the passes. It is most efficient to keep this option off, because if chosen, rendering time takes even longer.

FIGURE 34
Multi-pass rendering effects

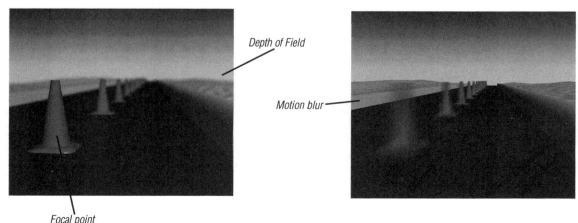

Lesson 5   Apply Depth-of-Field and Blur Effects

QUICKTIP

There is also a Depth-of-Field (mental ray renderer) option in the Effect drop-down list, which is beyond the scope of this lesson.

After you have enabled depth-of-field multi-pass effects, you can adjust the parameters for the depth-of-field effect in the Depth of Field Parameters rollout beneath the Parameters rollout. One of the most important things you can do is adjust the number of rendering passes by changing the number in the Total Passes box in the Sampling group. Note that rendering time increases with each additional pass. The Sample Radius is the radius of the circular shift of the camera during rendering that creates the blurring effect in the areas outside the focal point. Increase the number in the Sample Radius box to increase the blurriness and create a greater contrast in clarity between the focal point and its surroundings. The Sample Bias controls whether the blurring is weighted away from or close to the sample radius. If the Sample Bias is greater than the default of .5, the blur is closer to the sample radius and smoother in appearance, increasing the depth-of-field effect; at less than the default of .5, the blur is closer to the center of the camera's shift and is uneven.

As you adjust the depth-of-field parameters, with the Camera viewport active, click the Preview button in the Multi-Pass Effects group in the Parameters rollout to see a preview of the effect in the viewport. When you are satisfied with the result of the effect in the scene, render the scene. If you want to change the focal point of the scene, simply move the camera's target object and re-render (or re-preview) the scene. See Figure 35 for an example of the same scene previewed with two different focal points.

FIGURE 35
Previewed scene with two different focal points

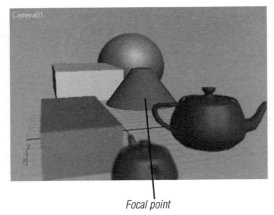

Focal point

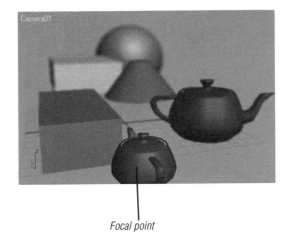

Focal point

Effects

Understanding Motion Blur

In a real-world camera, an image is produced by exposing a photo-sensitive surface (such as film) to light. If either the subject or the camera moves during that brief period of exposure, the image becomes blurred. This is a normal occurrence with photography and our eyes have become so accustomed to seeing motion blur that most people don't even notice it until it's missing. In 3ds Max, there are several methods you can use to add motion blur to your scenes. Motion blur created with multi-pass rendering causes anything that has changed position over time in an animation to appear blurry. In addition to motion blur created with multi-pass rendering, there are two other kinds of motion blur available.

Object motion blur works by rendering multiple copies of an object in each frame. The result is that the object appears to be blurry. Object motion blur gets calculated as the scanline renderer is rendering the scene. Object motion blur takes camera movement into account, but it does not blur environment background maps, so this means it's not really good for simulating the motion blur that would occur due to camera movement, if you are using a background map.

Image motion blur applies a smear effect to objects that are moving across the screen in an animation. The effect gets applied after the scanline renderer has rendered the scene, in the same manner as would a rendering effect. With Image motion blur you can blur environment background maps, so its use is preferable for creating moving camera effects.

Generating Motion Blur Effects

Generating motion blur with multi-pass rendering looks very nice, and you can get a preview of the blur in the viewport before rendering. But, as mentioned earlier, the downside is that you are looking at lengthy render times due to the many passes that the renderer must take. To add motion blur using multi-pass rendering, you need a camera in the scene. As you do with Depth of Field, click the Enable check box in the Multi-Pass Effects group of the camera's Parameters rollout. Once enabled, you can preview the effect in the camera viewport by clicking the Preview button. The scene will shift slightly as it does a quick calculation of the blur, and then will show you the preview. You could then further manipulate the motion blur in the Motion Blur Parameters rollout.

The second option for adding motion blur to an object is a two-step process in which you enable motion blur in the Object Properties dialog box for the objects that you want to blur, and then you enable it in the Render Scene dialog box before rendering. The Motion Blur group for an object is in the bottom-right corner of the Object Properties dialog box, as shown in Figure 36. In this group, make sure that the Enabled check box is selected, and then click the Image option button to enable Image motion blur for the object, or click the Object option button to enable Object motion blur for the object.

After you have set the motion blur for an object, open the Render Scene dialog box, click the Renderer tab to open the Renderer panel, and make sure that the Apply check box is selected in either the Object Motion Blur group or the Image Motion Blur group.

The Object Motion Blur group, as shown in Figure 37, gives you several options. The Duration (frames) parameter acts like a "virtual camera shutter." A value of 1.0 is like having the shutter open for the duration between one frame and the next. To increase the smearing effect, you could set a higher value, so the virtual shutter is, in effect, open for a longer duration. The Duration Subdivisions parameter determines how many copies of the object are made within the duration, as shown in Figure 38. The Samples parameter determines how many of the duration subdivisions are actually

FIGURE 36
Motion Blur group in Object Properties dialog box

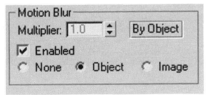

FIGURE 37
Object Motion Blur group in Render Scene dialog box

FIGURE 38
Animated sphere with object motion blur

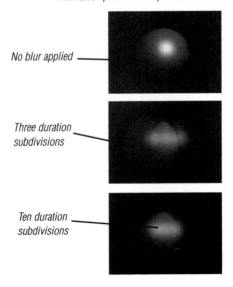

sampled. If this value is lower than the Duration Subdivisions value, the result is a grainy effect, because only some of the copies are sampled. If the values equal each other, the effect does not have a grain.

The Image Motion Blur group, as shown in Figure 39, has slightly different parameters. The effect does not use samples or duration subdivisions, so those options are not present.

The Duration setting is similar, though; increasing this value increases the smearing effect. Click the Environment Map check box to apply the blurring to the Environment Map. Click the Transparent check box to enable the effect to blur transparent objects that overlap, such as objects behind glass. Remember, though, that enabling this effect increases render time.

QUICKTIP

Another way that 3ds Max lets you apply image motion blur (but not object motion blur) to a scene is to add it as a rendering effect by adding the Blur effect to the Effects list on the Effects panel in the Environment and Effects dialog box. However, this is not really necessary because you can activate motion blur from the Render Scene dialog box without ever adding it as an effect.

FIGURE 39

Image Motion Blur group in Render Scene dialog box

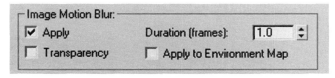

Lesson 5   Apply Depth-of-Field and Blur Effects

DISCREET 3D STUDIO MAX 10-39

Use multi-pass rendering effects

1. Open **MAX10-02.max**, then save it as **pylons**.

   In this scene, a Target Camera has a low angle on a row of pylons that stretch out along a desert highway.

2. Render the Camera viewport.

   The scene has no depth of field. The pylons farther away from the camera appear to be just as in focus as the closest one.

3. Minimize the **rendered scene window**, select the **camera** in the Top viewport, right-click back in the **Camera viewport** to activate it, then click the **Modify tab**.

   The camera's parameters are now available on the Modify panel.

4. In the Multi-Pass Effect group in the Parameters rollout, select the **Enable check box**.

   The Preview button becomes available.

5. Click the **Preview button**.

   The viewport shifts around a little to calculate the effect, then gives you a preview of the depth-of-field blurring in the viewport.

6. Render the Camera viewport again.

   This time, the scene takes 12 separate rendering passes to generate the depth-of-field effect. The focus is crisp near the first pylon, but gets softer for the pylons in the scene farther away from the camera.

   (continued)

FIGURE 40
Depth of Field multi-pass rendering effect

Third pylon in focus

FIGURE 41
Motion Blur multi-pass rendering effect

7. Minimize the **rendered scene window**, select the **camera target** in the Top viewport, then move it back near the third pylon from the camera.

8. Select the **camera** again, then in the Depth of Field Parameters rollout on the Modify panel, change the Sample Radius to **5**.

   This produces a more dramatic blur, increasing the depth-of-field effect.

9. Right-click in the **Camera viewport** to activate it, then render the Camera viewport.

   The scene renders and appears to be in focus near the third pylon, but has a softer focus in front of and behind that area, as shown in Figure 40.

10. Minimize the **rendered scene window**, click the **drop-down list arrow** in the Multi-Pass Effect group in the camera's Parameters rollout, then click **Motion Blur**.

11. Drag the **time slider** to frame **50**, then render the scene.

    The scene renders with the motion blur multi-pass rendering effect, as shown in Figure 41. The camera is in motion at frame 50, so objects that are moving in the frame appear blurry.

12. Close the **rendered scene window**, save the file, then reset 3ds Max.

You enabled the Depth of Field multi-pass rendering effect in a scene, rendered the scene, adjusted the target for the focal point of the scene, accentuated the depth-of-field effect by changing the effect's Sample Radius parameter, then rendered the scene again. You also enabled the Motion Blur effect in the scene, then rendered the scene again.

Render Object Motion Blur

1. Open **MAX10-03.max**, then save it as **bullet**.

   This is a scene of a bullet that has been animated to pass through the Perspective viewport over the course of 20 frames.

2. Drag the **time slider** to frame **10**, then render the frame.

   The scene is rendered and the bullet has no motion blur, as shown in Figure 42.

3. Minimize the **rendered scene window**, select the **bullet**, open its Object Properties dialog box, click the **Enabled check box** in the Motion Blur group to select it, click the **Object option button** to select it, then click **OK**.

4. Open the Render Scene dialog box (if necessary), then click the **Renderer tab**.

   (continued)

FIGURE 42
Bullet with no blur

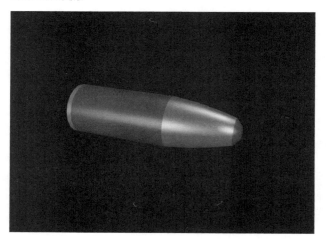

FIGURE 43
Bullet with object motion blur

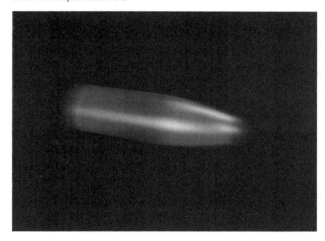

5. In the Object Motion Blur group, select the **Apply check box** (if necessary), then click the **Render button**.

   The scene is rendered with the default Object Motion Blur settings applied, as shown in Figure 43.

6. Minimize the **rendered scene window**, change the Duration (frames) parameter in the Object Motion Blur group to **1**, then click the **Render button** again.

   Now that you have increased the duration, the effect is more spread out, and thus blurrier.

7. Minimize the **rendered scene window**, render frames 5 to 15 of the active time segment to an AVI file called **bullet.avi**, then view the AVI file.

   The bullet passes the camera pretty quickly, but the motion blur adds a stronger sense of realism to the scene.

8. Close the AVI file, then save the scene.

You enabled Object Motion Blur in the Object Properties dialog box for the bullet, changed the parameters for the blur, then rendered the blurred scene to an AVI file and viewed it.

Rendering Image Motion Blur

1. In bullet.max, select the **bullet**, then open the Object Properties dialog box.

2. In the Motion Blur group, click the **Image option button** to select it.

   Notice that the Multiplier field in the Motion Blur group becomes active. This setting can be increased if you want to exaggerate the blurring effect.

3. Click **OK** to close the Object Properties dialog box, open the Render Scene dialog box, click the **Single option button** in the Time Output group at the top of the Common panel, then click the **Save File check box** in the Render Output group to clear it (if necessary).

4. Click the **Renderer tab**, in the Image Motion Blur group, make sure the **Apply check box** is selected, then click the **Render button**.

   The scene is rendered first, then two separate passes take place before you see the blur results, as shown in Figure 44. The multiple passes are blended, producing a smoother motion blur than the object motion blur.

(continued)

FIGURE 44
Bullet with image motion blur

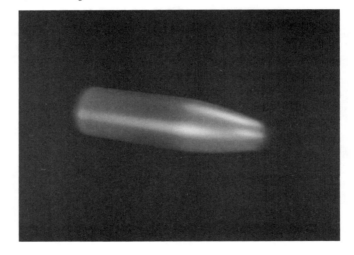

FIGURE 45

Bullet with increased blur duration

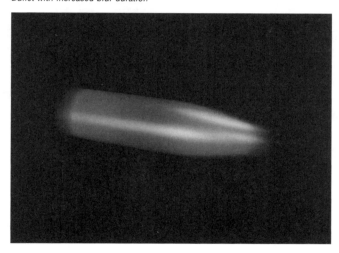

5. Minimize the **rendered scene window**, change the Duration (frames) parameter in the Image Motion Blur group to **1**, then click the **Render button** again.

   Again, increasing the duration spreads out the effect, producing an elongated blur, as shown in Figure 45.

6. Close the rendered scene window, save the file, then reset 3ds Max.

You switched an object from Object Motion blur to Image Motion Blur, rendered the scene, changed the Duration of the blur, then rendered the scene again.

LESSON 6

APPLY HAIR
AND FUR

What You'll Do

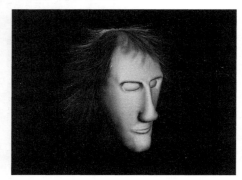

▶ *In this lesson, you will learn how to use the Hair and Fur modifier to create hair for a character head, and you will learn how to adjust the initial parameters of hair after it has been created. You will also examine the Style dialog box and learn the different tools you can use to style and cut the hair on an object.*

Creating Hair and Fur

With the new hair and fur feature of 3ds Max, you can generate realistic-looking hair and fur effects and use a host of parameters and tools to control how the hair looks and behaves. You can set up the parameters to achieve an extremely wide variety of hair and fur styles, but you can also use the effect to create things such as grass or other strand-based items.

At the core of the hair and fur system is the Hair and Fur modifier, which you apply to a mesh or spline object to grow hair on it. The modifier has many parameters that let you set up how the hair initially looks. To add hair to a model, select the model, and then apply the Hair and Fur modifier to the model from the modifier list. The Hair and Fur modifier appears in the object's modifier stack, as shown in Figure 46, with nine accompanying rollouts on the Modify panel full of parameters for manipulating the hair and fur. When the modifier is applied, red guide hairs appear all over the object, as shown in Figure 47. **Guide hairs** are how you manipulate bunches of hair; each acts as a control for a cluster of hair. To save display memory, only guide hairs appear in the viewport as you work with hair. When the scene is rendered, the rest of the hair shows up in the rendered scene.

To make hair appear only on a portion of the model, you can select objects at the Face, Polygon, or Element subobject level in the Hair and Fur modifier. To do this, expand the modifier in the modifier stack, and select one of the subobjects: click the Face, Polygon, or Element button in the Selection rollout on the Modify panel; or press [1] to enter Face mode, [2] to enter Polygon mode, or [3] to enter Element mode. Next, select the subobjects on the model on which you want the hair to appear. After you have done this, click the Update Selection button in the Selection rollout to update the distribution of hair. In Figure 48, guide hairs appear only on the selected subobjects.

FIGURE 46
Hair and Fur modifier applied

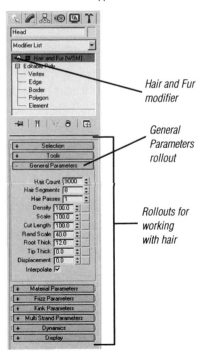

FIGURE 47
Guide hairs on head model

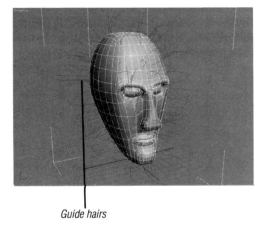

FIGURE 48
Hair distribution after updating selection

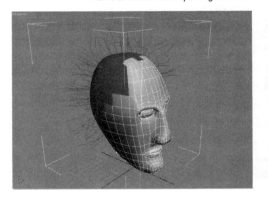

Adjusting Hair Parameters

To control the initial look of the hair created by applying the Hair and Fur modifier, you can adjust the parameters in the General Parameters rollout for the modifier on the Modify panel, as shown in Figure 46. Hair Count sets the number of hairs that are rendered. The maximum setting is 999999. The Hair Segments value determines how many segments and vertices each hair has. These segments are just like spline or primitive segments; the more you have, the more natural will the curves in the hair look. More vertices in the guide hairs also give you more opportunities for selecting and moving the hairs. Like with all modeling, you want to strike a balance between how many segments you need to make the hair look good without wasting geometry.

Increasing the Hair Passes value creates a more feathered, transparent quality, but also increases the render time. The Density setting acts as a percentage multiplier on the Hair Count. This setting has a map button that lets you control the density of hair based on the grayscale values of a map. Brighter areas of a map generally have more hair density and darker areas have less density.

The Scale parameter is a percentage multiplier for the length of the hair. Setting this value to 50, for example, decreases the current length of the hairs by 50 percent. This parameter is also mappable, with the brightest areas on an assigned map having a value of 100 percent scale, and the darkest areas having a scale factor of 0 percent. Cut Length is a percentage multiplier for the Scale value; you can also apply a map to this parameter. Rand Scale adds a random scaling factor to the hairs. A setting of 50 scales down 50 percent of the hairs randomly. A setting of 0 produces no random scaling.

> **QUICK**TIP
> To lengthen, shorten, or cut a selected group of hairs rather than all the hairs on the object, use the styling tools explained in the next section.

Root Thick adusts the thickness of hair at the root. Tip Thick adjusts the thickness of hair at the tip. The Displacement parameter affects the distance of the hair root from the surface of the object, making the hair seem to float above the surface.

Click the Interpolate check box to spread the hairs evenly among the guide hairs. When Interpolate is off, the modifier generates only one hair per triangular face in the mesh.

You can also use the Material Parameters rollout, under the General Parameters rollout on the Modify panel for the Hair and Fur modifier, to specify the coloring and material qualities of the hair. You can change the Tip Color or Root Color of the hair by changing the color in its color swatch or applying a map to the color by clicking the map button next to the swatch. When you define different colors for the hair at the tip and the root, the colors blend into each other across the hair. The Hue Variation value applies a variation percentage to the colors. With the default value of 30, the hair appears to have a natural variation in color. With a value of 0, the hair has no variation in color, and a value of 100 produces the highest amount of variation. The Value Variation parameter adjusts the variation of the hair brightness, also on a percentage basis. The Mutant Color swatch lets you define a color that appears randomly throughout the hairs. To adjust the amount of mutant hairs that appear with the hair, increase or decrease the Mutant % parameter.

Styling Hair

The Style dialog box is really more than a dialog box—it is a separate interface you can use to style guide hairs interactively, using the mouse. To access the Style dialog box, select the Hair and Fur modifier, open the Tools rollout on the Modify panel, as shown in Figure 49, and then click the Style Hair button. The interface opens, as shown in Figure 50, showing you the object with the

FIGURE 49
Tools rollout

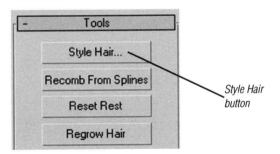

FIGURE 50
Style dialog box

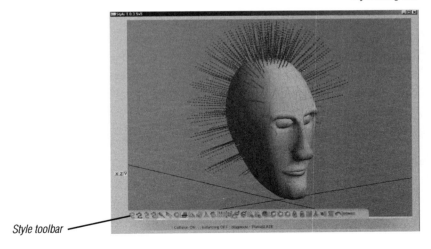

guide hairs in place. The Style toolbar, as shown in Figure 51, appears at the bottom of the screen. In this interface, you usually work in one of three different modes: Select mode, Brush mode, or Drag mode.

Select mode lets you select the hairs that you want to manipulate using a circular selection region. To enter Select mode, press [Esc] to exit whatever mode in which you are currently located, and then click and drag a circular region in the window over the hairs you want to affect. To select hairs as you drag, hold down [Ctrl]; to deselect hairs as you drag, hold down [Alt].

When you are in Select mode, one of four selection modes is in effect: Select by hair ends lets you manipulate the hair by grabbing only the end vertices of the selected strands; Select the whole strand selects every vertex in the hair; Select any hair vertex lets you choose specific vertices to select and work on; and Select any hair strand by its root selects only the vertices at the scalp. The selection mode determines how the hairs respond to the Brush and Drag tools. A hair whose whole strand is selected responds differently when brushed than a hair that has just its tip selected. To enter one of the selection modes, click the Select by hair ends button, the Select the whole strand button, the Select any hair vertex button, or the Select any hair strand by its root button. Try experimenting with each mode combination to see how the hairs react.

When you open the Style dialog box, by default Brush mode is in effect. **Brush mode** lets you drag the guide hairs to style them, the same way you might brush hair in the real world. To enter Brush mode, click the Brush mode button on the Style toolbar. If no hairs are selected, brushing the hair affects any hairs under the brush. To affect only a certain set of hairs, use one of the selection modes; in Figure 52, the brushed hairs are selected by whole strand. Next, size the brush by pressing and holding [B] and dragging (without clicking) in the viewport. As you drag the mouse up and down, the brush increases and decreases in size. Release [B] when you are happy with

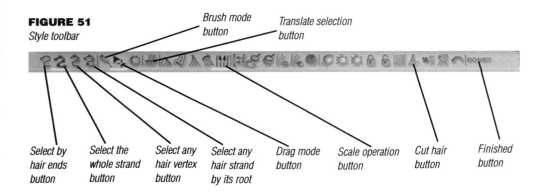

FIGURE 51
Style toolbar

Select by hair ends button | Select the whole strand button | Select any hair vertex button | Select any hair strand by its root | Brush mode button | Drag mode button | Translate selection button | Scale operation button | Cut hair button | Finished button

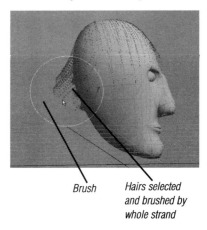

FIGURE 52
Brushing hairs selected by whole strand

Brush | Hairs selected and brushed by whole strand

10-50 AUTODESK 3D STUDIO MAX   *Effects*

the size. **Drag mode** lets you drag in the view to affect all of the currently selected hairs at once. To enter Drag mode, click the Drag mode button on the Style toolbar.

Drag mode simply drags the hairs (and all their vertices) in the direction you drag, while Brush mode tries to simulate the effect you would achieve with a real brush. When you are in Brush or Drag mode, you can also perform several different operations, such as scaling, rotating, or translating the position of the hairs. To **translate** in the Style dialog box means to affect the position of the hairs. To move the hairs as would a real brush, click the Translate button, then simply click and drag the hairs that you want to brush, as shown in Figure 52. To translate hairs in Drag mode, click and drag the hairs to drag them in the direction that you would like them to lay. In Figure 53, the hairs have been selected by whole strand and dragged in a downward direction. To scale hairs in Brush or Drag mode, click the Scale button, and then drag left or right to scale the hairs up or down. To rotate hairs in Brush or Drag mode, click the Rotate button, and drag left or right to rotate the hairs. Once you get the hang of it, it's a very intuitive way to design hairstyles for your characters.

QUICKTIP
When a mode is active, a little yellow line appears under its button on the Style toolbar.

Cutting Hair
Cutting hair is a fairly straightforward procedure in the Style dialog box. Select the hair that you want to cut, enter Brush mode, and then move the brush over the portion of selected hairs that you want to cut. Press [C] and the hairs that are currently under the brush are trimmed— or, rather, scaled, so the shorter strands still have the same amount of vertices. Alternatively, you can press the Cut button on the toolbar.

FIGURE 53
Dragged hair

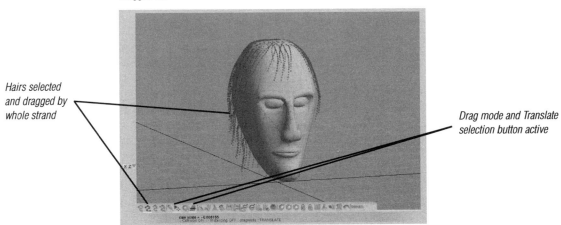

Hairs selected and dragged by whole strand

Drag mode and Translate selection button active

Lesson 6   Apply Hair and Fur

DISCREET 3D STUDIO MAX 10-51

Rendering Hair

When you have finished styling and cutting the hair, click the Done button on the far-right of the Style toolbar. The Style dialog box closes, and the hair guides appear styled in the viewport.

The last step is to render the scene. As soon as you apply the Hair and Fur modifier to an object, a Hair and Fur rendering effect automatically appears in the Effects list of the Environment and Effects dialog box. When the effect is selected in the Environment and Effects dialog box, as shown in Figure 54, you can adjust options that are related to the rendering process in the Hair and Fur rollout beneath the Effects list. The default settings in the rollout produce good results at render time, but one parameter you might want to be aware of is the Hairs drop-down list in the Hair Rendering Options group. The default Hairs setting is buffer, which uses the rendering engine of the hair and fur plug-in to produce the hair as an effect at render time. This option provides the real power behind hair and fur because it allows you to render millions of hairs with minimal memory requirements. The geometry option actually creates geometry for the hair at render time. The MR prim option is for use with the Mental Ray renderer.

Because Hair and Fur is a rendering effect, a rendered scene with hair first appears in the window without the hair, and then after two more passes the hair appears.

QUICKTIP
Hair and fur look much better in a scene that contains lights with the shadows turned on.

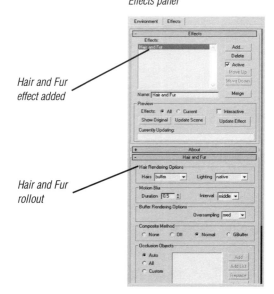

FIGURE 54
Effects panel

Hair and Fur effect added

Hair and Fur rollout

FIGURE 55
Selection Updated

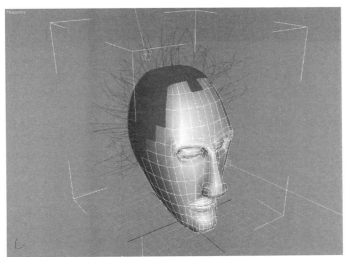

Apply the Hair and Fur modifier

1. Open **MAX10-04.max**, then save it as **hair**.

   This is a scene of a strange-looking head lit by two lights.

2. Select the **head**, click the **Modify tab** , click the **Modifier List list arrow**, then click **Hair and Fur**.

   The Hair and Fur modifier is applied, and in the viewport you see a man with hair all over his face.

3. In the Selection rollout on the Modify panel, click the **Polygon button** ■ to enter Polygon subobject level, then, using a combination of viewports, click and drag to select the areas of the head where you would like the hair to appear.

   TIP Click and drag while pressing [Ctrl] to select polygons, and click and drag while pressing [Alt] to deselect polygons.

4. When you have selected the area that you want, click the **Update Selection button** in the Selection rollout.

   TIP Click the Ignore Backfacing check box in the Selection rollout to ignore the polygons on the other side of the head when selecting, if desired.

   As shown in Figure 55, the guide hairs now appear only on the selected polygons.

   (continued)

5. Render the scene.

   The shadows are calculated first, then the scene appears in the window. After the renderer takes two effects passes, the hair appears on the head, as shown in Figure 56.

6. Minimize the **rendered scene window**, then save the file.

Adjust the hair parameters

1. In the General Parameters rollout on the Modify panel, change the Hair Passes to **2** and the Root Thick setting to **4**.

   Increasing the Hair Passes gives the hair a more realistic softness and transparency, and the hair will be thinner at the root.

2. Just below on the Modify panel, open the Material Parameters rollout, then change the Tip color to a light yellow and the Root Color to a darker yellow.

3. Change the Mutant % parameter to **20**.

   This randomly changes 20 percent of the hairs to the Mutant color of white.

4. Render the scene.

   The hair takes much longer to render this time, but the effect is more impressive, as shown in Figure 57.

5. Minimize the **rendered scene window**, then save the file.

You changed several hair parameters to add some natural variation to the hair color, then rendered the scene to view the effect of the changes.

FIGURE 56
Rendered hair

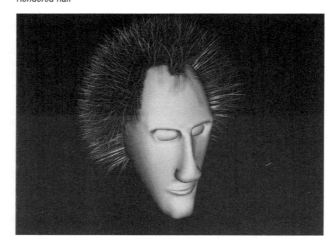

FIGURE 57
Adjusted hair

FIGURE 58
Hairs dragged down

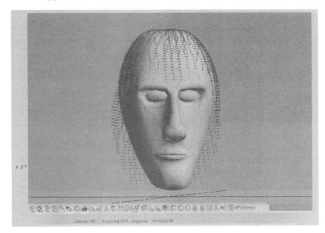

FIGURE 59
Brushed hair

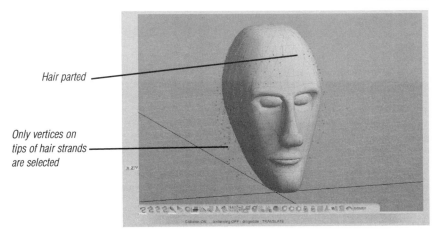

Hair parted

Only vertices on
tips of hair strands
are selected

Style the hair

1. Open the Tools rollout on the Modify panel, then click the **Style Hair button**.

   The Style dialog box opens, and all vertices on all guide hairs are selected.

2. Press and hold **[Alt]** while moving the **middle mouse button** to arc rotate the scene and take a look around the head.

   As you rotate, you get a good view of the hair from all angles.

3. Click the **Drag mode button** to enter Drag mode, then in the viewport, click and drag down to move down all the hairs.

   As you drag the hairs down, they conform more to the head, as shown in Figure 58.

   TIP Maximize the Style dialog box (if necessary) to see screentips for the buttons at the bottom of the screen.

4. Click the **Select by hair ends button** on the Style toolbar.

   You now see only the vertices at the ends of each guide hair.

5. Click the **Brush mode button**, then press **[B]** and drag in the viewport to decrease the size of the brush by about a third.

6. Click and drag over the hair that hangs down in front of the man's forehead, to style it a little. Try parting the hair, as shown in Figure 59.

(continued)

DISCREET 3D STUDIO MAX 10-55

Lesson 6 Apply Hair and Fur

As you click and drag, the hair responds by moving from the tip, as opposed to when the whole strand was selected. It might take some practice to get the hang of it, so go around his head and have some fun.

7. When you're done, press [Esc] to exit Brush mode and enter Select mode.

Scale the hair

1. In Select mode, click the **Select the whole strand button**.

   All the vertices on the guide hairs appear.

2. Arc rotate to a side view, then click and drag up near the base of the man's skull to select only the hair that hangs down at the back of his head.

   TIP Press and drag the middle mouse button to pan the view (if necessary).

3. Click the **Drag mode button**, then click the **Scale selected hair button**.

4. Click and drag in the viewport, dragging to the right to grow the hair, and to the left to shrink the hair.

   Leave the hair looking similar in scale to that shown in Figure 60. As you drag the hairs, they scale up or down. Only the selected hairs are affected.

You selected some hair by whole strand, entered Drag mode, then dragged to scale the selected hair.

FIGURE 60
Scaled hair

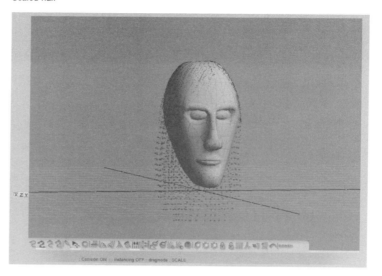

10-56 AUTODESK 3D STUDIO MAX

Effects

FIGURE 61
Cut hair

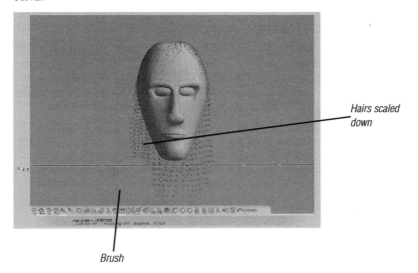

Hairs scaled down

Brush

FIGURE 62
Rendered hair

Cut the hair

1. Arc rotate to a front view of the head.
2. Click the **Brush mode button**, then press **[B]** and drag in the viewport to decrease the size of the brush by about a third.
3. Place the brush over an area that you would like to cut, then press **[C]**.

   The hair gets scaled down so that it seems to have been cut by the brush, as shown in Figure 61.
4. Go around the head, trimming back the hair in different places, then continue to brush and style the hair using the different techniques that you have learned.
5. When you are done, click the **Finished button** on the toolbar to close the Style window, then go back to the regular 3ds Max interface.
6. Render the scene.

   The hair is rendered in the scene, showing the updated style you have given the man, as shown in Figure 62.
7. Close the rendered scene window, save the file, then reset 3ds Max.

In Brush mode, you selected an area of hair to cut, then cut the hair. You continued to cut the hair as desired, exited the Style dialog box, then rendered the scene to see the results.

CHAPTER SUMMARY

In this chapter, you learned what atmospheric effects are, how to add them to scenes, how to limit some effects to a confined area, how to apply effects to individual objects, and how to adjust effect parameters. You learned what rendering effects are, how to add them to a scene, and how to preview rendering effects in the rendered scene window as you add and adjust them. You learned about the different types of lens effects, how to add them to scenes, how to apply them to lights using the Effects panel, and how to apply them to other objects by using a common object or material ID number. In addition, you gained an understanding of multi-pass rendering effects and how they add realism to a scene. You explored several methods for blurring objects in a scene. Lastly, you learned how to use the Hair and Fur modifier to create hair on an object, adjust its initial parameters, and style and cut the hair once created.

What You Have Learned

- How to add an atmospheric effect to a scene using an atmospheric apparatus
- How to add a fire effect, volume light, and fog to a scene
- How to adjust the parameters of atmospheric effects
- How to add lens effects to a scene
- How to preview rendering effects interactively
- How to use the Depth of Field and Motion Blur multi-pass rendering effects
- How to render Image Motion Blur and Object Motion Blur to create blur effects in a scene
- How to create hair using the Hair and Fur modifier and modify its initial parameters
- How to style, scale, and cut hair

Key Terms

Atmospheric apparatus An object that contains an atmospheric effect.

Atmospheric effects Effects in 3ds Max that look like things in the real world that don't have easily defined geometry or solid definition (e.g., fire and fog).

Guide hair Hair on an object that acts as a control for a cluster of hairs.

Image motion blur Effect that creates blurring in an animated scene.

Multi-pass rendering effects Visual effects created by rendering a scene multiple times, moving the camera's position a bit each time to create a level of blurriness in the scene that matches what you might find in a real-world photograph.

Lens effects Rendering effects that simulate the distortions of light that can occur through a camera lens.

Object motion blur Effect that creates blurring of an object in an animated scene by rendering multiple copies of an object in each frame.

Rendering effects Effects that are applied to a scene after it is rendered.

GLOSSARY

A

Absolute mode
In the Transform Type-In boxes, shows the exact position, rotation, or scale of an object along each axis.

Action safe frame
Denotes the area of the screen in which important objects and activity should be enclosed; outside of this frame objects may be cut off when shown on a TV monitor.

Active time segment
The part of the animation that the timeline shows. This is the segment that will be played when you click the Play button

ActiveShade rendering
Uses the default scanline renderer to display a preview quality rendering.

Ambient color
The color of an object where it is in shadow.

Animation
A sequence of still images that changes slightly from one image to the next; when viewed quickly and in order by the human eye, the images depict an object or objects moving or changing.

Anisotropic shader
A shader with elliptical highlights.

Array
A series of objects arranged along one or more axes.

Aspect ratio
The relationship of an image's width to its height.

Assets
The images, objects, textures, maps, and other elements in your scene.

Atmospheric apparatus
Contains an atmospheric effect within a specific volume. An apparatus can be created in one of three shapes: box, sphere, or cylinder.

Atmospheric effects
Enable you to produce effects that look like things in the real word that don't have easily defined geometry or solid definition. There are four atmospheres that you can apply to any scene: Fire, Fog, Volume Fog, and Volume Light.

Axes
Measure points in space. If you are looking at the axis tripod from the front, the x-axis runs from the origination point to the right, the z-axis runs from the origination point upward, and the y-axis runs from the origination point away from you.

Axis tripod
A representation of the x-, y-, and z-axes.

Axonometric view
A flat, two-dimensional (2D) view of your scene, displayed without perspective.

B

Bevel
To first extrude a polygon, and then adjust the size of the outer border of the polygon in order to create an angle.

Bezier controller
Produces a curve on any animated parameter when interpolating the values between two keyframes.

Bind
To attach objects that you want a space warp to affect to the space warp.

Bitmaps
In 3ds Max, maps that are static images (rather than calculated) are known as bitmaps, even though .bmp is only one of many file formats you can use.

Blinn shader
The default shader in 3ds Max, produces soft, round highlights.

Bones
Function as systems in 3ds Max; groups of objects that not only have geometry, but have certain behaviors as well.

Border
A sequence of edges that border a hole in the object.

Bridge
Connecting two subobjects using polygons.

C

Camera
Creates a viewpoint (or point of view) of a scene that is fixed in space.

AUTODESK 3D STUDIO MAX 1

GLOSSARY

Chamfer
Cut off a corner or edge of the object to make it more rounded.

Character rig
A combination of bones and special controls set up to make the process of character animation possible.

Closed spline
A spline whose starting and ending vertices meet to create a shape; for instance, a rectangle is a closed spline.

Compound controller
A controller made up of more than one controller.

Compound object
Produced when two or more objects are combined, with one object as the result.

Constraint
Causes the behavior of an animated object in a scene to depend on the parameters and/or behavior of a second object in the scene.

Context-sensitive Help
Accessed by pressing [F1], gives you information about the task at hand.

Control point
In a deformation curve, moving a control point up or down increases or decreases the scale of the shape at that location on the path.

Controller
A part of 3ds Max that handles all of the tasks associated with animating an object.

Copy
An exact duplicate of an object.

Cutting
Has the effect of running a knife across the surface of the object, resulting in new edges and polygons subdivided into smaller polygons.

Data transfer rate
The amount of time required to play a file.

Deformation curve
A red line that goes from the left to the right side of the deformation grid, connected by control points, showing the scale of the shapes used on the path from its start to end vertex.

Density
A shadow's darkness.

Depot
In a particle system, contains all of the actions (operations and tests) that are available for building events.

Depth-of-field effect
An effect in which the main subject of a scene is clearly in focus and the foreground and background are blurred.

Diffuse color
The color of an object in general lighting, neither in shadow nor direct light.

Direct light
Emits light rays parallel to each other in one direction.

Dummy object
A kind of helper object that doesn't have any parameters and doesn't render. Useful for linking to other objects to help you control them.

Edge
A line that is both the side of a polygon and connects two vertices.

Editable poly
An object broken down into polygons, renderable surfaces enclosed by sequences of three or more connected edges.

Element
In an editable poly, all of an object's polygons.

Emitter
The object that specifies the location from which particles originate.

Empty flow
When you build a particle system, a flow that contains only the global event and no local events at all. It offers you the option of building your flow from scratch.

End effector
The bone with the lowest position in the hierarchy. Useful in IK, because when you rotate or move the end effector, the positional or rotational data is inherited by the end effector's parents

Event display
In a particle system, where you build and connect events together to program the behavior of particles.

AUTODESK 3D STUDIO MAX 2

Event-driven particle system
A system that is dependent on a particular event taking place. For example, you can have particles collide with something and then spawn into new kinds of particles at the moment of impact.

Expert mode
Hides all user interface (UI) elements except the menu bar, viewports, and track bar.

Exploding
You can ungroup objects in a group by exploding it.

Extrude
To push a polygon out from an object, or make it project away from its original location.

Faces
The polygon that make up an object's surface.

Falloff
The transition between a light's hotspot to the unlit area, or in other words, from full intensity to no intensity.

Far attenutation
The setting for where a light goes from full intensity to zero.

Field of view (FOV)
The amount of the scene that is visible through the camera. Measured in degrees of the horizon.

Field-of-view cone
The light-blue pyramid shape that appears when a camera is inserted.

Floating palette
A movable window that lets you keep tools and panels open while you work in 3ds Max.

Focal length
The distance between a camera's lens and the surface onto which a scene is captured.

Forward kinematics (FK)
The process by which rotational and position data is inherited by the child from its parent, down the hierarchy.

Frame
Shows a scene at a specific point in time. A single image in an animation.

Free camera
A camera that takes in the scene that appears in the direction the camera is aimed, without sticking to a particular target.

Frozen object
An object that cannot be selected or adjusted in any way.

Gizmo
Geometry that appears on-screen within an object to help you manipulate the object.

Global event
The first event in a particle flow.

Glossiness
Shininess; determines the size of an object's highlights.

Goal display
Represents the end of the IK chain and is the object that you select in the viewports in order to animate the chain.

Grid
Helps you align and place objects in your scene. Represents the center of the 3D universe.

Hierarchy
A set of parent-child relationships between objects.

Home grid
Grid in the Perspective viewport.

Hot material
Material in a sample slot applied to an object in a scene is "hot." Any changes made to it in the sample slot are reflected in the objects in the scene to which it is applied.

Hotspot
The area of a light that is at its brightest, or full intensity.

IK solver
Calculates how all the bones in a chain should move when the end effector moves.

Image motion blue
An effect that applies a smear effect to objects that are moving across the screen in an animation.

AUTODESK 3D STUDIO MAX 3

GLOSSARY

In tangent
Defines the shape of an animation's curve as it comes into a keyframe.

Index of refraction
The rate at which real-world substances refract light. Also called IOR.

Initial flow
An action that you drag into the event display to get started building a particle system.

Inner envelope
In a skeletal rig, vertices that lie within the inner envelope are influenced in a rigid manner, meaning that when a bone rotates, those vertices inherit 100 percent of the movement.

Instance
A clone of an object that is affected by any modifiers applied to the original, and vice-versa.

Instanced geometry
Particles that are duplicates of other objects in the scene.

Interpolation
The process of generating intermediate values between known values in animation.

Inverse kinematics (IK)
The process by which rotational and position data is inherited by the parent from its child, up the hierarchy.

IOR
See Index of refraction.

K

Key
Marks a significant change to an object or to its position in a scene.

Keyable
An object for which you can create keyframes.

Keyframe
Two keys between which a change takes place in a scene.

L

Lathe
A spline that serves as the outline for an object that is symmetrical all around its axis.

Lens effect
A visual effect that makes a scene appear as if it is being viewed through a lens, which can distort light, for example by streaking it or blurring it.

Live area frame
Encompasses all parts of a scene that will be rendered.

Local event
In a particle flow, contains operators that only perform within the event (as opposed to a global event).

Loft
A compound object that is the result of combining one or more shapes with a path; the shapes are located along the path as cross-sections, and 3ds Max generates a surface between them.

M

Map
An image applied to a material.

Master control
Lets you move an entire skeletal rig at once.

Materials
Make it possible for an object to look nearly photo-realistic.

MAXScript
The 3ds Max scripting language.

mental ray renderer
Uses a more advanced rendering technique than the scanline renderer to generate photo-realistic images.

Meta particles
Generate a type of particle called metaballs.

Metaballs
Particles that blend into blobs when they collide with each other.

Metal shader
A shader whose highlights produce the appearance of a metallic surface.

Modeling
The process of creating realistic-looking objects in 3ds Max by "sculpting" them.

Modifier
Changes an object's surface by deforming it in a specified way.

Modifier stack
The modifier stack has an object at its base, and modifiers applied to that object appear above the object in the stack, in the order that the modifiers were applied.

AUTODESK 3D STUDIO MAX 4

Motion blur
An effect in which the movement of something in an animated scene, such as wings on a bird, is blurred to imply very fast motion.

Multi-pass effects
Visual effects created by rendering a scene multiple times, moving the camera's position a bit each time to create a level of blurriness in the scene that matches what you might find in a real-word photograph.

Multiplier
A light's intensity, or brightness.

Near attenuation
The setting for where a light starts at zero and goes to full intensity.

Nested group
When one group of objects is part of another.

Non-event driven particle system
A system that operates continuously and is not dependent on a particular event taking place, such as two particles colliding with each other.

Normal
Direction that a polygon surface faces.

Nub
Extra little bone that appears when you right-click to end the bone creation process. The nub is necessary when you apply inverse kinematics (IK) to a bone hierarchy.

Object motion blur
An effect achieved by rendering multiple copies of an object in each frame. The result is that the object appears to be blurry.

Offset mode
In the Transform Type-In boxes, enables you to enter a value to offset (move) an object relative to its absolute position.

Omni light
Emits rays in all directions.

Opacity
The amount of transparency in an object.

Opaque
Allows no light to pass through.

Open spline
Has a starting vertex and ending vertex that don't meet and is also called a path. An example of an open spline is an arc.

Operator
In Particle Flow, part of an event that is responsible for performing an action.

Orthographic view
A straight-on axonometric view of a scene, without any rotation.

Out tangent
Defines the shape of an animation's curve as it leaves a keyframe.

Outer envelope
In a skeletal rig, when a bone rotates, vertices within the outer envelope can inherit less than 100 percent of the motion, depending on where they lie within the outer envelope.

Paint Deformation
A feature that lets you push and pull the vertices of a surface up or down as you move the mouse pointer over an object.

Parameters
Settings that you can change to affect an object in a scene.

Parameters panel
Lets you change the parameters for the individual operators that make up an event.

Parent-child relationship
Determines how two or more objects interact with each other. For example, a parent object controls its children.

Particle Age map
Map with parameters that enable change in the appearance of the material applied to a particle over the life of a particle.

Particle flow
Determines how particles in a particle system affect one another.

Particle system
An object that generates clusters of many subobjects called particles.

Perspective view
Displays all three dimensions at once, resulting in a view that is not flat. Some examples of this kind of view are the Camera, Perspective, and Isometric User views.

Photometric light
Light whose parameters are based on the actual physical characteristics of light in the real world.

GLOSSARY

Pivot point
The point around which an object rotates

Point helpers
Enable you to change the position of the vertices of a spline while keyframing to animate the curvature of the spline.

Polygon modeling
The most common type of modeling in 3ds Max, in which you convert an object to an editable poly and then manipulate polygons to achieve a certain look or effect.

Polygons
Renderable surfaces enclosed by three or more connected edges.

Prerendered images
2D image files, either static images or animations, created from a 3ds Max scene.

Procedural map
A map produced by mathematical algorithm. Procedural maps generate a certain look or pattern on material, such as Checker or Marble, and have adjustable controls inside 3ds Max.

Quad menu
A menu that appears when you right-click in a viewport.

Radiosity
A calculation of the way light moves around a scene, from its first contact with a surface to its effect on other surfaces when it bounces in a different direction.

reactor
A 3ds Max toolbar that lets you simulate physical forces inside 3ds Max scenes.

Reference
A copy of an object that changes according to the changes made to the original. Changes to the reference don't affect the original.

Render
To convert a scene into a two-dimensional image or animation, using the materials, lighting, background, and environment settings you have put in place.

Rendering effects
Effects that you can apply to a scene after it is rendered to process the look of the output image in various ways.

Re-scale
To stretch or shrink an animation over a greater or lesser number of frames.

Resolution
The physical size of an image, measured in pixels.

Safe Frames
A feature in 3ds Max that lets you see how your scene would appear on a TV monitor.

Sample
To calculate an effect.

Sample slots
Squares in the top of the Material Editor, each of which shows a material as it would appear when applied to a sample object, with sample lighting.

Scanline renderer
Renders an image or frame one line of pixels at a time, pixels being the tiny dots of color that make up a digital picture on a computer monitor.

Scrub
A method for previewing your animation. You scrub by grabbing the time slider and moving it left and right as you preview your animation.

Segments
Straight lines that visually divide an area of an object. Segments don't actually divide an object into pieces; they simply break an object's surface down into smaller parts, so that the object might appear to be smoother or more flexible as the modifications to the object become more complex.

Selection region
A shape with a dashed-line border that appears as you click and drag over an area with the Select Object Tool active.

Selection set
A predefined group of selected objects.

Self-illumination
The level at which an object appears to glow from within.

AUTODESK 3D STUDIO MAX 6

Shader
Controls how the highlights on an object look.

Skeletal rig
A chain of bones used to bring life to a character model.

Skinning
Associating bones with certain parts of your character mesh.

Skylight
A photometric light that lights a scene as though it is a dome around the scene.

Slicing
Cuts an object as though a saw has run straight through the whole object in one direction.

Smooth tangents
Produce natural looking motions as you animate.

Snapping
The adjustment of an object's parameters, position, rotation, or scale using predefined increments.

Soft selection
Makes it easy to create and/or manipulate a contoured area on an object's surface, without having to transform each vertex in the area individually.

Space warp
An object that creates a force field effect that operates on other objects.

Specular color
The color of an object where it is reflecting the light source (i.e., is highlighted).

Specular level
Refers to the strength or intensity of the highlights on the object.

Spline
An object that is basically a line composed of at least two vertices connected by a straight or curved segment.

Spotlight
Emits light rays from a source as a single beam.

Standard flow
In a particle system, a flow that consists of one global event plus one local event.

Standard light
The simplest kind of light object in 3ds Max.

Standard material
When you apply this material, an object appears to have a single color applied to it, with standard reflective properties.

Standard particles
Predefined shapes that appear in the Standard Particles group, such as tetra, sphere, and cube.

Standard polygon primitives
The building blocks for most of the things you will create in 3ds Max. Also called Standard primitives.

Standard primitives
See Standard polygon primitives.

Submap
A map assigned to another map.

Subobject
A subset of an object's geometry.

Tangent
Refers to the shape of an animation curve as it is plotted from keyframe to keyframe.

Target camera
A camera that always focuses on a target object.

Target object
The object with which you want to align another object. Also the object on which a target camera focuses.

Test
In Particle Flow, part of an event that tests some condition and then, based on the results of the test, performs different actions on a particle and then passes it from event to event.

Tick
Each tick on the timeline represents a frame in your animation.

Time controls
VCR-like controls in the lower-right side of the interface designed to help you navigate your animation.

Time slider
Feature on the trackbar that tells you what frame of the animation you are viewing.

Title safe frame
Frame within which titles (or other wording) should remain in order not to be distorted by the slant of a monitor near its edges.

Track bar
Displays the frames in a scene, from 1 to 100 by default.

GLOSSARY

AUTODESK 3D STUDIO MAX 7

GLOSSARY

Track hierarchy
A way of viewing the parent-child relationship between objects and parameters in track view.

Tracks
Separate timelines for each parameter you can animate.

Trajectory
The line that starts where an object starts and follows the path of the object as it moves.

Transform gizmo
The gizmo that appears in an object to help you move, rotate, or scale an object.

Translucent
Allows some light to pass through.

Tweening
Interpolation, or the process of generating intermediate values between known values in animation.

Utah Teapot
First created by a computer graphics researcher named Martin Newell. Because of its irregular curves, as well as the hole in the handle, and the way it casts a shadow upon itself, it provided an excellent model for testing advances in 3D graphics.

Vertex
A point in space that defines the structure of an object or a polygon.

Viewports
Let you look at a scene from different angles and dimensions.

Weight
The amount of influence that a bone has over a specific vertex is called the weight of the vertex.

Weld
To permanently combine two vertices into one vertex.

Wire
To connect the events in an event-driven particle system.

Wireframe mesh
Displays an object as if it has been traced, but not filled in.

XRef objects
Externally referenced objects; objects that you can use in a scene that exist in another scene. This makes it easier for multiple people to work simultaneously on models that will ultimately appear in the same scene.

INDEX

3D Snap Tool, using, 2-76–2-77, 2-80
3ds Max
    animation. *See* animation
    customizing interface, 1-10, 1-36–1-39
    interface, exploring, 1-4–1-13
    introduction to, 1-2–1-3
    returning to default configuration, 1-9
    special effects. *See* effects
    starting, 1-11

Absolute mode, Transform Type-In boxes, 2-25, 2-31
action safe frames, 5-15
actions in Particle Flow, 9-34–9-36
active time segment, 6-23, 6-27
ActiveShade rendering, 7-8–7-13
adding
    See also inserting, instancing
    atmospheric effects to scenes, 10-4–10-11
    bone fins, 8-18–8-19, 8-22–8-23
    environmental effects to scenes, 10-4
    fire effects, 10-4, 10-9
    keys, 6-46
    lights to scenes, 5-20–5-29
    motion blur effects, 10-37–10-39
    objects to groups, 2-63
    rendering effects, 10-23–10-24
    star effects, 10-32–10-33
    text to scenes, 3-95
    XRef objects to scenes, 3-76, 3-80–3-81
Affect Hierarchy Only button, Adjust Pivot rollout, 2-71
Affect Pivot Only button, Hierarchy panel, 2-72
aligning objects, 2-84–2-89, 2-91
ambient colors, 4-5, 4-21–4-22
ambient lights, 5-53
Angle Snap tool, using, 2-78, 2-81
animating
    See also animation
    bones, 8-48–8-57
    cameras, 6-10–6-11

creation parameters, 6-14–6-15
lights, 6-16–6-17
materials, 6-13–6-14
animation
    See also animations
    3ds Max tools for manipulating, 6-2
    adding secondary motion, 8-49, 8-52–8-53
    assigning animation controllers, 6-52–6-59
    assigning constraints, 6-60–6-69
    capabilities of, 6-7
    configuring timing, 6-22–6-31
    creating loops, loop cycles, 8-49, 8-53–8-54
    Curve Editor, using, 6-42–6-51
    displaying trajectories, 6-6
    Dope Sheet, manipulating keyframes with, 6-38–6-41
    editing keys, 6-32–6-37
    editing playback properties, 6-25
    loops, creating, 6-55–6-56
    and particle systems, 9-6–9-7
    rendering. *See* rendering
    setting active time segment, 6-23, 6-27
    terminology, concepts, 6-4–6-5
    time display, changing, 6-24–6-25
Animation menu and submenus (fig.), 6-53
animations
    described, 6-2
    grouping, ungrouping, 2-63
    navigating with time controls, time slider, 1-33–1-35
    playing, 6-7
    rendering as video codec, 7-14, 7-17
animators, 6-4
anisotropic shader, 4-7, 4-25
applying
    See also assigning
    IK to bones, 8-26–8-27
    Lathe modifier, 3-113–3-114
    materials, 4-4–4-5, 4-10
    materials to objects, 4-13–4-14
    materials to particles, 9-25, 9-29–9-31
    materials to sample slots, 4-16–4-17

MeshSmooth modifier, 3-72–3-75, 3-77
modifiers to group of objects, 2-51
modifiers to objects, 2-47
modifiers to subobjects, 3-18–3-23
space warps to event-driven particles, 9-48–9-49
subobject modifiers, 3-21–3-22
Symmetry modifier, 3-74–3-75, 3-79–3-80
TurboSmooth modifier, 378
arc splines, creating, 3-96–3-97
arcs
    creating, 3-98
    modifying parameters of, 3-108
    as open splines, 3-93
arms
    animating with linked objects, 2-60–2-61
    creating, 3-86–3-87
arrays, creating, 2-53–2-55, 2-58–2-59
aspect ratio of images, 7-21
Asset Browser, 1-31
Assign Renderer rollout (fig.), 7-7
assigning
    See also applying
    animation constraints, 6-61–6-62, 6-64–6-65
    animation controllers, 6-52–6-54, 6-57–6-59
    bitmaps, 4-31
    maps to material components, 4-35–4-36, 4-46–4-47
    maps to materials, 4-30–4-33
    maps to other maps, 4-57
    Object ID numbers to objects, 10-29
    Particle Age map, 9-52–9-53, 9-57
    Smoke material, 9-60–9-61
atmospheric apparatus, creating, 10-5–10-6
atmospheric effects
    adding to scenes, 10-2, 10-4–10-11
    adjusting parameters, 10-12–10-21
attaching objects to groups, 2-63
attenuation
    fire effects, 10-15
    light, 5-33–5-35, 5-39–5-41

AUTODESK 3D STUDIO MAX 9

INDEX

Auto Key
    animation with, 6-4–6-5
    displaying trajectories, 6-6
    setting keyframes with, 6-5
Autodesk 3d Studio Max. *See* 3ds Max
AVI video files, 7-14, 7-15, 7-23, 7-27
axes described, 2-20
axis tripod
    described, 2-92
    in grids, 1-19
    and moving, rotating, scaling, 2-20–2-21
axonometric
    view controls, using, 1-16–1-17
    viewport described, 1-14

Bend modifiers, 2-42, 3-19, 3-20, 3-21
beveling
    objects, 3-36
    polygons, 3-42–3-43
Bezier Float controllers, 6-52
Bezier, Pierre, 6-52
Bezier vertices, corners, 3-105, 3-107, 3-110
binding objects, 9-16
Birth operator, particle flows, 9-39
bitmaps
    assigning, 4-30, 4-31
    file formats and uses (table), 7-15
Blinn, James, 2-7
Blinn shader, 4-7, 4-21, 4-25
Blizzard particle system, 9-5, 9-9–9-10, 9-19–9-21
Bone Tools floater, creating bones with, 8-12, 8-14–8-15
bones
    adding and editing fins, 8-18–8-19
    animating, 8-48–8-57
    applying IK to, 8-26–8-27, 8-30–8-31
    completing skeletal rig, 8-24–8-25
    creating, 8-4–8-5, 8-7–8-8, 8-14–8-15
    editing, 8-16–8-25
    fins, adding and editing, 8-18–8-19, 8-22–8-23
    moving, rotating, 8-6, 8-8

naming, renaming, 8-12, 8-15
repositioning pivot points, 8-17, 8-20
sizing, shaping, 8-17–8-18, 8-21–8-22
skinning, 8-38–8-47
using, 8-2
using SplinkIK solver, 8-28, 8-33–8-35
Boolean operators, using in searches, 1-40
borders
    bridging, 3-70–3-71
    bridging between two, 3-61–3-63
    chamfering, 3-32, 3-38
    extruding, 3-35
boxes
    cloned as instance (fig.), 2-56
    creating, 2-6, 2-9
    bounding, particles spawned as (fig.), 9-56
    modifying parameters of, 2-35–2-36
bridging borders and polygons, 3-61–3-63, 3-70–3-71
brightness, contrast effects, 10-23
Bubble and Pinch numbers, soft selection, 3-48–3-49
bump mapping, 4-60–4-61, 4-65–4-66

cameras
    adjusting parameters, 5-7–5-8, 5-10–5-11
    animating, 6-10–6-11
    changing viewports into camera viewports, 5-16
    positioning, 5-12–5-14, 5-17–5-18
    rotating, 5-14–5-15
    using, creating, 5-4–5-6, 5-9–5-10
    using generally, 5-2
    using Safe Frames feature, 5-15, 5-19
chamfering
    borders, 3-32, 3-38
    edges, 3-31–3-32
    objects, 3-30–3-33
    vertex and two edges, 3-37–3-38
changing
    See also converting, modifying
    ambient, specular, diffuse colors, 4-21–4-22
    animation time display, 6-29

bone names, 8-12
bone shapes, sizes, 8-16–8-17
display options, 1-17–1-18, 1-22
frame rate, 6-22, 6-23
light intensity, 5-36–5-37
particle shapes, 9-26
tangent types, 6-43–6-45
viewports, 1-14, 1-20–1-21
viewports into camera viewports, 5-16
character mesh, creating bones within, 8-10–8-15
character rigging, 8-2
characters, modeling, 3-82–3-91
Checker map, 4-48–4-49
Checkered Cloth material, 7-11
child objects and linked objects, 2-60–2-61
Cinepak codec, 7-16, 7-26
circles, creating, 3-94
Clone and Align tool, using, 2-86
cloning
    and aligning objects, 2-86–2-87
    and deleting keys, 6-36
    keyframes, 6-33–6-34
    objects, 2-52–2-59
closed splines, 3-92
closing arc spline, 3-94
codec, video, 7-14, 7-16, 7-17
color balance effect, 10-23
colors
    adjusting in maps, 4-32
    ambient, specular, diffuse, 4-5
    changing light, 5-30
    coloring objects, 2-32
    diffuse, 4-50–4-51
    editing material, 4-21–4-23, 4-26–4-27
    filter, mapping, 4-61
    and Material Age operator, 9-53
    and Particle Age map, 9-57–9-59
Command panel
    described, 1-44
    exploring, 1-8–1-9, 1-28–1-31
    Output Size group, 7-21
commands, finding hotkeys for, 1-41
Common Parameters rollout, 7-19
compound controllers, 6-52

compound objects, 3-114
compression, file, 7-16
computers crashing during rendering, 7-23
cones
    adjusting parameters, 5-31–5-33
    creating, 2-6–2-7
connecting vertices and edges, 3-57–3-58, 3-66–3-67
constraints, animation
    described, 6-60
    LookAt, 6-61, 6-64–6-65
    Path, 6-60–6-62, 6-66
context-sensitive Help, 1-40–1-43
control points, scaling objects with, 3-117
Controller window, 6-38
controls
    See also specific control
    axonometric viewport, 1-16–1-17
    master, for dummy objects, 8-29
    modifying parameters of, 2-37
    time, described, 1-32–1-33
converting
    See also changing
    objects into editable polygons, 3-4–3-6, 3-27
    primitives into editable polygons, 3-10
    splines into editable splines, 3-104–3-105, 3-109
    vertices, segments, splines, 3-105–3-107
copying
    objects with [Shift] key, 2-12–2-13
    maps, 4-34, 4-38
    modifier to another object, 2-50
    objects by cloning, 2-52, 2-87
Create panel
    creating bones with, 8-7–8-8
    using, 1-28–1-29
creating
    See also instancing
    animation loops, 6-55–6-56
    arrays, 2-53–2-55, 2-58–2-59
    atmospheric apparatus, 10-7–10-8
    bones, 8-4–8-5, 8-7–8-8, 8-10–8-15
    cameras, 5-4–5-6, 5-9–5-10
    characters, 3-82–3-91

edges, 3-56–3-57, 3-64–3-65
hair, 10-46–10-47
IK chains, 8-27
image file sequence, 7-23–7-24
keyboard shortcuts, 1-41
lines, arcs, helices, 3-98
link hierarchy, 2-65
loft compound objects, 3-114–3-116, 3-121–3-122
master controls, 8-36–8-37
materials for particle systems, 9-25–9-30
non-event particle systems, 9-5–9-7, 9-11
Particle Flow systems, 9-32–9-33
particle flows, 9-38
particle systems, 9-19–9-20
paths, 3-92–3-93
polygons, 3-56–3-57, 3-64–3-65
prerendered images, 7-5–7-6
rectangles, donuts, NGons, 3-99
rendering, and saving, 7-18–7-21
shapes, 3-94–3-95
space warps, 9-16–9-18
spherical deflector, 9-23–9-24
splines, 3-92–3-97, 8-31–8-32
standard primitives, 2-4–2-11
text splines, 3-96, 3-100
transformational clones, 2-53, 2-57–2-58
vertices, 3-56–3-57, 3-64–3-65
Creation Method rollout, using, 2-8, 3-96–3-97
Cube creation method, using (fig.), 2-8
current objects described, 2-85
Curve Editor, using, 6-42–6-51
Custom UI schemes, switching to preset, 1-36–1-38
customizing 3ds Max interface, 1-10, 1-36–1-39
cutting
    objects, 3-68–3-69
    polygons, 3-60–3-61
cylinders, creating and adjusting, 2-6, 5-31–5-33

data transfer rate, 7-16
deactivating maps, 4-37
decay, light, 5-33–5-35, 5-41–5-42

deflectors
    planar, creating and modifying, 9-25
    in space warps, particle systems, 9-17–9-18
    spherical, creating and modifying, 9-23–9-24
deforming
    loft objects, 3-116–3-117, 3-122–3-123
    objects with Soft Selection, 3-47–3-49
    Paint Deformation, 3-44–3-46
deleting
    See also removing
    keyframes, 6-33–6-34
    keys, 6-36
density of shadows, 5-44
Dent map, 4-49
depth-of-field effects, 10-22, 10-34–10-39
destination objects, 2-86
detaching objects from groups, 2-63
diagrams, particle, 9-34, 9-54
diffuse colors, 4-5, 4-21–4-22, 4-50–4-51, 6-13
diffuse lights, 5-53
direct lights, 5-20
directional lights, inserting, 5-27
displacement mapping, 4-58, 4-62–4-63
display options, changing, 1-17–1-18, 1-22
Display panel, using, 1-31
displaying
    grids in viewports, 1-8, 1-18–1-19
    scenes in real time, 7-4–7-6
docking
    ActiveShade window, 7-9
    Command panel, 1-9
    Main toolbar, 1-25
dollying cameras, 5-14
donut splines
    creating, 3-95
    extruding, 3-118–3-119
donuts, creating, 3-99
Dope Sheet, animation tool, 6-38–6-41
dots per inch (DPI) image resolution, determining, 7-17
DPI (dots per inch), 7-17
dragonbird character
    animating, 8-48–8-57
    creating, 8-10–8-15

AUTODESK 3D STUDIO MAX 11

dummy objects
    creating and linking, 8-28–8-29
    described, 6-60
duplicating. *See* copying
DVDs, rendering animations for, 7-14
dynamic particle systems, 9-18

Edge option, Create panel, 2-11
Edged faces option
    display option, 1-18
    in Perspective viewport (fig.), 1-23
edges
    chamfering, 3-30, 3-31–3-32, 3-37–3-38
    connecting with vertices, 3-57–3-58, 3-66–3-67
    creating new, 3-56–3-57, 3-64–3-65
    extruding, 3-35, 3-40–3-41
    of objects, 3-7
Edit Poly modifier, 3-5–3-6
Edit rollout, Modify panel, 3-33
Edit Spline modifier, 3-104
editable polygons
    accessing subobject levels, 3-6–3-9
    applying modifiers to subobjects, 3-18–3-19
    converting objects, primitives into, 3-4–3-6, 3-10
    extruding, 3-33
    selecting subobjects, 3-12–3-13
editable splines
    converting splines into, 3-104–3-105, 3-109
    inserting vertices into, 3-107
editing
    animation playback properties, 6-25, 6-30–6-31
    bone fins, 8-18–8-19, 8-22–8-23
    bones, 8-16–8-25
    key properties, 6-34, 6-37
    keys for selected objects in animation, 6-32–6-37
    map parameters, 4-48–4-49, 4-55–4-56
    material colors, 4-26–4-27

materials, 4-20–4-23
selection sets, 2-15
self-illumination and opacity of materials, 4-24, 4-28–4-29
shader parameters, 4-25–4-26
specular levels and glossiness of materials, 4-27–4-28
splines, 3-102–3-111
text in scenes, 3-95
effects
    See also specific effect
    adding to scenes, 10-2
    atmospheric, adding to scenes, 10-4–10-6
    atmospheric apparatus, creating, 10-5–10-8
    depth-of-field, 10-34–10-39
    lens, applying, 10-26–10-33
    rendering, 10-22–10-25
Effects panel (fig.), 10-24
elements described, 3-7–3-8
ellipse spline, creating, 3-94
emitters in particle systems, 9-4
empty flows in Particle Flow, 9-35
end effectors, 8-26
enlarging selection area, 3-15
envelopes, and skinning, 8-39, 8-44–8-45
European standard frame rate, 6-22
event-driven particle systems
    applying space warps to particles, 9-48–9-49
    described, 9-4–9-5
events
    in Particle Flow, 9-32
    splitting particles between, 9-37, 9-46–9-48
    wiring together, 9-32, 9-36–9-37, 9-44–9-46
exploding
    groups, 2-63
    nested groups, 2-67
explosion effects, 10-14
externally referenced objects. *See* XRef objects
extruding
    objects, 3-33–3-36
    polygons, 3-39–3-40
    splines, 3-112, 3-118–3-119
    vertices and edges, 3-40–3-41

faces of objects, 3-4–3-6
Facing shape, applying material to particles, 9-25
falloff values, light, 5-37–5-38, 5-31–5-32
far attenuation, light, 5-34
field of view (FOV) of cameras, 5-6
File menu, exploring, 1-4–1-6
file output
    adjusting options, types, 7-25–7-27
    effects, 10-23
    file formats, 7-14
    rendering parameters, 7-18–7-21
filenames for saving renderings, 7-20–7-21
files
    formats, 7-14
    opening, 1-5–1-6
    saving, 1-11
film grain effects, 10-23
filter colors, mapping, 4-61, 4-66–4-67
filtering keyframes, 6-19–6-20
Find Target test, 9-43–9-44
fingers, creating, 3-88–3-89
fins, adding to bones, 8-18–8-19
fire effects, 10-4, 10-9, 10-12–10-14, 10-17–10-18
FK chains, 8-26–8-27
flare effects, 10-27
Flat Mirror map, 4-59
flipping normals, 3-25–3-27, 3-29
floating palette, 1-9
focal length of cameras, 5-6
focal points of scenes, 10-36
fog effects, 10-15–10-16
forces and space warps, 9-16–9-17
forward kinematics (FK), 8-26
frame rate, setting, 6-26
frames
    animation, 6-4
    described, 1-44
    keyframes. *See* keyframes
    navigating with time controls, 1-32–1-33
    rendering subset, 7-20
    setting frame rate, active time segment, 6-22–6-23
    and track bar timeline, 1-10

free cameras, 5-6
free spotlights, creating, 5-22
freezing, unfreezing mesh objects, 8-11, 8-13
frozen objects described, 1-31
functions, hotkey, 1-41
fur effects. *See* hair

Geometric/Deformable space warps, 9-18
geometric shapes. *See* standard primitives
GeoSphere button, Create panel, 2-5
gizmos
   described, 2-92
   and moving, rotating, scaling, 2-21
   Wave (fig.), 6-12
global events
   in Particle Flow, 9-34
   wiring together, 9-37
glossiness
   of colors, 4-5
   mapping, 4-48
   of materials, editing, 4-27–4-28
glow effects, 10-26–10-27, 10-30–10-31
goal display in HI solver, 8-27
graphing objects, 2-62
Gravity space warp, creating and modifying, 9-22–9-23
grids
   deformation, 3-117
   working with, 1-8, 1-18–1-19, 1-23, 1-44
grouping objects, 2-62–2-64, 2-66
groups, attaching, detaching, nesting, exploding, 2-63
growing selection area, 3-15

hair
   adjusting parameters, 10-48–10-49, 10-54
   applying Hair and Fur modifier, 10-53–10-54
   creating, 10-46–10-47
   cutting, 10-51, 10-57
   and fur effects, 10-22

   rendering, 10-52
   scaling, 10-56
   styling, 10-49–10-51, 10-55–10-56
hands, creating, 3-86–3-87
helices, creating, 3-93–3-94, 3-98
Help, accessing, 1-40–1-43
HI (History Independent) Solver, 8-27
hiding toolbars, panels, 1-36
hierarchy
   link, creating, 2-65
   object, 2-61
   rotating links between objects in, 2-74–2-75
   subobject levels, 3-6
Hierarchy panel
   repositioning pivot points, 2-68–2-69
   using, 1-30
highlights
   mapping specular components, 4-47–4-48, 4-52–4-53
   specular, 4-23
home grid described, 1-19
hot materials, 4-14
Hotkey Map, using, 1-41–1-43
hotspot values, light, 5-31–5-32, 5-37–5-38

IK (Inverse Kinematics)
   applying to bones, 8-26–8-27
   chains, creating, 8-27
   Hierarchy panel option, 1-30
IK solver feature, applying to bones, 8-26–8-27, 8-30–8-31
image file sequence, rendering, 7-23, 7-28–7-29
image motion blur effect, 10-37
image resolution, determining, 7-17
images
   aspect ratio of, 7-21
   file formats and uses (table), 7-15
   prerendered, 7-4–7-6
   rendering effects, 10-22–10-25
   rendering image file sequence, 7-23–7-24
In tangents, 6-43, 6-51–6-52
Indeo codec, 7-16

index of refraction (IOR), 4-60
Inherit section, Hierarchy panel, 1-30
Ink 'n Paint material, 4-6
inner envelope, 8-39
inserting
   See also adding
   control points along path, 3-117
   omni lights, 5-28–5-29
   spotlights, 5-25–5-26
   vertices, 3-107, 3-111
instanced geometry described, 9-2
instances
   box cloned as (fig.), 2-56
   and clones, 2-52, 2-87
instancing
   See also adding, creating
   lights, 5-35, 5-42–5-43
   maps, 4-34
intensity, changing light, 5-30, 5-36–5-37
interfaces
   customizing 3ds Max, 1-10, 1-36–1-39
   loading customized user, 1-39
   restoring default user, 1-37
interpolation
   in animation, 6-4
   of hair, 10-49
inverse kinematics. *See* IK

JPEG (Joint Photographic Experts Group) files, 7-15, 7-23–7-24

Key Info dialog box (fig.), 6-34
Key window, 6-38
keyboard shortcuts, creating, 1-41
keyframes
   See also keys
   adjusting key timing and values, 6-45–6-46
   described, 1-32, 6-4
   filtering, 6-19–6-20
   setting with Auto Key, 6-5, 6-8–6-9
   setting with Set Key, 6-18, 6-20–6-21

INDEX

keys
   See also keyframes
   adding, 6-46
   adjusting in Dope Sheet, 6-38–6-41
   editing properties, 6-34, 6-37
   examining in Curve Editor, 6-47–6-48
   and keyframes, 6-4
   on track bar, 1-32

L

Lasso Selection Region button, 2-13
Lathe modifier
   applying, 3-112–3-114, 3-119–3-120
   described, 3-26
layered fog effect, 10-15–10-16, 10-20–10-21
lens effects
   applying, 10-26–10-33
   described, 10-22
lighting
   See also lights
   adjusting parameters, 5-30–5-35
   advanced effects, 5-51, 7-6
   angle of incidence, 5-33
   controlling surfaces with, 5-48–5-53
   radiosity, generating in scenes, 5-55
   use generally, 5-2
lights
   See also lighting
   adding to scenes, 5-21–5-24
   adjusting cone, cylinder parameters, 5-31–5-33
   animating, 6-16–6-17
   attenuation, using, 5-39–5-41
   changing intensity, color, 5-30, 5-36–5-37
   decay, attenuation, 5-33–5-35, 5-41–5-42
   and hair, fur, 10-52
   instancing, 5-35, 5-42–5-43
   projecting maps with, 5-49–5-51, 5-54–5-55
   shadows. *See* shadows
   types of, 5-20–5-21
   Volume Light effects, 10-4, 10-10–10-11, 10-14–10-15, 10-19–10-20
line splines, 3-96, 3-119

lines
   See also segments
   converting into editable splines, 3-104
   creating, 3-98, 3-101
   creating paths, 3-94
link hierarchies, creating, 2-65
linking
   master controls, 8-36–8-37
   objects, 2-60–2-61
   and unlinking objects, 2-64
links, rotating between objects in hierarchy, 2-74–2-75
List controllers, using, 6-62–6-63, 6-68–6-69
live area Safe Frame, 5-15
local events in Particle Flow, 9-35
locking
   color components together, 4-22
   soft selection, 3-49
loft compound objects
   creating, 3-114–3-116, 3-121–3-122
   deforming, 3-116–3-117, 3-122–3-123
LookAt constraint, 6-61, 6-62, 6-64–6-65
loops, animation
   creating, 6-55–6-56, 8-49
   creating cycle, 8-53–8-54

M

Main toolbar
   exploring, 1-7
   working with, 1-24–1-27
map bumpiness, using, 4-60–4-61, 4-65–4-66
map displacement, using, 4-62–4-63
mapping
   color components of Standard material, 4-46–4-47
   diffuse colors, 4-50–4-51
   filter colors, 4-61, 4-66–4-67
   reflection, 4-58–4-59
   refraction, 4-59–4-60, 4-64–4-65
   self-illumination and opacity, 4-54–4-55
   shadows, 5-45, 5-47
   specular highlight components, 4-47–4-48, 4-52–4-53

maps
   See also mapping
   assigning to material components, 4-35–4-36
   assigning to other maps, 4-57
   assigning to Particle Age map, 9-52–9-53, 9-57–9-59
   copying between components, 4-38
   deactivating, removing, 4-37
   editing parameters, 4-48–4-49, 4-55–4-56
   instancing, copying, swapping, 4-34
   navigating, 4-40–4-45
   projecting with lights, 5-49–5-51, 5-54–5-55
   reactivating or removing, 4-33–4-34
   types of, assigning, 4-30–4-33
Marble map, 4-49
master controls
   creating and linking, 8-36–8-37
   moving dummy objects with, 8-29
Material Dynamic operator, 9-52, 9-53, 9-59–9-60
Material Editor
   creating materials for particles, 9-27, 9-29–9-31
   navigation with, 4-41–4-42, 4-45
   with new material displayed (fig.), 4-17
   using, 4-10–4-11
Material/Map browser (fig.), 4-12, 4-17
Material/Map navigator, using, 4-40–4-41, 4-43–4-44
Material Static operator, 9-52, 9-54–9-55
materials
   animating, 6-13–6-14
   applying to objects, 4-13–4-14
   applying to sample slots, 4-16–4-17
   applying to scene objects, 4-18–4-19
   assigning maps to, 4-30–4-33
   assigning maps to components, 4-35–4-36
   creating for particle systems, 9-25–9-31
   described, 4-2
   editing, 4-20–4-23
   editing colors, 4-26–4-27
   editing specular levels of, 4-23
   'hot,' 4-14

mapping shader components, 4-46–4-57
material operators, using, 9-52–9-61
navigating, 4-40–4-45
rendering scenes, 4-7–4-8
setting up particles for, 9-55–9-56
shaders. *See* shaders
Smoke, creating and assigning, 9-60–9-61
use generally, types, 4-4–4-7
viewing, applying to sample slots, 4-10–4-13
Matte/Shadow material, 4-6
MAXScript reference guide, New Features Guide, 1-40
MAXScripting option on Asset Browser, 1-31
mental ray renderer, 7-6
menus, exploring 3ds Max, 1-4–1-7
mesh objects, freezing, unfreezing, 8-11
Mesh Select modifier
 applying, 3-72–3-75
 using, 3-19–3-20, 3-22–3-23
meshes, creating bones within character, 8-10–8-15
MeshSmooth modifier, 3-19, 3-77
meta particles described, 9-2
metal shader, 4-7
Mini Curve Editor (fig.), 6-43
modeling
 characters, 3-82–3-91
 described, 2-4, 2-92, 3-2
 efficiently, 3-72
 with splines, 3-112–3-117
 using references, 3-73–3-74, 3-77
modifier-based space warps, 9-18
modifier stack, working with, 2-42–2-45, 2-48–2-49
modifiers
 See also specific modifier
 animating, 6-11–6-12
 applying to objects, 2-45–2-47
 applying to subobjects, 3-18–3-23
 described, 2-42, 2-92
 Edit Poly, 3-5–3-6
Modify panel, using, 1-28–1-29, 2-32–2-33

modifying
 See also changing
 box, sphere, cone parameters, 2-35–2-37
 polygon objects, 2-32–2-37
motion blur effects, 10-22, 10-34
Motion panel
 assigning animation controller using, 6-57
 using, 1-31
.mov files, 7-14, 7-15
Move tool, using, 2-21–2-22
movement and linked objects, 2-60–2-61
moving
 bones, 8-6, 8-8
 clones, 2-53
 dollying cameras, 5-14
 keys, 6-32–6-33, 6-35
 objects, 2-21–2-22, 2-25, 2-26–2-27, 6-6
 pivot points, 2-70
MPEG (Motion Picture Experts Group) files, 7-15
multi-pass rendering
 described, 10-34–10-35
 using, 10-40–10-41
multiplier, light, 5-30

names
 changing bone, 8-12, 8-15
 filenames, 1-6
 of objects, 1-29
 selecting objects by, 2-13–2-14, 2-18
National Television Standards Committee (NTSC)
 aspect ratio standard, 7-21
 frame rate standard, 6-22
navigating materials and maps, 4-40–4-45
near attenuation, light, 5-34
nested groups, exploding, 2-67
nesting groups, 2-63
New command, File menu options, 1-4–1-5
New Features Guide, 1-40
New Scene dialog box, 1-4–1-5
Newell, Martin, 2-7

NGon
 adjusting number of sides, 3-102–3-103
 creating, 3-95, 3-99
Noise constraint, 6-63
Noise Controller properties (fig.), 6-68–6-69
non-event particle systems, creating, 9-4–9-7, 9-11
Normal modifier, 3-26
normals
 described, 3-24–3-25
 flipping, 3-25–3-27, 3-29
NTSC (National Television Standards Committee)
 aspect ratio standard, 7-21
 frame rate standard, 6-22

Object ID numbers, adding to objects, 10-29
objects
 adding atmospheric effects to, 10-6
 adding Object ID numbers for lens effects, 10-29
 adjusting segments on, 2-38–2-41
 aligning, 2-84–2-89
 applying materials to, 4-13–4-14, 4-18–4-19
 binding, 9-16
 camera. *See* cameras
 chamfering, 3-30–3-33
 changing appearance with modifiers, 2-42–2-51
 changing parameters of, 2-32–2-33
 cloning, 2-52–2-59, 2-91
 compound, 3-114
 converting into editable polygons, 3-4–3-6
 creating standard primitives, 2-4–2-11
 current, target, 2-84
 destination, 2-86
 displaying trajectories, 6-6
 dummy, creating, 8-28–8-29
 dummy, described, 6-60
 externally referenced. *See* XRef objects
 extruding, 3-33–3-36

INDEX

filter colors, mapping, 4-61
frozen, described, 1-31
grouping, 2-62–2-66
keyable, 6-19
linking, 2-60–2-61
modifying polygon, 2-32–2-37
modifying using Modify panel, 1-28–1-29
motion blur effects, 10-37
moving, 2-26–2-27
names of, 1-29
parents, children, 1-30
renaming, recoloring, 2-32–2-33, 2-35–2-36
reorienting in relation to pivot points, 2-73–2-74
repositioning in relation to pivot points, 2-70, 2-72–2-73
resizing, 2-24
rotating, 2-28
scaling, 2-29–2-30
selecting, 2-12–2-19
slicing and cutting, 3-68–3-69
space warps, 9-16–9-17
transforming with Transform Type-In box, 2-30–2-31
XRef, using, 3-75–3-76
Offset mode, Transform Type-In boxes, 2-25
omni lights, inserting, 5-20, 5-28–5-29
opacity
    adjusting intensity of application, 4-33
    mapping, 4-48
    of materials, editing, 4-5, 4-24, 4-28–4-29
Opacity Checker map, 4-57
opaque materials, 4-5
open splines, 3-92
operators
    defining actions in events, 9-35–9-36
    defining for particle flows, 9-39–9-43
    material, using, 9-52–9-61
    particle system, 9-35–9-36, 9-39–9-42, 9-49–9-50
    using Boolean in searches, 1-40
orientation, aligning objects by, 2-89
Orthographic view described, 1-44

orthographic viewport, 1-14–1-15
Out tangents, 6-44, 6-51–6-52
outer envelope, 8-39
Output Size group, Common panel, 7-21

P

Paint Deformation, using, 3-44–3-46
painting, soft selection, 3-54–3-55
palettes, floating, 1-9
panels
    See also specific panel
    on Command panel, 1-28
    hiding, 1-36
paper size, Print Size Wizard settings, 7-30–7-31
parameters
    adjusting camera, 5-7–5-8, 5-10–5-11
    adjusting cone and cylinder, 5-31–5-33
    adjusting fire effect, 10-12–10-14
    adjusting hair, 10-48–10-49, 10-54
    adjusting layered fog effect, 10-20–10-21
    adjusting light, 5-23–5-24, 5-30–5-35
    adjusting objects, 2-32–2-33
    adjusting particle system, 9-4, 9-7–9-10, 9-14–9-15
    adjusting spline, 3-102–3-103
    animating creation, 6-14–6-15
    Blizzard particle system, 9-20–9-21
    changing object's with Spinner Snap tool, 2-83
    described, 2-92
    editing map, 4-48–4-49, 4-55–4-56
    editing shader, 4-20–4-21, 4-25–4-26
    fog effects, 10-16
    modifying arc, star, 3-108
    modifying box, sphere, cone, 2-35–2-37
    rendering, 7-18–7-21
    of standard primitives, 2-4
Parameters section, Hierarchy panel, 1-31
parent-child relationships
    in linked objects, 2-60
    of objects, 1-30
PArray particle system, 9-5, 9-9–9-10
Particle Age map, 9-57–9-59

Particle Flow systems, creating, 9-32–9-33
particle systems
    adjusting parameters of, 9-7–9-10
    adjusting Spray parameters, 9-11–9-12
    changing particle types, 9-28
    creating Blizzard, 9-19–9-21
    creating materials for particles, 9-25–9-30
    creating non-event, 9-5–9-7, 9-11
    creating Super Spray, 9-13–9-14
    described, 9-2, 9-4–9-5
    Find Target test, adding and defining, 9-43–9-44
    splitting particles between events, 9-46–9-48
    using material operators, 9-52–9-61
    using space warps, 9-16–9-25
    wiring events together, 9-32, 9-36–9-37, 9-44–9-46
    working with particle flows, 9-32–9-51
Particle View
    using, 9-34–9-35
    writing events together in, 9-32
Path constraint in animation, 6-60–6-62, 6-66
paths
    adjust options, 6-67–6-68
    and open splines, 3-92
PCloud particle system, 9-5, 9-6, 9-9–9-10
Percent Along Path parameter, Path constraint, 6-62
Percent Snap tool, scaling objects with, 2-78, 2-82
Perspective view described, 1-44
Perspective viewport
    controls, using, 1-17
    described, 1-14, 1-15
    displaying different (fig.), 1-20
photometric lights, 5-20
Pinch and Bubble numbers, soft selection, 3-48–3-49
pinning the modifier stack, 2-44
pivot points
    bone, repositioning, 8-17, 8-20
    of objects, 1-30
    working with, 2-68–2-75

AUTODESK 3D STUDIO MAX 16

planar deflectors, creating, 9-25
planes
    creating, 2-4–2-5
    with pulled vertices (fig.), 3-46, 3-50
    with pushed and pulled vertices (fig.), 3-45, 3-50
playback, animation, editing properties, 6-25, 6-30–6-31
playhead. *See* time slider
playing animations, 1-34–1-35
point helpers in SplineIK solver, 8-28, 8-29
points, pivot. See pivot points
polygon
    modeling, 2-4
    objects, modifying, 2-32–2-37
polygons
    beveling, 3-36, 3-42–3-43
    bridging, 3-63, 3-70–3-71
    creating new, 3-56–3-57, 3-64–3-65
    described, 2-5–2-6, 2-92
    editable, 3-4–3-6
    extruding, 3-33–3-34, 3-39–3-40
    normals. *See* normals
    slicing and cutting, 3-59–3-61
Position Object operator, particle flows, 9-40
positioning
    cameras, 5-12–5-14, 5-17–5-18
    hair, 10-51
    Main toolbar, 1-24–1-27
    objects with snap tools, 2-80, 2-88
    pivot points in relation to objects, 2-68–2-69
Preference Settings dialog box, setting Undo levels, 1-7
previewing
    effects interactively, 10-31–10-32
    rendering effects, 10-24–10-25
primitives
    See also standard primitives
    converting into editable polygons, 3-10
Print Size Wizard, 7-3, 7-30–7-33
printing, 7-30–7-33
procedural maps, 4-30
production rendering, 7-8

projecting maps with lights, 5-49–5-51, 5-54–5-55
pyramids, creating, 2-6
push and pull vertices, 3-50–3-51
pyramids
    grouping, ungrouping, 2-66
    linking, 2-64

Quick Align tool, using, 2-85–2-86, 2-90
Quicktime .mov files, 7-14, 7-15

radii, adjusting for objects, 2-33
ray effects, 10-27
Re-scale Time dialog box (fig.), 6-24
re-scaling animation time, 6-24–6-25, 6-28
reactivating maps, 4-33–4-34
reactor toolbar, using, 1-7
Real Time check box, 6-25
real-time rendering, 7-4–7-5
real-time viewport, texture display in, 7-4
recoloring objects, 2-32, 2-35–2-36
rectangles, creating, 3-94, 3-99
Rectangular Section tool, 1-26–1-27
Redo tool
    Main toolbar button, 1-24
    using, 1-7
Reference Coordinate System list (fig.), 6-21
references
    and clones, 2-52
    modeling using, 3-73–3-74, 3-77
reflection, mapping, 4-58–4-59
refraction, mapping, 4-59–4-60, 4-64–4-65
regions
    of ActiveShade viewport, updating, 7-13
    selection. *See* selection regions
relaxing vertices, 3-46, 3-51
removing
    See also deleting
    maps, 4-33–4-34, 4-37
renaming objects, 2-32, 2-35–2-36

Render Output File dialog box (fig.), 7-22
Render Scene dialog box, 7-18–7-19
rendering
    ActiveShade, 7-8–7-13
    creating and saving, 7-18–7-21
    effects, 10-2, 10-22–10-25
    file output, 7-14–7-17
    generally, 4-8, 7-2
    hair, 10-52
    image file sequence, 7-23–7-24
    multi-pass, 10-34–10-35, 10-40–10-41
    object motion blur, 10-42–10-45
    particles, 9-8–9-9
    with Print Size Wizard, 7-30–7-33
    real-time, prerendered images, 7-4–7-6
    renderer types, 7-6–7-7
    scenes, 7-22
reorienting objects in relation to their pivot points, 2-73–2-74
repositioning
    bone pivot points, 8-17, 8-20
    objects in relation to their pivot points, 2-70
    object's pivot points, 2-72–2-73
    pivot points in relation to objects, 2-68–2-69
resetting 3ds Max, 1-13
resizing
    gizmos, 2-21
    objects, 2-24
    standard primitives with [Ctrl] key, 2-6
    viewports, 1-12–1-13
resolution, image, 7-17
restoring default user interface, 1-37, 1-39
Revert to Startup Layout command, Customize menu, 1-37
reviewing subobject levels, 3-11–3-12
rigging skeletal, 8-2, 8-24–8-25
Right hand rule, 1-19
ring effects, 10-27
Rotate tool, using, 2-20, 2-22–2-23
rotating
    animation object, 6-55–6-56
    bones, 8-6, 8-8, 8-26
    cameras, 5-12, 5-14–5-15
    and Lathe modifier, 3-113

AUTODESK 3D STUDIO MAX 17

INDEX

links between objects in hierarchy, 2-74–2-75
objects, 2-22–2-23, 2-25, 2-28, 2-70
objects with snap tools, 2-78, 2-81
wings using forward kinematics, 8-30
Rotation operator, particle flows, 9-41

S

Safe Frames feature, using, 5-15, 5-19
sample slots
    applying materials to, 4-10–4-13, 4-16–4-17
    viewing materials in, 4-15
sampling effects, 10-13
Save File As dialog box, 1-5–1-6
saving
    files, 1-5–1-6, 1-11
    renderings, 7-18–7-21
scale, aligning objects by, 2-89
Scale tool, using, 2-20, 2-23–2-24
scaling
    See also resizing
    atmospheric apparatus, 10-8
    hair, 10-56
    images, 7-21–7-22
    keys, 6-46
    objects, 2-23–2-24, 2-25, 2-29–2-30
    objects with control points, 3-117
    objects with snap tools, 2-78, 2-82
scanline renderer, 7-6
scenes
    adding atmospheric effects to, 10-4–10-6
    adding fire effects to, 10-4, 10-9
    adding lights to, 5-21–5-29
    adding text to, 3-95
    adding XRef objects to, 3-76, 3-80–3-81
    applying material to objects in, 4-18–4-19
    creating cameras in, 5-9–5-10
    creating new, 1-12–1-13
    described, 1-44
    designed with Particle Flow (fig.), 9-33
    generating radiosity in, 5-55
    lighting by overshooting, 5-38–5-39
    linking objects in, 2-61
    previewed, with two focal points (fig.), 10-36
    rendering, 4-9, 7-4–7-6, 7-22

schemes, Custom UI, 1-36–1-37
screen resolution, setting, 1-24
searching
    Help index, 1-40
    using Boolean operators, 1-40
see-through mesh, 8-10–8-11
segments
    active time, 6-23
    adjusting on objects, 2-38–2-41
    converting, 3-106, 3-109–3-110
Select Object tool, using, 2-12–2-13
selecting
    editable poly subobjects, 3-7–3-9, 3-12–3-13
    multiple subobjects, 3-14
    objects, 2-12–2-19
selection area, growing and shrinking, 3-15
selection regions
    described, 2-92
    selecting multiple objects using, 2-17
    selecting objects using, 2-12–2-13
Selection rollout options, 3-9
selection sets, creating, 2-14–2-15, 2-19, 2-92
self-illumination
    adjusting intensity of application, 4-33
    mapping, 4-48
    of materials, editing, 4-5, 4-24, 4-28–4-29
Set Key, setting keyframes with, 6-18, 6-20–6-21
shaders
    editing parameters, 4-20–4-21, 4-25–4-26
    types of, 4-7
shadows
    mapping, 5-45, 5-47
    modifying parameters of, 5-44–5-45
    soft vs. hard-edged, 5-24
Shape Instance operator, particle flows, 9-41
shapes
    adjusting fire effect, 10-12–10-13
    and closed splines, 3-92
    creating, 3-94–3-95
shiny materials, 4-5
shrinking selection area, 3-15
sides of objects, adjusting, 2-38, 2-41
skeletal rigs, creating, 8-24–8-25

Skin modifier, applying, 8-38, 8-42
skinning
    adjusting skin envelopes, 8-44–8-45
    adjusting vertex weight, 8-39–8-41, 8-46–8-47
    described, 8-2, 8-38
    envelopes and, 8-39
    testing deformation, 8-43
skylights, 5-51
slice function, Modify panel, 2-33–2-34
slicing
    objects, 3-68–3-69
    polygons, 3-59–3-60
Smoke material, creating and assigning, 9-60–9-61
smoothing parameters, setting, 2-33–2-34
snapping tools, working with, 2-76–2-83
Snow particle system, 9-5, 9-7
Soft Selection
    deforming objects with, 3-47–3-49
    painting, 3-54–3-55
    using when moving vertex, 3-52–3-53
space warps
    applying to event-driven particles, 9-48–9-49
    creating Gravity, 9-22–9-23
    described, creating and modifying, 9-16–9-18
specular
    colors, 4-5, 4-21–4-22
    highlight components, mapping, 4-52–4-53
    level of material, editing, 4-23, 4-27–4-28
Speed operator, particle flows, 9-41
spheres
    creating, 2-4–2-5, 2-9
    modifying parameters of, 2-36–2-37
    slicing, 2-33–2-34
spherical deflector, creating, 9-23–9-24
Spinner Snap tool, using, 2-79, 2-83
spinners, using, 2-79
SplineIK solver, using, 8-28, 8-33–8-35
splines
    applying Lathe modifier to, 3-119–3-120
    converting into editable splines, 3-104–3-105
    converting to lines, curves, 3-106–3-107

AUTODESK 3D STUDIO MAX 18

creating, 3-92–3-97, 8-31–8-32
extruding, 3-112, 3-118–3-119
inserting vertices into editable, 3-107
modifying parameters of, 3-102–3-103
splitting particles between events, 9-37, 9-46–9-48
spotlights, inserting, , 5-20, 5-25–5-26
Spray particle system, 9-5, 9-7–9-8, 9-11–9-12
stack, modifier, 2-42
Standard material
    applying maps to, 4-31–4-33
    mapping color components of, 4-46–4-47
    mapping reflection, refraction, bumpiness, 4-58–4-61
    using generally, 4-6–4-7
standard particles, applying materials to, 9-2, 9-25
standard primitives
    creating, 2-4–2-11
    described, 1-8, 2-92
star effects, 10-27, 10-32–10-33
star splines, 3-96
stars, modifying parameters of, 3-108
starting 3ds Max, 1-11
static images, 7-5
streak effects, 10-27
styling hair, 10-48–10-51, 10-55–10-56
submaps described, 4-49
subobjects
    applying modifiers to, 3-18–3-23
    described, 3-6
    levels, reviewing, 3-11–3-12
    selecting multiple, 3-14
    slicing and cutting, 3-60
    transforming, 3-16–3-17
Super Spray particle system, 9-5, 9-9–9-10, 9-13–9-14
surfaces, controlling appearance with lighting, 5-48–5-53
swapping maps, 4-34
switching to preset Custom UI schemes, 1-36–1-38
Symmetry modifiers, 2-68, 3-79–3-80, 3-82

T

tangents, types of, changing, 6-43–6-45
Taper modifier, 3-11–3-12, 3-23
Taper settings, bone, 8-18–8-19
target cameras, 5-5
target objects, 2-85
target spotlights, 5-22, 5-52
Target Weld button, 3-59
teapots
    creating, 2-7–2-8, 2-11
    scaling, 2-29
television aspect ratio, 7-21
testing
    events, conditions, 9-36
    targets, in particle flows, 9-43–9-44
text splines
    creating, 3-96, 3-100
    described, creating, 3-95
textures and rendering, 7-4
ticks, time, 6-24
TIFF file format, 7-14–7-15, 7-32–7-33
Time Configuration dialog box, 6-23, 6-29
time slider
    navigating frames with, 1-32–1-33
    and track bar timeline, 1-10
    using, 1-32–1-33
timeline on track bar, 1-32
timing, configuring animation, 6-22–6-31
title safe frames, 5-15
toolbars
    hiding, 1-36
    Main, exploring, 1-7
    reactor, using, 1-7
tools, snapping, 2-76–2-83
torso, character, creating, 3-84–3-85
toruses
    creating, 2-6–2-7
    self-illuminated (fig.), 4-24
track bar
    exploring, 1-10, 1-44
    playing animation (fig.), 6-7
    working with, 1-32–1-33
Track View, using, 6-38–6-39
tracks
    animating one at a time, 8-48
    hierarchy, 6-38
trajectories, displaying object's, 6-6
Trajectories section, Hierarchy panel, 1-31
transform gizmos, using to manipulate objects, 2-21, 2-62
Transform tools, snap tools, 2-76–2-83
Transform Type-In boxes
    transforming objects with, 2-30–2-31
    using to move, rotate, or scale objects, 2-25
transformation keys, Auto Key animation, 6-5
transformational clones, creating, 2-57–2-58
transforming subobjects, 3-16–3-17
translucent materials, 4-5, 4-24
transparent mesh objects, 8-10–8-11
tubes, creating, 2-6–2-7, 2-10
TurboSmooth modifier, 3-19, 3-74
tweening process, 6-4
Twist modifiers, 2-42, 2-68, 3-20

U

Undo tool, 1-7, 1-24
undoing actions, 8-7
unfreezing, freezing mesh objects, 8-11, 8-13
unlinking objects, 2-64
User Reference Help system, 1-40
'Utah Teapot,' 2-7
Utilities panel, using, 1-31

V

vertices
    chamfering, 3-30, 3-37–3-38
    connecting with edges, 3-57–3-58, 3-66–3-67
    converting, 3-105–3-106, 3-109–3-110
    creating new, 3-56–3-57, 3-64–3-65
    described, 3-7
    extruding, 3-35, 3-40–3-41
    inserting, 3-111
    inserting into editable splines, 3-107
    pushing and pulling, 3-44, 3-50–3-51

AUTODESK 3D STUDIO MAX 19

relaxing, 3-46
relaxing pulled, 3-51
weight, in bones, 8-39, 8-40–8-41
welding, 3-58–3-59, 3-67–3-68
video
   See also animation
   frame rate standard, 6-22
   rendering animation as codec, 7-14, 7-17
viewing
   materials in sample slots, 4-10–4-11, 4-15
   normals, 3-27–3-28
viewpoints of cameras, 5-4
viewports
   ActiveShade, updating window, 7-13
   changing, 1-20–1-21
   changing into camera viewports, 5-16
   controls, adjusting views with, 1-16
   described, changing, 1-4, 1-14, 1-44
   exploring, 1-7–1-8
   resizing, 1-12–1-13
   vs. camera viewports, 5-4–5-5
   wireframe, 1-17–1-18
views
   See also specific view
   adjusting, 1-14
   types of, 1-14
Volume Fog effects, 10-4
Volume Light effects, 10-4, 10-10–10-11, 10-14–10-15, 10-19–10-20

W

Wave gizmo (fig.), 6-12
Web site, Autodesk 3d Studio Max, 1-2
weight of vertex, 8-39, 8-40–8-41
welding vertices, 3-58–3-59, 3-67–3-68
Window/Crossing Selection toggle, 2-13
Wireframe display option, 1-17–1-18
wiring events together, 9-32, 9-36–9-37, 9-44–9-46

X

x-axis, moving object in relation to, 2-22
XRef objects
   adding to scenes, 3-80–3-81
   using, 3-75–3-76

Y

y-axis, 2-21

Z

z-axis, 2-21
zoom controls, axonometric view, 1-16–1-17
zooming on viewport, 1-21, 1-22